BONIFACE WIMMER

LETTERS OF AN AMERICAN ABBOT

EDITED BY JEROME OETGEN

SAINT VINCENT ARCHABBEY PUBLICATIONS
LATROBE, PENNSYLVANIA
2008

Library of Congress Cataloging-in-Publication Data
Wimmer, Boniface, 1809-1887.
   [Correspondence. Selections. English]
   Boniface Wimmer : letters of an American Abbot / edited by Jerome Oetgen.
       p. cm.
   Includes bibliographical references and index.
   ISBN 978-0-9773909-4-6 (pbk. : alk. paper)
   1.   Wimmer, Boniface, 1809-1887--Correspondence. 2.   Benedictines--United States--History. I. Oetgen, Jerome, 1946- II. Title.
BX4705.W58A4 2008
271'.1073--dc22

                                   2008040717

Printed in the United States of America
Saint Vincent Archabbey Publications
300 Fraser Purchase Road
Latrobe, Pennsylvania 15650-2690
http://www.stvincentstore.com

Book design by Liz Cousins, Saint Vincent Archabbey Publications
Cover photo: Courtesy of Saint Vincent Archabbey Archives
Cover design: Rev. Vincent de Paul Crosby, O.S.B.
Back cover: Kim Metzgar, Saint Vincent Archabbey Publications
Copyeditors: Rev. Omer U. Kline, O.S.B., and Rev. Chrysostom Schlimm, O.S.B.
Editorial Assistants: Laura Gerhart and Kelly Bridges
Saint Vincent Archabbey Publications
Proofreader: Judy Regula
Photo credits: Courtesy of Rev. Brian Boosel, O.S.B.,
Saint Vincent Archabbey Archives

TABLE OF CONTENTS

ABBREVIATIONS

c	copy
encl	enclosure
Eng	English
frag	fragment
Ger	German
Ital	Italian
Lat	Latin
o	original
OSB	Order of St. Benedict
RB	*Rule of St. Benedict*
trans	translator

ARCHIVES

APH	Archives of St. Martin's Archabbey, Pannonhalma, Hungary
ASA	Archives of Scheyern Abbey, Scheyern, Germany
ASBA	Archives of St. Benedict Abbey, Atchison, Kansas
ASBC	Archives of St. Benedict Convent, Erie, Pennsylvania
ASBM	Archives of the Abbey of St. Benoit, Maredsous, Belgium
ASJA	Archives of St. John's Abbey, Collegeville, Minnesota
ASMA	Archives of St. Meinrad Archabbey, St. Meinrad, Indiana
ASPA	Archives of St. Procopius Abbey, Lisle, Illinois
ASPR	Archives of St. Paul's Outside the Walls Abbey, Rome
ASVA	Archives of Saint Vincent Archabbey, Latrobe, Pennsylvania
NAUS	National Archives of the United States, Washington, D.C.
RAB	Royal Archives of Bavaria, Munich, Germany

TRANSLATORS

ABi	Anselm Biggs, O.S.B.
ABu	Aaron Buzzelli, O.S.B.
AH	Alcuin Hemmen, O.S.B.
AHo	Alexius Hoffmann, O.S.B.
AS	Anthony St. Pierre, O.S.B.
BB	Bede Babo, O.S.B.
BS	Bernard Sause, O.S.B.
CB	Clement Bloomfield, O.S.B.
CW	Clarence Weber, O.S.B.
CZ	Conrad Zimmerman, O.S.B.
FF	Felix Fellner, O.S.B.
GB	Gerard Bridge, O.S.B.
GE	Gonzaga Englehart, O.S.B.
GM	Gregoria Mueller, O.S.B.
GS	Gertrude Schmitz, O.S.B.
HW	Hugh Wilt, O.S.B.

IB	Imelda Bauer, O.S.B.
IG	Incarnata Girgen, O.S.B.
JM	Jonathan Murrman, O.S.B.
JO	Jerome Oetgen
KB	Kurt Belsole, O.S.B.
LK	Leopold Krul, O.S.B.
MN	Margretta Nathe, O.S.B.
MS	Meinulph Schmiesing, O.S.B.
PB	Peter Beckman, O.S.B.
RG	Rhabanus Goetz, O.S.B.
SB	Simon Bischof. O.S.B.
VH	Vincent Huber, O.S.B.
VS	Vera Slezak
WM	Warren Murrman, O.S.B.
WT	Wilfred Theisen, O.S.B.

PUBLISHED SOURCES

ABR14   Giles Hayes, O.S.B., ed., "Documents: Early Bayley-Wimmer Correspondence (1854-1857)," *American Benedictine Review* 14 (1963): 470-93.

*ABR*20   Edward E. Malone, O.S.B., trans., "A Long Lost Letter of Boniface Wimmer," *American Benedictine Review* 20 (1969): 309-20.

*ABR*26   Walter Sauer, "Unpublished Viennese Letters of Benedictine Missionaries," *American Benedictine Review* 26 (1975): 374-77.

Annalen   *Annalen der Verbreitung des Glaubens.* Munich, 1847-1855.

AugsP   *Augsburger Postzeitung.*

Berichte   *Berichte der Leopoldinen Stiftung.* Vienna, 1847-1855.

Bridge   Gerard Bridge, O.S.B., *An Illustrated History of St. Vincent Archabbey.* Beatty, Pa.: Archabbey Press, 1922.

Burg   Remigius Burgemeister, O.S.B., *History of the Development of Catholicity in St. Marys: 1844-1919.* St. Marys, Pa.: Privately Published, 1919.

CinW   *Cincinnati Wahrheitsfreund.*

*Conf*6   Warren Murrman, O.S.B., trans., "Wimmer to von Reisach," *Benedictine Confluence* (St. Vincent Archabbey) 6 (Winter 1972): 19-24.

Ellis   John Tracy Ellis, ed., *Documents of American Catholic History*. Wilm-
             ington, Del.: Michael Glazier, 1987, I: 279-88.

Fell   Felix Fellner, O.S.B. *Abbot Boniface and His Monks*. 5 volumes. La-
             trobe, Pa.: Archabbey Press, 1956.

Girgen   Incarnata Girgen, O.S.B., *Behind the Beginnings: Benedictine Women
             in America*. St. Joseph, Minn.: St. Benedict's Convent, 1981.

KathK   *Katholische Kirchenzeitung*. Baltimore.

Kohler   Hortense Kohler, O.P., *The Life and Work of Mother Benedicta Bauer,
             O.P.* Milwaukee: Bruce, 1937, pp. 101-05.

Math   Willibald Mathäser, O.S.B., *Bonifaz Wimmer O.S.B. und König Lud-
             wig I von Bayern*. Munich: J. Pfeiffer, 1938.

Morkin   Morkin, M. Louis, and Theophane Seigel. *Wind in the Wheat*. Erie,
             Pa.: McCarty Publishing, 1956.

*Scrip*17   "Wimmer Letters," *The Scriptorium* (St. John's Abbey) 17 (1958): 53-
             64.

*Scrip*18   "Wimmer Letters," *The Scriptorium* 18 (1959): 69-82.

*Scrip*19   "Wimmer Letters," *The Scriptorium* 19 (1960): 61-83.

StudM   *Studien und Mitteilungen zur Geschichte des Benediktiner-Ordens und
             seiner Zweige*. Munich.

*SVJ*3   Vincent Huber, O.S.B., "Sportsman's Hall and St. Vincent Abbey," *St.
             Vincent's Journal* 3 (1894): 203-04.

Wand   *Der Wanderer*. St. Paul, Minnesota.

CORRESPONDENTS

AMBERGER, JOSEPH. Cathedral rector in Regensburg, Bavaria, and a benefactor of the American Benedictines.

AUGSBURGER POSTZEITUNG. Daily newspaper of Augsburg, Bavaria.

BARNABO, ALESSANDRO CARDINAL (1801-1874). Secretary and then Prefect of the Sacred Congregation for the Propagation of the Faith.

BAYLEY, JAMES ROOSEVELT (1814-1877). Bishop of Newark (1853-1872) and Archbishop of Baltimore (1872-1877).

BRAUNMÜLLER, BENEDICT, O.S.B. (1825-1898). Successor to Utto Lang as abbot of Metten.

BURKHARDT, SCHOLASTICA, O.S.B. (1832-1881). Prioress of the Benedictine priory in Erie, Pennsylvania.

CASARETTO, PETER, O.S.B. (1810-1878). Reforming abbot and president of the Italian Cassinese Congregation (1852-1858). He founded the Cassinese Congregation of the Primitive Observance in 1872 and served as Abbot General of that congregation (1872-1876).

CASSINESE CONGREGATION. Benedictine congregation in Italy with which the American Cassinese Congregation was affiliated in 1855.

CHRISTOPH, AEGIDIUS (GILES), O.S.B. (1830-1887). Monk of St. Vincent who served as prior at St. Vincent and at St. Benedict Priory, Atchison, Kansas.

CONRAD, FROWIN, O.S.B. (1833-1923). First abbot of the Swiss-American abbey of Conception, Missouri (1881-1923).

DI MAROGNA, DEMETRIUS, O.S.B. (1803-1869). Monk of St. Vincent, where he was prior 1854-1856; leader of the Benedictine mission to Minnesota in 1856.

DUBUIS, CLAUDE M. (1817-1895). Bishop of Galveston, Texas (1862-1892).

DUSMET D'AMOURS, JOSEPH BENEDICT, O.S.B. (1818-1894), Archbishop of Catania, Sicily (1867-1894), elevated to cardinal 1889, beatified 1988.

EDELBROCK, ALEXIUS, O.S.B. (1843-1908). Second abbot of St. John's Abbey, Minnesota (1875-1889).

ENGLBRECHT, CELESTINE, O.S.B. (1824-1904). Monk of St. Vincent Abbey; member of the original Benedictine colony in Pennsylvania.

FEEHAN, PATRICK A. (1829-1902). First archbishop of Chicago (1880-1902).

FOFFA, CHRYSOSTOM, O.S.B. (1830-1899). Monk of St. Meinrad Abbey, Diocese of Vincennes, Indiana.

FRANSONI, GIACOMO FILIPPE CARDINAL (1775-1856). Prefect of the Sacred Congregation for the Propagation of the Faith.

GIBBONS, JAMES CARDINAL (1834-1921). Archbishop of Baltimore (1877-1921). In 1876, when bishop of Richmond and vicar apostolic of North Carolina, he invited the Benedictines to establish a monastery and college in North Carolina.

HAINDL, BENEDICT, O.S.B. (1815-1887). Monk of St. Vincent Abbey and member of the original Benedictine colony in Pennsylvania. He served as prior in St. Marys, Pennsylvania, in St. Cloud, Minnesota and at St. Vincent.

HENNI, JOHN MARTIN (1805-1881). First Bishop (1844-1875) and then first Archbishop (1875-1881) of Milwaukee.

HINTENACH, ANDREW, O.S.B. (1844-1927). Prior at St. Vincent Abbey (1876-1886) and Wimmer's successor as archabbot (1888-1892).

HOFFMANN, ILDEPHONSE, O.S.B. (1829-1873). Monk of St. Vincent who was drafted and served in the Union Army during the Civil War.

JAEGER, JOHN NEPOMUCENE, O.S.B. (1844-1924). Monk of St. Vincent Abbey who became first abbot of St. Procopius Abbey, Chicago (later Lisle, Illinois).

KAGERER, CANON JOSEPH. Priest of the cathedral chapter of Munich and a member of the board of directors of the Ludwig Missionsverein.

KATHOLISCHE KIRCHENZEITUNG. German Catholic newpaper published in Baltimore, Maryland.

KILGER, JULIAN, O.S.B. (1855-1939). Monk of St. Vincent Abbey.

KINTER, MAURUS, O.S.B. (1842-1928). Editor of the Benedictine journal *Studien und Mitteilungen zur Geschichte des Benediktiner-Ordens und seiner Zweige*; monk of the Abbey of SS. Peter and Paul, Raigern, Austria.

KOCARNIK, WENCESLAUS, O.S.B. (1845-1912). Founding pastor of the Bohemian (Czech) parish in Omaha, Nebraska, and monk of St. Procopius Abbey.

KRAMER, AMANDUS, O.S.B. (1827-1889). Monk of St. Vincent Abbey.

KRUESZ, CHRYSOSTOM, O.S.B. (1819-1885). Archabbot of St. Martin's Archabbey, Pannonhalma, Hungary.

LACENSE, PLACIDUS, O.S.B. (1802-1887). Monk of Metten Abbey and director of the Royal Educational Institute (the Ludwigs-Gymnasium).

LANG, UTTO, O.S.B. (1806-1884). Abbot of Metten, succeeded Gregory Scherr.

LEISS, RUPERT, O.S.B. (1795-1872). A novitiate classmate of Wimmers at Metten. Abbot of Scheyern Abbey.

LEO XIII, POPE (1810-1903). Reigned as pope from 1878 to 1903.

LINCOLN, ABRAHAM (1809-1865). Sixteenth President of the United States (1861-1865).

LORAS, MATHIAS (1792-1858). First bishop of Dubuque (1837-1858).

LUDWIG I (1786-1868). King of Bavaria and benefactor of the Benedictine mission in the United States.

LUDWIG MISSIONSVEREIN. The Bavarian mission society that provided substantial funds for the Benedictine mission in the United States.

MARTY, MARTIN, O.S.B. (1834-1896). Swiss-born first abbot of St. Meinrad Abbey, Indiana (1871-1880). Later bishop of the Dakota Territory (1880-1889), Sioux Falls (1889-1895), and St. Cloud (1895-1896).

MEYRINGER, JOSEPH. A clergyman in Bavaria and cousin of Wimmer.

MITTERNDORFER, THOMAS, O.S.B. (+1860). Abbot of the Abbey of Kremsmünster, Austria.

MÜLLER, ADALBERT, O.S.B. (1842-1906). Monk of St. Vincent Abbey, later prior of the Abbey of Sant' Anselmo, Rome.

MÜLLER, JOSEPH FERDINAND (1803-1864). Chaplain to the court of King Ludwig I of Bavaria and general manager and treasurer of the *Ludwig Missionsverein*; one of the principal benefactors of Wimmer and the Benedictine mission in the United States.

NEBAUER, ILDEPHONSE, O.S.B. (1768-1844). First prior of St. Michael's Priory, Metten, after the restoration in 1830.

NORTHROP, HENRY P. (1842-1916). Vicar apostolic of North Carolina (1881-1883) and bishop of Charleston (1883-1916).

OBERKAMP, RUDOLPH VON. Member of the Central Committee of the *Ludwig Missionsverein.*

OERTEL, MAXIMILIAN. Editor of the *Katholische Kirchenzeitung* of Baltimore.

OSTENDARP, BONAVENTURE, O.S.B. (1856-1912). Monk of St. Vincent and founding member of St. Mary's Abbey, Newark, New Jersey. Ostendarp was a painter who had studied in Bavaria and who worked in the Beuronese style.

PESCETELLI, ANGELO, O.S.B. (1809-1885). Abbot of Farfa and procurator general of the Italian Cassinese Congregation. From 1855 to 1884 he also served as procurator general for the American Cassinese Congregation.

PIERRON, EDWIN, O.S.B. (1846-1930). Monk of St. Vincent Abbey.

PFRÄNGLE, HILARY, O.S.B. (1843-1909). Director of St. Vincent College (1872-1886) and later abbot of St. Mary's Abbey, Newark, New Jersey (1886-1909).

PITTSBURGH CATHOLIC. Official newspaper of the Catholic Diocese of Pittsburgh.

PIUS IX, POPE (1792-1878). Reigning pope when St. Vincent was founded (1846). He raised Saint Vincent to the dignity of abbey (1855).

PUCCI-SISTI, AUGUSTINE, O.S.B. (1810-1886). Monk of the abbey of St. Paul's Outside the Walls, Rome; procurator general of the Italian Cassinese Congregation, titular abbot of St. Clement's on the Tiber, and Roman procurator for the American Cassinese Congregation 1884-1886.

REGER, MICHAEL. Priest of the Diocese of Regensburg, Bavaria, dean of the cathedral chapter, and vicar general of the diocese.

REISACH, KARL AUGUST CARDINAL VON (1800-1869). Bishop of Eichstätt (1836-1846), Archbishop of Munich-Freising and president of the *Ludwig Missionsverein* (1846-1855), cardinal and official of the Roman *curia* (1855-1869); a major benefactor of the Benedictine mission in the United States.

RIEDERER, DOMINICA, O.S.B. (1834-1896). Prioress of the Benedictine priory in Erie, Pennsylvania.

ROBOT, ISIDORE, O.S.B. (1837-1887). Monk of the French abbey of Pierre-qui-Vire who became prefect apostolic of the Indian Territory and founder of Sacred Heart Abbey (later St. Gregory's Abbey), Oklahoma.

SCHERR, GREGORY LEONARD, O.S.B. (1804-1877). Abbot of Metten (1840-1856) and later Archbishop of Munich (1856-1877). As abbot of Metten, Scherr gave Wimmer permission to undertake the mission to the United States.

SEIDENBUSCH, RUPERT, O.S.B. (1830-1895). Monk of St. Vincent who served as prior in St. Marys, Pennsylvania, in Newark, New Jersey, and at St. Vincent. He was elected first abbot of St. John's Abbey, Minnesota (1866) and named bishop of the Vicariate of Northern Minnesota (1875).

SIMEONI, GIOVANNI CARDINAL (1816-1892). Cardinal Prefect of the Sacred Congregation for the Propagation of the Faith.

SMITH, BERNARD, O.S.B. (1818-1892). Monk of St. Paul's Abbey Outside the Walls, Rome, and professor at the Roman College of the *Propaganda Fide*. He became a titular abbot and served as the American Cassinese Congregation's Roman procurator from 1886 to 1892.

STADER, BONIFACIA, O.S.B. (1858-1920). Nun of the Benedictine priory in Newark, New Jersey.

STILLINGER, JAMES AMBROSE (1801-1873). Priest of the Diocese of Pittsburgh, pastor of Ss. Simon and Jude Parish, Blairsville, Pennsylvania, and former pastor of St. Vincent Parish.

DER WANDERER. German Catholic newspaper published in St. Paul, Minnesota.

WIMMER, LUKE, O.S.B. (1825-1901). Monk of St. Vincent and nephew of Boniface Wimmer.

WOLF, INNOCENT, O.S.B. (1843-1922). Monk of St. Vincent Abbey who became first abbot of St. Benedict Abbey, Atchison, Kansas (1876-1922).

WOLTER, PLACIDUS, O.S.B. (1828-1908). First abbot of the Abbey of Maredsous, Belgium.

WOOD, JAMES F. (1813-1883). Fifth Bishop and First Archbishop of Philadelphia (1860-1883).

YOUNG, JOSUE MARY (1808-1866). First Bishop of Erie, Pennsylvania (1854-1866).

ZIEGLER, GREGORY THOMAS, O.S.B. (1770-1852). Benedictine abbot of Wiblingen in Suabia who became bishop of Linz, Austria (1827-1852). He was one of the principal early benefactors of Wimmer and the Benedictine mission to the United States.

ZILLIOX, JAMES, O.S.B. (1849-1890). Monk of St. Vincent Abbey who served as novice master and seminary prefect before becoming first abbot of St. Mary's Abbey, Newark, New Jersey.

INDEX OF LETTERS

ACKNOWLEDGEMENTS

The letters of Benedictine Archabbot Boniface Wimmer (1809-1887) are note-worthy for two reasons. Not only do they provide important details about the early history of the Benedictine Order in the United States, but they also shed significant light on the nineteenth-century history of the American Catholic Church, particularly with respect to Catholic immigrants and Benedictine missionary activity among them. The present volume, commemorating the 200th anniversary of Wimmer's birth, consists of translations and English originals of 200 of the most important letters the Archabbot wrote between 1832, the year he entered the Benedictine monastery of Metten in Bavaria, and his death in Latrobe, Pennsylvania, in 1887.

Some of Wimmer's letters were published in his lifetime, but most remained unpublished and untranslated until the twentieth century when a few appeared in German and American publications. Chief among the editions of Wimmer's German correspondence was Father Willibald Mathäser's *Bonifaz Wimmer O.S.B. und König Ludwig I von Bayern* (Munich: J. Pfeiffer, 1938), which included letters exchanged between Wimmer and King Ludwig I of Bavaria from 1846 to 1868. Translations (often partial) of other letters appeared in historical studies by Benedictine historians Vincent Huber, Gerard Bridge, Alexius Hoffman, Felix Fellner, Colman Barry, Peter Beckman, and Incarnata Girgen (among others); and translations of complete letters appeared in such journals as *The American Benedictine Review*, *The Scriptorium*, and *Benedictine Confluence*.

Wimmer was a prolific letter writer who took great pains to inform his correspondents in the United States, Bavaria, and Rome of the progress of the Benedictine mission to America. In doing so, he brought into sharp focus Benedictine activities in the United States at a time when an historic surge in immigration was redefining the character of the American Catholic Church. These letters, therefore, contain a trove of information and insight not only about Wimmer and American Benedictine history, but about American Catholic history as well.

The Wimmer papers in the archives of Saint Vincent Archabbey, Latrobe, Pennsylvania, include more than 1500 of Boniface Wimmer's letters. Some of them are originals but most are copies made by monastic researchers from originals in European and American archives. Among those who helped collect these letters was Wimmer himself, who kept copies of some of his more important correspondence and commissioned several of his students in Rome to make copies of the Latin letters he sent to the Holy See between 1846 and the mid-1880s. Father (later Abbot) Vincent Huber, for example, copied letters in the archives of the Congregation for the Propagation of the Faith while a student in Rome in the 1880s, and his work, together with that of the early archivists of Saint Vincent, Fathers Edward Hipelius, Augustine Schneider, and Oswald Moosmüller, formed the basis of the collection that now exists.

In the 1930s, Father Felix Fellner visited Europe and photocopied hundreds of Wimmer letters in the archives of the *Propaganda Fide* and the Abbey of St. Paul's Outside the Walls in Rome, as well as in the archives of Metten Abbey, Scheyern Abbey, and the *Ludwig Missionsverein* in Bavaria. Fellner was an indefatigable researcher who collected from both European and American archives the copies and originals of those letters that form the bulk of the collection. In the 1960s, when Father Matthew Benko was archivist at Saint Vincent, a new effort was begun to gather letters that had not already been included in the Wimmer letter collection. With the assistance of archivists in Benedictine communities throughout the United States, photocopies of additional letters were added to the collection at Saint Vincent. Among the most important of these were the letters at St. John's Abbey, Collegeville, Minnesota, and St. Benedict Abbey, Atchison, Kansas, where Father Colman Barry and Father Peter Beckman had made extensive use of them in researching and writing the early chapters of their histories of those two communities.[1]

---

[1] Colman J. Barry, *Worship and Work: St. John's Abbey and University 1856-1956* (Collegeville, Minn.: St. John's Abbey Press, 1956); and Peter Beckman, *Kansas Monks: A History of St. Benedict's Abbey* (Atchison, Kans.: Abbey Student Press, 1957).

The next step was to transliterate those letters written in the unfamiliar German script into the more accessible Roman script. The work of transliteration was carried on by Father Rhabanus Goetz and Brother Lambert Berens when Father Omer Kline succeeded Father Matthew as archivist. In 1968, Brother Philip Hurley, assistant archivist, began the arduous task of re-cataloguing all the Wimmer papers in the archives of Saint Vincent in order to facilitate their use by researchers. About this time, Archabbot Egbert Donovan of Saint Vincent initiated an effort to translate those letters written in German and Latin (which constituted the vast majority) into English. Dozens of translators from American Benedictine communities of men and women were recruited for the task, and hundreds of letters were translated. Translators whose work is included in this volume are listed on page vii—viii above and noted at the end of each letter.

In editing these translations, I have tried as much as possible to respect the judgments of the individual translators with regard to interpretation and English style, making substantial changes only when upon comparison with the original letter it was clear that a particular translation was inaccurate. For the most part, the translators (and the editor) have followed the example of the tenth-century Anglo-Saxon Benedictine Abbot Ælfric of Eynsham who, when translating the works of the Latin Fathers into English, noted that he intended to provide his readers with a "clear sense of the original rather than a slavishly literal version." The reader, of course, should keep in mind that, except for a few letters written in English, these are indeed translations and suffer from the limitations of that genre. Professional historians and researchers will want to consult the originals, and for that reason, I have noted at the end of each letter the locations of both the original and the copies used.

The letters in this volume are a selection and represent only a fraction of the collected letters and papers of Boniface Wimmer. I made extensive use of the Wimmer collection in the archives of Saint Vincent Archabbey when writing both the biography of Wimmer and the history of the archabbey,[2] and the reader may find those works useful in understanding the context within which the letters in the present volume were written.

Acknowledging that flaws in this edition are the fault of none but myself, I am pleased to take this opportunity to express my appreciation to Father Omer Kline and Father Chrysostom Schlimm of Saint Vincent, as well as Father James Flint

---

[2] Jerome Oetgen, *An American Abbot: Boniface Wimmer 1809-1887*, revised edition (Washington, D.C.: Catholic University of America Press, 1997) and *Mission to America: A History of Saint Vincent Archabbey, the First Benedictine Monastery in the United States* (Washington, D.C.: Catholic University of America Press, 2000).

of Saint Procopius Abbey, Lisle, Illinois, each or whom reviewed the letters in this volume with a careful and critical eye and provided astute and judicious suggestions for improvements. I would also like to thank Liz Cousins and Kim Metzgar of Archabbey Publications for the care and professionalism they brought to the task of turning the often confused and confusing manuscript I gave them into a coherent and attractive book. In addition, I want to express my gratitude to Archabbot Douglas Nowicki, Father Vincent Crosby, Father Campion Gavaler, Father Brian Boosel, and indeed the entire community of Saint Vincent Archabbey, whose support and assistance throughout the long process of editing these letters made the work a reality. I acknowledge with sincere thanks the many researchers, archivists, and translators who over the past decades helped make Wimmer's correspondence accessible to a broader public. Their quiet, unassuming efforts were often astonishingly productive. All of them, working separately yet collectively, made publication of this volume of Boniface Wimmer's correspondence possible. Finally, and especially, I want to thank my wife Cecilia and my daughters Mercedes and Teresa for their love and patience throughout the course of my work on the Wimmer letters. They gave me the time and space I needed to accomplish the task while providing indispensible support and valiantly enduring my enthusiasm for nineteenth-century monks and monasticism with inexhaustible good humor and constant wry commentary that always kept things in clear-sighted perspective. I owe them an unpayable debt which, *deo volente,* I will somehow find a means to repay.

Jerome Oetgen

INTRODUCTION

The 200th anniversary of Archabbot Boniface Wimmer's birth falls within the Jubilee Year 2008-2009, announced by Pope Benedict XVI to mark the 2000th anniversary of the birth of St. Paul. The fact that these two celebrations are occurring concurrently is a happy coincidence and reminds us of some salient parallels between the life of Wimmer and the life of St. Paul. Like St. Paul, Wimmer was a missionary who preached the Gospel over a wide geographic area. He was a community builder who traveled extensively and established Christian communities everywhere he went. He was a man of strong faith whose zeal and single-minded devotion to duty strengthened the Church of Christ. He was a prolific letter writer who through his persuasive correspondence urged and inspired those to whom he wrote to remain faithful in the face of adversity. Was it mere accident, or perhaps a subtle hint of providential design, that he began his work in the United States at a church dedicated to St. Vincent *de Paul,* or that his second major missionary undertaking occurred in the Diocese of St. Paul?

The late John Tracy Ellis, dean of American Catholic historians in his day, called Wimmer the greatest Catholic missionary of nineteenth-century America. Reading Wimmer's letters provides evidence that Ellis had a point. Standard histories of the American Church, however, tend to undervalue if not neglect Wimmer and the Benedictines' contributions to the development of Catholicism in America. This historical undervaluation is not limited to American Benedictines. To a great extent, historians of the Catholic Church in the United States have treated institutional religious life in general and religious orders (of both men and women) in particular as incidental to the narrative of American Catholic history. This is unfortunate for many reasons, but especially because of the incontestable importance that religious orders have had from the beginning in the life of the Catholic Church in this country. One thinks of the Franciscans in Florida and California, the Ursulines in Louisiana, the Jesuits, Sulpicians, and Carmelites in Maryland, as well as the profound impact that religious orders have had on the faith of American Catholics virtually everywhere. Hardly any Catholic diocese in the United States could have succeeded in its mission to teach and sanctify the faithful without the contributions, and often the essential contributions, of at least one, and frequently many, religious orders. Hardly any Catholic congregation in America could have grown into a community of faith without the support and influence of priests, missionaries, and/or teachers from religious orders. The pastoral care provided to the American Catholic community by virtually every bishop since John Carroll has benefited, often in dramatic ways, from the support of nuns, brothers, and/or priests of religious orders.

Numbers never tell the full story, but it is interesting to note that by 1880, only 34 years after Wimmer and his eighteen companions arrived in Pennsylvania, nearly 900 Benedictine monks and nuns were working and praying in 60 monasteries in the United States. These monastics served 138 parishes where they provided pastoral care for 44,000 souls, operated three major seminaries, six colleges, and 63 elementary schools, and educated an estimated 7,000 students. By 1880, Benedictine monks and nuns served in 21 American dioceses and vicariates apostolic (out of a total of 70), located in 20 states and territories of the Union (see *Album Benedictinum 1880*). Most of the Benedictine monks and nuns who carried out this work of pastoral care, evangelization, and education in nineteenth-century America regarded Boniface Wimmer as their founder, their leader, and their inspiration. The work continues. Today, American Benedictines who trace their roots back to Wimmer serve in more than 20 American states, as well as in Canada, Mexico, Puerto Rico, the Bahamas, Colombia, Brazil, Taiwan, and Japan.

Boniface Wimmer was a Benedictine priest from the Bavarian abbey of Metten who came to America in 1846 to establish the Order of St. Benedict in the New World, to evangelize the immigrants, and to preserve and strengthen their Catholic faith by providing them with pastoral care and formal education. The Benedictines had already experienced a long and notable history in Europe when Wimmer introduced them to America. They had founded centers of spirituality, learning, and culture throughout the Old World; and, for nearly thirteen centuries, these centers had made unparalleled contributions not just to the dissemination, but at times to the very survival of Christian civilization in the West. During the early Middle Ages, for example, Benedictine communities, and the schools attached to them, had kept the light of Christian faith and classical learning alive as barbarian tribes descended upon Europe, destroying the fabric of the old Roman civilization. Europe and the Old World owed a great deal to the Benedictines. Wimmer's intention was to make the New World indebted to them as well.

The Benedictine tradition that Wimmer brought with him on his mission to America in 1846 was founded on such values as a firm and practical faith, a deep respect for history and tradition, a sense of community, and a life-long commitment to hard work and frequent prayer. Wimmer's single-mindedness and persistence—which some called his perseverance and others, his stubbornness—were manifest throughout his life. He set out as a missionary in 1846, and forty-one years later was still at it. He was deeply conscious of his participation in a tradition, in a history by which he himself had been shaped and which he, through his life's work, would reshape and confirm. He saw his work in America as a continuation of the work of the eighth- and ninth-century Benedictine missionaries in Europe, who brought the twin lights of faith and education to a period called the Dark Ages and who evangelized and essentially Christianized the northern part of the continent. Wimmer was quite specific about his relationship to history. "When we consider North America as it is today," he wrote in 1845, "we can see at a glance that there is no other country in the world that offers greater opportunities . . . , no other country that is so much like our old Europe was. [In America one finds] immense forests, large uncultivated tracts of land in the interior, most fertile lands . . . . The [people] are scattered, uncultured, ignorant, hundreds of miles away from the nearest priest . . . . In a word, the conditions in America today are like those of Europe 1000 years ago, when the Benedictine Order attained its fullest development and effectiveness by its wonderful adaptability and stability." [To the *Augsburger Postzeitung*, November 8, 1845, page 16]

Wimmer was born in the first decade of the nineteenth century, a time when Europe experienced the devastation of invasion, war, economic uncertainty, and spiritual decline. The Christian faith was at low ebb in its history. It was a time when the enemies of religion manifested their disdain more through cynical indifference than active persecution and when relativism, materialism, and secularism were embraced as the new gospel by the people who counted. Only the "simple-minded," the dreamers, those prone to "outdated" thinking actually believed in the gospel of Christ. The sophisticated, the educated, the enlightened European at the time regarded Christianity as perhaps a curious historical relic, but certainly as something that had no relevance in the modern world.

As so often happens in history, however, it was precisely at the moment when Christian faith was at low ebb that a spiritual awakening took place. In the third decade of the nineteenth century, when Wimmer was a young man, a revived spiritual commitment to Christian faith arose in Europe to counter the secularism and materialism of the Enlightenment. One manifestation of this awakening was the revival of Benedictine monasticism in Italy, France, and Germany, a monastic revival that confronted a rampant secularism and reasserted those Christian values that for centuries had formed the spiritual and intellectual foundation of Western culture. Like St. Paul, Wimmer became a convert to this reawakened Christianity. Then, after an apprenticeship of prayer, work, and spiritual formation, again like St. Paul, he became a missionary.

From the beginning, education had played an important role in Benedictine tradition. Schools were an essential part of the monasteries from the earliest times, and there had developed in them a heritage of humane and liberal learning centered on such Benedictine values as stability, community, hospitality, and moderation, all nurtured within an ambience of faith, hard work, and prayer. "We intend to establish a school for the Lord's service," St. Benedict wrote in his sixth-century monastic *Rule*. "In drawing up its regulations, we hope to set down nothing harsh, nothing burdensome."

Wimmer's aim was to imitate the models of his Benedictine predecessors and to establish strong, stable communities devoted to the service of God, the pursuit of learning, the preaching of the Gospel, and the education of youth. He believed that America was fertile soil for the planting of this ancient Benedictine tradition and that the tradition itself would contribute a new and vital spiritual energy to the young nation. In 1849, he wrote: "I have determined that our monasteries should not be simply schools for religion and learning, but should also serve as custodians of the fine arts and thus foster greater appreciation for culture, and protect our fellow countrymen from the mercenary spirit of the Americans who can think of nothing but how to make a living." [To Ludwig I, St. Vincent, July 23, 1849, page 92]

With the aid of eighteen young recruits from Bavaria,[3] he established at Saint Vincent in Pennsylvania the Benedictine community he had envisioned. Then for the remaining forty years of his life he worked tirelessly to strengthen the monastery and school in Pennsylvania and to establish others throughout the United States. From Saint Vincent, he founded Benedictine communities and schools in

---

[3] In several of his letters, Wimmer says that 19 men accompanied him to America, but the names of only 18 survive, which suggests that one must have left the community shortly after arriving in the United States.

Minnesota, Kansas, New Jersey, Texas, Illinois, Iowa, Nebraska, Colorado, Virginia, Kentucky, Alabama, Georgia, Florida, and North Carolina. By 1887, when he died, he was recognized throughout the American Church as an outstanding missionary, ecclesiastical leader, builder, and educator—a worthy successor of St. Paul, the prototype, and of St. Boniface, his patron and the Benedictine missionary who had introduced Christianity to the Germanic tribes in the early Middle Ages.

Wimmer emerged at a moment in history when Christian Faith was regarded as passé; when relativism, materialism, and spiritless rationalism were dominant in the world. How did he respond? With boldness and intelligence, with strong faith and a deep understanding of history, and with an ability to look at the world with an impressive clarity of vision. It also helped that he was stubborn. He came from a region in Bavaria where the people, like those of New England, are still famous for their stubbornness and where in Wimmer's day a popular Latin aphorism—*omnis sanctus pertinax*, "every saint is stubborn"—reflected the kind of respect that stubbornness based on principle produced. Wimmer himself quoted the aphorism with some frequency (see, for example, Letter #178 to Kilger, July 18, 1885, page 522).

There are countless stories that illustrate Wimmer's strong will and stubbornness. He refused, for example, to take no for an answer when his superiors in Bavaria repeatedly denied him permission to go to America as a missionary. Then, when he finally received permission and had arrived in America, he stubbornly refused to be dissuaded from his purpose even when every Catholic leader he consulted in New York told him that his intention to establish a monastery and school in the rural districts of western Pennsylvania with inexperienced and untested recruits from Bavaria was pure folly and doomed to failure. His later missionary foundations in Minnesota, Kansas, North Carolina, and elsewhere, moreover, would never have succeeded had it not been for his stubbornness.

Wimmer's stubbornness, like St. Paul's, led to success in his farsighted missionary endeavors when others saw only the prospect of failure. It also, at times, got him into trouble. This was most obviously the case in his encounter with Mother Benedicta Riepp, another stubborn Benedictine, who under Wimmer's auspices came from the Bavarian abbey of Eichstätt with a small group of nuns to establish the first monastery of Benedictine women in the United States.

Wimmer had invited the nuns to America, and when they arrived, he supported them with food, shelter, money, advice, and prayer. To help them establish stable communities, he sought to unite their monasteries with the monasteries of men that constituted the new American-Cassinese Congregation. Mother Benedicta had other ideas and sought to create a Benedictine presence in the United States independent of Wimmer. The result was a conflict whose details and ramifications continue to be debated by historians in the twenty-first century. When he attempted to assert his authority over the sisters, Mother Benedicta went to Europe where she denounced his alleged high-handedness to the Pope. Abbot Boniface countered with a denunciation of Mother Benedicta's alleged insubordination.

The judgment of Rome was unsatisfactory to both sides. The Holy See withdrew the communities of American Benedictine women from the authority of Wimmer and placed them under the authority of the bishops of the respective dioceses in which their monasteries were established. These bishops had little understanding of Benedictine tradition or the charism of Benedictine life and often made decisions affecting the sisters' lives and work without taking into consideration their communities' monastic character. Upon her return to America, Mother Benedicta surrendered her position as prioress and affiliated herself as an ordinary nun with the Benedictine community of women in Minnesota. Her move to Minnesota was followed almost immediately by her tragic death from tuberculosis, the scourge of communities of American Catholic nuns throughout the nineteenth century.

Wimmer's victory was Pyrrhic. Mother Benedicta and he appear to have reconciled before her death, but because of the controversy, Abbot Boniface is sometimes regarded by modern-day critics as an authoritarian misogynist who hounded Mother Benedicta to her grave. Is he guilty of the charge? We must remember that he was a man of the nineteenth, not of the twenty-first century, and was conditioned by his culture and his age to believe in the essentially hierarchical nature of society, both human and divine. For Catholics of the nineteenth century, the Church was hierarchical, monarchal, and patriarchal. Abbot Boniface viewed himself as having been given a sacred trust that burdened him with the responsibility of protecting and exercising the Church's authority over the Benedictines—men and women—in America. When he perceived anyone challenging that authority (as he thought Mother Benedicta had done), he responded firmly and unequivocally. Does this mean that he was the cruel anti-feminist he has sometimes been made out to be? Certainly not.

There are at least two sides to every story, and much has been said about the conflict between Abbot Boniface and Mother Benedicta that the founding sisters and brothers of the Benedictine Order in America would not have agreed with. The fact that his correspondence with the sisters after the controversy with Mother Benedicta, and theirs with him, are filled with expressions of mutual respect and affection points to the reality that he was not regarded by the sisters as a tyrant. Nor was he one. His letters to the sisters over the years, some of which are included in this book, reveal a generous confrere and father concerned about the welfare of the sisters and eager to do what he could to support them and their work. In a letter written towards the end of his life, he warmly acknowledges that their prayers and intercessions on his behalf were probably the only thing that would count in his favor on the Day of Judgment. Six months before he died, he wrote a friend in Bavaria:

> *It has pleased the good Lord to use me, unworthy as I am, as an instrument to bring our Order to America. He chooses the weak and the foolish of the world in order to confound the mighty. Still, as you know, I must not rest on that and am often in great anxiety about the end of my life. Nevertheless,* I trust in His infinite mercy and in the prayers of so many … religious women for whom I opened the door to the religious life. *[To Kagerer, June 28, 1887, page 542] (Emphasis added.)*

Abbot Boniface had great love for the sisters, and they for him. Indeed, he did everything in his power to help them, as they did everything in their power to help him.

When Wimmer was a young priest stubbornly attempting to convince his superiors to allow him to become a missionary in America, his confreres at Metten mockingly called him the community's *Projektenmacher*—the "plan-maker," the unrealistic visionary, the Don Quixote whose extravagant projects were bound to fail. Wimmer *was* a plan-maker, but he was no romantic dreamer. Nor was he history's slave, seeking to recreate in the present the rose-colored image of an idealized past. His pragmatism and his ability to look at the world around him with a clear and sharp vision, made him recognize that while he had been shaped by history, it was his responsibility to take the inheritance he had received and create from it something different, something new, something rooted in the past but inexorably focused on the future. His mission to America involved drawing strength, insight, and wisdom from the past in order to transform the present by prayer, hard work, and strong faith. Wimmer was a planter, a cultivator of trees. He said: "People plant trees, although they know for certain that their fruits will benefit only the next generation." [To Scherr, July 22, 1843, page 7] His plan called for planting saplings all over America. Many of them grew to become great monasteries, centers of evangelization, oases of Benedictine spirituality, learning, and education.

Possessing an outspoken character, Wimmer was frank and sometimes intemperate in his language. "I speak plainly," he said, "even in Latin." He once referred to the bishop of Pittsburgh as an "Irish scoundrel," but he struggled to check his tongue and his temper, and always expressed genuine remorse after such outbursts. He faced opposition and betrayal from some of those in whom he had placed his greatest trust, but showed uncommon magnanimity towards those who opposed him. "I have been accustomed to every kind of treachery and ingratitude," he wrote, "and would be tempted to be a misanthrope if I had not learned to make God alone witness of my intentions and actions." [To Seidenbusch, September 21, 1868, page 318]

Wimmer was a man of strong faith—faith in himself, of course, but above all faith in God. When the students who were to accompany him to America expressed their fears and doubts about the wisdom of leaving their families and homeland and accompanying him to an unknown fate, he reminded them of the cross of Christ. He wrote:

> *We should consider it a great privilege that God deigns to use us as instruments in founding an institution which, if the foundation is well laid, will confer untold benefits on the people of the United States . . . . If these are your sentiments, you will never have cause to regret having followed me [to] America. The main reason is not that you are in quest of beautiful surroundings, a comfortable home, or a life of ease, but rather that you are seeking the opportunity to carry the cross of self denial after the crucified Jesus, to save or regain souls that otherwise would be lost and for which His blood would have been shed in vain." [To Clerical Students, February 19, 1846, page 26]*

Many years later, when he had nearly completed his life's work and had time to reflect on what he and his companions had accomplished, he wrote one of those same students who had been reluctant to come to the United States, but who had come and who for forty years had been a Benedictine monk and missionary in America:

> *No one imagined us capable of accomplishing anything significant, and yet we did accomplish something. God's grace was obviously with us. . . . May unbounded thanks be given to God a thousand times, for He chose and made use of us as instruments for the execution of His designs. . . . Inasmuch as things have come this far only with the evident protection and grace of God, so may we not expect from ourselves success in the future, but again only from the grace and protection of God, who cannot fail us so long as we work not for ourselves, but for Him, for His holy Church, for the Order, and for souls. [To Englbrecht, July 24, 1887, page 547]*

The letters in this volume reveal a man of many facets—dedicated priest, conscientious monk, inspired community builder, successful land speculator, enthusiastic farmer, shrewd businessman, wily ecclesiastical politician, fearless risk taker, loyal ally, formidable adversary, outspoken but fair-minded opponent, indefatigable correspondent, wise counselor, generous friend, compassionate confrere, forgiving father, tireless missionary—and a "plan-maker" who when at last he came to the end of his life was reluctant to stop making plans. There were still monasteries to be founded, converts to be made, immigrants to be evangelized, young people to be taught, missions to be accomplished. Like St. Paul, however, he turned his thoughts in the end from earthly plans to eternity. "Let us pray for one another that we shall be saved," he wrote a friend not long before his death. Like St. Paul, he fought the good fight; he finished the race; he kept the faith. And when it was time to go, he handed the work over to his successors, his spiritual sons and daughters in the communities he had built and inspired. It is a mark of the ultimate success of Wimmer the plan-maker, and of God's blessing upon the plan, that his work, performed now by those spiritual sons and daughters, continues.

Jerome Oetgen
Feast of St. Benedict
July 11, 2008
Washington, DC

1832-1844

TO ILDEPHONSE NEBAUER   1

Altötting, May 22, 1832

Reverend and Dear Father Prior: I have had the secret desire for a long time to enter a monastery, partly to atone for the grave faults I have committed in the past, partly to amend my life for the future, and partly to work for the greater honor of God, no matter how weak my strength. In the monastery under your supervision and in union with virtuous and well-educated men, I could work out my own salvation as well as that of others. Divine Providence itself seemed to work toward the realization of my desire and to prevent misunderstanding. Immediately after my ordination, I was transferred to Altötting without having asked for this assignment. Here I learned to value the common life that I had lived in the seminary at the *Gregorium*, Munich, for two years, and for one year in Regensburg. I have learned the necessity of the common life. At the same time, I had experiences that one can have only here.

Since my decision called for departure on the 24th, I informed my confessor Father Neuhaus about it. He approved and encouraged me to go ahead. At that time, the Reverend Director[1] wrote you for information about the new house at Metten and about the prospect of my entering the monastery there. At that time, I wanted in all humility and obedience to present you with my petition to enter the monastery. I also wanted to talk the matter over with some of my friends who

---

[1] Father Joseph Albrecht, superior of the diocesan community at Altötting.

had the same intention. However, I did not want to inform them of my desire. Meanwhile, the parish of Unterneukirchen, an hour and a half distant from Ötting, suddenly became vacant, and I was installed as administrator until the bishop's curia in Passau made other arrangements. I had to stay there seven weeks until a permanent successor took my place.

This incident did not alter my decision. As soon as I returned to Ötting, I drew up a new petition stating my reasons and sent it to the bishop of Regensburg.[2] If he approves, I will send you my humble request, so that after his approval,

Rev. Ildephonse Nebauer, O.S.B.

my entry into your monastery will not be refused because of personal unfitness.

I will take the liberty to present you with the certificates of my studies at the *Gymnasium* and *Lyceum* in Regensburg and at the university, as well as the work I have done in the care of souls. If perhaps the number of those who are to be accepted into your monastery is filled already, then I would humbly beg you to notify me so that I can make arrangements accordingly. Meanwhile, I am eagerly awaiting an answer from the bishop, begging the Lord that He may make His will known to me so that I will know whether I will be so fortunate as to be called forever. Your most obedient son, Sebastian Wimmer

Ger   oAMA   cASVA   transCZ,MS   *Scrip*17(55-56)

---

[2] Johann Michael von Sailer (1751-1832), bishop of Regensburg from 1829 until his death on May 29, 1832.

TO ILDEPHONSE NEBAUER   **2**

Altötting, July 16, 1832

Venerable and Dear Father Prior: Praise be to God! I have returned safely to Öt-ting from my travels. I conferred with Bishop Wittmann[3] in Regensburg about my plan to enter a monastery. After more information, he approved my plan and told me that in God's name I should put it into effect, for neither flesh nor blood urged me to do it. In addition, since neither my dear mother, brothers, nor sisters expect any support from me, I will meet with no objections from them in proving my firm resolution.

Since my purpose and vocation in life seem to be from God, I come with a most humble and submissive request. I wish hereby to apply formally for admis-sion into the monastery over which God has placed you as prior. Please do not consider my total unworthiness and worthlessness, but rather my sincere and holy resolution to serve God in the most agreeable and profitable manner for my eternal salvation. Please allow me to enter, live, and die in the Order of St. Benedict under your guidance and supervision. That you may better understand my humble request, I submit the reasons that led to my decision. There are three reasons, and I shall state them briefly.

They grew out of the conception I had of a monastery and the monastic life in general. The founders of religious orders, and especially the father of monks, St. Benedict, seem to have had no other purpose than to erect an institution wherein they themselves and their followers would (1) do penance for sins committed, (2) preserve themselves as much as possible from sin, and (3) find motivation and means to do good.

Consequently, my reasons are threefold:

(1) To do penance for my many sins of the past by which I have offended God. Thus by judging and punishing myself, may God not judge and punish me. I have often misused my freedom. Now I offer it to God as a sacrifice so that I no longer possess freedom as men generally do whereby they can do what they want. I do not want any other will than the Rule of St. Benedict and the will of my future spiritual superior.

(2) Flight from the world and its dangers. I know very well that if I wanted to avoid all temptations, I would have to leave the world entirely. I know that wherever I go, the tempter accompanies me. I am also quite aware of the fact that, by assuming a more severe way of life, I take upon myself obligations

---

[3] George Michael Wittmann (1760-1833), succeeded Bishop Joseph von Sailer on July 25, 1832 after serving as coadjutor bishop of Regensburg since 1822.

that as a secular priest I would not have. I also know that by disobeying or by obeying only partially I would sin. I have often found the truth of the psalmist's words, "With the good I have been good, and with the bad I have been bad." I expect to find good in the monastery, more good at least than bad. I believe that with God's grace I can become good with them, for I am not good now.

(3) Conversion of morals by the common work and action of all the members of the monastery. In the world, I am entirely left to myself. However, I should be a city on top of a high mountain, visible from afar, a great attraction and protection to all strangers. However, I feel so weak, so unsure of myself, so desolate, so downcast, for I cannot be what I know I should be. I should be a light placed on a lamp stand, so that all in the house may see; but if the light itself is darkness, how can it shine? I should be the salt of the earth that prevents decay wherever applied. I should not weaken. I am so lukewarm, so poor, so needy. I need the salt myself before I can be salt to others. My weaknesses will be made strong from the strength of the other monks in the monastery. My weaknesses will be made bright from their spiritual lamp. My lukewarmness will be made warm by their zeal and fervor. The rule of the monastery will prevent me from misusing my freedom and will give me the means to do only good. Everything in the monastery is arranged around the daily praise and service of God. I am convinced that all I do, if it is according to the *Rule*, is profitable when done out of obedience, something I cannot say of many deeds I did while in the world.

Therefore, I can gain in every case once I have the good fortune of living in a monastery. At the same time, I consider it an undeserved good fortune and distinction, for I know very well that I bring nothing with me, and that what I want to be, I must acquire first in the monastery. I have thought much about what I have written and am absolutely convinced of the truth of these statements. The reasons I have stated here could easily be elaborated upon if space would permit. They are not only grounded in my knowledge and conviction, but are also the concern of my heart, which tells me that this is something necessary and counsels it as such, as well as something which must be acted upon and carried out to the full.

Before God and my conscience, I am not aware of any other purpose for my holy resolution. If I believed that I was looking for something other than the honor of God, I would never have applied to the monastery since I was dissuaded from all sides and would not have had the smallest external need. The question of whether I am fit for the monastic life is important to me insofar as it is a question of whether I have a vocation to that life. If my vocation had not been decided already, I would not have dared in the least to take it for granted. However, since God is calling me, I trust in Him that He will give me the necessary strength to follow my vocation and to cooperate faithfully with the will of His grace. This I believe myself able to do.

Since I do not have a right to form a judgment in this regard, and since I am the least capable of judging, for you alone have to decide it, I leave it entirely to your discretion to consider whether my reasons are sufficient to stand the trial and are satisfactory enough to warrant my acceptance. Once again, I take the liberty to request humbly that you consider my motives and in your wisdom judge them as genuine so that you might permit my acceptance into your monastery, to be among the number of those who have the grace to attain their salvation under your guidance.

At the same time, I humbly beg you to set the time for my entry into your monastery. With boundless love and devotion, ever ready to obey your will, I submit myself to any trials necessary to prove my obedience to the Rule of the Order and to you as my future superior. Your most obedient son, Sebastian Wimmer

Ger   oAMA   cASVA   transCZ,MS   *Scrip*17(56-58)

TO GREGORY SCHERR   3

Munich, December 8, 1841

Lord Abbot: We have received with mixed feelings the information that Weltenburg is to be restored.[4] First, we are deeply grateful that His Royal Majesty, the noble restorer of our Order in Bavaria, interests himself in promoting the success of the Order to such an extent that he plans to restore another monastery. On the other hand, it is distressing to think that His Majesty wants Weltenburg to be restored. After hearing all the information about the place and its location, about the people who visit Weltenburg for forbidden pleasures and entertainment, how can one be interested in choosing this place for a monastery? We are sad to hear of it, for we are convinced that Weltenburg, rather than becoming a training school

---

[4] Wimmer and others wanted to restore the Benedictine monastery of Mallersdorf, 20 miles southeast of Regensburg. King Ludwig I planned instead to restore the monastery of Weltenburg on the Danube. This letter was written by Wimmer and signed by six of the Metten monks teaching at the Royal Gymnasium in Munich.

for the Order, will be a great hindrance for the Order, and if we have to staff it, it will be [the Order's] grave unless God works a miracle.

If the unhealthy location of the monastery prevents anyone from joining it, who then will go to Weltenburg and what benefit will the Order receive from it? A seminary for boys? Who will see them come, these unfortunates, who during the time of flood cannot step over the threshold and go outside for two weeks at a time or longer? Or who during the rough winter, when great snowstorms have blocked the roads, will have to break their own paths? Who would want to be prefects over them and suffer terrible anxiety every day when they take a walk, fearing that one may drown in the Danube, close by, or fall down from the rocks? Concerning the pastoral care, on weekdays there are no more than six people in church. On Sundays and Holy Days, no more than 150 to 200. Terrible and poor roads, snow in winter, water in spring will all cut us off from the rest of the world. Water and snow are in the inner rooms of the monastery for weeks at a time.

As for the novices, who could imagine successfully starting a novitiate there, what with the noisy uproar of the countless guests, the loud cries and proverbial cursing of the boatmen on the Danube, and the boating and singing of the visitors? All this will disturb not only our daily peace but also our nightly tranquility. The spirit of quiet solitude and contemplation that characterizes the tranquil surroundings will be lost because of the partying, sojourning, and conversations of visitors. Concerning the economic disadvantages, the monastery will never be rich enough to entertain all the visitors who will come, and in a short time, when the canal is completed, the number of visitors will increase to a multitude that will have to be given hospitality.

The fact is that it is entirely mistaken to spend thousands of florins for the purchase and renovation of [Weltenburg] when the money can be used to much greater advantage elsewhere. Certainly, His Royal Majesty, if informed about the location and conditions of Weltenburg, would have never made that choice. His Majesty always acknowledges your wisdom and respects your judgment. No one could enlighten him better than Your Grace. You can and should speak to him. The matter has to do with a calamity that can either occur or be prevented, a calamity that menaces the future of the Order. We place our most submissive petition before Your Grace that you advise His Majesty against the plan to restore the monastery of Weltenburg, and that he use the sum of money intended for Weltenburg to restore Mallersdorf or another monastery. P. Boniface Wimmer, P. Benno Sulger, P. Augustine Hafer, P. Anton Vischer, P. Michael Preisser, P. Isidore Braun, P. Anselmo Dunfle

Ger   oAMA   cASVA   transFF

The reason you give for it, namely, that there is no necessity for the trip, can be easily refuted. During the past few days, the bishop of Pittsburgh,[12] to whose diocese I intend to emigrate, was here himself. He left for Vienna two days ago. He came here especially to find priests for his German people. Similarly, the court chaplain, Father Müller,[13] whom I also visited, has requests from Wisconsin in the United States that are far more pressing than the bishop's. Just in case you are inclined to doubt me, I gladly offer written proof.

For three consecutive years, I have been put off from one year to the next, and this year I have been completely shoved aside. It is just as if I were a child with some caprice that will easily pass away if one just stalls a bit. A man is as good as his word. That is the way I see it, and you can consider it in no other light either. At any rate, I will take every legitimate path to reach my goal. Consideration for Metten can detain me even less. As has recently been shown by Father Anthony's dismissal, an action nobody here can understand, Metten has no need of more members.

For a long time I have given much and even daily thought to this journey of mine. I understand all the difficulties: local, physical, and moral. I have also often considered that it would be presumptuous to think of forcing oneself on God as if one had a missionary vocation. I have not forgotten to ask Our Lord with prayer and pleading whether my underlying motive might not be to escape from obedience, or the desire to become a superior myself. Yet I have never to my knowledge been plagued by these ambitions. On the contrary, the result of my soul searching is always the same: my poor, forlorn countrymen stand before me and call for help. I should and want to help as best I can. I desire to go—as firmly as can be desired—with several others or alone, whichever is possible and convenient. I will not rest until I have succeeded.

I also feel shame for my Order in this affair. I ask you to see only one aim in all my labors: to have as many Benedictines as possible in Bavaria and to save as many monasteries as possible. This is my secret aim. If you can make yourself see it, as His Majesty[14] did, you will admit that I am more interested in the good of our whole Order than anyone else. Really, I think of this more than I am able to say. Just lately, I heard again from the court chaplain Father Müller that the Premonstratensians of Wiltau have established a monastery in North America. One priest has been there for several years. Now their abbot has sent him two more.

---

[12] Michael O'Connor (1810-1872), who became first bishop of Pittsburgh in 1843.

[13] Joseph Ferdinand Müller (1803-1864), court chaplain to King Ludwig I and general manager of the *Ludwig Missionsverein*.

[14] King Ludwig I of Bavaria.

The next question is, what religious order is most adapted for the American missions, not to convert the native Indians but to provide for the spiritual needs of German immigrants?

As far as I know, the only religious in the strict sense of the word now found in America are the Jesuits and Redemptorists. The missionaries of the Middle Ages–Benedictines, Dominicans, and Franciscans–are not yet represented in the New World, except by a few individuals who do not live in monasteries.[17] The Jesuits devote their energies principally to teaching in colleges; their students are mostly from the higher classes of society and many of them belong to Protestant families. Many Jesuits are also doing excellent work among the Indians, and others have charge of congregations in cities near their colleges; but while they accomplish much in their sphere of labors, they can do little for Germans, because few of them speak their language. The Redemptorists are doing noble work for our countrymen in the United States. In cities and in thickly settled rural districts, they have large congregations and do what they can for others as traveling missionaries. Some secular priests likewise go about among the scattered Catholics doing good, but they naturally and necessarily concentrate on cities where there is a large Catholic population.

We see, therefore, that much is being done in America, very much, indeed, when we consider the small band of priests and the difficulties under which they labor. However, as yet nothing has been done for the stability of the work because no provision has been made for an increase of German-speaking priests to meet the growing demand for missionary laborers. It is not difficult to see that secular priests, whose labors extend over a district larger than a diocese, can do nothing to secure reinforcements to their own number; but why have the Redemptorists and Jesuits not accomplished more in this line? By his vows, neither the Jesuit nor the Redemptorist is bound to any particular place, but must always be prepared to leave his present position at the command of his superiors, and may also request, if not demand, his own transfer for weighty reasons. This has many advantages, but for America, it seems to me also to have disadvantages; for the successor of the one who has been removed will require a long time to become acquainted with all the circumstances with which his predecessor was familiar, and even the uncertainty as to how long he will remain at any particular place will be an obstacle in his way. Moreover, the fact that Jesuits generally receive only the children of rich families, many of whom are Protestant, into their institutions, because

---

[17] Wimmer was unaware that Edward D. Fenwick, O.P. (1768-1832), first Bishop of Cincinnati, had opened St. Rose Priory near Springfield, Kentucky, in 1806 as the first Dominican monastery in the United States.

they depend upon them for their sustenance, and the fact that the Redemptorists are by their statutes required to devote themselves to missionary work and can, therefore, not be expected to take charge of seminaries, give us no reason to hope that the spiritual needs of Americans, particularly of German-Americans, will be provided for by native German-speaking priests. Moreover, in the event that the mission societies of Europe should unexpectedly be rendered incapable of supplying money or reinforcements in priests, the situation would become even more serious. Even supposing that everything remains as it is, we cannot hope to have an efficient supply of priests as long as we have no means of securing a native clergy for the United States of America; for the number of those who are educated at Altötting[18] or elsewhere in Germany is not in proportion to the continually increasing emigration to America, not to speak of the natural increase of Germans in America itself. Jesuits and Redemptorists are, therefore, doing noble work in America and their number should be increased as much as possible; but they will scarcely be able to remove the chief cause of the deficiency of German-speaking priests. We need not speak of the Dominicans and Franciscans. There are very few German Dominicans, and the present social condition of America seems not to call for Mendicant Friars.

We now come to the Benedictines, who so far are not represented in the United States. In my opinion they are the most competent to relieve the great want of priests in America. In support of my opinion, I will adduce some facts, but I must again state that I have not the remotest intention of belittling the efforts and successes of other religious orders. On the contrary, I am desirous of seeing them labor in the same field, side by side with the Benedictines.

History abundantly proves:

(1) That we owe the conversion of England, Germany, Denmark, Sweden, Norway, Hungary, and Poland almost exclusively to the Benedictines, and that in the remaining parts of Europe Christendom is deeply indebted to them.

(2) That the conversion of these countries was not transient but lasting and permanent.

(3) That this success must be ascribed to the fact that the Benedictines are men of stability; they are not wandering monks; they acquire lands and bring them under cultivation; they become thoroughly affiliated to the country and people to which they belong, and they receive their recruits from the district in which they have established themselves.

---

[18] Site of a seminary for missionary priests located in the diocese of Passau, Bavaria. Wimmer had once served as a secular priest at the famous Marian shrine of Altötting.

(4) That the Benedictine Order by its *Rule* is so constituted that it can readily adapt itself to all times and circumstances. The contemplative and practical are harmoniously blended; agriculture, manual labor, literature, missionary work, education were drawn into the circle of activity which St. Benedict placed before his disciples. Hence, they soon felt at home in all parts of Europe and the same could be done in America.

When we consider North America as it is today, we can see at a glance that there is no other country in the world that offers greater opportunities for the establishment and spread of the Benedictine Order, no country that is so much like our old Europe was. One finds in America immense forests, large uncultivated tracts of land in the interior, fertile lands that command but a nominal price. Often for miles and miles no village is to be seen, not to speak of cities. In rural districts no schools, no churches are to be found. The German colonists are scattered, uncultured, ignorant, hundreds of miles away from the nearest German-speaking priest; for, practically, they can make their homes where they please. There are no good books, no Catholic papers, no holy pictures. The destitute and unfortunate have no one to offer a hospitable roof. The orphans naturally become the victims of vice and irreligion. In a word, conditions in America today are like those of Europe a thousand years ago, when the Benedictine Order attained its fullest development and effectiveness by its wonderful adaptability and stability. Of course, the Benedictine Order would be required to adapt itself again to circumstances and begin anew. To acquire a considerable tract of land in the interior of the country, upon which to found a monastery, would not be difficult. To bring under cultivation at least a portion of the land and to erect the most necessary buildings would give employment for a few years to the first Benedictine colony, which should consist of at least three priests and ten to fifteen brothers skilled in the most necessary trades. Once the colony is self-supporting, which could be expected in about two years, it should begin to expand so that the increased number of laboring hands might also increase the products and revenues to be derived from the estate. A printing and lithographing establishment would also be very desirable.

Since the *Holy Rule* prescribes not only manual labor and the chanting of the Divine Office for all, but also that the monks should devote several hours a day to study, this time could be used by the fathers to instruct the brothers thoroughly in arithmetic, German grammar, etc., thereby fitting them to teach school, to give catechetical instruction and in general to assist in teaching children as well as adults. Such a monastery would from the very start be of great advantage to German settlers, at least to those who would live near it. They would have a place where they could depend upon hearing Mass on Sundays and hearing a sermon in their own language. They would also have a place where they could always be sure to find a priest at home to hear their confessions, to bless their marriages, to baptize their children, and to administer the last sacraments to the sick if called in time. Occasionally the Superior might send out even the Brothers two by two to hunt up fallen-away Catholics, to instruct children for their first Communion, etc. All subsequent monasteries that might be established from the motherhouse would naturally exercise the same influence.

So far, the services rendered by the Benedictines would not be extraordinary. Any other priests or religious could do the same, except that they would not likely be able to support themselves without assistance from Europe, whereas a community of Benedictines, once firmly established, would soon become self-sustaining. Such a monastery, if judiciously located, would not long remain isolated. All reports from America inform us that the German immigrants are concentrating themselves in places where churches have been erected or where a German-speaking priest has taken up his residence. This would also be found, and to a greater extent, if there were a monastery somewhere with a good school. In a short time, a large German population would be found near the monastery, much as in the Middle Ages villages, towns, and cities sprang up near Benedictine abbeys. Then the monks could expect a large number of children for their school, and in the course of time, as the number of priests increased, a college with a good Latin course could be opened. They would not be dependent upon the tuition of the students for their support, which they could draw from the farm and the missions (though these would not be a source of much income in the beginning). Thus, they could devote their energies to the education of the poorer classes of boys who could pay little or nothing, and since these boys would daily come in contact with priests and other monks, it could scarcely be otherwise but that many of them would develop a desire for becoming priests or even religious.

I am well aware that to many readers these hopes and expectations will appear too sanguine, since all efforts at securing a native American clergy have hitherto failed so signally. We must, however, remember that the annals of the missions as well as the oral reports of priests who have labored in America, inform us that these efforts were more theoretical than practical, that there was a desire of making such efforts, but that they were not really made, and that those that were really made were more or less restricted to the English-speaking clergy, and that in general there were neither sufficient means nor sufficient teachers to train a native German-speaking clergy. It is said that the young American is not inclined to devote himself to the sacred ministry because it is so easy for him to secure a wife and home; that the American has nothing in view but to heap up the riches of this world; that fathers need their sons on the farms or in the workshops and, therefore, do not care to see them study. Nevertheless, let me ask, is it not the same here in Europe? Are the rich always pleased when their sons study for the priesthood? Are all Germans in America well-to-do or rich? Are they not as a rule the very poorest and to a certain extent the menials of the rest? Moreover, is the first thought of a boy directed to matrimony? Is it any wonder that he should show no inclination for the priesthood when he sees a priest scarcely once a year; when divine services are held in churches that resemble hovels rather than churches, without pomp and ceremony; when the priest has to divest himself of his priestly dignity, often travels on horse-back, in disguise, looking more like a drummer than a priest; when the boy sees nothing in the life of a priest but sacrifice, labor, and fatigue?

All this would be quite different if boys could come in daily contact with priests, if they received instructions from them, if the priest could appear to advantage, better dressed and better housed than the ordinary settler, if young men could learn from observation to realize and appreciate the advantages of community life, if they could learn to understand that while the life of a priest requires self-denial and sacrifice, his hopes of great reward are also well grounded. Yes, I do not doubt that hundreds, especially of the lower classes, would prefer to spend their lives in well-regulated monasteries in suitable and reasonable occupations, than to gain a meager livelihood by incessant hard labor in forest regions. Let us remember that here in Bavaria from the year 740 to the year 788 not less than 40 Benedictine monasteries were founded and the communities were composed almost entirely of natives from the free classes who had enjoyed the advantages of freedom in the world and could have chosen the married state without any difficulty or hindrance. Why should we not reasonably expect the same results in the United States where conditions are similar?

Such a monastery in North America would not draw its recruits exclusively from the surrounding country, but also from the great number of boys who during the voyage or soon after their arrival in America lose their parents and thereby become helpless and forsaken. An institution in which such unfortunate children could find a home would undoubtedly be a great blessing for that country; and where could this be done more easily than in Benedictine monasteries as described above, in which young boys could not only attend school, but also do light work on the farm or in the workshops and according to their talents and vocation become priests or at least educated Christians and good citizens. Surely, many of these would gladly join the community as brothers or priests, and thus repay the monastery for the trouble of educating them. In this way, a numerous religious clergy could soon be secured, and then some of the fathers might be sent out to visit those Catholics who scarcely ever see a priest. Occasionally at least they might preach the word of God and bring the consolations of religion even to those who live at a great distance from the monastery. Small congregations could be established, and the seminary could soon furnish a goodly number of secular clergy.

Where could the Benedictines be found to establish such a monastery in North America, and where are the necessary means for such an undertaking? The writer is informed that there are several fathers in the Benedictine Order in Bavaria who would gladly go upon such a mission, and with regard to brothers there would be no difficulty whatever. Within a few years, not less than 200 good men have applied for admission into one of our monasteries. It is well known that of those who are studying for the priesthood, many are joining the Redemptorist Order simply because it offers them the hope of becoming missionaries in America.

The necessary funds could easily be supplied by the *Ludwig Missionsverein*. Bavaria annually pays 100,000 florins into the treasury of this society. Would it be unfair to devote one tenth of this sum to the establishment of monasteries in America, especially since just now hundreds of our own nationality are seeking homes in the United States, and consequently the money contributed would be used to further the interests of Germans in general and our countrymen in particular? Could better use of such contributions be made? Could anything appeal more strongly to our patriotism? Is it right that we should continually look after the interests of strangers and forget our own countrymen? Moreover, whatever would be done for the Germans would advance the well-being of the entire Church in America. We must not stifle our feelings of patriotism. The Germans, we hear often enough, lose their national character in the second or third generation. They also lose their language because like a little rivulet they disappear in the mighty stream of the Anglo-American population. Is this not humiliating for us Germans? Would this sad state of affairs continue if here and there German centers were established to which the stream of emigration from our country could be systematically directed, if German instruction and sermons were given by priests going forth from these centers, if German books, papers, and periodicals were distributed among the people, if German boys could receive a German education and training, to make themselves felt in wider circles?

Let us therefore no longer build castles in the air for our countrymen in America. Let us provide for their religious interests. Then their domestic affairs will take care of themselves. Benedictine monasteries of the old style are the best means of checking the downward tendencies of our countrymen in social, political, and

religious matters. Let Jesuits and Redemptorists labor side by side with the Benedictines. There is room enough for all and plenty of work. If every religious order
develops a healthy activity within its own sphere, the result will be doubly sure
and great. North America will no longer depend upon Europe for its spiritual
welfare, and the day may come when America will repay us just as England, converted by the Benedictines, repaid the continent of Europe.[19]

Ger   o*AugsP*   cASVA   Ellis(I:279-88.)

TO GREGORY SCHERR   9

Munich, January 26, 1846

Esteemed Father Abbot: No one is sorrier than I that you have been troubled
with gout in your fingers for so long. Like everyone else, I am sorry that you

Fr. Peter Lemke

have to suffer, but I more than others because I
have a special interest in pursuing the vocation
approved by you for which I have longed and
prayed for such a long time. If you cannot write
a few lines yourself to console me, a few lines
from a confrere would suffice. I ask for nothing
more than a simple statement or repetition of all
that we have written and discussed, namely, that
you release me for the purpose of contributing
to the spreading of our Order in America by the
founding of one or several monasteries, and that
I will be released forever if I succeed in founding a monastery as large as Weltenburg, and that
you authorize me to do so. It would be better still
if you would notify Rome and assign me to this
work as the tool of your own intention, but if you
are unwilling to do that, at least give me the writ-
ten authority to do it. If you refuse to do even that, then I must respectfully ask

---

[19] Wimmer refers here to the historic fact that England, converted to Christianity by monks from
Italy at the end of the sixth century, sent English monks to German lands in the eighth century to
convert the people there. The leader of the English monks in the conversion of Germany was St.
Boniface.

for a "yes" or "no" so that I will know what to do and what not to do. Otherwise, I will do wrong on all sides.

I received a letter from Father Lemke[20] who informed me that in anticipation of my arrival, he has promised the bishop of Wisconsin,[21] 300 miles farther inland in America, that he would come to him next spring to minister to the Germans who are entirely abandoned there. At the same time, he wrote that he was seeding 25 acres with wheat so that we will not lack the necessary sustenance for our company. He has also enlarged the house so that we will have enough room. I replied that I could not come before autumn since I cannot leave the parish, but that I will come at that time. Father Müller[22] continues to urge me to go and supports me as much as he can. He says that secular priests from Europe, with few exceptions, are not good missionaries and usually have little success. Only monks can help. Whoever knows the conditions will be of the same mind. That is why we must do something.

I will not turn back now, and if I cannot work there as a Benedictine, I will do so in a different habit, as I have told you previously. I will not alter my plans and intention. If you do not trust me or think that I cannot govern a monastery (which I will not dispute), and if this is the only thing you fear, then let someone else accompany me. No matter what his name is, I will be glad to serve under him, but something must be done—of this I am firmly convinced—and it must be done by us. My road can be made difficult but cannot be blocked. I can be held back and slowed down but not stopped. I go my way because I firmly believe that God wills it. He who has removed so many difficulties already will also remove the others that I see coming. Therefore, I respectfully request a written reply to the following points: (1) whether I am dismissed permanently, (2) whether I will be given the authority to found a monastery of our Order, (3) whether I am permitted to accept suitable brothers and novices for this monastery, (4) whether you yourself will apply for permission to found a Benedictine monastery or shall I have to apply for it as I originally planned.

I cannot be satisfied with the permission given earlier because that permission no longer covers my present plans. Encouraged by some confreres and by Father Müller, I have told Father Neuhaus[23] that for the present I will submit so that in the end I will be certain that I can make the journey. What I have said should not

---

[20] Peter Henry Lemke (1796-1882), the German missionary in Cambria County, Pennsylvania, who had invited Wimmer to establish a Benedictine community in the diocese of Pittsburgh.

[21] John Martin Henni (1805-1881), bishop of Milwaukee.

[22] Joseph Ferdinand Müller (1803-1864), manager of the *Ludwig Missionsverein* and court chaplain to King Ludwig I of Bavaria.

[23] Wimmer's confessor, a secular priest.

be considered the words of a subordinate to his superior designed to obtain his object by obstinacy, but rather to prove to you that I am not acting by caprice or by a sudden inspiration. I know what I am doing, and I earnestly consider it as the strictest obligation. With all my heart I would prefer to have my present superiors send me rather than simply dismiss me. As a last resort, if they prove pitiless, I will join another order in which the superior will fulfill my desire. I do not want a higher rank, God knows, but only the missions.

I must make another request. Please revoke your order that I preach every Sunday while the other fathers preach only on feast days. We do not have sermons on feast days. That would leave the others idle while I do all the work. [Text missing] I know and hope that I will not be able to do it. I did not merely advise him; I also helped him in a friendly way. Yesterday I gave the eighth sermon for him. Besides me, Father Ferdinand is the only one who has ever preached for him. I will preach again next Sunday and, if necessary, every Sunday, but I suffer greatly from this, for I have three hours of English studies. I admit that I cannot put myself wholeheartedly into my work adequately if I have to give the sermons on Sunday. Naturally, I can never do anything for the lesson preparations, nor enough for the sermons on Sundays, for it is a different thing to preach to students than to preach to farmers.

Money and time count very much where I am. I cannot be as good a priest as I should if I have to study French besides. I have to help in religious exercises too, and I have something else to do, as last year. I also have to hear confessions. Where do I get the time to do it? But if it has to be done, I will do it....

Hoping for an early reply and decision, I remain with the greatest respect, your most devoted, Boniface Wimmer

P.S. I am very sorry if I have grieved you in any way.

Ger   oAMA   cASVA   transFF

TO CLERICAL STUDENTS   **10**

Munich, February 19, 1846

My Dear Candidates: In reply to your communication regarding our proposed mission to America, I wish to submit the following. If I rightly understand the tenor of your letter, you wish to inform me that as matters now stand you are not satisfied with the mere prospect of becoming Benedictines and missionaries in America, but that you are anxious to know whether I intend to take you with me at once, or leave you in the Institute until you complete your regular course of studies, or send you to one of our monasteries to become acquainted with the *Holy Rule*. You also intimate that unless you first live here under the *Rule*, you might later regret the step that you are planning to take. I can even see the beginning of wavering in your resolution to follow me. I do not find fault with you for submitting these questions, and in response, I wish to send you the following reflections for your serious consideration:

(1) You must above all be determined to become priests and good priests.

(2) You must be determined to become religious not only to be united to Christ more closely and follow Him more faithfully, but, if necessary, to do more for Him, to suffer for Him, and not by any means to go with the intention of becoming priests more easily or, still less, to escape temporal cares.

(3) The vocation to the priesthood in itself is a great grace, and that to the religious state a greater one, because it is a state of perfection, and that to the missionary life still greater, because it is an apostolic vocation.

(4) We should consider it a great privilege that God deigns to use us as instruments in founding an institution that, if the foundation is well laid, will confer untold benefits on the people of the United States. If you consider this well, you will not put yourself forward without vocations. If, however, you feel the call within you, you will not allow yourselves to be deterred by obstacles from following this impulse, because the greater the sacrifice, the greater the reward. We will be able to say to Our Lord with Peter, "Behold we have left everything and have followed you; what therefore will we have?" Undoubtedly he will give us the same answer that he gave to Peter, recorded in the Gospel of St. Matthew, chapter 19, verse 28 ["I tell you this: in the world that is to be, when the Son of Man is seated on his throne in heavenly splendor, you my followers, will have thrones of your own, where you will sit as judges of the twelve tribes of Israel"].

Charles Martin Geyerstanger (1820-1881), one of the four clerical students who accompanied Wimmer. He was the first Benedictine ordained in the United States.

If these are your sentiments, you will never have cause to regret having followed me when you are in America. The main reason is not that you are in quest of beautiful surroundings, a comfortable home, or a life of ease, but that you are seeking the opportunity to carry the cross of self denial after the crucified Jesus, to save or regain souls that otherwise would be lost and for which His blood would have been shed in vain.

What I know of America I have learned only from hearsay and from what I have read. I must be prepared to meet all possible emergencies. I am giving up a comfortable and honorable position and cannot reasonably expect another. I am leaving behind relatives who are poor and therefore stand in need of me. I am parting from kind superiors and confreres who honor me and only reluctantly allow me to go. I am renouncing a position in which everything is well ordered to enter upon an entirely new state of life in which everything has to be started anew and be put in order. I do this because I am interiorly urged, although I take upon myself difficulties, cares, and hardships. My heaviest burden will be that I must carry out my plans with men whose willingness, confidence, and vocation have first to be tested.

You see, therefore, that I have no advantage over you. I am willing to take you along because I am confident that you will gladly share my joys and sorrows in the service of God and our neighbor. If you join me, you must be animated by the same confidence in me. If you cannot have this confidence in my integrity, my honesty, my zeal, my experience, and my determination, do not go with me. Under such conditions, you would not obey, and I could not keep you. We must all be animated by a mutual love and confidence in one another. Perhaps next to confidence in God, these qualities will often be the only means to console and support us in our difficulties and hardships. Through harmony, small things grow; through dissension, great things are destroyed.

To that end, you should consider it a privilege to be allowed to take part in a work like this. I will be glad to have good and zealous helpers, but you must not imagine that you are doing me a favor by going with me. The reception into a religious order is something that must always be sought and asked for, no matter how welcome an applicant may be to a community. For this reason, do not go with me to please me, but on the contrary, consider yourselves fortunate and honored if you are found worthy to take part in such an undertaking. God is able to raise up children of Abraham from stones. He made Paul out of Saul. If my undertaking is from Him, He will send me co-laborers, wherever they may come from. I am sure of this. Therefore, I will not persuade or entice you to go and thus render you unhappy if you have no vocation. You will never have cause to cast this up to me. I do not know the future. I only show you the cross. If you take it upon your shoulders, very well. Do not, however, complain afterwards when from time to time you feel its weight. Jesus said to his apostles, "Behold, I have told you beforehand," and "Behold, I send you as lambs among the wolves." If you are frightened when you hear their howling and see their gnashing teeth, then stay at home. If with the grace of God you have not the courage to do and suffer these things for Him, to go wherever obedience requires, to allow yourselves to be used as willing tools, then do not enter the monastery and by no means go with me to America. It is true that in America men are free to profess whatever religion they please. Non-Catholics are more numerous, powerful, and wealthy than Catholics. We cannot tell how long they will respect the laws. It is possible that they may persecute us and put us to death. I can vouch for nothing. I am prepared for everything. Whoever wishes to follow me must also be prepared.

As you desire to go with me, it will not be necessary to complete your course of studies. In America, no one will ask you whether you have completed your entire course of studies. However, if you wish to finish it, it must be done before July, and I hope to obtain this favor for you. The preparations for it will have to be made here. Moreover, I would not advise you to enter a monastery here to make your novitiate before you leave. You would soon become accustomed to many things that you will not find in America, and this would result in unpleasant comparisons. I know of a religious community that receives no one who belonged for even an hour to another community.

Whether it would be better for you to accompany me or to remain and continue your studies is a difficult question to answer. Although I have given the matter much thought, I am unable to say which is preferable. If you wish to accompany me at once, I will take you along without much ado, but your decision must be made soon because I will have to make arrangements accordingly, as two may have some difficulty getting released from army service. You will have time to become acquainted with the *Holy Rule* before you leave. As soon as the copies I ordered arrive, we can begin instructions immediately. It will not take long to read it and you need not fear it, for it is very moderate. You must also obtain the consent of your parents and guardians. Only after I have a written statement of this will I be able to arrange matters with the government, and I must do so before Easter.

Each one will take along what he possesses. Whatever may be left after the fare to America has been paid will be his until he makes his religious profession. After that, it will belong to the community. However, if one has poor relatives, he may leave it to them, according to the *Holy Rule*. He who has little will take little. Let each one endeavor to get as much as may be required to secure an outfit, namely, the necessary books, a habit, clothing, etc. The money that I have will be sufficient for a time if we work a little. Work in the fields and other hard work will naturally devolve upon the lay brothers, but at times, we may be obliged to lend a helping hand. The housework, apportioned according to each one's physical condition and with regard to the fact that they are preparing for the sacred ministry, will fall to the lot of the clerics. When I begin to explain the *Rule*, I will inform you of the order of the day, insofar as it may be determined at present. The details can be arranged only after our arrival. We will have everything that can reasonably be expected: a house, clothing, food and drink (at least good, fresh water). We will have time for prayer, meditation, and study, for practice in teaching and preaching, and for other useful occupations so necessary to ward off the evils that result from idleness.

If to all this everyone adds good will and cherishes a kind regard for his brother, then our little monastery will be a veritable paradise. Even if suffering, sickness, poverty, or persecution should occasionally be our lot, as they are not wanting in any place, still they will be like pepper and salt to season the monotony of our daily routine. They will remind us that there is nothing perfect here below and that we must carry the cross of affliction because the road to heaven is narrow and thorny. Let there be no Judas among us. Let no temporal considerations motivate us. Let not ambition be our goal. Do not render my life or yours miserable through such aims. If you feel that you are weak, it is no disgrace to stay at home, but to come along without being animated by pure and holy intentions would be acting the part of Judas.

From this, you know my opinion in the matter. Consider well whether you are satisfied with what I have said. May God guide you in your decision. I will not entice you, nor will I tempt you to go, but I will take you along if you desire to follow me. P. Boniface

Ger   cASVA   transFF,GB   Fell(V:41-44)   Bridge(60-64)

TO THE *LUDWIG MISSIONSVEREIN*   11

Munich, February 26, 1846

Esteemed Central Committee of the *Ludwig Missionsverein*: For many years, I have had a great desire to work for the Catholic Church in the United States. In my thoughts, I am frequently occupied with the problem of a continuous supply of priests, especially of priests who are able to speak and to understand German. Since there is a shortage of these priests in America, I believe the best remedy would be the founding of monasteries of our Order. Benedictines, because of their broad purpose of self-sanctification and their wide interest in the care of souls, in education, study, and research, could fulfill the many needs of the Catholic Church.

The most important problem for the founder of a monastery is that of support. In order to attain the necessary stability for a foundation, it must have a regular income that should not be diminished except under extraordinary circumstances, and then only for a short time, and should never be entirely exhausted. I have, therefore, obtained a substantial amount of land from which we hope to attain our livelihood by manual labor, as did our Benedictine ancestors. Under this plan, which should be profitable, we will find it possible to accept poor boys to be formed and educated for the priesthood. Of course, this would not materialize during the first years because great expenses would be incurred in erecting the necessary buildings; but I hope in time, especially after the community has increased, to open a school in which young boys of well-to-do families would be formed and pay for their education.

The property on which to build the monastery was given to me by a note dated June 15, 1845, by the missionary Mr. Lemke.[24] He did not inform me about the price of this land. I, therefore, do not know what to expect. Meanwhile, he did speak of 8,000 florins for the real estate. Before his departure, he also spoke of selling the cattle and the buildings at auction. I hope his next letter will give me the information I need. Nevertheless, I would like to accept Mr. Lemke's property, under favorable circumstances, since 100 acres of it are under cultivation and planted for this year, and next year's grain requirement has been taken care of. Moreover, the necessary farm buildings and at least one small house are already there. A community of about 700 Germans has also settled there.

My very reverend lord abbot[25] was hesitant about allowing me to leave because we ourselves are short of personnel, and he would not allow me to go as a simple missionary; but in the hope that more could be accomplished by founding a monastery, he finally consented to give permission as the recommendation below indicates. Since I myself do not have the means to carry out my plans, however, I am forced to turn for support to the mission society that is known for the invaluable help it has given to Catholic missionaries and especially the loving kindness it has shown for our German settlers in America. I venture, therefore, to submit to the esteemed central committee my most humble request for a gracious grant of the necessary funds for making the first foundation of a Benedictine monastery in

---

[24] Father Peter Henry Lemke (1796-1882).
[25] Gregory Scherr, O.S.B., of Metten (1804-1877).

the United States, for the purpose stated above. I leave to your kindness and wise judgment the amount of money required. I will certainly strive to make the best use of the amount provided, and I promise to promote the purpose of the mission society. An account of the money expended will be rendered.

I confidently hope that my good will and the unselfishness of my intention will not be misinterpreted and will bring me the necessary support. I remain with respect and submission to the honorable central committee, your obedient servant, P. Boniface Wimmer, O.S.B., Prefect and Professor of the Catholic Educational Institute [Munich]

[Attachments]

Copy [Lat]

> *With this document I freely dismiss Boniface Wimmer, a professed monk of this house in good standing, to this end: that he may labor in the American missions for the honor of God and the salvation of souls and that with legitimate authority he may establish one or more monasteries of the Order of St. Benedict. Nor do I intend to revoke this permission except for grave cause or unless the project fails. Metten, February 14, 1846. Gregory, Abbot*

[L.S.] A true copy
Jos. Ferd. Müller, Business Manager

Copy [Ger]

> *On the advice of Dr. Michael O'Connor, bishop of Pittsburgh, I assure P. Boniface Wimmer, O.S.B., of his acceptance and that of several lay brothers into the diocese of Pittsburgh. I also pledge to give to him on his arrival in America a tract of land with the necessary buildings to allow him to live according to his Order. Munich, June 15, 1845, Pet. H. Lemke, missionary authorized by the bishop of Pittsburgh*

A true copy
Jos. Ferd. Müller, Business Manager

Ger   oALMV   cASVA   transIG

TO GREGORY SCHERR   **12**

Munich, March 16, 1846

Esteemed Lord Abbot: The reply from Propaganda[26] arrived almost at the same time as your permission. Of course, it contains permission only for my going personally to the missions and not permission to found a monastery. After your first permission to leave, I did not want to apply to Rome for it, but later I was induced to do so by Father Neuhaus and also by Father Augustine's answer.[27] The latter also told me that at present I should apply only for permission to go to the missions, hoping to get the rest later on. He was afraid that if I waited any longer I would lose a year's time. A reply to the petition to found a monastery could come only after your permission to do so had arrived. I left a request for its approval by Rome at the Nunciature. Only the Nuncio[28] considered it inopportune to write so soon for it and advised me to write for permission first to the bishop of Pittsburgh.[29] After that, he would write to Rome himself. This permission could also be obtained when I am in America.

My letter may arrive in Pittsburgh in a few days, but I cannot expect a reply before the end of April. As there is no doubt that the permission will be granted, I should start now to prepare for the journey. I have to take care of a lot of correspondence with my future novices and have many things to think about, but I am not anxious or sorrowful. Six thousand florins have already been formally approved for me by the *Ludwig Missionsverein*. I am also expecting a letter from Lemke any day.

I must decide how many persons I can take with me, depending on how far our money will go. Besides Enzensperger and Krammer,[30] who are still to be ordained over here, another theological student from the university and five very good ones from the upper classes want to go with me. Some of the others who want to go I am leaving behind to follow later, partly because there are too many, and partly because I do not trust them, even though they have excellent testimonial letters.

---

[26] The Sacred Congregation for the Propagation of the Faith, the Vatican Congregation from which Wimmer sought permission to go to the United States as a missionary.

[27] Neuhaus, a secular priest, had been Wimmer's confessor before he entered the monastery. Father Augustine was probably Father Augustine Hafer, O.S.B., of Metten.

[28] Archbishop Carlo Morichini, papal nuncio to the kingdom of Bavaria.

[29] Michael O'Connor (1810-1872), bishop of Pittsburgh .

[30] The last named is probably Amandus Engelbert Krammer (1827-1889) who though not among the original pioneers joined Wimmer's community in America in 1851. Enzensperger is unidentified.

At least 12 brothers, who will be employed in the fields and in the house, will go with me according to my present plans. I am also to recruit and take along 12 brothers for the monastery in Wisconsin that three Premonstratensians from Wiltau have recently established. Their abbot cannot find candidates in Tyrol because emigration is taking a heavy toll there. Accordingly, he notified Father Müller, who in turn asked me to hire the necessary men, farm hands, gardeners, masons, etc. The only requirement is that the men be good.

At Easter, I must see whether I can get someone to donate the necessary altar linens. This will be my last vacation trip. Therefore, I will be able to get to Metten only at Easter time. I would like to ask for 1,000 florins in Mass stipends. I already have the exact data on the journey. I will start from Würzburg, go to Rotterdam by river steamer, and from there to Havre by boat, then from Havre to New York by sailing ship. It will cost 75 florins. If at all possible, I must set out about St. James's Day [July 25], for otherwise we would be caught by the dangerous September storms. There is still enough time, but I have many things still to attend to. I beg for your mementos and a good visit among my confreres. Please continue your accustomed favor and kindness. I will always be your most respectful and thankful, P. Boniface

P.S. At first, I had intended to take action against Baron von Schenk, but now I think it is better to wait. The minister will defend us.

Ger   oAMA   cASVA   transCZ,CW   *Scrip*18(71-72)

TO GREGORY ZIEGLER   13

Munich, June 9, 1846

Right Reverend Bishop: Having waited, not without some concern and anxiety, for news of how my letter to you would be received, my joy and surprise was so much the greater when I received Your Grace's most kind letter of May 30. I rushed through the lines at once with impatience and could hardly believe my eyes as I read of the generous support you are prepared to give my undertaking.

I also suppose it more than mere accident that I received your letter on my namesday [June 5, the feast of St. Boniface] immediately after Holy Mass. It was as if the great and holy apostle of Germany, the founder of so many famous monasteries, especially in Bavaria, had himself written to me through Your Grace. I must not be fearful or anxious about whether the work that lies before me is great, and the material and personal strengths for its completion small. The ancient

God, who is pleased to be served by weak instruments for the accomplishment of His purposes and to whom all honor alone is due, still lives and knows means and methods sufficient to help the weak in ways no one expects. I must not lose sight of my single goal–the greater glory of God–and I am confident that I will gain His protection. One must be prepared to contend with many obstacles, but through courage, perseverance, and confidence in God, one will overcome them all.

Thus has your paternal kindness on June 5 enriched an unforgettable day for me, an epoch in the history of my endeavors for the missions. I wasted no time informing my abbot about it and faithfully copied your handwritten letter to send him, for I no longer allowed the manuscript out of my hands for any reason. If, as I confidently hope, I found a monastery with God's help, in its archives the original letter will be the most treasured document. I quite happily leave to my abbot further, more detailed communications with Your Grace–communications, which at my humble request will doubtless begin promptly. Although in your kind letter you left untouched the questions my own letter raised–the breviary and the choir prayer of the brothers–these matters nonetheless have great importance for me inasmuch as I do not consider myself competent to rule on them without at least having heard the advice of higher authorities. Since you are such an authority yourself, I would value your opinion, even more because you are a Benedictine, who knows the condition and needs of the Order, and a high priest. Thus, Your Grace will consider it completely natural that I continue to cherish the hope that you will send an answer to the questions referred to above before the press of time–I will leave here on July 20–makes it necessary for me to decide the matters myself.

I want to express my wholehearted thanks to Your Grace for the kindness and loving sympathy you have shown me and my enterprise. Many with whom I have discussed my plans have shown themselves skeptical. Still, I have found some who have encouraged me, among whom is our gracious and good king,[31] who in a lengthy audience on June 4 urged me on with the most vigorous approval, consented to my plan in all respects, expressed his heartfelt joy over it, and promised his strongest protection and support.

Because it is no longer possible for me to do so in person, I hope that Your Grace will accept the written assurances of my warmest gratitude and filial loyalty, with which in deepest reverence and subservience this letter ends. Your Grace's most submissive son, P. Boniface Wimmer, Professor and Prefect

Ger   oADL   cASVA   transABu

---

[31] Ludwig I of Bavaria.

TO GREGORY ZIEGLER   **14**

Munich, June 30, 1846

Right Reverend Bishop: I was sorry to hear yesterday that my abbot[32] had still not conferred with you on the matter of my mission. The abbot planned to travel to Linz himself but was repeatedly prevented from doing so. However, in the first few days of the coming month, this week in fact, he will make the trip, according to his letter to me.

In the meantime, I take the liberty of passing along to Your Grace a letter I just received from the missionary Mr. Lemke. He has decided on the place where I will establish myself. His bishop[33] has also promised to send me a letter soon. It is true that the bishop has spoken of a restriction (expressed to me in an earlier letter I did not receive, so it was probably lost), but since he says that the matter will be easily resolved, I presume it is about testimonials from my own bishop, which I failed to send with my request for acceptance. Mr. Lemke's letter reads:

St. Joseph's, May 28, 1846

Dear Friend: Yesterday I received your letter of April 2. You speak of two letters you had written me, but I know of only one, and in that one you still give me absolutely no definite information about our business. Perhaps one was lost. I am heartily pleased that the matter is now finally in order. As for the questions you put to me, I can say nothing with certainty in reply. I will sell you at once the entire property I have built up with much trouble and care over the last ten years. It consists of about 400 acres of land, of which over 100 are under cultivation. Plenty of uncultivated land exists around here. One piece of 300 acres, which borders mine, I have more or less purchased, but I did not sign the agreement because I did not know whether I could rely on your coming. Meanwhile, it will not run away from us, and I think it best to wait until you are here. At that time, we will have my property evaluated by three impartial men expert in these things. I have considerable livestock, moveable goods, and furniture, and expect a bountiful harvest. If you want to add it all up, the whole thing will no doubt amount to somewhat over $4,000 (i.e. 10,000 florins). Of this, however, I spent $1,000 that I received from the Leopoldine Foundation[34] expressly for this community. Furthermore, $1000 does not have to be paid at once, but may be paid

---

[32] Gregory Scherr, O.S.B., (1804-1877) abbot of Metten.
[33] Michael O'Connor (1810-1872), bishop of Pittsburgh.
[34] The Austrian Catholic mission society.

gradually in annual installments of $200. I will not only remain here until you arrive, but perhaps will also spend the entire winter with you in order to help you at the beginning, for people, when they first arrive from Europe, are often like infants just emerged from the womb, or like people just fallen to earth from the moon. Perhaps I will become a Benedictine myself, or build myself a hermitage in your vicinity, for the world is thoroughly repugnant to me. In addition, in case I go, I will be leaving a real treasure here for you, namely a lad, born in this country of German descent, who has a vocation to the monastic life if ever a man had one. He speaks English, knows the land and its ways, and is skillful in every kind of farm work and carpentry. Your coming is generally known around here, and all are longing to see the sons of St. Benedict swinging axes in the American forests as they did a thousand years ago in the German forests. Kindly give Fr. Müller[35] the enclosed receipt from O'Mealy. God be with you! If you do not write me any more from Germany, then write me at once from New York, where I will go to meet you. Yours, Peter H. Lemke

I had already discussed this purchase with Mr. Lemke last year and provisionally settled the matter with him. This year, however, as I received no answer from him for four months, I almost began to doubt the sincerity of Lemke's promise. In order not to arrive at last at the settlement in the greatest difficulty because of uncertainty, I had recourse, through the mission administrator, Court Chaplain Müller, to several Redemptorist missionaries in America for information about where a Benedictine monastery conforming to my plan could best be established. They recommended the state of Illinois, diocese of Chicago, where I had decided to move. Now, however, I am staying with my earlier destination: St. Joseph's settlement, Cambria County, Pennsylvania, diocese of Pittsburgh, in the beautiful Allegheny Mountains, at the origin of the Susquehanna River, seven hours from Loretto where Prince Gallitzin[36] worked so long and so profitably that almost the whole county is Catholic. The place is indicated in Dr. Salzbacher's travel accounts.[37] The place has much to recommend it over distant Illinois. Settling there

---

[35] Joseph Ferdinand Müller (1803-1864).

[36] Father Demetrius Augustine Gallitzin (1770-1840), an émigré Russian aristocrat, was one of the first Catholic priests ordained in the United States. From 1799 until his death, he worked in Cambria County, Pennsylvania. Known as the "Apostle of the Alleghenies," his cause for canonization is under review.

[37] In 1842, Canon Joseph Salzbacher of Vienna made a trip to the United States on behalf of the Austrian Leopoldine Foundation to ascertain the condition of German-speaking Catholics in America. His report, *Meine Reise nach Nord-Amerika in Jahre 1842*, published in 1845, stimulated Wimmer's ideas about how best to serve German Catholics across the ocean.

would be much easier for me because I will find a house with farm buildings and a wooden church. Likewise, I will have a nice harvest and a nice garden. In addition, it is only a day's journey by train from Philadelphia, almost midway between that city and Pittsburgh. Thus it is very well situated for a monastic motherhouse, where new arrivals can first become acclimatized and then, if others follow later, can turn westward with the flow of immigrants. Moreover, Pennsylvania has many German inhabitants, and though from a pastoral perspective there is less to do here because the Redemptorists have already settled the region,[38] there is always more to do for education. Then from Pennsylvania, one could easily explore, over time, the question of where still another monastery could be suitably located. On the other hand, in Chicago, I would have to begin quite at the beginning, and everything would be new at first. Because of this, my brothers might lose courage. In addition, the climate in Chicago is warmer, and Germans would find themselves less suited and less healthy for that reason.[39]

The price of land in Pennsylvania is, I admit, markedly higher. However, one can take advantage of the fact there is a large city nearby and that communication with the coast is very good and rapid. I believe therefore that Your Grace will also agree with my decision. Perhaps [Lemke's] letter will give you the information you desire about the land I hope to purchase. In any case, I believe Your Grace should be familiar with the letter because with it a new undertaking in a new era of development has begun. There are many details in the letter that resolve the difficulties that from the beginning have hindered the way, difficulties that the finger of God, everywhere manifest, interceded in solving. May the Holy Spirit at all times guide me, that I may always and everywhere perceive this finger of God, heed it, and go only where and as far as it points me.

This letter will also bring a bit of news to my abbot, but because I assumed he probably would not have received it, I did not send it to him. I hope that from your discussion with my beloved superior, Your Grace will also draw the conclusion that I did not decide on the missions in order to become a fugitive or to free myself from the constraints of the monastery or out of ambition or other worldly motives, but rather because as long as I have been a Benedictine and a priest I have felt the desire and inner drive for missionary work, and indeed for many years sought through petitions and presentations to procure (though in no way to extort) permission to follow this desire. Likewise, the remaining matters that I felt I needed to communicate about my earlier circumstances and efforts will also be confirmed throughout.

---

[38] German Redemptorists were serving parishes in Philadelphia and Pittsburgh.

[39] Where Wimmer got the idea that Chicago was warmer than Pennsylvania is unknown.

Because my companions (17 brothers, two of them third-year theologians and one a priest) and I have not yet completed preparations for the journey, our departure from Munich may be postponed until July 22, and our embarkation from Havre de Grace can thus take place only on August 8. I will not fail, unless I become too bothersome, to provide Your Grace with news periodically from America about the new little monastery, if it pleases God to let me succeed. For students and laymen who may want to follow me next year, news will not be lacking.

With the humblest prayers for your blessing, I commend myself most submissively to your continued good will and close with deepest respect. Your most humble and obedient, P. Boniface Wimmer, O.S.B., Prefect in the Royal Educational Institute [Munich]

Ger   oADL   cASVA   transABu

TO GREGORY SCHERR   15

Munich, July 16, 1846

Right Reverend Father Abbot: I have already received a letter from the bishop of Linz.[40] He mentioned your letter, but to my regret he said nothing at all about the travel fare, other than that he would contribute his goodly mite to the success of my endeavor. Nor did he say anything about the breviaries, etc. Thus, since I cannot scare up enough copies of the Maurist breviary, I will have to use the common one, much as I dislike it, unless I can find some of the other at St. Stephen's.[41] Nor can I immediately get the fare for my novices–five clerical students and two lay brothers–nor for the parish priest and myself. Thus, my cash-on-hand will turn out to be quite meager indeed. Added to this, Krammer[42] still has some debts that must be paid.

I now have two places where I can settle: either in St. Joseph's, Pennsylvania, with Lemke,[43] or at St. Mary's, Illinois, in the diocese of Chicago, where Bishop Quarter[44] wants me. I have the 6,000 florins from the *Missionsverein* on hand. I also have the dismissorials from Regensburg with the *prima nota* and a letter of

---

[40] Gregory Ziegler, O.S.B., (1770-1852) bishop of Linz, Austria, one of the principal contributors to the Benedictine mission to America.

[41] St. Stephen's Abbey, Augsburg.

[42] Probably Amandus Krammer, O.S.B. (1827-1889), who entered the novitiate at St. Vincent in 1851.

[43] Father Peter Henry Lemke.

[44] William Quarter, bishop of Chicago 1844-1848.

recommendation from the local bishop here. All that we need for the voyage and the initial accommodations we have. Of course, this outlay cost me 1,200 florins, but some rich lay people have reimbursed me for most of it. With regard to the church, I have been quite amply provided for. Without my asking—but encouraged mostly by my penitents—acquaintances and strangers, people of high rank like Baroness von Abel, the Princess of Löwenstein, the Baroness of Würzburg, Baron von Wibeking, the Countess of Rechberg, etc., and people of lower rank have contributed church linen, altar vessels, and money, amounting to about 300 florins.

Now I must again humbly ask to be acknowledged, formally and in writing, as the superior of the mission, so I may have the necessary ecclesiastical authority over my people, and will be able to prove my legitimate jurisdiction to my future ordinary. I dislike having to make such a request, but it is necessary that some ecclesiastical title be added to the name "the Reverend Boniface." If not, authority can hardly be upheld in the land of freedom. Except for this, I believe everything is taken care of, provided that the Holy Spirit, who is, of course, the most important element, is on our side. Certainly, God will not wholly deny the prayers full of faith and confidence offered to Him on my behalf by many devout souls in many places.

I have closed my account and will leave here on July 24 or 25. I go forward to life or death, whichever pleases God. I hope that in the future I will not lose the courage and confidence that have never left me and in times of difficulty have even become greater. *Dominus pars hereditatis mei et calicis mei* [the Lord is the portion of my inheritance and my cup], which when I am given it to drink will most probably be quite bitter. I have not merited anything better. May God, through the merits of His Son, be willing to forgive me for all those things I meant to do well but did badly. Most of all, may He forgive me the evil that I have deliberately willed or done.

I trust also in your fatherly and fraternal love for me. Again, I humbly beg your forgiveness. I have asked pardon, similarly, of my other confreres for any offenses by which I might have scandalized them. I have received numerous proofs of their brotherly love and indulgence, which are so much the more meritorious for them insofar as I am wholly unworthy of such treatment. I earnestly beg them all to continue in this sincere brotherly love. I shall always remember them in my prayers for the absent brethren. I especially beg you that my future foundation be admitted into the family of monasteries for which prayers are said at Metten, that fraternal charity might increase among us.

Now I must close, for the day after tomorrow I must face the *absolutorium*. Professor Höfler is the *commissario*. I do not yet know whether I will be able to write again before my departure. Certainly, however, I will write from Havre just before we embark. All my novices except one, Wolfgang,[45] are full of confidence. He is like an old woman who can never make up her mind. If he does not back out by himself, I will advise him to do so. He does not have firm confidence in God or in me, and for a decision such as this, one needs both.

Most likely, you will be able to arrange with Bishop Ziegler everything that can be settled now. My reports from America will enable you to complete this successfully. I recommend myself to your continued favor and kindness. I remain with sincere and grateful love, Your Lordship's most humble son, P. Boniface Wimmer

Ger   oAMA   cASVA   transCZ,CW   *Scrip*18(74-75)

TO GREGORY ZIEGLER   **16**

Mainz, July 30, 1846

Right Reverend Bishop: It was not possible for me to answer from Munich Your Grace's kind letter because I was too much preoccupied with preparations for my departure. Despite the many important affairs with which you are occupied, I ventured to ask for a response to my most humble inquiries. That I have been stubbornly persistent has its basis merely in the implicit confidence I place in your highly regarded experience, knowledge, and ecclesiastical spirit, and is in no way out of disdain for my superior. I am well aware of what is customary at Metten. However, that custom has not existed long, is neither proven nor approved of in all respects, is not in accordance with original usage, and, besides, conditions at Metten are completely different from what they will be in America. [At Metten] there are only three lay brothers, while I have 16 of them. On the other hand, there are many priests and clerics at Metten, while I have only five.

If the prayer life of the lay brothers is neglected, it will be a grievous error. Our breviaries are few. If all do not pray the breviary, the choir in America will have to be held at different times and by turns, because with the modest space in the church and the house, one party would disturb the other. After careful consideration, I have therefore decided that the brothers must also pray the breviary. I was confirmed in this decision by a lengthy discussion with a pious and learned

---

[45] Unidentified. In the end, he did not accompany Wimmer to America.

confrere in Weltenburg, and by a passage in the writings of St. Alphonsus Ligouri who believed that difficulties arising from the lay brothers' ignorance of Latin can be avoided by providing short summaries of the main ideas in the psalms, so that during the recitation of the Divine Office, they might be thoroughly occupied with attitudes of love, trust, praise, and worship.

Unfortunately, in my haste I have been able to collect only six breviaries for the clerics. Hence, I had to grab up some Einsiedeln editions. Whether the Maurist edition might be better, I will have to decide later because I do not know the Maurist [breviary] well. Should Your Grace favor the Maurist edition, I would gratefully accept and could use thirty copies. In that event, I could receive them through Court Chaplain Ferdinand Müller of the *Ludwig Missionsverein*. (He lives in Munich, in Maxburg.) If not, then I will find other means.

Through my abbot, I received while in Munich 200 florins from Your Grace designated as travel money. For this generosity, as well as for all the other unde-served expressions of your good will and favor, I wish humbly to express my affec-tionate, loving thanks. May we never fail to pray for the reward of heaven. With God's help, I hope not to disappoint the confidence and hopes of my benefactors, sponsors, and friends. If these hopes are fulfilled, Your Grace will not regret hav-ing found the cause that I represent worthy of your attention, participation, and gracious support.

With intense awareness of my poverty, feeling the need for the pious prayers of all God-pleasing people, I commend myself once again to your remembrance before God and remain, with feelings of deepest gratitude, in respectful devotion and childlike reverence, Your Grace's most humble and obliged, Rev. Boniface Wimmer, Superior of the Benedictine Mission to America

Ger   oADL   cASVA   transABu

TO GREGORY SCHERR   17

On Board the Packetboat Iowa at 50° Longitude,
September 1-11, 1846

Right Reverend Lord Abbot: Upon my arrival in America, I will likely have more than enough business to attend to. Therefore, while still aboard ship, I want to give an account of my ocean experiences. Then when we land, I will only have to complete it. We set sail at noon on August 10. Because of the unfavorable wind, a steamboat towed us about a mile and a half out of the harbor. There we floated. Only a slight breeze was stirring, hardly enough to flutter the sails. Two other three-masters and several smaller boats had been towed from the harbor with us. Very slowly all moved in a southwesterly direction, close to the southern shore of the beautiful bay upon which Havre is situated. We could see far up the Seine River Valley. At Havre, the river's mouth is about twelve miles wide. Strictly speaking, it is no longer a river here, since the color of its water differs from the sea only near its bank.

Towards evening, we were probably 15 or 18 miles from the city. We were steadily approaching the French coast near the dangerous Calvados. Finally, when the two lighthouses on the heights near Havre were lighting their mighty flames, the captain turned the ship northward. The wind having risen during the night, the next morning we found ourselves near the English coast close to Portsmouth. We soon made a quick turn southward. By evening, we could again see the coast of France and the lighthouse at Cape Beaufleur. The sails were then reset for sailing north-northwest, and by morning, we saw the English coast near Cape Portland. Immediately the ship again turned southward, and Thursday morning [August 13] we once more sighted the French coast, Cape la Hague, and the Isle of Aurigny about four and a half miles away. Then after the sails had been reset and the ship put about, we headed north once more. Before long, a storm arose. It lasted all that evening and night and nearly drove us into the bay of Plymouth. The captain remained on deck continuously. I was there with him until late at night and very early in the morning. I could not sleep anyway, since my bed was constantly tossed back and forth. When day broke, we saw the English coast about a mile and a half away and the mountains that encircle the bay [of Plymouth]. To our left we saw that lonely rock, Eddystone, in the sea. Upon it stands a slender tower that serves as a lighthouse. Then, the storm still raging, quick orders were given to reset and turn the still usable lower sails. In a few moments, we were again sailing southward, the treacherous rock on our right and the coast behind us. Now at last we sped along. The storm soon subsided and towards evening, we were finally driven out of the English Channel. We could tell this by the color of the water, for it looks green in the North Sea and the Channel. In the ocean, it looks almost inky black or at least very dark blue and appears green only in the breaking waves and the spray at the ship's bow. On Saturday evening [August 15], we saw the coast of Ireland, but not very clearly since the sky was overcast. About Monday noon, we again saw Ireland because contrary winds had once more swept us north. A driving north-northwest wind, which tilted the ship precariously to one side, followed. The ship rocked so much that all tumbled head over heels upon each other and no one was able to walk or stand up.

All passengers with few exceptions became seasick during this storm. Whole families just lay there, so sick they felt they were dying. Wherever we stood or walked, we saw and heard people vomiting. It was especially appetizing when, sitting at table, one after another quickly ran to regurgitate what they had just swallowed. The cabins where the sick, lamenting and shrieking, vied with one another at vomiting, were just as bad (excuse my words!). Although I used to be bothered by such scenes, I steadied myself this time and so far, the ocean cannot boast of having overcome me. On the contrary, I can eat and drink more than ever. I am now quite convinced that I will not become seasick, but even among my own group many succumbed to it. The locksmith, the gardener, the stonemason (Mr. Sailer[46]), and the mechanic (Mr. Kreis[47]) have been sick from the beginning of the voyage. Others, such as my nephew,[48] the cook, the tailor, etc., did not get sick at all. They cooked not only for the rest of us, but also for those who were entirely helpless.

From this, Your Lordship can see that the ship is sailing very slowly and that there is little of the pleasure trip in a sea voyage. We have had favorable wind for only two days. During the rest of the time, the wind has been more or less contrary, and thus only partially useful. On two days, we even lay becalmed for several hours. It was especially true on the feast of the Holy Guardian Angels, when we had wonderful weather, but unfortunately no wind. I thought of Metten while renewing my vows to Our Lord. In spirit, I renewed them in union with all my confreres there.

Nothing else worth mentioning has taken place aboard ship. So far, we have seen only a few ships during the voyage. We saw a herd of porpoises three times, and they accompanied our ship for several hundred paces. On the feast of the Guardian Angels, we also saw several larger fish in the distance. Daily we see swallows, fish hawks, and some sea plants. Otherwise, there is only the immense water surface, which several miles away appears much higher. Thus, we always seem to be sailing with our three-masted ship in a little valley. Incidentally, our ship is an excellent sailboat. It has outsailed every ship we have met.

On August 17, I discovered that there was on board with us a nephew and a relative (with his wife, sister-in-law, and mother-in-law) of the Frenchman Piguet, founder of the colony at St. Mary's in Illinois. Meeting these people was most

---

[46] Joseph Sailer (1820-1891), one of the brother candidates.

[47] Unidentified. Presumably one of the brother candidates who abandoned the mission shortly after its arrival in the United States.

[48] George Wimmer, another of the brother candidates. He joined the monastery but did not remain.

welcome for many reasons. The bishop of Chicago has entrusted the spiritual ministration of St. Mary's to me.[49] I can now get excellent information regarding that region and my future position there. These were items about which I still had much to learn. If I go there, I will find a two-story house plus a church. There will also be about 200 acres of real estate, which will be left to me *gratis*, along with the house.

Still it irked me that these people were always near us and never hinted that they were Germans. (They are Alsatian.) Every day they heard the three of us, i.e., the Reverend Max from Wiltau,[50] the Reverend Edmund von Hall,[51] and myself, speaking in German. I personally am little inclined to serve a French speculator, even though Germans form the majority in his colony. Furthermore, my German sensibility is opposed to living closely with Germans who are ashamed of their language and origin. The situation here has lately altered quite a bit. These people are now quite friendly and eagerly seek our company and companionship. Nonetheless, if I can arrange something at St. Joseph's with Mr. Lemke, I would rather go there than to Illinois. My next letter, which I will write soon, will bring you further information in this matter.

With regard to food and drink, life on board ship is good. At 8:00 am, a bell rings for rising. Breakfast at 9:00 am consists of coffee or soup, cold meat, fried mutton, warm ham, and some cereal. At 12:00, the noon lunch of soup, cold meat, and cheese is served. The dinner or main meal comes at 4:30 pm. At this meal, the captain at the upper end of the table and the lieutenant at the lower end pass around small cuts of various kinds of meat: beef (very well preserved), pork, goose, duck, or chicken. There are also three or four kinds of cereal foods. Dried plums, raisins, hazelnuts, coffee, etc., are served in great abundance. There is also good Bordeaux wine in sufficient quantity. The meal lasts at least an hour. A Negro and a mulatto cook the food, two mestizos have charge of the cellar, and a German waits table. Everything is prepared in the English style and is not much to our taste. At 8:00 pm, we have supper served with tea, to which we add milk, and pastries. We go to bed whenever we choose, usually not before 10:00 or 11:00 pm.

---

[49] William Quarter, bishop of Chicago (1844-1848), had offered Wimmer the French colony of St. Mary's in Illinois to establish his monastery. For a while, Wimmer considered going there rather than to Pennsylvania.

[50] Father Maximilian Gärtner, O. Praem., the Norbertine monk who was leading a group of missionaries to Wisconsin.

[51] Unidentified.

The salon and the individual cabins are very elegantly furnished. The floor is covered with carpets and all the doors are of precious, polished wood. The beds are quite narrow but good; they are always double-decker beds, and we are just able to sit up in them. The women's cabins have their own salon, which is not open to us. We are situated one story higher than the common folk. None of them is allowed either to enter a cabin or to come onto the cabin deck. During days of fair weather, these people are invariably on deck. When they sleep or eat, and in rough weather, they remain in the steerage below our feet. Below them is the freight and thousands of huge rocks that serve as ballast. One hundred and seventy-four persons in this steerage area have paid their way. Three got on board as stowaways and were discovered only far out at sea, when it was too late to turn back. One of them, a tailor's apprentice, has to feed and care for the chickens, geese, and ducks as punishment. The second young fellow has to look after the cow and the pigs. The third is a woman who has to do washing. Two thieves, French brothers, also got aboard. They ransacked the trunks in the lowest part of the ship and stole several sets of keys, gold watches, and other precious articles. These they hid in several strongboxes bound like books. A sailor discovered them by accident. They were taken into custody and locked in the lowest part of the ship. They get out into the fresh air only during the daytime. One of our countrymen from the Bayreuth region stole 600 florins from the strongbox of a compatriot but was soon caught. Because he confessed and returned the money, he was set free. The people in steerage are remarkably diverse in character. There are several good families living next to some disorderly young men and other people. Among these latter are six females from Württemberg, two of whom are real models of impudence. Others have lice, which they gladly share with their neighbors.

My 19 men are together and finish out the row on one side toward the window in the back part of the ship. Luckily, they are numerous; otherwise, they would not fare so well. According to my instructions, they pray a rosary, aloud and kneeling, every morning, afternoon, and evening. At first, there were difficulties. Some of their fellow passengers laughed, others whistled or sang, and still others did something else. However, with patience, earnestness, and, when necessary, measures of greater firmness, they grew more peaceful. By now, their prayer is proceeding quite well. I must admit that the many Jews on board are quite tolerant. It was several Württembergers and Frenchmen who needed to be threatened. We especially felt like stuffing their mouths when they purposely disturbed us. After a while, even some of the better sailors participated. To be sure, I am very well satisfied with all my companions.

The kitchen covers the main deck on both sides of the foremost mast. It smokes fearfully, and there are just too many cooks. It is really a cross to have to cook there. Potatoes and ham are the principal foods. Water is scarce and of poor quality. The wine is already weak and sour. Hard biscuits in place of bread are not appealing. Coffee without milk is hardly good for anyone. Everyone longs to see land, but that won't be granted us for ten or twelve days.

We did not forget to celebrate His Majesty's namesday.[52] In addition, I often think of Augustine, that old fox, who used to give me such a hard time.[53] I won't soon forget either of these two days. On August 25, an extremely strong wind tilted the ship sharply to one side. We had a very restless night. In the morning, I felt as though all my bones were broken from the tossing. On the night of St. Augustine's feast, a mighty storm raged that lasted until noon the next day. It was so bad that the waves often washed the deck, and again all our patients had a relapse.

Down in our cabins, we have been especially annoyed by three boys and a little child. They constantly run, quarrel, fight, and yell. Because of them, I can hardly get anything done when the weather prevents me from going up on deck. Nevertheless, I managed to review my entire English grammar again, and even squeezed in a certain amount of regular reading. The four students handle the breviary quite well already. They pray the entire office aloud in common.

September 11

On September 2, we came very close to a disaster. We were near the coast of Newfoundland, where many boats are engaged in cod-fishing. The sea is only 200 feet deep there and is shrouded with a heavy fog. We could hardly see 60 paces ahead. Suddenly we rammed into a beautiful little three-masted fishing boat anchored there. As soon as the sailor on watch yelled, "A ship!" everyone leaped forward to loosen the sails and thus check the ship's forward movement. However, it was not possible. We were going too fast. Neither boat could swerve out of the way, since the fishing boat was anchored, and we were speeding with the wind. It was about 3:30 pm. Horrified, we awaited the crash. I expected that one or both ships would go to the bottom. Then came the collision. Our ship rebounded. The other, being smaller, had its side rammed in. Its rear mast snapped off like a brittle stick when the yard lines and sails of both ships became entangled. On our ship, a plank up front was ripped away and the figurehead on the bow, a life-sized wildman, was demolished. This was the only damage we suffered. Whether or not the

---

[52] The feast of St. Louis, August 25.
[53] The feast of St. Augustine of Hippo, August 28.

other ship suffered any further damage, I cannot say, because we quickly lost sight of it again in the fog. Thus, we escaped with a good scare.

What took place in the early morning of August 28 was a little more comical. The storm tore off a crosspiece from the mast. The crosspiece hit the deck next to the kitchen with a terrific crash. Since the latter was just then emitting much smoke, someone assumed that something was burning inside. He yelled into the steerage, "Fire!" All the people there were still in bed, but in a flash, they came rushing up to extinguish the fire and to save themselves. The first to bound up the stairs was a seventeen-year-old Jewish boy. He had hardly set his foot on deck when he fell backwards and landed solidly on his posterior. There he lay sprawled out on the deck. His first movement was to stick his hand back there to see if everything was still intact. Over on the other side, one of my men, Mr. Geyerstanger,[54] dashed up in his underpants, trousers in hand. He leaned against a handy water barrel so that he could slip into his trousers, but try as he might he couldn't do it because of the pitching ship. When he saw it was a false alarm, he had to beat a retreat in his white underpants. There were many other such incidents also. I still laugh when I recall them.

Now after two windless days we are having wonderful weather with a good wind. We are still 200 miles from land. We have seen several whales in the distance and a large shark quite near. On the eve of the Nativity of Mary [September 8], we were surrounded by schools of large fish intent on paying honor to "The Star of the Sea." On September 10, we saw some very fine northern lights. Today is a wonderful day.

Every day now, I have long discussions regarding St. Mary's with the Alsatians I mentioned above. One of them even drew me a diagram of the layout. I can plainly see that the site will not be adequate unless Mr. Piguet adds about two or three hundred more acres of land to it. I explained this and received a definite promise. The vivid description these people have given me regarding the lamentable religious situation in Illinois scarcely permits me to abandon St. Mary's. Still I don't want to relinquish St. Joseph's. Certainly, Mary and Joseph belong together. I will give my reasons and plans in my next letter. For now, I can only report that I have definitely decided to go first to St. Joseph's and there await and accept whatever the future has to offer. I certainly hope to celebrate the Queen of Heaven's namesday in New York.

---

[54] Charles Martin Geyerstanger (1820-1881), one of the four clerical students accompanying Wimmer. He was the first Benedictine ordained in the United States.

All my men are now quite well except the locksmith, Mr. Wittmann from Kelheim,[55] who is still suffering somewhat. With the hope of seeing land soon, all the hardships of the voyage are forgotten. All are happy to have made the trip. They are also full of courage, expecting everything to go well in the new world because there are enough of us to help ourselves in all things as far as work is concerned. As for myself, I am burdened only with uncertainty as to my destination and future work. However, this worry too will soon be over.

Since I am sure that Your Lordship wants to know as soon as possible whether and how we crossed the ocean, I have written these lines. I did it with great pleasure since I was with you in spirit while writing. I now look much healthier and feel stronger than I did in Munich. I have God alone to thank and beg Him to grant me good health in the future, at least until others can take my place and continue the work that has now begun. Not only because we are now far from each other, but also because we are united in a common love of God, let us seek and greet each other in Him and also in the most Blessed Hearts of Jesus and Mary. With a most grateful love and loyalty, Father Boniface

Ger   oAMA   cASVA   transCZ,CW   *Scrip*18(76-82)

TO JOSEPH MÜLLER   18

Mount St. Vincent, October 26, 1846

Reverend Court Chaplain: When you see the name of the place where this letter is written, and the date, you will probably say, "Why is he not at St. Joseph's?"[56] We changed our residence and are now 50 miles southwest of that first colony in one of the most beautiful and salubrious spots in America for a Benedictine monastery. The most reverend bishop[57] offered me two farms of 315 and 150 acres. They are the foundation of Father Brouwers,[58] a pious missionary who lived here towards the end of the last century and donated them for the support of the pastor to minister to the Catholics who are scattered over the whole county. The bishop also wishes me to start a seminary as soon as possible to educate young men for

---

[55] Placidus James Wittmann (1814-1867), one of the brother candidates.

[56] St. Joseph's church in Cambria County, Pa., where the Benedictine missionaries first settled.

[57] Michael O'Connor (1810-1872), bishop of Pittsburgh.

[58] Theodore Brouwers, O.F.M. Cap. (1738-1790), founder of Sportsman's Hall parish, which became St. Vincent.

St. Vincent College, Beatty, Pa.
St. Vincent's in 1846.

Saint Vincent as it appeared when Wimmer
and the Benedictines arrived in 1846.

the priesthood. At present there is no such institution in the country,[59] but such a
school is most necessary for the Church in the United States. Boys of the wealthier
classes usually study for secular professions. For this reason, almost all the secular
clergy are of foreign birth: Irish, German, French. The whole diocese of Pittsburgh
has only one native-born American priest,[60] and he, although of German descent,
understands little of the language of his ancestors. Other dioceses are in a similar
condition. Therefore, priests are not only too few for the number of people, but
being foreigners often do not have the confidence of their parishioners. Moreover,
they themselves come to understand the mind of the people only gradually, especially if in mixed populations they speak only one language.

The Irish and German Catholics usually live close together, and when the pastor, even if he resides among them, speaks only one language, one part of the
congregation seldom hears a sermon or is without spiritual assistance in the confessional and when sick. What is still worse, almost all the schools are controlled
by non-Catholics. Therefore, missionary seminaries, not in Europe, but here in

---

[59] Wimmer means here that there is no Catholic seminary exclusively for German-speaking students.
[60] Father James Ambrose Stillinger (1801-1873), a native of Baltimore. Stillinger served as pastor of
St. Vincent from 1830 to 1843 and at the time of this letter was pastor of SS. Simon and Jude parish
in Blairsville, thirteen miles from St. Vincent, and vicar general of the diocese of Pittsburgh.

America, will be the only means of solving the problem. Our people are so well convinced of this that no other method is ever mentioned. Such institutions must be established on American soil. Likewise, everybody concedes that only a religious order can maintain such seminaries for poor boys because such institutions must have a sufficient and assured income. Lay brothers by their work can provide this support. Unfortunately, endowments are so far non-existent. Thus, only an order that has lay brothers can hope to succeed at present. A mendicant order cannot carry out such a plan because it possesses no property. Therefore, the situation that confronts us calls for an older order that in addition to its priests also has lay brothers. This is the Benedictine Order with its varied membership. Here our Order has all the opportunities to rise to new life. I defended this theory in Bavaria, and now I am glad to find it confirmed here by experience.

How far this Benedictine foundation corresponds to those ideals, only the future can tell. Everything is dependent upon the blessing of God who can give both the inspiration and the fulfillment. Anyone who considers the meager means with which we have made the start might have misgivings about the success, but as history teaches, everything that God does begins slowly, proceeds gradually, and often succeeds contrary to human plans and expectations.

With respect to myself, nobody can be filled with greater fear than I. Yet we must remember that God can raise children of Abraham from stones. This is the basis of my hope and confidence. The foundation is laid, the beginning made, the temporal support given—not only for me and my companions but also for others who are willing to work with us. What we need most now are good priests, or such who soon can become priests and who have a true vocation for religious life. I do not doubt that the Lord will send them because He knows best what is most necessary here.

Although our community is not yet fully organized, we are keeping the following order as well as we can. We rise at 3:45 am to meet in the parish church where at 4:00 am I say Matins and Lauds with the four students in the choir loft while the brothers recite one-third of the Rosary and other prayers in the sanctuary. At 5:00 am, when the sign is given, meditation begins and lasts an hour. After that, I say conventual Mass. This is followed by a frugal breakfast for the brothers while we [Wimmer and the clerical students] recite Prime, during which the *Martyrology* and a chapter from the *Holy Rule* are read. The rest of the morning, the brothers work and the students attend classes or study, with a short interruption at 9:00 am, when we recite the Minor Hours.

At 10:45 am, all are called again to the church for adoration of the Blessed Sacrament and particular examination of conscience. At 11:00 am, we take dinner, after which the students have a short recreation and the brothers receive instruction in the religious life. At 1:00 pm, the brothers recite the second part of the Rosary and then work until 5:00 pm. During that time, the students have classes or lectures, which are interrupted by the recitation of Vespers at 3:00 pm. All attend spiritual reading or the explanation of the *Holy Rule* from 5:00 to 6:00 pm, followed by supper. Then a second recreation or housework until 7:30 pm, when the brothers recite the third part of the Rosary and we say Compline. Finally, common night prayers and general examination of conscience conclude the day. At 9:00 am all retire. . . . [letter incomplete]

Ger   oALMV   cASVA   transFF   Fell(I:76-79)

TO GREGORY ZIEGLER   19

Mt. St. Vincent near Youngstown,
Westmoreland in Pennsylvania
November 5, 1846

Most Reverend Bishop: From the attached letter of the bishop of Pittsburgh,[61] Your Grace is informed that I have successfully crossed the ocean and, furthermore, have already found a place excellently suited for a motherhouse of our holy Order. Indeed, I went first to St. Joseph's[62] and spent time there with my 19 confreres (two of whom were separated from us during the trip). From September 25 until October 16, I was happy to stay there, but when I was unable to come to an agreement with the owner of the property[63] because of the excessive price and difficult terms, an offer came just in time from the bishop of Pittsburgh, as though sent from God.

   Mount St. Vincent (as the place where I now am is called) lies in Westmoreland County in Pennsylvania, in the diocese of Pittsburgh. It is 22 hours away from St. Joseph's but only 16 hours away from Pittsburgh, and is located in an uncommonly beautiful and fertile region not far from the Philadelphia-Pittsburgh highway and only half an hour from the little town of Youngstown, through which the highway passes. It is situated on a pleasant hill that slopes gently down to a valley

---

[61] Bishop Michael O'Connor.
[62] St. Joseph's church, Hart's Sleeping Place, Cambria County, Pa., was the first place that Wimmer and his companions settled. They remained there only three weeks, moving to St. Vincent at the invitation of Bishop O'Connor.
[63] Father Peter Henry Lemke.

*A stained glass window depicting Wimmer's arrival is
located in Saint Joseph's church, Hart's Sleeping Place.*

on the east, south, and west sides but climbs higher towards the northwest. It is
not a village but a wilderness with only a church and, perhaps 50 paces east of it,
a building presently occupied by seven Sisters of Mercy and 18 pupils whom they
instruct. South of this building, perhaps 60 paces, lies the farmhouse, and west of
this a new house intended as a schoolhouse, where I will live with my men until
the sisters and the founder depart on April 17.

All about lie our fields and meadows, and beyond that our woods, a genuine
oak forest. The farm buildings are miserable, but the others were built quite recently of brick. A monastery could be built here, such that none lovelier could
easily be found. Only ponds are missing, and I can easily provide them, although
then I would have to sacrifice our lovely meadows. However, the best choice for
them would be on the south side, if I can buy the land for it from my next-door

neighbor. Then a mill could also be set up. My neighbor to the north sold his property of 300 acres for $20 or 50 francs per acre. Much of that property would be quite suitable. Besides these two houses, one sees only four others at some distance because although the view on three sides is vast and beautiful, hills and bush hide the desolate places, and besides, there are not many villages in America. Within the cloister, there is a well with a pump. Also, next to the farmhouse is a running spring.

Now this is where the most reverend bishop long desired to establish a religious community that in addition to the care of souls would also maintain a minor seminary. He found none, however, until I came. Hence, he received me with the greatest joy, offered me the entire diocese, urged me to settle down here, and promised to give me the property for the Order if I would settle here. It certainly cannot become our property in such a way that we could dispose of it at will or sell it or use it for anything we like, because a bequest was made by a German missionary named Brauer[64] that from its revenues at least one priest could be supported who would undertake the care of souls for the Catholic settlers nearby. The bishop of the diocese, at his discretion, can give the property to whoever fulfills this condition.

Half the local Catholics who live within a radius of five to seven hours are German, the others Irish. In a common effort, they built the large and beautiful church in 1835 for about $8,000, of which a few thousand remain to be paid off from the pew rent, which amounts to $700 annually. The schools are all in the hands of the Protestants, and since my people cannot yet speak English, and everyone here wants to learn English, I cannot do much about it, although something should be done as soon as possible.

I am the only German priest in the whole county, which numbers 42,000 inhabitants, almost all originally German though scarcely more than 2,000 are Catholic. Not many more colonists are expected here because the place is already fairly well populated and is already costly. However, there is good reason to hope for converts. Had there been German priests here, one would hardly have found so many people who had lost their faith, which unfortunately until now has not been such a rare occurrence. For that reason, the place is already important, but even more important because it is very well suited for a minor seminary since Pittsburgh, where 7,000 German Catholics and as many Irish Catholics live, is not far away.

---

[64] Theodore Brouwers, O.F.M. Cap. (1738-1790), the founder of Sportsman's Hall Parish. On Brouwers and the early history of St. Vincent parish, see Omer U. Kline, O.S.B., *The Sportsman's Hall Parish, Later Named Saint Vincent, 1790-1846* (Latrobe, Pa.: Saint Vincent Archabbey, 1990).

In America, one must seek Christians in the cities, not in the country, just as in the time of the Roman Empire when heathen *pagani* were despised because those country folk were the last to be converted to Christianity. The cities are where most of the boys are who have the desire and disposition for studying, provided one gets them at 12 or 13 years of age. The country folk, on the other hand, having no domestic servants, use their sons for labor, and the girls work only in the home. The Redemptorists in Pittsburgh told me they could provide several talented, well-behaved lads for me every year, if I could take them in *gratis*. I think we could handle about 50 of them, especially if I could buy some more land and with a growing staff of priests set up a seminary for paying students. Since the bishop still has 10 properties similar to St. Vincent in his diocese, they could, after a brief time, become so many monasteries. In addition, if even a few boys found an education in each, think of the results! Other orders that do not have brothers to do the farming would have to hire servants who must have [?] dollars a year salary. Most orders cannot afford that, but we can, as is generally supposed here, if the brothers do well. Until now, I have not had the least cause to doubt it, since my men, the seventeen[65] that I now have, are all animated with the best spirit.

Our order of the day is as follows. At 4:00 am, we go to the church where I pray Matins and Lauds with the four students and the lay brothers capable of it. The others pray the rosary. From 5:00 to 6:00 am I hold meditation with all the men. For this, the untrained lay brothers have books. At 6:00 am, we have Holy Mass, after which the brothers take a little broth, but I pray the Minor Hours with the students and take no breakfast. The lay brothers then work until 10:45 am while the students have *lectio* and then study. From 10:45 until 11:00 am, we have particular examination of conscience in the church. Lunch is from 11:00 to 11:30 am. There is free time until 1:00 pm, a period also used for lessons because, if possible, I would like to have them all in the choir. At 1:00 pm, the lay brothers pray another rosary in the church and then go to their work until 5:00 pm. I have Vespers at 3:00 pm, then a lecture, and then from 5:00 until 6:00 pm explanation of the *Holy Rule* and spiritual reading. At 6:00 pm, we have dinner, after which there is free time until 7:30 pm when Compline and the rosary close the day.

We eat meat twice a week. We have only water to drink. All are satisfied, all confess and receive communion weekly, and I see with joy that the best spirit prevails among us. I need ten workhorses and many supplies, without which I am in trouble if no help is given because I lost several thousand with the trip and mov-

---

[65] Two of the lay brothers had become ill on the journey from New York to Pennsylvania and remained in Hollidaysburg, Pennsylvania, until they recovered and rejoined the community at St. Vincent.

ing back and forth. With the coming of spring, I must begin reconstructing the farm buildings, that is, the shed and stables, and build a suitable place to house my men. Then the monastery will be expanded. For the present, we will build a smithy and a scriptorium and various facilities. We still have the nicest warm days for doing this.

With this report of my experiences thus far, I pledge the assurance of my deepest respect and subservience, and the most affectionate entreaty for the continued good will of Your Grace. Your humble, most obedient, Fr. Boniface Wimmer (called) Superior of the Benedictine Mission in America

Attachment [Lat]

November 5, 1846

Rev. Michael O'Connor,
(1810-1872),
bishop of Pittsburgh.

I have named the Reverend Boniface Wimmer, O.S.B., pastor of the church of St. Vincent near Youngstown in this diocese. The pastor has the right to an estate of 500 acres, which when well cultivated seems to me sufficient to support 50 or more monks. For the present, the estate is the property of the pastor. I am prepared, however, to regulate the matter in such a way that the superior of the Benedictine monastery to be established here will always be pastor and have full and complete rights to this property. From the fact that the estate has been given to the pastor there arises no other obligation than that he attend the pastoral care of the neighboring Catholics, either he himself or through another. As soon as the Benedictine fathers are ready to take over this church permanently, I will transfer the rights in such a manner that neither civil nor ecclesiastical laws can disturb them. I gladly give [the Benedictines] permission to establish in this diocese other monasteries in which they might lead a monastic life and devote themselves either to the education of youth, both for the secular and clerical states, or to engage in the care of souls. Michael O'Connor, Bishop of Pittsburgh

Ger   oADL   cASVA   transABu

TO THE *KATHOLISCHE KIRCHENZEITUNG* OF BALTIMORE 20

Mount St. Vincent, December 14, 1846

Maximilian Oertel, Editor: I arrived in New York on September 15 of this year and on September 30 at St. Joseph's, Cambria County, Pa., where I stayed with all my people until October 16. I came to this place (Mount St. Vincent) because I discovered that St. Joseph's afforded a livelihood for only a small community even though the Most Reverend Bishop O'Connor considered it the best location for a foundation of the first Benedictines in the United States. I found Mount St. Vincent more suitable for the cradle of the Benedictine Order in the New World.

My reasons for settling here were not only to establish religious life in a monastery that would labor for the pastoral care of the souls of my German people (until they became thoroughly acquainted with the English language), but also to extend this care to English-speaking Catholics, and especially to educate German boys for the priesthood (and, in time, also Irish boys). This project will be undertaken on a small scale next year.

My community, upon arriving in America, consisted of only four students (one of whom will be ordained this year) and fifteen lay brothers who are presently with me. Since then the community has been increased because the Reverend Father Michael Gallagher, who voluntarily resigned the pastorate of this same parish but remained here as assistant pastor for the English-speaking parishioners, joined our Benedictine Order on the feast of the Immaculate Conception.[66] Furthermore, Father Nicholas Balleis[67] of Newark, New Jersey, who came from St. Peter's in Salzburg, made the generous decision to devote all his energies toward establishing our Holy Order in the United States, to which he has already given so much honor and fame by his former labors. I have most graciously cooperated with him and hope, with the grace of God, that still more priests will become available and that, in due time, the Benedictine Order will plant deep roots.

All credit goes to the Most Reverend Bishop O'Connor for permission to transfer to the more suitable place, Mount St. Vincent, for the foundation of the Benedictine Order in America, and certainly the entire Order will always be grateful.

---

[66] Gallagher (1806-1869) remained at St. Vincent until June 1847, when he left to join the Augustinian Order in Philadelphia.

[67] Nicholas Balleis, O.S.B. (1808-1892), was pastor of St. Mary's church, Newark, N.J. He had come to the United States in 1836 and worked as a missionary among Germans in Pittsburgh and New York. He was one of the priests Wimmer consulted upon arrival in America. At the request of Balleis, Wimmer and the Benedictines of Saint Vincent took over St. Mary's parish in 1856 and established a priory that in 1884 became St. Mary's Abbey.

Fr. Boniface Wimmer, Superior and Pastor at Mount St. Vincent, Youngstown, Westmoreland Co., Pennsylvania

[P.S.] On the third Sunday of Advent Fr. Gallagher publicly received two adult Protestants into the Catholic Church.

Ger   cASVA   transIB   *Katholische Kirchenzeitung* (Baltimore), December 25, 1846

TO KARL VON REISACH   21

Mount St. Vincent's, March 1, 1847

Most Reverend Archbishop: Before my departure from Munich, Your Grace had the kindness to receive me in a long audience and to hear a report on the purpose and aim of my trip and the manner of its execution and–what was no small encouragement to me–to approve my project. Since then everything has gone better than expected. I attribute this to the power of the Holy Sacrifice of the Mass that you had the graciousness to solemnly celebrate before the journey, and for this reason, I will not forget that our mission stands in close relationship to Your Grace. What I proposed in Munich (which after long and mature consideration I have always considered a necessity) has not been lost from my sight:

(1) Monastic life was my first aim. I have organized it here and am confident enough to say that in no Bavarian Benedictine monastery is the *Holy Rule* more exactly observed than among us. My merit in all this (if I may say so) is nothing other than that I explain the *Holy Rule* to my people and tell them what they have to do. I have found in all of them a joyful compliance, which has not slackened for a moment, to lead a life pleasing to God according to the trusty *Rule* of St. Benedict. In this regard, I cannot thank God enough that, driven by His Holy Spirit, such a considerable number of staunch people have gathered around me. If all are not equally industrious and thoroughly permeated by their vocation, most are, and these have such a salutary effect through word and example on others who are not so advanced in the spiritual life that they gladly follow. Now I believe and fear that he who goes about seeking souls to devour will not pass us by, but with God's grace I hope that he will find none who would be his victim, or at least that the misfortune of one individual will not be the ruin of all.

(2) The second thing I sought was to provide pastoral care for our German compatriots. To devote this help exclusively to Germans could not be my inten-

tion. Had it been, then better insight into local circumstances would have convinced me that this would not be feasible, or at least not out in the countryside where, in my opinion, Benedictine monasteries should chiefly be. Besides, there is hardly a single larger congregation that is completely unmixed. Except for St. Marys,[68] I know of none in the East. There are a few smaller ones in the western states, but I could not take any of these into account since for more than one reason it was necessary to establish my foundation near a secure settlement as soon as possible.

In America, Germans and Irish, or anglicized Germans, usually live mixed with one another, and usually the Germans are in the minority. Even at St. Joseph's,[69] where I originally wanted to go, and where in fact I went for a while, there is no purely German Catholic population. It is very mixed. The missionary there, Father Peter Lemke (who now has been relieved of his duties), utterly disappointed me in this and in many other things. The only thing he told me that was true was that there are only Catholics there. They are predominant in Cambria County and close themselves off from the Protestants. Since I found it to be no place for me and since I had to give up the station, at least for the present, for reasons of self-preservation, I did not hesitate to take over the parish of St. Vincent at Youngstown, although this is neither unmixed German nor sharply separated from the Protestants. I found [at St. Vincent] a base more certain than hardly any other place in America, which offered me the material means for founding a monastery.

If the Germans are not in the majority [at St. Vincent], they constitute half the population. In fact, except for about 18 or 20 Irish families and some converts, all are of German extraction. After the death of the founder of this mission, who was a northern German Franciscan by the name of Brouwers,[70] two German priests took charge; both were very bad. One took money belonging to the parish and disappeared; the other had to be forcibly driven off by the Protestant magistrates because he wanted to appropriate the benefice established by Brouwers.[71] From then on, English-speaking priests had the

---

[68] The German colony of St. Marys, Elk County, Pa., established by German settlers in 1842.
[69] A Catholic colony in Cambria County, Pennsylvania.
[70] Theodore Brouwers, O.F.M. Cap. (1738-1790).
[71] The two priests were John Baptist Cause, O.F.M., and Francis Rogatus Fromm, O.F.M., Cap. For the pre-Benedictine history of the St. Vincent Parish, see Omer U. Kline, O.S.B., *The Sportsman's Hall Parish, Later Named Saint Vincent, 1790-1846* (Latrobe, Pa.: Saint Vincent Archabbey Press, 1990).

pastoral care. (One of these, Vicar General Stillinger,[72] is the son of a native of Cologne. He speaks German, but never preaches in that language, although he has many Germans in his care.)

It has developed in the course of time that most of the German children hardly understand the language any more. Only the children of new immigrants (about 12 or 15 families from the Würzburg and Baden regions) have managed to retain their mother tongue. I can therefore say that I preside over a German, if not purely German, congregation. Besides the German Catholics, many German Protestants live here. In fact, they constitute the majority of Germans. Many of them attend my talks, so in its origin and direction my mission is to the Germans and extremely important for the Germans, and will contribute essentially toward keeping the Germans German.

This will be even more the case when other parishes can gradually be established from here, which is my plan. My smaller farm (160 acres), an hour and a half from here, promises to become a very fine parish from which one or two priests with four or five lay brothers would find sufficient sustenance. In Greensburg, the county seat, three hours from here, a Catholic church is being built and is already under roof. Many Germans live there and many more in the neighborhood. It has no endowment yet, but it could obtain one through bequest or purchase. Two and a half hours beyond Greensburg in the little town of Adamsburg live five Catholic and many Protestant families. The same number live in the neighborhood. I have 19 other such towns in my charge. Nine German families, 14 miles on the other side of the mountain, also want me to build a German church.[73] They can come here only rarely. I cannot get to them very easily but will visit them when the harsh winter is over, because the German Protestants there have also invited me to preach to them. I bring this up only because, as I gather from a letter from Bavaria, the notion reigns there now and then that I have let myself be misled by the Irish and to some extent have betrayed the Germans.[74]

---

[72] James Ambrose Stillinger (1801-1873), diocesan vicar general, was pastor of SS. Simon and Jude Parish in Blairsville, thirteen miles from St. Vincent, when Wimmer and the Benedictines arrived. He had served as pastor of St. Vincent from 1830 to 1844.

[73] These Catholics lived in the Ligonier Valley, east of St. Vincent on the opposite side of Chestnut Ridge.

[74] Wimmer had received reports from Bavaria that his move to St. Vincent from St. Joseph's had not pleased the directors of the *Ludwig Missionsverein*, who intended their contributions to support German, not Irish, Catholics. Father Joseph Ferdinand Müller, general manager of the mission society, for example, had written to warn Wimmer "not to neglect the Germans." (See ASVA:

(3) The third thing I have attempted to do is to educate German boys for the clerical state. Until now, I have not been able to think much about this. Still, I have already accepted one German boy who wants to study, and after Easter, the Redemptorists of Pittsburgh will send another. However, here too I must admit that I have modified my original plan somewhat and propose not to limit myself to German boys. In fact, I have already taken in an Irish orphan. The reason for this modification is my better insight into local circumstances. Everywhere in America, Germans live among English-speaking Germans or Irish or Americans. Because they are so poor, German Catholics in rural areas cannot create their own ecclesiastical communities, build churches, or support German clergymen; and even if they could, there are not enough German priests to serve all the German immigrants.

Because this situation will continue as long as new immigrants arrive, most German communities must depend on Irish priests. However, since the Irish priests' own people constitute the majority of the population, the Germans are often abandoned. Things would be different if the Irish priest could speak and preach in German, or the German priest in English. This could be accomplished if English and German boys were educated by teachers who have a command of both languages, and it would be to the advantage of the Germans if the teachers were German. If I therefore educate an English boy for the priesthood and at the same time teach him German (and they learn both languages easily!), then I am also educating him as a German priest. In the same way, in the German boy I am educating an English priest. The result would be that many small German communities would receive a German-speaking priest who also understands English and who otherwise, without a knowledge [of German], would never be able to obtain this position. Thus, I will kill two flies with one blow. I am considering, therefore, educating principally German boys, but according to circumstances Irish boys as well, and by doing this, I am not acting unpatriotically. In fact, I profit insofar as the Irish bishops will not then view our Order with suspicion. I will also contribute to the unity of Catholic [ethnic] groups, which because of the intended or actual prejudice of one side against the other have often in the past brought the work of the Church to ruin for all. For the same reason I have happily received the Irish priest Michael Gallagher into our Order.[75] For while I do

Müller to Wimmer, Munich, November 5, 1846.) Wimmer's letter to von Reisach answered these objections.

[75] Father Michael Gallagher (1806-1869), Wimmer's predecessor as pastor of St. Vincent, had relinquished his position when the Benedictines arrived and joined the monastery as a novice. He left the community in June 1847 and went to Philadelphia where he became an Augustinian.

not consider integrating large numbers of the two nationalities in our monastery to be advantageous, yet it would be good if after a while one or the other German would enter an Irish monastery and vice versa. Yet I will gladly let myself be convinced otherwise.

With regard to my–our–material situation, it strikes me as secure for the present, as I already had the honor to mention in my report to the central committee [of the *Ludwig Missionsverein*]. With the people I have now, I can subsist here; but I am not satisfied with this since nothing would be accomplished [with mere subsistence], and I have not traveled so far just for that. If something worthwhile is to be achieved, then several, many, very many monasteries must be founded, and this can easily happen, as I have said before. However, to achieve this goal I need more financial support and more land so that 50-100 men can live here, of whom a few could be sent elsewhere as colonists from time to time, being replaced by new recruits. Once the operation is underway and God gives his blessing, 4,000-6,000 florins yearly would mean a new foundation could be made almost every year, and in a short time, most dioceses would have monasteries of our Order.

I beg therefore most humbly that for this year Court Chaplain Müller be authorized to send at least the travel money for me, the four students, and two brothers, and half fare for two other brothers, since I counted on it and made plans accordingly. For the present, I am not only limited and handicapped in my undertakings, but in many ways pressed and endangered. I also beg Your Grace most earnestly to cover the travel expenses of any qualified student or layman who should follow me, but who himself cannot raise the money for the trip.

At the same time, I earnestly ask your blessing and pious remembrance at the Holy Sacrifice, so that peaceful reflection, constancy, and prudent zeal, which are so necessary here, may be richly granted me by the Lord of all gifts, so that I may bring about many things for His honor, which has always been my intention. With deepest respect, I am Your Grace's most obedient, P. Boniface Wimmer, Superior, O.S.B.

Ger   oALMV   cASVA   transWM *Conf6*

TO JAMES A. STILLINGER   22

St. Vincent, March 23, 1847

Very Reverend General Vicar[76]: I give me
the honour, to invite you to the first holy
Mass, which one of my brothers, Rev. Martin Geierstanger,[77] whom the Bishop has had
the goodness to ordinate last days in Pittsburgh, on the festival of the Annunciation of
the B.V. Maria in our church will say at ½
11 o'clock. If you had the time, it would me
make the greatest pleasure, if you would be
so kind to have the english preaching according the circumstances of this day, and so assist
to the young priest in offering the holy sacrifice. There shall be no guests in our house,
but my brothers and perhaps Mr. Binkele,[78]
who wished to get word of the time of his first

Rev. James A. Stillinger

holy Mass. For the case, that you should be prevented, I beseech you at least to
keep me and the young novice-priest in your pious memory before God, that the
benediction of S. Benedict and his Spirit may be poured out over him, who is the
first priest flower of the Benedictine Order in America.

Approve ye the most sincere resurance of my excellent esteem, with which I
remain, Your Reverence, devoted P. Boniface Wimmer, O.S.B.[79]

Eng   oASVA

---

[76] This is the earliest surviving letter that Wimmer wrote in English and is printed here without cor-
rections. The recipient was Father James Ambrose Stillinger, pastor of SS. Simon and Jude Parish,
Blairsville, Pa., and vicar general of the diocese of Pittsburgh. Stillinger had earlier been pastor at
St. Vincent.

[77] Charles Martin Geyerstanger, O.S.B. (1820-1881), was one of the four clerical students to accompany Wimmer to America. He was ordained to the priesthood by Bishop Michael O'Connor
on March 18, 1847, the first Benedictine priest ordained in the United States.

[78] Unidentified.

[79] Stillinger accepted the invitation and preached in English at the Mass.

TO GREGORY ZIEGLER   **23**

St. Vincent, August 11, 1847

Most Reverend Bishop: On February 28 of this year, I received from my abbot[80] the wonderful news that Your Grace, in addition to the generous travel grant of 200 guilders, had most kindly allowed an additional 1,000 guilders for my support. At the same time, I was directed to report how and in what currency I could safely receive this sum. Because I would have preferred to receive the money itself rather than the inquiry, I answered the abbot the next day, but I do not know whether my letter was lost or perhaps mislaid. Later I learned through Court Chaplain Müller[81] in Munich that the abbot was sending me the money, but since then I have not received it, nor any further letter from Metten, so that I remain in complete uncertainty about it. I am not writing this to complain about anyone, because I know very well that the abbot has done and will do what is in his opinion best. I thought it necessary to write, however, because Your Grace rightly expected to receive a receipt and my hearty thanks for the donation and would certainly judge me guilty of ingratitude should you not hear from me. I have not written until now because I wanted to acknowledge and thank you for the donation when it arrived.

I want to report that my undertaking is proceeding, with God's grace, on a quiet and satisfactory course. So far, I am completely satisfied with my lay brothers, and no less so with the students, though among them is one whom I am thinking of not allowing to take vows because he is very lazy and peculiar. From an unexpected corner, I had some trouble, which for several months placed in doubt whether or not I could remain here. My most reverend bishop[82] expected me to accept gratis in the seminary I am thinking of opening next year as many Irish boys as Germans. I was surprised by this because upon my arrival I had openly expressed, both orally and in writing, the intention of establishing a German seminary. Moreover, the bishop, when he called me to St. Vincent and handed this post over to me—as Your Grace knows from his explanation attached to my earlier letter[83]—did so without demanding further obligations from me beyond the care of souls. Hence, I did not agree to this condition, and even less to some

---

[80] Gregory Scherr, O.S.B., of Metten.
[81] Joseph Ferdinand Müller (1803-1864), general manager of the *Ludwig Missionsverein* and chaplain to the court of King Ludwig I.
[82] Michael O'Connor of Pittsburgh.
[83] See Wimmer's letter to Ziegler of November 5, 1846, page 52.

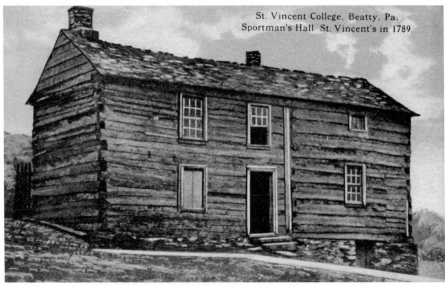

St. Vincent College. Beatty. Pa.
Sportman's Hall St. Vincent's in 1789.

Sportsman's Hall, the oldest building at Saint Vincent when
Wimmer and the Benedictines arrived in 1846.

others calculated to make German Benedictines and German money exclusively, or chiefly, serve Irish interests, as so frequently happens here.

Mr. Balleis,[84] whom I consulted, insisted that I should leave this place without further ado and settle elsewhere. Bishop Henni of Milwaukee,[85] the only German bishop here, assured me of a potential foundation in his diocese. We negotiated, but I did not want to give up this place unnecessarily because it really is very beautiful, healthful, and excellently situated for a monastery, furthermore because it was purchased in the 1790s by a German missionary,[86] and finally because the Germans in this region, within a radius of up to 20 hours, would otherwise, once again, be deprived of all help. However, for greater assurance, I demanded of the reverend bishop that St. Vincent be incorporated as a parish and given over perpetually to the Benedictine Order. With regard to the seminary, I made the concession that I would enroll and instruct free of charge those boys whom the bishop may want to send us for training in the religious life, but that he must pay an annual fee for board that must at least compensate for their expenses. Concerning discipline and teaching methods, I reserved full freedom for the Benedictine

[84] Nicholas Balleis, O.S.B., (1808-1892), pastor of St. Mary's Church, Newark.
[85] John Martin Henni (1805-1881), bishop of Milwaukee.
[86] Theodore Brouwers, O.F.M. Cap. (1738-1790), who purchased the St. Vincent property (then called Sportsman's Hall) in 1790.

Order, and I set the condition that we pledge ourselves to offer only as many courses as we have qualified professors in the house to teach, and that we could never be bound to call up or take professors from elsewhere whenever the most reverend bishop might want to send students to us. I also made papal endorsement a condition for any agreement. He vigorously objected to this last item but in the end conceded. The formal written document was promised in two copies. I could not and cannot concede more, and more could not justly and practically be demanded. If he keeps his word, then I remain. If not, then I go to Milwaukee.

This affair has resulted in a certain delay, but there is no danger, not even materially. Nevertheless, I am sorry to say that I have now become suspicious, and for that reason have a mind not to erect the monastery on this site but in the neighborhood, and to purchase an adjacent estate of 300 acres and on this to establish both the institution and German interests securely. Of course, I need money for this. Both in Germany and America, the Germans are convinced that they can be helped only by means of a German seminary in this country. Hence, I will not be discouraged. I can acquire two properties that adjoin ours, one of 294 acres and the other of 150 acres. An acre of 42,000 square feet costs around $25 or $28 cash . . . [text indecipherable] . . . I suppose the best. The price therefore is much less, and credit is available, because ready cash is scarce here.

The wheat harvest was small. The other harvest, however, was good, so that we are secure for next year even though Father Prior Peter Lechner is bringing me 18 fresh men.[87] Peace in the house, bread and wholesome water, enough work and joy in addition, and the conviction that a beautiful and great purpose is being realized—what more is needed? With the arrival of the prior [Lechner], our operation, which depended until now on my own personality with all the consequences, will gain so much more stability, since he is a lovable person, a learned priest, a pious religious, and an excellent pastor of souls, and we have known each other for the longest time. Without him, I might not be able to bear the burden of affairs, nor even to look after them properly, for in addition to the management and organization of such a large house, the preparations for a vast construction program, the daily distribution of work for so many men, the novitiate, the extensive correspondence that makes its claim on me, I must travel up to two or three hours every day, often as far as 16 to 20 miles, and once a month go 34 miles in order to visit the formerly neglected German community in Indiana, a mission that requires 14 hours of travel at a stretch and costs me three days.

---

[87] On August 18, 1847, a week after Wimmer wrote this letter, Father Peter Lechner, O.S.B. (1805-1874), prior of the Bavarian abbey of Scheyern, arrived at St. Vincent with 18 recruits for the lay brotherhood.

Monastic observance continues at home. Nonetheless, I leave with anxiety, and my [brothers] worry and wait patiently for me, uneasy and longing for my return, because I have a strongly Protestant region to ride through. I always wear my clerical dress on trips in order to make the Protestants acquainted with it. They believe the Catholic priest a kind of devil, and last winter I convinced them, by permitting an inspection, that we have no horns, which until then they believed. These were Mennonites! Those who live closer to us, of course, were not so foolish. They often visit our church and attend my sermons. Gradually, I hope, it will become easier and doors can be opened there as well. Protestantism here is by no means a definite religion with definite dogmas. Each believes what he likes, and in a single family, there are not rarely three or four religions represented. Or they have none at all. They live without baptism, church, faith, and divine services. It is pitiful and heartbreaking. [Faith] is also strongly lacking among the Catholics, though not as much. Most are fervent and cling to us with childlike love.

Oh! It is so difficult to see such misery and not be able to help! Pray, Most Reverend Bishop, to the supreme Shepherd of souls, that He may not fail to look down on my weak endeavors to serve His ends and to achieve them, that He may not disdain to enlighten and strengthen me through His Holy Spirit so that I may with discretion and prudence, with strength and perseverance, lay the first foundations upon which the new structure of our holy Order may be erected here for the glory of God, for the consolation of our holy Church, for the blessing of this world and the next, for the glory and splendor of the holy Order itself. I ask that Your Grace bless our new foundation and me. I remain in deepest respect and profoundest gratitude, Your Grace's most humble and obedient, P. Boniface Wimmer, Superior of the Benedictine Mission

P.S. I request that you make no use of this letter for public leaflets. I feel the lack of a good library severely. Good books of theology are not to be had for money here. Please do not forget us in this. Because of the high postage for letters, I have thoroughly used every bit of space for writing.

Ger   oADL   cASVA   transAS

TO RUPERT LEISS   24

St. Vincent, October 12, 1847

Right Reverend Abbot: I have long intended to write you, and should have done so sooner, as soon, in fact, as I learned that the first assistance from Bavaria would come from Scheyern in the person of your dear prior.[88] However, there was always one thing or the other that had to be put in order. The tasks are extraordinarily numerous; correspondence keeps me busy; often there is not a penny in the house to pay the postage–and so I kept procrastinating, at the same time hoping that Your Grace would receive news of my foreign adventure from my confreres in Munich to whom I always sent my reports for Metten. Now, however, I can no longer keep silent, although I would have liked to await the outcome of one piece of business before I write. It has to do with money. Since February, I have been expecting the remainder of the travel expenses Father Müller[89] promised me, as well as the gift from the bishop of Linz.[90] Instead, I received only an inquiry from Metten as to how I wanted the money sent. I replied but have still received nothing–and that was on March 1! Now it is October 12 and still I have nothing!

The prior [Lechner] was supposed to bring the money. Instead of the gold offered him, he took the draft and had it cashed by the Redemptorists in New York. When they recalled it, it was accepted only on credit, that is, it would be paid in London, for which it was made out. This was made known to me around September 3, after repeated urgent letters from me. Since then I have heard nothing more, but indirectly I learned from someone else that the superior of the New York Redemptorists thinks I have nothing to fear. Still, however, I am without money.

The prior's company of 17 brothers and five others brings us to a total of 50 men in the house–and for that reason quite a variety of necessary items must be purchased: stoves, crockery, bedding, and clothing. This is only one inconvenience, but it retards and hinders me greatly and provides me almost no help, for among the new arrivals there is only one whom I can use as a builder. Nevertheless, this year there is no more time to build because I had to devote the fair weather entirely to preparing for the new guests in order merely to be able to live in some sort of comfort. In addition, this autumn the weather has been bad to an unprecedented degree–continuous rain–something most unusual here in this season. Now it doesn't matter, however, and even if the draft for almost 2,000 florins

---

[88] Father Peter Lechner, O.S.B., (1805-1874) prior of the Bavarian abbey of Scheyern, arrived at St. Vincent on August 18, 1847, with 17 recruits for the lay brotherhood. In his letter (#23) to Bishop Gregory Ziegler of August 11, 1847, above, Wimmer states that Lechner planned to bring 18 "fresh men" to St. Vincent. His reference to "17 recruits" in this letter suggests either that in the previous letter he was including Lechner among the number or, if there were indeed 18 lay brother candidates in the original group, one withdrew before reaching St. Vincent.

[89] Joseph Ferdinand Müller, general manager of the *Ludwig Missionsverein* and one of the most devoted supporters of the Benedictine mission to America.

[90] Gregory Ziegler, O.S.B. On this gift, see Wimmer's letter to Ziegler of August 11, 1847, page 64.

should be lost, still the sky won't fall in. In any event, today I am about 100 per cent stronger and better off with my community than I was a year ago. I only ask, if it wouldn't be too much trouble, that you kindly inform Court Chaplain Müller that as of today I have not received a penny of the money he sent and that I do not know anything about it. At first, I was a bit put out, but I soon understood that it is a wholesome lesson for me to expect help from God alone and, if I have done my best in accord with my weak energies, to entrust all the rest to Him in a childlike manner.

From the start, humanly speaking, my undertaking was a daring one, if not foolhardy. It could not succeed without special aid from heaven. I have built on this aid, and all that has since happened has only confirmed me in my confidence, because everything proceeded better than I expected, at least it turned out better, even if from the beginning it often had a doubtful outlook. All that I have since experienced and seen justifies not only the usefulness but also the necessity of the enterprise. What need, what misery from the religious point of view prevails here can be recognized only when one sees it, and one perceives it more and more the longer one can observe.

I have not yet converted any heretics, but quite often, at their request, I have preached to them in various places and have brought some pretty near the Church. Moreover, I have confessed people who had not been to confession since 1800 and have brought back to the Church people who had not belonged to it for years. I have baptized children from ten to fourteen years of age as well as adult so-called Catholics. The more I get to know the more remote parishioners, the more wretchedness I find: entire families without baptism, without the knowledge and practice of prayer, without any religion, even though born of Catholic parents; people who have never been to confession, never gone into any church, even a Protestant one. Moreover, these families, many of whom have long been lost to the Church, usually become clans, as I have often found, because all marry, and thereby increase the number of our enemies! Or half the children are Catholics, the others Methodists, Presbyterians, brothers or not, often from three to four sects together! How can one who has a heart and a love for God and his fellow man regard this with indifference? One must do what he can and make sacrifices. God will reward our efforts. We must exercise compassion in order to experience it! We must work so that no one, in error through no fault of his own, dead without baptism, can ever complain and say, "I was not helped when I could have been, I was not enlightened on the way, even though there were more than enough persons who could have educated me and wanted to!" I ask you, have compassion on us if the salvation of so many souls who will otherwise be lost concerns you, if also the growth of our holy Order interests you, since only through the missions will our Order again acquire new grace from God, new life, the approval of good people, and its former importance. With 100 brothers, I can accomplish nothing, but with only a single priest much. Send at least one more if you can, or earnestly beg the other abbots to come to my aid by sending priests. Especially under existing circumstances, this is very necessary.

Father Nicholas Balleis from St. Peter's in Salzburg, who has a beautiful church with a residence and garden in the city of Newark, New Jersey, and who is the only German priest there, wants to go to Germany to recover his health. Thus, he needs a German priest as a substitute. If we do not supply the help, he must request a secular priest from the bishop of New York–something he does not want to do. Immediately after our arrival, this confrere of ours placed himself under obedience to me and asked to be a Benedictine again. Much as I could use him here, still I could not recall him from Newark, not only because of his congregation, for which he needed three priests, but because the church and all that belongs to it is his private property. It could be a very fine monastery, a hospice for confreres from overseas, and it is well situated for an academy. [Newark] is half an hour by steamer from New York and five hours from Philadelphia, where more than 30,000 Germans live. Newark itself has more than 25,000. Father Nicholas now wants to keep this property for the Order and transfer it to me. Furthermore, it is required by local law that he turn the deed over to me by a will valid in law. He also needs the consent of Bishop Hughes,[91] which he expects to obtain quickly and will "shortly" request. He has taken care that in the event of his sudden death, his property will not go to the state. Some years ago, he drew up a will in which he made over the deed to the bishop with the condition that he should turn it over to a religious institute. This will is in the custody of a priest, and the bishop knows nothing about it. Of course, he must now make another one, if he cancels this one and the bishop accepts us, but if I cannot provide for him, he cannot do all this so easily and with so good an excuse. Therefore, four weeks ago he asked me whether I could not send him Father Peter, at least for six months. I spoke with the latter and he consented. Now, however, it is almost impossible for me to let him go, for what am I to do alone among 50 brothers, ten of whom are students? On the other hand, I cannot possibly let that opportunity slip by, which is of the utmost importance for our Order. Expecting now that either my abbot, as he has promised, or Your Grace will surely assist me this year with at least one priest, I promised to send the prior to Newark and to leave him there during the absence of Father Nicholas. However, if the abbot of Metten does not keep his word, as

---

[91] John Hughes (1797-1864), bishop and later archbishop of New York.

has so often happened,[92] then I am alone and must shelve one enterprise: the care of souls or the monastery. Suppose I become sick or die?

October 15

I have just now experienced a real novelty, which leaves in the air the question of how long I shall be here. After Easter, I argued with the bishop because he demanded I take into my seminary Irish boys as well as German, just as many Irish as German, free of charge–and even accept an Irish priest as their prefect– even though at the time of my arrival and of his invitation he had not mentioned a word of this and knew from me, orally and in writing, that I came to educate German priests. I was on the point of leaving, but finally, after three months and much writing back and forth, we agreed to the extent that I promised to accept Irish boys, but only for payment and without an Irish prefect. We also agreed that I would retain full freedom with respect to the educational program and discipline of the school.

Today, I was again at odds with him for the following reason. Without consulting the congregation and allegedly at his own expense, my Irish predecessor[93] erected two buildings here, one of which he intended to use as a school house, the other as a rectory, which the Irish nuns, who now have their convent half an hour from here but who for a while lodged here, might use as accommodations. The cost came to more than $1,100. A year ago, he resigned in my favor and promised me his harvest *gratis*, but when I came with the brothers, he demanded payment for it because otherwise he could not pay his debts. He even entered our Order, only to leave again at Pentecost, claiming he could not endure it, which he really proved. He is no longer young. Now more and more debts have come to light. I was gradually able to assess the church accounts and saw that, instead of paying debts, he had assigned all the construction costs to the church or congregation respectively. I spoke rather frequently about this with the bishop. He investigated and ascertained the truth but decided that [Father Gallagher] had acted with good intention and that his debts had to be paid by me–that is what he intended–or by the congregation. I declared frankly that I would pay nothing and several lay persons of the congregation declared the same thing. Trustees were then named, before whom the matter was laid, and it was politely explained to me that if the congregation did not assume the debts, there was no other recourse than to reinstate the resigned pastor in his parish so that he could pay a little at a time– and, of course, to dismiss me. This should have terrified me, but I don't become

---

[92] In fact, the following year Abbot Gregory sent two priests, Thaddeus Brunner, O.S.B., and Adalbert Pums, O.S.B., from Metten to assist Wimmer at St. Vincent.
[93] Father Michael Gallagher.

Saint Xavier's in 1855.

frightened easily and repeated that I would not pay. Now I am curious as to who will pay. Hardly the congregation. The bishop wanted to take the place away from me for the time being. He had in his hands the deed of incorporation, which I had earlier asked for and obtained and which he had promised to sign! He did not sign today, but gave it back to me. Soon afterwards, he sent over a messenger from the convent[94] and demanded it back. He said he would sign it at once when he had settled the matter, but instead, I sent back the reply that the affair had now assumed such a form that I no longer regarded that deed as a basis on which I could build the first Benedictine monastery in this place. I spoke first with the prior, and he agreed with me. Therefore, most likely I will not be here long. I am torn between Newark and Wisconsin, to which the German Bishop Henni[95] has earnestly invited me three times. I thought of St. Teresa and intend to have nothing further to do with this Irish scoundrel. In reality, this changes nothing at all

---

[94] St. Xavier's Convent, the home of the Sisters of Mercy half an hour from St. Vincent.
[95] John Martin Henni (1805-1881), the Swiss-born bishop of Milwaukee.

except the place. We are best under Germans, and never again will I have anything to do with acting as a pastor for the Irish.

P.S. October 31. You see that, in anger, I wrote in a somewhat too German manner. Now I am calmer and not resentful. On October 16, I visited the Germans in Indiana [Pennsylvania] 35 miles away, as I do every four weeks. Determined to leave here, I looked around there for a place and three were offered me, one of which (425 acres together with buildings) cost $8,000 (20,000 florin). The others cost less, but in order to have a choice I traveled from there farther north (82 miles) to St. Marys [Pennsylvania] to our dear fellow countrymen. The three contractors (Benziger, Eschbach, and Schrötter[96]) happened to be there, as well as the superior of the teaching brothers of Nancy, who intends to settle there, so that three orders (with the Redemptorists), besides the teaching sisters (Miss Pronath is there), are represented. I was very urgently invited to move there and was offered *gratis* as much land as I wanted and wherever I wanted. I explained that I wanted a valley, through which flowed a small stream that could operate a mill and irrigate gardens. Such a spot was found nine miles from the town, and there, where it empties into the Clarion, a beautiful river navigable by raft, I intended to establish the center of the new foundation. However, I left three days later without a firm decision because I did not know whether the bishop would endure me in his diocese if I left St. Vincent or whether he would not again pose unacceptable conditions. Moreover, the three men offered me 40 miles from St. Marys, where they have much land, a splendidly equipped farm without any conditions, if I wanted to go there. This, of course, would be to their advantage because then they could sell the surrounding land more quickly and at higher cost. If I depart from here, I must divide my flock and leave one-half under the prior (if he does not go to Newark) at Indiana or on that farm. With the other half I intend to go to the valley and cut down and burn the forests in a struggle with wolves and bears and rattlesnakes, which still dwell there, as do deer and elk (weighing 600 pounds). If the bishop is opposed, then I shall go to Wisconsin. One reason why I so unhesitatingly accepted the challenge is this: if no priests are sent to me (and Müller writes to me that despite repeated promises none is coming from Metten), and if I have to send the prior away again, I must completely neglect the monastery and live by pastoral work. Hence, I prefer to bury myself in the deepest woods and live for my brothers, doing no pastoral work until we have settlers around us. To be sure, there is something very sad about all this: Germans and Irish want to keep us and there is much to be done, much to be gained, but alone and without help, I can do nothing else. On the one hand, the Order must

---

[96] The founders of the German colony of St. Marys, Pennsylvania.

have permanent and incontestable property; on the other, the first Benedictines here must be thorough Benedictines. Of course, for this, unfortunately, I know I am not the man, but my people have every confidence in me. They fear and love me, readily follow me, love prayer (many are real men of prayer), and pray daily for me, and so I hope that for a second time God will make a teacher out of an ass, as in Balaam's time.

I cannot possibly abandon Newark because it is too important and valuable to us. If the Bavarian abbots want to let me dangle alone in suspense, I may still struggle for three or four more years until my students are priests. Meanwhile, however, hundreds may lose their faith. Children may die without baptism. Heresy may grow fat on the offspring of Catholics left without help–I can do nothing about it. One must live in America in order not to find such statements exaggerated, but that is the situation.

Meanwhile, my draft has arrived, and no one is happier than the prior. In this, I perceive the providence of God. Had it come sooner, I would have built a sawmill and would not now be able to leave so easily. I have reported the latest developments to Müller, but please do not give the matter any publicity, although instead of damaging our affairs it improves them. I am in exactly the same situation as we once were at Augsburg.[97] At precisely the right time, I freed myself from the snares in which I was to have been cunningly entangled. Please, most humbly ask the abbot of Metten and Müller in my name for the speedy dispatch of Mass stipends (at least 1,000) in case my letter went astray. Do not forget! I continue to be well, praise God! So is the prior. I send kind regards to the entire community, especially to those I know. They must pray earnestly for their absent brethren. Surely, the united prayers of so many pious souls in beautiful Bavaria will sustain me in my situation–difficult, dangerous, complicated, and filled with responsibility as it is. I ask your blessing and kiss your hand, which has so often blessed me. With the most heartfelt respect, Your Grace's very grateful, P. Boniface

Compliments to the prior and to all at Scheyern.

P.S. November 9. Last week I was in Pittsburgh to cash the draft from the bishop of Linz and two others that came from Müller and to shop for all sorts of things for the winter. While there, I spoke again with the bishop, who had written me once more in the meantime. However, I left without a decision. Meanwhile,

---

[97] In 1835, Wimmer and Leiss had been sent to Augsburg against their will to help restore the abbey of St. Stephen's. At the time, it seemed as if Metten would be suppressed and that the Metten monks would be forced to transfer their vows of stability to the new abbey, but Wimmer orchestrated an opposition movement, obtained the support of leading churchmen, and succeeded in saving Metten. See *An American Abbot*, 25-30.

there has been a small revolution. The congregation, not only Germans but also English, do not want to let us go. It is really difficult to do. I am in great perplexity. I have racked my brains with plans, as the question required. I finally came up with one that makes it possible for me to keep this place and, incidentally, also to accept the others. For the bishop repeatedly expressed orally and in writing his keen regret that I intended to leave here, but he also declared that I could settle in his diocese wherever I wanted, in one or in several places at the same time. Now I have decided, under certain conditions and with caution, to leave here the necessary personnel but to take the others to St. Marys or to the other farm I have been promised. (I still have to go there for the first time, next Saturday.) In order not to incur expenses, I am building nothing here for the present but am turning over a part of my income to liquidate the debt, while on the other hand the congregation must make a loan without interest in order to pay the interest and debts of the church. In this way, I will later be assured the income from the pew rent and thus will be indemnified again. Of course, I must first write the bishop, but I am sure he will agree. The congregation, in a well-attended meeting, acknowledged the necessity as well as the usefulness of my proposal and will do their part, although they are not very well off.

If I do not receive two priests, however, I cannot carry this out and must either remain here with all the brothers or go away with all of them because wherever there are brothers there must be at least one priest. Here there must be at least two. If I have to wait for my students to be ordained, I may wait for three or four more years. In that time, I could have three or four monasteries. Perhaps this would have been a quite welcome recourse for certain gentlemen who wear the habit, as I do. Because of its beautiful and salubrious location, this place, if we retain it–and we are now in a position to do so–would be very suitable for our clerical novitiate, Newark for a trade center and a high school, Indiana for an educational institution, St. Marys for a brothers' novitiate. All of America is open to us! Of course, out in the countryside we live much more poorly than in the cities. In the countryside, however, we live more securely, and all people, all Germans, all priests agree that only through our Order, if it takes an interest in the young, will the hole be filled which until now no one could fill–the absence of an institute to educate German (and perhaps also Irish) priests. Therefore, hindrances become only one more spur for me to work so that something may be accomplished, even though I cannot speak of real hindrances but only of difficulties, which have to accompany every such undertaking. The real obstacle is the lack of priests, but I am convinced that the dear Lord, who never forsakes an honest German, will still bring out all the Bavarian Benedictines if they are unwilling to come individually. He who has eyes, let him see! Today I am threshing my wheat. I have harvested more than 2,000 bushels of corn–enough for 100 men and 100 hogs. A thousand greetings to my confreres. I could use Father Corbinian and Father Martin at once. P.B.

My address the entire winter, that is, until Easter in any event, is Rev. Mr. Boniface Wimmer at St. Vincent near Youngstown, Westmoreland County in Pennsylvania. Via Cherbourg-New York. We need one or two good carpenters, well-equipped. The brothers are very well behaved. Everything is sound. They are willing to go to St. Marys or anywhere else.[98]

Ger   oASA   cASVA   transABi

TO KARL VON REISACH   25

Mount St. Vincent, March 3, 1848

Most Reverend Archbishop: I hope Your Excellency has learned through Vicar General Dr. Windischmann–provided that my letter on the matter reached the right place–of the difficult situation in which I found myself a few months ago. Just as in the story of Laban and Jacob, the bishop[99] ten times changed the conditions under which he wanted to transfer this place to me for all time, whereas in the beginning he had made no conditions at all. When after much bargaining I believed him to be finally at his goal, there came a new condition, so that I decided irrevocably to drop the negotiations and move to a new place. When it really became serious, the bishop then withdrew all his conditions with the exception of the single one, that I assume the $800 debt of my predecessors,[100] half payable in four years, half in six, while the bishop himself assumed the remaining $300 on his account. I submitted to this because to stay was the only thing possible and to leave would have caused the bishop as well as my predecessors and the whole parish great damage. It would also have postponed the development of our Order here for at least several years. For until I could have prepared as much tillable land and habitable buildings in the wilderness as I already found here, several years would have slipped by and far more than $800 would have been lost. It is

---

[98] In the end, Wimmer remained at St. Vincent with the majority of the community. He later established priories in St. Marys (1850), Indiana (1852), and Newark (1857).

[99] Michael O'Connor (1810-1872), bishop of Pittsburgh (1843-1860).

[100] Fathers Michael Gallagher (1806-1869) and James Ambrose Stillinger (1801-1873), Wimmer's immediate predecessors as pastor of St. Vincent.

certainly a very beautiful idea to build a Benedictine monastery in a primitive forest, but in reality, it is very difficult when the men working together are not pure saints and holy men. Then I received the following document in duplicate:

[Lat]

> *Michael O'Connor, by the grace of God and the Apostolic See, Bishop of Pittsburgh, to all whom it concerns, peace in the Lord. When Father Boniface Wimmer, O.S.B., came from Metten in Bavaria to this country, possessed of the necessary authority to establish a Benedictine monastery in which boys, especially Germans, would be educated for the clerical state, and when he sought permission from us to make that foundation in this diocese, we granted our approval to this petition and assigned to him the property and church of St. Vincent in Westmoreland County where he might canonically establish such a monastery. We granted further that the superior of this monastery would always be pastor of the church at St. Vincent, that we would establish him in the pastorate as soon as his election or nomination had been announced to us, provided that we knew of no canonical impediment [here it originally read "and we knew nothing to be present to hinder it"]. With this office, he assumes all the rights and obligations that accompany it (among which is the right to the two estates which the Reverend Theodore Brauer[101] granted in his will to the pastor of the church of St. Vincent). He or any of his confreres who with our approval is assigned the care of souls will be subject to us and our successors in all things pertaining to that care and will be held accountable in the same way as other pastors of this diocese. In the confirmation of which we give these letters and sign them with our own seal. St. Vincent, December 6, 1847.*

Now to be sure this document leaves much to be desired with respect to decisiveness and exactness. However, it gives me what I primarily need, namely, security that as long as Benedictines are here, they will be in possession of this parish and benefice, and since this benefice is incorporated with the state, and consequently can never be alienated from its purpose, the endowment is as safe as any private property can be.

I gave a copy of the document to Bishop Henni,[102] who had most kindly offered me his services to take it to Rome for confirmation. If this happens, then I can consider the monastery here as legally existing, and the Benedictine Order then has a firm base in the United States. I have presumed this confirmation and

---

[101] Theodore Brouwers, O.F.M. Cap. (1738-1790), founder of Sportsman's Hall Parish, which became St. Vincent.

[102] John Martin Henni (1805-1888), bishop of Milwaukee.

am preparing to erect a seminary building in addition to the monastery building. Much could have already been done in this regard during the past year had uncertainty not always held me up.

I have every reason to be satisfied with my people. The student Karl Spiro ran off, but he himself had doubted his vocation from the beginning and only the most pressing arguments of one of my confreres in Munich had moved me to accept him. In addition, a lay brother, John Kreis, left while I was on a trip to see Father Nicholas Balleis[103] in Newark, but he returned after three weeks, asked most humbly for readmission, and was received again; but as a consequence, all the students and brothers who had come with me immediately pressed me after my return from Newark, out of fear that they might also in a storm of temptation slide away, to let them make solemn vows. Partly in order not to weaken their zeal, partly because it is also necessary for me to be able to rely on a certain number of them, I granted their petition, but only insofar as I let them make simple profession (on February 25), and this only until the completion of their second year of novitiate (October 24, 1848), after Father Peter[104] had taken pains to make clear to them the importance of this step. Only one, the novice-priest Martin Geyerstanger,[105] was not permitted to make profession because during the course of the past summer he had given me reason for apprehension. A lay brother was also refused because he, along with three later arrivals, once had the desire to become a hermit. Both willingly accepted this humiliation and declared their readiness to stand by my decision. Several weeks ago, an experienced philologist, Schuderer, came and requested admittance, but he is so troubled and confused that only a miracle could make a monk out of him. Yesterday a certain Van der Grün[106] arrived from Munich by way of Baltimore and requested admittance. We will accept him after a period of testing shows that he is truly called to the monastic life.

So far this year our farm has been able to provide the food we need. With this year's anticipated harvest and with the significantly increased herd of cattle, I hope also to be able to raise enough money to purchase our clothing, provided no major problems arise. I must spend about $300 to buy sheep and cattle. However,

---

[103] Nicholas Balleis, O.S.B. (1808-1892), a Benedictine missionary from St. Peter's Abbey, Salzburg, Austria, who had come to the United States in 1836. He was pastor of St. Mary's Church, Newark.

[104] Peter Lechner, O.S.B.

[105] Charles Martin Geyerstanger, O.S.B. (1820-1881), one of the pioneer students. Ordained on March 18, 1847, he was the first Benedictine priest ordained in the United States.

[106] Odilo Vandergrün, O.S.B., became a novice and was ordained in 1850. He was dispensed from vows and left the monastery several years later.

to live from the farm alone would be almost impossible here because one can sell almost nothing for cash. We can only trade farm products for goods. Yet in a large house, there are always many essential articles (iron, etc.) that one can get only for cash. Pastoral work in the country brings in little, so teaching must provide for most of our needs. Therefore, my most zealous endeavor is to have a seminary as soon as possible in order to bring coin into the house, even if the students cover only expenses and the teaching were given *gratis*. I am ready, as I have had the honor to report earlier, to admit English boys for payment. Not only my bishop, but also the bishop of Philadelphia[107] sends me candidates. Because they want to become priests, I have considered charging only expenses if they are poor.

After the seminary, the construction of a steam-powered gristmill claims my attention because the local one is not always available and is in any event inactive during the summer. It will cost me a little less than $1,000. If I had a mill to serve my house and the neighboring convent of Irish sisters,[108] it would bring in more than the whole pastoral care. I would then not need to send brothers so often to the local mill. A sawmill could be easily linked to it. The steam pump costs only a little more than $300 in Baltimore. It requires no substructure, as I convinced myself with my own eyes, but is portable and can be erected on any level place. If I cannot accomplish this next summer, I can at least do it the following spring.

Good God! (Your Excellency will think) the man is nothing more than a farmer! What sort of monk is he? What kind of superior? Ach! I often think the same thing, but I cannot help it. Even if one lives poorly, one still has to live, and there must be someone who is concerned about the farm, who manages it. This burden is not the smallest part of my troubles, but it is the most dangerous because I enjoy it. The fact that I do it for the Church, for a good purpose, and to fulfill a great need will surely excuse me a little. On the other hand, I am prevented from becoming a mere farmer by the pressure and unavoidable necessity of attending to the pastoral care of souls. The joy of pastoral work compels me to limit my agricultural activity to mere supervision, direction, and management of the enterprise, while the brothers, according to their talents and skills, carry out the appropriate work under my direction, especially since I must be absent from home on the missions two to five days at a time.

Meanwhile my prior[109] handles the purely monastic and disciplinary matters. I cannot thank God enough that I am still quite well, although I really lead a very toilsome life–perhaps even because of that. Likewise, I find my previously

---

[107] Francis Patrick Kenrick (1796-1863), bishop of Philadelphia.
[108] St. Xavier's Convent, one mile from St. Vincent, where a community of Sisters of Mercy lived.
[109] Father Peter Lechner, O.S.B. (1805-1874).

expressed views perfectly justified, that a missionary is only sure of himself when he belongs to a monastery to which he can and must always return and where the regular practice of monastic life continually refreshes, purifies, and strengthens his spirit.

Whether through the result of my negotiations with Bishop O'Connor everything was achieved from my side that was expected in Munich, I do not know. Yet I believe I surrendered nothing in the German interest or in the Order's interest and generally acted according to what duty, conscience, my position, as well as the situation and circumstances, demanded of me. To discuss all this in a letter would be too lengthy and probably superfluous since everyone must realize that the chief consideration is to have a place immediately that I can call mine, upon which I can maintain and organize myself and from which I can spread out with my people. All this counseled me to stay here if I could do so with honor. Moreover, the Order and the German mission have gained in the parish benefice a property that after a few years is already worth some $20,000. It can never be taken away from us once the episcopal incorporation receives papal approval because this property is designated not for the maintenance of the church but of the pastor, and he will be appointed only by ecclesiastical authorities.

The education of English boys with German boys is financially useful to the monastery. It will facilitate introducing our Order into all dioceses, is of service to general Catholic interests, and is highly useful to both Germans and English. A priest who does not understand English can hardly be useful here, and one who does not also speak English is less than half-effective. The instruction of English boys forces my novices to learn English. The German boys learn it through their contact with the English boys, and the English boys learn at least enough in their contact with German classmates and professors that they will be able to hear confessions in German.

At the end of January, I made a trip to Newark (New Jersey) and Baltimore. An offer of 1,000 acres in St. Marys[110] has been made to me should I desire to settle there. On the other hand, Father Balleis in Newark continues to ask me to send him a priest so that he can transfer his beautiful property there to our Order, to which he himself belongs. I wanted to speak with him before I negotiated with Mr. Benziger,[111] and thus I went first to Newark. We agreed that I would send him my novice priest at least for a while and a brother as cook. He himself would act as prior with the consent of the bishop of New York.[112] This consent is not yet

---

[110] The German colony of St. Marys, Elk County, Pennsylvania, 120 miles north of St. Vincent.
[111] One of the trustees of the German colony at St. Marys, Pennsylvania.
[112] John Hughes (1797-1864), bishop of New York (1842-1864).

given, but Father Balleis wrote me that the bishop received the request favorably and informally permitted the sending of a priest and brother.

At the same time, he expressed interest in having two priests from me for two parishes in New York itself, with whose pastors he is not satisfied. I can therefore confidently suppose that he will find the introduction of our Order in his diocese useful, since he offers me more than I can accept. Meanwhile, however, nothing will come of the takeover of Newark for the moment since Father Balleis, because of a scrupulous conscience, does not consider himself suitable to be prior and at present wants only help and not the foundation of a regular little monastery. I do not agree with him. He also expressed doubt about whether I have authority to name him prior since my undertaking was only private. Finally, he expressed concern about his future, when he becomes incapable of serving and when his property (a frame church with a few lots and a house) becomes the property of the Order. He expressed all this for the first time in his recent letters. Prudence and respect bid me under such circumstances to counsel him to stay on as he has done until now and exercise his Benedictine loyalty simply through this: that he eventually make his will out to the Order. His response to this advice I do not yet know.

After the agreement with Father Balleis, I could make Mr. Benziger no promises this year, but I demanded (provided I was wanted in St. Marys) in addition to the 1,000 acres of land (i.e., virgin forest), $50 annually for each of the five to seven brothers for at least three years, as well as the first buildings for them. Then, when I am able to send several brothers and form a congregation, I will expect the construction of a parish house and a sufficiently large church on a spot where I can also build a monastery. The last request caused some doubts, and the affair has been postponed with the explicit understanding that we will discuss the matter later and come (we hope) to an agreement. I could not demand less. Nowhere does a pastor build the parish house and church himself, even less so when he is certain that he will not receive a penny from the parish for ten years, which is what is to be expected in St. Marys. The 1,000 acres are now worth $1,000. If I send only one priest who would not have a penny for sustenance, although each priest in the diocese receives at least $300 a year, it would cost me $900 in three years, and I could easily spend $100 on travel in three years if I visit there a few times a year. There must be two priests there, however, or really three for the sake of a community, which moreover would be entirely senseless at the beginning because they are desperately needed in other places where parishes have already been formed. They could at the same time earn something elsewhere. I would therefore suffer a considerable loss and would receive only a paltry income after many years. Benziger and company will profit by at least $300,000 if they can sell all the land, and it will not be anything for them to build a church for a religious colony that would draw immigrants. If negotiations are resumed, I will also demand maintenance for each priest until the parish is strong and able to provide the necessary support. Land has also been offered to me elsewhere, but because I now know from experience how much the beginnings cost, even living in poverty and need, and that one cannot live from the farm alone, I do not want to be given any if there is not already a congregation there that needs a priest and can support him. I would rather buy a nice farm somewhere else that pays.

Your Excellency may perhaps want to accuse me of not being patriotic, but one must also learn to speculate and reckon. One cannot count on gifts and contributions in this country. The American gives nothing for nothing and believes he has given his clergy everything when he pays his pew rent, which unfortunately does not always happen either. The motto here is not as in Germany "God help you" but rather "Help yourself." Nonetheless, the Catholics, and especially the Germans, do a lot for religion by way of "subscriptions," but only insofar as the subscription is for a cause that benefits them and not primarily the clergy. Thus, they build churches and schools wherever they are able, especially in the cities, but that is voluntary, though a pressing need. Moreover, in the cities, they have money, or if they have little on hand, they can earn it. In the rural areas, they do not have any money, much less than in Bavaria. In order to obtain money, they want to receive pay for the smallest services. In the cities, priests have a good income because they have large congregations. The many baptisms and weddings mean something, and the pew rent brings in a lot. In the country, it is worse, and only the Irish priests can make any headway as moneymakers, appealing to the sixth law of the Church, which stands in all English catechisms: "You must contribute to the support of your clergy." Almost every Sunday, as long as the Irish priest[113] was with me, money came onto the table at the end of the sermon. I cannot do that. My parishioners have the right disposition about it, but I cannot get anything. All the more so because I am rumored to be rich since I can feed so many people and not go into debt. Germans and English would rather live off me than give so that I can live. I always find myself overcharged or cheated when I trust anyone even slightly. In this way, I have learned to speculate and reckon, and I now understand the American motto "Help yourself."

Whoever wants to get ahead goes to the city when they can, be they priest or layman, but the cities are not the place for us. In order to help ourselves we need a

---

[113] Father Michael Gallagher, Wimmer's immediate predecessor as pastor of St. Vincent.

farm that gives us what we require and a little more besides, so that we can obtain everything necessary. In addition, we need at least some income from stole fees (Masses, baptisms, marriages: one receives nothing from IOUs and written promises but often receives them as payment) and seminaries, where the poor sit next to the rich who can and must pay. Where one or the other of these two cannot be combined with the farm, we can hardly exist. I say "hardly" because on a very large farm (of 1,000 acres or more), where one can maintain a significant number of animals, specifically sheep, it may be possible, and it will certainly be the case when I can exchange my products for cash, but until now I have not been confident that I can find a sure market, and many years will pass before virgin forest can be turned into productive land.

That is the reason that I will not soon go to St. Marys unless I can count on good conditions or support from Bavaria. For we would lack there, both at the beginning and for a long time, the three factors necessary for economic success: (a) a farm with productive soil, (b) income from the pastoral care, (c) opportunity for operating a boarding school (on account of the isolation of the place). One cannot count on the last factor for several years, not before the railroad reaches there, inasmuch as there will be no profit until not just poor boys, but boys who can pay can be instructed. The same holds true for the pastoral care as long as the colony has no resources. The farm could yield a minimum amount of food after two or three years if I temporarily send six or seven brothers to clear the forest, but the necessary construction of a gristmill and sawmill, as well as of the necessary buildings, demands substantial expenditures, and before 400 to 500 acres of woods are changed into fields and meadows and a large herd of cattle is procured, money must also be spent for clothes for the brothers, etc. A regular income of about 5,000 florins for four or five years should bring the foundation to the point where it could maintain itself.

It is certain that through the foundation of a monastery, Catholic settlers will be drawn into a sparsely settled region, and that through the foundation of a monastery in a sparsely settled, but fertile and healthy region, a predominately Catholic population will develop. It is this view that makes it advisable to seek out such regions, but it is just as certain that many Catholics who live among Protestants are lost or become totally indifferent without the help of priests. On the other hand, many better Protestants would become Catholics again if they had the opportunity to be instructed and converted. Then the conversions in each parish would be more numerous than the apostasies, for the latter occur almost exclusively in parishes without pastors. This calls for a foundation where Catholics already live, and even more so, since these need a priest and can contribute to his

Father Demetrius Gallitzin

support. In places where small colonies have just begun, however, the priest has to wait for the people and may sooner have to give than to receive.

The question continually arises whether it would be better to follow the stream of immigration or lead it. The first is the easier and more natural thing to do. In its favor would be patriotism, if it were possible to retain the German language in this way and bring about a large concentration of Catholics. I cannot yet declare myself decidedly in favor of this approach, even if I had the personnel. The best would be to allow Providence to rule and to lay hold where the need is greatest and the circumstances make it easiest. In the older states, it is at any rate impossible to make the German language predominant or even equal to the English. Even in St. Marys the children are speaking English already. It is desirable that English or German be spoken exclusively. Only because of the stream of Germans now arriving is it necessary to have German priests–the ones born here understand English better than German. Even though Lancaster, Bucks, and other counties were almost exclusively populated by German Protestants and German was virtually the only language spoken, and even in recent times they have had German schools, nevertheless before another generation passes English will be spoken there almost exclusively just as it is everywhere else!

A foundation in St. Marys would be much easier, were it not 116 miles away from here. One could be made a day's journey away for half the cost. Therefore, I wanted and still want to make a foundation in the neighboring county of Indiana, near the city of Indiana. For $8,000, of which only $2,000 would have to be paid in cash and the rest in yearly installments of $1,000 or $2,000, I could get a property of 420 acres with excellent farm buildings. The German Catholic congregation there is small, but would soon increase by itself and through new arrivals, since land is still cheap. At the same time, we would be closer to the German parishes in Cambria County, the only county where Catholics predominate (through the long residence of Gallitzin[114]). We would then be 35 miles closer to St. Marys and could reach it if we made a foundation from Indiana at Brookville in Jefferson County. Bishop Henni wants me to come to Wisconsin, but I cannot consider that before I have three priests to put at his disposal in a place so far away.

These are just plans, desires, ideas. We must first have one place that is certain and secure. If we prosper here, then it will not be difficult to make a new foundation elsewhere. An excellent spirit still exists among the brothers and students, even if the same spirit does not exist in all (which cannot be expected in 50 men). Certainly, our poverty has a great deal to do with it. We have little more than bread and water for nourishment, with the difference that we drink the water fresh and take bread with our soup, especially in Lent. Outside of this season, we have meat four times a week, but only once a day, and not much at that. Throughout the winter, we have had no vegetables other than beans. (The potatoes rotted and cabbage was scarce.) The bread was two-thirds corn meal and stone hard. One has to have a healthy stomach for this kind of bread so as not to burst. We will have more vegetables next year since we have prepared a nice garden, and the bread will be better because we are planting more wheat and rye. We can eat fruit when the trees I have been planting grow. In addition, in the future there will be some cheese on fast days since I have 18 cows already and believe I can maintain 30. Such a large number of brothers will hardly always be necessary, although in their place the students are increasing. There are now 35 brothers, three students, nine philosophers and theologians, one German beginner to be joined at Easter by a second, and the priests. We have already received word that others will be coming.

With regard to profession, I have decided after much deliberation to do it this way: the new arrivals–brothers or students–will remain for a while in the monastery without the habit, that is, until we can get to know them better and discover whether they are called. However, this will not be more than one year. Then they will make a one-year novitiate. Should they complete this satisfactorily, then I would like to let them make simple vows and then after the second year, solemn vows according to the following formula:

[Lat]

> *In the name of our Lord Jesus Christ, Amen. In [year], on [day], I [name] of the diocese of [name] promise chastity, poverty, obedience, and the conversion of life according to the Rule of St. Benedict and the Constitutions of this*

---

[114] Father Demetrius Gallitzin (1770-1840), the "Apostle of the Alleghenies."

monastery, before God and all the Saints whose relics rest in our monastery,
and in the presence of the Reverend Father [name], as long as I shall persevere
in the said monastery, not intending to leave by my own will. If, however, it
should happen that the superior of the said monastery should expel me from
it because of bad conduct, in that sole case would I be free and absolved of all
obligation of vows and of religion. In testimony whereof, etc.

This formula was prescribed for the brothers of the Congregation of St. Vitonus by Pope Alexander VII on July 30, 1666, and it seems to me to be the most suitable because it gives the good brother full security but allows full freedom to the superior to get rid of a bad one without his later being bound in conscience. Since the monastery is not yet recognized by Rome, I do not know whether I can ask for permission to use this formula. There is still time.

Thus, I close my long report. I commend myself and my people to Your Excellency's prayers, graciousness, and good will, being ready to fulfill any wish or command as far as I can, and I sign in deepest respect, your most obedient servant, P. Boniface Wimmer, O.S.B., Superior.

Ger   oALMV   cASVA   transWM

TO GREGORY ZIEGLER   26

St. Vincent, June 11, 1848

Most Reverend Bishop: Overburdened with business as I am, I still owe you an apology for writing so seldom, especially after receiving so many strong demonstrations of Your Grace's continued paternal concern for the welfare of the poor Benedictine colony in the distant forests of America. I presume that my abbot[115] from time to time supplements my neglect–at least I have asked him to do so and have always reported to him faithfully.

Yesterday I received a bill of exchange for the 600 gulden Your Grace kindly sent as a present for us. The letter was dated January 21 but just reached me now. I must therefore send an immediate expression of my deepest thanks for this generous new gift. Perhaps if I make you a report from our region that is of the delightful, comforting sort, it will be all the more appropriate under the circumstances,

---

[115] Gregory Scherr, O.S.B., abbot of Metten.

since the recent painful news surely fills Your Grace's kind heart with anxiety, sorrow, and grief.[116]

I reported earlier in my correspondence that after initially favorable relations with our most reverend bishop,[117] much trouble occurred on account of certain demands he made to which I could not possibly agree without betraying the German cause and giving up the independent status of the Order. I was of the opinion that I would have to move on and had sadly made arrangements to do so when finally, on December 6, 1847, the bishop yielded and placed the matter securely to rest by a formal, written document with regard to our continued possession of the place. He also retracted his demands. I ended up having to accept a debt of $800, half of which I have to pay in four years, the other half in six years. This is a completely unjust burden, but for the sake of peace, and in order to spare the bishop embarrassment, I entered into it, leaving it to Providence how I will fulfill the obligations I have assumed.

At last, I can seriously think of making long-range plans. During the winter, we cut down timber, broke stones, procured sand and lime, excavated a cellar, and the like. Since spring, we pressed and baked bricks (the masons are very busy), laid out a beautiful vegetable garden, planted some hundred and forty-odd fruit trees. Next autumn we will have enough space to increase our 40 people by 20 more. As long as my money lasted, I continued to increase the livestock, so that I now have 10 horses, 19 cows, 4 oxen, and enough young cattle, sheep, and pigs. At the same time, we cleared 20 acres of land and did everything to ensure the livelihood of the brothers.

Since Lent, I have ridden through my parish in all directions and have visited all the remote families in their homes. I discovered many for the first time who had never seen a priest, and I have established seven new stations where I can say Mass, preach, baptize, etc. in private homes at least a few times during the year. As far as I know, they are the remotest points of my parish, where I find Catholics 75 to 80 miles from one another. On the last excursion, 52 miles from my church, in a place where there has never been a permanent priest, I inquired in two directions about other families I had heard of. I will look for them the next time I go there. Certainly, there are many others out there, among them, unfortunately, many fallen-aways. Without priests, they become all too easily the prey of Presbyterians or Methodists, and seldom do they return. I hope with God's help that the situation will no longer occur in our parish that the salamander grows fat by the chil-

---

[116] Wimmer refers here to the success of liberal revolutionaries in Bavaria who had succeeded, among other things, in forcing King Ludwig I to abdicate.

[117] Michael O'Connor, bishop of Pittsburgh.

dren of God. On the other hand, we are making conquests, especially among the German Lutherans. If I could give them more attention, much could be hoped for, but until I have more priests, I can do little for them, for until now, I am the only traveling pastor of souls in the whole district. My father prior[118] is at home playing the role of professor for the senior students. The novice priest[119] cannot be employed very much, and I am therefore not letting him take vows with the rest. So I must do alone what can be done. For several weeks, I was at home only two days back to back. Otherwise, I am seldom at home.

A bad chair is usually my bed, on which I sleep sitting up. Sun and moon are my road guides in the beautiful oak forests. My shield is my Jesus, whom I always have near me. I also carry everything I need to offer the Holy Sacrifice of the Mass. Thus, my horse is a wandering chapel. I remain healthy and have never yet encountered any serious misfortune. I always ride in my habit. I understand English to the extent that I can preach, though just barely, hear confessions, catechize, and argue with the Protestants, for which there is always opportunity along the way. In this country, where there is true freedom, many people do not like Catholics. Some who live in regions where they have never seen one imagine the Catholic priest to be a monster, of whom they are afraid, like children elsewhere are of the boogeyman. Nevertheless, when they see that we, too, are like other people, only more well behaved and cultured, then we are allowed to pass quietly; indeed we may even be invited in as a guest, or at worst be laughed at. It will not be long before these incredible prejudices of the Americans will disappear and Catholicism will begin to gain attention and plentiful conversions will occur. Soon the Church will grow, and the growth will be in multitudes as more priests are available.

Three of the brothers have run off from me, also one student who was sent to me. On the other hand two brothers have joined and a new student as well. I now have ten theologians and philosophers as well as four beginners from America. I could not accept several who applied because of a shortage of space and provisions.

The brothers are getting on well with one another. On February 24, I permitted two who came along with me to make simple vows, as well as three theologians,[120] so that I now have a proper monastery. Four of the brothers have been set up as deans over the others in order to supervise the discipline. Two others are in charge

---

[118] Peter Lechner, O.S.B.

[119] Charles Martin Geyerstanger, O.S.B.

[120] The two brothers who took simple vows on February 24, 1848, were Joseph Sailer and Engelbert Nusser. The three students of theology were Benedict Haindl, Placidus Döttl, and Celestine Englbrecht.

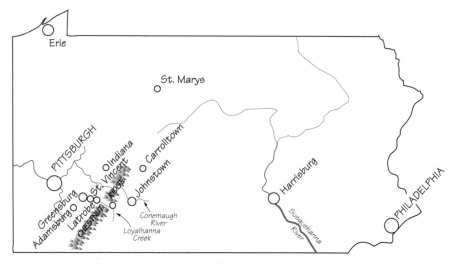

A map of Pennsylvania.

of the field and construction jobs so that I need only give my commands and the work then gets underway even when I am not at home. Prior Peter Lechner manages discipline and spiritual affairs in the best manner possible and is an excellent teacher and superb man of the Order. Thus, we live in peace and joy and seclusion from the world, partly with spiritual exercises, partly with physical labor in beautiful silence, hoping our dear God will bless our efforts and allow the small mustard seed to grow into a large tree. Until now God's blessing has been with us, and I can hold out, survive with all my people, even if my fatherland forgets me.

Recent events [in Bavaria] are a hard blow for me because they rob me of all hope of support from there, and this will naturally make it impossible for me to admit poor boys for study. Still, I do not want to despair, and God will not abandon me because I work only for Him and for His holy Church. My confreres in Bavaria, who earlier pitied me and predicted little success, are gradually beginning to understand that I indeed chose the better part, that I was perhaps sent out to America as quartermaster. I can hope in the course of the year to embrace several of them as companions in my need and in my toils. I only fear that others will take from them beforehand what they promised me, but it does not matter. Love has enough room, and they must eventually come happily to America.

Repeating my heartfelt thanks, I close with the sincerest wish that the Comforter, the Holy Spirit, in the midst of all present confusions and hardships, and those that are yet to come, may support, comfort, and strengthen Your Grace.

Strife in the quarreling Church is nothing new. Now it has taken another form. The damage will be great, but also the benefits, because light and darkness part company. In deepest veneration and service, Your Grace's eternally grateful, P. Boniface Wimmer

P.S. We suffer from a significant shortage of good theological works, especially on polemical and historical themes. We have nothing at all of the works of the holy fathers. Apart from these, there is also a shortage of musical instruments, particularly of a grand piano, which is atrociously expensive here but which we need very much. I have barely enough Mass vestments, but as soon as we have more priests here, these will also be in short supply, especially because there are more and more churches being built. Last year three were built and consecrated in our neighborhood.[121] We have only two chalices, the two that I brought.

Ger   oADL   cASVA   transAS

TO RUPERT LEISS   27

St. Vincent, March 12, 1849

Right Reverend Abbot: For your namesday, though very late, I wish every good thing for yourself and your whole community, because your happiness certainly consists in this: that all your people are happy. Unlike on previous occasions, this time I do not intend to ask any favors–would it help anyway? Rather, I intend to apologize for the favor granted–the sending of Father Peter [Lechner]. I was not sufficiently grateful nor was I satisfied. After the much, I have also asked for the more. I know now why the more has not come since Father Peter, when I accompanied him to St. Joseph's[122] (where he is to establish a new little monastery), made known to me that he had written you complaining about me because of the students' work.[123] I will not wonder any more. I will also not ask or complain any more.

Nevertheless, we still have never seriously fallen out. He has never knowingly and intentionally obstructed me. I did not and do not abandon my opinion that

---

[121] In 1847-1848 congregations in Greensburg, Saltsburg, and Ligonier had built churches under the direction of Wimmer.

[122] St. Joseph's Parish, Hart's Sleeping Place, Cambria County, Pennsylvania.

[123] Wimmer and Lechner had disagreed over the appropriateness of the Benedictine students doing manual labor. Wimmer insisted that they should work in the fields and thus contribute to the maintenance of the community while at the same time learning the value of manual labor. Lechner argued that by working in the fields they had less time to study.

students, too, must work "in case of necessity." My purpose is not to have many priests as soon as possible, but to discover how to make it possible that thirty to forty students, together with brothers and priests, can live with good management on a piece of land like ours here! If I know that and can achieve it, then soon there will be no further dearth of priests here.

However, Father Peter holds that one can live on air or on five to ten acres of land. I was pleased that on several occasions I was able to give him an opportunity in his new position to moderate these whims and to learn that only God can make something out of nothing. He has no distress there, but he needs money, much money despite much work, and that delights me. At first, he seemed to regard his station as a kind of exile, but I could not do otherwise. There was no one else whom I could send—and it was good for him.[124] In addition, he is not alone, there is another priest, Martin,[125] with him. Now he has settled down again and is very cheerful.

I visited him just recently. We are 55 miles or 22 hours from each other. There are six of them, more than 60 of us. For many it is too strict, for others it is not strict enough.[126] Leonard and Krebs whom Father Martin recommended are no longer here. I certainly have no enviable life, full of troubles and anxiety and responsibilities. Nevertheless, the good God seems to compensate for my wretchedness. Everything proceeds in such a way that one has to say "Forward!" The thing is practicable in and for itself, and after a couple of years nothing will be needed but a capable man who, combining a spiritual life with extraordinary skill, will stamp the whole with the proper spirit. There are many flexible tools, if only they are used well. I scarcely have time to think of Germany, and I am glad that I am here. I do not know whether the Lord will accept the various unfortunate circumstances [I have experienced] since my arrival here, and for almost a whole year, as a sufficient trial, or whether still more and greater ones are imminent. Nevertheless, things are relatively so good with me that I am uneasy about this. By chance Metten is now represented by me, Scheyern by Father Peter, Weltenburg

---

[124] After their disagreement, Wimmer sent Lechner to Carrolltown, Pennsylvania, to establish a priory at the site of St. Joseph's Church.

[125] Father Charles Martin Geyerstanger, O.S.B. (Father Martin) had spent a short time at the priory of Weltenburg before joining Wimmer as a clerical candidate.

[126] A second disagreement between Wimmer and Lechner had to do with monastic observance. Lechner wanted to create a more contemplative form of monasticism at St. Vincent, with strict enclosure and greater attention to liturgical practice, silence, study, and prayer. Wimmer, while recognizing the importance of these monastic values, was concerned about the practical problems of creating a viable community, establishing a seminary to train German-speaking priests, and attending to the pastoral care of the Catholics in his charge.

by Father Martin, and St. Stephen's (Ottobeuren) by Father Andrew Zugtriegel.[127] Metten has sent help and in due course Scheyern will too, if it can. Meanwhile, thank God for what we have. Please greet all the confreres most cordially and have me remembered by name to the Brothers of the Heart of Mary. I remain, with most sincere devotion, Your Grace's most obedient, P. Boniface

Ger   oASA   cASVA   transABi

TO KING LUDWIG I   **28**

St. Vincent, July 23, 1849

King Ludwig I

Most August, Most Mighty King! Just three years ago, at the audience that Your Royal Majesty so graciously deigned to grant me before my departure for America, Your Highness urgently charged me to preserve and promote here, with all vigor, the German language, culture, and life, and to strive to train devout and learned ministers for our holy religion, in whose cause Your Highness has already built a temple in the fifth continent.[128] May Your Royal Majesty permit me now to make a brief report on how I have up to this time complied with the task Your Highness assigned me.

When I left Munich, I was accompanied by four students and fifteen laymen. Of the latter, some were peasants, others of the middle class. All of them, however, wanted to be lay brothers in the Benedictine Order. Now, after three years, I am superior of a Benedictine mission that already numbers three houses, two in Pennsylvania and one in New Jersey.[129]

---

[127] The Bavarian monasteries had finally sent assistance to Wimmer. In addition to Fathers Peter and Andrew, Father Thaddeus Brunner, O.S.B. would soon arrive from Metten and take charge of the Latin school at St. Vincent.

[128] In 1844 Ludwig I had contributed 2,000 florins for the construction of a church in New Zealand.

[129] St. Vincent in Westmoreland County was the principal monastery in Pennsylvania. The other was St. Joseph's in Carrolltown, Cambria County. The house in New Jersey was St. Mary's Church,

Of the first two, the best one is situated in the beautiful mountainous county of Westmoreland, 250 miles west of Philadelphia and 40 miles east of Pittsburgh. We have here a rather large and roomy building with five priests, three clerics in minor orders, six who are studying theology or philosophy, and 36 lay brothers, all belonging to our Order. We have in addition a small minor seminary where this year there are 13 poor but talented German boys. Next year more than twice that many will be housed and taught free of charge. Three young men studying for the secular priesthood also enjoy with my novices their education and board without cost. Besides schoolwork, my priests and I must undertake the care of souls, without any outside help, in the two large counties of Westmoreland and Indiana, and to some extent in neighboring counties as well. The lay brothers take care of the buildings and do the farm work (there are 315 acres of good farmland). The farm is the source of our livelihood, which is very meager. Our second house located in Cambria County, with two priests of the Order and three lay brothers, ministers to souls and operates a school for Germans in Cambria, Blair, and Huntingdon counties.

The third house was founded just this year after the Council of Baltimore, at which I was the first to represent the Benedictine Order.[130] This foundation is in Newark, only nine miles from New York, and numbers two priests of the Order along with one brother. It has a splendid location on a hill overlooking the city (with 32,000 inhabitants), with a view of the bay and the towers of New York, the commercial metropolis of America.

The two priests are engaged in the care of souls in the local city parish, which has a rather large congregation. As soon as there is an increase in personnel, and provided we have sufficient funds, we shall have to consider founding a German school since there are over 150,000 Germans in the nearby cities of New York, Philadelphia, and Baltimore. Even so, my confreres not only in Newark but also in Carrolltown in Cambria County have undertaken the training of gifted boys to prepare them for higher education.

Thus, in a short period of time and with very limited means at our disposal, we have opened for the Benedictine Order a vast field of activity. In the first place, to be sure, our efforts are directed mainly toward the training of good, qualified German priests, since history always shows that without a zealous and well-educated

Newark, the parish founded in 1842 by Father Nicholas Balleis, O.S.B., of St. Peter's Abbey, Salzburg, Austria. Balleis had come to the United States in 1836 as an independent missionary and had submitted himself to Wimmer's jurisdiction when the Bavarian Benedictine mission arrived in the U.S. in 1846. In May 1849, Wimmer sent Father Placidus Döttl, O.S.B., one of the newly ordained priests at St. Vincent, to assist Balleis in Newark.

[130] In May 1849, Wimmer attended the Seventh Provincial Council of Baltimore during which he was named Benedictine Provincial in the United States.

clergy not only the spirit of religion, but also true human culture and real patriotism disappear from the people at large. Indeed, the budding beauty of the North American Union faces an awful fate in the next generations if, in the meantime, the strength of the Catholic Church has not grown to the point where, through her faithful disciples whose lives are guided by sound principles, she can became a mighty bulwark against the evil spirit of the various nonsensical forms of heresy and unbelief. I say this, O Royal Majesty, because it is forever true, and false liberalism would like to contradict it, that even the noblest concern for freedom, if it stems from purely human principles, begets nothing but egoism, whereas religion and genuine Catholicity provide the real key to patriotism. It is for this reason that our principal concern is the training and education of young Germans so that they may become good priests.

It is quite true, however, that along with this, we are working directly and indirectly for the preservation of the German language, culture, and life, and also to maintain an affectionate concern for the fatherland. We are not alone in our efforts, for the Redemptorist Fathers and recently the School Sisters [of Notre Dame] are working for the same end in the cities with great success.[131]

I am convinced that Your Royal Majesty always welcomes with the greatest pleasure anything done for the good of Germany and Holy Church, and that Your Highness, not content with that, also gladly becomes involved with the work yourself and strongly promotes it. On the strength of this conviction, I trust I am merely presenting to Your Royal Majesty a golden opportunity to exemplify this German and Catholic spirit, brilliant signs of which are everywhere in evidence, when I venture the most humble petition for your most gracious support in our endeavors. In making this petition, I humbly call attention to the fact that not only money but also other things would be very gratefully accepted, such as books on theology, philosophy, and history; sacred vessels or vestments; drawing materials; music books and music primers; ecclesiastical pictures or altar-pieces, etc. For we are in need of all these things, to a greater or lesser extent, and they cannot easily be obtained in this country. I have determined that our monasteries should not be simply schools for religion and learning, but should also serve as custodians of the fine arts and thus foster greater appreciation for culture, and protect our fellow countrymen from the mercenary spirit of the Americans who can think of nothing but how to make a living. It is dire need that compels them to think this, and example, we know, is contagious.

---

[131] Wimmer maintained communications with the German Redemptorists in New York, Baltimore, Philadelphia, Pittsburgh, and St. Marys, Pa. In St. Marys he had also made contact with the Bavarian School Sisters of Notre Dame.

Meanwhile, I certify in advance that all that you give will be used conscientiously for the specified purpose, that is, for the Germans and their interests, and for devout Catholics. I also would like to inform you that, when sending anything, the easiest and surest way of its reaching us is through the *Ludwig Missionsverein* in Munich, via Philadelphia or Baltimore. With filial confidence and fervent aspirations for the grace and favor of Your Highness, I bid you farewell. Your Royal Majesty's most humble, most loyal, and most faithful, P. Boniface Wimmer, Superior of the Bavarian Benedictine Mission in the United States

Ger   oRAB   cASVA   transBB   Math(10-12)

1850-1854

TO RUPERT LEISS

St. Vincent, March 27, 1850

Your Grace: Father Peter[1] is no longer under my authority but under yours, and soon probably no longer under yours either. Listen to the course of events. My earlier complaints are probably still in your memory. When the founding of the monastery[2] was completed, he hit on the notion of becoming a Trappist and disseminated it, as he had done with his notion of the founding of a monastery, in private conversations with novices and brothers. A certain Wohlfahrt,[3] a former Capuchin candidate and a private student without prospects, an eccentric, but otherwise a good man, who wanted to "live absolutely in the strictest order in the world," had either imparted it to him or had been taken in by him. He was his penitent and was, in any event, fortified and defended in his determination to become a Trappist by Father Peter. Since he had already made simple profession, I refused his request to go to Gethsemani (the Trappist monastery in Kentucky)[4] in order to ask for admittance and dissuaded him from leaving. Father Peter defended him, took no account of his vows, and held he could go and be accepted

---

[1] Peter Lechner, O.S.B.
[2] The priory in Carrolltown, Pennsylvania.
[3] Jerome Wohlfahrt, O.S.B., a young cleric who had come from Bavaria to join the monastery at St. Vincent.
[4] French monks of the Cistercian Order of the Strict Observance (Trappists) had established the monastery of Gethsemani in Kentucky in 1848.

even without my consent–which I denied. Nevertheless, I allowed him to speak on this matter to the bishop[5] so that he might ask admittance, and when he obtained it, I let him go. He was a good musician and his departure was therefore felt, although I was not unhappy to see him go because of his obstinacy, in which he persisted because of his limited insight and poor judgment.

This was around Michaelmas. He soon wrote to the prior. The letter came while I was with the brothers in St. Joseph's and was publicly read in the refectory by Father Andrew (of Ottobeuern)![6] He knew well how to exploit the sensitive issue among my brothers by stressing that the Trappists make solemn profession after one year (which, despite pressing demands, I have not yet granted and do not intend to grant any time soon) and that everyone is admitted. This did not fail to produce a considerable effect on some and to revive the agitation that had subsided. Having returned home, I was of course very indignant at what Father Andrew had done, and that the prior had permitted him to do it. I soon heard that four novices, penitents of his, among them my two best and now my only musicians, were preparing to leave for Gethsemani. Since my words were of no use, I bade them go, but before they went, Father Peter declared that he, too, wanted to go, and now I learned that he had long known of their decision, approved it, but had said nothing to me. I replied that he could not go without your consent, even more without a dispensation etc., but to no purpose. He got ready, but the day before he intended to leave (the others, meanwhile, had gone to Pittsburgh to await him), he came and said he could not go. Something was holding him back, as formerly at Scheyern,[7] and so he stayed once more, but the whole community knew of it.

Now, I thought, things would be quiet again, but after a few weeks, I heard that a letter from Wohlfahrt had come to him, which he read to some, but he did not speak of it to me. I kept silent and had no harsh thoughts, although I had to conclude that he was keeping up a secret correspondence.

On Palm Sunday, I had to celebrate Mass at Saltsburg, 16 miles from here. On leaving [St. Vincent] I said I would not return home before Tuesday because I intended to travel 20 miles farther to Indiana, where a nephew of mine was causing embarrassment on the outside similar to what the prior [Lechner] was

---

[5] Michael O'Connor of Pittsburgh.

[6] Andrew Zugtriegel, O.S.B., who had come from the Augsburg monastery to assist the Benedictine mission at St. Vincent. Zugtriegel soon left St. Vincent and went to Germany where he joined the Trappists. He became abbot of the Trappist monastery of Oehlenberg in Alsace and continued a long correspondence with Wimmer.

[7] Before coming to America, Lechner had once considered leaving the Benedictines at Scheyern to become a Jesuit.

causing inside.[8] Since the Annunciation is celebrated here as a holy day on March 25, and several people wanted to confess, I had to spend the night in Saltsburg. On Monday I offered Mass there and then went home so as not to be absent too long. When I arrived, the prior asked permission to go to Pittsburgh to speak to his friend Dr. Bosl[9] (with whom he continually corresponded) before he left Pittsburgh. I granted it because I always sought to keep him in as good a humor as possible, but in the evening after Compline my Father Placidus[10] came to my room and told me that the prior had again received a letter from Wohlfahrt. He had then sent for him as his confessor, had fallen on his knees before him, and had asked his opinion with regard to his joining the Trappists. Wohlfahrt had written that he would be accepted and his vows would be no obstacle, etc. Father Placidus, who like all my priests and clerics and a great majority of brothers is sincerely devoted to me, was startled by such an overture because of the recent irritations, and said he did not dare give an opinion in this matter.

I slept little that night and pondered long on what I should do. I foresaw that he would not pay attention to my remonstrance. He had virtually ignored your paternal letter to him, which he showed me and which I copied. I saw that the letter writing and the conspiring would never end and that I would have no peace so long as he was in the house. A few days earlier, before the letter arrived, he had turned his attention to the Milwaukee theologians studying here and called upon them to join him and found a monastery with him! Perhaps you think I am joking, but dear Peter is really like a banner on the roof, and, in understanding and ideas, a child.

Perhaps it would be more politic to leave him alone. He will only make himself ridiculous by parading his fantastic plans and little by little lose all prestige. Moreover, his teaching is extremely pernicious, for if it is true, as he boldly maintains before novices and brothers, and was and again is about to show through example, that every religious, even after solemn profession, can enter a stricter order without the knowledge and against the will of his superior, then no superior is secure, especially with respect to simple vows. He also taught that whereas the superior could not dismiss any subject without the most serious reasons, each could freely leave him! My arguments against this claim, which I have had to insist on to him privately and publicly, have, it is true, made him hesitant, but they

---

[8] Wimmer discusses his nephew's embezzlement of funds intended for the mission at St. Vincent later in this letter. This incident was the beginning of the famous brewery controversy that brought Wimmer into conflict with Bishop O'Connor of Pittsburgh.

[9] Superior of the Redemptorists in Pittsburgh.

[10] Placidus Döttl, O.S.B., one of the pioneer students at St. Vincent who was ordained in 1849.

have not converted him. Hence, he wanted to go to Pittsburgh to consult Father Bosl and, as he told Father Placid, the bishop. Nevertheless, I had to expect that in his present mood, he would become a Trappist or, after a short while, the old dance would begin again. In order, then, not to be always beaten down and appear as the vanquished, but rather to stand forth as avenger of the infringement of order, I decided to dismiss Father Peter the next morning and restore him to your authority. Just as I left the altar, however, I was summoned to a dying man one hour's journey from here, and by the time I got back Father Peter had gone. He had travel money, for he had received six Mass stipends (three dollars) and had kept them.

I then wrote a dismissorial letter with the statement that he had returned to his own superior, but honorably and with the best recommendation. In an attached letter, I explained the reasons to him and advised him to go to Father Balleis in Newark and from there to write you and execute the change legally if he believed himself called. I would give him money for the trip to Newark but not to Gethsemani. I sent this to Father Bosl in Pittsburgh, from whom he obtained it, and I reported to the bishop. At the same time, I forbade him my house unless he were obedient.

It is difficult and vexatious that it has to come to this, but I had no alternative. I must have peace. He cannot truthfully say that there is no order and discipline here, that nothing is suitable, nothing goes forward. What is not properly ordered because of deficiencies in the locality will not be changed. We have built a house 60 feet long, 40 feet wide, and three stories high, which attached to the old one, is now 100 feet long. It is finished except for the attic, which is still to be constructed. This year I will add 36 feet and in another year, I will add to the front. Then our monastery will be as long as the monastery at Scheyern. A brick barn, 60 feet long, 40 feet wide, and 40 feet high up to the roof, was built in the autumn and is large enough for the harvest. Twenty boys obtain a good education. There are 15 philosophers and theologians. Four clerics will soon be ordained. In a radius of 30 to 40 miles, we have pastoral care of the Germans and often of the English also. Choir prayer and the brothers' rosary take place regularly. The nocturnal silence is strictly observed. Meditation and the examinations of conscience are diligently performed, as is spiritual reading. Fresh water is our only drink. Our food is ordinary fare. No priest or cleric takes breakfast (nor do I), apart from the prior. I gladly allowed him this and prescribed it because of his infirmity. If the brothers work out of doors, they are required to take breakfast on my orders–the prior opposes this–because I want good work and cannot have brothers here just for fasting and prayer. He gave his lectures most diligently. Because I lost all my musicians because of the prior, I have hired a layperson to whom I must give $100 for food and clothing. The boys sing and fiddle and even play the piano and organ quite well. Enclosure is strictly observed with regard to the outside. I still have to allow women in the parlor and kitchen because on Sundays the people, especially mothers, often need a little breakfast if they come from a distance and are fasting, but on workdays no one comes in. It is unavoidable that I am often away (especially since, because of the bishop's unrelenting pressure, I sent two priests to St. Marys[11]). Therefore, I appointed a prior and dean, but it cannot be said of me that I have traveled or ridden only for pleasure, and if I can ever reach my monastery, I travel all the way home, often at 10:00 or 11:00 at night.

I had a bad year, full of conflicts, inside and out. A nephew of mine, who was supposed to bring me money, embezzled 1,000 florins. Since he no longer had it, I could not get it from him. He bought a brewery in the expectation of a good marriage. It fell through. I loaned him money in order to make it possible for him to pay the 1,000 florins or be able to pay it myself. Since he again displayed an inclination to seek his own advantage rather than mine, I threw him off the premises and kept the brewery for myself. As a precaution, I had the bill of sale made out to me. This caused me much thought and anxiety, but still I saved my money and hope sometime to be able to erect a small monastery there (in Indiana, Pennsylvania). Frequently, I have not had a dollar in the safe and 80 mouths in the house to feed. In addition, the consciousness of being surrounded by false confreres, the constant opposition, the endless series of impractical proposals, the perpetual complaining when I cannot conjure up everything–this is difficult. Still, I am unremitting, always well, and delight in the Lord, for it is also a comfort to suffer, especially when suffering comes not from wickedness but from well meaning but misdirected zeal. I know indeed that this is the case with the prior, but there I had to prescribe limits, because otherwise the devil could only have made the chasm wider and finally caused a break, and perhaps that is what is happening. As God wills it, but I cannot help it. I need my prestige and hence must maintain it. I do not know what he is engaged in. I hope he does not completely forget himself but remains in Pittsburgh as a professor in the diocesan seminary, where one is now needed. Later I want to report further, but I would advise you not to recall him home, because he will not willingly go or will not go at all and because, for all his piety, he is difficult to manage.

Perhaps it is different with you, but he regards me as beneath him in every respect, in behavior, in learning, and in age, and he cannot do so with regard to you in any respect. He has that unfortunate disposition of imagining as perfect

---

[11] The German colony of St. Marys in Elk County, Pennsylvania.

anything that he does not have, and just as at Scheyern the Jesuits were his ideal, so here the Trappists are. He is a man of feeling such as few are. I love and honor him, but he has caused me more grief, chagrin, and harm than my worst enemy could have done. However, if I have not acted properly as superior, or if I have acted too tactlessly against him and you, please excuse me on the grounds of necessity and good will. I saw and see no other way. I thank you for your kind assistance and your good will, but God preserve me from helpers who instead of gathering merely scatter, instead of inculcating the customary generally impose the extraordinary, instead of cooperating always want to reform and construct after their own ideas! So far, I have no reason to alter or discard the plan I am following, but I am so disposed that I could easily adopt another, according to circumstances. Moreover, if God is with me, the devil may do as he wishes–Mount St. Vincent is really a thorn in his side–and it will surely pass. What I need this year are $2,000 and 20 good students. If I do not get them, the sky will not fall in. I would need absolutely nothing for St. Vincent if I had not been forced to make that purchase because of my nephew's rascality.

May God grant you good times, vigorous health, and limitless, prosperous activity. I sign with sincerest respect, Your Grace's most grateful, P. Boniface

P.S. We received very late that breviary and the four dollars for my nephew Alois,[12] who will be ordained after Easter. Thank you so much. God bless you.

Ger   oASA   cASVA   transABi,VH   *SVJ3*

TO GREGORY SCHERR   **30**

Mount St. Vincent, August 14, 1850

Your Grace: I was unable to answer your letter of February 26 earlier than today. I received the money from the bishop[13] in due time and have thanked the old gentleman in writing. If you happen to have any Mass stipends left over, please do not forget me. I am very happy that you have built such a beautiful monastery and that Metten is advancing so rapidly. I am very eager to hear who will be the abbot of St. Boniface[14] and am hoping that it will be Father Placidus.[15]

---

[12] Luke Aloysius Wimmer, O.S.B. (1825-1901), came to St. Vincent in 1847.
[13] Gregory Ziegler, bishop of Linz, Austria.
[14] St. Boniface Abbey, Munich.
[15] Father Placidus Lacense, O.S.B.

My Father Peter[16] is no longer here, as you may have already heard. I have shut the door to him. He was in Pittsburgh, but having tasted enough of that place, he has now gone to Milwaukee. Father Andrew,[17] the Suabian, intended to join the Trappists, and inasmuch as he had submitted a release from his abbot, I let him go. You may have already heard this through the court chaplain.[18] He enticed three brothers to follow him—my master of works directly and explicitly, and two others indirectly. I did not give Father Peter permission to leave. During that time, I fought with him by letter until he was exhausted. The bishop himself,[19] together with Fathers Bosl and Haftenscheid,[20] relying on the writings of St. Alphonsus Ligouri, shared the same opinion, namely, that a solemnly professed monk, without asking for or receiving the permission of his superior, could join an order of stricter observance. For a long time, I could use only arguments dictated by common sense to oppose this view, but then I found an excellent edition of the decrees of the Council of Trent (Chapter 51 "Concerning Religious," Session 25, fourth declaration), which declared that only "with the approbation of the monastic chapter and for a well-established cause etc." could permission be granted. Even more explicitly, in the fortieth discourse of Cardinal de Luca's *Annotations on the Decrees of the Council of Trent*, it is stated that such permission may not be granted at all "without the approbation of the Sacred Congregation of Religious" and that the Sacred Congregation would then contact the monk's superior who, if a transfer were to be granted, would determine the Order which the supplicant could join.

Despite all this, he still did not believe me until he himself in his readings came across a similar case in a French text where it was stated that by a special decree of Pope Clement XIII the matter was reserved to the Holy See. At that point, the whole comedy took a ridiculous turn. Father Andrew, whom my Trappists had followed most eagerly, was the first one to run off [from the Trappist Abbey at Gethsemani, Kentucky]. It seems they had to go to confession through an interpreter. Others followed him, though a few remained because they did not have the money to leave. The most enthusiastic of all (the private student Wohlfahrt[21]) was the first to return to St. Vincent, just as he was the first to go to Gethsemani. They found that there was a less strict enclosure there than here, and they were

---

[16] Peter Lechner, O.S.B. (1805-1874).

[17] Andrew Zugtriegel, O.S.B., of St. Stephen's Abbey, Augsburg.

[18] Joseph Ferdinand Müller (1803-1864), chaplain to the court of King Ludwig I of Bavaria and general manager of the *Ludwig Missionsverein*.

[19] Michael O'Connor (1810-1872), bishop of Pittsburgh (1843-1860).

[20] Redemptorist priests in Pittsburgh.

[21] Jerome Wohlfahrt, O.S.B.

especially shocked by the heartlessness towards the sick. During their sojourn, three brothers in solemn vows ran off. These events forced even my hot-headed Peter to admit that he had erred.

Father Andrew, being aware of his guilt, did not want to come back, but I threatened him with severe punishment for his obstinacy, and he finally returned the day before yesterday from Louisville where he had been staying since he left Gethsemani. I do not want to keep him here. I do not need such scoundrels. I made him aware of how we stand with each other and will send him back to St. Stephen's where his abbot can let him go where he pleases.[22]

Father Peter still had ideas about founding a monastery, which his abbot[23] killed in his last letter to him. He has ordered him back to his monastery, allowing him only one more year in America. In the papers he left behind, we found a petition to the Holy See dated June 20, 1845, regarding a monastery he planned to establish under a new rule for religious. All this I have to send to the abbot of Scheyern for his information. No wonder he was so busy here. His plan was to found his own monastery and to destroy mine. He would have done this had I not used every means possible to defeat his efforts. He did not expect this. I have now experienced sufficiently what it means to live with false brethren. Only God knows what I had to suffer this past year. He helped me, and everything intended for my shame and destruction turned out in the end to increase and strengthen my reputation, both inside and outside the house.

I do not know yet what to do with those who were deceived. One of them I rejected out of hand upon his return. Concerning the other three, I held consultations with my community. They were in favor of taking them back, but as novices. However, I am very much afraid that I will bring the enemy back into my house if I accept them. What I suspected is now certain. Fathers Peter and Andrew blatantly advised them inside and outside the confessional to leave, and not only them. They also enticed some of the most highly-trained brothers–the tanner and the saddler, for example. The joke cost me $500 and in many ways held me back in the work of building.

Your Father Thaddeus[24] is in no way better. He is doing nothing that would disgrace a priest, but he is trying everything in his power to deprecate the monastery,

---

[22] Father Andrew Zugtriegel returned to St. Stephen's Abbey, Augsburg, and later transferred to the Trappist Abbey of Oehlenberg in Alsace, where he became abbot. In later years, Wimmer carried on a cordial correspondence with him.

[23] Rupert Leiss, O.S.B. (1795-1872), abbot of the Bavarian abbey of Scheyern.

[24] Thaddeus Brunner, O.S.B., a priest from Metten who had come to assist Wimmer at St. Vincent.

to raise suspicions, and to make life sour for his brethren by unspoken opposition. For the present, Father Lemke[25] is his close friend, to whom for months in his loneliness I had given food and shelter. Now in gratitude he is agitating against the Benedictines, possibly because I had warned both Father Thaddeus and Father Celestine[26] to be careful of him. Not only would I gladly permit your Father Thaddeus to return home, I am asking you to recall him and to send the travel expenses. Four weeks ago, he was here[27] trying in some way to surrender, i.e., making conditions under which he would stay. These conditions were nothing less than that I should give up my whole plan for the brothers and their agricultural work to be the main source of income so that I can erect a seminary for poor boys who want to become priests. He wants me to accept his plan, i.e., to build a seminary for rich boys who are able to pay $100 a year, and thus make our life here easier. Naturally, I rejected his plan. To accept it, I would have had to become a traitor to my own cause, to the *Missionsverein*, and to the Church. Besides, I do not have the professors for such a project. Moreover, Father Thaddeus, who wanted to become the director, is the last person fit for that position because through negligence he has failed to learn even enough English to hear confessions. With all their cleverness, these gentlemen do not know what they want. They hardly know what they are saying, and they want to tell old Father Boniface, a man with all kinds of experience, what to do. That won't happen either today or tomorrow.

You console me in your letter by saying that things will improve by and by. I do not know what reports you have received, but in this, Father Abbot, I am telling you the absolute truth: our situation is not bad. It is good, very good. If I were to listen to Father Thaddeus, I could bring in $5,000 (12,000 to 13,000 florins) this year, but I already have my buildings and my people, and I am able to have them without that money. I came here not for the rich Englishmen but for my poor countrymen, and toward that end I prefer to suffer some distress and a meager income for the opportunity to give my young priests time for their education rather than to serve the world and enjoy a large income. Am I wrong in doing so? Must I be ashamed of my poverty? We are not in such great need anymore thanks to the bishop of Linz and, of course, my incomparable friend, the reverend court chaplain.

In just the past few days I have been bargaining for a large farm of 300 acres for which I have offered $9,000 (or about 24,000 florins), half of which will be

---

[25] Peter Henry Lemke (1796-1882), the German missionary who had invited Wimmer to Cambria County, Pennsylvania, and who in 1852 entered the novitiate at St. Vincent.

[26] Celestine Charles Englbrecht, O.S.B. (1824-1904), one of the pioneer Benedictine students.

[27] Wimmer had assigned Brunner to the priory in Carrolltown, Pa.

due on April 1, 1851, and the other half two years later. Everyone realizes that I can count on help from abroad, so I have sufficient credit to raise this money. At least I reasonably hope so. Last spring my financial distress was enormous because my nephew Matthias caused an embarrassment for which I was not prepared. Just as the prior and the other stranger priests caused me problems inside the house, so he brought me untold misery and embarrassment outside the house. I did not expect to be swindled. If he had only listened and not overstepped all bounds of reason, prudence, and justice, everything could have been settled smoothly, but I was to have a year full of bitterness, insult, and worry in that I had to be crucified by my spiritual brothers and my own nephew. Nevertheless, I succeeded in my struggle with him. The victory is mine, and all the rascals who were against me and were trying to shout me down are silenced, including the fellow whom the devil brought from hell just to set everything in motion against me, and an unhappy priest, poor Stauber,[28] who had cooperated with him because of his conviction that I was the cause of his suspension.

Recently I myself came into conflict with my bishop because I had recalled my priests from St. Marys for the reason that I needed them at home. I also did not want to become a tool of the bishop and the land company for their greedy plans. Because of that, he was very angry with me since the plans he had for the sisters in St. Marys were frustrated. There suddenly followed a prompt demand that I at once sell, rent, or close down the brewery in Indiana.[29] I could do none of these three things without suffering a huge loss. For that reason, I did not submit to the bishop's demands. I calmly gave him my reasons, but in order to please him I promised that when time and circumstances permitted I would either sell or rent the brewery because in fact I myself was anxious to get rid of it. A disagreement ensued (and continues). I went from the defensive to the offensive and from the fact to the question of principle. Namely, I stated that the Benedictines in North America surely have the same rights as others (the Redemptorists, the Jesuits, the Vincentians), wherever they are living, to drink beer, and while I never really thought of building a brewery because my stomach can still digest water, that might not always be the case with the stomachs of my confreres. In the rural districts, you cannot get good beer. It is either not very good or too expensive. Because of that, we have to make it ourselves, and since it would cost too much

---

[28] Unidentified.

[29] Wimmer's nephew, who had embezzled funds sent to St. Vincent from Bavaria, had with his uncle's assistance bought a brewery in Indiana in order to repay the money he had embezzled through the profits he earned from beer sales. The nephew failed in the beer business, whereupon Wimmer took over the brewery in an attempt to make it profitable. Bishop Michael O'Connor, a temperance advocate, opposed the Benedictines' involvement in the beer trade.

to brew it only for ourselves, we must consider brewing it for others as well. It would not cost us anything, and besides it would mean a great resource for the management of the kitchen and the seminary. All over the world monks have their breweries and vineyards and sell what they do not need for themselves. You find nothing against it in Canon Law or in the Decrees of Trent. We are not living in China or Turkey. We are not speaking of a new right here, but rather of the right to brew beer and have a tavern. If the bishop does not permit it, I will assure him that he will not see many Benedictine monasteries in his diocese. In the two we already have,[30] I am convinced that we have the right to do what is not forbidden but permitted within the limits of the *Holy Rule* and Canon Law. For quite some time I have been waiting for an answer to my letter. It appears the bishop has cooled down and I hope he will soon be my friend again.

Such is the case with me. Everything is aimed at my poor self, but I have also become cooler than before, and for that reason I am not so easily bent. *Intus pugnae et foris.*[31] The dear Lord has given me harsh lessons and opportunities to know the world and its inhabitants.

For three weeks, my whole house has been struck with illness, one after the other. It is a kind of flu or influenza or cholera that has pinched me since last Saturday, but it is improving. The real cholera is in the neighborhood, but not in the monastery.

The cock is crowing a second time already. I have to close. Perhaps later I will have time to add a "Let us rejoice" to all these tales of woe. If not now, then another time. Pray for me and my household, and ask your people to pray for us. My affairs are in good shape, but it is extremely important that the devil give us a rest by not interfering so much. Our harvest was very good. If you know someone who wants to buy a brewery and can afford it, a brewery that will earn him 5,000 florins and change (in cash), he would have a wonderful opportunity here.

Cordial greetings to Father Subprior and all the old and young fathers. For the Methodist Carl I can do nothing. Since my first notice, I have not heard anything. With me at present are Fathers Benedict Haindl, Placidus Döttl (the prior), Charles Geyerstanger, Maurus Zacherl, Luke Wimmer, Odilo Vandergrün (recently ordained). Father Celestine [Englbrecht] is with your Father Thaddeus [Brunner] in Carrolltown. In addition, there are here: a German theologian and two English ones who give my priests two-hour English lessons every day. The boys are on vacation. We expect no less than 30 of them this year.

---

[30] At St. Vincent and Carrolltown.
[31] There are battles inside and out.

The petition to the Holy Father with regard to an abbey I shall send in the near future to the court chaplain. It is an absolute necessity that our monastery receive recognition from Rome and be confirmed as an abbey. Please be assured that by this petition I do not have in mind being appointed abbot but that I merely request that the monastery be made an abbey. Please do not fail to acknowledge that my intention is honest. I am not envious of anyone for the miter and crosier. If nothing but ambition motivated me, I would have followed Father Xavier[32] long ago. (I am not implying that ambition moved my dear confrere.) As long as I am wise, as long as I am able, and as long as it is the will of God, I shall keep on fighting right and left, putting my trust in Him for whom I do battle, who was always on my side and helped me to final victory.

I do not like sending my young priests outside, but sometimes circumstances require an exception. I call them home in due time for the spiritual exercises.

The German monsters, whom the revolution floated across to us, are furiously shouting here against priests and monasteries. They want to devour us all, but that is nothing new. A squadron of them would not terrify us, in our fortress on the mountain. Upon the advice of Father Lemke, we brought double-barreled shotguns along for hunting bears, and we can use them to shoot holes in the skins of these anarchists. We are still riding on horseback through the countryside in our habits! For the present no one dares make an attempt on us because there are 2,000 Irish railroad workers throughout the county who have so much respect for us that they even kiss the footprints we leave when we walk. That's the truth!

I am very grateful for your well-intentioned advice that I not make any criticism of my confreres public, but I have to say that letters of mine, in which I discussed similar cases and which were not for publication, were printed anyway. It was done with a bad intention. I myself, to my great embarrassment, have seen some of my own letters in print that were written in private. Surely, you will not give me the consolation of making public my letters intended for you. As a result of an earlier incident I came into conflict with the Redemptorists, especially with the sensitive Dr. Bosl, the intimate friend of my man with similar ideas.[33] I was unable to understand his rebuke until I discovered that I was supposed to have printed in the public papers the statement that "the Redemptorists have it easy, sitting around in cities and having a good time." I did not say that, and if I wrote something like it (I really can't recall), I wrote it privately and did not mean to do any harm.

---

[32] Probably Father Xavier Sulzbeck, O.S.B., of Metten.
[33] A reference to Father Peter Lechner.

The student from Vienna who was announced has not yet arrived. Probably the "Reds" could not use him. Otherwise, they would not have sent him to me.

One day you will see me at Metten bringing a regiment along. You wrote, "The money requested follows." That means I can expect more money since I have not received it yet. I am still waiting for the grammars. The letter from Offenburg I have sent to Miss Elise. We often correspond with each other. P. Boniface

Ger   oAMA   cASVA   transRG

TO KING LUDWIG I   31

Munich, April 18, 1851

Most Gracious King and Lord: In accordance with my promise, I most respectfully submit to Your Majesty the enclosed accurate sketch of our monastery at
Mount St. Vincent that I just received. Father Luke,[34] who drew it, depicted the
monastery from the southeast since this gave him the opportunity to represent
all the buildings together, although by doing so, the whole is out of proportion
and one is not given a true picture of the relative position of the individual buildings.

What you see first is the church with the cemetery behind it. The tall building
along with the smaller addition to the right of the church is the monastery, which
is parallel to the church. In the center of the open space before the church, there
is a large mission cross. The small building near the fence is the blacksmith shop.
The somewhat larger building with four windows is the schoolhouse. The large
three-story building contains, in the American style, the stables on the ground
floor and the barn above it. Between the barn and the schoolhouse, one can see
the gable of a small building, which was the first dwelling of the earlier German
missionaries. The road runs from the barn down the hill between two hedges
(called here "fences"). You can see Chestnut Ridge in the distance, the last range
of the Allegheny Mountains. It will be a great pleasure for me when I reach the
point where I can most respectfully lay before Your Royal Majesty, by means of
subsequent sketches, a still more faithful picture of the whole structure, showing
at the same time the progressive development of the basic idea underlying the
whole construction. I hope that our monastery proves to be a powerful support,
not only for religion, but also for German learning, art, and language.

---

[34] Luke Aloysius Wimmer, O.S.B. (1825-1901), was Wimmer's nephew.

To make all this possible, it is above all necessary that it enjoy a formal stability just as much as a material stability. Your Royal Majesty will remember from my previous report that the land and ground on which the monastery stands was actually purchased 70 years ago by a German Franciscan[35] who in his last will and testament bequeathed it for the support of his successor in the church there. Later it was formally recognized by the state as Catholic Church property, but then it fell entirely into English hands where it remained for 23 years until it was given over, through me personally, to the Benedictine Order by the present bishop of Pittsburgh, Dr. Michael O'Connor. Through the incorporation of St. Vincent Parish into the Benedictine Order, this land became the property of the Order in perpetuity. It was of the greatest importance to me that this transfer by the diocesan bishop receive papal confirmation. I was glad to receive this confirmation by papal decree through the *Propaganda Fide* on July 23, 1848.

This, however, was not sufficiently formal either for me or for the bishop of Pittsburgh. Therefore, to put an end to all doubt and anxiety, I directed a new presentation of this matter to his Eminence Cardinal Fransoni[36] and even thought of going to Rome myself in order to hasten and expedite matters and to entreat his Holiness that St. Vincent, already declared through a formal decree to be a monastery enjoying all the rights and privileges as such, be formally elevated to an abbey since the necessary number of monks are already there or shall be when I return home, and since furthermore with the broader expansion of our Order in America, in order to preserve unity and proper subordination among the various superiors, it is necessary that the superior of the monastery be one who enjoys a higher ecclesiastical position and greater authority.

I faced a problem, however, because on the one hand it appeared to me to be an offense against decorum if I were the one to make such a move, since it could be attributed to ambition and self-promotion. On the other hand, from the time when Your Royal Majesty became truly the founder of our monastery through the most gracious gift of 10,000 florins and a valuable library, it appeared to be entirely in the nature of things that just as after the restoration of the Benedictine monasteries in Bavaria Your Highness yourself had a share in the merit, and in the honor and glory as well, so also in history you should stand out as the founder of the first Benedictine abbey in America.

I have given up the idea of a trip to Rome and presume instead to make this humble petition. May it please Your Royal Majesty to propose [to the Holy See]

---

[35] Theodore Brouwers, O.F.M. Cap., who purchased the land in 1790.
[36] Giacomo Filippe Fransoni (1775-1856), prefect of the Sacred Congregation for the Propagation of the Faith.

that the Benedictine monastery, Mount St. Vincent, in the diocese of Pittsburgh, in Westmoreland County of the State of Pennsylvania, whose canonical erection was already confirmed through a papal decree from the *Propaganda* on July 23, 1848, be formally declared an abbey; and that the landed property belonging to the church there for the support of the priests, and also the parish house itself, as they were handed over in perpetuity by Dr. Michael O'Connor, bishop of Pittsburgh, to the Benedictine Order, so also should belong to the same irrevocably.[37]

Since Your Royal Majesty must be concerned that your endowment, as far as possible, continue to be used for its specified purpose, and since I myself can assure you, in all sincerity, that I have been led to make this most humble petition by no other motive than the security and furtherance of my undertaking for the welfare of our German countrymen in America, therefore I am confident of your most gracious guarantee for the same. With feelings of the warmest gratitude and of the most faithful affection and devotion, I bid you farewell with the most profound respect and loyalty. Your Highness is our most gracious protector and founder, and I, Your Royal Majesty's most humble, most loyal, and most faithful, P. Boniface Wimmer, Superior of the American Benedictine Mission

Ger   oRAB   cASVA   transBB   Math(25-28)

TO KING LUDWIG I   32

Mount St. Vincent, September 4, 1851

Most Gracious King and Lord: Since my last most humble report I have had the opportunity to meet personally with the bishop of my diocese[38] and to speak about matters concerning our monastery. On August 27, I was in St. Marys,[39] the German colony that with few exceptions is inhabited mostly by people from Old Bavaria and the Upper Palatinate. I have now definitively undertaken the care of souls in this colony and have come to a firm resolution and decision to establish a Benedictine monastery there. For this purpose, the bishop handed over to me 745 acres of land formerly occupied by the Redemptorists. Upon their withdrawal from the colony, this land became the property of the congregation, whereupon the congregation handed it over to the bishop.

---

[37] Upon the intervention of the Bavarian government, the Holy See confirmed St. Vincent as a canonical monastery in 1851 but delayed elevating it to the rank of abbey until 1855.

[38] Michael O'Connor of Pittsburgh.

[39] The German colony of St. Marys, Pennsylvania.

These 745 acres are now the property of our Order with no obligation or condition other than that the Order be responsible for the care of souls in the colony. Two fathers have now begun to carry on this work there. I have entered into special negotiations to acquire some additional pieces of land intermingled with our property. In addition, I have made proposals to some private individuals, whose homes would be too close to the monastery we have projected, to give up those homes for which they will be compensated either with money or with land further away. I had to act in this way; otherwise, I would not feel properly oriented in my surroundings and our lay brothers could not very well work at cultivating the land if in the midst of it or very close to it there were living the heads of German families with their wives and daughters.

For the present, I have gained nothing by accepting this land. Rather, I have lost a great deal, first because the cultivation of the land involves much toil and labor, and second, because a monastery and church must be built, since both were burned down a year ago. The very fact that no one was willing to espouse the cause of the Germans there was motive for me to do something in the hope that through an unflagging will and a dogged determination I might find myself in a position whereby I could at least, little by little, bring something to pass that would be a credit to the German name and the Catholic Church. The bishop himself was much pleased to see that finally the religious needs of the congregation were addressed and permanent provision for the people had been made.

He told me that His Eminence Cardinal Fransoni[40] wrote him asking for an explanation of why he had refused to use the full authority accruing to him, which empowered him to make a formal declaration that our monastery has been canonically erected and is to be recognized as such.[41] He said that he immediately explained to the cardinal that he never intended to refuse the final, formal recognition of our monastery as one enjoying full canonical status and independence, but that he was simply waiting for a decision from Rome about a question that is quite familiar to you, namely, whether in America monasteries are authorized to have breweries and sell beer at retail.

In the enclosed letter to Cardinal Fransoni I have discussed this problem and refuted the objections that were raised. I made the point that the judgment handed down in this matter by the Irish-American prelates was entirely one-sided and biased since these gentlemen usually ignore the Germans entirely, in spite of the

---

[40] Giacomo Filippe Fransoni, prefect of the Sacred Congregation for the Propagation of the Faith.

[41] O'Connor was reluctant to have an independent monastery within his jurisdiction and had postponed promulgation of the Roman decree establishing St. Vincent as a canonical priory. Wimmer had complained of this to the Holy See through Bavarian diplomatic channels.

fact that in the non-slave-holding States we form one-half and in some cases even the majority of the population. (Cardinal Fransoni wrote to Count von Spaur[42] of "certain prominent ecclesiastics of those provinces close to the bishop," by which he could only mean the two archbishops, Hughes of New York and Purcell of Cincinnati, both of whom are Irish and were in Rome at the time). We are entitled to have our ideas of justice and decency receive some consideration.

Furthermore, I let His Eminence know that I did not come to America to brew beer, and in fact had not given a thought to building a brewery. It was purely accidental that I had to defend and justify myself for possessing and running a brewery because I was compelled to take over a small one, far from the monastery, in order not to lose a considerable amount of money.[43]

Hence, I hope there will be no further obstacle from any quarter to prevent the erection of an abbey. I hope too that with the papal confirmation and its formal recognition by the bishop, our position will in a very short time be fully secure, if indeed Your Royal and Most Gracious Majesty will be so kind as to deign to employ Your Highness's name and influence for the cause.

This, then, would be my plan: that in every diocese the smaller houses would be governed by priors, all of them under the jurisdiction of an abbot. Then when the Order becomes more widespread, all the abbots should be united in one congregation so that by a union of their energies and resources, in the interests of both Church and nation, against heresy and unbelief and against English usurpation as well, they may enter the arena with greater strength. Finally, I venture the humble petition that Your Royal Majesty forward the enclosed report to Rome through the Royal Bavarian Embassy, since I cannot otherwise be certain of its safe arrival.

With the most sincere assurance of my faithful affection and devotion and with deepest respect, I bid you farewell. Your Royal Majesty's most humble, most loyal, and most faithful, P. Boniface Wimmer, Superior

Ger   oRAB   cASVA   transBB   Math(30-33)

---

[42] The Bavarian ambassador to the Holy See.

[43] A nephew of Wimmer had embezzled money sent from Bavaria for the monastery at St. Vincent. To assist him in repaying what he had stolen, Wimmer helped his nephew finance the purchase of a brewery and tavern in Indiana, Pennsylvania. When the enterprise failed through the nephew's mismanagement, Wimmer took over the operation. Bishop O'Connor objected strenuously to the Benedictines' brewing beer and operating a tavern, and he opposed the elevation of St. Vincent to abbatial status until the matter was resolved. Wimmer gave up the tavern but insisted that it was a traditional practice of Benedictines in Bavaria to brew beer. The case was presented to the Holy See which, influenced by the intervention of the Bavarian government, declared that the monks of St. Vincent could brew beer but could distribute it only wholesale. St. Vincent eventually became an abbey in 1855.

TO KARL VON REISACH **33**

St. Vincent, January 1, 1852

Your Excellency: When I find time to send New Year's greeting only on the day itself, I can blame only the huge amount of urgent business and the American custom of disregarding New Year's congratulations with the result that those who are used to formalities almost forget this duty. In the week before Christmas we had two German and three English Redemptorists here giving a mission in our church. There was no thought of writing then, and before that, I had to make trips to St. Marys and to Philadelphia. That kept me away for three weeks.

May God strengthen Your Excellency anew for what promises to be a fateful year–1852. May He continue to bestow upon you all the graces and blessings he has until now so abundantly poured upon you and your good intentions, endeavors, and labors for the sheep and the lambs in your care. May He crown your efforts for your flock with comforting results for God's honor and for the salvation of others, as well as for your own joy. May He give you strength so that you do not succumb to the strenuous work of your office.

The past year has brought us a dangerous guest, namely, Kossuth,[44] who not only acted as a revolutionary but also preached and worked as a Protestant against the Catholic Church. The Catholic press naturally came forward with a determination and frankness seen only here in America. The best English newspapers are against him, but our mob is for him and sympathizes with him, no doubt because of his hatred for the Church. It is quite possible that his presence will not be without evil effects here. Lola Montez[45] came with him, but as his opponent since she openly denounced him as a humbug and a swindler. In the countryside, we feel less the impact of such events that electrify the cities, though we are pained by the recurring experience of a demon blinding the people so that even those who can see do not see or understand and are blown about by every wind. Even our Senate has lowered itself so far as to strew incense before this braggart in order not to spoil their image with the mob.

---

[44] Lajos Kossuth (1802-1894), Hungarian revolutionary and liberal reformer who for a short period after the revolution of 1848 led an independence movement to separate Hungary from the Austrian empire. When the movement failed, he was driven into exile. The U.S. government invited Kossuth to visit America and sent a Navy frigate to bring him to the United States.

[45] The Irish courtesan who posed as a Spanish dancer and whose love affair with King Ludwig I of Bavaria helped bring about the monarch's abdication in 1848.

Nothing very important or new has occurred since my last letter except that on December 6 Böld, Huber, and Wohlfahrt[46] were ordained priests. They have to wait two more months for their faculties. The bishop[47] examined them very thoroughly, especially in apologetics in which Böld answered pretty well, but more by guessing than from knowledge of basic principles. We are now 12 priests and shortly expect the missionary, Count di Marogna,[48] who lately asked for admission. Of these 12, eight are here at home; two are in St. Marys with two brothers; one is with the missionary Lemke[49] and six brothers in Carrolltown, and for three weeks one has been in Indiana with three brothers.

I believe I told you in my last letter why I took St. Marys back. I was there myself in August and again at the end of October. Then about the middle of November, I sent the brothers there. Incidentally, the company gave me about 80 acres of land, which I needed to round out my possessions, to establish connections between the large sections, and to isolate myself from the new city and from the colony. I had to buy several lots in the former city. Others I had to exchange for lots in the new city, which the company had previously given me. Of the seven houses that had to be removed, I bought four. For the remaining three I am still in the process of negotiation. I will probably need $2,500 for all this. Then we will have a nice estate. However, as usual, it is not totally free, for after the withdrawal of the Redemptorists, the bishop accepted it under the condition that it be used for ecclesiastical, charitable, and educational purposes, though with permission to use it for only one of these purposes exclusively or to sell part of it. With these stipulations, he gave it to me and to the Order in trust–as our property to be sure, yet restricted by the conditions to which he had agreed. The Redemptorists were even more restricted than we were, for we at least can use the income from the investment for the German colonists, if not immediately, then as soon as I have time to cultivate the land.

The church must be built next spring. Only the Lord knows where I will get the means. At present, I have only $400 available. The construction of a monastery is less pressing since in case of need we can live in the temporary house built for the

---

[46] Ildephonse Böld, O.S.B. (1826-1855), Utto Huber, O.S.B. (1819-1896), and Jerome Wohlfahrt, O.S.B.

[47] Michael O'Connor of Pittsburgh.

[48] Demetrius Charles di Marogna, O.S.B. (1803-1869), a Bavarian nobleman of Italian descent who had served as a secular priest in Illinois before applying for admission to the monastery at St. Vincent. Di Marogna became prior at St. Vincent and in 1856 led the Benedictine mission from St. Vincent to Minnesota.

[49] Peter Henry Lemke.

School Sisters,[50] but we must work on the mill because the colonists need it badly. Currently many have to go 16 miles to have their grain ground because there is only one mill in the colony and it cannot take care of all. Besides, the mill must be the source of our income, the main source at that.

If I had my wish, I would get Benedictine sisters there. If not them, then School Sisters. But I would prefer the former since they follow the same *Rule* as we do. This would make it much easier for spiritual guidance. Moreover, I am too committed to my Order not to desire spreading it among the other sex. Candidates who are conversant in English are not lacking here. If we had only two choir sisters and one lay sister, we would soon have enough. I still firmly maintain that the old religious Orders, ours above all, if they renew themselves, emerge from their rigid seclusion, and adopt a more flexible form of life, have as much chance for permanence, power, and discipline as the republican orders.[51] In my opinion, we are to each other as the Church is to religious sects, as the limited monarchy is to a republic.

In St. Marys the company gave me five acres in the center of the city where the [sisters'] monastery will be built. This is so that all communications between monks and nuns can be observed but all unnecessary business be prevented. Our monastery will either be rather far from the city–in the direction of the mill–or where the buildings stand. I do not know yet.

Indiana has caused me more grief and vexation than all the other places. I had a buyer for the brewery, a former parishioner from Stephansposching[52] whom I thought I could trust completely, but he too has cheated me and caused me considerable loss. He had started to make another purchase, which he hoped to complete with my help and by which he would have cheated me even more. Being aware of this, I declined to help him. That is, I loaned him no money and consequently he was forced to let me join him as a partner in order to rid himself of the business. In this way, I gained a very good farm of 310 acres at $1,620, which before long, after my brothers cultivate the land, will have a value of $6,000, but while I was absent Father Benedict, my subprior, let himself be misled to partly loan and partly stand good for $600 that I have never recovered. The earlier losses

---

[50] Bavarian School Sisters of Notre Dame had worked in St. Marys for a time but were forced to withdraw from the mission because of financial problems. The monks from St. Vincent were given their former convent.

[51] The Jesuits, Redemptorists, and other modern religious orders, like republics, elected their leaders for determined periods of time. Benedictine abbots traditionally served for life. This may be why Wimmer referred to the former as "republican orders."

[52] Before coming to America, Wimmer had served for a time as curate in Stephansposching in the diocese of Regensburg, Bavaria.

in Indiana were made good and were sufficiently covered by new acquisitions. Now I have turned the brewery into a monastery, rented out half the farm, and let the brothers take care of the other half. I will start brewing after I have secured a brewmaster. We will brew only for our own use. To others we will sell by the barrel for cash. The bishop has nothing against this anymore. The next thing to do is to send a second priest to Indiana so they can work together. All this will cost a lot of money, much more than I have. Therefore, I must earn more. I must go forward. We must grow from year to year. That lies in the nature of things. I make the debts and the budget. God and Your Excellency will provide the income. With this in mind I am with deepest respect and submission, your most humble and obedient, P. Boniface Wimmer

Ger   oALMV   cASVA   transGE

TO THOMAS MITTERNDORFER   34

St. Vincent, March 24, 1853

Right Reverend Abbot: The court chaplain, Joseph Ferdinand Müller of Munich, and the abbot of Metten, have long since acknowledged my receipt of the legacy of Bishop Ziegler[53] through your kind offices. For my part, I have neglected to send an acknowledgement because the court chaplain expressed in his letter the hope that I would possibly be favored with a letter from you. Although other commitments have prevented me, I will wait no longer to make a respectful and grateful acknowledgement of the bishop's legacy to the amount of 3,030 franks and 45 kronen. My earlier correspondence has already revealed my financial difficulties. Hence, it is unnecessary to remark that Your Grace, through your benevolent intervention and good offices in sending the money, has proved most helpful to me and my community. You have bound us under the obligation of the greatest thanks.

I have set up a perpetual anniversary foundation for Bishop Ziegler in our monastic church because he really became one of the founders, not only because of his last will, but also through his earlier sizable annual contributions, which never amounted to less than 500 franks. In the beginning, when I had no credit and was often in the direst need, he made up for many thousands! I feel his loss very deeply. Only a person who knows what it means to have a friend when one is in need can understand this loss. I was completely unknown to him personally. I

---

[53] Gregory Thomas Ziegler, O.S.B., bishop of Linz, Austria, who died on April 15, 1852.

had never seen him nor he me until I was in Linz two years ago, but before I left Munich on my mission to America, I made my plan known to him and requested his advice. He thought well of the idea and immediately offered me generous support, promised to give me further assistance, and fulfilled his promise faithfully. All of us, and especially myself, are bound in every way to everlasting thanks and will never fail to fulfill this sacred obligation. I do not know whether he has perhaps specified other obligations for me or my community in his legacy, but I want to submit most obediently if this should be the case. I would ask that you graciously inform me about the matter at your earliest convenience. He himself had already spoken to me about the anniversary, and we have already fulfilled the memorial service most solemnly in all our churches, as I believe I have already mentioned–but I will be happy to fulfill his other wishes if he gave expression to any at all.

Since I last wrote you, nothing of real importance has happened here–still, one thing occurred that, if not very interesting, is nevertheless new. I have lost another priest and a brother through death, both of them in St. Marys. Father Maurus Zacherl,[54] who came from Kaufmühl, near Regensburg, was a priest only two and a half years and had been assigned to the priory in St. Marys almost a year ago especially to provide for the outlying German communities in the rough, sparsely settled Clearfield County, and when he was at home, to look after an Irish settlement in Kersey. He devoted himself to this hard work with intense zeal and dedication. Every month he was gone from the monastery weeks at a time because he had to ride horseback 40 to 60 miles, and in doing so had to sleep in wretched huts, and especially in damp weather and during the winter, he had a great deal to endure. The Allegheny Ridge cuts through this county at different points, and the traveler must often ride 15 to 20 miles before he sees even one house.

At the end of October, after one of these mission journeys, Father Maurus returned to the monastery very ill. He paid no attention to his condition for a couple of weeks, but finally had to take to his bed and developed typhus, which killed him in a short time–on the first Sunday of Advent. He was beloved by all everywhere he was known, by Catholics and even by Protestants, with whom he came into frequent contact on his journeys, but especially at St. Marys itself. By his untiring efforts to promote peace and harmony, he brought people who had been estranged from one another into complete reconciliation and unity.

The first news of his illness gave me an inkling of the probability of his death. For that reason, I immediately asked our bishop to ordain two of our theologians who had completed all the requirements: Amandus Krammer, the theologian

---

[54] Maurus Quirinus Zacherl, O.S.B. (1827-1852).

from Linz, and Augustine Wirth from Würzburg.[55] After the ordination, I went immediately with Father Amandus to St. Marys, doubtful whether we would find Father Maurus alive. Although unaccustomed to traveling, Father Amandus bore up well under the hardships the first day, but by evening of the second day, he was exhausted. It went well again on the third and fourth days and we reached St. Marys safe and sound on December 4. While we were still on the way, I received news of Father Maurus's death and burial.

At St. Marys, two priests and 14 brothers all live in a small farm house made of rough planks fitted together without plaster or mortar and without clothes closets. Father Amandus had a good reminder of death since he had to sleep the very first night in the room where Father Maurus died. It had been cleaned and made up, but we newcomers still felt the strong smell of death. Father Prior, Father Amandus, and I sat down to talk with one another about the last moments of our dear confrere's life, and in order to get the odor of death from tongue and nose, I permitted a bottle of wine to be set out and cigars to be lit, because I was anxious about Father Amandus. He had not yet celebrated his first Mass and prepared himself for it in the quiet of the next few days, while I devoted myself to the foundation and discussed with Father Prior the needs of the buildings, its roof, and so on. On the feast of the Immaculate Conception [December 8], Father Amandus celebrated his first solemn Mass, during which the members of the poor community did their best to participate in the festivity. The following day I rode back home.

Everything had gone along well in the meantime, but just before Christmas the nerve fever broke out among the brothers [in St. Marys] and three of them contracted it at the same time. Upon receiving this news, I immediately sent a third priest, Father Odilo Vandergrün, with instructions to isolate the sick into an unoccupied house in the neighborhood. In a short time, two others were added to the three, and one after the other they all became sick to the last man, so that at one time only three of the 17 could make it to meals. There was no doctor in town, and none in the neighborhood. Fathers Prior and Odilo practiced homeopathy and also played doctor. For the most part, they managed to prevent a real outbreak of the fever, and of the five seriously ill, only the youngest and strongest died, Brother Leo Sitzberger from Wilshofen.

The three priests were also sick, one after the other, but in all cases, they recovered after only several days when the infection and bronchial catarrh ran its course. When I next came to St. Marys in mid-February, only Brother Meinrad

---

of Switzerland[56] was still sick. In his case, the fever settled in the lungs, which is usually fatal. After giving him a thorough examination for all the symptoms (I am head of all the homeopaths in western Pennsylvania), I prescribed phosphorous and then mercury, and the fellow, a most lovable young man, was cured and is again chopping trees. The sickness has upset all our plans. The priest and brother I lost were both first-rate persons who showed much promise. All winter long very little could be done because half were sick and the others needed to attend to them, but the Lord is God and His holy will at all times adorable.

King Ludwig of Bavaria gave our Benedictine Sisters 8,000 franks to build a small convent. This gift lifted an enormous burden of debt from me, for otherwise, I would have had to defray the cost of the building. Through this grand gift, his majesty, as in the case of an earlier gift of 10,000 franks for my monastery, merits the sincerest thanks of the Americans, as through his foundations in Bavaria he has merited the thanks of all Bavarians and Benedictines everywhere.

Our good sisters[57] live in just as miserable a house as my confreres, but they are also just as satisfied and as frugal as the priests and brothers are. They teach the girls in the school with great zeal and have already made the beginning of a small academy in which so far they are instructing six girls, among whom are three orphans. On my last trip to St. Marys, I brought them four additional girls, one of whom understands only English, the other three English and German, so that the girls, according to the wish of their parents, can be instructed in English as well. In summer, I shall take still others, so that they can choose the best teachers out of their number. I must provide living expenses. For me and for them there will be other cares as well.

Our seminary now stands at 70 students and grows almost every week. It is impossible for me to consider all who apply, for the majority cannot pay any tuition. I must first cultivate and procure means of support, and then I will be able to proceed. In spite of all my needs, I have begun building a gristmill at St. Marys because it is needed by my brothers and by the colony, and here I will also begin after Easter to build a steam mill which, not counting our labor, will cost about $2,000 or $2,500. Since the millers here charge a tenth, I am losing too much by not having a mill.

---

[56] Meinrad Bischof, O.S.B. (1828-1904).

[57] In July 1852, three Benedictine nuns from St. Walburga Convent, Eichstätt, Bavaria–Benedicta Riepp, O.S.B. (1825-1862), Walburga Dietrich, O.S.B. (1804-1877), and Maura Flieger, O.S.B. (1822-1865)–arrived in St. Marys, where they established a convent and school. See Ephrem Hollermann, O.S.B., *The Reshaping of a Tradition: American Benedictine Women 1852-1881* (St. Joseph, Minn.: Sisters of the Order of St. Benedict, 1994), 55-69.

The two priests from Einsiedeln[58] arrived at the beginning of February. Father Ulrich seems to have grown into the kind of person to whom a weighty undertaking, such as the founding of a monastery, can be entrusted. They spent about a week in our monastery and left on the feast of St. Scholastica [February 10] for Vincennes, their next destination. I gave them advice and recommendations to the best of my knowledge and conscience. May the holy Virgin guide their efforts successfully and protect them. My confreres and I have entered the Union of Prayer. I hope that it will bring new life and fresh activity to our holy Order.

Since I have three priests in St. Marys, we have taken over the care of souls in Warren County. Father Odilo is in charge. The county lies in the extreme northern part of our state, up toward Lake Erie. There are not many German Catholics in the region, and they live far apart. That makes the pastoral care so much the more difficult. The priest must ride 56 miles to reach Warren, the county's principal city. On his very first trip, Father Odilo almost drowned because a bridge over a swollen stream broke with him. Both priest and the old horse reached the opposite side safely, but the horse was seriously injured in one leg. It was in January, and although it was not extremely cold, the poor missionary, thoroughly drenched, almost froze to death because he had to travel ten miles before he came to a house. A short time ago, another of my priests, Father Henry Lemke,[59] going to the druggist at night, suffered a heavy, crushing bruise when his horse stumbled and fell on top of him.

The last time I rode to St. Marys to accompany the four candidates for our Benedictine sisters, I myself escaped a similar danger in a rather remarkable manner. I did not take the straightest and shortest route, but a detour of almost 100 miles, by which I could return on the train in a few hours so that I would not lose time. In Lewistown, we had to take the stagecoach, or post coach, which left from there only once a week, Wednesdays, over the Alleghenies toward St. Marys. I had made my arrangements in advance so that I would arrive in ample time at Lewistown, but during the night the train was delayed ten hours at one place because a rail was broken and could not be immediately replaced. I was quite provoked because I knew well that I had now missed the post coach and lost a whole day and

---

58 These were Ulrich Christen, O.S.B., and Bede O'Connor, O.S.B. They had come to establish a daughter house of the Swiss Abbey of Einsiedeln in the state of Indiana, a house that became St. Meinrad's Archabbey, the first monastery of the Swiss American Congregation. See Albert Kleber, O.S.B., *History of St. Meinrad Archabbey 1854-1954* (St. Meinrad, Ind.: Grail Publications, 1954), 29-62.

59 Lemke was the missionary who had invited Wimmer to western Pennsylvania in 1845. In 1852 he became a Benedictine at St. Vincent. Wimmer assigned him to his former mission station in Carrolltown.

would have to take our own cart. That is the way it all happened, but how happy we were as we drove over the mountains the next day to learn that the post coach, which fortunately had no one aboard, overturned, so that, had we been on it, we would certainly not have come through the ordeal without serious injury.

They are still at work in our neighborhood constructing the railroad, although the Central Railroad from Philadelphia to Pittsburgh has already been completed. On this main line, they are laying a second track, and to its right they are building a private road towards our Indiana priory and to the left, away from Greensburg, another line towards Wheeling, a famous port town on the Ohio River in Virginia. Thousands of Catholic Irish are employed on these projects. We have to care for them pastorally, near and far. Every Sunday, two or three priests must ride horseback to different places along the railroad or travel by train to the largest settlements where the Irishmen eat and sleep, in order to offer Mass, preach, baptize, and so on. These Irish are a people unto themselves. Always disunited among themselves (the northern and southern Irish), they do not get along very well with the Germans or the Americans either. They generally hold fast only to their Faith and live like gypsies winter and summer in houses of rough planks, which often do not have a single window or a chimney. The unmarried among them gather in large numbers and move as groups from one end of the United States to the other. When one railroad or canal is completed, individuals among them buy a piece of land with the money they have saved, and once firmly settled on their own property either work at founding a new community or at increasing one already established. They are given to drunkenness in which there is no lack of brawling. This reproach does not touch the greater number of them, and even the drinkers are very much to be excused because they have to work hard, receive no beer, and easily become intoxicated from whiskey or brandy, which they often must drink because of the unwholesome water. Otherwise they are well behaved and chaste, especially their daughters, who are not distinguished by their beauty. They do far more for the Church and the priests than the Germans do, but the Germans do far more for the schools. I really like them very much and have become deeply indebted to them during the two years they have been in our neighborhood, but they cause us a lot of trouble day and night by seeking medicines for the least physical indisposition. When they are not feeling well, they immediately send for the priest, who must then often play the part of doctor for them as well. With the great faith of these good people regarding the power of the priest, he often becomes a true wonder worker through prayer and sacramentals.

At present, a powerful religious movement is going through the countryside hereabouts. The Protestants and unbelievers see our growth and cannot prevent it. The Catholic Church has greatly increased in the number of priests, churches, monasteries, teaching institutions, and members. Through the strength and ability of the Catholic priests, as well as the prominent and eminent talents of many bishops, we have won much respect and influence. In order to hide their inner deterioration and conceal their superficiality and weakness, our adversaries, who really are not very clever, fall into anxiety, fear, and frenzy at the same time. Every insignificant incident they believe they can build up to the harm of the Catholic Church is used, suitably garnished and decked out, in order to make a weapon against the Catholics.[60]

For eight months the affair with the Madiai in Florence[61] has been making the rounds in all Protestant and political newspapers in order to make Catholics hated and scorned as enemies of religious freedom. The rascals know perfectly well that there is nothing to the whole incident, but they lie and egg others on, always hoping that something of their accusations will stick. They have no feeling and capacity for truth and honor, nor any shame. Hence, they act according to the usual pattern, and when they do not find Catholics refuting their statements, they go on lying.

On the other hand a number of our bishops, notably Archbishop Hughes of New York and Bishop O'Connor,[62] have launched a crusade on the school and teaching questions,[63] and in a series of open letters on the subject have taken to task the politicians and heretics for their inactivity, hypocrisy, and injustice. They have done so with a forthrightness and candor that is possible only in a country where freedom of the press is complete. Naturally enough, this has caused heated controversies in which we will really not win anything for the time being, and in which the long history of heresies may again argue themselves to death because they can neither withstand the truth nor the dialectics of our church leaders, but

---

[60] Anti-Catholic, anti-immigrant nativist groups such as the "Know-Nothing" Native American Party were particularly active in Pennsylvania during this period.

[61] In January 1853, American newspapers reported that the Duke of Tuscany had sentenced Francisco and Rosa Madiai, Italian converts to Protestantism, to fifty-six months in prison, allegedly for conducting a Protestant bible meeting in Catholic Florence. The religious freedom case became a cause célèbre in the United States. See New-York Daily Times, January 21 and February 24, 1853, and Richard Shaw, *Dagger John: The Unquiet Life and Times of Archbishop John Hughes of New York* (New York: Paulist Press, 1977), 273-76.

[62] John Hughes, archbishop of New York (1797-1864), and Michael O'Connor, bishop of Pittsburgh (1810-1872).

[63] The "crusade on the school and teaching questions" was an attempt by Hughes and other members of the American Catholic hierarchy to obtain access to funds from the state school tax for the support of Catholic parochial schools. See Wimmer's discussion of this in his letter of July 4, 1853, below.

still they will not handle the matter honestly and hence must carry the humiliation of an evil conscience.

Enough for the time being. If the Austrian Benedictines were only a little more closely united with the Americans, I could readily see to it that they would receive detailed information about our public and church life, which would be not only interesting but truly useful as well.

Repeating my warmest thanks and commending myself to Your Grace in all obedience, and greeting all my reverend confreres in a spirit of deep friendship, I am, with deepest respect and submission, your most humble and devoted, Father Boniface Wimmer

P.S. The priest G. Niedröder from Linz has turned over a new leaf. A German priest advised him to have recourse to me. I accepted him, even though at the time I had no place to put him. I sent him to the Redemptorists in Pittsburgh, who gave him asylum until I could do something for him. I hope we can reconcile him once more to God and to the Church. I am enclosing a letter from him. It is a grace to be able to help these wayward priests and bring them back to the right path. We usually have one or two of them here—some Irish, some German—doing penance and learning discipline.

Ger   oAKA   cASVA   transBS

TO KING LUDWIG I   35

St. Vincent, July 4, 1853

Most August, Most Mighty King! Most Gracious King and Lord! Although in a detailed report to the Central Committee of the *Ludwig Missionsverein*, printed in the *Annals of the Missions*,[64] I have presented a complete description of our lot and situation in this country, I still believe it my duty to report most humbly on this matter directly to Your Royal Majesty, for it may prove to be of particular interest.

I received the communication concerning the intervention of the royal Bavarian ambassador to the Holy See with regard to the brewery and in response I offer herewith to Your Royal Majesty my most sincere thanks for the royal favor on the part of both of you. Almost at the same time, through His Eminence Cardinal

---

[64] The *Annalen der Verbreitung des Glaubens* was the annual publication of the *Ludwig Missionsverein*.

Fransoni,[65] news reached me about the steps taken by the royal ambassador, with the remark that the Holy See settled this affair in such a way that he believes the Benedictine Order can henceforth, in accordance with that decision, regulate the matter in a way that is most beneficial to the Church herself. At the same time, I was advised that the bishop himself [66] would inform me of the decision. However, he gave only general information, namely that Rome granted permission to make beer and to sell it, but not at retail, either directly or indirectly, that is, through someone acting in our name. The main objective was realized in this decision, but it leaves many things still rather vague, on which time and experience will no doubt shed some light. For the present, I did not want to push the bishop any further in the matter since he was rather upset by his setback, and I for my part, overall, had every reason to be satisfied with the decision. Moreover, we are still drinking nothing but plain water, as we do not have the time to build a brewery [at St. Vincent]. We are nevertheless enjoying good health. Only the elderly and the more feeble among the fathers and brothers find it rather hard to be without some strong invigorating drink, especially in summer when they have to work hard in the burning heat, and also on fast days (which occur three times a week) when we have neither fish nor eggs nor cheese but invariably only a thin broth and sauerkraut, or beans or sliced apples with Bavarian noodles.

The cardinal makes no mention in his letter about the elevation of the monastery to the rank of abbey. The bishop, however, wrote saying he is not against it. On the contrary, were I to draw up more precise statements about the relation of a priory to the main monastery and, in addition, if I were to draw up a list of our statutes (as I intended to do), he would then gladly send the statutes to Rome with his recommendation for approval and propose at the same time the erection of the abbey itself. Since, however, I had a pile of other things to attend to, I have not yet been able to do anything in the matter, and to some extent I am also unwilling to do anything. For it is very difficult to lay down something as a rule before you have found out by experience that it is beneficial and feasible. Also, I would not like to have it said of me that I managed to make myself the abbot, since until now my confreres would have had no other choice than elect me. This year, on August 15, Father Demetrius (Charles), count of Marogna,[67] will make his solemn profession. He is more worthy and more capable of the office of abbot than I am. I will then not delay the draft of the constitution and statutes any longer and

[65] Giacomo Filippe Fransoni, prefect of the Sacred Congregation for the Propagation of the Faith.
[66] Michael O'Connor of Pittsburgh.
[67] Demetrius Charles di Marogna, O.S.B., (1803-1869) a secular priest and Bavarian nobleman who entered the monastery at St. Vincent in 1852.

will do my best to leave the responsibility of the whole matter in your hands.[68] I must mention further, as worthy of note, that the bishop, on behalf of the Holy See, has made me officially and formally superior of the now formally recognized monastery, and in this way, by the same authority, I have been dispensed from my vow of stability so that I am now only an honorary member of the monastery of Metten. In any case, I want to live and die on the mission, for the cause of religion. Nothing else could bind me to this country, to which, if I had the choice, I would prefer Bavaria a thousand times.

I have acquired nothing further since my last report. The 3,600 acres of land (an acre being equal to 42,000 sq. ft., not 4,200 sq. feet as the *Annalen* say) are now for the most part free of debt. Only in St. Marys and in Indiana are they still in arrears. I had to make great sacrifices there. For the last two years, all the subsidies coming out of Munich have been expended on St. Marys, and even that does not suffice. Now we are building a mill there that should be ready about the end of August. It is truly a blessing for the colony as well as for us. Also at St. Vincent, we want to build a steam mill this year since we are without waterpower here, especially in the summer. All the necessary preparations have already been made. The actual building, however, can be started only after the harvest (which began here eight days ago). On both buildings, the brothers do all the work that is not properly the task of the millwright or the machinist. Yet for the mill in St. Marys, the iron work and stones alone cost me $800, or 2,000 florins. The steam engine for the mill in that place costs $950. The whole thing will come to $2,500 for the one at St. Marys, and the same for the one at St. Vincent, so that the construction will cost $5,000.

I could not have undertaken the construction of these two buildings had not Your Royal Majesty so graciously deigned to assign the sum of 8,000 florins to be used for the erection and building of a convent for the Benedictine nuns in St. Marys.[69] They, of course, were not in a position to begin immediately the construction of their convent since the whole colony had its mind set on the completion of a new church, which was already under construction. The people wanted to finish this construction and so could not allow any interruption. Accordingly, the nuns were very willing to loan me the royal gift, which for the present they could not make use of anyhow, on condition that I take care of the expenses for

---

[68] Wimmer intended to rely on the king and the Bavarian government to influence a favorable decision in Rome with respect to the elevation of St. Vincent to abbey status.

[69] Wimmer's decision to divert the money donated by King Ludwig to purposes other than the building of a convent in St. Marys caused serious difficulties between him and the Benedictine sisters in the years to come.

the purchase of such household furnishings that were of immediate necessity, and then, as time allows, to apply the rest of the money to the construction of their convent. Meanwhile the nuns are living in a frame building that the corporation had built originally for the School Sisters who were in St. Marys in the time of Baron von Schrötter[70] but later left, together with the Redemptorists. At the time I took possession, the corporation left this building to me. Until now the lower floor was used as a church, while the upper floor along with the adjacent buildings were used by the nuns as living quarters and as quarters for the school. When the furniture was purchased for this building, care was taken that the nuns would be able to use this furniture again in their new convent. The necessary arrangements for the building of this convent should be made in late autumn and winter so that by next spring they may proceed at once in earnest with the actual construction. There is no material to be found in the vicinity of St. Marys that can be used for the baking of bricks. There are only thin layers of split rock that we can use for building. There is also a lack of good sand, not however of limestone. We have here, let me add, an abundance of the finest building timber.

The nuns' convent will be located in the middle of the new city, which is being laid out on a rather small scale, and will be added to the new church, which will be 115 feet long and 60 feet wide. My masons, carpenters, and cabinet-makers will be occupied all summer long in order to put up the building. In this way, the nuns get a convent, whereas I earn for myself some 1,000 florins for my work, which I otherwise would have had to do for nothing. For it should be noted that this poor congregation had achieved something extraordinary and remarkable in the building of their church, and so could not be in a position to build a convent for the nuns. Since I was instrumental in getting them to come here, it therefore became incumbent upon me to help them build. Therefore, Your Royal Majesty, through your generous endowment, has shown very great kindness not only to the good nuns but also to me and my confreres. I do not fear to have acted contrary to the noble intention of Your Royal Majesty if, without prejudice to the parties concerned and with their full knowledge and consent, I have handled matters in the manner described in this report. Naturally, in a country where a skilled worker earns along with his food $1 a day (= 2 florins and 30 kronen), and where a wagon driver wants the same pay for every horse, that is, $1 a day (= 2 florins and 30 kronen), the nuns, even with the royal donation, would not be in a position to put up a building that would include all the rooms needed for a motherhouse, a girls' school for the colony, and an educational institute. However, I do not have to pay out any money in wages; therefore the thousands of dollars that

---

[70] One of the founders of the St. Marys colony.

remain after the furnishings of the convent have been paid are truly a donation for us also, for which I hereby express to Your Royal Majesty the most sincere thanks in the name of all my confreres!

Two nuns and one lay sister came to St. Marys from St. Walburga[71] and since then have taken in 12 candidates, 11 of whom were born in this country and one of whom came over from Bavaria. It seems that at St. Walburga they were not pleased to learn that the mother superior here,[72] at my urging, has already opened a novitiate, inasmuch as they were of the opinion that the local convent should be regarded as a branch house of St. Walburga and so should be ruled from there. That would be about as practical as the Austrian arrangement whereby a general giving orders in actual combat is made dependent in his maneuvers on the royal war council in Vienna. Even at the risk of being abandoned entirely by St. Walburga, I myself pressed for the erection of a proper novitiate and the establishment of self-government so that we could meet the crying needs here for the religious instruction of the youth of the female sex as soon as possible and as far as possible. I do hope the people in Eichstätt will appreciate the reasons I have given. Since the convent receives annually from the school tax (here this tax must be paid by every adult male, married or single, lay or cleric) only $200 (a little over 500 florins), the burden of support for so many persons falls consequently and as usual upon me. It is, however, for this reason that I construct mills. For this reason, I clear the land with my brothers, so that many of us, and many more still, may live in order to fight for God and His holy Church, for justice and order in this country, and also to gain followers. In this matter, I indeed hope to be motivated more by trust in God than by the merely probable results of artificial estimates and calculations, while not engaging in speculative ventures or neglecting the wise precepts of good domestic economy. My confidence has indeed been sorely tested on many occasions, but I was never disappointed because of it. Often I did not even have a cent and no hope of any money at all, and that at a time when some urgent payments had to be made. Repeatedly, however, the money arrived at the right moment and from a source that was entirely unexpected. Last winter it was Your Majesty who by your donation for St. Marys saved me from the greatest embarrassment, since I had to pay several thousand dollars within a short interval, and without the 8,000 florins, I would not have had the money to meet these payments. Therefore, I was able to fulfill the obligations I contracted, to pay my debts on time, to maintain my credit, and with this credit to enter upon new undertakings.

---

[71] Mother Benedicta Riepp, Mother Walburga Dietrich, and Sister Maura Flieger had come to St. Marys from the monastery of St. Walburga, Eichstätt, in July 1852.
[72] Mother Benedicta Riepp, O.S.B.

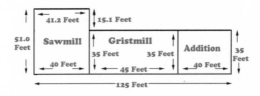

Saint Vincent Gristmill
Plan View

1. Gristmill erected in 1854.
2. Sawmill was erected in 1855 (one story).
3. In 1880 second story added.
4. Addition to east in 1883 was 35 by 40 feet.

The floor plan of the Saint Vincent Gristmill, including later additions.

In America everything is done on credit since there is not much cash around and still less ready cash. If you have credit, you are rich. Your wealth is as great as your credit. The more one ventures to do things on credit, provided his transactions turn out well, so much more credit will be given him. It is not therefore a rare thing to see even a poor man, who is shrewd and clever, become extremely wealthy in the space of a few years. The American people often appear to be like compulsive gamblers. Everyone gambles. Everyone takes risks as far as he can. Many thereby lose everything, but many succeed, just as with luck in the game of dice. However, they always try their luck again, if not in the place where they are known, at least in some other place, or in another state, with some other line of business or in some other manner, as the case may be.

It is awful, however, to see how often the ordinary folk and people of the poorer class are swindled. On the other hand, you also see some sharp swindlers outwitted by others still more clever. Nevertheless, a huge swindle is not looked upon as something disgraceful. On the contrary, it is rather like a diploma awarded for cleverness, or, as they say, a feather in one's cap. People who have been tricked view such trickery as the farmer looks at blight or a hailstorm. It is something accidental. It is a chance one must take and there is no protection against it. After all, one usually will do the same thing to another if he can get away with it, or if he happens to be hard pressed. This spirit of reckless chance-taking, along with such lack of concern for others, underlies the egoism that is so noticeable in the American character and that may be called the key to the tremendous and truly amazing advances in every area in this country. Such progress is made so easily because the existing laws allow the widest scope to individual initiative. Everyone can do as he pleases with his own property, and on his own land or ground, so long as he pays the various taxes, such as the state tax, the county tax, the poor tax, and the school tax. In addition, if he is running a business, he must pay the current business taxes, which are rather high. Anyone can buy or sell as he pleases (except in the case of the death of a marriage partner). He can reside wherever he wishes and can run any business he likes. There is no definite apprenticeship for the beginner, no specific training period for the doctor or lawyer, or for the preacher. Finally, there is no compulsory military service except in the case of an attack upon our country. Thus, all things remain open to all, everywhere and always. That is to say, everyone can try his luck at anything. Talent, energy, and luck count for success in everything. Most people have no religion. Instead, they adhere to the party from which they expect the most at the time of the elections and the handing out of appointments. How can you put any limits on the capabilities and achievements of such a people, especially, if as is actually the case, they are richly and highly endowed by nature!

Among people of this sort and in such a country, O Royal Highness, life is so different that you cannot act in the same way here as in Bavaria where people are known for their goodness and straightforward simplicity. If you have intelligence, you must put it to use. One cannot remain still. You must move forward, venture upon new enterprises even though it means taking great chances, with this difference, however, that to cover for any failure, provision must be made that all will not be lost or that the consequences may not be disastrous for other people. In religious matters, there is the same frenetic activity that characterizes the life of the people. We see signs of religious activity springing up everywhere: cathedrals and seminaries, hospitals and orphanages, monasteries and convents, educational institutions, and, of course, churches and schools. One cannot say that Catholics here are lagging behind other groups. Rather, they are far in advance if you consider the meager resources at their disposal. The big question is, who appeals to the young, up-coming generation in such a way as to have a rightful claim on it?

It is now no longer a question of victory or defeat for either Catholicism or Protestantism.[73] That question has already been settled. It seems to me that Protestantism can be traced almost entirely to the moral laxity of priests or to the greed of certain pompous individuals who speak grandiosely. The former end up with women and the latter gain the coveted possessions of the clergy. As to the reaction of the common people to Protestantism, the bad element among them will readily embrace it since it caters to their sensuality. The better ones among them, however, would find it so repulsive that only compulsion could get them to embrace it. In matters of doctrine, its inconsistencies and lack of logic could never survive a confrontation with Catholic truth. Untruth, calumny, and historical falsifications succeed in an intolerant atmosphere where truth is not allowed a hearing.

In America, however, where there is full freedom of the press and everyone is free to speak out, where not only the church but also the speaker's platform, the shopkeeper's stand, or the soapbox in the street can serve as a pulpit, it is easy to get to the root of the matter and uncover the lurking falsehood. Protestantism had its heyday when there were no Catholics here, or as long as Catholics were held down by repression and were without priests to serve them. However, as freedom spread throughout the country and bishops and priests grew in numbers, and with the advent of the Catholic press and the uncovering of the humbug imposed upon Protestants by their preachers, such as that Catholic priests have horns or claws or cloven hoofs, which Protestants could see for themselves was not true, and, finally, since priests have now been put in a much better light historically thanks to some good historical works on the subject, a truly remarkable change has taken place. Hence, with respect to Protestants, only the most stupid of them still dance and croak in the meetings of the Methodists (and there are still quite a large number of these). In the same way, many bigoted and fanatical members still identify with the Calvinists, who in this country are divided into various sects and generally go under the name of Presbyterians. Usually, however, the well-informed and unprejudiced members of the hundred or so sects in our land are inclined to believe nothing whatsoever. This group of unbelievers makes up

---

[73] Wimmer's discussion of the conflict between Catholicism and Protestantism in the paragraphs that follow can best be understood within the context of the historical events taking place at the time. By mid-century a resurgence of anti-Catholic nativism had occurred in the United States, and even some distinguished Protestant leaders had begun to attack the Catholic Church openly and viciously. See Ray Allan Billington, *The Protestant Crusade: 1800-1860* (Chicago, 1938); Carleton Beals, *Brass-Knuckle Crusade: The Great Know-Nothing Conspiracy, 1820-1860* (New York, 1960); and James Hennesey, S.J., *American Catholics: A History of the Roman Catholic Community in the United States* (New York: Oxford University Press, 1981), 124-27.

more than half the population of the Union, that is, over 12 million people! This is something dreadful, the more so since it is readily predictable that the youth, for the most part, will fall in with this group, whereas it is just as certain that the majority of Protestants, including many preachers, who on the surface still appear to be Protestants, are Deists at heart, and for the most part even atheists.

Thus, Catholicism has nothing whatsoever to fear from Protestantism. That is, the latter, to be sure, does us injury whenever it can and in every way possible, underhandedly and openly, with the result that it grows worse and we become better. It is defeated and it cannot deny it. It foresees that in a short time it will be all over with Protestantism unless Catholicism can be repressed. It realizes that it must allow for its own self-contradictions unashamedly and even indefensibly. Hence Protestantism is continually representing the Church as the enemy of freedom and as a constant danger to the state in order to provoke the multitude of unbelievers against us. In short, it wants freedom, of course, for itself, but none for us, and thus shows the same kind of inconsistency found in its doctrines. Pretending to be zealous for freedom, it wants to deny it to others.

However, the majority of the people (even unbelievers) are really in favor of freedom for all. It happens to be our good fortune that the various Protestant sects are forever quarreling among themselves and are very jealous of each other. Thus, there is little danger that legal exemptions will be granted or that restraining laws will be passed, since each group is afraid that once you give in to laws of this kind, they might well be used more frequently by the strong to exploit the weak. About this, there can be no doubt.

With the unbelievers, however, it is different. They abide by the letter of the Constitution and still reach their goal, namely, through the school. The public schools, that is, those supported by the state, are, without exception, indifferent in matters of religion. In these schools, it is not allowed, it is in fact against the law, to make any mention whatsoever of religion, except such things as pertain to natural religion and morality or might be reckoned as such.

No one is bound to go to school or to send anyone to school. Yet if any child wants to go to school, he must attend the public schools because there are no others. In these schools, they learn reading, writing, arithmetic, geography, history, etc., but no catechism. A priest or minister dare not put one step over the threshold of a schoolroom. The fundamental reason underlying this very popular law is the diversity of the religious sects. It is estimated that mutual peace among the sects is better served if all of them are barred from the schoolroom. Even though you are free to attend church, the church is usually very far away, and with ministers and priests rather scarce, and parents generally incapable or careless and negligent when it comes to religious instruction, there is nothing to prevent the youth from becoming religiously indifferent and for the most part even irreligious. This will be more and more the case as long as the present school situation remains as it is.

In view of this, German Catholics in the cities and elsewhere (and recently the English as well) have undertaken to build their own schools alongside their churches at their own expense. They have also paid the salaries of their own Catholic teachers and are still doing so. All of this the state allows. Since, however, they must still pay the school tax (in addition to what they have to give for the support of their own Catholic schools), many parents have decided to send their children to the public schools anyway, thus avoiding having to pay for the building and maintenance of Catholic schools as well as for the support of their teachers. In this way, we have lost many children. The resources of smaller congregations are generally too meager to construct their own schools and to pay the salaries of the teachers, and so they are compelled to send their children to the public schools if they do not want them to grow up in complete ignorance, only to be saddened by the sight of their little ones falling victims to heresy and unbelief, especially in places where there is no priest.

Because this unnatural alternative for Catholics—of having children who are either unbelievers or heretics (in places where Protestant influence is predominant) or completely illiterate—is in direct opposition to true freedom, our bishops have sought from the various state governments redress and justice, suggesting that either the school tax be lifted or a distribution of the tax revenues be made to the various denominations in proportion to their contribution. In this way, each denomination would look after its own needs in the matter of schools and teachers. A public discussion of this problem is now taking place in the press, with ardent supporters and strong antagonists about equally divided. We have not given up hope that justice will be done for the Catholics.

In the meantime, however, as I mentioned above, we are striving to set up everywhere churches and schools at our own expense in order to get a firm hold on the youth so as not to have to abandon them to unbelief. In this respect, we have done our utmost, and it is almost unbelievable how much has been accomplished, partly through the support obtained from the *Missionsverein* and partly through our own resources. The major seminary attached to our monastery numbered 28 students at the end of the current year. (The seminary closed its school year on July 4.) In the minor seminary there were 70 students. Several hundred children were prepared for the sacrament of Confirmation, some in the congregations belonging to us, others among the Irish workers along the railroad, most of whom are heads of families. Moreover, in the local parish [of St. Vincent], two new churches are to be built, one in the small town of Ligonier, the other in the village of Derry. We had a very hard time collecting the money for these churches. In the Indiana mission, a small church is to be built on the Mahoning River, entirely at our own expense. The brothers are helping as much as they can in the building of the church at St. Marys, and our sawmill supplies the lumber *gratis*. Furthermore, only a short time ago we contributed $300, and $250 before that. Churches will also be built in three places belonging to the St. Marys mission, namely, in Centreville, Williamsville, and Coopers Settlement, for which two priests stationed there, Fathers Odilo Vandergrün and Amandus Krammer, collected rather generous contributions.

Such is the case more or less everywhere, both in the country and in the cities. If only we had enough priests! I lost two of my priests in one year. One returned to Germany and the other died in St. Marys of a nerve disease that he contracted because of the hardships he suffered from the cold, damp climate of that rough and rugged country.[74] The brothers contracted it from him, and thus the monastery was truly a hospital all winter long since one after another, priests as well as brothers, succumbed to the fever, with only one exception. It is noteworthy, however, that only one brother died.[75] Twice I had to ride on horseback to St. Marys in order to get the advice I needed and to help with my homeopathy.

The following were ordained to the priesthood: Amandus Krammer, Augustine Wirth, and Rupert Seidenbusch (who came from Munich). In addition, two secular priests made their profession for the Order,[76] and Father Demetrius di Marogna will make his profession on August 15. Besides the sickness I just mentioned, the only other misfortune we met with was a big hailstorm that destroyed two-thirds of our wheat and caused about $30 worth of damage to windowpanes. It was, however, a complete surprise to me when I came upon an enemy against whom, I must admit, I am no match and who can still do me a great deal of harm. The following will identify the adversary to which I refer.

The royal Bavarian government has uncovered an old law dating to the time of the so-called Enlightenment whereby subjects of the kingdom of Bavaria are forbidden to take their legitimately obtained fortunes to monasteries outside the country. This law was already enforced on two occasions against people who wanted to emigrate to this country. The first case was that of a lay brother. Bavari-

---

[74] Jerome Wohlfahrt, O.S.B., returned to Bavaria to become a Capuchin, and Maurus Zacherl, O.S.B., died on November 28, 1852.
[75] Leo John Sitzberger, O.S.B. (1832-1853), died on January 23 in St. Marys.
[76] Peter Henry Lemke (1796-1882) and Joseph Billon (1801-1861).

an officials would not let him have his fortune because he entered a monastery here. However, he absconded with it. The second case concerned William Moosmüller,[77] the son of the royal Bavarian gamekeeper who wanted to be a priest in the Benedictine Order here. He provided bail of 1,000 florins because he was still subject to military service and then wanted to take the rest of his considerable fortune to the monastery. He received a court order from the trustee, however, that, by virtue of the above-mentioned law, no remittance is to be allowed. I did not receive him into the Order because I do not see why I should hand over to the royal treasury some three to four thousand florins, money to which it has no just claim. The enforcement of such a law in this modern day and age, and against a person emigrating to America, when you consider that otherwise any rascal is permitted to take his money there for any purpose he likes, appears to me an awful anachronism

Bonifaz Wimmer, Erzabt von St. Vincent in Pennsylvania, *written by Oswald William Moosmüller, a monk of Saint Vincent Archabbey.*

that would not have come to pass in Your Majesty's government. Moosmüller is a well-behaved young man, having reached his majority three months ago. He is studying here but has not received the habit. He wrote again not long ago for his money under the title of emigration but got nothing! It almost appears as if people are permitted to bring their money here for the support of the revolutionary funds of Mazzini, Kossuth, and Kinkel but not to help build up the culture, education, and Catholic life of the Germans. In Baden they helped me get out of

---

[77] This was Oswald William Moosmüller, O.S.B. (1832-1901), who came to St. Vincent as a candidate for the priesthood in 1852. Moosmüller, solemnly professed in 1855 and ordained in 1856, was one of the most outstanding Benedictine missionaries in the United States and a noteworthy historian. He wrote the history of the Benedictine mission in the United States (*St. Vincenz in Pennsylvanien* [Regensburg, New York, and Cincinnati: Friedrich Pustet, 1873]) and a biography of Boniface Wimmer (*Bonifaz Wimmer, Erzabt von St. Vincent in Pennsylvania* [New York: Benziger, 1891]). See Jerome Oetgen, "Oswald Moosmüller: Monk and Missionary," *The American Benedictine Review* 27(1976), 1-35.

the country, whereas in Bavaria they imposed a ban on secular possessions against our monastery!

We have enlarged and beautified our monastery considerably, as can be seen from the small sketch I am pleased to enclose. The monastery is seen here from the northwest, facing the nearby railroad. There are almost 200 of us who live in this building, which, with the exception of a public building in Lancaster, is now the largest to be seen from the railroad between Philadelphia and Pittsburgh (a distance of about 325 miles). How deep and ardent is my wish that much good may emanate from this monastery for us Germans, for the Catholic Church, and for the country in general!

One of these days, I will make a trip to New York and visit the royal Bavarian consul there. I already asked him on a previous occasion to see that Your Royal Majesty would get a good map of the United States. In case he has not yet sent it, I will indicate on it the scenes of our various fields of activities. I am also enclosing a catalogue listing the Catholic churches in the United States, in which material pertaining to our monasteries is found on pages 127-29. Since then, however, there have been many changes in the monks at the individual mission stations and, as mentioned above, there has been an increase in the number of students. Your Royal Majesty will find the perusal of these statistics of the American Church rather interesting in view of the fact that Your Highness has been pleased all along to bestow such lively interest upon these same missions. Undoubtedly, an abundance of honor and blessing will redound upon Your Majesty as well as upon Your Highness's royal family.

I forgot to mention that both houses of the [Pennsylvania] legislature, along with the governor of our state (who by the way is of German descent; his name is Bigler[78] and his brother is governor of California), at the last session, on a motion of the Catholic delegates, incorporated the Benedictine Order as a legal corporation in the state of Pennsylvania.[79] Here in this country this is the greatest and most reliable form of recognition legally possible. The main advantage of this recognition lies in the fact that the actual and currently accepted head of the Order is also officially recognized by the state as such and therefore can bear his own special seal. In addition, the incorporation carries with it a guarantee from the state recognizing the Order as a moral person with legitimate title to ownership of the property of the Order. It should be noted that the law gives no recognition to Church wealth as such, but to private wealth only, that is, such as

---

[78] William Bigler was governor of Pennsylvania from 1852 to 1855.

[79] The Benedictine Society of Westmoreland County was incorporated by the state of Pennsylvania on April 19, 1853.

belongs to either physical or moral persons. Thus through episcopal, papal, and state recognition, our future existence and stability have been given the greatest possible assurance. We shall endeavor to serve both Church and state to the best of our ability, either directly or indirectly. That we are of service to the state also from a material standpoint is seen from the fact that today we must pay $200 (or 500 florins) in property taxes, whereas upon my arrival here I had to pay only $16 (or 40 florins). Since taxes are levied in accordance with a yearly appraisal of real estate, this enables us to measure the improvement of our property since it has come into our hands. At the same time, it furnishes proof that republics like ours are no less expensive than monarchies. The lord abbot of Metten has property that is better and larger than I have here (considering especially the monastery at Metten), but the direct assessments he has to pay are hardly as much as the taxes I have to pay, apart from my additional taxes.

In conclusion, I have another request. May Your Royal Majesty be pleased to accept with your customary grace my most sincere and most respectful congratulations as well as those of my entire community of 14 priests, 80 brothers, and 28 novices on the occasion of Your Highness's namesday[80] and to kindly accept from us wishes for many years to come. With profound sentiments of reverence, gratitude, and devotedness, I bid you farewell. Your Royal Majesty's most humble and most loyal, P. Boniface Wimmer, Superior of the Bavarian Benedictine Mission

Ger   oRAB   cASVA   transBB   Math(44-57)

TO POPE PIUS IX   36

St. Vincent, December 10, 1853

Your Holiness: The Benedictine monastery of St. Vincent in Westmoreland County, Pennsylvania, has three dependent priories in Indiana, Carrolltown, and St. Marys of the same state. The first is 28 miles from the monastery with a resident pastor and three lay brothers. This house is established on a farm of 300 acres near the town in which we also have a few lots. At the second place, 50 miles away at Carrolltown, three fathers are stationed. They are in charge of a large mission field, primarily settled by German farmers. The monastery farm of 1,100 acres is managed by lay brothers. In St. Marys, which is 115 miles from the motherhouse, three fathers are likewise taking care of an extensive parish and a number of missions in the adjacent territory. Nine brothers are cultivating a large farm given to

---

[80] The feast of St. Louis was August 25.

the Order in trust for the congregation. A fourth place, St. Mary's Church in Newark, New Jersey, is administered by a Benedictine father[81] of St. Peter's Abbey, Salzburg, Austria. He has already expressed his desire to transfer it to the Order, but owing to a lack of men, I have not been able to accept it so far. St. Vincent itself has a seminary, a novitiate, and a college with seven fathers stationed there. Thirty-three students are taking ecclesiastical courses, and 45 are preparing for secular professions. One priest is pastor of the church connected with the monastery, and as far as possible, all the fathers assist in the neighboring missions, some along the central railroad as far as 90 miles away. All this will be per-fected and extended if the monastery is raised to the

Pope Pius IX

rank of an abbey. Holy Father, with child-like confidence we beseech you to grant us this petition, which is prompted by the purest motives. P. Boniface Wimmer, O.S.B.

Lat oAPF cASVA transFF Fell(I: 187)

TO GREGORY SCHERR 37

Latrobe,[82] Pa., February 28, 1854

Your Grace: You have probably received my letter of the middle of December. I have no other reason for writing now than the occasion of your namesday.[83] I send you my most cordial congratulations and my wish that you remain in the best of health both in body and soul and that for a long time to come you may be blessed in promoting and presiding over your great community, whose glory and reputa-tion was reported to me even from Hungary[84] some time ago. Despite the fact that I no longer belong *de facto* to Metten, I still belong to it *in affectione*. It makes me happy to hear of all the great and edifying things being done and achieved there.

---

[81] Father Nicholas Balleis, O.S.B.

[82] Latrobe, three miles north of St. Vincent, was established in 1852 as a stop on the main line of the Pennsylvania Railroad and was incorporated by the State of Pennsylvania in 1854.

[83] March 12, the feast of St. Gregory the Great.

[84] Presumably in correspondence from St. Martin's Archabbey, Pannonhalma, Hungary.

Such news breathes the spirit of Metten, the true Benedictine spirit that surpasses everything. I wish you the greatest possible success in your work for the glory of the Benedictine Order, a glory manifest also here, in Austria, in Hungary, and in Switzerland.

The number of my priests will increase in the near future by the ordination of two deacons. Five acolytes will restore "the succession," until now interrupted.[85] During the month of January, we had missions in Carrolltown and St. Marys. Father Seelos,[86] a Redemptorist, was retreatmaster in the former, I myself in the latter. If you have the impression that I can give conferences only about agriculture and livestock (since in your last letter you say that my mission reports are always too much about economics and not enough about pastoral concerns), you would be badly mistaken.

In the opinion of most people, I am still preaching fairly well. If that were not the case, then how can you explain that my people have such respect for me, that a certain "tremor" surrounds me when I am at home, and that everything is more exact and better run than when my prior, Father Demetrius,[87] is in charge. You still do not want to understand me correctly. I report on our economic and financial conditions for the simple reason that from the beginning my main point and purpose was always to build our Order in such a way that it would have a solid foundation and be able to do much good and more good than all the other orders, which despite their efforts cannot equal us. All the rest I presume as consequence and corollary. Learning and pastoral care are attended to with all zeal and energy wherever Benedictines enter the field. To erect a German seminary was my aim. It has been fulfilled to a great extent. In any event, were I to die today, any other person could bring it to perfect achievement.

Bishop Neumann[88] was here, as I have already written you, and made a very remarkable statement. He said that ours is the first and only and best German seminary in America. These were his words. That makes me somewhat proud—not that it is my doing or important because of my work but because Benedictines brought it into existence and put it on a permanent footing. Before long, the

---

[85] Wimmer means here that five acolytes will be ordained deacons and continue to the priesthood, maintaining a continuous succession of ordinations at St. Vincent each year (except 1853) since 1847.

[86] Francis Xavier Seelos, C.Ss.R. (1819-1867), superior of the Redemptorists in Pittsburgh. He was beatified by Pope John Paul II in 2000.

[87] Demetrius di Marogna, O.S.B. (1803-1869), whom Wimmer appointed prior at St. Vincent shortly after his solemn profession on August 21, 1853.

[88] John Nepomucene Neumann, C.Ss.R., bishop of Philadelphia. He was canonized by Pope Paul VI in 1977.

future will understand its importance. Without economy, however, it could not exist, and that is the reason that I always write in my reports about financial conditions. After all, I receive acknowledgements and thanks for it. In this regard, the abbot of Einsiedeln[89] sent me most cordial congratulations. By this, I do not want to imply that your criticism has caused me displeasure. I only want to make this statement, and not a different one. To avoid the scandal of concentrating on unimportant things, I shall report more about the care of souls.

At present, I am working to obtain for our monastery the right to elect an abbot. In this regard I wrote to Rome, to our congregation (i.e., the Propaganda Fide), and to Cardinal Morichini,[90] who answered immediately that he will make use of his influence with the Propaganda so that it will not turn against us. Let us hope that the nuncio[91] was convinced that suspicions of our alleged actions against the bishop[92] were without any foundation. If our petition is not granted, you have papal authority to declare that the title "Superior" is the highest that the head of a Benedictine community in this country can bear. I want to have the matter settled formally. In any case, though, I shall resign in order to make room for my esteemed and dear Father Prior. I shall stay at his side as advisor, with my suggestions, in case he has need of me, and will work productively. I am still robust and in good health, but my eyesight is not so good any more. My memory is getting weak, and to a certain extent my hearing also. I am becoming slow and bad tempered and see myself going downhill, the evening approaching. Naturally, I do not deserve to rest on my laurels, but I want to heal the wounds and damages inflicted on the battlefield.

Often I am not satisfied with myself, and this is getting worse. When I see that circumstances are improving outwardly, I more and more come to the conviction that another man should be at the head of this undertaking. In fact, I am suffering so much in this regard that I am disgusted with everything. I am tired of living. Unlike in the past, I avoid the society even of my brothers. At home, I am most of the time by myself. I never have free time or go to recreation, and if I have to make an exception and do so, the aftertaste is most bitter. I think I should become a hermit on our ridge so that I can be undisturbed and indulge my inclination to

---

[89] Henry Schmid, O.S.B., who had recently sent monks to the diocese of Vincennes, Indiana, to establish an offshoot of the Swiss abbey of Einsiedeln.

[90] Formerly apostolic nuncio to Bavaria, Carlo Luigi Morichini (1805-1879) was an official of the Roman Curia in 1854.

[91] Archbishop Gaetano Bedini, the Holy See's special envoy to the United States, who visited St. Vincent in December 1853.

[92] Michael O'Connor of Pittsburgh.

solitude more easily. I should try to become a saint but do not have the necessary courage to do it.

This feeling of depression does not hold me back from being active in the work to be done and expanding my thoughts and endeavors towards the present as well as the future, but it has made me so cold and apathetic towards everything that is going on in the world that I would like to lie down and die, if only I could hope to be certain of a blessed welcome in the other world. The enormity of all the human misery and destruction that comes from everywhere, and my inability to resist, has had much to do with my mental condition. One does not often receive consolation or cause for exaltation. In all the German papers (more or less) and in not a few English ones here, one finds not only gross unbelief and the most obdurate heresy, but also open and unreserved hatred for God. What misery! To work and build dams against the flood of destruction is something worthwhile, but how long it has lasted already! How weak is the resistance, how few the means, how frustrating to see that we are not doing enough, not even half enough of the good that is our duty to do. Who can bear it?

Were I at Metten, perhaps I would run off to fight the real as well as the Christian Mohammedans and to help clean up the world of these parasitic insects. Only here one must make himself a bystander, unable to do anything but lose his temper. You read in the newspapers how all over the country they insulted the nuncio.[93] In Pittsburgh, it seemed that it would come to violence. All the German Catholics were provided with arms. On the last Sunday, a German ruffian tried to lay hands on the nuncio as he was leaving St. Patrick's church, but mistakenly grabbed the bishop[94] instead. Luckily, I was not there, but in the evening, I drove with Father Holzer in front of him to the German orphanage in the suburb of Allegheny and back. There was general apprehension of an assault upon his person. He was warned that it might happen on another occasion, but he said, "Let it happen." I also carried a weapon in the event of an attack. It would have been frightful.

I have around me good people, many of them very good, some really excellent–a great consolation indeed. My brothers are pure gold. My young priests all behave very well; they are obedient, submissive, studious. Some of them are preaching in English as well as German to everyone's satisfaction, especially Father

---

[93] Archbishop Bedini had encountered vocal and sometimes violent anti-Catholic demonstrations during his visit to the United States. See James F. Connelly, *The Visit of Archbishop Gaetano Bedini to the United States of America, June 1853—February 1854* (Rome: Libreria Editrice dell'Università Gregoriana, 1960).

[94] Michael O'Connor.

Augustine.[95] They are all heaping honor upon honor on us. Even old Lemke[96] is doing his share.

We are still drinking nothing but fresh water. For supper we have no more than soup and mush. On feast days only soup, vegetables, and noodles, and meat only once a day if it is available. Brother Remegius is a skilled goldsmith and is making chalices, monstrances, etc.; Brother Cosmas[97] is an excellent cabinet maker and architect; Brother Peter[98] is doing an excellent job as supervisor of the steam mill. Father Luke[99] is bringing to completion the restoration of the paintings and is doing it with great zeal. A few days ago, he began work on a damaged painting. He took the whole picture from the canvas and put it on a new one for the purpose of restoring its beauty. Not long ago I sold a small statue of the Madonna he had made and got $50 for it. His pupil Koch[100] is advancing rapidly in painting. Our orchestra is excellent. Thus, art and learning go together in the house, peace and joy, contentedness and study, zeal for souls near and far. There are students in our seminary from New York, Baltimore, Buffalo, Milwaukee, and St. Louis–that is, from 500, 700, 1,500 miles away–and never have I lacked means to provide for them. Three weeks ago, I did not have even $10, and now I have $2,000 again. Strange to say, hail, fire, famine cannot damage us. When I received news that the mill [in St. Marys] had burnt down, I was with the Dominican sisters and had just made final arrangements for them. After many irksome and prolonged negotiations, I arrived at the point where they could settle themselves formally in Williamsburg [New York].[101] [The destruction of the mill] was my reward. It was the revenge of the devil because the good sisters are such a great hindrance for him. They now have 243 children in their school, more than half of whom had earlier gone to the Protestant school or to no school at all. The same thing has happened to me elsewhere, where we now have flourishing parishes in good standing. Thus, it is in St. Marys, where a dozen parishes have already come into

---

[95] Augustine Wirth, O.S.B

[96] Peter Henry Lemke, O.S.B.

[97] Cosmas Wolf, O.S.B. (1822-1894).

[98] Peter Seemüller, O.S.B.

[99] Luke Wimmer, O.S.B. (1825-1901).

[100] Paulinus Koch, O.S.B.

[101] In 1853, Wimmer had helped Dominican nuns from Regensburg, Bavaria, settle in Williamsburg (later Brooklyn), New York. See Eugene J. Crawford, *Daughters of Dominic on Long Island* (New York: Benziger Brothers, 1938); and Oetgen, *An American Abbot*, 124-30.

existence. Likewise, in Carrolltown where my first adversary eventually became my confrere.[102]

I often wonder how my people allow themselves to be commanded by me. I transfer them from place to place without regard for their clearly stated desires, and disagreeable assignments are often made. Yet when I say go, they go; come, they come. If I wrinkle my brow, everyone gets out of my way. What would these good people do if they had a Wittmann as their superior?[103]

Four railroads are about to be built near St. Vincent to which several hundred Irish will be called for work. The railroads will bring money in, also a lot of work– but not just a little danger for younger priests. Fathers Wirth, Seidenbusch, and Englbrecht[104] are busy serving the railroad workers. I must appoint a fourth but do not know who yet. I had in mind erecting some buildings this year, but it will first be necessary to clear the fields. Then I will finish the steam sawmill and build a small brewery here if I can. In St. Marys, I shall soon start again on the mill. I have to furnish a great deal for it because of its importance. We must be more careful in the future that such a disaster does not repeat itself.

On February 10, I gave the habit to four postulants. Our bishop, who was transferred to Erie, is now back in Pittsburgh and his successor went to Erie.[105] On January 20 and February 26, we had terrible thunderstorms. After that, there was more snow and ice. We have had so little rain for the past eight months that water is becoming scarce.

Best regards to all my confreres. I recommend myself to their prayers. Repeating all my best wishes, I remain in sincere affection and deepest respect, Your Grace's most obedient, P. Boniface Wimmer

Ger   oAMA   cASVA   transRG

---

[102] Peter Henry Lemke, O.S.B. (1796-1882), had invited Wimmer to Pennsylvania in 1845. Wimmer's earliest relations with him were marked by conflict and controversy. In 1852, Lemke entered the monastery at St. Vincent and became a Benedictine.

[103] George Michael Wittmann (1760-1833), bishop of Regensburg, was Wimmer's teacher and counselor who urged the young priest to pursue his monastic vocation. Wittmann was widely regarded in southern Bavaria as an inspired spiritual leader and after his death, a saint.

[104] Augustine Wirth, Rupert Seidenbusch, and Celestine Englbrecht.

[105] When the new diocese of Erie was established 1853, Michael O'Connor of Pittsburgh was named bishop and Josue Mary Young chosen to succeed O'Connor in Pittsburgh. At the urging of both O'Connor and Young, the Holy See soon agreed to reappoint O'Connor to Pittsburgh and assign Young to Erie. See Robert G. Barcio, *A Cathedral in the Wilderness: A History of the Diocese of Erie 1853-1920* (Erie, Pa.: The Diocese of Erie, 1991), 44-45.

TO KARL VON REISACH **38**

St. Vincent, August 7, 1854

Alphonse John Heimler, O.S.B., served as president of Saint Vincent College from 1862 to 1872.

Lord Archbishop: I received with gratitude the message that we will be remembered again this year with a generous stipend of 7,000 florins from Your Excellency. Through this help, the holes made last year by various endeavors and accidents will again be partially patched. Current problems, to which I fell heir because of hail, fire, and rising costs, have not caused any lull in our work because here credit is often as good as cash. I simply had to open one hole in order to patch another, and in this way, I got by well enough. The number of students in the lay and religious seminary increased each month and will grow even more next year so that I will again have to extend our house by 53 feet.

H. Jacker[106] arrived here safely, and on July 3, he was invested. Until now, he is well and satisfied except that he is somewhat concerned about his dismissorials if, because of his emigration, his father has to pay the stipend. When the new school year begins (September 1), I will use him as a teacher so that he can make himself useful. A certain Heimler from Regensburg also arrived recently. He is an excellent student, but unfortunately, was born without fingers on his right hand. Though he surely cannot become a priest, he can become a cleric and an outstanding professor.[107] Like Noah's ark, all sorts of creatures from everywhere gather under our roof. Often, too, useless creatures, who disappear after a while or get thrown out, come. To him who knocks, the door is opened. Some leave soon, others only after months. Some even return and are admitted again. Whoever stays is good.

---

[106] Unidentified.

[107] Alphonse John Heimler, O.S.B. (1832-1909), was ordained a priest in 1857 after Wimmer arranged for surgery on his hand and for a dispensation from Rome to allow him to celebrate Mass with deformed fingers. He became, as Wimmer predicted, an outstanding professor at St. Vincent and eventually president of St. Vincent College.

Things are expensive this year, and the price of food is rising even more after the bad harvest. On poor soil, people did not even get seed for the winter grains, especially wheat. On good soil, they got only a half or a third of the usual crop. We are far behind, and what is worse, after a very cold, dry winter we have had an exceedingly hot summer. In June and July, we had 95 to 98 degrees Fahrenheit almost constantly in our hills (for we live on hilly land). A few times, we even had 100 degrees in the shade. This so-called "beating heat" made us itch all over our bodies, which was nearly unbearable. Everything dried up. The streams disappeared. The mills stood idle. Even well water became scarce. Every day I use seven bushels of flour, and five bushels (or one barrel) cost $10. Often we lacked flour. How badly off I would have been without the steam mill! The millers here grind the grain only once and as a result make only fine flour but no coarse flour. The rest goes into bran. My miller (Brother Peter Seemüller from Fürstenfeld) handles this differently for us. He grinds coarse flour too, and so it goes twice as far. However, we also mix corn with the flour for our bread, and we get by fairly well. I had very little to grind because the crops were poor. However, according to moderate estimates, the mill saved me $1,000 this year. This will likely not represent a large gain since I will need to buy grain, but then our expenses will be smaller. Hay is the most expensive item this year, but I have enough. During the winter, we fenced in our woods and were able to graze our herd there until harvest time, while other farmers had to use their clover fields for grazing. In this way, we substituted fodder for hay. Nevertheless, we will get only 70 loads of hay when we could easily have had 130. The corn was hopeless until July 31 when a good rain helped very much. Since then we have had more rain, but the harvest will be poor. The potatoes have nice foliage but have not yet sprouted. As for vegetables, we will have only pickles and a few beans. It is just as bad in Indiana. In St. Marys, it is pretty good. In Carrolltown, it is still better. When all is said and done, I will again be able to feed and clothe 200 people, if I do not have another fire. The mill that burned down is again half rebuilt. The parish eagerly helped with teams and hands. The rascal who very likely started the fire has gone to Harrisburg. The mill will cost me another $2,000.

The new bishop of the new diocese of Erie on Lake Erie, Josue Young, a convert, was at St. Marys for a visitation and confirmation from July 12 to July 16. He ate with the sisters and lived with the brothers. The superior[108] did all she could to show him hospitality and to entertain him. Father Amandus Krammer (from Linz) wrote a nice song for the bishop's visit. Father Leonard Mayer (from Württemberg) set it to music, and the novices Benedicta Burkhart, Bonifacia Cassidy,

---

[108] Mother Benedict Riepp, O.S.B. (1825-1862).

Josepha Bärkle, Luitgarde Butz, Bernarda Weidenberner, and Hildegarde Renner sang it very well in the refectory. He enjoyed it all very much, although he is not a lover or a good judge of music. In the evening, 12 of my students gave him a concert with wind instruments. He liked this so much that he finally asked for "Yankee Doodle," which he really enjoyed. He also took a two-hour ride with me and two other priests through the settlement in order to see all the marvels of St. Marys. On July 15, the sisters' exhibition took place, and he distributed prizes to the girls, speaking to them fittingly and impressively in English and German. On Sunday, we had a pontifical service at which I gave the main sermon, but he gave another appropriate talk in English and German before Confirmation. He is a very fine, pious man, some 50 years old, very tall and strong, and an American without prejudice against the Germans. He is very poor and has an extremely poor church. I would like to recommend him to the consideration of Your Excellency, if I may do so. He gave me (that is, "the Benedictine Society," as we are legally called) the deed to the parish church, the school, and the sisters' land (seven acres), of which Bishop O'Connor only wanted to give us the management. Since he did not even have a *pluviale*,[109] I gave him one as a gift. True, it is not nice enough for a bishop, but it is worth more than 100 florins. I promised I would collect money from my people for a nicer one. He wished to have Benedictines from here come to Erie because he was so pleased with our performance, especially in building. The sisters had packed him sandwiches and cake for the journey, but unfortunately the driver forgot them, and as I later heard, he did not have enough to eat that evening in Williamsville, a horrible place. The whole community here did what it could to honor him and make his stay pleasant.

It becomes increasingly clear that the prejudice commonly held against Americans—that they do not want to become priests—is unfounded. I am sure that in a short time I will have 100 boys, or as many as I can accommodate, who want to become priests, and only a few will prove unfaithful in this resolution. Here, as everywhere else, they come from the middle class or from the poor. If they cannot study [because of lack of money], then, of course, there will be few priests. If we meet with no great misfortune, we will go far with buildings and agriculture each year, so that we will always be able to take pupils. Without a doubt, St. Marys, because it is in another diocese, will soon be a rival of St. Vincent, and similar efforts will be made there.

I believe I already reported that we would take over Butler and Butler County, where Father Utto and Father Kilian[110] are stationed with a lay brother. I also pro-

---

[109] A liturgical cope.
[110] Utto Huber, O.S.B. (1819-1896), and Kilian Bernetzeder, O.S.B. (1818-1887).

cured 207 acres of land, together with a house and barn, 45 minutes from here, for $2,500, of which the first $500 must be paid only after five years and then $500 every two years. I must permit two boys to study here *gratis* for it and may not rent out any of it. This makes it cheap since its approximate value would surely come to about $4,000. Otherwise, things are going along in the normal way. Most of us are well, happy, and satisfied. Next to me, Father Demetrius[111] is most in demand in the house. During the heat wave, he was sick a few times. I have only five priests here with me until more are ordained. Everyone is overworked, especially on Sundays, when two, and sometimes three have to go out.

We are in a bad political situation. The Protestant bigots and egoistical nationalists found a secret meeting place with a secret society called the Know Nothings. From there they work madly against foreigners, especially against Catholics. Lies and slanders and every type of attack are used against bishops, against the orders, and especially against priests and religious. One has to see it to believe it. Their aim is to stir up the people to persecute us or to provoke us to attack so that there will be a reason for a fight. We remain calm. Thus, they will not succeed but be defeated. Our good Bishop O'Connor[112] was recently slandered. One can understand lies, but to bear them is nevertheless hard. Therefore, we find the Church Militant everywhere. Its freedom is still only on paper, and she can use it only with difficulty. "Not peace, but the sword."

May God reward your goodness to us. We will beg Him to do so daily. With sincerest regards, your most submissive, P. Boniface Wimmer

P.S. Father Demetrius is very happy to know that Princess Therese is in the monastery, and he respectfully sends his best regards.

Ger   oAAM   cASVA   transMN

TO GIACOMO FRANSONI   39

St. Vincent, December 18, 1854

Your Eminence: Humility may counsel us not to present our case so strenuously, but this question is of the greatest importance for us. We are firmly convinced that the success or failure of a Benedictine monastery, the admission or rejection of the Order in the United States, and the development or ruin of our missionary seminary depend on the approval or refusal of this request. Our monastery cannot

---

[111] Demetrius di Marogna, O.S.B. (1803-1869), was claustral prior at St. Vincent.
[112] Michael O'Connor of Pittsburgh.

last much longer without a permanent head, and if the monastery must be given up, the institutions connected with it will come to naught.

Perhaps Your Eminence, who assured us repeatedly of your paternal protection, is wondering why we put so much stress on the word "abbot." If the saying is true, "where your treasure is there is your heart," who could be surprised that we love what we accomplished with so much labor? Moreover, because as Benedictines we look upon our Order and upon our monastery as the treasures closest to our hearts, we are seeking to advance both in every way. If other religious orders and societies have canonical superiors in accordance with their monastic principles, why should not we wish to enjoy the rights and privileges of our Order?

We know very well that the abbatial dignity is a favor that we cannot demand but must humbly ask for. Yet, when was such a favor denied if solicited with great humility and good reason? Why is it refused to us "when the Sacred Congregation usually approves and confirms everything that is good"? What can we answer our benefactors when they ask us about the present state of affairs at St. Vincent? Who would not be discouraged or disheartened after so much has been achieved with so much zeal?

Your Eminence, this condition renders everything uncertain for us. This state of affairs is becoming unbearable because many believe that during the coming winter, Europe may again be involved in war and recourse to the Holy See will take a long time, and may become difficult if not impossible. Therefore, with the deepest respect I must state that we are forced to send this petition, not to promote our honor, but (as we all believe) to advance the cause of our monastery and even the propagation of the faith in the United States.[113] Your Eminence's most obedient and humble servant, Boniface Wimmer, O.S.B., Superior

Lat   oAPF   cASVA   transFF

---

[113] Wimmer's letter was accompanied by a petition to Pope Pius IX, signed by the capitulars at St. Vincent, requesting abbatial status for their monastery. See Felix Fellner, *Abbot Boniface and His Monks* (Latrobe, Pa.: Privately Published at St. Vincent Archabbey, 1956), I: 192.

1855-1859

TO GREGORY SCHERR **40**

On Board the *Canada*, February 8, 1855

Most Esteemed Right Reverend Abbot: I received your last letter in the middle of January, just as I was ready to make my journey to Europe. It is fortunate that I got it in time to approach the district judge formally. By resolution of the chapter, I must go to Rome because my more excitable young monks do not want a superior any more but an abbot. One year ago we sent a petition in this regard to Rome but received no response except a fine letter saying that we should behave ourselves and that the outcome would be as we desired, but that the matter was so important that it would have to be considered carefully before an answer could be given. After no answer came, they insisted that I not rest but pursue the matter, and with that, I repeated my petition on December 18 of last year. Because the political situation [in Europe] threatened war, they now insist emphatically that I go at once and present the petition in person. I waited only for the return of Bishop O'Connor from Rome. When he returned, I met with him and from our conversation concluded that he was not in favor of our petition and that he had even used his influence against our most earnest request. After that, I could not be held back any longer.

On January 25, I left St. Vincent for Newark, and on January 30 I went from Newark to Boston and from there to Liverpool where I hope, God willing, to land on February 13 to visit my English confreres, and then via London and Brussels to arrive in Munich on Shrove Tuesday to see once more the fools and clowns who are not at home beyond the ocean. Naturally, I intend to transact some business. I have with me some small California golden eagles which I want to exchange for two-headed eagles and lions.[1] I also have American securities that I will exchange for money, which I am authorized to do. I hope to have good luck in this even if I do not obtain the diploma. That is, even if our monastery does not receive the title of abbey, I hope to return to my home across the ocean in a few months with a menagerie of two-headed eagles and lions. Thus, I take the liberty of notifying Your Grace, in all humility, so that you will be prepared for my mission and be ready to rid yourself of such beasts, since you will not be safe in regions populated by them unless you hide behind locked doors.

I do not know how soon I shall be in Metten, but I do not intend to stay long in Munich and want to rush through Bavaria as fast as possible so that I can be in Rome in time to attend to my principal business, that is, the raising St. Vincent to an abbey and the obtaining for the community the legal authority to elect an abbot. I also want to settle some particular questions with regard to the *Holy Rule*, etc. Perhaps you will have something for me to do at Metten. I shall be glad to give you my assistance, but in any case, I beg you for a few days lodging if all the cells are not occupied. I hope to see all the confreres in the best of health, especially my dear Father Subprior and Father Charles. I did not think to see you so soon. It looks as though I am destined to be a *mobile perpetuum* and not to observe stability until I am enclosed in the tomb I have in mind to build some day.

Thus far, we have had a very enjoyable voyage, except that on February 3, a very heavy storm rose from the southwest and lasted for 12 hours. Our old *Canada* endured, though with pants and groans. It was in the region where the *Arctic* went down. I felt that a thousand devils were howling to bring us to the same misfortune. Such a musical *forte* evoked in me a particular and general examination of conscience, and the sharp spray, like ice blown in one's face, was good holy water. My stomach did not get upset but withstood nausea and dizziness as the ship pitched and rolled. *Ergo* Pater Bonifacius is coming again, in person, with this letter. Prepare ye the way of the Lord, because for love of Him, he is making a long and dangerous voyage.

---

[1] Bavarian and Austrian coins.

Cordial greetings in advance. Very soon, you shall see (as ever) how deep a respect for Your Grace has P. Planifacius[2] Wimmer

Ger   oAMA   cASVA   transRG

TO DEMETRIUS DI MAROGNA   41

Rome, April 9, 1855

I arrived here the night before Maundy Thursday (four days from Munich, not counting three days in Einsiedeln, one in Genoa, and one in Livorno) and have been here with our confreres since Holy Saturday.[3] The abbot is Pappalettere, but they have another older abbot here, Theoduli, who comes from an aristocratic Roman family. Besides this, there is a third abbot, Pescetelli, now general procurator of our Order, a very capable and dear man. There are about 20 capitulars, 5 brothers, and 25 students. My room overlooks the hills and Frascati, and the Passionist monastery on top of its hill lies beautifully before me. However, the area is so unhealthful that windows may be opened only when the sun is high. We are one hour from the city. The basilica (monastery church) of St. Paul's

Demetrius di Marogna, prior at Saint Vincent. He led the mission to Minnesota in 1856.

is far more beautiful and larger than that of St. Boniface [in Munich]. I prefer it to St. Peter's. The grave of St. Paul the Apostle is unusually beautiful. It is right in front of the presbytery. What splendid marble pillars and Corinthian capitals! Even statues of St. Benedict and St. Scholastica are found here in marble on the

---

[2] A Latin wordplay on Wimmer's name. As Bonifacius means "doer of good," so *Planifacius* means "maker of plans." Long before he went to America, Wimmer had been nicknamed by his confreres at Metten *Der Projektenmacher*, "the plan-maker" or "quixotic visionary." He often used the term in self-deprecation.

[3] Upon his arrival in Rome, Wimmer had been invited to stay at the Abbey of St. Paul's Outside the Walls by Abbot Angelo Pescetelli, whom the Sacred Congregation for the Propagation of the Faith had named as the American Benedictines' advocate in the case of St. Vincent's elevation to abbey status. Pescetelli became a staunch defender of the American Benedictines and a close friend of Wimmer's.

epistle side altar. In still another chapel is a second St. Benedict, seated and beautifully done by the greatest contemporary sculptor.

We rise at 6:00 am and meditate from 6:30 to 7:00 am. Then we have Prime
and Masses. Breakfast (a little coffee or chocolate) follows and then work. At
11:00 am, a high Mass is sung by the choir. Tierce takes place before this, Sext and
None afterwards. At noon, we have soup, a little meat, very good vegetables, hard-
boiled eggs. After the meal, I have a cup of black coffee and a little weak wine with
water in the community room. At 1:00 pm, we take a little siesta, and at 3:00 pm,
we have vespers, sung by the choir. (The little students, some of whom are only
nine years old, sing along.) After this, we take a walk. At 9:00 pm, we have the
evening meal, after which we recreate for 15 minutes. At 10:45 pm, all go to bed.
We have readings at meals and silence in the corridors. My bed is a straw sack.
Our rooms have no heat and only a small window.

There isn't much fuss. The abbots participate in everything and are very intimate with the capitulars. All are like children toward each other. There are three
Germans here. One of them is already ordained, one is a theologian, one is still
young.[4] Besides these, there are a Spaniard, two Australian Benedictines (who
quarreled with Archbishop Polding[5] and won him over), one English Benedictine,
and two French brothers. I feel bad because I am supposed to speak Italian all the
time and don't know much. However, I want to learn more. I will soon move to
San Callisto near St. Peter's,[6] because in the summer all go there because of the
bad air. I'm already quite homesick and will have to stay here probably three more
months. All for the honor of St. Benedict!

Nevertheless, there is something good in all this because we are making acquaintances and finding supporters. Abbot Pescetelli already defended our cause
on March 12. Cardinal Barnabo[7] did not look on it with favor. The opposition

---

[4] The three Germans whom Wimmer refers to probably included Anselm Nikes, O.S.B., and Placidus Wolter, O.S.B., who had joined the community of St. Paul's Outside the Walls in 1852 and
1855 respectively. Later, two of Placidus Wolter's brothers, Maurus and Hildebrand, also joined the
Roman community. Hildebrand died in Rome in 1858. In 1862, Placidus and Maurus returned
to Germany and founded the monastery of Beuron. Anselm Nickes remained a monk of St. Paul's
Abbey until his death in 1866.

[5] John Bede Polding, O.S.B. (1794-1877), an English Benedictine who became first archbishop of
Sydney, Australia.

[6] San Callisto's monastery in Trastevere was the Roman residence for monks from the abbey of St.
Paul's Outside the Walls. On this and subsequent visits to Rome Wimmer stayed there because it
was close to the Vatican offices where he had to conduct his business.

[7] Alessandro Cardinal Barnabo, secretary of the Sacred Congregation for the Propagation of the
Faith, which had authority over affairs in the American missions.

of the bishop[8] is described as "typical of American bishops"! They want no abbots, at least not with miter and crosier! We, however, are spoken of honorably and kindly. I found out something. Someone other than myself is to be chosen as more suited to govern. It is not you. It will have to be someone younger.

As yet, I haven't made any calls, but we do have powerful and good friends, and among the three main people–the cardinal protector Antonelli, Barnabo, and Count Hohenlohe[9]–we are mightily supported. The chief advisor[10] is our best friend. Thus, we hope and pray hard that our just cause will triumph. The Australian, English, and American Benedictines all have important business before Propaganda at the same time! We had been regarded as dead, and now we have new life in three parts of the world. I did not know that there are Benedictines in South America. Now I hear there are many in Brazil.

My last letter was very little comfort, I'm sure. I am sorry to know you are in need and having difficulties. I eagerly await news from Munich about the money. If only Mrs. Hilbert receives her due! As much as possible make the most of the railroads to Wheeling and St. Marys when they are built, and plant many potatoes wherever possible on the Ridge.

Are all the fathers well? And all the brothers and students? I hope all do their duty and especially perform their singing and praying diligently. I am often with you in prayer and even more in my desire, for I find doing nothing unbearable.

I left Munich on March 27 after congratulating Abbot Rupert of Scheyern[11] and receiving 200 florins from him for my travel expenses. The confreres there were very kind. At 4:00 pm, I was in Lindau, at 6:00 pm across Lake Constance in Rohrschach, and at 8:00 pm in St. Gallen. On March 28 at 6:00 am, I was in Einsiedeln[12] and immediately offered holy Mass for myself and our entire house in the chapel of the miraculous Madonna. The same on Thursday and Friday. On Friday afternoon, the abbot[13] took me to Brunnen on Lake Lucerne. There I offered holy Mass on Saturday with Father Karl Brandeis, who accompanied me. I

---

[8] Michael O'Connor of Pittsburgh.

[9] Cardinal Giacomo Antonelli (1808-1876) was papal secretary of state; Gustaph Adolph Hohenlohe (1823-1896), a German nobleman and Vatican official who later became papal chamberlain (1857) and cardinal (1866).

[10] Presumably Abbot Angelo Pescetelli, O.S.B., who advised the Propaganda Fide on matters pertaining to the American Benedictines.

[11] Rupert Leiss, O.S.B., abbot of the Bavarian monastery of Scheyern and Wimmer's novitiate classmate at Metten. The congratulations were for Leiss's namesday, March 27.

[12] The Swiss Benedictine abbey of Einsiedeln had established a community in the diocese of Vincennes, Indiana, in 1853.

[13] Henry Schmid, O.S.B., abbot of Einsiedeln.

took a steamer on Lake Lucerne at 8:00 am to Flüelen and the mail coach from there over the St. Gotthard Pass. There was no snow in Bavaria but plenty in Switzerland. We soon had to take sleds, and at first only four-seaters, to Andermatt, where we arrived around 3:00 pm. Surrounded by glaciers, this is a frightening place in the winter. We had a fine meal of wild snow grouse and excellent wine for three francs. From there we had only a two-seater, that is, we sat facing each other. The driver sat in front, half way up, one foot stretched out in order to prevent tipping. Our six sleds zigzagged up frightening heights over very deep snow. Other sleds came down meeting us, which was very difficult. We went down so fast that we often shuddered with fright. At 6:00 pm, we were already at the foot of the Airolo. There we again took wagons. At noon, we were in Bellinzona, at 1:25 pm in Magadino, at 2:00 pm in Arogno, at 4:00 pm in Navara. From there we went by rail and were in Genoa at 10 pm. We left there the next day at 8:00 am. Then we went on the Castor to Livorno. We stayed from 5:00 am until 4:00 pm. In the evening, we went to Civitavecchia, where we arrived at 5:00 am. At noon we left, and at 12:30 pm, we were in Rome. The weather was nice on the Gotthard Pass, but then it became rainy and cold. There was much snow, and in the Apennines, there is still snow. I slept in a chair on my first night in Rome. Every room was occupied. The next two nights I had a room without a window.

Several fathers from Einsiedeln will travel to Vincennes soon. Among them is the dean.[14] Receive them as best you can. Let them see the farm and the Ridge as well as Carrolltown. The abbot wishes it. They treated me most hospitably at Einsiedeln, and I am sure an intimate relationship will develop between them and us. In addition, the Benedictines here wish to have us in their congregation. Pescetelli thinks we should elect abbots first for three years, then for six years. Only after that should they be abbots for life. In the Cassinese Congregation, the abbots are elected for six years, not by the capitulars but by the general chapter. It has its good and bad points. This may be applicable to a congregation but hardly to a single house.

Today we visited the church where St. Bernard and Eugene III lived. Franciscans are there now. It is a very unhealthy place! There is a poor basilica with a nearby chapel. From it, one can see the prison in which St. Paul was a captive and the pillar on which he was beheaded. One can also see the fountains that sprang up in the three places where his bouncing head rested, each about 20 feet from

---

[14] The monks from Einsiedeln who went to the diocese of Vincennes, Indiana, in 1855 were Athanasius Tschopp, O.S.B., and Chrysostom Foffa, O.S.B. They joined other monks from Switzerland who had arrived there in 1853 and 1854. In Indiana, they established the monastery of St. Meinrad, which became the first abbey in the Swiss-American Benedictine Congregation.

the next one. We drank the water. The water of each fountain had a different taste. Ach, what one feels in such a spot, which is entirely forsaken and forgotten! (I have already seen the Holy Father twice.)

One needs no breviary here. They have choir stalls around the high altar, another choir in the chapel near the high altar, and two upstairs. Everywhere are office books with large musical notations. Everyone uses these. Only three lamps burn in the choir, one on each side for the abbots. In the middle is a large box that contains the office books. On it, there is a large lectern on which the books are placed. A lamp burns in front of it. The fathers and boys stand around this lectern and sing from it and respond to the readings, which are read out of a large lectionary in front of the abbot, after which the reader returns to his stall and is seated. The 25 little fellows sing along with full-throated song.

I could write more specifically about our problem, but this is enough for now. You may share this letter with the fathers, but do not divulge what I wrote about the bishop to anyone. Now I can see why he did not want me to go to Rome! Here one can hear *sub rosa* many things of which one may not speak. So do nothing further with the monastery. Two things–that St. Vincent become an abbey and that it elect an abbot–have been asked for, and I press these causes mightily. The election can take place only after our problem is settled. It is possible that three monks will have to be proposed for abbot and that the Holy Father will then choose one. There was some discussion of this. Since I am the main agitator and there is concern that we will succeed in becoming an abbey, another will likely be proposed as abbot, and since I have already proposed one, there will probably be three names in all.

Archbishop Polding from Sidney, Bishop Brown[15] from England, and Paulinus Heptonstall, our provincial in England, were at dinner today. I talked with the latter for an hour. I spoke much with Brown too and want to see Polding as well. It was interesting for me. Brown and his Benedictines wanted to establish a chapter so that English will always have at least one Benedictine bishop, and they succeeded! Our situation is being discussed much in Rome in higher circles. They thought today that it would come up in three weeks. Next week the Australian, the following week the English, and the third week the American Benedictine problem will be taken up. I don't think it will be too late after you receive this letter for you to organize some small devotion in the evenings for the successful outcome of this business.

But enough for now. I will write again in a few days so that you will always know what our hopes or fears are. Don't work too hard and get whatever you

---

[15] Bishop Thomas Joseph Brown, O.S.B., of Newport, England.

need. Greet all the confreres both in and out of the monastery. Also, greet Messrs. Kuhn, Gillespie, Lebus, Elders, and Heads. With all love and regard, P. Boniface

Ger   oASJA   cASVA   transMN

TO KING LUDWIG I   42

Rome, June 4, 1855

Most Gracious Lord and King: I received the letter of your assistant von Gmainer of Ascognano on May 26 and thank you most sincerely for the good news it contains, as well as for the gracious courtesy that prompted Your Majesty to undertake personally the support of the just cause of my monastery. I am no longer worried that it will not triumph and am happy that we will become an abbey without the burdensome conditions the bishop[16] wanted to impose upon us. This view is held quite generally, although nothing definite can be predicted until the meeting to be held before June 29 is over.

Concerning me personally, Count Hohenlohe[17] thinks that I will definitely not become abbot because Cardinal Barnabo[18] told him that I had written too harshly and should expect to receive a penance for it. It is true. I speak plainly, even in Latin, but I used expressions which any educated man uses when he has to defend right against wrong. I had reserved even stronger language in case of necessity, which now, fortunately, no longer exists. If I deserve punishment because of this, it is agreeable to me because I do not have a guilty conscience. It would be no penance for me if I did not become abbot. I never desired it. I never sought it. I myself suggested my prior, Father Demetrius di Marogna, to the Propaganda as abbot. Among pagan Greeks and Romans, we have examples of faithful dedication to a good cause without regard for honor or recognition in the eyes of the world. Therefore, I suppose, even a Benedictine will have enough selflessness to dedicate himself with all his strength to the growth of his monastery without expecting or even desiring to be its abbot! It is enough for me to know that I never have deserved the spurs. When I do not ride, I do not need them.

However, this entire matter is only conjecture, and the penance could be something else. If only they treat the monastery well, I will be content. Otherwise, I would do what I threatened to do: I would leave the monastery and the diocese

---

[16] Michael O'Connor of Pittsburgh.

[17] Count Gustaph Adolph Hohenlohe, Vatican official who was named cardinal in 1866.

[18] Alessandro Barnabo, secretary of the Sacred Congregation for the Propagation of the Faith.

and build a new one under a just bishop, one in which I could live my vocation in peace. If I did that, I would, I am sure, suffer great damage, but the bishop would suffer even more damage, and disgrace besides.

We regretted the sudden departure of Your Majesty because the Pope had set the following day, Friday, as a day on which to pay his return visit, which was no longer possible after your departure. At the time he brought Holy Communion to Archduke Max a week ago, he wept hard and long! Next Friday or next Sunday, I will have an audience with him. After that I will go to Subiaco and perhaps also to Monte Cassino. As soon as this business is settled, I will go to Munich.

I did not want to neglect to thank Your Majesty personally and to wish you a very happy trip. However, since I saw that Your Highness was very busy, I did not wish to disturb you and left immediately. Baron von Verger[19] will speak strongly in the name of Your Majesty on behalf of our monastery and its needs to Cardinal Antonelli,[20] who is also general protector of the Benedictine Order. In this way, His Holiness will also learn of our monastery and its problems. Thus, all preparations have been made for the storm, and the enemy will, no doubt, have to surrender!

Again, expressing sincerest thanks and deepest appreciation, I recommend myself to your favor and kindness and remain with deepest respect and humble submission, Your Royal Majesty's, most obedient, P. Boniface Wimmer, O.S.B., Superior

Ger   oRAB   cASVA   transMN   Math(69-71)

TO KARL VON REISACH   43

Rome, July 2, 1855

Your Grace: To my delight, I am writing this letter to follow the sweet call of duty by thanking you most profoundly for your generosity in sending my dear Father Prior[21] 5,000 florins. By doing so, you have alleviated many, many problems for him. Now I am more reconciled to my fate of having to sit around here for two months. A thousand thanks.

On June 19, I finally had the audience with the Holy Father for which I had waited so long. I was supposed to be at the palace at 10:30 am and was there at

---

[19] Ferdinand von Verger, Bavarian ambassador to the Holy See.
[20] Cardinal Giacomo Antonelli (1806-1876), papal secretary of state.
[21] Demetrius di Marogna, O.S.B.

10:00 am in a borrowed *cuculla* and a personal servant behind me. There were only four others in line for audiences. Archbishop Cullen of Dublin was with the pope for an hour, then Cardinal Tosti for another hour, and then I was called. I had prepared myself with great care for what I wanted to say. The Holy Father was sitting in a small room in front of a desk. He was busy writing when Count Talbot introduced me. His Holiness wore a common white habit like a lay brother. I could hardly find a place to genuflect three times. I tried to kiss his foot, but he reached out his hand for the kiss. After that, he gave me a sign to take a place opposite him, which I did, though I continued standing. The pope called me "abbate" and asked me what language I preferred to speak, Italian or Latin. I chose Latin because I am more acquainted with it, but he continued questioning me in Italian, so I answered in Italian as best I could. He was in very good humor and very kind in his treatment of me, like a father. He even spoke about our beer affair and said that the retail trade would not be for the best. I answered, referring to what is allowed in Germany, and said that I was not so much concerned about the fact but rather the principle and was now satisfied since Rome had sent instructions and I now know where I stand. I said we stopped [brewing] at once and since then are drinking fresh water. Whether we can keep it up is another question. At that, he laughed heartily saying, "Yes, yes, St. Paul wrote to Timothy to use mixed wine for his weak stomach. Water alone would never do on a permanent basis." Then the talk turned to the number of members of our community. He was pleased to hear about the large number of novices and seminarians and said that much good could be done with them. After some other questions, he let me know that he now knew what he wanted to know. He dismissed me graciously. Naturally, as a result I did not say much of what I had in mind and heart, but seeing that he was very busy, even writing from time to time during our conversation, I did not have the courage to disturb him any further. I asked for the apostolic blessing and then left. After me, an older priest from Naples went in. Naturally, I was not exactly satisfied with the audience because I did not have the opportunity to say what I had prepared to say. Nevertheless, I was glad to see the Holy Father in good humor and to leave him in the same spirit. Two days later, I heard from Count Hohenlohe[22] that he was pleased with my conduct and my report.

I hoped to have the honor of speaking to him again at St. Paul's,[23] but in vain. He arrived at 10:00 am along with the duke of Brabant and his wife and the king of Portugal and his brother with their magnificent entourage. After the High Mass

---

[22] Gustaph Adolph Hohenlohe, Vatican official and advisor to Pope Pius IX.
[23] The abbey of St. Paul's Outside the Walls, which the pope visited on the feast of St. Paul (June 30).

by Monsignor Bedini,[24] the poor Benedictines had to stay in the background as His Holiness led the duchess and noble ladies around the church, showing them some of the salient points of architecture, while Cardinal Antonelli[25] entertained the noble gentlemen. After that, they went to breakfast. The only guest at the table with them was the abbot. We had the privilege of looking at them. A visit to the relics chamber followed lunch and then they left. We did not have an opportunity to kiss his foot. The Holy Father was in good humor and a jovial mood.

On the feast of St. Peter [June 29], I attended the High Mass and saw the illumination but not the *girandola*. Vespers at both St. Peter's and St. Paul's lasted two hours. Except for the splendid music, it was somewhat tiresome.

With regard to my own business, I know as a certainty only that it will not come up for discussion this month. Last month, there were two sessions, one on June 18 and the other on June 28. In the last, the Irish affair was settled. Archbishop Cullen had already left before it took place. Then I was to have my *referendum*, but only for me. They did not have a general session, so I have to wait until two others are finished. They promised to distribute my papers this Saturday, but I do not believe it. It will not be the first time that a promise has not been kept. It seems that another session will not be held before the end of the month. Then after ten days, I shall be notified of the outcome. It seems I will not be able to leave Rome before the end of August.

Concerning the main point–the abbey–Monsignor Barnabo[26] at least is of the opinion that it is certain. With that, I must be satisfied for the time being. He has permitted me to write him privately to find out what he thinks in particular matters. Bishop O'Connor of Pittsburgh has written several times. For the most part, he has withdrawn his demands, which is naturally very much in my favor. Now I have less reason to fear danger from that side.

In general, I am in good health. The hot season began a few days ago, but it is no hotter than at St. Vincent. Nonetheless, the strange meals, the miserable wine, the lukewarm water, the fruit on the table seldom fully ripe–none of this contributes to good health. More than once, I had to take refuge in my homeopathic drugs. With regard to meals here, Casaretto[27] did not have to introduce a reform since they were always taken in common. To my great surprise, we had strict fast

---

[24] Archbishop Gaetano Bedini, who had visited St. Vincent in December 1853.

[25] Giacomo Antonelli, papal secretary of state.

[26] Alessandro Barnabo, secretary of the Sacred Congregation for the Propagation of the Faith.

[27] Abbot Pietro Casaretto, O.S.B., monastic reformer who became president of the Italian Cassinese Congregation in 1852 and abbot general of the new Cassinese Congregation of the Primitive Observance in 1872.

and abstinence for three days before the vigil of Peter and Paul. By the way, I cannot reconcile myself to Italian devotions and do not have much confidence in their piety. It is far from deep-rooted.

Tomorrow I go to Subiaco to venerate the relics and saints. I have heard so much about the place that I cannot hold back my curiosity any longer. Casaretti is at present in Piemonte. I would like to go to Monte Cassino also but cannot for fear of not having enough money, since they may charge me here too much for room and board. Cardinal Morichini[28] has invited me for a visit. I might accept if I travel via Ancona. Your Excellency's most grateful, P. Boniface Wimmer

Ger   oAAM   cASVA   transRG

TO DEMETRIUS DI MAROGNA   44

Rome, July 29, 1855

Dearest Confrere: Our case was presented to the cardinals on July 23 and voted on unanimously. This evening at 10:30, the result will be given to the Holy Father and tomorrow early, at about 7:30 am, I will be informed definitively. The following cardinals were our judges: Fransoni, Mattei, Patrizi, Ferretti, Marini, Barbarini, Brunetti, and Roberti. Macehi, Amat, Altieris were sick or absent. I went around with the procurator general, Abbot Pescetelli, in order to pay my respects to all individually and to give them the necessary information that circumstances might require. Marini, a special friend of our bishop,[29] was our reviewer (*ponente*). Ferretti, the pope's nephew, who is the principal *poenitentiarius*, and for that reason seldom attends sessions in Propaganda, refused to accept the position since he thought he would not be able to attend the meeting. Altieris, who stoutly defended me in the beer controversy, having understood these things better from the time he was nuncio in Vienna, was out of town. So neither Ferretti nor Altieris was available to be *ponente*.

Six questions were considered according to the six proposals made by the procurator general. Of these, I believe the last one was modified beforehand. The interpretations of these, when printed, made a large document. Mine alone, which I will be happy to share with you upon my return, is from page 47 to 110 in *quarto* print. We had much to discuss with the cardinals, much to defend, many arguments to make in opposition to theirs, etc. This was especially necessary with

---

[28] Carlo Luigi Morichini, former papal nuncio to Bavaria.
[29] Michael O'Connor of Pittsburgh.

regard to our reviewer, who wanted to find enmity toward our bishop in my explanations. In the meantime, they were all in good humor, especially Ferretti, who couldn't find enough words to praise us. He at once gave his full consent to all six points. Still, he urgently advised for the sake of peace that we make a sacrifice and take two of the bishop's students *gratis* each year. I agreed to do so if all else would be granted us.

It seems that the whole matter went according to Ferretti's suggestion. After the meeting, Barnabo told me that all were unanimous. On the day before yesterday, I heard from very good sources that all six proposals were granted with the stipulation that we keep two of the bishop's students *gratis*. Tomorrow I will hear the details. My arrangements are now such that I can leave here in a week (August 8) and on August 14 will arrive in Munich. If for any reason my return home is either necessary or desired, I will comply and come at once. If not, I will try to collect a little money, which may take two or three months. So please write how everything is at home.

I was very sorry to hear of the death of our dear confrere Ildephonse![30] On July 23, I immediately began to say the nine Masses for him. Since May 18, I have celebrated 55 Masses. Please cross these out in the ledger. Before May 17, I celebrated 77, as I have already written. Very likely, you have already noted these. You will be troubled because of the vacancy in Carrolltown, especially because Father Celestine[31] is sick. Perhaps it will be best to send Father Celestine back and call Father Augustine[32] in as pastor so that he can preach in English at home on the two Sundays when there is an English sermon. On the other two Sundays, he can go to Greensburg. It is not necessary that a resident priest be there, especially if the railroads do not advance any more. Then we should tell the bishop that it is time he took the English preaching away from us. In the meantime, Father Odilo[33] could take care of the farther mission as before, but if you have already arranged otherwise, then let's leave it that way. Tomorrow I will write to Carrolltown and St. Marys too with regard to money, etc.

You say you would like to have some priests ordained. I have nothing against it provided there is someone who has passed his examinations satisfactorily. Otherwise not. I would prefer to give up Butler in order to have the priests there at our disposal, for the bishop is complaining everywhere that our priests, with the

---

[30] Ildephonse Böld, O.S.B., prior in Carrolltown, Pa., had died on June 14, 1855, when he was thrown from a horse and suffered a broken neck.

[31] Celestine Englbrecht, O.S.B.

[32] Augustine Wirth, O.S.B.

[33] Odilo Vandergrün, O.S.B.

exception of three or four, have very limited knowledge. I do not like to see that. I am afraid Father Valentine[34] likes to drink too much coffee, which is poison for one in his condition. Greet him sincerely for me and express my deep sorrow to him about his failing health. I hope the milk cure will restore him. In addition, tell the young men to ride slowly so they don't break their necks one after another. Not always hop! hop!

It is very warm here now, and the cholera is all around (but not in Rome). I am well and can't complain about anything except that I am always thirsty because there is no fresh water and the bad, watery wine is so tepid. On a recent Sunday I visited the seven churches, which is a 20-mile trip. I perspired much and swallowed a lot of dust but suffered no harm otherwise. I was on foot from 1:30 pm until 8:00 pm. If all goes well, I want to do this again after having made my last courtesy calls on the cardinals and the pope. In the meantime, I am copying all kinds of things that can be of use or interest to us. I will buy some things for presents and souvenirs if there is money left. I hope to have in my possession these sacred things and the decree about the abbey by next Saturday and to bring them along. The cardinals voted for our cause unanimously, and the Holy Father will surely not disapprove.

You can well imagine how happy I am that I am free once more and can travel homeward again. It is true, I became accustomed to everything and was less lonesome, but I have counted the days with great longing. Let us be glad that God arranged everything. We now have a very good reputation among everyone here. I succeeded in destroying prejudices and erasing the blemishes attributed to us without in the least stepping on anyone's toes. Even if we do not achieve everything we want, it will not matter. Our cause is regarded as a just and worthy one. However, in order not to sadden the bishop, they might object to one or the other point, as, for example, the congregation, exemption, etc. However, we will definitely receive them eventually if not now.

Let us be sure that nothing is said about the bishop, that he is in no way angered or given a reason to complain. We have won many good and powerful patrons even among the cardinals of the Propaganda Fide. Even old Fransoni[35] said to me, "Now the case is ripe for the abbey." In the circle directly around the pope all admire the fact that we have so many brothers. The brothers will be no less proud that the Holy Father and the cardinals read their names and duties individually. I hope all prayed diligently. I do believe that the happy outcome of our cause is

---

[34] Valentine Felder, O.S.B.

[35] Cardinal Giacomo Filippe Fransoni, prefect of the Sacred Congregation for the Propagation of the Faith.

the result of the pious prayers all of you together sent to heaven. Let us continue to pray that the bishop will also understand that he has nothing to fear from us. Avoid all exterior show that could be interpreted as a whoop of victory. Perhaps the bishop was, and is, a cross that God permitted to test us for our own good. God always leads to victory through reverses. Bishop Wittmann[36] often said that the first to hinder St. Benedict and banish him was a bishop. Therefore, we should not be surprised that misunderstandings, troubles, and sorrow play a role in our monastery.

Let the filling of positions be temporary until I come home, and if Celestine goes to Carrolltown, he should not neglect the account book but should turn in all monies and calculate well. Father Henry[37] could, if Celestine cannot, take over money matters for the time being, if he wants to handle them according to my instruction.

July 30, at 2:00 pm.

St. Vincent is an abbey! Father Boniface is abbot. We will educate the bishop's students charging only board, which will cover our costs. The bishop can visit and supervise his own students as apostolic delegate, but not ours. All according to the statutes of the Bavarian Congregation! This is the report from the Holy Father. May God reward and bless him for it. Sincerest regards to all. Most devotedly, Boniface

Ger   oASJA   cASVA   transMN

TO KING LUDWIG I   45

Munich, August 19, 1855

Most Gracious King and Lord: In the life of a great and good king, such as you are, Your Majesty, there are surely few days which are not distinguished by some act of special importance and far-reaching influence, whether it is in the realm of politics or religion, whether it concerns art or science, whether it is in the hidden and unnoticed realm of human kindness and unknown benefaction. Many such days in the life of Your Royal Majesty are already entered into the memoirs of history. Others will, and can, be entered only when the great results that must derive from the noble and wonderful efforts of Your Majesty become known. Some things that are now misunderstood will then be understood. Things that are

---

[36] George Michael Wittmann, deceased bishop of Regensburg.
[37] Peter Henry Lemke, O.S.B.

now judged with prejudice will then be entirely approved. Things that are now left unnoticed or overlooked will then be brought to light. That which before was not respected because it did not show outwardly, even though it was good and noble in itself, will then be seen in its true value and will be deservedly praised.

Undoubtedly, a matter that will give Your Majesty all the more honor since it was not expected belongs to this category–namely, that during your most recent visit to Rome, Your Most Sovereign Majesty personally decided to risk your name and reputation for the Bavarian Benedictines in America in order to protect them against the unjust attacks of an Irish bishop[38] and to help them achieve their just rights. This royal action, even if only those directly concerned knew it, will always be one of the most beautiful and beneficial acts recorded in the memoirs of a king. At the same time, however, it is an act that can scarcely remain unnoticed because of its effects. Through it, the definitive introduction and establishment of the Benedictine Order in America was brought about. This will be of the greatest religious, intellectual, and artistic consequence for that land, and for the German population in the United States, especially, it will be a national mainstay.

There is not the least doubt that Your Majesty deserves all possible praise for having achieved this goal through your personal intervention. The bishop knew so well how to close the net in which he wanted to catch us, that it would have been impossible for me to tear it entirely. Now, however, the tide has turned: the atmosphere, previously so unfavorable, has changed into a favorable one for me. Even his own best friends among the College of Cardinals in Rome recognized the bishop's injustice and encroachments as such, and considered as necessary and acceptable measures against them. All his demands were refused. The Order was granted the freedom to develop, and the monastery is entirely safe, as far as ecclesiastical affairs are concerned. At the meeting of the Congregation for the Propagation of the Faith on July 23, the cardinals assembled there at the request of the secretary, Monsignor Barnabo,[39] unanimously decided the following:

(1) That St. Vincent will be an abbey;
(2) That it is withdrawn from the bishop's jurisdiction (in other words, it is exempt!) and placed directly under papal jurisdiction;
(3) That the abbey, along with its daughter monasteries, will form an American Congregation with the statutes of the former Bavarian Benedictine Congregation;

---

[38] Michael O'Connor of Pittsburgh.
[39] Alessandro Barnabo, secretary of the Sacred Congregation for the Propagation of the Faith.

(4) That this American-Bavarian Benedictine Congregation will be affiliated with the Benedictine Abbey of Monte Cassino, so that it will have a representative in Rome in the person of the procurator general of the Cassinese;[40]

(5) That the monastic school will be open to the bishop for his students provided that they pay their expenses. Only in connection with his own students can the bishop act as apostolic delegate, making criticisms about conduct and progress. In the matter of caring for souls, the Benedictines are subject to the bishop according to the common law and customs that exist in America;

(6) That the introduction of our many lay brothers is approved.

On July 30, the Holy Father approved these decisions of the cardinals and all they include. At the suggestion of Monsignor Barnabo and the cardinals, he made me first abbot with pontifical rights on August 5. That is more than I expected, even more than I dared ask for. It is true; I requested that plans for the formation of a future congregation be initiated at once so that the youthful strength of the Order would not be dispersed, but I did not dare hope for the favor, though I had desired it. The cardinals, however, made the decision on their own. They wanted to give Your Majesty joy, and they wanted to protect the Benedictine Order against the attacks of the bishop.

Thus, through an act of marvelous condescension, Your Majesty gave great advantage to religion and to the German situation across the ocean. Because of this, Your Majesty became, indeed, the founder of the first American Benedictine abbey, of the first all-German independent educational institution in America! Not only the chroniclers of the abbey and of the monasteries branching from it, but also the ecclesiastical and educational histories of the United States of America will one day gratefully recognize the great service of this beautiful royal action.

May Your Majesty, please, permit me to be the first to express my sincerest joy at this action. As a Bavarian and a Benedictine, I have always loved Your Majesty with such childlike affection that whatever redounds to Your Majesty's honor and glory always made me sincerely happy. As much as the joyful result of Your Majesty's intervention for the success of our cause makes me happy, I am equally happy that at the same time it contributes greatly to the honor and glory of Your Majesty. Therefore, I most humbly beg leave to express my sincerest, warmest gratitude for it. Aside from my own self, the least important person, my venerable old Order has received an immeasurable benefaction from you by what you have done for it. A completely new part of the world has been opened to it as a setting for its activity, one to which hundreds and thousands who could otherwise not

---

[40] Abbot Angelo Pescetelli, O.S.B., was the procurator general of the Italian Cassinese Congregation.

receive a solid religious and scientific education are now directed. The Order can accomplish immeasurable good there, and you can be assured that this house will make real contributions to history.

For me it is a pleasant coincidence that I can express my sincere joy and heartfelt thanks for your efforts, crowned by beautiful success, just now, directly before your namesday,[41] because, undoubtedly, it is a special joy for Your Majesty to appreciate the results of your efforts. It also gives me an opportunity to humbly add my sincerest good wishes for this beautiful day, which is a happy feast for every Bavarian.

May Almighty God, who has raised up Your Majesty so wonderfully on this earth, who has given you so many noble gifts of mind and body, and who has guided you so wisely through His Holy Spirit so that you are and continue to be the pride and joy of a good people and the comfort of His holy Church, grant you many happy returns of the day. May you continue to accomplish many more great, noble, and good things according to your desires. May you, by honoring God, one day as surely receive the heavenly crown of eternal glory, as you are worthy of wearing your earthly crown. The many thousands of blessed Benedictines in heaven will certainly mightily support the pious wishes and prayers that the living Benedictines daily offer for the temporal and eternal welfare of their greatest benefactor, the restorer and protector of their Order in both hemispheres.

I had returned home from Rome only a few days ago when I learned firsthand the outcome of our cause without, however, receiving the papal brief concerning it. It was a personal concern of mine to inform Your Majesty of it at once. Now I am going to the places necessary in order to be ready to sail from Bremen with several brothers and students and five Benedictine nuns from St. Walburga's on October 5 and after a long absence to see my confreres who, I suppose, already have news of the happy resolution of our important question.

In the name of all my confreres, I again humbly repeat my sincerest good wishes and heartfelt thanks, and I close with faithful love and grateful submission to Your Royal Majesty. Your most submissive and obedient, Boniface Wimmer, Abbot of St. Vincent

Ger   oRAB   cASVA   transMN   Math(71-75)

---

[41] The feast of St. Louis was August 25.

TO DEMETRIUS DI MAROGNA   **46**

Munich, August 22, 1855

Dearest Confrere: Very likely, you did not receive one of my letters, but I hope you have received at least two from me. Your last one of July is here before me. On August 6, I left Rome and came here via Genoa and Einsiedeln on the evening of August 14 at 11:00 pm.

I must add something to my last report to you. It is true I have nothing written in my hands yet, but it will very likely be as Barnabo[42] told me. Thus, the monastery is an abbey and is exempt. We will form an American Congregation under the statutes of the Bavarian Benedictine Congregation. The abbot will be canonically elected for life and approved by the pope. We are affiliated with the Cassinese Congregation so as to have a representative in Rome. Our institute of lay brothers is approved. With regard to the seminary, we must accept the bishop's[43] students, but he has to pay their expenses. He can visit his own students as apostolic delegate, but only his own. He has no jurisdiction otherwise. With regard to the care of souls, we are, of course, subject to him under the law existing in America for diocesan and religious order priests. It is the best that could be done.

I am abbot but only for three years. After three years, we will have our first election and whoever is elected will be abbot in perpetuity or until death. As I wrote you the last time, Barnabo told me in the presence of Abbot Theoduli[44] I would be abbot for life. He thought this himself, as did the cardinals. When I saw him to thank him, Cardinal Mattei asked me whether I would pontificate for the first time at St. Paul's or in Munich. On the feast of St. Dominic [August 4], when I said Mass with the Dominicans, Cardinal Ferretti introduced me to all present as the first abbot in America. The others did likewise. However, after two days I found I was not abbot as I had already written you and Father Müller.[45] I was teased and ridiculed about it quite a bit. Barnabo himself was greatly embarrassed, and I was more than a little embarrassed too because of what he, having just come from the pope, said. The pope had already approved the decisions of the cardinals when he told me. I would have been ridiculed in Munich and America too had I not really been abbot.

---

[42] Alessandro Barnabo, secretary of the Sacred Congregation for the Propagation of the Faith.
[43] Michael O'Connor of Pittsburgh.
[44] Retired abbot of the abbey of St. Paul's Outside the Walls.
[45] Joseph Ferdinand Müller, chaplain to the court of King Ludwig I and general manager of the *Ludwig Missionsverein*.

However, the situation was this. The procurator general[46] had already given his report on our petition in six points before I arrived in Rome, as I wrote in my first letter. He did this before he knew that the bishop had not suggested me as abbot. According to the proposals he made, the bishop suggested someone else who, according to the description given, could have been no one but Father Benedict.[47] He was the bishop's candidate. I had suggested you. The procurator completed the trio and suggested me while defending me as well as possible against the reports of the bishop. However, he went no further except that he tried to secure me against opposition from outside forces, making a definite proposal that I be abbot. My advisor Monsignor Vespasiani in general held to the six points and made his suggestions according to them with one exception: he considered the suggestions I had made regarding the seminary, the statutes, and the length of time for the abbot to hold office. You see, he wanted abbots to hold office for three years only. However, I saw enough of these Italian abbots and insisted that the abbot be abbot for life, according to the statutes of the Bavarian Congregation; but I did not expect that I would be first abbot. Since the advisor and procurator held to our petition in which we asked not for an abbot but for the election of an abbot, nothing else was suggested. All the cardinals voted for an abbot in perpetuity and for me as first abbot, without seeing to it that this notion was added to the suggestions, the *dubiis* as they call it. Thus, these were brought to the pope as they were, and they were approved by him. Accordingly, the abbot should have been elected at once.

When the mistake was discovered, nothing was left to do but to leave things as they were or to bring them to the pope once more. Barnabo and the procurator would have preferred the latter and I the former, although I was angry at first because I thought I had been fooled, until Barnabo convinced me otherwise. I had already arranged for a farewell visit with the pope and the day was already set. In any event, the procurator and my advisor were backing down, and the latter was very fearful I would speak up at the audience. However, I did not. I was received very kindly by the Holy Father. I thanked him in the name of our monastery and presented a young German who would come with me to America (Andrew Michel). He dismissed us both most kindly with his blessing, again extending his hand to me to kiss. Barnabo presented the business to the pope two days later, telling him of the mistake and suggesting that according to the suggestions of the cardinals the pope make me abbot for life.

---

[46] Abbot Angelo Pescetelli, O.S.B.

[47] Benedict Haindl, O.S.B. (1815-1887), prior in St. Marys and one of the pioneer Benedictine clerical students to come with Wimmer to St. Vincent in 1846.

However, the pope did not do that. "It won't do," he said. "A week ago I decreed the abbot should be elected freely, and today I should decree Father Boniface as abbot! I cannot contradict myself. All I can do is this: let the election be postponed for three years and let Father Boniface be abbot in the interim so that the monastery is not without a head. If he is then elected, let it be in perpetuity." Therefore, I have the privilege of being the first, last, and only American triennial abbot. Another unusual thing is I am abbot *infulatus* but *sine benedictione*[48] like the Cassinese and French.

This happened on the evening of the feast of the Blessed Virgin Mary *ad Nives* [August 5] at 11:30. On the feast of the Transfiguration [August 6], I learned of it and left Rome on the same day. My Italian abbots were very happy, yet they were sorry to see that I asked for and succeeded in obtaining an abbot for life, while they have ruling abbots for only six years. I was satisfied with the results because the Holy Father wished to give the monastery free choice, and the bishop cannot say the pope made me abbot when he himself failed gloriously in preventing it and in gaining approval for all his stipulations and demands. Besides, it would have taken seven months to elect an abbot, to review the election, to approve the one elected, and to send approval back to America. In the beginning, they really intended to publish only a simple decree about these decisions, as I wrote you. However, Barnabo later thought it best to publish a brief, which we will not receive for six weeks and which I will wait for here. A triennial abbot *per se* is one thing of which I cannot approve, although the French have them. For example, Abbé Guéranger,[49] after he was elected three times, became abbot in perpetuity. All the cardinals were of my opinion and thought it wiser to go back to the old *Rule*.

As for the creating of an abbot, I was altogether passive, entirely out of the picture. I would have accepted the honor had I received it because I soon saw that things would have taken much longer otherwise. I feared war might break out and that in this way the election could not be approved for a long time. Likewise, I knew from many capitulars that they would elect me anyway. Finally, all my friends advised me to end the affair once and for all. I myself did not want to ask for it for obvious reasons. Perhaps it was a mistake that I did not merely stop with our petition and refuse to accept the abbacy, but the above reasons were against it. I could not and would not gainsay the pope, and so things are as they are. I hope

---

[48] That is, Wimmer has the right to wear the abbatial regalia (the *infula*) but will not receive a formal liturgical blessing.
[49] Abbot Prosper Guéranger, O.S.B. (1805-1875), Benedictine reformer and restorer of the abbey of Solesmes.

all is according to God's will and the best interests of the monastery. The fact that we received this decision astonished everyone in Rome, Einsiedeln, and here. It also surprised the archbishop[50] and nuncio with whom I dined today. Yesterday I wrote King Ludwig for his namesday and mentioned it. Bishop O'Connor will hear of it through Barnabo. The latter and Cardinal Ferretti were especially kind.

I enclose $400. Send $200 of it to St. Marys. I hope to receive enough to pay bills here and to bring some along.

You will understand, I know, that I want to hurry home, but I fear I cannot return before November. I would like to put the Moosmüller case and other money matters in order before I come. Politically, things sound bad. It is better when all is secure. Naturally, too, I would like to bring the papal brief along so that I can show it to all, black on white. Father Luke[51] will receive everything he ordered. Many books, vestments, pictures, and several thousand cards are coming for the brothers and students, and, if possible, money. In short, I still have much to do, to buy, to count, to pack, to beg, to send, before I come home. I hope everything will be all right.

Pitzer asked whether O'Connor has received the paintings he asked for and asks that the others he sent be sold and the money sent to him. And now, a thousand greetings. I hope all will be satisfied with what we accomplished and with my efforts. I did what I could in the best of faith. I asked the help of all who could help me. I explained, protested, and insisted in German, Italian, and Latin as well as I could, orally and in writing. Do not be concerned about me. I am still well and now am eating well again, but pray for me that I continue well in body and soul. Work together in holy love, cheerful obedience, trust, and peace. Rome has honored us wonderfully. Do not let them shame us by saying to those who belittled us that we do not deserve it. Let us show that we are neither ignorant nor base nor dangerous people who threaten the Church. Do not let the complaint be made about me that I exaggerated or lied when I praised the priests, clerics, and brothers on account of their good behavior, zeal for souls, diligence, peacefulness, reverence for their superiors, etc.; and you, Father Prior, please do what remains to be done in my name according to the *Holy Rule* as you see fit, and be assured of my sincere thanks in advance. Read this letter to the capitulars at a chapter meeting. To the brothers read only what you think best and emphasize well, as I have said before, that there are to be no cries of triumph over the bishop. Peace be with you all, especially with the bishop. With sincere love, your devoted, Boniface

---

[50] Karl von Reisach, archbishop of Munich-Freising.
[51] Luke Wimmer, O.S.B., Abbot Boniface's nephew and professor of art at St. Vincent.

P.S. I have received power from Rome to receive the formal emigration for all the brothers who will inherit money. That is, Bernard and Michael, if they do not already have it. Do not forget. If it does not arrive soon, it must have been sent to the court chaplain.[52] Brother Remigius should make a crosier, a very simple one, because it is prescribed by Alexander VII that the pontifical gear of abbots should be simpler than that of a bishop. The capitulars should not forget their obligation to secrecy outside the chapter.

Ger   oASJA   cASVA   transMN

TO GREGORY SCHERR   47

On the Ocean, November 21, 1855

Father Abbot: I am sorry I had no time to write you from Munich, but I do not want to wait until I get back to St. Vincent, and for that reason I am sending this letter off from the Banks of Newfoundland. First, my warmest thanks for all the love and excellent treatment I experienced in abundance at Metten and at every place where the flag of Metten is hoisted. I traveled without difficulty from Munich to Regensburg where I remained three days in order to see His Excellency the bishop,[53] who was on visitation. I did not get to Weltenburg because the district judge, Mr. Sartory von Abersberg, a fellow-student, held me back for a whole day at Meyringer's. I was at Scheyern for two days where I found the most congenial hospitality. I spent practically the whole day conversing with the abbot[54] more or less exclusively and did not fail, upon your request, to urge him to vote for the congregation. During our conversation, I became aware of his dislike for the idea of a congregation, a dislike that springs from that ill-famed decree of 1834 by which St. Stephen's was made the head of all the Bavarian Benedictine monasteries and given charge of the discipline of the congregation. I showed him that this decree–still on the books since it has never been revoked–could be used by a hostile government against the Order but that its value would be certainly lessened if the monasteries were to unite themselves in a congregation and by doing so place themselves under the Holy See. This is the truth. I believe I was able to convince him so that he will not cause any more difficulties. Likewise, I convinced Abbot

---

[52] Joseph Ferdinand Müller.
[53] Valentine von Riedel, bishop of Regensburg.
[54] Rupert Leiss, O.S.B., abbot of Scheyern, who, like Gregory Scherr, had been a novitiate classmate of Wimmer's.

Haneberg[55] to join, but he will do so only if he does not have to make heavy expenditures for sending his ten novices elsewhere. Such a condition is not advisable, and I consider it unnecessary because King Ludwig will surely contribute 1,000 florins for keeping ten novices a year in a common novitiate at Weltenburg. A common gymnasium in Munich has to be another principal point. I needed much time to get his consent. You will have to try your best.

My stay in Munich was not too pleasant because I had diarrhea and there are so many philologists among the reverend confreres that an American philistine had no chance in the evening to enjoy a real conversation with them. Besides, in the evening there were always strangers who inhibited me from having a good time. I received the apostolic brief before I left. I showed it to his grace the archbishop, Seinsheim, the dean, and the vicar general and was congratulated from every side. The *Missionsverein* made a copy of it, and likewise I made a copy for you through the kindness of Father John.

I believe you were afraid that I would leave behind a considerable sum on your account for you to pay, but I did not make much use of my "honorary member's" right. Two very beautiful miters were furnished *gratis* by Beuerberg; gloves, shoes, stockings by the court chaplain;[56] I bought a *tunicella* and *mozzeta* and crosses, so I have enough. The crosier will be made by Brother Remigius, and then the abbot will be ready. I forgot my buckled shoes at Metten so I had new ones made without latches. I left my hat, pants, and overcoat in Munich, because they were worn out from traveling, and ordered new ones at Angner for which you will receive a small bill of 80 florins on your account. I could not pay this myself because my books were closed and all my cash had been exchanged for drafts. Surely, you will be kind enough to take care of this small matter. "The poor you will always have with you, but me you will not always have." Likewise, I am asking you to pay the 20 florins interest every year in order to fulfill the wish of the lady benefactor about whom we spoke.

I left Munich on October 26, Eichstätt on October 27, and on October 29 arrived in Bremen with five Benedictine sisters, two Ursulines, one brother, and a young boy who had been put in my charge at Waldkirchen. From there I went by steamer to Bremerhaven on November 1, and on November 2, we were at sea. Already on the first day, we encountered a terrible storm that made all my people sick. After 24 hours, the weather calmed, and on November 4 at noon, we entered Southampton. We remained there three days. On November 7 at 3:00 pm, we left and are now, after 14 days, still a thousand miles from New York. The weather

---

[55] Boniface Haneberg, O.S.B., abbot of St. Boniface Abbey, Munich.
[56] Joseph Ferdinand Müller.

has been agreeable on only two afternoons. Otherwise, the storm has roared day and night continuously and furiously. The winds have been against us so that we cannot make any progress. On November 13, it was very bad, but the worst was on November 16, 17, and 18 when during the day we could not go forward. The decks were covered with waves so that we lived in the greatest danger of everything breaking into pieces. The waves were 50 or 60 feet high. The roar of the wind was ghastly. The ship cracked and squeaked as if it would at any moment shatter to bits. Sleeping was out of the question. You could not stay in one place, walk, or sit down. In a word, these were terrible days with rain, hail, and bitter cold. Fortunately, I had bought in Southampton two large woolen capes and with these and my overcoat, the sisters covered themselves and went up to the deck. Otherwise, they would have frozen half to death. The seawater poured over us and made us look like millers because when it dried, it formed a salty white shell, like an egg.

This sea voyage is the most terrifying I have ever experienced, and it is only through luck that we have narrowly escaped death. On board are a Jesuit provincial and two Irish priests. Today we were to have reached New York. There is another storm in the west, and if things remain like this, we will not arrive for eight or ten days. This *memento mori* impresses us most vividly. God's will be done. Still, I am confident that I will see my people once more, but I am ready to sacrifice the joy of seeing them again and to offer everything I wish for, strive for, and hope to achieve with my poor strength [to the Lord]. At best, we shall arrive in New York this Tuesday (November 27). I will have to stay there for three days, so I will not reach St. Vincent before December. If you receive this letter, I shall be safe. I beg and pray that you keep me in your good and prayerful memory. With a thousand greetings to all the confreres, and the most sincere affection and respect for Your Grace, I am most gratefully, Abbot Boniface

Ger   oAMA   cASVA   transRG

TO GIACOMO FRANSONI   48

St. Vincent, December 18, 1855

Your Eminence: Your kind letter, the apostolic brief that raised St. Vincent to an abbey, and the papal decree appointing me abbot of this monastery for three years reached me while I was still in Europe. Indeed, these documents gladdened our hearts by reminding us of the great benefits we have received from the Holy Father and the kindness that Your Eminence shows for us. They gave us new courage to make progress in religious life and to extend our missionary work.

Certainly we would not be worthy of these favors and benefits if we were not eager to show by word and deed our gratitude to the Holy Father and to the Sacred Congregation. As far as I am concerned, I shall do the best I can to exercise the power with kindness and show humility in sacred functions in order to render the title and authority of abbot injurious to no one. On the contrary, I will strive as an abbot to bring benefits to the Order and the Church.

The Most Reverend Bishop O'Connor very kindly answered the letter in which I announced my arrival and promised to visit him as soon as possible. In his answer, far from being displeased with the decision of the Holy See, he expressed full satisfaction that everything had been arranged and defined so wisely and so exactly. In his opinion, however, there is a passage in the papal brief that is not clear. He fears that later doubts or controversies may arise over the phrase: "In the monastery of St. Vincent itself, a monastic seminary will be maintained into which secular clerical students should be admitted for whom only board is paid." The most reverend bishop believes that this sentence is too general because it does not specify that only students of the bishop [of Pittsburgh] are to benefit from the concession, and he asked me to submit this question to the Sacred Congregation.

As it was my intention that our seminary, under our direction and administration, should, as far as we are able, offer the bishop every means and opportunity to educate his clerical students in our monastery, and although everything seems clear to me, I humbly ask the Sacred Congregation to interpret this sentence so that no further doubt is possible. I would express it in these words: "A monastic seminary should be maintained in which also clerical students for the priesthood whom the bishop wishes to send be admitted."

The number of students need not be mentioned because we will receive as many as he wishes to send, always with the condition that we do not demand anything else for their education and board beyond our expenses. As the most reverend bishop wishes to add a few words to this inquiry, there is no reason for me to say more.

Your Eminence, allow me to express once more my heartfelt gratitude for the favors that you granted us so graciously, for which not only I but also our whole community will always be grateful. With the most humble submission to the Holy Father, to the Sacred Congregation, and to Your Eminence, I am, with the most profound reverence, your most humble servant, Boniface Wimmer, Abbot of St. Vincent

Lat   oAPF   cASVA   transFF

TO CHRYSOSTOM FOFFA[57]   **49**

St. Vincent, January 2, 1856

Reverend and Dearly Beloved Confrere! Krälin arrived here with your letter. His case was a real problem and left me in a quandary, partly because there was no room for him in the seminary and partly because he came in the middle of the school year. He will simply have to fulfill the condition for admission set by Father Prior,[58] which is, that he continue in the lay state until he is ready to be enrolled in a class, that is, at the beginning of the school year.

As for my abbatial dignity, there is little to add. Since we petitioned for an abbey and the election of an abbot, I could not very well do anything that would help bring about my personal elevation. Neither did I want to.[59] Hence, I was made abbot for only three years in order that the monastery would not be without a head during the long time required for the election and confirmation of an abbot. Whoever is elected after three years will be abbot for life and will be confirmed as such by the pope. We are forming a congregation modeled on the statutes of the former Benedictine Bavarian Congregation and affiliated with the Cassinese Congregation, which therefore classifies us as exempt religious. This arrangement with many lay brothers is a great asset. The seminary problem has been adjusted in accord with law and justice so that the bishop[60] has nothing to complain about on that score. We have received a special papal brief concerning this matter. We can certainly congratulate ourselves on this decision, which occasioned much surprise both in Rome and in Munich. Bishop O'Connor is also satisfied with it. The

---

[57] The recipient of this letter, Chrysostom Foffa, O.S.B., was one of three priests at the Benedictine Priory of St. Meinrad in the diocese of Vincennes, Indiana. The priory had been founded in 1854 from the Swiss abbey of Einsedeln. St. Meinrad became the nucleus of the Swiss American Congregation. See Albert Kleber, O.S.B., *History of St. Meinrad Archabbey 1854-1954* (St. Meinrad, Ind.: Grail Publications, 1954).

[58] The prior of St. Vincent was Demetrius di Marogna, O.S.B.

[59] In December 1855, Wimmer had returned from an extended trip to Bavaria and Rome where he had successfully petitioned for the elevation of St. Vincent to the rank of abbey.

[60] Michael O'Connor (1810-1873), bishop of Pittsburgh (1843-1860).

bishop of Erie and Archbishop Purcell[61] have extended me their congratulations, all of which goes to show that the fear of our exemption giving offence was wholly unwarranted.

To my great sorrow, on my way home I learned in Einsiedeln of the illness of the prior, Father Athanasius.[62] I am glad to hear now that he is on the road to recovery. The abbot of Einsiedeln appeared to be anxiously concerned about him. What you say in your letter, that I should send you a dozen serviceable men, if it is not said in jest, will certainly remain in the category of a pious wish. I have, it is true, many lay brothers, but the kind you are looking for are not plentiful with me either since we must build continuously. Moreover, at present our masons are very busy setting up the arched ceilings for the cellar of the new building that we are putting up this year. They are also roughcasting the rooms, and in the spring, it begins all over again since there is nothing else to be done. In spite of our steam sawmill, we are not able to saw enough lumber. I could perhaps spare one black-smith, but to get organized in such a line of work would cost a lot of money.

It is my opinion that after a while you will get plenty of brothers, once it be-comes known that you admit such people into your community. In the mean-time, however, the best thing to do is rent out the farm, mill, etc., and be satisfied with your income, although there will be no profit in it for you. It does not pay to have a lot of lay brothers if you have no seminary, since a farm alone, by itself, would hardly be a paying proposition. All that brothers are good for is to do away with the need for outside help. A brother, however, hardly earns his board. Only our millers and tanners bring in money. The craftsmen and wagon repairmen save only on wages and wagon expenses. Up until now, I have every reason to be glad if I can meet the cost of the food, for which I must often pay a considerable sum—in the last year, for example, several thousand dollars. You can make money only from the care of souls or from a seminary with paying students, but to maintain a seminary for non-paying students, such as most of my seminarians are, you need a good farm, for which, of course, brothers are necessary.

Nevertheless, if I can be of help to you in any way, I am ready to do your bid-ding. We, moreover, will probably send a small colony out West this year. Our numbers are growing so fast that we have to think of migrating. It will be the same with you after a few years—monastic foundations should never be hurried. I noticed this earlier in Bavaria and experienced it again here in this country. One should be careful not to lose patience. Though one sows in tears, he shall reap in

---

[61] Josue Mary Young (1808-1866), bishop of Erie; John Purcell (1800-1883), archbishop of Cincin-nati.
[62] Athanasius Tschopp, O.S.B., was prior of St. Meinrad Priory in Indiana.

joy. Only let the seed be sown and the plant will not fail to appear, even if it is slow to sprout and slow to ripen!

Kindly convey my most friendly greetings to the prior and the other reverend confreres. Be assured of the special esteem and trust I hold for your reverence. Most devotedly, P. Boniface Wimmer

Ger   oASMA   cASVA   transBB

TO MATHIAS LORAS   50

Latrobe, Westmoreland, Pa., February 8, 1856

Right Reverend Bishop, Dear Sir: I have received both of your letters dd. 10 & 15 of Jan. and thank you kindly and heartily for their content. I beg and hope you will have it in your power after a while to give me the desired information about the girl which gave occasion to my letter. I shall be very thankful to the Rev. gentleman, whom you charged with the trouble to take sight of her affairs.

With regard to our intended settlement, I have a notion to send F. Prior[63] to the West in the coming spring as an explorator. Whether we can do anything this year, or not, depends on circumstances. We must go into the West, and our Bishop does not like it at all; also there is plenty of chance in the East to make new establishments; but in the West there are more Germans and fewer priests. This is the cause driving us to the West.

Of course, we won't be obtrusive in [any] way and won't go where we are not needed or welcome. With regard to the recommendation of that respectable clergyman mentioned in your last favour, I have only to say that I do not know whether or how much trouble we have given to our Bishop. The Bishop himself could tell this the best. But if the Rev. Gentleman says: "by their distillation of beer, sending it to Pittsburg city for sale"–he says a thing that is not true; for we never have been distilling beer, and never have been sending it to Pittsburg for sale.

Nevertheless, there is something on this thing, and this is the following. A relative of mine was trusted, emigrating to this country with $800 belonging to me; but he kept the money for his own use, bought a small brewery in Indiana town, 30 miles from the Monastery of St. Vincent, broke up, and I had no way to recover my money without my buying the property. This I did, and the man who had attended to the brewing business before, took charge afterwards again,

---

[63] Demetrius di Marogna, O.S.B. (1803-1869).

first as a renter, and then for my own account, until I could get a chance to sell the property. Of course, it was a great trouble to me. Bishop O'Connor had no objection against my buying the house with the view to recover my money, but objected when I told him that the man who attended to the brewing did so on my account, he thinking I could not do it without sin, and I defending [that] I could because in Germany, Austria, Belgium, and indeed everywhere all Monasteries not only male but even female, and of all orders, Benedictines, Jesuits, Carthusians &c had and have yet Breweries and are selling beer. As to the fact, I was quite willing to stop at the earliest opportunity possible; but as to the right or principle, we could not agree. The Bishop himself wanted me then to bring the question before the Apostolic See: whether it would be lawful for Religious in this country to distill and sell beer or not? The answer was: They could distill it and sell it, but only in barrels, i.e., only in wholesale, but not in retail, if this would give occasion to a concourse of many men, and to excesses, sins &c.

It may seem a laughable affair to bring such a question before the Apostolic See, but for us it was truly important. We are now 10 years in this country; all of us have been used to drinking beer; here we have it not: it is too high in price to buy it for so many–(we were [at] that time 100 men; now we are 150, not accounting 100 scholars); but it is cheap if we would distill it ourselves; however if we dare not sell any, we can not afford either to brew it for our own use, it being yet too costly; and always being obliged to drink fresh water and nothing else is a thing which no religious orders, even not the Trappists, Carthusians, and Paulans, are obliged to do. Therefore all religious orders, except Capuchins and Franciscans, were allowed everywhere to sell the wine of their own vineyards, or the beer of their own distilleries, in order to have from the profit of the sale their own drink *gratis*, and not only in barrels, but (of course not in the monasteries and by their own friars) even in retail in taverns kept for that purpose.

Now long ago before the decision was communicated to me, I had stopped the business (which was never carried on by a lay brother, but only by laymen, and 30 miles distant from the Monastery, on a very small scale and in the same way as it had been usual in the house for 30 years, the license not being on my name); I had done so with a loss of more than 3000 $ since I could not sell the house anymore without the business, and the house is now the residence of a priest of our order who attends to the congregation in Indiana town and county.

When I was in Rome last summer even the holy Father plagued me a little in an audience I had with him, about the beer-affair. I replied, "Holy Father you have a good saying about your Benedictines brewing and selling beer; but you forget that we don't drink any these 9 years, and that we have no brewery." "Germans and not drinking beer," he replied; "that is much." "Yes, indeed," I said; "until now we could do so, being young; but when we grow older, we will probably be in the necessity to drink beer." "Of course," he said. "S. Paul also wrote to S. Timothy he should take a little wine for his weak stomach, and so you must have something"– and he laughed heartily.

This is the fact, Right Rev. Bishop, of which 6 years ago many a good joke was made by Temperance-men, who indeed brew no beer, but drink strong ales, spirits and wines, and preach temperance to the hard working classes. I may have been imprudent in getting my hands into that business, but I could hardly help, and from the notions I have of that business I could positively not foresee any difficulty or scandal, except from the temperance men; and with regard to these men, I only say, I divide them in 2 classes–in fools and in hypocrites; and I could easily defend this thesis. The Apostolic See has at different times and repeatedly declared against this temperance system, which is of no catholic character. *Mania a pater* [undecipherable] not known in countries where wine or beer is in use; [undecipherable] is the only [undecipherable] of whiskey and strong liquors in general. The Turks, Chinese &c have no beer, no wine, but drink the *opium*; our heretics forbid wine and beer, and get *poisonous liquors*.

But I came not to write an apologie for beer or wine; it was only to answer the report of that R. gentleman that I wrote this.

For the rest I would beg leave to say that we had not yet time to brew beer for our own use and less for sale; for we were these 9 years busily engaged to get up large buildings for ourselves and for our boys or scholars. But it might be the case that after a while I might get up a building for distilling beer for our own use and for those who would like to get any from us. Likewise we have recommended a vineyard which is much promising; if we succeed, we might after a few years be able to drink sometimes a little wine also, or to sell some. Also we built a fine steam grist and saw mill, where we do a great deal of grinding and sawing also for other people, and are selling planks. Likewise we have a tannery and are selling leather in large and small quantities.

Otherwise we have a regular gymnasium, a complete philosophical and theological course, an excellent music-orchestra, a painting and drawing school with a rich material, and all around in the Diocese of Pittsburgh, Erie, and Philadelphia partly, the German Catholics are under our care, and in many stations also the Irish and Americans. Not everything is in a regular way yet, but we are striving with our best efforts to finish the Monastery and College. Of course, we could commence in the West only with 2 or 3 priests and a few brothers, wheresoever we might settle, and it would take several years before we could get up a Monastery or anything like it. We have not com[undecipherable] and with money, as our College is for the poor; but I would not despair of good success if we find a suitable place and many Catholics to attend to. Still, we can take our time, and so also the Right Reverend Bishops can take their time before they open [for] us their respective Dioceses.

It was manifestly the will of God that I settled in this Diocese, though I had also a call to Chicago from R.R. Bishop Quarter.[64] No doubt God will let us know through his vicars on earth where he will have us if we have to think of finding a new place.

A religious order stands in need of the confidence and benevolence of the Bishop, and in return a Bishop will earn a great deal of advantage from a well organized religious corporation; still there are regards for both of them that must be kept in view; which, Sir, I do not think hard, if you want to know the men who would come to be your assistants in the vineyard of the Lord. Therefore, I thought it necessary to speak frankly and to say what is our practice now and what may be our practice afterwards. *Nil nisi quod traditum est.* We enter only into the paths of our fathers of old. We are Germans, but not so obstinately as not to conform to the genius of the country, if it be a good, a Catholic one; we have our countrymen, but not exclusively; we serve willingly the Bishops, whilst we try to observe our rule; and grant slowly the preference to other orders, already established here, but try not to [be] behind them.

With the sincerest respect and profoundest reverence, I remain, Right Reverend Dear bishop, your most humble servant, Boniface Wimmer

Eng   oADD   cASVA

TO GREGORY SCHERR   **51**

St. Cloud, Minnesota, November 3, 1856

Reverend and Gracious Archbishop: I have never before written you from such a great distance. I have already informed you that I sent a group of monks to Minnesota, which is in the extreme northwest section of the United States. Father Demetrius di Marogna was appointed superior of the group, and was assisted by

---

[64] William Quarter was bishop of Chicago between 1844 and 1848. In 1845, he had invited Wimmer to settle in his diocese.

two recently ordained priests and two brothers. On the advice of Bishop Cretin of St. Paul, the capital of this territory and also the residence of the bishop, they settled near St. Cloud, eight miles from St. Paul, 46 degrees and 54' north latitude. This land was bought from the Indians two years ago and then occupied by white immigrants. Almost exclusively German Catholics settled our county [Stearns County]. They have already erected little wooden churches in St. Augustine, St. Cloud, Sauk Rapids, Jacobs Prairie, and Richmond. St. Cloud, the young capital of this county, is about a mile long and has about 50 houses. However, it will expand a great deal this winter and next spring. The steamships are able to come only ten miles above St. Paul, up to St. Anthony, but then the river drops suddenly. The river there closely resembles the falls of the Rhine by Schaffhausen. From St. Anthony smaller steamboats are able to continue on to St. Cloud, while immediately above this city, near Sauk Rapids (another new town) the river again becomes quite rough. Beyond this, ships can travel only when the water is extremely high. The river at this narrow stretch is still 600 feet wide, rapid, and swift, but because of the sandbars, it is not navigable at ordinary depth. Our monastery is very close to the city, only 60 feet from the river, from which we also obtain drinking water. There are many islands in the river, which teem with wild ducks. We have been eating duck every day since I arrived. Otherwise, we would not have anything except potatoes, bread, and black coffee because we do not even have a cow.

The monastery is built in a rather odd style: 72 feet long, 12 feet wide, and one story high. One part was constructed of stone and the other of boards. It has three cells, a refectory, a kitchen, a small chapel, a carpenter's workshop, and a guest room. All the doors open directly on the outside. The barn, a rectangular building, has two stone walls ten feet high. The roof is formed by wooden rafters crossing the frame of the building. On top of the rafters, straw and hay are piled. There two horses and two oxen are housed. There are no doors, and there is absolutely no room for a threshing floor. Three acres of land are fenced off near the buildings, and along the lowlands of the river are wild plums, hazelnuts, and tall bushes that make the land almost impassable. Towards the west, the land rises to a height of 100 feet and is densely wooded with oak, poplars, aspen, and ash. Most of the trees are not healthy, however, because they have been damaged by frequent fires. On a higher level, the prairie begins, level land heavy with grass. A little oak tree grows here and there, also burnt at the bottom. Occasionally large funnel-shaped pits can be seen which are nearly always, not only during the rainy season, filled with water. Throughout all of Minnesota there are several thousand (some say 10,000) such ponds (some larger and some smaller). They are, however, frequently small lakes.

Our property here consists of 320 acres (that is, one-half an English square mile) west of the river. Along the river, an abundance of rich black soil has accumulated. On the plains, the ground is just as black but not more than a foot deep. Then comes sand. The land should be very productive, however. When my people came here, the whole prairie was white with strawberry blossoms, and a little later, red with the strawberries themselves. When these died, many thousands of other flowers bloomed. Among them are some that are found only in the horticulturalist gardens of Bavaria. Now dead grass can be seen, which easily catches fire. Around St. Paul, thousands of haystacks were burned because of such fires. The hay was stacked in the open since they did not yet have suitable haylofts. Consequently, most of the farmers had to sell their cattle because they could not feed them over the winter. The bishop himself was afraid that he would have to sell his two horses, which he needs for hauling wood, traveling, and other duties. Hay is so expensive that the innkeepers charge half a dollar for one feeding of two horses. My monks have about as much as they need, if it does not burn on them.

The above-mentioned 320 acres of land form, as they call it here, two claims of 160 acres each. It was the property of two elderly brothers, Ludwig and Wilhelm Rothkopp, who came from the Prussian Rhineland. They were among the first immigrants to settle here, and each took 160 acres as his own since every immigrant was allowed to occupy that much. At that time, the land was not surveyed on the west side of the river, but since then it has been surveyed and will soon be sold by the government. The price for each acre is $1.25, or $200 for 160 acres and $400 for 320 acres. Each settler is allowed to occupy 160 acres, wherever he wants, if another does not already own it. He must build a little house, where he can live, and must put part of the land under cultivation. Then he has the first right to purchase it when the government decides to sell it–at a price of $1.25 per acre. However, he can sell it even before he himself has formally bought and paid for it, provided that he can prove that he had it in his possession at one time. That is what these two brothers did. Because their claims lay so close to a navigable river and a town, the speculative Americans had already offered them $3,000 for the claims. Still, the brothers would not sell but gave it *gratis* to the prior on condition that he pay the government within the prescribed time the $400 and that the monastery support and clothe both of them for the rest of their lives. In return for this, they do whatever work they can, since they are both over 60 years old. In addition, the monks were also required to educate their nephew and niece. I consider this a real gift, since the land has already increased two thousand dollars in value, and we have been offered $5,000 for it. In a short time, if St. Cloud becomes a large city (as every indication points), it will be worth ten times more.

Father Prior and the two younger brothers repeatedly asked me to send a few priests and several brothers. They also asked me to accompany them in order to determine whether we could acquire more land ten miles west of St. Cloud for a future monastery. I assented unwillingly to both requests, since they required a great deal of time and money, and I have little of each. When, however, I presented the matter in chapter on October 8, the chapter unanimously recommended that I come myself and take priests and brothers with me. This I did, selecting Brothers Wolfgang Beck, Roman Veitl, and Vincent Hörmann from Indiana, and Father Alexius Rötzer from Butler. Besides these, I took Paul Stenger, who is finishing theology and is a professed monk, and a lay brother, Veremund Erhard.[65] I traveled with them on October 15 to Pittsburgh and from there on October 16 to Cleveland. Then we crossed over the great lake[66] (which at this time of the year is very stormy and extremely dangerous). After we reached Detroit, we continued on to Chicago, and then up the Mississippi to Dunleit,[67] which lies across the river from Dubuque. I arrived there on a Saturday evening. We immediately boarded a steamboat for St. Paul. After traveling a day and a night, we reached St. Paul on Thursday at 11:30 am. At that point, the Mississippi is an imposing stream. The high hills that hedge in the river form a valley seven miles wide. Not even in the valleys of the Rhine and the Danube or any other place have I seen such a unique change of scenery. The old castles are absent, but occasionally a picturesque village appears in which commercial activities are flourishing, even though they were only recently established. An idea of their importance is indicated by the fact that a little plot of ground 50 feet wide and one hundred feet long usually costs between $2,000 and $5,000 as soon as a few houses are built.

The river flows a little further into a lake, which is called Lake Pepin. The lake is 40 miles long with no beach to speak of. At one place between two ranges of hills, it stretches to a width of about five miles. However, this lake is inferior to the impressive Lake Vierwalterstätter in Switzerland and the large Lago Maggiore in northern Italy, with their majestic surroundings. In many respects, however, it surpasses both of these. Incidentally, we rode on this lake for four hours. Above

---

[65] Wolfgang Beck, O.S.B. (1805-1879), Roman Veitl, O.S.B. (1820-1893), Vincent Hörmann, O.S.B. (1821-1911), Alexius Rötzer, O.S.B. (1832-1860). Paul Stenger, O.S.B., and Veremund Erhard, O.S.B., did not persevere in monastic life.

[66] Lake Erie.

[67] An important port on the Illinois side of the Mississippi River, Dunleit came to be known as East Dubuque, Illinois.

the lake, the river is definitely smaller, and at St. Paul, it is no wider than the Danube at Abeih. North of St. Paul there is a prairie, the greatest attraction of which is the magnificent waterfall at St. Anthony. St. Paul itself lies high above the river on a limestone bed. It has a beautiful location. There are already 10,000 inhabitants, and it will undoubtedly be one of the largest cities in the country. The bishop is already building his cathedral, and the basement (which is being used as a school) is finished. He himself lives in a large brick house, the first story of which serves as a church and school, the second as a kitchen, and the third as living quarters for him and his priests. He was on visitation when I arrived. The next day I set out from there with the mail wagon, reaching St. Cloud at midnight on the Feast of the Holy Archangel Raphael. However, Father Prior was not at home but in St. Paul. We passed each other on the road but were not even aware of it. The prior had to buy flour and meat there for the winter, since they only had a few supplies in St. Cloud, and what they had was too expensive.

While awaiting his return, I accompanied Father Bruno Riess and Father Cornelius Wittman to St. Joseph (another little town ten miles west of St. Cloud). The next day we went into the so-called Indianbush with two men who were well acquainted with this area. We wanted to look for a piece of land near the stream Wettel where we might in the future establish a large monastery. For the present, we chose a section (or 640 acres) of which the greater part was woods while the rest was heavy brush and a beautiful meadow of wild hay along the Wettel. We scratched ourselves miserably as we walked Indian fashion through all these thorn bushes. Then we came to the meadow where the grass was so tall that we could hardly get through. These four claims were registered under the names of the four brothers whom I had brought along. We are still going to take four more claims (640 acres or one square mile) for Father Alexius, Frater Paul, and the two brothers, Benno Muggenthaler and Patrick Greil, who were here before. To carry out these plans, four men are going to mark off the claims tomorrow and put up a cabin on each claim. This will give us legal proof that this land has already been settled. Next spring we have to begin farming the land. Right now, these claims will only cost us a day's work, but when we have to buy the land, they will cost $1,600 or 4,000 florins. We also have 240 acres near St. Joseph, which Father Bruno acquired in his name and which will cost $300. The price for the land in St. Cloud is $400. Altogether, we need about $2,400 or 6,000 florins. Father Prior has already petitioned the government for the beautiful, heavily-wooded isle that lies directly across from us in St. Cloud. He wants this land because we do not have much wood on our 320 acres, and besides, wood will soon be a very scarce and expensive item. We will naturally need a lot of wood at the monastery since the extremely cold winter lasts six months. If we get this land, we have to pay for it, which means another 4,000 or 5,000 florins, or at the most 6,000. Our plan is to erect a school, the first one in this area. The monastery should be built in St. Joseph or in the Indianbush so that the professors might provide for and administer to the spiritual needs of the surrounding communities. A large piece of property would furnish support for both of these activities. I can easily staff it with ordained monks. In the case of brothers, however, it is more difficult since none has applied for admittance for some time. However, the situation will probably improve soon, as we shall receive a few candidates from the poor boys we take in. The majority of them, giving evidence of a vocation, remain with us.

I hope that Your Excellency will approve and support this venture. I am fully aware as you warned me in your last letter of the hazards of too-hurried expansion, and I am not overlooking the dangers that exist for the young priests. My zeal is so impatient, however, that I do not want to delay. We live in youthful, young-blooded America, where everything grows faster than in the decadent countries of Europe. In the last ten years, I have worked constantly for the rapid growth of the monastery. For that reason, I have brought in so many persons that I have neither food, rooms, nor work for them at home. Furthermore, several bishops have written me from other areas asking for help, just as our German people cry for priests. What, then, should I do? Finally, the main purpose for my coming to America was so that our monasteries would be seminaries for the German Catholics of this country. St. Vincent is already fulfilling this role. This year it has again furnished eight Benedictine priests and two diocesan priests, besides three candidates for the diocesan seminary. It will continue, I hope, to do so on a larger scale. The United States is an immense country. Not all who wish to attend school can come to St. Vincent. Consequently, we will have to establish several monasteries and seminaries. Through them, those who live in this materialistic society will be instructed to despise all their earthly possessions and thus more easily devote themselves to the service of God. Therefore, I cannot carelessly allow myself to pass up any occasion as opportune as this. We are not worried about our debts. I trust the Mission Society will always provide for us. Other organizations of both rich and poor people do occasionally the same work. We work and live as economically as possible. The Catholics in this region help as much as they can. Why, then, should funds ever be lacking?

Just a few weeks before I decided to go to Minnesota, I had intended to build a sawmill in Carrolltown. We have a magnificent growth of trees there, over 700 acres, which so far has not served any practical purpose. Various circumstances, especially our lack of time and money, prevented us from constructing the mill. It would cost at least 1,000 florins, even though the brothers would do most of the work. If ever finished, it would afford us a substantial yearly income with which I could pay the debts, or at least the interest, or enlarge the seminary at St. Vincent. My whole life is devoted to establishing a good preparatory seminary for worthy Benedictines and diocesan priests. This work is my only joy, for which I tirelessly write, study, and beg. Although it is already quite large and productive of much good, it is still far from what I want it to be. Perhaps I will not live to see it finished, but I will do all in my power to bring it to completion. However, it must sprout new branches before it can reach maturity, since nothing lasts long in this world. To provide for this, new foundations have to rise up.

These are the most pressing needs. Tomorrow I am riding back to St. Paul, and on November 10, I will sail on a steamship to Dunleit because no ships sail later than that. Usually the river freezes about the middle of November. It is 800 miles from here to Dunleit, and 1,000 miles to Pittsburgh on a straight road. I had intended to go down to St. Louis and then go up the Missouri to Kansas, where Father Henry Lemke was supposed to have begun a monastery, but it is too late now, and it costs too much money. The trip here cost me $250. I bought a cow for $45 and a sow for $20. Besides, I brought with me a monstrance, a ciborium, a chalice, and a censer–which cost me $100. Moreover, I have to leave some money for the monks. Then there is my return trip to be paid for. All this comes to a sum of $600, a huge amount for a poor abbot.

I received part of your donation of 7,000 florins some time ago and the rest will probably surprise me in a huge sum upon my return to St. Vincent. I will send my receipt along with my sincere gratitude immediately. I also take this opportunity to express on behalf of myself and the German people our heartfelt gratitude to Your Excellency for your generous donation. From this report, you can see that I will need just as large a sum next year. It will be used for the exact purposes for which it has been designated: to improve the present minor seminary, to build a new one, and to take care of the pastoral needs of our German people who would be without priests if it were not for us. I humbly ask Your Excellency, as president of the *Ludwig Missionsverein*, and the esteemed central committee, kindly to remember the American Benedictines in your next year's budget.

There is no excess of stipends in your diocese. Otherwise, I would have offered to take some of them myself. The five priests here, and ten of the fourteen at St. Vincent, have no stipends at all. If we had enough of them, we would not need any donations at all. Those Masses for which we have no special intention are offered for our benefactors. In this way, we repay their charity.

In closing, I assure you that everything fares well in the monastery and in the various priories. The priests and brothers are devoted to their holy vocation. They emulate one another in their zeal for the care of souls and in teaching. Fraternal charity and good will regulate their lives. When occasion demands, they willingly sacrifice themselves, performing all things for the praise of God. As happened last spring, clerics and lay brothers again answered my plea at once to come to remote and rugged Minnesota. One almost envies those who have received such blessings, although from their letters it is evident what hardships they have suffered. May this disposition always characterize the American Benedictines!

I will finish this letter at St. Vincent since by that time I will have a few more things to tell you. I wrote it here, however, because I can scarcely find time for such a long epistle at home.

St. Vincent, November 14, [1856]

After I had taken care of my business in St.Cloud, I drove back with Father Prior to St. Paul, which I left by steamboat on Saturday afternoon at 1:00 pm. On Sunday at 1:30 pm I was already in Dunleit, took an early train to Pittsburgh, arriving there on Tuesday at 9:00 pm. On Wednesday, November 12, I was safe and sound at St. Vincent, after a four-week absence.

A big stack of letters lay on my desk upon my arrival. I quickly glanced through them to see if I could recognize the writing. I came across a bulky letter from Munich–apparently from Baron von Oberkamp.[68] "Alleluia! It contains money from the Society," I thought, opening it with joyful expectancy. Indeed, it did contain 7,000 florins in two checks–not from the Society, however, but from a truly generous donor. This was none other than our good King Ludwig, the august restorer of our holy Order in Bavaria and the noble patron of the monks in America. May God preserve him and reward him a thousand-fold.

Once again, my hopes were fulfilled. So quickly! In such an extraordinary manner! Once again, I can pay my debts and make more debts. I can undertake some noble works for the honor of God and welfare of my confreres because I can maintain my credit. I just barely manage to make ends meet, always in need, yet rich–*semper egentes et omnia possidentes* ["always needy but possessing everything"]! If only the mission money were added to this, I would be greatly relieved of the burden of keeping up on interest payment. Because of the crop failure, price increases, and construction of the mill, the interest has increased immensely within the last year.

---

[68] Baron Rudolph von Oberkamp, business manager of the *Ludwig Missionsverein*.

On my way back, I met the bishop of St. Paul, Dr. J. Cretin, a beloved and eminent prelate. He presented me with a written declaration in which he not only empowered me to establish a monastery in his diocese in Stearns County, but even expressly stated that this was his most ardent wish. He promised to do all in his power to ensure the success of the undertaking. In addition, he earnestly desired that we should establish a monastery at Crow Wing,[69] 80 miles north of St. Cloud, to take care of the needs of the Indians who live on a government reservation. At present, I could not accept this proposal because the German people are dearer to me than the wild redskins. However, if my novices persevere, we will have opportunities to work with them in Crow Wing or perhaps somewhere else, if it is the will of God that I should live to do this.

There is no other news. In the presidential election, we favored the Democrats who won the election for honest Buchanan.[70] He attributed his election in the three deciding states of Pennsylvania, Indiana, and Illinois to the Catholics. As before, the Democrats have protected us from the Know-Nothings. All the enemies of the Church, especially the red Forty-Eighters,[71] were on Fremont's side. Excitement and tension were very great towards the end of the election.

I wish you a happy New Year and recommend myself to your prayers. Your most humble and obedient servant, Boniface Wimmer, Abbot

Ger   oALMV   cASVA   transSB,WT   *Scrip*17 (56-64)

TO PETER CASARETTO   52

Carrolltown, December 11, 1856

Right Reverend Lord Abbot and President:[72] I had intended to write Your Grace sooner and to give you an account of the successful and happy outcome of my business in Rome last year, so that you would be aware of it, but time did not

---

[69] Crow Wing was the site of Father Francis Pierz's first mission church in Minnesota. Father Pierz arrived in Minnesota in 1852 to work among the Indians.

[70] In the 1856 presidential election James Buchanan, a Democrat, won against John Fremont of the Republican Party and Millard Fillmore of the American (or Know-Nothing) Party

[71] The Forty-Eighters were free-thinking Germans who emigrated to America after the abortive revolutions of 1848 in Germany. These Germans revolutionaries continued the anti-Catholic campaigns in the United States that they had begun in Germany.

[72] Abbot Peter Casaretto, O.S.B. (1810-1878), was president of the Cassinese Congregation, with which the American Cassinese Congregation was affiliated.

permit me to do so until this moment. I therefore hasten to write you now in order to inform you:

(1) That the monastery of St. Vincent in Westmoreland County, Pennsylvania, in the Diocese of Pittsburgh, founded with the permission of my abbot, Gregory Scherr (recently named archbishop of Munich), and with the approval of Bishop Michael O'Connor of Pittsburgh, was earlier recognized by the Holy See and has just been declared an abbey;

(2) That the monks of the abbey have been granted the right to freely elect an abbot;

(3) That the abbey and its priories have been constituted as a congregation which follows the statutes of the former Bavarian Benedictine Congregation and which has been placed under the protection of the Holy Guardian Angels; and

(4) That in accordance with the wishes of the bishop, the monastery has established a seminary to educate both religious and diocesan candidates for the priesthood, though it remains a monastic institution.

Despite serious difficulties, the invaluable assistance of the procurator general of the Cassinese Congregation, Abbot Angelo Pescetelli, and the powerful intervention of King Ludwig I of Bavaria resulted in our success. In addition, I cannot give enough praise and thanks to his eminence Cardinal Barnabo, secretary of the Sacred Congregation of the Propagation of the Faith, who presented my case and defended it before the cardinals. Subsequently his holiness, Pope Pius IX, reviewed the recommendations of the council of cardinals and gave his approval to the abbey, to the free election of the abbot, to the creation of an exempt congregation affiliated with the Cassinese Congregation, and finally to the establishment of an independent seminary. The Holy Father confirmed all this in an apostolic brief dated August 26, 1855.

Nevertheless, in order to avoid any difficulties at the beginning of the new abbey's existence, the Holy Father, following the advice of the most eminent cardinals and in accordance with the recommendation of the procurator general, decided that I should become the first abbot of the new abbey for a period of three years. I did not consider myself worthy of this honor, but I could not refuse it. My confreres believed that I was the best person suited for the job since I best knew the state of our affairs. Of course, all my confreres are my disciples and my sons.

It is hardly necessary to say that our success brings great joy not only to us American Benedictines but also indeed to all American Catholics. It is generally acknowledged that the Benedictines in America have devoted themselves selflessly and successfully until now not only to the education of young men for the clerical state but also to the care of souls. Our work of education especially brings us honor and esteem because no other institution such as ours exists that accepts and educates poor students *gratis*.

Therefore, both the laity and the clergy rejoiced when they learned that our monastery had become an abbey. Everyone recognized that the existence of the Benedictine Order in America depended upon our monastery becoming an abbey. Without this, the future of our Order in America was in doubt. However, with the abbey, the Order is secure, and with the seminary, in which the poor who aspire to the priesthood can receive an education, the institution is secure.

While in France, the bishops were opposed to the establishment of an exempt Benedictine congregation; in America, the bishops congratulate us, and more than one of them has requested a colony of our Order.

Thus, it happened that after my return from Europe, we held a general chapter at which both the solemnly professed monks and the lay brothers (who number 110) renewed their vows according to the statutes of the Bavarian Congregation. At this chapter, we also considered the establishment of a new monastery. We decided to send a colony to work among the German immigrants in the vast territory of Minnesota, in the extreme northwest of our republic, near the source of the famous Mississippi River. We did this in response to a request of Bishop Joseph Cretin, who again and again asked for our help.

In the month of April, Father Demetrius, Count di Marogna, who was then prior at St. Vincent, went with two clerics about to be ordained, Father Bruno Riess and Cornelius Wittmann, and two lay brothers to Minnesota. They arrived there after a three-week journey on the Ohio and Mississippi Rivers. Bishop Cretin received them in the diocesan see with great joy and honor, and after examining the two clerics, ordained them to the priesthood. Since the number of priests and brothers was not sufficient for the work, I myself, after taking counsel with my confreres, traveled to Minnesota and on October 15 arrived there with Alexius Rötzer, a cleric ready for ordination, and four lay brothers, to give solace and help to our confreres there and to see with my own eyes what had to be done. It was a journey of 2,000 miles, most of it by rail, though I had to travel briefly on the deep Mississippi. We had to travel quickly because the winter in these northern forests and lake-covered regions descends suddenly in November, and we were concerned that the snow would make our return impossible.

God has truly blessed the American Benedictines. In ten years, we have established our monastery in Pennsylvania, together with another priory in the Diocese of Pittsburgh and one in the Diocese of Erie. Now we have established a third priory among the wild Indians in the heart of North America by following those

Catholics who have recently (in the last two years) begun to immigrate to this barely known but most beautiful and fruitful territory. Thus, even there, true religion inserts its foot with Benedictine stability into a place where the desire for material gain and money compelled unstable men to go. In the past year, nine of our clerics have been ordained priests, and we expect an equal number to be ordained in 1858. May God grant that a similar number of priests from our seminary be ordained in subsequent years. We have a hundred students and will be able to accept more if unforeseen calamity does not strike.

I make this report to Your Grace not to boast but so that you will rejoice with us and give thanks to God for his great and unmerited blessings on our venerable Order. If Abbot Gregory and his monastery of Metten can rightly claim to be the author of this success, so also can the Cassinese Congregation claim to be in truth the patron of our congregation. For without the outstanding help of the very reverend procurator general, the tender sapling of our monastery would have hardly grown into such a tall tree, which now extends its branches broadly and invites and collects many under its shade. It is no more than just, therefore, that I acknowledge this publicly and solemnly render our fervent thanks to you and to your congregation, begging that you will acknowledge us as your sons and continue to regard us as worthy of your protection.

If you do not think it inappropriate, I ask that you share this letter with your general chapter so that in this way we might form a closer bond of fraternal charity between American and Italian Benedictines, and perhaps increase in some measure the propagation and consolidation of our Order. Commending myself and all my confreres to you and to your general chapter, I remain with reverence and veneration Your Grace's obedient servant, Boniface Wimmer

Lat   oASPR   cASVA   transJO

TO RUDOLPH VON OBERKAMP   53

St. Vincent, September 18, 1857

Reverend Sir and Friend: For a long time I have heard nothing from you, but I myself have not reported anything special to you either. You received news some four weeks ago, I hope, about a joust, albeit unbloody, between me and the former venerable superior in St. Marys, Benedicta Riepp. She defeated herself and cleared the field. By this time the prioress of St. Walburga[73] has also received letters and reports from various authentic sources, so that I had to intervene to show that Benedicta is a good nun but not, therefore, a good superior. The confusion that meanwhile arose among the sisters because of the stupid actions of Benedicta I quickly resolved by establishing suitable prioresses everywhere: Theresa Vogel in St. Marys, Scholastica Burkhardt in Erie, and Emmerana Bader in Newark.[74]

Our missions in Minnesota and Kansas are prospering splendidly. True, the fathers must suffer much want and discomfort, but they have a very beautiful and blessed field of labor that is constantly expanding. Three priests are in Atchison, Kansas: Fathers Augustine Wirth, Henry Lemke, and Casimir Seitz, with Brother Paul in Doniphan on the Missouri.[75] The Indian missions, which have been offered to us by Bishop Miège of Kansas,[76] are also there. I will have to go there myself to see if we can accept them.[77] Our affairs in St. Cloud, Minnesota, are not proceeding well, but the fathers are respected and sought wherever they show themselves. In fact, almost half of the huge territory is under our care. Father Demetrius is prior; Fathers Benedict Haindl, Cornelius Wittmann, Clement Staub, Bruno Riess, and Alexius Rötzer are his assistants,[78] and there are eight brothers. Recently six sisters from St. Marys also went there, but this was premature. They will have a hard winter.

Nine priests were ordained this year for our Order: Father Casimir in Kansas, Father Eberhard Gahr in Newark, and seven others at home on May 28, namely, Fathers Wendelin Mayer, Alphonse Heimler, Magnus Mayer, Othmar Wirtz, Otto Kopf, Leo Rau, and Louis Fink.[79] They are all good, worthy, and able men. I have written to you, I think, that I took over the German parish of St. Mary's in New-

---

[73] Mother Edwarda Schnitzer, O.S.B., prioress of St. Walburga Priory, Eichstätt.

[74] Theresa Vogel, O.S.B. (1834-1886), Scholastica Burkhardt, O.S.B. (1832-1881), and Emmerana Bader, O.S.B. (1829-1902).

[75] Augustine Wirth, O.S.B. (1828-1901), Peter Henry Lemke, O.S.B. (1796-1882), Casimir Seitz, O.S.B. (1829-1867), and Paul Pfeifer, O.S.B. (1807-1868).

[76] John B. Miège, S.J. (1815-1884), vicar apostolic of Kansas.

[77] The Benedictines were unable to accept the Indian missions in the Kansas Territory because of their other commitments.

[78] Demetrius di Marogna, O.S.B. (1803-1869), Benedict Haindl, O.S.B. (1815-1887), Cornelius Wittmann, O.S.B. (1828-1921), Clement Staub, O.S.B. (1819-1886), Alexius Rötzer, O.S.B. (1832-1860), and Bruno Riess, O.S.B. (1829-1900).

[79] Eberhard Gahr, O.S.B. (1832-1922), Wendelin Mayer, O.S.B. (1832-1881), Alphonse Heimler, O.S.B. (1832-1909), Magnus Mayer, O.S.B., Othmar Wirtz, O.S.B. (1831-1874), Otto Kopf, O.S.B. (1832-1907), Leo Rau, O.S.B. (1829-1861), Louis Fink, O.S.B. (1834-1904), Odilo Vandergrün, O.S.B. (1827-1887).

ark. It happened around the middle of April
when I sent Fathers Valentine Felder[80] and
Eberhard Gahr there. Unfortunately, Father
Valentine died tragically in a terrible accident
in New York on May 28. He was run over by
a train. Father Rupert Seidenbusch[81] is now
in his place. I have also taken over Bellefonte
in the Diocese of Philadelphia. Fathers Odilo
Vandergrün and Louis Fink are there.

Newark, only nine miles from New York
and on a bay, will become a very important
place. For the moment, it is only a heavy burden for me. It must be entirely rebuilt. The
cemetery was filled. There was no house for
the priest. The church, almost finished, cost
over $24,000; a new cemetery, $2,000; three
small houses, close to the church, which we
bought, one for the rectory for the priest and
another for the nuns, cost $8,000. The last
$10,000 goes on the bill of the Benedictines.
The parish is building the church. The ex-

Father Bruno Riess, O.S.B.,
(1829-1900), early Benedic-
tine missionary in Minnesota.

penses of the trip of seven sisters from St. Marys to Newark, their setting up house
there, one piano, etc., comes to almost $400.

In Erie, the sisters had to teach classes in the old Church of Our Lady. Because
of the elevation and the cold in winter, that would certainly have killed them. I
pressed the bishop to give them this church. He promised to do so. Then I made
arrangements that before winter the church would be rebuilt, i.e., in such a way
that it will now be a two-story building. The cost of this is $500 to $600. Who
will pay? In St. Marys, Benedicta left behind nothing but debts and ran off with
the money. In Minnesota, there are six sisters and one child. Twelve intended to
go there in accordance with the wishes of the superior. Half of them would certainly have starved or frozen to death had I not prevented their going by contact-
ing Bishop Young.[82] It is not possible to live on the income from the school there,
and my fathers have nothing themselves because the grasshoppers again destroyed
everything. If you or the *Missionsverein* do not help, things will be difficult. I am
very anxious to hear how much will be allotted to us this year. My abbey is really

[80] Valentine Felder, O.S.B. (1830-1857).
[81] Rupert Seidenbusch, O.S.B. (1830-1895).
[82] Josue Mary Young (1808-1866), bishop of Erie.

a child of the *Missionsverein*, and the *Missionsverein* must not be ashamed of it. I hope it will also care for it in a special way and continue to support it strongly.

Please be so kind as to pay the court chaplain[83] 427 florins, and Mr. Unkraut in [Bremen] $46 for the wine he sent me, because we do not know where we can procure any reliable Mass wine here. Our school has more students than last year. That includes several paying students who do not want to become priests. There are 11 novices, 11 professed clerics, 13 scholastics or postulants. B. Brunner finished his novitiate but almost died of chest cramps. He was sick for three months. He wanted to make profession immediately, but I am still concerned that all is not yet right. I promised to help him become a priest since he wishes it in any case. If he is a Benedictine, that can also happen. We would have more novices, but our novice master, Father Peter Baunach,[84] a [former] Redemptorist, is extremely strict with his novices, so that it irritates quite a few. However, I wish all things according to the *Holy Rule*; therefore it is better to have fewer and these few good.

We have had a very blessed year for crops, but costs are high. We are all well, with few exceptions. Among the brothers, there arose a spirit of mistrust and dissatisfaction that caused many to leave or forced me to dismiss them. I lost $2,000 because of it. By far, most stood firm and true, as always. The devil tries all kinds of ways to harm us. Yet the material loss in such cases is always replaced by spiritual gain, in that the proven ones reveal themselves and the chaff is separated from the wheat. I now have too few brothers. In Minnesota I could use as many as I have at home. Cooks are especially needed.

Once the budget of the *Missionsverein* is planned and the treasury finds itself in a healthy condition, may I ask you to send a good part of our portion? In addition, I hope the poor Benedictine sisters will surely receive something. They are, in fact, in great want at all four stations where they are now.

If I travel to Kansas this fall, you will receive a long letter as soon as my business allows me to write. I have, in fact, much to do and must travel a great deal for my priests and my sisters. The worst thing about this is that I still lack support and must fight constantly against deficiencies in money, time, and health to help them! That is the way it goes—and it is proper, too.

Recommending myself most humbly to your benevolence and your pious prayers, I sign myself with special devotion, your most humble, Boniface Wimmer, Abbot

Ger   oALMV   cASVA   transIG   Girgen (105-108)

---

[83] Father Joseph Ferdinand Müller (1803-1864), chaplain to the court of King Ludwig I and former business manager of the *Ludwig Missionsverein*.
[84] Peter Baunach, O.S.B. (1815-1868).

TO CASSINESE CONGREGATION   **54**

St. Vincent, March 16, 1858

Very Reverend Father Abbots, Dear Confreres: As you come together to hold your general chapter, a confrere abbot from North America greets you. Although I am not a member of your venerable assembly, I nevertheless am closely bound to you. I am head of a young Benedictine congregation that Pope Pius IX, now gloriously reigning, established in the United States of America by an apostolic brief published on August 26, 1855. This congregation follows the statutes of the former Bavarian Benedictine Congregation and sought successfully to be affiliated with your celebrated Cassinese Congregation.

This affiliation, unless it is merely in name, seems to imply that according to the intention of the Holy Father a twofold relationship exists between the Cassinese and American Benedictines. Certainly as the junior and weaker brethren, we look to you not only as our seniors and fathers but also as our patrons and protectors. We will need and implore your counsel when we have questions and we will seek your help when we face difficulties. On the other hand, we ask that you deign to acknowledge us as adopted sons, to befriend us, to protect us, and to instruct us. You may equally expect from us our due respect and, should necessity require it, our mutual support. Since small things grow and discord diminishes through friendship, it is necessary, especially in these days when we Benedictines confront such great obstacles and challenges, that all Benedictines firmly unite in congregations and that these congregations turn to your congregation as their center of gravity. It is also important that each congregation be represented by a procurator in Rome, the center of Catholicism. Most reverend confreres, you have well satisfied your duty towards us (if it is possible to speak of it as a duty) by naming as our procurator that most distinguished man, Dom Angelo Pescetelli,[85] who has earned the highest esteem of all American Benedictines.

Almost three years ago, our monastery of St. Vincent, the first Benedictine monastery in this part of the world, was elevated to the rank and dignity of an abbey, and the capitulars obtained the privilege of electing an abbot by majority vote. In addition, the monastery and its priories were formed into an exempt congregation. Bishop Michael O'Connor, our ordinary, attempted to use his authority to prevent us from receiving these privileges, but the distinguished procurator general, acting as our advocate, defended us strenuously, wisely, and successfully. Contrary to everyone's expectations, he managed to achieve the unanimous approval of the eminent cardinals to our petitions, an approval that the Holy Father

---

[85] Abbot Angelo Pescetelli, O.S.B. (1809-1885).

most graciously confirmed. In one stroke, he obtained for us the abbey, the right of electing an abbot, and the exempt congregation, and he did this at a moment when our monastery was in great danger of dissolving had we not obtained these privileges. His motive for helping us was the purest fraternal charity. He acted solely out of zeal for the advancement of our holy Order and not because he hoped for or had been promised money. This was very apparent to me and my confreres.

However, this service was not all that the indefatigable and generous procurator did for us. He then proceeded to obtain several other benefits for us. He obtained permission for Father Alphonse,[86] who has a crippled hand, to be ordained and to say Mass without distributing communion. In another case, when the bishop did not want to grant orders beyond the subdiaconate to one of our clerics, the procurator obtained a decision from the Holy See that established the cleric's right to be ordained deacon and priest. Similarly, in the matter of the abbot's right to pontificate, he ensured our success, and in several other questions of great importance, he made use of his erudition and expertise in canon law to obtain for us what was needed. In many small matters too, such as the buying and sending of breviaries, diurnals, textbooks, etc., which required tiring effort, he demonstrated the greatest kindness, understanding, and benevolence towards us.

I am profoundly grateful for all that he has done, and I want to express publicly my deepest thanks to our beloved procurator general for the services and benefits he has bestowed on us. I will always be in the greatest debt to him, and to you too, my most reverend confreres, in whose name the procurator has acted. From this, it is clear that I have attempted to complete the work given me while at the same time seeking the best counsel and advice possible. I ask your indulgence in allowing me to report to you the progress of our monastery and our Order in the United States.

Eleven and a half years have elapsed since I was sent from the monastery of Metten in Bavaria by Abbot Gregory Scherr,[87] who is now archbishop of Munich, in order "to establish one or more monasteries of our Order." Bishop Michael O'Connor[88] received me most cordially. I had with me four students and fifteen lay brother candidates. I had the idea of using many lay brothers in the forests of America to cultivate a farm that the monastery would acquire. The work of the brothers on this farm would provide food for the monks as well as for the boys being educated for the clerical state. In the following year, 1847, Father Peter

---

[86] Alphonse Heimler, O.S.B. (1832-1909).
[87] Gregory Scherr, O.S.B. (1804-1877).
[88] Michael O'Connor (1810-1872).

Lechner,[89] a confrere from the Abbey of Scheyern, arrived with twenty additional lay brothers. The Bavarian Mission Society sent me an annual subsidy of 2,000 *scudi*. I inaugurated monastic life here on October 24, 1846, although we had only a small house with two rooms. One room served as an office and study hall, the other as a kitchen, refectory, and infirmary. We all slept above the rooms, under a bare roof. In addition to instituting monastic life in strict accordance with the statutes of the Bavarian Congregation, we undertook pastoral work, especially among a great number of German immigrants who had intermarried with English-speaking Catholics and who lived here without a pastor. In size our parish was more a diocese than a parish. Our brothers prepared all the materials necessary for building a good-size monastery–stones, bricks, lime, lumber, planks. They cultivated the fields, cut down the forest, etc. As soon as we had constructed a small house and some of the students were ordained priests, we began a seminary for boys. By working, progressing, and never hesitating, we gradually grew in numbers, usefulness, and effectiveness. From the monastery at St. Vincent, we built priories in Carrolltown, St. Marys, and Butler, and in these three places, we had almost exclusive charge of German Catholics. Our seminary, moreover, grew day by day.

When the community had grown to 21 priests and a large number of lay brothers, it became necessary for our monastery to obtain the rank of abbey and for the abbey to be governed by an abbot, lest confusion, disturbances, and irregularities occur. We therefore sent a petition to the Holy Apostolic See, and I went to Rome to promote our cause. I was helped extensively in this matter by the procurator general, as I indicated above. After my return from Europe, I called all the capitulars from their mission stations to a general chapter. I reported to the chapter about my journey and the matters I had attended to. I read and briefly explained the statutes of the congregation, as much as time allowed, and then we all renewed our vows in accordance with the statutes. Thus, we have entered upon a new era for our Order in America.

Since then we have grown even more. Now our priests number 38, although four have died prematurely. There are 15 clerics, of whom five will be ordained to the priesthood after Easter. There are 12 novices, 16 scholastics (or postulants who wear the habit), more than 100 brothers, and 105 seminarians from the early grades through theology. Besides the priories in Carrolltown, St. Marys, and Butler, we have a priory in Bellefonte (Diocese of Philadelphia); another in Newark, New Jersey, on the shores of the Atlantic Ocean; another in Doniphan, a new city on the Missouri River in the Territory of Kansas; and another in St.

---

[89] Peter Lechner, O.S.B. (1805-1874).

Cloud near the banks of the Mississippi River in the Minnesota Territory. We have recently established a priory in Covington, Kentucky, on the Ohio River, and as soon as five clerics have been ordained after Easter, I will send two of the senior fathers to Omaha City, capital of the Nebraska Territory, a territory recently occupied by Americans settlers. Nebraska neighbors the territory of the Mormons and is a place where the wild Indians still live. Three hundred Catholic families live without a priest in Omaha City. There is only one priest for the whole territory, and he lives 90 miles from Omaha City. These Catholics asked their bishop, J.B. Miège,[90] who lives in Kansas, to send them a priest, but he had none to send. So they wrote me, as did the bishop, and I agreed to send them a priest as much for the sake of religion as for the sake of the expansion of our Order. A seminary for boys has already been established in St. Cloud. This is its first year, and it has eight students. Four months ago, a German parish in the city of St. Paul, capital of Minnesota, was transferred to our care. Both in St. Paul and in Shakopee, Minnesota, I have been compelled to add an additional priest to the ones residing there because I must respond to the pastoral needs of the faithful throughout this enormous region. At the moment, the priories have only two priests each, but without any doubt the number of the faithful will grow, and with God's help some of these communities will develop into abbeys over the next ten years, especially in Minnesota, Kansas, and Nebraska. In these places, we have already acquired ample property, with fertile land, and we will easily be able to acquire more. In Minnesota, we have six priests and 11 lay brothers. I will send three more priests there after Easter. The war with the wild Indians is over. The famine, which resulted from the terrible devastation of the locusts and which seriously affected our people, has ended. I will probably be able to send at least three more priests there after the ordinations in 1859, and then we will be able to establish an abbey in Minnesota.

Of course, there is danger that our missionary fathers, while they are preaching to others, may themselves neglect the *Rule*. To avoid this, I always send them in pairs to their mission stations, and in another year, I hope to send a third priest to each station. One must always be on guard lest the discipline of the *Rule* be neglected. The *clausura*, strict poverty, common recitation of the Divine Office (if they are at home), meditation, *lectio divina*, frequent confession, etc. have been firmly established and are faithfully practiced. Moreover, the priests are not transferred from place to place unnecessarily. Thus it is that up until now we have enjoyed an excellent reputation and have been invited by archbishops and bishops to establish new monasteries, even though exemption is one of our conditions!

[90] John B. Miège, S.J. (1815-1888).

The Benedictine tree has now extended its branches from the shores of the Atlantic Ocean to the farthest frontier of American civilization. We are turning east, west, south, and north. In Pennsylvania, we have fixed our roots at Mount St. Vincent. New shoots have been planted in Covington (Kentucky), Kansas, Nebraska, and Minnesota. Soon these shoots will become vigorous young plants, strong and fruitful. I myself have visited the vast territories of Minnesota and Kansas, first in 1856 and again in October and November 1857. I wanted to see with my own eyes what had to be done. I have no doubt whatever that Minnesota is an especially congenial and promising land for our Order. At the moment there is neither a bishop[91] nor another religious order to assist that territory. We are the only ones there. We can do a great deal in Minnesota in the areas of pastoral care and the education of youth (both for the world and for the clerical state), even though we have begun if not in great poverty, certainly in great need.

I have also introduced the nuns of our Order in America. Their first priory was in St. Marys, a German colony. This convent grew in numbers and then established smaller convents of ten or twelve sisters in the city of Erie (1855), a diocesan see; in Newark (1856), a large city and also a diocesan see; and in St. Cloud, Minnesota. Now not only men but also women sing the praises of God in a land where among 27 million inhabitants, only five million are Catholics; and from among the 22 million non-Catholics, only 12 million are Christians from various Protestant denominations. All the rest are infidels, descendants of Christians who now deny Christ. The future success of religion in this country depends on the Christian education of youth. Our Benedictine sisters teach in public schools and private academies and promote the values of a Christian republic. With the exception of our priories in the large cities of Newark, Covington, St. Paul, and Doniphan, our monasteries are situated in places that have large and splendid farms that bear abundant fruit and that in the future will bear even more.

Every beginning is difficult, but through hard work, patience, and perseverance, we overcame many difficulties and managed to increase and prosper. Now, at the abbey alone, we are able to provide food and clothing to more than 250 people every day, not to mention the many visitors we receive. In all our houses, we observe strict poverty. We hold all things in common. We enjoy meat only rarely on Sundays at supper. We have neither wine nor beer. We hardly know fish or cheese. Our missionaries in Minnesota eat potatoes, a little bread, and preserved meat, but they do not have vegetables because the locusts destroyed everything. Our library is not large, but our church is spacious enough and lovely. In our school,

---

[91] Bishop Joseph Cretin (1799-1857) of St. Paul had died the previous year. His successor, Thomas Grace, O.P. (1814-1897), would not be named bishop until 1859.

we teach classical and modern languages, as well as dogmatic and moral theology, ascetics, and the liberal arts, especially music and painting. In mathematics, physics, and astronomy we lack good professors and good instruments, and until now I have been unable to correct this defect.

You now see, Most Reverend Confreres, that as far as possible we are working hard to be, or certainly to become, true Benedictines. In our monastery, in the missions, in the care of souls, in literary studies, in promoting the liberal arts, in the splendor of the public liturgy, in the education of youth, in the construction of our own buildings by our own hands, in the cultivation of our fields, in the spread of our Order's fame among heretics, infidels, and Catholics, and even among the barbarians, we serve among the standard bearers of the clerical army, as soldiers without pay, reaping the harvest with our own hands.

I must also mention the generosity of the faithful, and especially the generosity of King Ludwig of Bavaria[92] who in the beginning bestowed a gift of 10,000 florins on me, then gave another 8,000 florins, followed by further gift of 3,000 florins. After that, he granted me 3,000 florins each year so that I could establish these new institutions. This excellent prince restored our Order in Bavaria after his father had destroyed it. He did no less for our Order in America and deserves the thanks and prayers of all sons of St. Benedict.

These then are a few of the things that we have accomplished. There are many more things, of course, that we must do. An abbey has been created with a congregation and with the privilege of exemption. We have grown in the spirit and in our own self-assurance. We have earned the good opinion of the people, and God has most generously granted us increase. Neither the bishops nor the civil authorities, nor the lay people, have impeded our progress. We have had a free hand in promoting and spreading our Order. Indeed, nearly all the bishops of this country have written me to ask that I establish monasteries and educational institutions in their dioceses. We have already established houses in the dioceses of Pittsburgh, Erie, Philadelphia, Newark, Covington, Leavenworth (Kansas), and St. Paul (Minnesota). We are spread out over a distance of 3,000 miles.

Perhaps the members of your general chapter will not be pleased to learn that we have established such small monasteries. If this is the case, then I ask you to remember (1) that there is great danger in delay if thousands of the faithful are without pastors; (2) that I can hardly send more than two priests to any place because I do not have more priests; (3) that there is neither sufficient food nor sufficient housing for more than two priests in the mission stations; (4) that it costs a great deal of money for me to send even two priests to the far-off missions with

---

[92] King Ludwig I of Bavaria (1796-1868).

altar vessels, books, vestments, etc.; and (5) that I have been compelled to send some out to the missions each year because the mother house does not have room for so many. Twelve priests are enough here for the school, the pastoral work, and the choir because all the clerics, novices, and postulants join us in the choir.

Pray, therefore, for us that among so many labors and dangers we may not lose the spirit of our Order, the spirit of prayer, of meditation, of internal recollection, of mortification, of humility, and of obedience. Pray that where erudition is lacking, experience, vigilance, and knowledge of the saints may make up the deficiency; that where the *clausura* is not possible, the fear of the Lord may still be preserved; that where happy success enriches the soul, modesty and holy discretion may drive away pride and rash behavior. Pray that we may be worthy sons and worthy members of your noble family! Receive my warmest, most grateful, most tender thanks for the benefits you have bestowed on us through the most worthy and zealous father and procurator general, Abbot Angelo Pescetelli, and grant that he who serves your congregation so faithfully may continue to carry on his most generous work for ours.

Since I sent Abbot Casaretto[93] a copy of the apostolic brief by which the abbey of St. Vincent and the congregation were erected, it is hardly necessary for me to send another now. However, I do not want you to think me negligent, so if there is anything I have failed to do in my effort to show my love, my reverence, and my respect for you, please inform me so that I might fully satisfy my duty to you. Moreover, if in this report you do not find a Cicero but rather a barbarous German who among the pressures of work and business hardly finds the hours to describe all the things that come to mind, at least I have attempted to inform you of those things that God has deigned to do through me for the increase of His greater glory. For indeed, my prayer, like yours, is always: May God be glorified in all things!

With the deepest reverence and filial love, I will always be, Most Reverend Fathers, your most humble confrere, Boniface Wimmer, Abbot and President of the American Benedictine Congregation

Lat   oASPR   cASVA   transJO

---

[93] Peter Francis Casaretto, O.S.B. (1810-1878).

TO ALESSANDRO BARNABO   **55**

St. Vincent, July 4, 1858

Your Eminence: Shortly after I had written the Sacred Congregation for the Propagation of the Faith for instructions regarding the election of an abbot,[94] I received your letter dated March 17 concerning the religious woman Benedicta Riepp.[95] I do not think I can provide the required information better than by going to the root of the matter. Let me make it clear. I did not take control of the cloister, the profession, or the discipline of the nuns. Rather, let me ask whether or not as abbot and president of the Bavarian American Benedictine Congregation I hold jurisdiction over not only my brothers but also over the nuns of our Order in America as well? I always thought and acted as if I held jurisdiction over the women religious of our Order in this country, and after stating her doubts, even my adversary [Riepp] admits that I have this jurisdiction. Therefore, if I do not question the jurisdiction and if this formal lawsuit does not question it, then there is no reason for litigation between Sister Benedicta and me. I have done nothing about which she can complain. Moreover, she has not acted so imprudently that I have been forced to complain about her, until she brought these charges against me.

I regret that I have to write so much about this matter and to take up so much of Your Eminence's time and patience, but I can hardly clarify the matter in a few words. I therefore beg Your Eminence to hear what I have to say. From document number 13 of those I showed the Sacred Congregation for the Propagation of the Faith when I was in Rome, it is clear that I introduced Benedictine women into the Diocese of Pittsburgh with the permission of Bishop O'Connor.[96] Three of them came with dismissorial letters from the bishop of Eichstätt,[97] namely

---

[94] Wimmer wrote Cardinal Barnabo on April 18, 1858, for instructions for the procedure of electing a lifetime abbot of St. Vincent. See Oetgen, *An American Abbot*, pp. 179-83.

[95] Benedicta Riepp, O.S.B. (1825-1862), first superior of the Benedictine women in the United States. Wimmer's letter to Cardinal Barnabo is one of three important letters he wrote defending his actions in his controversy with Mother Benedicta Riepp. The others were to Father Joseph Ferdinand Müller, court chaplain to King Ludwig I (Pittsburgh, July 24, 1857), and Baron Ludwig von Oberkamp, business manager of the *Ludwig Missionsverein* (November 27, 1857). These letters are translated and printed in Incarnata Girgen, O.S.B., *Behind the Beginnings: Benedictine Women in America* (Saint Joseph, Minn.: St. Benedict's Convent, 1981), 86-99 and 113-21. For a discussion of the controversy, see Ephrem Hollerman, O.S.B., *The Reshaping of a Tradition: American Benedictine Women 1852-1881* (Saint Joseph, Minn.: Sisters of the Order of Saint Benedict, 1994), 91-220, and Oetgen, *An American Abbot*, 196-226.

[96] Michael O'Connor (1810-1872), bishop of Pittsburgh.

[97] George von Oettl, bishop of Eichstätt, Bavaria.

Benedicta Riepp, Walburga, and Maura.[98] The superior was Benedicta, a woman
26 years old. She had only a few more years in life than I at that time had in the
priesthood. This happened on July 15, 1852. I sent the three sisters to our priory
in St. Marys, about 115 miles from the abbey, where a colony of German Catholics lived. I wanted them to lay the foundation of a monastery there and apply
themselves to the education of girls. I gave them a house that had been built for
the School Sisters[99] and that the School Sisters had lived in for several years. It now
belonged to me, and my confreres lived in it. The School Sisters had left St. Marys
because of their poverty. At the same time the Redemptorists, who had lived and
worked there for several years, also left for the same reason–poverty. Indeed, St.
Marys is an extremely difficult place, situated in the middle of an immense forest.
The Redemptorists spent a great deal of fruitless time there and lost $3,000 as
well. Nevertheless, because of the misery of our German people and the constant
pleas of Bishop O'Connor, I accepted the place. With much expense, great labor,
and not a few trials, I improved the place so that now a religious institution for
men and another for women flourish there. Moreover, the colony is now, if not
the first, certainly the second most important place, politically and religiously, in
the Diocese of Erie (to which it belongs).

Thus, we turned our house over to the sisters. My brothers moved into two
other houses that I quickly obtained. Your Eminence can easily understand that
the house where the sisters lived was not a splendid structure. Nevertheless, it
was at the time, and still is, spacious enough and suitable for the sisters. It had a
proper cloister, a vestibule for receiving secular guests, a choir, a chapel, garden,
etc. Nothing was lacking that was required for the establishment of a monastery.
Neither priests nor brothers nor lay people entered it. Nor did the sisters have any
contact with our brothers. The truth is that in order to wash their clothes etc., the
sisters had to go outside the cloister, and in the summertime after supper, they
sometimes went for a walk outside the cloister (though this was not a practice that
I established). Nevertheless, they always acted in such a way that no one could
find fault with them. The house was not in the town but about a mile distant, as
it still is. There the sisters' confessor, the bishop (who visited the monastery only
once in six years), and I myself were received not in the vestibule but in a room a
little farther inside the convent. The vestibule was less appropriate because of the
frequent visits by lay people, but we always took proper precaution that two or
three sisters were present.

---

[98] Walburga Dietrich, O.S.B. (1804-1877) and Maura Flieger, O.S.B. (1822-1865).
[99] The Bavarian School Sisters of Notre Dame, who for a while had worked in St. Marys,
Pennsylvania.

Thus, while they did not observe the strictest *clausura*, nonetheless they did observe the same *clausura* as they were accustomed to in Germany, a clausura fully in accordance with monastic observance. The nuns did not have contact with anyone who did not belong to the monastery without the presence and permission of the superiors. From the beginning until now, they were not able to have a stricter *clausura*.

As I have said, I gave the sisters their house and recognized our Benedicta as head of the monastery for an indefinite period time, with the same title I had in those days, namely "superior." I wanted her to be mother to all the sisters of the Benedictine Order just as I was father to all the brothers. It was my intention that wherever the brothers erected a monastery, the sisters, if possible, would follow them and help them in the missions by establishing institutions for the education of girls. We therefore soon began to receive novices. They were all accepted by the superior, either directly or when I recommended one or the other to her. Thus, either the candidates themselves or I always sought permission from the superior for a novice to be admitted to the community. Whatever is said to the contrary is a pure lie. However, when after two years the number of novices and sisters in simple vows had grown to 30, I prohibited the superior from accepting any more without my permission. I was right in doing so, for the entire annual income of the sisters amounted to only $250 from the public school and $400 from the Mission Society in Munich, a total of around $650 dollars (or 650 Roman *scudi*), or about $21 dollars per year for each sister's food and clothing, which was obviously not enough. Therefore, the onus of making up the difference and of providing for them fell on me. I had to supply the bread, the meat, the clothes, etc. If I did not want to do so, or was unable to do so, they would have had to take on a debt that they could not repay. No one denied that I had both the right and the obligation to prevent the reception of more sisters than could be fed.

The superior was displeased that I prohibited new novices from being accepted, and if I am not mistaken, she took in eight or nine more postulants, one of whom I had specifically rejected. She convinced the sisters' confessor to give the habit to the one whom I had prohibited from receiving it. Thus the number of sisters grew to 45. I do not need to demonstrate that this manner of behavior is contrary not only to the canons but also to prudence and good sense.

This was the first difficulty that occurred between us. The second soon followed. Shortly afterwards, when I had returned from Rome, she decided to send a colony of her sisters to the city of Erie. She received a request to establish a convent of German nuns in a place where there were some German inhabitants. The nuns were invited to care for the girls of the parish. Sister Benedicta, without knowing any of the details of this important undertaking, immediately agreed to accept the invitation. I strongly opposed the move for various reasons. I knew, for example, that Sister Scholastica,[100] the mistress of novices and instructor of the junior sisters, would be forced to go to Erie as superior. Without a doubt, this would have resulted in a great loss to the monastery in St. Marys. However, it was in vain that I objected. Against my wishes and advice, she sent five sisters to Erie so precipitously that neither the pastor nor Bishop Young[101] were at home and the sisters had to spend three weeks in a private home. The bishop was on visitation and the pastor was collecting money for the new church, and neither expected the sisters! Moreover, Sister Benedicta sent Sister Scholastica with two novices and two sisters in simple profession, and again she persuaded the confessor (having ignored me) to approve her decision. The two novices had to teach in the public school. The sisters lived in a small house that the pastor had formerly occupied. The house was cloistered, but to get to the school they had to go outside the house and walk veiled through the public street, which was very improper.

Shortly after this, the third difficulty arose when I removed the prior, Father Benedict Haindl,[102] and put another in his place.[103] This made the superior very angry. Several reasons, however, compelled me to make this change. First, Father Benedict had often asked me to relieve him of the burden of being prior of the monks and confessor of the sisters. Second, I had recently sent the prior of St. Vincent[104] to Minnesota and did not have a better man to replace him at the abbey than Father Benedict. Third, the superior had completely subjected Father Benedict to her will. Father Benedict is a good and extremely mild-mannered man who is able to refuse nothing asked of him. Sister Benedicta, on the other hand, is very clever, forceful, ill-natured, and stubborn. She might not have learned rhetoric from Demosthenes, but she has the ability to persuade anyone she wants to do whatever she pleases. A thousand times a day she called Father Benedict to the convent. She did nothing without his advice, though at the same time she did everything she wanted to do. Thus, she persuaded him, as I noted above, to permit her to disobey my orders. Father Benedict became weary of this. The brothers began to complain. The parishioners began to gossip because often when they went to see him, Father Benedict was summoned away to the sisters' convent. He

---

[100] Scholastica Burkhardt, O.S.B. (1832-1881).

[101] The pastor of St. Mary's Church, Erie, Pennsylvania, was Father Francis J. Hartmann; the bishop of Erie, Josue Mary Young (1808-1866).

[102] Benedict Haindl, O.S.B. (1815-1887).

[103] The new prior in St. Marys was Rupert Seidenbusch, O.S.B. (1830-1895).

[104] The prior at St. Vincent was Demetrius di Marogna, O.S.B. (1803-1869).

was a captive and did not know how to resist. Let me not suggest that there was anything wicked going on. Father Benedict is an excellent religious, mature in years and above all suspicion. Nonetheless, it seemed to me necessary to remove him for the reasons mentioned above.

What a war that caused! What complaints! What tears and petitions! I remained unmoved, however, and did not change my decision. Benedict became prior at the abbey, and Father Rupert Seidenbusch became prior in St. Marys, where he also became confessor for the nuns. The bishop was informed of this change. Now, while Father Benedict had frequently gone to the convent to give advice to Sister Benedicta, Rupert was never called except to hear the sisters' confessions. Not only that! When the superior spoke of him in front of the sisters, she did so with contempt and irreverence, so that many humble souls in the convent were scandalized. In addition to the superior, there was another sister who did not like the new confessor. This was Sister Willibalda,[105] a solemnly professed nun who had come from Bavaria. These two sometimes failed to go to confession and consequently they often did not go to Holy Communion. Lest they have an excuse, I permitted them to go to confession to either of the other two priests I had in St. Marys, but even this changed nothing. This aversion (dare I say "hate"?) toward the confessor continued as long as these two nuns remained in St. Marys.

Thus, these two things–the establishment of the new convent in Erie and the aversion to the confessor–led to many grave problems in the convent in St. Marys. When Sister Scholastica, the mistress of novices and an excellent religious, was sent away, Sister Willibalda was put in charge of the novices. She excelled in music but not in the ascetic life, and she had no knowledge of holiness.

When I returned to America from Rome, I brought four other sisters with me. I knew nothing of these problems in St. Marys. The confessor of the nuns at Eichstätt, however, Father T. Schmidt, a Jesuit and a friend of mine from student days, commented to me about Sister Willibalda in this way: "If you want to know what she is like, imagine a very clever student skilled in the art of deception and there you have our Willibalda." This person was now mistress of novices. In a short time she was running the house and began to rule over the superior, whom she led by the nose. She instructed the novices and junior sisters neither in music nor in ascetics nor in zeal. They passed their time doing useless things. Everyone surrendered herself to these useless things. Frequently they complained to me of this situation in the confessional (for I was their extraordinary confessor), but no one dared complain openly. Gently and moderately at first, then candidly and firmly

---

[105] Willibalda Scherbauer, O.S.B. (1828-1914).

later on, I pointed out to the superior and the mistress of novices, both inside and outside the confessional, what seemed to be happening in the convent. However, it was in vain. Day by day matters became worse. They took the two little girls of an Irish woman into the convent, one about three years old, the other hardly weaned from her mother's breast. There was no obligation, no need, no reason to do this. These infants disturbed the whole house with their crying day and night. Our Benedicta and Willibalda played with them (especially the smallest one). They kept them in their cells. They brought them into the choir. Anyone who spoke against this behavior, complaining that it disturbed the silence, devotion, and meditation of the monastery, did so in vain.

Soon afterwards, factions sprang up in the convent. Some of the professed sisters were no longer able to restrain themselves. They made it known to the superior that they could not abide the state of affairs any longer. They were upset that some spoke of the confessor and of me contemptuously. Now the hatred of the superior and Sister Willibalda turned against these sisters, and they began to persecute them. The result was that two of them, Emmerana and Walburga,[106] considered returning to their home monastery at Eichstätt. Others who were more timid groaned bitterly under the yoke of oppression. Great dissatisfaction reigned in the monastery.

I did not know what to do. Then it occurred to me that it might be a good idea if some of the junior sisters, or rather all who according to the *Rule* were prepared to make final profession, should be admitted to solemn vows in order (1) that there might be more sisters in the chapter to consider important matters; (2) that among them there might be those, more advanced in the spiritual life, in age, and in knowledge, who could take on the cloistral offices that were not filled; and (3) that the whole convent might be better organized, chapters could be held, etc. Thus, the junior sisters could see what should be done in practice if later they were transferred elsewhere. I also wanted the superior to act according to the *Rule* and not to govern the monastery arbitrarily.

Therefore, I urged that the junior sisters be allowed to make solemn profession, especially since they all desired it. The superior agreed and called a chapter. From those who were ready for profession, she admitted only five favored choir sisters to solemn vows. She rejected all the English-speaking sisters and the others whom she suspected (as she said) of being friendly to me. Fine. These five favorites pronounced solemn vows on March 21, 1857, but I knew well that with them I would not be able to achieve my goals in this matter. They were good nuns

---

[106] Emmerana Bader, O.S.B. (1829-1902), and Walburga Dietrich, O.S.B. (1804-1877).

but very timid, and they would certainly never dare to say a word against the superior.

Until then I had always wanted St. Marys to become the motherhouse for all future monasteries of the nuns of our Order. Now, however, I doubted that anything good could come from there, and when I called together my confreres in chapter, we all thought it best to establish a monastery of nuns elsewhere, independent of St. Marys, and afterwards transfer the novitiate there. Perhaps I erred in this. Perhaps it would have been better had I followed the advice of the confessor, Father Rupert, and deposed the superior and then either by election or by my own authority put another in her place. However, I could not have done this without great troubles and serious dissension. I could not have done this even though Sister Benedicta had been named superior not by the bishop but by myself, and she had already held the office for five years. No, I could not have removed her without open war and the use of force. A commotion could not have been avoided unless I had expelled her from the monastery. I therefore preferred to take another route. I asked for some sisters to go to our mission in Minnesota. Sister Benedicta agreed. I asked for those who had not been allowed to make solemn profession. Some she permitted to go, others she refused. Then I named Sister Emmerana superior of the group, but Sister Benedicta refused to allow this. When I insisted that she be superior because she was one of the senior sisters, because she was discontent at St. Marys and was considering, as I mentioned above, returning to Bavaria, and because she was a good, hardworking sister whom I did not wish to lose, Sister Benedicta continually and impertinently resisted (even though she could in no way restrain her since Sister Emmerana had pronounced solemn vows in Bavaria and had not been dispensed from her vow of stability). I then demanded that a chapter be held and that all the sisters, both solemnly and simply professed, be summoned to it in order to decide the matter by majority vote. She called the chapter, though unwillingly, and Father Rupert and I went to it in the refectory. Here I explained the matter to the sisters and told them to consider it carefully. Then Father Rupert and I left. When I returned again to the monastery after supper, the superior informed me that all the sisters had cast their votes in my favor. Therefore, after a few days I left St. Marys with six sisters and accompanied them to our priory in Indiana where they stayed in a suitable house under the care of Father Ulric,[107] who was pastor in Indiana. There they began to prepare for the journey to Minnesota.

I had decided to send the six sisters to Minnesota not only for the reasons I stated above, but for another reason as well. It was very difficult to provide so many

---

[107] Ulric Spöttl, O.S.B. (1831-1859).

sisters in St. Marys with food and clothing because the place was very poor. At the same time, only a few sisters were needed in St. Marys, and there were many there who had little to do, among whom were some rebels who were waging war in the community. Certainly, under these circumstances I should have been able to demand that some of them be transferred, and since I had to provide food for them, it was only appropriate that I should have a say in naming their superior.

I did nothing by force or against the *Holy Rule* or sacred canons. Nor did I lead anyone away who did not want to go. Rather, voluntarily and with joy they left the monastery in order to exchange it for another. Nor did I lead any more away than were necessary, and I left more in the monastery in St. Marys than were needed there. The ones I took away, moreover, left with the consent of the whole convent. Whatever the superior has written to the contrary is either a distortion of the facts or an undiluted lie.

When these six sisters were sent not to Minnesota but to our new priory in Newark, where both the parishioners and Bishop Bayley[108] desired them, Sister Benedicta humbly and appropriately wrote to me and asked that I give her permission to go to Minnesota with ten or thirteen sisters. She said that on account of the humiliation she had experienced in St. Marys, she could achieve nothing there, but that with God's help she would begin anew in Minnesota and do well there and try to satisfy me in all things. I believed that she wrote sincerely and from the heart, and although the tenor of her letter had something of the flavor of the secret pride that was characteristic of her, nonetheless I did not want to refuse her since in another place and with some sisters who were attached to her she might indeed be successful. Therefore I gave her permission to go to Minnesota, on condition, however, that she not take ten or thirteen sisters with her but only six or seven because any more than that would have a hard time finding food in a new territory that the wild Indians had only recently left. In addition, I told her to remain in St. Marys until my confreres in Minnesota had informed me that they had made all the necessary arrangements for the arrival of the sisters and until I had received permission from the administrator of the diocese (Bishop Cretin[109] having recently died).

Her letter did not say what she truly felt. She hid the evil in her heart, which afterwards I learned from those in whom she had confided. Through my letter, which I wrote carefully, she clearly understood that she had lost the authority she presumed over all future monasteries and that she would never be raised to the abbatial dignity in St. Marys as she had hoped. She probably feared that I would put

---

[108] James Roosevelt Bayley (1814-1877), bishop of Newark.
[109] Joseph Cretin (1799-1857).

another in her place, or at least that I would force her to observe the *Rule* much more strictly than she had observed it over the previous two years. Therefore, she was determined to destroy the monastery that she was no longer to govern and in which she could no longer live in comfort as she wished. She tried therefore to take with her not just ten or thirteen, but as many sisters as possible. She wanted to take with her all the outstanding members of the community, the talented ones and those who because of their erudition could take charge of public schools. Those who were weak or sick or useless for teaching she would leave behind. Even more than before, she spoke against Father Rupert and myself.

Then, in order to raise money, she held a fair at which, as is the custom in these parts, the sisters sold various items, clothes, embroidery, etc. that they had made by hand. They even sold the musical instruments that they could not easily carry with them to Minnesota. The poor sisters had to work day and night, even on Sundays. More than ever before the choir and the religious exercises were neglected. There was no daily order. Since they often worked until after midnight, they did not get up until after six in the morning, etc., etc. They still did not have permission from the diocesan administrator in Minnesota, but they expected that permission to come at any time and meanwhile made certain that they would be ready so that when the time came they could quickly leave St. Marys. For three continuous months, they had neither choir nor the common table. Everything that constitutes a monastery was neglected, which caused great pain and sorrow for all the good sisters.

Father Rupert made these things known to me by repeated letters. He urged that I go to St. Marys at once and stop these things from happening. I therefore went again on June 5, the day of the fair. When I arrived, I discovered that the refectory and the chapel (with the Blessed Sacrament removed) had been turned into exhibition halls where diverse items were on display for public sale and where raffles were being held. The sisters were mixing with lay people in order to show what they had for sale and to guard the items. In a classroom outside the cloister, candies and cakes were being sold not for the sisters but by them. Thus, they were compelled to wander out among the lay people. To be sure, necessity requires that rules sometimes be broken, but this was not a necessity, and even if it were, there were postulants and candidates present who could have been negatively influenced by all these things. In addition, there were secular women in the town who could have taken on this business on behalf of the sisters. Nevertheless, as much as all this displeased me, it had already begun and I was hardly in a position to stop it without giving great scandal. I therefore said nothing but rather tried to find some advantage in the situation. So I joined the crowd, and when the occasion presented itself, I spoke with some of the sisters and admonished them not to leave the monastery so rashly and incautiously, not to follow the mother superior without my previous permission. I told them that a great deal of suffering and misery would befall them if so many of them went to Minnesota. I told them too that by going to Minnesota they would gravely harm their own monastery in St. Marys, especially if they left without a valid reason and without permission.

However, I had hardly returned to my abbey from St. Marys when I received a letter from Father Rupert saying that Benedicta, with 13 sisters, $800, and nearly all the valuables of the convent, had left the monastery under conditions that raised the greatest din and gave the greatest scandal to the faithful. Only 25¢ remained in the treasury, together with $400 in debts. She did not even appoint a superior to take her place. Thus, she left everything in the greatest confusion. I returned speedily to St. Marys to straighten things out.

My patience was nearly exhausted, for I had been compelled five times in the preceding six months to make the long journey to St. Marys on account of this malicious woman. I usually had to spend 12 or 14 days at a time there. Now I had to go again. When I arrived, I appointed Sister Theresa as temporary prioress and made Sister Walburga, the senior nun, subprioress, and Sister Edwarda novice mistress.[110] I then called a chapter and told the sisters what had to be done. I restored mutual trust among them after listening to their complaints. I again introduced the daily order, with choir and regular spiritual exercises, and I arranged things so that the convent would be well ordered. Father Rupert was again received by the sisters to advise them, to have authority over them, and to give them instructions. Thus after much tribulation, joy, peace, concord, and regular discipline returned to the monastery, and we achieved good where diabolical cunning had brought bad. This happened on July 6, 1857.

I did not know where Benedicta and her companions had gone. I thought that she might be in Erie, so I sent a letter to the bishop of Erie[111] making him aware of what had occurred and asking him to prevent more than six sisters from going to Minnesota. The danger was that they would perish from hunger and hardships there, because for two successive years the locusts had eaten all the grain in Minnesota. I also knew that if 13 sisters traveled to Minnesota together, all the money they had would be exhausted on the trip. My brothers in Minnesota lived in the greatest poverty and would be able to do nothing for the nuns. They were all living in a new colony which because of the devastations of the locusts

---

[110] Theresa Vogel, O.S.B. (1834-1886), Walburga Dietrich, O.S.B. (1804-1877), and Edwarda Redant, O.S.B. (1832-1859).

[111] Josue Mary Young (1808-1866).

was poverty-stricken. The bishop of Erie agreed and kept five of the sisters who were still in Erie from leaving. Six had already gone to Minnesota, and Benedicta herself, together with a companion, had returned to Bavaria on the pretext, as I learned from the bishop, of collecting money to establish a girl's academy in Erie! What hypocrisy! What lies! What illusions! Under this pretext, she won over the kind-hearted bishop, who knew nothing of what had gone on before. Benedicta thus received a letter of recommendation from him with which she hoped to raise money, not for the proposed academy in Erie but for a monastery in Minnesota, where Father Demetrius and Father Benedict were. She thought she could easily win them over, for in Erie she feared the pastor, Father Hartmann, who was the sisters' confessor. A strong and energetic man, he would not have put up with the scandalous behavior of these women. She did not complain of me to the bishop, but she did tell him that she wanted to go to the Holy See to learn the limits of my jurisdiction.

Your Eminence, I am a person who cannot remain angry with anyone for long, and I have never been vindictive. Therefore, as long as Benedicta sinned only against my authority, I easily ignored it, and even now, I ignore the fact that she is spreading lies against me in Bavaria and before the Holy See. She has cost me much time–not just days, but weeks and months–and much money, but I have borne it all with a calm soul and never spoke to her harshly or bitterly. Much less did I do so in front of her sisters. When her sisters came to me to complain about her (and almost all of them did so), I urged them to be patient and to pray that God, the guardian angels, and St. Benedict not permit the monastery to be ruined. I frequently excused her on account of her weak health. However, when I saw and heard that she was prepared to destroy the monastery in St. Marys, which I had sweated over, which I had spent so much money on, which I had watched over with such care, which was so necessary and useful for the Catholics of the colony, which was an ornament for the whole diocese, and which would perhaps become of great importance for all of America, I was not able to restrain myself from doing everything in my power to thwart her and to proceed against her.

I therefore wrote the archbishop of Munich[112] and the bishop of Eichstätt,[113] informing them of what had occurred and of what I had done and asking them not to give her money because out of vengefulness she was attempting to suppress the existing monastery and because she was not a suitable person to establish anything. Because of my letters, she received nothing, not even money so that she

---

[112] Archbishop Gregory Scherr, O.S.B. (1804-1877).
[113] George von Oettl.

and her companion could return to America, unless the prioress in Eichstätt[114] gave it to her so that she would not be compelled to keep her any longer at St. Walburga's. She raised serious complaints against me to the archbishop, who saw through her. Moreover, the bishop of Eichstätt, who originally sent her to me, refused to admit her into his presence and did not allow her to stay in her native monastery. Even the sisters sent to America from Eichstätt repudiated her of their own accord in a long and extensive report. The bishop of Eichstätt then sent her complaints to the Holy See while at the same time sending an order to the prioress in St. Marys that she should obey me and seek my advice on all matters.

The complaint she raised against me to the archbishop of Munich was sent to me. If I were to judge it kindly and in the spirit of charity, I would say that it contains many imaginary things that she fabricated from her suspicions and from the suggestions made to her by the Devil and by Sister Willibalda. Because of this, I should easily excuse her. In addition, however, the complaint contains many transparent lies, malicious insinuations, and distortions of fact that admit of no excuse. It is sufficient for me to declare solemnly that the complaint contains no truth whatever, and this I am able to prove, if required, with witnesses and facts. I do not know what accusations she sent to Rome, although the articles to which I must respond appear to be the same ones she sent to the archbishop of Munich.

It is clear that if the Holy Apostolic See wishes to investigate the full truth of this matter, or if it does not have confidence in my testimony, it will be necessary to order Bishop Young of Erie to conduct a more thorough inquiry into it. St. Marys is situated in his diocese, and several nuns remain there. Others live in Erie, in Newark, and in Minnesota. It is not appropriate for me to conduct the investigation myself, but I would indeed demand it if my own testimony is found wanting since I know that among the sisters, clerics, and lay people who have knowledge of these matters there are none who would not thoroughly vindicate me for acting as I have done.

As I noted at the beginning of this report, this affair is a question not so much of deeds but of law and jurisdiction. This religious woman wished to shake off the yoke under which she thought herself to be because, as I said, I sometimes imposed my authority when she did not do what she should have done or when she did what she should not have done. She would not have made her complaints unless she had hoped to resist me. Because she doubted whether she could resist me legally, or whether she could acquire her independence, she went to the Holy See, hoping that with luck she would be able to obtain a favorable decision. Indeed, she hid behind the bishop of Erie, and if she could have managed it, she would

---

[114] Edwarda Schnitzer, O.S.B. (1815-1902).

have brought about a war between him and me over the question of jurisdiction. This question of jurisdiction, Your Eminence, must be resolved lest similar or graver scandals result, but I will raise this question in a separate petition.

There are now other things I must raise in order to resolve the matter at hand. I will first proceed with my narrative, and then I will respond to those articles that I have not already dealt with in this report.

After Sister Benedicta's departure for Bavaria, the sisters left in Erie did not know which of them was superior. Sister Scholastica had been superior in Erie until then. Benedicta, however, wanted Scholastica to go to Minnesota and Sister Alexia[115] to be superior in Erie. However, when the bishop, at my request, refused to allow more sisters to go to Erie, the question arose, who would be superior? They therefore wrote to me asking that I visit them and, as I had done in St. Marys, put things in order among them. I did not want to accept the invitation because I was worried that the bishop would be annoyed and because I had never formally exercised any jurisdiction over the sisters in Erie. I therefore asked whether they wanted to be under my authority. If not, I would not take them into my care. If on the other hand they acknowledged my authority, I would go to Erie and organize them according to the *Holy Rule*. I then asked directly what they would do if Sister Benedicta returned again, whether they would follow her or follow me. When they declared that they would always regard me as their highest authority in this country, and not Benedicta, I visited them in September. I made Sister Scholastica prioress for three years and named Sister Alexia subprioress. I also made inquiries into the events that had transpired.

I arranged for them to live in a small house with a small garden, though they had title to neither the house nor the garden. This house was situated on the left side of the church. The school was on the right side of the church. They were therefore compelled to walk through the public street whenever they went to the school or the church. They had their choir in the oratory inside the cloister, however. Another building in which there was a small Catholic public school was located in front of the church. It seemed completely satisfactory for them, and I arranged to get this small building at little cost. Surrounding the building is a spacious field where the sisters can have a lovely garden and where they can take walks without being seen. I spoke with the bishop, who has always been very friendly toward me, and with the pastor, who is the nuns' confessor, and arranged for the building and surrounding land to be obtained in trust for the sisters in such a manner that they will have the permanent right to use the property. The building will become a monastery and will have a school for girls and a chapel. The sisters will be able to

---

[115] Alexia Lechner, O.S.B. (1827-1891).

go directly to the church without having to walk through the public street. Everyone agreed most willingly to these arrangements. The bishop promised money to help adapt the building to the sisters' needs. I established for the sisters the same daily order that I had prescribed at St. Marys, a daily order fully consonant with our statutes. I wanted both the men and women of our Order to have the same statutes, with appropriate changes being made because of differences between the sexes. All the sisters, no less than the pastor and the bishop, were happy with these arrangements. They rejoiced that their status was no longer uncertain and particularly that the discipline of the *Rule* had been established.

Even the sisters in Minnesota wrote me a very humble letter asking that I come to help them because they were virtually destitute. I did not consider them as daughters belonging to the family. Several of them wrote me individual letters asking forgiveness, confirming their faithfulness, and imploring my help. The fiery Sister Willibalda was still there. She was the woman who shared with Benedicta the blame for all their tribulations. Like the prodigal son, poverty and misery had reduced them to reason. Actually, they were all innocents, more deceived than perverse.

Therefore, I went to Minnesota, not chiefly because of the sisters but rather because of the missions that we have in St. Paul, in Shakopee, in St. Cloud, etc. I saw the sisters, and the first thing I did was to harshly rebuke Sister Willibalda in front of the whole community of sisters as much for her maliciousness, frivolity, and perversity as for her wickedness. She tried to put all the blame on Benedicta or some other sisters. Nonetheless, with many tears (perhaps crocodile tears) she asked for forgiveness and I granted it.

Not only because the locusts had brought great misery to this province, but also because money was scarce and the people insecure, which made it difficult to borrow money, my confreres living in Minnesota were able to do almost nothing for the sisters. As I noted above, nothing had been prepared for them before they arrived, and the diocesan administrator and my prior were astonished when suddenly six nuns with a ten-year-old orphan girl (who had been instructed in music and whom they had brought from St. Marys without telling her relatives) showed up saying that I had sent them. They placed them in a house for $250 a year that had no wall and was not separated from the neighboring houses. The church was outside the town and very distant. Likewise the school, which was above the church. Only a few girls went to the school. The greater part of their money had been expended on the journey. The most valuable part of their baggage had been lost. They were without food, without protection. Like my brothers, they had almost nothing to eat, only apples, a little bread, and coffee without milk. I pitied them, but I was able to do very little for them. I instructed my confreres whenever they could to bring them wood for the stove etc. (because the winter is harsh and long in Minnesota) and to urge the more prosperous residents to help them in every way possible. They had divine office and they observed the *clausura*. (That is, they permitted no one to enter their house, and they remained separated from the townspeople, with the exception of the girls who were in the school or whom they instructed in music in the house.) The people held them in great honor, Catholics and non-Catholics alike. As far as I could see, there was peace and harmony among them. Because they did not have a superior, I proposed Willibalda to them as prioress. I thought it better for her to be prioress than no one. No one else was suitable for the position. All the other sisters were much younger than Willibalda and inferior to her in knowledge and ability. I told her privately that she had the ability and knowledge to be prioress and that it would not be my fault if matters did not turn out well because of her immaturity and negligence. Until now I have heard no complaints about her. Meanwhile the parishioners have built a house for the sisters next to the church. The sisters overcame great difficulties and did very well in the school. I would have been able to do more for them this year if I had wanted, but I preferred that they stand on their own.

In the month of January 1858, I again went to Erie, invited by the nuns, in order to admit them to solemn profession, which according to the *Rule* they had the right to receive. Since they did not have a chapel, the profession ceremony had to take place in the parish church. I invited the bishop to preside, while I assisted, and he accepted. In the profession document, my name was placed after the bishop's. Since because of the vow of stability our nuns had to have their own property, I would not have admitted them to solemn profession unless the bishop had promised to give them the old church, with the adjacent property and land (which was very suitable and valuable) as soon as the experts had drawn up the necessary documents.

Now Erie has its own priory. There is a second in Newark, where a prioress has been named for a three-year term and where I will provide the sisters with a house. A third is in St. Marys, and a fourth, similarly, will develop in Minnesota, provided that the sisters there manage their affairs properly. If not, I will send them back to Erie or St. Marys. Thus from one monastery four have been established. Thanks to divine providence, the efforts of the Devil to ruin and destroy all these monasteries have been in vain. Had I not defended the work tirelessly and with a firm hand and had I not resisted pride and disobedience, without a doubt it would all have collapsed and been ruined in a conspicuous scandal.

This then is a brief history of the introduction of the nuns of the Order of St. Benedict in America. Now I shall say a little about article four, concerning economic affairs. In St. Marys, as I said above, I gave the sisters a temporary house, which belonged to them. The temporary house was spacious enough. Other structures were close by, including a new schoolhouse. The superior enlarged it and expanded the kitchen so that 40 sisters, with some postulants and 18 pupils, could live there comfortably. Since they had an income of only $250 from the school and $400 from Bavaria, arrangements had to be made so that they would not have to buy milk, wheat, vegetables, and meat. Therefore, my brothers began to work their fields for them so that they would have vegetables. My brothers likewise planted grass and hay for them to provide for five cows (or as many as they wanted to have). Moreover, they cut wood and dug coal for the sisters and carried it to the monastery. From the gristmill, they provided all the flour needed for bread and for the table. The superior gave money for the grain when she had it, but everything the sisters needed was provided for them whether or not they had money to pay for it. In return, the sisters washed clothes for the fathers and brothers. They made new clothes and repaired old ones, and they prepared bread in their bakery for the brothers and for themselves. Thus, the sisters and my confreres helped one another, but they were not engaged in trade with one another. If anything was given or received, it was given and received without recompense.

Last year, the sisters hired a married workman who did nearly all the heavy work for them. I have reason to believe that he did many bad things. When he heard anything the brothers might have imprudently said, he reported it to the superior, which caused her pride to be offended. The sisters complained bitterly that the superior spent hours talking to this man.

Thus, it was possible for 40 sisters to find everything necessary for their community, even though the regular income of the monastery could provide for only three or four sisters. Every year I had to make great sacrifices, which I did willingly for the common good of our Order. Because it was hardly possible for me to build a new monastery for the sisters from my own resources, I received, with the help of a friend, 8,000 florins from King Ludwig[116] to do so. I received the money, not the sisters, but I received it for the purpose of building a monastery for them. At the time I received this money (1853), there were only a few sisters. The house they occupied was spacious enough and suitable in every way. It was not necessary to build another house for them at once, nor was the place in which I intended to build it available. It was still a dense forest. In addition, for 8,000 florins, or 3,000

---

[116] King Ludwig I of Bavaria (1786-1868). The friend Wimmer refers to was Father Joseph Ferdinand Müller (1803-1864), business manager of the *Ludwig Missionsverein.*

dollars, I could not have built a bigger house for them than the one they already had. Besides, I had to buy another house for my confreres, which cost me $1,400, because we had given our house to the sisters. The two houses into which the brothers had moved after the arrival of the sisters were too far from each other and otherwise unsuitable. In addition, in that same year, I began to build a gristmill, which was necessary not only for both monasteries but also and especially for the whole colony, and before doing anything else I had to complete it. After we had expended $5,000 and a year of labor on the gristmill, an arsonist burned it down. We therefore had to devote another year of work and another $5,000 to rebuild the mill. The result was that I was unable to build a monastery for the sisters at that time. Then, when the parish church was consumed by fire, the parish Mass on Sundays and feast days had to be celebrated in the house where the sisters now lived. It was necessary because of the great inconvenience this caused the sisters to build a new church. I planned to build the church in the middle of the town, in a place that belonged to me that was still covered with trees. Then I wanted to build the monastery for the nuns next to the church so that they could easily go to Mass and have frequent access to the Blessed Sacrament for their spiritual comfort. For two years, the parishioners, together with my brothers, expended all their strength to construct a solid, spacious, and beautiful church (134 feet long, 60 feet wide). During this time, it was impossible to build a monastery. Seven acres of forest belonging to me around the church still must be converted to fields by cutting down and burning the trees. This must be done before a monastery and garden can be prepared for the sisters. It is shameless for Sister Benedicta to present these matters as she has done and to imply that I would not give the sisters the money sent by the king. I myself have already informed the most pious king about this matter, and he has not objected to what I have done. The money was given not just for the sisters but also for me so that I might be able to build the monastery for the sisters more easily. I have already spent much more than 8,000 florins on the sisters. I can prove that easily, and that should suffice as a response to this article.

Concerning solemn profession, let me say the following. It is well to remember that there are many things required for solemn profession, according to the canons and the decrees of the Holy See, which in our little monasteries are not yet, strictly speaking, present, and if the rigor of these decrees and canons must be applied, we would hardly be able to have solemn profession in this generation. I certainly do not question the wisdom of the Church's laws or the Church's authority, though some do. I take the Church's authority very seriously. At the same time, however, I think that if the spirit of the law of the Church is kept constantly in mind, and if moral certitude exists that those things which the canons prescribe and which vows require are strictly observed, everything is sufficient as far as the Church's authority is concerned even if it is impossible to fulfill the letter of law. The Holy See appears to agree with me in this since it allows many things in America that it seldom permits in Europe, and this is certainly a wise and correct approach, promoting the advantage and success of the Catholic faith.

I therefore summoned the Benedictine nuns from Bavaria and did so with the approval of the bishop. I assigned a place to them. I gave them a temporary house. I appointed a superior for them. They instituted monastic life according to the *Holy Rule*. They were found pleasing to others, and novices came who, when they finished the novitiate, took simple vows. Almost all these novices were poor. With hard work and at great expense they were instructed for many years in literature, languages, music, and embroidery until such time as they were capable of instructing others in these same arts. They knew from the *Holy Rule* that Benedictines take solemn vows. They desired to do what the *Rule* permits. They lived a holy life. They found peace in the Order, which they had sought in vain in the world. They tasted and they saw how sweet God is. Why wonder if under these circumstances they desired to consecrate, devote, and surrender themselves entirely and perpetually to God? Why wonder if they wanted to possess Him fully? On the other hand, the superiors wanted to have something more certain than changeable vows to depend on so that they might retain and call their own those whom they loved so much, whom they educated with such care, whom they had acquired for their community with so much labor and expense. Until then the sisters could leave as easily as they entered. Nearly all young girls in this part of the world, unless they have some serious deformity, can easily find husbands if they want to marry. If the sisters did not want to marry when they were in the world, and after two or three or four years in the monastery if they still did not want to marry, and if they were no longer of an age when young girls here normally get married, why deny them solemn vows? When water is present, why deny baptism? What benefit is there in making them wait until they are 35 years old, or on the point of death, as one of the bishops at the Baltimore Council proposed? Surely, at the point of death, when they hardly know the difference between men and women, they are not thinking any more about marriage, but certainly virginity made secure at last at the moment of death is a pitiable thing. I have always believed that Our Lord Jesus Christ gave the evangelical counsels not to the moribund and decrepit but above all and especially to the young. Let him follow these counsels who is able to do so.

Impressed by these arguments, Your Eminence, I admitted the sisters to solemn vows. I did not compel them to take these vows. I did not force them. I admitted those whom I knew well to be virgins, those who were of such character as made me confident that there would be no danger of their leaving the monastery to marry. With regard to their material security, I knew that they would receive everything necessary by working in the school. With regard to the *clausura*, I knew that if there was a problem because of local conditions, my brothers and I would be zealous in arranging all things according to the *Rule*.

If the superior had not given me such trouble over the past two years, if she had not caused so much uncertainty for so long, I would already have sought from the Holy See formal confirmation of the monastery in St. Marys. When I was in Rome, I began the process. Later, however, I was forced to postpone it until a more opportune time. These then are in general the things that I must report to you concerning this troublesome matter. I do it in good faith. I have before my eyes nothing other than the honor of God, the glory of our Order, and the advance of Christianity. Nonetheless, it would not surprise me to learn that I have done badly or that I have erred. I willingly submit all these matters to the judgment of the Holy Apostolic See.

Sister Benedicta recently returned to America after an eleven-month absence and is now living in the monastery in Erie. From there she recently wrote me a thankful and prayerful letter. Concerning her, I should note the following:

(1) She is no longer superior of the monastery in St. Marys. She was in charge there because I made her superior, but she left that monastery voluntarily, having asked for and obtained permission from me, because, as I said, she was able to do no further good there and because she wanted to establish a monastery in Minnesota, a region 1,300 miles from St. Marys. She is therefore no longer superior in St. Marys. She wrote a lie when she wrote that she was superior in St. Marys. By legitimate authority, as I believe, and because of necessity, I established Theresa Vogel as prioress in St. Marys for a three-year term according to the *Rule*. She is a sister who recently made solemn profession, a prudent virgin, pious and well-educated, who until now has governed the monastery well.

(2) Moreover, Benedicta cannot be superior in Erie because when she sent Sister Scholastica there, Sister Scholastica was named superior. Later five others, who were kept back from the expedition to Minnesota, joined Erie. Thus, ten sisters, some simply professed, some solemnly professed, are there. Because of necessity, and at the unanimous request of the sisters, I established Sister Scholastica as prioress there for a three-year term. She has already received four novices, and she manages affairs there in an excellent manner. Thus

Benedicta can hardly become superior in Erie until Scholastica's three-year term ends.

(3) The place to which she now belongs is St. Cloud in Minnesota. She wanted to go there. She sent her sisters there. Therefore, she should go there! However, even there Sister Willibalda is now prioress for a three-year term. Since she is neither in age nor in knowledge inferior to Benedicta, and in terms of her ability to govern she is certainly no less capable, it will cause no injury to Benedicta if she subordinates herself to Sister Willibalda. It seems to be little enough if after such grave calumnies and offenses committed against me I seek this single satisfaction–that she do what she wanted to do in the first place: that is, go to Minnesota and learn to obey. Her companion on the journey to Europe, Sister Augustina,[117] who pronounced simple vows for a year, has not renewed them. She is a virgin of good character who got involved with this affair not through perversity but through ignorance. If she wishes to renew her vows, it is fine with me. She can join one of the communities in Newark, St. Marys, or Erie, if any wishes to accept her.

Bishop Young of Erie does not want to have anything to do with this matter until he receives instructions from the Holy See. I learned this in a letter I received yesterday from Sister Scholastica. Father Hartmann, the pastor in Erie, sent me a letter when Benedicta suddenly reappeared saying that he would strenuously defend Scholastica in the office of prioress. As I noted above, Benedicta sent me a conciliatory letter and asked that I see her in Erie, which I certainly will not do unless I have to go there to eject her in the event that she causes any further disturbances. If the bishop gives her protection, I will immediately send my sisters in Erie back to St. Marys because they do not want to live with her. Nevertheless, I am certain that the excellent bishop, because of his friendship toward me, will not do this. Since it is not possible to receive instructions from the Holy See quickly, I consider it necessary that I work diligently to prevent scandal. Because everything is peaceful, I do not want this litigious woman to foment and incite new discord among the sisters. From a letter that the prioress in Eichstätt sent me, saying that she had given 600 florins to Benedicta and her companion in order that they could return to the monastery in St. Marys, I infer that perhaps Benedicta herself, or perhaps her former superior, wanted her to return to the monastery in St. Marys. However, in no way will I allow her to go there, not even in the role of subordinate, because all the sisters are opposed to her.

It is clear that new discord and divisions will occur unless Sister Benedicta goes to Minnesota. For five years, she was superior, and for three of these years she did

---

[117] Sister Augustina Short, O.S.B. (1834-1902).

well enough, but for the last two years, she did badly. For no just cause, she made a very long journey to Bavaria, although she was bound to a strict *clausura*, and she left everything in the greatest confusion. She expended a great sum of money on her journey, leaving her monastery in great poverty and deep in debt. She expressly declared by word and deed that it was her intention to destroy the monastery she had governed for five years. Would it not be rash to put this woman in charge of that same monastery once again? Would it not be a mistake to permit her to be restored to an office that in every way she has abused and that she has voluntarily resigned? If she wished to know the limits of her authority and of mine, what stopped her from seeking a decision from the Holy See? If she wanted to go to Germany, why did she not say so and simply do it? Why did she proceed with so much noise, with so many lies?

But why say more? I have already tried Your Eminence's patience enough. I do not want to anticipate the instructions of the Holy See. I have already explained the whole matter in a letter to Abbot Angelo Pescetelli,[118] procurator of our Order, because I wanted to have his opinion. I did not want to appeal to the Holy Apostolic See, partly because my authority was sufficient to control this rebellious woman, partly because I did not want to bother the Sacred Congregation with these matters, and, finally, partly because it seemed necessary to give the monasteries of our nuns more time to develop before seeking definitive rules for them. The procurator approved everything I had done and did not hesitate to say, "The rebellion of Mother Riepp has to be regarded as the work of the Devil."

I have obeyed the command of Your Eminence and have clearly and distinctly presented here all the facts, from which my views concerning monastic affairs can be easily seen. It has always been my goal to do as our Holy Father Benedict exhorts us and to ensure that everyone follows the *Rule* in all matters. My intention has been to establish, to implement, and to fulfill all things according to the *Rule* inasmuch as my strength and my opportunities permitted. I am fully conscious of the fact that I must seek and strive for the common good and not pursue merely my own honor and my own will. Perhaps I acted with a certain presumption with respect to solemn profession, but I did not do wrong intentionally. As for the rest, I do not hesitate to assert that, except for a brief period, the spirit of religion has flourished in St. Marys, in Erie, and in Newark, and it will continue to flourish in these monasteries to the greater honor and glory of God.

---

[118] Angelo Pescetelli, O.S.B. (1809-1885).

Recommending myself most humbly to the gracious benevolence of Your Eminence, I am, with profound reverence and submission, Your Eminence's humble servant, Boniface Wimmer, Abbot O.S.B.

Lat   oAPF   cASVA   transJO

TO ANGELO PESCETELLI   56

St. Vincent, September 18, 1858

Very Reverend Procurator General, Dear Friend: Only recently did I receive the letters of July 25 and August 20 that you so kindly sent me, and I want to respond quickly. Today we held the election for a lifetime abbot. Since nothing is more bothersome than an uncertain and suspended status, I called a general chapter, which preceded the election. That all might proceed in the spirit of charity and according to the will of God, I invited Father Francis Xavier Weninger,[119] a German Jesuit who is expert in giving missions and conducting spiritual exercise, an extraordinarily saintly man, to give us a spiritual retreat. He came on September 11 and gave the retreat for four hours each afternoon through September 17. We were all highly edified.

When the retreat was over, and after I had read them your latest letter, all the capitulars addressed me in one voice, urging me to allow the election to proceed. The arguments against holding the election were: (1) that I had received no response from Rome concerning my inquiries; (2) that there was no one present who could preside at the election; (3) that some of the capitulars who lived far away and who had been invited to the election had not come and had not nominated procurators. On the other hand, the arguments in favor of an immediate election were: (1) that the capitulars present numbered 29 priests and five subdeacons; (2) that among those present were all the priors, namely those from Carrolltown, St. Marys, and Butler in the Dioceses of Pittsburgh and Erie; from Bellefonte in the Diocese of Philadelphia; from Newark; from Covington; from Doniphan in Kansas and St. Cloud in Minnesota. The priors of Doniphan and St. Cloud were authorized to act as procurators for some of the monks who were not able to attend. Father Francis Cannon from Nebraska had nominated a procurator. Letters nominating procurators were missing from two capitulars in Kansas and three in Minnesota. One missionary in Erie sent his vote through the mail without sealing it, and so it was voided (by me). Of the 48 eligible to vote, five had not named

---

[119] Francis Xavier Weninger, S.J. (1805-1888).

procurators and one had sent a voided ballot; (3) that several of the fathers had come to the general chapter only after overcoming great difficulty and at great expense; and (4) that all of them insisted upon holding the election.

On the morning of the election, we convened in the chapter room after singing a Solemn High Mass of the Holy Spirit. I ought to mention that I had invited Bishop O'Connor[120] to preside at the election. He came to the abbey but declined to preside. Instead, he persuaded me in the presence of the capitulars to preside and to select two capitulars to assist. I followed his advice after the capitulars added their voices to his. Three tellers were then chosen by majority vote. All those eligible to vote swore an oath that they would elect a worthy person, and the three tellers swore that they would not hamper the election. The novices wrote out the oaths to ensure that no one swore falsely. Three times the name of each person eligible to be elected was read aloud, i.e. the names of those who were older than 30 years of age and who had no canonical impediments. Then after another prayer to the Holy Spirit, the capitulars proceeded to vote. The votes were written on pieces of paper and placed in an urn. Then, in the presence of all, the tellers opened the pieces of paper and read the results. On the first ballot, 38 votes were cast for Boniface; Father Utto Huber[121] received two votes; Father Benedict Haindl[122] received one; and one ballot stated, "Let the Pope decide." Five eligible voters failed to name procurators, and one vote was voided because it had arrived in the mail unsealed. A total of 48 eligible votes was therefore accounted for. An absolute majority was 25 votes. I was then declared abbot for life by acclamation, and the capitulars solemnly led me into the church where the election was concluded with a solemn benediction and *Te Deum*. Afterward, I wrote out the protocol, which everyone will sign. I will then send it to the Sacred Congregation for the Propagation of the Faith for confirmation.

It is hardly necessary to report that before the election I told all present that they were under no obligation to choose me, but rather that they were bound by oath to elect the person whom they considered most worthy, because not only the future of the monastery but also the future of the whole Order in America depended on the election. I will not deny that the universal and sincere expression of confidence that my confreres revealed to me in the election has moved me deeply. It is a reward for the many tribulations and labors that I have frequently had to endure and suffer for the welfare of our monastery. I feel both honored and consoled.

---

[120] Michael O'Connor (1810-1872), bishop of Pittsburgh.
[121] Utto Huber, O.S.B. (1819-1896).
[122] Benedict Haindl, O.S.B. (1815-1887).

In any event, if the Pope confirms the election and I retain with God's help the name and burden of abbot, I will never abandon my efforts to work strenuously and firmly, so long and as much as I am able, for the greater glory of God, for the prosperity of the Catholic Church, and for the honor and expansion of the Benedictine Order. In a few days, I will send the acts of the election to the Sacred Congregation. Meanwhile, please, if you are able, inform His Eminence[123] of these events so that he will not think that I conducted the election in contempt of the authority of the Holy See by acting before I received a response from the Curia to my doubts and questions. Otherwise all things were done according to the sacred canons, and there is no doubt that of the votes not cast, most would have gone to me, just as among those that were cast, only three did not go to me, and one of those was mine.

I can no longer think of moving to Minnesota now. At the general chapter on September 20, we voted to raise the priories in Kansas (Diocese of Leavenworth) and Minnesota (Diocese of St. Paul) to independent status. In a short time, they will be ready to become abbeys. I am not able to ask the bishop to give me the abbatial blessing, and if I were able, I would not want to ask him because I am little interested in the external trappings of the office. I am doubtful, moreover, whether it is something that should be done at all.

There is no more news except that of the two priests I sent to Nebraska, Bishop Miège[124] of Leavenworth kept one in Kansas so that he could care for the Germans there and build a church for them (for which purpose the bishop has obtained 1,500 *scudi*). The other priest, Father Francis Cannon,[125] an Irishman, is alone in Nebraska where he has established himself in Omaha City, the capital of that Territory. I would not be surprised if Father Demetrius[126] (who voted for Father Benedict through a procurator) became bishop of St. Paul. Father Pelamourgue, who was nominated as bishop, has refused the dignity and has strongly recommended Father Demetrius. Perhaps I will travel to Minnesota again in the autumn. The Devil is putting up many obstacles for us in St. Cloud, obstacles that can be better dealt with by an abbot than by a prior. Nevertheless, I am reluctant to make the long journey, which can be very dangerous, especially when traveling on the Mississippi River. Three months ago, a steamboat exploded because of the negligence of one of the crew, and more than 120 people (including two priests)

---

[123] Cardinal Alessandro Barnabo, prefect of the Sacred Congregation for the Propagation of the Faith.

[124] John B. Miège, S.J. (1815-1884), of Kansas.

[125] Francis Cannon, O.S.B., eventually left the Benedictine Order and returned to Ireland.

[126] Demetrius di Marogna, O.S.B. (1803-1869).

lost their lives. (One was superior of the Daughters of Charity and the other, superior of the School Sisters of Notre Dame.) In addition, one of our former lay brothers lost his life in the explosion. Fifty ships a year are lost on American rivers because of sinking or fire or explosion or striking tree trunks in the water, and many hundreds of people die.

I read with great pleasure what you wrote about our Brazilian confreres. I heard the good news from England from Father Heptonstall,[127] but they are unable to publish the breviary for another year. In Bavaria King Maximilian[128] will not permit our Benedictines to establish new monasteries or restore old ones. Perhaps God allows this so that more Bavarian Benedictines will come to America. Because of the new transatlantic telegraph, I am able to speak with you from my cell, should I wish to have several hours of conversation with you at St. Paul's or St. Callistus. I would prefer, of course, to see you in person, and the election provides me a good and plausible excuse for a journey. Nonetheless, I am unable to leave my monastery for a long period unless it is absolutely necessary.

It seemed as though we were going to have an abundant harvest, but since June 13, a continuous drought has dimmed that happy prospect. We are not in great need, but we lost most of our corn crop and now have to pay high prices for corn and wheat. We have almost no potatoes and only a few vegetables. Our pastures have no grass.

For the last five days, we have seen a great comet in the sky. Its tail points north; every day it seems to turn more towards the south. Please write me whether Father Alto[129] can stay with you for one or two years (you can determine the charge) so that he might continue to study theology. I am happy that you are working seriously on your literary work. We must learn today so that we can write and teach tomorrow.

I send greetings to Cardinal Barnabo, Cardinal von Reisach, Abbot Theoduli, Father Nikes, the Wolter brothers,[130] and all the confreres who know me. I have sent you the news of the election before anyone else. See how dear you are to me and how much I esteem you. Please press for the confirmation after the acts of the election arrive. Everyone here sends warmest greetings to you. With the kiss of

---

[127] Cuthbert Heptonstall, O.S.B. (1804-1867).

[128] Maximilian II (1811-1864), son of King Ludwig I.

[129] Alto Hörmann, O.S.B. (1829-1867).

[130] Karl August von Reisach (1800-1869), Paul Theoduli, O.S.B., Anselm Nikes, O.S.B. (1825-1866), Maurus Wolter, O.S.B. (1825-1890), and Placidus Wolter, O.S.B. (1828-1908).

peace and with many thanks for all your prayers and pious works on our behalf,
Boniface Wimmer, Abbot[131]

Lat   oASPR   cASVA   transJO

TO JOHN MARTIN HENNI   57

St. Vincent, November 6, 1858

Most Reverend Bishop, Gracious Lord: I must ask pardon a thousand times for
answering your letter of August 7 only today. Our election for a lifetime abbot was
approaching and that prevented me from answering sooner. Then followed the
general chapter, the necessary reports to Rome, etc. Thus, because of the pressure
of duties, I completely forgot about Marathon.[132] I have already received two
letters from Marathon regarding the matter, but I did not answer either for the
same reason–i.e., I did not want to do anything about this without your knowledge. I remarked to a few people from Pittsburgh (who came here for the same
purpose), which perhaps led them to believe that I would at once send a priest
if Your Grace would permit it. However, I did not say that. I have three priests
in Newark, New Jersey, three in St. Marys, Pennsylvania, and a fourth priest for
the men who are building the railroad. There are three priests in Butler (near
Pittsburgh), two in Carrolltown, one in Indiana, and one in Greensburg not far
from the abbey. Then there are three in Kansas (Doniphan), eight in Minnesota
(St. Paul, Shakopee, and St. Cloud), and, finally, one in Omaha City, capital of
Nebraska. Besides these, our professors from the monastery take care of many parishes. Here at home are myself, Father Prior, the subprior, the novice master, the
chaplain, the director of the Latin school, and two other professors. In all, there
are nine priests and five subdeacons here.

Father Henry Lemke[133] went on a business trip to Europe. Altogether, we have
43 priests who are fully occupied, especially those who are at the monastery. I
have neither a procurator nor a secretary and therefore must impose on the prior
and burden myself more than I should. I was hoping that one of my older monks

---

[131] Because of irregularities in the procedure of the election of Wimmer as lifetime abbot of St.
Vincent, the Holy See merely reappointed him to a three-year term. He did not become permanent
abbot until 1866.

[132] German settlers in Marathon, Wisconsin, had asked Wimmer to send a priest to take charge of
the parish there.

[133] Peter Henry Lemke, O.S.B. (1796-1882).

*Father Augustine Wirth, O.S.B.
(1828-1901), first prior of St.
Benedict's Priory, Atchison, Kansas.*

would be elected abbot and either leave me alone or allow me to be of service as a professor or as procurator, but with the exception of two votes, they all wanted me to be their abbot (on condition that the Holy Father would approve). I must therefore necessarily do my best to justify their confidence in me and try to accomplish what still has to be done.

In the general chapter, I insisted that Minnesota and Kansas become independent priories, which would make them better able to pursue the interests of the Order and the care of souls, as well as largely relieve me of my burden. By a majority vote Father Benedict Haindl[134] was elected prior in Minnesota and Father Augustine Wirth[135] in Kansas, both for three-year terms. By this action the American Benedictine Congregation came into being, which was already taken for granted in the apostolic decree of August 26, 1855.[136]

The common novitiate and common house of studies for the entire congregation remain at St. Vincent, where the buildings will represent more and more a well-established monastery, although there will always be much to be done. There are 90 young men in the seminary, not counting our scholastics, novices, and clerics. It costs much and the gross income is only $3,000 because most of the students are poor.

From all this you will understand that at present two requirements for making a new foundation are lacking, namely, priests and money. One can easily see that the good people of Marathon are not able to do much for the priest, even if I were able to send them one. Moreover, it would be worse if I sent only one to a place so far away from here. Against my will I have only one in Nebraska. Bishop Miège[137]

---

[134] Benedict Haindl, O.S.B. (1815-1887).

[135] Augustine Wirth, O.S.B. (1828-1901).

[136] The Holy See had created the American Cassinese Congregation in 1855, but at the time, there was only one independent monastery (St. Vincent) in the new congregation. It was not until the priories in Minnesota and Kansas became independent that the number of independent houses reached the number required by canon law for a congregation.

[137] John B. Miège, S.J. (1815-1884), vicar apostolic of Kansas, whose jurisdiction included the Nebraska Territory.

outwitted me. I sent two priests to Nebraska, but he kept one in Leavenworth, probably hoping that I would send another one to Omaha City. I did not do that, and could not, because I had no one to send. I will be obliged to send one as soon as we have another ordination. He and Father Tracy will be the only priests in that enormous territory.

I keep hoping that I will be able to found a monastery in Wisconsin since there are so many Germans in that state. I want to do it also because I was invited by a bishop[138] to whom I feel indebted for the support he gave me in Rome at the time when I was trying to have my monastery raised to the status of abbey. I want to go to Wisconsin when I make my next trip to Minnesota. I had intended to do so last fall, but the time was too short, since I had to go to Kansas from Minnesota. We ought to have stopping places between here and St. Paul. If that is necessary, then we will manage it. It is my plan to follow the westward movement of the people. Our stations on the Mississippi River, the St. Peter's River, as well as those on the Missouri and Platte Rivers, serve well as such stopping places.

Assuring you of my willingness to serve you, and with deep respect and submission, I am Your Grace's obedient Boniface Wimmer, Abbot.

Ger   oAAMwk cASVA   transAH

TO KING LUDWIG I   **58**

St. Vincent, July 25, 1859

Most Serene, Most Benign King and Lord: I have just received the letter issued by Your Majesty's high council on May 29 and hasten to express to Your Royal Majesty my most humble gratitude for its gracious contents. It is indeed gratifying and comforting to me that Your Majesty is convinced of the honesty of my intentions and the integrity of my dealings. It grieved me very much that I was obliged to write as I did, but I had to do so in self-defense. However, it is not necessary to remark that our Benedictine sisters in general are not responsible for the disloyal and undutiful behavior of their former superior.[139] It is always difficult to find good superiors, even for monasteries, and an audacious, energetic woman,

---

[138] Henni himself.

[139] King Ludwig had written in response to Wimmer's letter to him of April 9, 1859, explaining his decision to use for other purposes the money sent by King Ludwig to build a convent for the Benedictine nuns in St. Marys, Pennsylvania. The "former superior" was Mother Benedicta Riepp, O.S.B. (1825-1862), who had led the first group of Benedictine nuns to America in 1852.

if she does not possess the discretion becoming to the female sex, can cause more inconvenience than an unruly man.

Thanks be to God that in Erie, in St. Marys, and in Newark we have excellent convents. The one in Erie especially deserves to be commended because the sisters living there are good. They are also very poor. Without having discussed the matter with the pastor or with the bishop,[140] the superior, Benedicta Riepp, originally sent five choir and lay sisters there, not only without my advice but also against my expressed wishes. She left them, then, to their fate, which in fact was severe enough. I need only to remark that their income from August 1858 to the end of January 1859 was only $85, and that from this, 13 persons had to survive in a wretched wooden house. Peculiar relations with the parish prevented both the bishop and the pastor from doing anything to obtain property for them. I too could not help them, so I finally accepted the offer of the bishop and placed two of my priests in the parish. Then, as incumbent in the parish, I could alleviate their needs and build a suitable house and provide a better income for them. Erie is an important city on Lake Erie, the only inland port in Pennsylvania. It has a beautiful location, and I hope that in the future we will have one of our most beautiful priories there.

On the day before Corpus Christi, Bishop Odin[141] of Galveston, Texas, came to St. Vincent and urgently begged me for three priests for his immense diocese. There are many Germans from the Rhineland in that region, some of whom immigrated there 15 years ago. For a long time they had no priests at all. Later the Franciscan Friars Minor from Bavaria assisted them, but the Franciscans left, for what reason I do not know. The famous Jesuit missionary Father Xavier Weninger[142] suggested to the bishop that he resort to me, and so he did. Not without great reluctance, I allowed myself to be persuaded to give up three fathers. Only a short time before, I had promised two priests for Erie, but because several of the fathers volunteered for this hard mission and supported the request of the bishop, I permitted three priests and two brothers to go. Fathers Alto Hörmann, Peter Baunach, and Aemilian Wendel departed on July 1.[143] The towns of San Antonio, Castroville, Neubraunfels, Friedrichsburg, D'Hanis, etc., and a few near the Mexican border, will be the first scenes of their activity. Later a monastery will

---

[140] Father Francis J. Hartmann was pastor of St. Mary's Church, Erie, Pennsylvania, where the Benedictine sisters were located. Josue Mary Young (1808-1866) was bishop of Erie.

[141] John Mary Odin, C.M. (1807-1870), bishop of Galveston.

[142] Francis Xavier Weninger, S.J. (1805-1888).

[143] Alto Hörmann, O.S.B. (1829-1867); Peter Baunach, O.S.B. (1815-1868); and Aemilian Wendel, O.S.B. (1832-1901). The lay brothers who went to Texas at this time were Michael Böhm, O.S.B., and Norbert Rossberger, O.S.B.

be founded at San José, which lies between San Antonio and Castroville. We were given 600 acres of land for this purpose.

On June 5, I introduced three Benedictine nuns to Covington [Kentucky]. They arrived there from Erie with their mother prioress.[144] Thus, at the same time that I am involved in a war with a few refractory, unruly, and stubborn nuns [in Minnesota], I am also attempting to build houses for others and am endeavoring to open up new avenues for expansion. Ingratitude must not be allowed to prevent one from doing as much good as one can and as is possible, and the innocent must not be made to suffer with the guilty. The orders of Your Royal Majesty concerning the 3,000 florins will be conscientiously executed.

I must mention that a great misfortune has befallen us. We had a killing frost on June 5, and again on June 10, that destroyed our winter wheat. No farmer within a circumference of 100 miles will get even his seed back. Besides the wheat, the corn (our principal grain crop) was also ruined. We planted it again, and if we have a good fall, we might get a harvest from it. If not, I do not know what I will do. A frost at this late date and at this latitude (40 degrees) is unheard of. The western part of Pennsylvania and the eastern part of Ohio have been laid waste by it. With the wheat alone, I will lose $2,000. The rest of the country, fortunately, had a first rate harvest. Immediately after the frost, we cut the wheat and planted buckwheat, beans, potatoes, and beets of various kinds, so that we can harvest at least something. St. Marys, Carrolltown, and Indiana[145] unfortunately suffered as much as St. Vincent, so we all will have to buy bread for our monasteries. God will help and bless what remains all the more.

With regard to the war, it seems that the whole English press is for France and against Austria, while generally the German and radical press favor Austria. The whole population is therefore affected very unpleasantly by reports about the battles, so much the more as it becomes evident that it is Austria's lack of determination and energetic leadership that wins the battles for France. That Germany, in particular Prussia, is again following the tactics of 1795, instead of preventing the outbreak of the war by boldly stepping forward, makes a very bad impression on all. It is hardly believable that the Corsican would have dared to unsheathe the sword had the Germans risen as one man for a common cause. It can easily be foreseen that Napoleon, a man without conscience, without honor and without a sense of duty, facing such hesitation and selfishness on the part of the German

---

[144] Mother Scholastica Burkhardt, O.S.B. (1832-1881), prioress at the Benedictine convent in Erie, Pennsylvania. The first Benedictine sisters in Covington, Kentucky, were Alexia Lechner, O.S.B. (1827-1891), Salesia Haas, O.S.B. (1827-1880), Ruperta Albert, O.S.B. (1836-1926).

[145] The Abbey of St. Vincent maintained dependent priories in these Pennsylvania towns.

powers, everywhere had the advantage. Everyone realizes this and feels it, and the consequence of it can be only intimidation and a second subjugation under the French and Russian overlords, or a revolution that will bring every country under one rule so that with combined forces they will be able to cope with foreign intrigues and attacks. May the Lord in His infinite goodness ward off from our fatherland the great impending misfortune.

Recommending myself in humblest reverence to Your Royal Majesty, I am your most obedient, Boniface Wimmer, Abbot

Ger   oRAB   cASVA   transGE   Math (125-30)

1860-1864

TO THE *PITTSBURGH CATHOLIC*

St. Vincent, February 26, 1860

Dear Sirs: A friend of mine handed me a copy of the *Dispatch*[1] of the 20th inst., drawing my attention to a "Queer Story," telling that recently, while "Mass" was being celebrated in Latrobe, the Spirit of some Priest or Saint appeared and communicated the information to the *Assembly*, that it was all a misapprehension about *"Purgatory,"* no such place of intermediate state of probation existing, and worse than all, that but two Priests had yet found their way to Heaven.

The truth is that at St. Vincent's Abbey, near Latrobe, a Novice saw from the 18th Sept. until the 19th Nov., 1859, every day, from eleven to twelve o'clock a.m., or from twelve to two o'clock at night, the apparition of a Benedictine Monk in his full festival dress. After all, he asked him, in the presence of another member of the order, what he wanted. The spirit then answered that he had been suffering seventy-seven years already, because he had not said seven *Masses* of ob-

---

[1] On February 20, 1860, the *Pittsburgh Dispatch* had reported the sensational story Wimmer describes in this letter. The abbot responded by sending this response to the *Dispatch*, to the *Pittsburgh Catholic*, and to other English and German newspapers. The "ghost story" was a fabrication of novice Paul George Keck. Bishop Michael O'Connor of Pittsburgh urged that Keck's alleged visions not be given credence, but others in the United States, Bavaria, and Rome took them seriously. The result was a major scandal that Wimmer describes in his letter of June 20, 1863, to Cardinal Alessandro Barnabo of the Sacred Congregation for the Propagation of the Faith (see below). For a detailed discussion of the episode, see Oetgen, *An American Abbot*, pp. 256-79.

ligation; and he had appeared to seven other Benedictines, at different times, and had not been heard; and that he would have to appear after eleven years again, if *he* would not help him. He wanted then seven "Masses," said for him, besides this the Novice should, for seven days, observe the strictest silence and retreat, and more, he should say for thirty-three days, each day three times, the "Fiftieth Psalm," barefooted and his arms stretched out.

This was done from the 21st Nov. till the 25th Dec., when the last Mass was celebrated, and the Ghost disappeared. During this time he had appeared several times again, exhorted the Novice most impressively, to pray for the *Souls in Purgatory*, since they suffer very hard, and consequently are very thankful to those who concur to their redemption; and, sad enough, said that of the five Priests who had already died at the *Abbey*, no one was yet in Heaven, but suffering in *Purgatory*.

This is in substance the facts that gave origin to your strange report; we give it as much credit as it deserves; but this report is correct. B. Wimmer, Abbot

Eng   *Pittsburgh Catholic* (March 17, 1860)

TO UTTO LANG   60

St. Vincent, May 17, 1860

Right Reverend Father Abbot, Dearest Confrere: I was not able to answer your last letter until now because of pressing business. Your cleric will be very welcome, but because he writes of having trouble with his stomach, he might not be fit for our abbey. Our meals are still very rough, especially on fast days. We drink neither beer nor wine, although in the near future I shall start building a brewery. In some of our priories, the food is even worse than here. In other places–such as Newark, Erie, and Covington–it is much better, but I am afraid he might not find what he is looking for, and until he knows English, we cannot assign him to outside stations. Father Henry[2] speaks of him in his letter and says he is ready to transfer to St. Vincent. I have nothing against it. I just want to make it clear to him that he cannot expect too much. The mission life, in reality, offers few attractions, though there will be plenty of work for him to do. Still, I do have a dread of hypochondriacs and candidates that lack mental stability.

Father Henry has rendered me extraordinary service. I only wish he would bring many robust brothers so that our forests could provide more daylight. We

---

[2] Peter Henry Lemke, O.S.B. (1796-1882), who was visiting Europe at the time.

get plenty of students. This year two were ordained priests, of whom one, Father Theodore von Grunder, joined Father Alto Hörmann in Texas where Brother Gamelbert Daschner is stationed. The other one, Philip Vogyt, went to Father Augustine Wirth in Kansas.[3] In addition, we have 24 clerics, i.e. students in philosophy and theology. Three of them will be ordained this year; the others, next year and the following year. Of these, seven will be appointed to Minnesota and four to Kansas. We have only three novices at present, but toward the end of the school year (in July), others will enter the novitiate. We have some 20 scholastics. As a result, I have no need for a new generation, though I am always in need of money.

[In June] a frost killed our whole winter wheat crop. I got only half a bushel and now must buy wheat at a cost of more than $3,000 (8,000 florins). It was the same in Carrolltown, Indiana, and St. Marys. We had to buy wheat everywhere because for a radius of 100 miles, everything was killed by the bitter cold. This year there is wonderful outlook on nature. May it please God to keep it that way. Otherwise, it will be very bad for us because we feel the pressure of not having money. Everywhere commerce and business are at a standstill, and at the same time, there is not enough on the table for certain hypochondriacs. Something has to be done. In such cases, all the trouble is piled on the poor abbot. Nevertheless, we must move on. Forward, always forward, everywhere forward. We will not be held back by debts, by difficult times, by an unfortunate year. Man's extremity is God's opportunity.

I did not sell an excellent stallion even though I was offered $600 (1,500 florins).

Everywhere there is a need for priests, both in the East and especially in the Far West. Often I must turn down an opportune offer for the simple reason that I do not have the people or do not want to divide the work of my priests. Churches are being built all over, sometimes very beautiful ones. The kingdom of God is increasing in a wonderful way despite attacks from all sides, especially from the German Freemasons. They are devilish people.

With regard to your congregation,[4] let me quote the old axiom, "Here is as much as I know and have heard from Rome." The congregation is *ipso facto* exempt, and if the right of visitation is given to the bishop, it is only for extraordi-

---

[3] Theodore von Grunder, O.S.B. (b. 1834); Alto Hörmann, O.S.B. (1829-1867); and Gamelbert Daschner, O.S.B. (1817-1870). Philip Vogyt, O.S.B., did not persevere in the monastic life. Augustine Wirth, O.S.B. (1829-1901), was prior at the Benedictine priory in Kansas.

[4] The Bavarian Benedictine Congregation, restored in 1858 with Abbot Utto Lang of Metten as abbot president.

nary cases in his role as apostolic delegate. Nevertheless, your priests engaged in pastoral work are under the jurisdiction of the bishop. He can make visitations in your parish church as well as in your monastic churches because they are at the same time parish churches.

Remember the rescript from our former procurator general, Abbot Angelo Pescetelli of the Abbey of St. Paul's-Outside-the-Walls in Rome. I sent you a copy. You should have weekly theological conferences so that the bishop has no reason to interfere. In addition, submit yourself to him in pastoral matters with great care so that he does not intrude into your monastery. If you want more information, and do not have them on hand, order the two works by Ferraris and Giraldi, both published in Rome. That is where I got mine.

Last winter we had much sickness. Father Alexius Rötzer[5] died in Minnesota from bronchitis in the form of consumption. In addition, two gallant brothers died, Anthony Kohler and Sennon Moran.[6] Since winter, I have started nothing new, although I sent Father Oswald Moosmüller[7] to Rondout in the state of New York in order to do pastoral work among the many Germans who were not being cared for. In Erie, Father Prior Celestine Englbrecht[8] erected a small convent for the Benedictine sisters at a cost of $5,000, and in St. Marys, Father Aegidius Christoph[9] is doing the same for $8,000.

I am very happy that my old confreres are still alive and in good health. Do you pray for me? Ever since we had to redeem an old German Benedictine who had been in Purgatory for seventy-seven years,[10] I have regularly made a memento for our confreres with sincere intensity–especially for our deceased abbots, whom no one remembers, but we should also pray for our living abbots.

I seldom think of Metten, though I never forget it at Mass. In the holy sacrifice of the Mass, we find real consolation in a life full of trouble and suffering, of crosses and adversity. Let us meet each other there, under the cross. There is little time, though we must always take courage, gather fresh hope, and have confidence that is firm as a rock. With the kiss of peace for all, and especially for Your Grace, I am your most obedient servant, Boniface Wimmer

P.S. Perhaps the prior could give me some definite information about his *Manual for Religious*. Is it still for sale? Where? I would like to buy several copies and

---

[5] Alexius Rötzer, O.S.B. (1832-1860).

[6] Anthony Kohler, O.S.B. (1818-1860), and Sennon Moran, O.S.B. (1824-1860).

[7] Oswald Moosmüller, O.S.B. (1832-1901).

[8] Celestine Englbrecht, O.S.B. (1824-1904).

[9] Aegidius (Giles) Christoph, O.S.B. (1830-1887).

[10] See Wimmer's letter of February 26, 1860, to the *Pittsburgh Catholic*, page 232.

introduce our novices to it. Naturally, it has to be translated into English because of the lack of knowledge of German.

Ger   oAMA   cASVA   transRG

TO KING LUDWIG I   **61**

St. Vincent, December 12, 1860

Your Royal Majesty, Most Benign King and Lord: The year 1860 was in many respects an unhappy and fateful one, and as it ends, it seems to be making room for an even sadder one. As the year comes to a close, I feel compelled to offer Your Royal Majesty most reverently my best wishes for the coming year. I greatly fear that we are moving toward very evil times, which the Christian must consider not just as an accident or as the result of political forces, but rather as a judgment for the evil and a purifying trial for the good. Human wisdom cannot avert it, and even if it could, human wisdom is not present to do so for the Lord blinds those whom He wants to punish. Nor can human courage overcome evil times, nor profitably use them. There is nothing to do but resist evil by all possible means and bear it in such a manner that it will profit us. We must pray and implore God to protect and strengthen the good and enlighten them so that they may endure the trials manfully and meritoriously, supporting the weak and restraining the evil as much as possible.

Your Majesty, I always offer the holy Mass established for you in our monastery. With all the fervor of my heart, I constantly recommend to Almighty God all the cares of your noble heart, all your desires and needs of body and soul, the temporal as well as the spiritual well-being of your royal house. In the future, I shall do so even more urgently and zealously. May God's Providence direct everything for the best. May His grace comfort and strengthen you in all disagreeable circumstances so that your merits before God may increase and your crown of immortality become the more glorious.

With regard to conditions here at St. Vincent, I have nothing unusual to report. On the political horizon, dark clouds gather from all sides. There is still hope that they will scatter again, but probably only after they have spent themselves in a violent storm. The Democratic Party, known here as a conservative party and to which a majority of Catholics belong, lost out in all the northern states.[11] The

---

[11] The presidential election of November 1860 had resulted in the victory of Abraham Lincoln and the Republican Party.

consequence is a violent agitation in the South, which is making preparations to secede from the Union. If that happens, a further consequence will follow in a short time: war between the North and the South and most likely a rebellion of the slaves in the South and mob rule here in the North. In America, as in Italy, the secret societies and their hatred for the Church were the deciding factors. Abolition of slavery was only a pretext. Catholics are naturally strong and sincere supporters of the abolition of slavery, but not in a manner that allows the slaves to become masters and the masters, slaves; nor in a manner that causes masters to lose their slaves and their land at the same time; nor so that these still mostly pagan barbarians suddenly become full-fledged citizens with the right to vote. Because they easily fall prey to the corrupt methods of those who buy their votes, they can turn into a very destructive mob. What the Church will gain or lose through all this remains to be seen. The real enemies of the Church all sided with the Republicans, people such as the 1848 revolutionaries from Germany and the rest of Europe.

As for us Benedictines, we had a very good harvest everywhere. We have more students again in our seminary than we had some years back. We took over the German congregation in Richmond, the capital of Virginia, and lately also the German congregation of Nashville, the capital of Tennessee. Both are slave states. I sent three more priests to Texas, where we now have six priests laboring among the Germans, and two more to Minnesota, where nine are working. In Minnesota, they already have a flourishing boys' seminary. Kansas, too, received a third priest, and a fourth one is preparing to go there. Five were ordained to the priesthood, but to my sorrow, I also lost two who died in the prime of their lives.[12]

The very latest news is that we finally have a brewery. On Christmas, we shall for the first time drink our own beer. Only after great difficulties did I complete the building. I had to get barrels and other necessities partially on credit. Construction of the two convents for the Benedictine sisters in Erie and St. Marys began last year, but the buildings were completed and occupied only this year. The abbey has again been considerably enlarged. On the farm, we have also made notable progress.

It is the wish and pressing request of Bishop Grace[13] that we found a mission among the fierce Sioux Indians next spring. I assented, but can do so only if I receive support from the *Ludwig Missionsverein*. To begin such a work costs money. The long journey of 2,000 miles, furnishings, provisions, tools for handicrafts

---

[12] The priests who died in 1860 were Alexius Rötzer, O.S.B. (1832-1860), and Bede Bergmann, O.S.B. (1832-1860).

[13] Thomas Grace, O.P. (1814-1897), bishop of St. Paul, Minnesota.

and agriculture, etc., are expensive. We are to instruct and train these Indians in agriculture, trade, and industry.

Your Majesty can see from all this that the Benedictines understand the spirit of the times and respond vigorously. Great hardships and annoyances are not lacking, but on the other hand, there is also encouragement and appreciation. The government in Washington very recently permitted us to have our own post office on our monastery grounds so that now our address is simply "St. Vincent, Westmoreland County, Pennsylvania." The large Pennsylvania Railroad Company likewise has lately given us, on our monastery property, a freight station on their railroad line so that we now need to go or drive only a few hundred feet when we travel by train or ship goods or haul shipments from the depot. This is a great material advantage for the monastery and especially for the seminary.

Thus, our monastery gains more and more in spiritual significance and outward importance. If, as I confidently pray and most sincerely wish, Your Majesty lives many years, I hope with God's continuing blessing to be able to inform Your Majesty year after year of the expansion of our field of labor, of the founding of new houses, of the erection of new mission stations, and of other such ventures. The most beautiful abbeys in Sicily and Italy have again been secularized. Let us hope that in this land more will arise anew and bring honor to Your Royal Majesty, their first founder!

In closing, I repeat my heartiest wishes for every possible blessing and thank you most sincerely for all your gracious benefits. I sign and recommend myself in humble reverence and humility, Your Royal Majesty's most obedient, Boniface Wimmer, Abbot and President of the American Benedictine Congregation

Ger   oRAB   cASVA   transGE   Math(137-140)

TO MARTIN MARTY   62

St. Vincent, March 30, 1861

Reverend and Dearly Beloved Confrere: It was a real pleasure to hear from you again. It is not a surprise to me that you too are feeling the pressure of the hard and difficult times. They are being felt everywhere. What you have done concerning your jubilee was highly commendable. People would like to hear something about you occasionally. Let us know now and then something about St.

The Right Reverend Martin Marty, O.S.B., who became the first abbot of Saint Meinrad Abbey in 1870.

Meinrad,[14] especially about the good quality of the soil there and the healthy surroundings, which eventually will help to attract buyers. If conditions are favorable, you might lay out a small town as we did in Carrolltown, which numbers already some thirty homes. Lots valued at $50 to $75 for half an acre could be sold in the beginning for only $20 or $25. These people will then gladly take five or ten acres of land and will pay well. The land, however, should be very close to the church and the monastery. Stores and inns will spring up sooner than you may imagine, followed by an influx of blacksmiths, carpenters, and tradesmen who after a while will become rich and so attract more people. If you do otherwise, the going will not be easy. If you cannot purchase the land, then rent it for one third of its yield, but have it done legally with a document drawn up by a lawyer. It is better to be on the safe side than to end up with nothing at all, and try to elevate the standards of the school, even if it does not bring in much profit or none at all. At least it will keep money in circulation. In addition, it will command respect and yield spiritual profit.

Al. McCarthy was here for several years. I had to dismiss him since his health was so poor that he was of no use except to serve as prefect (a sort of overseer) for the boys. He was enrolled among the scholastics, but not yet among the novices. Other than that, I believe he is a good man.

My original plan was to set up the Order on its ancient footing, so that not only the brothers but also the priests and students would do manual work. I saw very soon that with the priests it would not work out so well. The students who were studying for the Order, however, had to lend a hand in planting and reaping corn,

---

[14] Martin Marty arrived at St. Meinrad from Einsiedeln in September 1860, six months before this letter was written, and immediately took charge of the small community as prior. Monks of the Swiss Abbey of Einsiedeln had established the Priory of St. Meinrad in the Diocese of Vincennes, Indiana, in 1854. In 1870, it became an abbey, and Marty was elected its first abbot. See Albert Kleber, O.S.B., *History of St. Meinrad Archabbey 1854-1954* (St. Meinrad, Ind.: Grail Publication, 1954), 128-48.

in helping with the haymaking, and with the harvesting in the spring and fall. I tried it out also with poor non-German students, and the result was a decline in the number of applicants.

The lay brothers as a rule are received here as guests for some months. During that time, they must follow the brothers' daily routine. Then they receive the habit. After one year they make their simple profession, and after four years solemn profession. Should they in the meantime give grounds for complaint, the solemn profession will be postponed or never granted at all. I had to expel a couple of bad characters with solemn profession.

When a man wants to become a brother, I make it clear to him that he is to receive no pay for his work, and he must sign a declaration before witnesses to the effect that in consideration of the spiritual benefits from the Order's daily Mass, reading, instruction, etc., he cannot demand any compensation should he later on decide to leave the Order or is compelled to do so. This precaution is necessary.

By the way, I could not have founded the monastery without the brothers, and most likely, you will not be able to either, for it requires from the very outset a regular order of the day. It is not the building, but the people who make up the monastery, who live the monastic life together. Two or three priests busy with the care of souls or teaching do not constitute a monastery because they cannot hold to the daily order. If several brothers are present, it will be all right. On October 24, 1846, when the fifteen brothers who came with me across the ocean received the habit, I introduced the order of the day that is still in force. They rise daily at 3:45 am, go to church at 4:00 am where they pray one rosary with the litany and read one chapter from the *Holy Rule*. Then they go and make their beds, clean up their rooms, light the fire, feed the horses, etc., until 5:00 am. Breakfast is at 6:00 am, after which is conventual Mass. Then they work until 10:45 am. Particular examination of conscience takes place from 10:45 to 11:00 am. Dinner with table reading takes place from 11:00 am, followed by a visit to the Blessed Sacrament in choir. Recreation follows. (Some have to feed the horses and cows and wash them etc.) From 1:00 to 1:30 pm, there is a second rosary with the litany, then work until 5:00 pm. From 5:00 to 6:00 pm, there is spiritual reading followed by supper with table reading. They have recreation from 6:30 to 7:30 pm. Some again have to feed and wash the horses and cows. At 7:30 pm, there is a third rosary with litany followed by a general examination of conscience. All have to be in bed by 9:00 pm at the latest. The same order is followed to this day in the priories at St. Marys and Carrolltown. In the summer, meditation is from 5:00 to 5:30 am, afterwards breakfast and work. In the evening, there is work until 5:30 pm. Spiritual reading is from 5:30 to 6:00 pm. During the harvest time, they will be

The rules of Saint Vincent Seminary.

working much later so that spiritual reading will be omitted or begun much sooner while meditation is omitted.

I follow the same order with my students. We rise at 3:45 am, pray *Matins* and *Lauds* from 4:00 to 5:00 am, have meditation from 5:00 to 6:00 am, then *Prime* at 6:00 am followed by Mass, breakfast, *Terce*, and *Sext*. We have particular examination of conscience from 10:45 to 11:00 am and Nones after a visit to the Blessed Sacrament. Vespers at 3:00 pm, *Compline* at 7:30 pm, then general examination of conscience and sleep.

Thus, I have a monastic community that, in spite of many trials from within and without, is growing ever stronger. When I am not at home, everyone still follows the regular course. I would experience this thing time and again. Some of my fathers do not like the idea of having so many brothers around. I notice that those who think and act this way are always such as have no love for strict order. Nevertheless, if they could enter upon an order of the day together with several priests and students, it would be all right.

I applied as early as 1848 for recognition of my community as a monastery and got it. I believe it is sufficient if you state the number of your reverend confreres (even if not all of them are living in the monastery) and the number of brothers. Then you should declare the approximate value of the principal properties in your possession, not forgetting to mention the debts incurred through the purchase of land. Mention both brothers and students and also what congregations are under your care. The recognition will come more surely if you have your petition delivered through the Swiss chaplain (I do not remember his name exactly) or better yet, through the procurator general of the Cassinese Congregation, Abbot Angelo Pescetelli, abbot of St. Paul's in Rome, who has done me so many great favors. You should of course realize that you will have to observe some definite statutes, probably of the Swiss Congregation.

If you are fearful of contracting overwhelming debts, I would advise you to discontinue any further building at St. Meinrad and start rather with a seminary in Terre Haute. Should I be able to find a buyer for you, it will be my pleasure.

If I can otherwise be of service to you, rest assured that I am always ready to do so. Only do not lose courage! We indeed have a lot of valuable property, yet we are struggling constantly with heavy debts. For a big farm you need a big farmer, otherwise things will get worse instead of better. Cattle raising is more profitable than corn growing. The raising of pigs is the best paying proposition because they multiply more rapidly. Wherever you have good pasture and a light winter, horned cattle will also be a paying proposition. What requires the least amount of work and is yet sure to bring in a profit is no doubt the ideal. Good congregations, however, are the best of all, better even than a college because board and tuition are often not paid if you do not take a firm stand as to advance payment.

With the greatest affection and esteem, I recommend myself to your prayers and those of your confreres. Your devoted confrere, Boniface Wimmer, Abbot

Ger   oASMA   cASVA   transBB

TO KING LUDWIG I   63

St. Vincent, June 4, 1861

Most Serene Highness! Most Benign King and Lord! Perhaps no one knows better than I what demands the Church and our friends and benefactors are justified to make of me, and likewise, no one knows better than I how much is still to be done before I am fully what I should be. Your Royal Majesty is so gracious that at every opportunity you speak of my "zealous" endeavors for the healthy growth and prosperity of the Order of St. Benedict, and I am almost ashamed of it–although I regard such gracious recognition rather as a gentle admonition than as praise. Nevertheless, I am deeply grateful to Your Royal Majesty, and it gives me great consolation in the midst of so much and at times such gross misunderstanding and lack of appreciation to be recognized for my good will to serve the Order by a person of such high dignity as yourself. Yes, Your Majesty, zeal is definitely needed to do justice to my position. The abbatial dignity may appeal to ordinary ambition, but the abbot of St. Vincent is in every way in circumstances that ordinary ambition does not care for and does not seek. Only unselfish zeal and sincere sacrifice on behalf of the welfare of the Order can carry this burden.

For four years, things have grown constantly worse. The outbreak of civil war made our misery complete. For quite a while, no one believed that war would occur. Public opinion was always for preserving the Union, but most people were very emphatic in voicing their intention to let the secessionists leave peacefully in the hope that later they would unite again with the North, rather than to force them to stay in the Union. The thoughts of the President,[15] however, were unfortunately otherwise. He wanted to restock Fort Sumter in the harbor of Charleston with new provisions. The secessionists who surrounded the harbor naturally could not tolerate this, took the fort by storm and thus, *de facto*, opened the war with the Union, and we are thus suddenly thrown into a civil war that the President thoughtlessly provoked and that the southerners, equally thoughtlessly, accepted. After that, all business stopped. All factories ceased to operate. Most of the banks discontinued redeeming their notes *in specie*. The banknotes in the different states were either entirely worthless or greatly discounted. Nobody wanted to pay. Few were able to pay. Those who had money on interest withdrew it, etc. In short, there exists such chaos and utter confusion and helplessness that one can hardly imagine it.

We suffer immensely from these conditions. There are some 20 boarders in our seminary from the South, with which we are now at war. All connections, i.e. correspondence, with the South are suspended and forbidden, and we can get neither letters nor money from their parents. I cannot send them back because the distance is too great and the journey would have to be made by sea. Therefore, I must board them without receiving any pay. I am in the same difficulty with many other boarders from the seacoast whose middle-class parents were rather well to do in ordinary times but who through this stoppage in everything are now without income and without money. I really do not know how I can satisfy my obligations, the more so since my creditors want their money.

In such straits, I can turn my eyes only toward Bavaria. The *Missionsverein* has again promised me the usual subsidy, and I wait with great eagerness. This, however, will not suffice this time because too much of my regular income is lacking. Therefore, I dare again to beg Your Royal Majesty, most reverently, to take St. Vincent once more into consideration at the distribution of mission alms. After receiving so many proofs of your most serene benevolence and graciousness, I ought not dare to petition again for support. Only a short time ago I did not think that I would get into such great stress and embarrassment so suddenly. The confluence of various combined unfriendly relations and tensions and ruinous destructive conditions force me to seek help wherever I can hope for it. Therefore, I entreat you most humbly to graciously excuse my temerity.

---

[15] Abraham Lincoln (1809-1865) was President of the United States from 1861 to 1865.

Today I am going to Chicago, a large, chiefly German, industrial city on Lake Michigan in the state of Illinois. Bishop Duggan[16] asked me to take over the German parish of St. Joseph, which has been without a priest for some time. I intend to fill the vacancy with two priests. Chicago is 500 miles from St. Vincent and is a major center of German Freemasons and Forty-Eighters.[17] These have caused Catholics throughout America much suffering, so there will be a great deal of work and a great deal of difficulty awaiting us. Formerly Chicago was a rich city. At present, there is great want there too, but we must disregard all these things. We must take care of our Catholic brethren. Lately I had four of my clerics ordained to the priesthood, and in the autumn, I will have three more ordained. Thus, I can very well spare a few older priests. Chicago also forms a convenient halfway point and meeting place between St. Vincent and our missions in Minnesota and is also important for that reason. His Excellency Archbishop Scherr of Munich and the Reverend Court Chaplain Müller[18] will probably write me a good lecture once again about taking on a new place because they fear we are spreading ourselves too thin, but I cannot worry about that. The Benedictines here in America must be missionaries again as they were everywhere hundreds of years ago. In the future, when the bishops have had time to supply sufficient secular priests, then the Benedictines too will have had time to enlarge their stations, to strengthen them and develop them into regular monasteries and so become a support to the secular priests as at present they are a support to the forsaken lay people.

Yes, I could probably save myself many a worry, unpleasantness, and pecuniary embarrassment if I were to take fewer novices and expand less. Then I would have no debts, need not importune others with petitions for support, etc. However, when I hear the complaint of Our Savior–"The harvest is great, but the laborers few"–I cannot refrain from trying to do all that is possible to supply what is lacking.

The war will hardly touch our monastery, although the southern border is only a two days' journey distant from us. For as it is probable that we cannot force the South to submit, so it is just as improbable that the South will invade our own land. However, I have a priest in Richmond, the capital of Virginia, whose con-

---

[16] James Duggan (1825-1889), who served as bishop of Chicago from 1859 until his hospitalization in 1869.

[17] "Forty-Eighters" were European revolutionaries who had participated in the failed revolutions of 1848 and then immigrated to America.

[18] Gregory Scherr, O.S.B. (1804-1877), archbishop of Munich; and Joseph Ferdinand Müller (1803-1864), chaplain to the court of King Ludwig I. Both were benefactors of Wimmer and the American Benedictines.

quest the famous General Scott[19] is now contemplating. Both armies are stationed near the city where soon they will come to an important battle.[20] How my poor confrere will fare I do not know. Congress will soon convene and perhaps a peaceful settlement is still possible.

Once more, I beg Your Majesty most humbly, if at all possible, not to forget me in my needs and be convinced that all that comes to us, little or much, will be well used. With sentiments of deepest gratitude and most loyal affection, I remain Your Royal Majesty's most humble, loyal, and obedient, Boniface Wimmer, Abbot

Ger   oRAB   cASVA   transGE   Math (142-45)

TO JOSUE MARY YOUNG   **64**

St. Vincent, September 25, 1861

Most Reverend Lord, Your Grace: I have received and read through the contents of the apostolic letter from the Sacred Congregation for the Propagation of the Faith dated July 13 of this current year, which you kindly sent me. A similar letter, or one of the same tenor, also came to our most reverend bishop,[21] who informed me about it. Indeed, I have invited him to come to the abbey and inquire of each lay brother what in the final analysis their views are about the things that Brother Joseph Sailer accuses me of.[22] The bishop came with his secretary, Father Stiebel[23] and privately interviewed each brother. He then sent their responses to the Sacred Congregation. I am sorry that you did not receive this letter before you went on your visitation to our priory in St. Marys, for indeed you would then have been able to examine the brothers who live there, and in their depositions you would have been able to discern very easily whether the things that are thrown at me are true or false. You also have our fathers in your diocesan see. They will certainly

---

[19] General Winfield Scott (1786-1866).

[20] The Battle of Bull Run took place on July 21, 1861, six weeks after Wimmer's letter to King Ludwig I.

[21] Michael Domenec, C.M. (1816-1878), bishop of Pittsburgh.

[22] Brother Joseph Sailer, O.S.B. (1820-1891), one of the pioneer monks at St. Vincent, had brought charges against Wimmer in Rome of injustice and arbitrariness in dealing with the lay brothers of the abbey. For a discussion of this episode, see Oetgen, *An American Abbot*, 235-39.

[23] Stiebel was a Pittsburgh priest of German heritage who could interview the brothers in their own language.

be useful witnesses to the reasons for my actions, especially since Father Prior[24] is one of the first who came with me from Bavaria to America at the same time as Brother Joseph Sailer, whose morals and disposition he has seen through.

Nevertheless, because you put such great confidence in my truthfulness, and because my explanation of things seems to satisfy you, I wish to state simply:

1) This matter has not been raised by any other lay brother whatsoever, only by Brother Joseph Sailer alone. None of the other brothers knew anything about the affair. Thus all the brothers and this Joseph Sailer himself positively and candidly declared, having been expressly interrogated about this affair.

2) It is a pure lie (a) that I conduct myself arbitrarily towards the lay brothers; (b) that the lay brothers can be easily dismissed after pronouncing religious vows in the Order; (c) that some of the lay brothers, having come to America, were ejected from the monastery and currently, left to themselves, live in great danger. This can be proven not simply from the testimony of the remaining brothers but also from the declarations of the chapter fathers.

It is true that two of the brothers were dismissed from the Order after making solemn vows, but one of them, Sebastian Connadi by name, was not so much ejected, as rather, when he himself left the Order and for four months loitered in St. Louis and afterwards returned to the abbey, he was not received again because he truly did not belong to the abbey but rather to the independent priory in Minnesota. Bending to his most insistent prayers, I sent him back to Minnesota. I therefore did not eject him, but gave him permission first to go back to the priory in Minnesota. When he himself left this priory and for a few months loitered in St. Louis (I do not know by what means) and then, without my permission, returned to St. Vincent, I did not receive him but sent him back to Minnesota.

Whether this be a crime, let others judge. I, however, confess that I do not understand how the discipline of the *Rule* can be sustained if anyone is permitted to travel freely here and there, to cause the greatest scandal, to disturb the peace and quiet of the whole congregation, etc. Moreover, this brother was most negligent and intolerable to all, to such an extent that not a few brawls between him and the other brothers occurred. Because of this, even the prior in Minnesota[25] did not receive him when he came again to him from St. Vincent. Certainly, it is upon the prior in Minnesota that the accusation of Brother Joseph should fall in this case.

---

[24] Celestine Englbrecht, O.S.B. (1824-1904), prior in Erie, Pennsylvania.
[25] Othmar Wirtz, O.S.B. (1831-1874).

Another of the brothers expelled from the monastery was Brother Albert Hör-mann.[26] I expelled him because repeatedly and after formal warning and express threat of ejection, he entered the home of a certain widow (of George Kuhn) eight miles from the abbey and asked her for her oldest daughter's hand in marriage, pretending that he was compelled to this by a certain angel that had appeared to him. He made the same petition repeatedly, three times, to the aforesaid widow. What am I supposed to do with such a man? What would you do? Must I restrain those, whom I am not otherwise able to restrain, through force? American law does not permit the use of force against its citizens. Was it not easier to send this brother away?

Neither the miserable Albert nor the sluggish Sebastian, however, remain in great danger. For Albert, after a few months, penitently returned to the monastery and was again received as a servant by the bishop of St. Paul,[27] the bishop having petitioned that I set [Albert] free, to which I readily assented, and if the bishop wishes him (being penitent and reconciled) to associate again with our confreres in St. Paul, there is no doubt that they would receive him. Certainly, in the house of the venerable bishop he is in no danger. After solemn vows, he thought that he was secure and that all things were permissible for him. He therefore cared little for obedience. Expelled from the Order, he bore himself better because he had to take counsel with himself.

I still have three other brothers whom I would gladly expel if I could. Among them is my accuser, Joseph. I say "if I could," because it was never my opinion that I could expel them for any reason that pleases me, but only for something serious, or for the gravest reason, and only after all admonitions and all penalties of the *Rule* had been tried without effect. This I have always said to all the fathers, as well as to the brothers before profession, and even in the novitiate. Therefore, no injury occurs to the willing.

I also discussed this with the most reverend cardinals of the Sacred Congrega-tion for the Propagation of the Faith when I was in Rome in the year 1855, and they did not disagree or object. Nevertheless, I am threatened now because a great inquisition has been instituted over a simple matter, and indeed, because of the calumny of a single brother who writes deceitfully in the name of all (no one else

---

[26] Brother Albert Hörmann of Nieder-Geroldshausen, Bavaria, was one of three blood brothers who became lay brothers at St. Vincent. The others were Vincent Hörmann, O.S.B. (1821-1911), and Thaddeus Hörmann, O.S.B. (1817-1897). After being expelled, Albert never returned to St. Vincent.

[27] Bishop Thomas Grace, O.P. (1842-1921), of St. Paul, Minnesota.

signed). The *Holy Rule* and the Statutes have been violated and held in contempt, unknown to the abbot and the chapter.

However, without a doubt it thus pleases God that they, from whom I should have expected all the most powerful help in the government of so large a family, in various ways are increasing the difficulties that beset me from all sides and that, without a doubt, will defeat me unless the same adorable hand, which before struck me down, supports me at the appropriate moment and raises me up.

I rejoice that you found the state of things in St. Marys, as far as both our nuns and our brothers are concerned, satisfactory to you. I hope always to know that as far as possible your spiritual sons and daughters of our Order merit your benevolence. Concerning the station at St. Severin, I do not know what I shall do. It is always dangerous to expose a single religious with a single lay brother [to the world], and I doubt very much if Father Charles[28] is fit to head that parish. Nevertheless, I will consider the matter more carefully in order to try to satisfy your desire.

Returning sincere thanks to you for so many favors conferred on me, and wishing you all prosperity, I sign with the greatest reverence, Boniface Wimmer, Abbot

Lat   oADE   cASVA   transLK

TO ALESSANDRO BARNABO   65

St. Vincent, October 7, 1861

Most Eminent Cardinal Prefect: Although you have not required me to provide a response in the accusations made by the lay brother Joseph Sailer[29] against me, nonetheless, I thought it necessary to write in order that a suitable remedy might be prescribed for the presumed evils this brother has complained of. Although you can easily see that what he has said against me is false and absurd, still a response is necessary in order to cure the imaginary fears of some of the brothers and to put an end to their presumption.[30]
1) Some of them fear that their solemn vows are not valid; that is, that their
   solemn vows are no more binding than simple vows and that they can be
   arbitrarily dismissed either by me or by my successor (if another abbot is

---

[28] Charles Geyerstanger, O.S.B. (1820-1881).
[29] Joseph Sailer, O.S.B. (1820-1891).
[30] This episode, sometimes referred to as the "insurrection of the brothers," is discussed in Oetgen, *An American Abbot*, 235-39.

elected), although publicly and privately I have declared a hundred times that solemn vows are perpetual vows and that those in solemn vows can be expelled from the monastery only for serious crimes and unyielding disobedience, according to the ancient *Rule* of St. Benedict (chapter 28) and in conformity with the practice of the bishops in America towards their clergy. Indeed only a few of the brothers are unsettled and affected by this fear, namely those who do not have a true vocation, those who are attracted to the monastery more on account of the food than for the sake of their salvation, those who rightly feel that they might be expelled because they do not lead a truly religious life. These brothers themselves are accustomed to stirring up the others, and among the worst offenders is Joseph, along with two or three other malcontents.

Brother Joseph Sailer, O.S.B. (1820-1891), one of the original band of monks who came with Wimmer to St. Vincent from Bavaria.

2) Therefore, they speak of laws and statutes, and in fact they actually think those statutes which are favorable to them are unjustly held back from them by me. In part, they want similar or equal statutes as the priests, which would give them the right to determine the regimen of the Order, to elect officials including the abbot, and to have active and passive rights. In a word, they want to be members of the chapter, like the priests.

This is clear, if not from their own words and deeds, certainly from the complaints of the excellent Joseph, who does not complain about the lack of time for praying, for meditating, for participating in spiritual exercises, or that the *Holy Rule* is not observed or is not able to be observed. No, no. He does not care about how to live a proper monastic life, about how to observe his vows. Rather he cares only about equality between brothers and fathers. He complains only that the brothers do not have their own monastic cells. (I might point out that for 12 years the priests in the monastery did not have their own cells either because the monastery was built in stages. It still is not finished.) Joseph also complains that the brothers are looked down upon, which is not true. He complains that they have to work as hard as slaves, but in fact they work seven or eight hours a day, according to the *Holy Rule*. He complains that they do not know what rights they have. He complains that they can be expelled, etc. For these and other grave matters, he seeks a remedy.

This is truly the height of arrogance for a lay brother to desire to rule, to desire to be equal to the priests, to demand rights and privileges that are contrary to canon law. What is more, if one can believe it, he accompanies his assertions with pure lies, calumnies, and distortions, which he has rashly dared to send to the Sacred Congregation. Indeed, his arrogance appears in the fact (a) that he has sent these accusations against me secretly; (b) that he wrote with total disregard for procedures, since this matter should have come first to the visitators, the president, and the general chapter of the congregation. By all means, one should always have the right of appeal to the Holy See, but what would become of the authority of religious superiors if every humble brother could refer his case to the Sacred Congregation? Imagine how great a burden would fall on the Sacred Congregation from the American Benedictines if each of the 130 lay brothers should feel free to write? To be sure, I am far from the desire to challenge the right of the Sacred Congregation to receive such appeals, but I myself have such great reverence for the college of cardinals that I write to them only when the responsibilities of my office or grave matters require it. I truly believe it a disgrace that an uneducated brother should be rash and bold enough to do so; (c) that he wrote to you in the name of all the brothers. This is absolutely false since none of the brothers were aware of what he was doing, and several would have vehemently opposed him had they known. Such action is strictly prohibited by the *Holy Rule* (chapter 69) and is highly offensive and presumptuous. This brother holds no office among the brothers. He is a servant in our minor seminary and nothing more.

I could respond to each one of the complaints of this brother, but it would be too wearisome to do, and Your Eminence would become tired of reading it. Nevertheless, I am not able to restrain myself from observing that the Devil has his docile disciples everywhere and that he can make demagogues even of lay brothers, just like revolutionaries who complain of oppression by their legitimate rulers, of the privileges of the nobility, of being deprived of rights and liberties, etc. Thus, rebels call for constitutions, equality for all, and liberty. Thus, they justify, vindicate, and praise rebellion and call themselves patriots, etc. Brother Joseph calls obedience slavery and vituperates against his superiors if they deny him anything. He inveighs against priests because they have special privileges. He condemns them as enemies of the brothers. He justifies the flight of apostates, and he himself assumes the honorable role of protector and liberator, first by writing to the Sacred Congregation for the Propagation of the Faith and perhaps later, if he should be successful and receive the power, by winning the souls of the brothers over to himself.

What a great triumph for him already that there has been an investigation conducted by the bishop of Pittsburgh![31] In fulfilling his duties, the bishop and his secretary came to the monastery and interviewed all the brothers privately concerning the complaints leveled against me. It was no small humiliation for the abbot that his words and deeds were subjected to such an inquisition because of the complaints of one of the brothers! By no means do I find fault with the bishop. He did not come to attack me, but rather he demonstrated the best of faith. Nor do I complain that he was ordered to conduct the investigation, for truly an abbot should be more humble, submissive, and obedient than a lay brother. Nonetheless, I do fear very much, and suspect, that this visit was not helpful. The rule of the common man, recently established in France and applied in Italy, has produced very dangerous fruits, and especially in a new order, or in a branch of an old order newly established, it will produce the same dangerous fruits. When the good are silent and the wicked speak, the violent bear the kingdom away.

There are those who think I have been too good to the brothers and that after my death, or if someone else is elected abbot in my place, no one will be able to govern them so well. My priests, at least some of them, think that I am too indulgent towards the brothers, and in fact, it displeases many of the priests that we have so many brothers. On the other hand, the Sacred Congregation for the Propagation of the Faith seems to think that I am an austere, harsh, and stubborn man who cares for nothing but carrying out his own designs.

It is not appropriate for me to judge myself, but in fact, the truth is found between these extremes. Without the brothers, I could have built neither the monastery nor the seminary. Many of them are very good. Some are excellent, but they are not all saints. A few lack a true vocation and are bad. It would be a grave loss if a decree were issued limiting the number or changing the status of the brothers, but it would also be a grave danger and a great loss if a decree in favor of the brothers was issued that was prejudicial to the abbot and the priests. The sacred canons, the *Holy Rule*, our statutes, justice, and fairness should determine the outcome of this case.

Therefore, I humbly ask:

(1) That the solemn vows that the brothers have taken after three years of simple vows be duly declared solemn vows, which in fact they are since they have all the effects of solemn vows;

(2) That solemn vows notwithstanding, the brothers (like the fathers) may be expelled from the monastery, in accordance with the tenor of our ancient *Rule*, on account of atrocious crimes such as theft, adultery, fornication, drunken-

---

[31] Bishop Michael Domenec, C.M. (1816-1878).

ness (which in America is especially odious), brawls, etc.; or on account of persistent disobedience. Such expulsion would come after the spiritual measures and punishments prescribed by the *Rule* have been applied, with the consent of the chapter, with the right of appeal, and after the person has received three warnings. All solemn vows have been made under these conditions. The reason is that under civil law it is impossible to incarcerate or otherwise restrain offenders in this country;

(3) That the lay brothers not have rights, which they previously had, in the general chapter or in the chapters of the independent monasteries; and that new brothers be either denied the right to solemn profession or that their profession be made for a specific number of years;

(4) That the vows of those who have been expelled still be in effect, as clearly must be the case, until they obtain a dispensation, which is not easily granted.

I ask these favors so that the fears and uncertainties that trouble some of the brothers may be resolved.

In order that the door of the brothers' arrogance may be closed, I also humbly request:

(1) That Brother Joseph be justly punished for his boldness, temerity, and wicked spirit in submitting these complaints;

(2) That the brothers be admonished to obey the abbot, the visitator, the president, and the general chapter, to whom they should submit their complaints in the future;

(3) That insofar as the statutes are concerned, they pertain to the priests alone, as in fact is the case, and that only those that deal with spiritual things apply to the brothers, namely Chapter II, 1; Chapter IV, 2 and 3; Chapter V, 1, 2, and 3; Chapter VI, Chapter VII, and Chapter VIII–with the necessary changes having been made, however, since the statutes were created for the priests and do not in all cases apply to the lay brothers.

All this has been explained to the brothers repeatedly. Each year in the winter, when they are all gathered inside the monastery, the subprior gives them conferences. Indeed the lessons about the meaning of vows prepared for the clerical novices in Latin have been translated into German and are read and explained to both the professed lay brothers and to the lay brother novices. I dare to assert with a clear conscience that in no other monastery are the spiritual and temporal needs of the brothers better attended to than in ours, but because the lay brothers, properly speaking, are not monks, it must not be expected that those who are accepted in the monastery chiefly to work and to take care of the temporal needs of the community can lead a contemplative life, as some of them (namely Joseph's friends) contend. The facts prove, however, that the hardest working brothers are the most devoted to spiritual things, while on the contrary those who complain that they have too much work reveal themselves to be slackers in their spiritual duties.

Before ending this long letter, I would like to observe that my accuser has brought calumny not only against his abbot but against his confreres as well. Anyone who reads his petition of complaint would think the brothers at St. Vincent are in a near state of revolt against their abbot, but the truth is that all the brothers, with the exception of a very few malcontents who are accustomed to murmuring, live here in the greatest peace, serve God by working and praying, and practice among themselves all the virtues. News of these complaints would come among them like a thunderbolt from a clear sky and would provoke the greatest indignation among them all.

It is not because I am unable to govern the brothers without the help of the Holy Apostolic See that I have written this most humble petition, but rather because now that the accusation has been made, it must be carried to a conclusion. The question has been raised and considered. It is necessary that a response be made.

Committing all these matters confidently to the wisdom of the Sacred Congregation for the Propagation of the Faith, I continue to be, in reverence and submission, Your Eminence's most humble servant, Boniface M[aria] Wimmer, Abbot O.S.B.

Lat   oAPF   cASVA   transJO

TO JOHN MARTIN HENNI   66

St. Vincent, April 22, 1862

Most Reverend Lord Bishop: Through Ignatius L. Lebling I received from the *Ludwig Missionsverein* $238.70, to be forwarded to you, as you perhaps have been informed. Today I sent this sum to you through Adams Express in good Pittsburgh money. I hope you realize you did not lose anything. If I had had the time to go to Pittsburgh, I would have sent you a check from the bank, but I am always overloaded with work and can therefore seldom get away. Be so kind as to give a receipt for the money so that I can prove that you received it.

If Your Grace should be going to Rome, may I ask that you kindly give my regards to my friend the Swiss Chaplain, who did so many favors for me when I was there. I intended to write him but never had the opportunity. I wonder whether the Benedictines of St. Paul's-Outside-the-Walls delivered my greetings. I would also like to ask you to give my kind regards to His Eminence, Cardinal Reisach.[32] He has always been my benefactor, and St. Vincent owes its existence to his kindness. I am greatly indebted to him.

For many months, I have been awaiting a report from our procurator general, Abbot Angelo Pescetelli, concerning the outcome of some business that was submitted to the Propaganda almost a year ago. Perhaps it will only be settled when our own Bishop Domenec[33] goes to Rome. He will be there next year. My monks and I are not in his good favor, I am sorry to say. He thinks I am too German. Bishop O'Connor[34] made allowance for the Germans and was happy to have the Benedictines care for the German Catholics, because then he did not have to provide clergy for the German parishes.

Bishop Domenec, when speaking to a farmer some time ago, said that he would have driven us out of the diocese long ago if he could! A few of his Irish friends, it is said, made the bishop believe that the Benedictines are gaining too much ground and that the abbot regards himself as a kind of German bishop in his diocese! This misunderstanding will, I hope, change in time. The abbot has so much to do regarding his own monastery that he does not want to undertake anything outside his domain, and the Lord Bishop will eventually learn who serves him sincerely, and who does not.

It is possible that I myself may have to go to Rome, perhaps next fall. It depends on circumstances. I no longer like going to Europe, although it may easily happen that America will also become an unfortunate country. In any case, it will never again be what it was. I am convinced that even if the North wins this time, the country will be divided into two or three republics or states, and that could happen soon because here everything happens so fast.

Your Grace must certainly have heard and read about our apparition a few years ago. The affair caused a great sensation inside and outside our monastery, and because I believed in it, it exposed me to many troubles and even persecution from many sides, but mostly from some of my own people. Even good friends could not refrain from regretting my actions and expressing their opinion. Without getting information from me, Bishop O'Connor published an article in which he

---

[32] Karl August von Reisach (1800-1869), archbishop of Munich from 1847 to 1855, and now a member of the Roman *Curia*. He had been an early benefactor of Wimmer and the American Benedictines.

[33] Bishop Michael Domenec of Pittsburgh (1816-1872).

[34] Bishop Michael O'Connor (1810-1872), Domenec's predecessor as bishop of Pittsburgh.

presented the affair as fiction or delusion. The poor brother who played the leading part as the deliverer of a poor soul from Purgatory could not for some time remain in the monastery, and for me, also, life was very bitter.

The incident has meanwhile been irrefutably verified, and a Nemesis has pursued the principal opponents in rapid succession. As a result of the deliverance of a poor soul who had suffered in Purgatory for 77 years, events have occurred that have had most important and beneficial effects not only for St. Vincent but also for our whole Order, and that are far more miraculous than the deliverance of the poor soul. These effects are not yet publicly known. However, they will become known in time.[35]

Now, without intending it, my short report on a money matter has become a long letter, and because of this, I missed the post. I ask forgiveness and sign myself, in deepest respect and submission, and humbly asking for your blessing, Your Grace's most obedient servant, Boniface Wimmer, Abbot

Ger   oAAMwk cASVA   transIG

TO KING LUDWIG I   67

Newark, December 2, 1862

Most Serene Highness! Most Benign King and Lord! It has been a long time since I have been able to send Your Royal Majesty a report. Both last year and again this year I waited in vain for publication of the *Catholic Almanac*, which always carries a general survey of ecclesiastical affairs in America, but again this year there was no almanac because of the war in the South and the interruption of all communications that prevents information from the South from reaching us. It is simply impossible to receive anything from that section of the country.

In our congregation nothing, or at least not much of special significance, has happened. Quietly and undisturbed, we continue what we have begun, intent upon gradually raising our educational institutions to higher levels and bringing them to the standards they should have so that they will not be merely schools for the training of a few people for our Order and for the secular clergy, but will be institutions that through the efficiency of their teachers and the thoroughness of their instruction will fulfill all the necessary requirements and even surpass all expectations. I

---

[35] On the alleged apparitions of Paul George Keck and their aftermath, see *An American Abbot*, pp. 256-79. Wimmer was eventually forced to repudiate Keck and his "visions." See Wimmer's letter (page 270) to Cardinal Barnabo, June 20, 1863.

have, therefore, appointed as professors the best-equipped members of our Order. The majority of them received their training in German institutions of learning. I sent one of our exceptionally talented priests, Father Edward Hipelius,[36] a native of Lower Franconia (Bavaria), to Rome to further his education, and upon his return, he will set up an outstanding school here. I also intend to send two clerics in minor orders to Rome to become well grounded in learning, especially in the fields of philosophy and theology, and later to teach these subjects in our school. Their names are Fr. Adalbert Müller and Fr. Innocent Wolf.[37] Both are very talented and so young that it will be several years before they can be ordained, though they will have already completed their philosophical studies before leaving for Rome. The priest as well as the two clerics are to stay in the reformed monastery of Abbot Peter Cassaretto at St. Ambrose in Rome in order not to lose anything in monastic discipline while they make progress in the arts and sciences. The expenses for each of the three boarders amount to 100 *scudi* annually, besides their expenses for books, clothes, etc. The trip to Rome comes to $150 per person. This is a great expense for the monastery—more than $300 per head, or nearly $1,000 for all three. I am going to ask the *Ludwig Missionsverein* for support in this endeavor, and if I do not get it, or get only a part of it, may I not invoke the generosity of Your Royal Majesty? To whom else can I turn? There is no one who has helped the Benedictine Order so perseveringly, so magnanimously, so successfully as Your Majesty!

I hope that within a short time I may have the pleasure to report to you that our priory in Minnesota has been raised to the status of abbey. At least we petitioned the Holy See for its elevation after the last general chapter at St. Vincent, on September 15, 16, and 17 of this year, and we hope the Holy Father will grant it since the priory already has nine fathers, three young clerics, and several brothers, and has, moreover, some very imposing property, procured with the 3,000 florins Your Majesty so graciously deigned to give us!

Immediately after the general chapter, I left for Minnesota to hold the chapter for the election of a prior or, in the event, of the abbot. The unanimous vote fell on the present prior at St. Vincent, Father Othmar Wirtz,[38] a native of Zurich and a convert. Since then he has assumed his post. It is a sad time in this otherwise

---

[36] Edward Hipelius, O.S.B. (1836-1900). One of the bright stars in the American Benedictine constellation, Hipelius left the monastery several years after returning to St. Vincent and became a diocesan priest.

[37] Adalbert Müller, O.S.B. (1842-1906), and Innocent Wolf, O.S.B. (1843-1922), went to Rome in 1866 and completed their studies in 1870. Wolf became first abbot of St. Benedict's Abbey, Kansas, and Müller, after teaching theology at Saint Vincent for several years, returned to Rome to become a professor at the Collegio di Sant' Anselmo and eventually prior of the monastery there.

[38] Othmar Wirtz, O.S.B. (1831-1874).

blessed and happy Minnesota. The wild Sioux Indians had shortly before perpetrated awful cruelties and devastations. Yet our institutions there have not suffered from them, though our parishes lament the loss of two or three human lives, while hundreds of Protestant neighbors were cruelly murdered!

On this occasion, I founded in the small town of Shakopee, on the St. Peter River, a small colony for our Benedictine nuns by taking with me from St. Marys [Pennsylvania] two choir sisters and one lay sister and introducing them there in order to give them charge of the school, to the great joy of the English and the German Catholics. The new convent has its own peculiar history. It was first a cow barn, then a horse stable, then a priests' dwelling, and now a sisters' convent. In the present emergency, it is adequate for its purpose.

In St. Cloud I also visited the older Benedictine convent whose earlier superior, Sister Benedicta,[39] caused me so much grief. She died last year. Since then everything has gotten back on the right track. With the present superior,[40] I actually could make the necessary arrangements for establishing from there (St. Cloud) a small Benedictine convent in St. Joseph.

On my return journey, I visited our second college, in Sandwich, a city in English Canada. It is called Assumption College. I took it over just last fall when it was in a condition of total decay. The first year we could get only ten students. This year we had forty-six, and the number of boarders is still increasing. Sandwich, though a small town, is the seat of a French-Canadian bishop.[41] The Catholics of the diocese are French and Irish, but very close to it, right on the shores of the river (the Detroit River), lies the large, mainly German city of Detroit, the capital of Michigan and likewise a bishopric with a bishop's residence. This makes Assumption College a highly important place because it is the only institution where the Catholic youth of both dioceses can obtain a Catholic education. The bishop donated the buildings together with one hundred acres of good land, in such a way, however, that we cannot sell it. I have three priests and two clerics there with several brothers who until now have won the full confidence not only of the respective bishops but also of the neighboring inhabitants.

During my absence in Minnesota, and while on visitation to the various priories, troops were levied and four of my lay brothers were drafted into the army though they had already made solemn profession. This forced me to hurry to Washington to see the President and from him to procure their release. My representations achieved the desired result. It was decided that monks of St. Benedict

---

[39] Benedicta Riepp, O.S.B. (1825-1862).

[40] Willibalda Scherbauer, O.S.B. (1828-1914).

[41] The bishop of Sandwich (later London), Ontario, was Pierre Adolphe Pinsonnault.

would be exempt from military service so that in the future we shall no longer be vexed in this respect.[42]

Leaving Washington, I made a short detour to Newark where I used the momentary rest to finish this report to Your Royal Majesty. I am exceedingly happy to learn from the newspapers now and then that Your Majesty enjoys good health. May God be pleased to keep Your Highness vigorous and well for many more years, for the consolation of the poor, for the ornament of Bavaria, and for the welfare of Holy Church! Tribulations cannot bow down your great soul but can only increase your merit! In most humble submissiveness and loyalty, I am Your Royal Majesty's most devoted and grateful, Boniface Wimmer, Abbot

Ger   oRAB   cASVA   transBB   Math 154-58

TO SCHOLASTICA BURKHARDT   **68**

Covington, Ky., February 7, 1863

Dear Reverend Mother Prioress: I would like very much to be in Erie on Tuesday to greet you in person on your namesday [February 10, the Feast of St. Scholastica], but since I cannot be present, accept my written wishes. I shall ask St. Scholastica to storm heaven for their fulfillment. I know that you wish for nothing more than to serve and to glorify God, to please your heavenly bridegroom, and to give Him much pleasure; to train and lead many true and loving brides to Him, and, as now, in the earthly choir, so some day to sing sweet songs of praise eternally in heaven, to delight in and enjoy His presence. I wish that, by His grace, all this will come to pass here on earth and in heaven.

Recently I went to Kansas on a visitation and came near to arriving either injured or dead. Twenty-nine miles from Steubenville all coaches without exception leapt over a 65 foot embankment. The baggage cars went into a thousand pieces. The sleeping coaches were burnt. Our coach, the next to the last, was burning also, but the fire was extinguished, and–wonderful to say!–only one man had a broken arm and two others received less serious injuries. All the others escaped with minor wounds. At first, I felt nothing at all, but afterwards (and now) it feels as if I slammed my forehead quite hard against something. My left hip and

---

[42] Wimmer had managed to obtain only a brief exemption for his monks. The following year a stricter draft law resulted in the conscription of other monks. See his letter (page 267) of June 10, 1863, to Abraham Lincoln.

shoulder are also affected. Brother Franz,[43] who was with me, also received minor injuries to his feet and back. Because the cliff was not only very high but also very steep, we all fell head over heels on top of each other, i.e., we were in a heap from the floor to the ceiling. Yet the coach did not turn over twice. That is, it did not roll. Otherwise, it would have broken, and then many would have been seriously injured or even killed.

This happened about 7:30 pm, after we had our supper in Cadis Junction. There I heard from the innkeeper that the morning train had left the track several miles back from the junction. All the passengers received minor injuries. As we returned to the coach, I related this to the brother and thanked God that our train had arrived about seven hours late in Latrobe, or we would have been on the morning train. Then I began to pray in silence and to place us under the protection of the holy guardian angels when suddenly it went bump! bump! bump! and we, too, tumbled down into the deep ravine. The angels surely helped. Otherwise, you would perhaps not have seen me again.

After we had removed the two over-turned stoves and extinguished the flames at either end of the coach, we extricated ourselves and climbed the high and steep embankment in the hard frozen snow. Only when we looked down into the ravine and saw the wrecked coaches did we realize the danger we had escaped.

Let me be included in the prayers of your pious children so that, God willing, I shall make this long trip safely, quickly, and with success. Perhaps I shall see you then on my return. Your most devoted, Boniface Wimmer, Abbot

N.B. The lard, no doubt, has arrived. It was sent last week via freight cars.

Ger   oASBC   cASVA   transGS

TO GREGORY SCHERR   **69**

St. Vincent, February 26, 1863

Your Grace: The many labors with which I am always burdened have prevented me from writing to you before this. Since your namesday is near, however, I must join in spirit with the many people for whom this is a day of rejoicing and most respectfully extend to Your Grace the heartiest good wishes of both my confreres and myself. For some months I had hoped to convey them to you personally, as in 1855, since many important matters demanded such urgent attention that it

---

[43] Francis Stelzle, O.S.B., (1832-1898).

appeared I would have to go to Rome again, but the political situation in our country has been so dismal for such a long time that if the President does not become more reasonable, a revolution will break out in the North, the consequences of which no one can foresee. Under these circumstances, I do not consider it a good idea to leave my monastery and my confreres for several months. Besides, one of my younger confreres is in Rome,[44] and he can take care of my business to a great degree.

We held our second general chapter, a small gathering, last September. Only two independent priors–Father Augustine Wirth[45] from Atchison, Kansas, and Father Benedict Haindl[46] from St. Cloud, Minnesota–and I (each with a delegate from our respective monasteries) attended the deliberations, but over and above this, all the priors from the priories dependent upon St. Vincent, and many other capitulars, had assembled. Before the event, we held a week of devotions, then three days of the chapter at which we proposed the elevation of the priory at St. Cloud to an abbey and the elevation of the prior, who is to be elected at St. Cloud, to an abbot. Moreover, we suggested that San José in Texas become an independent priory with Father Alto Hörmann[47] as the first independent prior. We issued various decrees on discipline and studies, which we have sent to the Holy See for confirmation.

Then the election of a permanent, lifetime abbot had to be held because four years ago my election was not confirmed by Rome (because of an error in procedure), that is to say, it was confirmed for three years and then extended for one year, but when all the summonses to the election had been sent out, and the distant priors with their delegates were already on their way, I received a notice from the procurator general[48] that contained a recommendation from the prefect of the Propaganda Fide[49] that the election be postponed until the capitulars living in the rebel states could attend. This was to avoid the possibility that the election might later be overturned if everyone did not have the opportunity to vote.

To the great chagrin of everyone present, the election had to be postponed once again. Because the uncertainty and vague situation had begun to be quite detrimental, one of the priors suggested that since there could be no election,

[44] Edward Hipelius, O.S.B. (1836-1900), a priest from Saint Vincent, was studying in Rome at the time.

[45] Augustine Wirth, O.S.B. (1828-1901).

[46] Benedict Haindl, O.S.B. (1815-1887).

[47] Alto Hörmann, O.S.B. (1829-1867).

[48] Abbot Angelo Pescetelli, O.S.B. (1809-1885).

[49] The prefect of the Sacred Congregation for the Propaganda Fide was Cardinal Alessandro Barnabo.

the chapter should petition Rome to appoint a lifetime abbot. Thus, it happened (without my being present) that a petition was composed to His Holiness that I should be made abbot of Saint Vincent for life. This petition was signed, with few exceptions, by everyone. Its outcome remains to be seen. To me, it seems extremely peculiar that the Holy See has so many doubts about sanctioning my lifetime administration of Saint Vincent. I have been most strongly tempted to resign. I have even told the procurator general of this intention. Since to resign would be detrimental to my self-respect, however, I have decided not to do it. Very recently, I heard that Rome will probably again deny the request because of complaints from one or several American bishops who want no lifetime abbot in America. The Order will certainly be the loser in this. A denial will impede the abbot in the exercise of his office and inhibit his effectiveness.

After these deliberations, I had to make another long journey to Minnesota in order to preside at the election of a prior and perhaps an abbot. The choice fell unanimously on my prior, Father Othmar Wirtz,[50] who left for Minnesota several days later. I visited my more remote western priories–Chicago, Covington, our Assumption College in Canada, and Erie. In the meantime, many new things happened that permitted me to pass judgment on the ghost story (rumor of which continues to grow).

Frightful things had been spread abroad with regard to this story, both in America and even more in Germany. Very few of these tales had any foundation. In a nutshell, I had reported a long time ago to the procurator general all the revelations and visions. I doubted many very strongly, but I considered several as authentic since many prophecies were fulfilled exactly, and several real miracles have been worked. For example, a noticeable cure, the conversion of a calloused sinner on his deathbed, etc. Since the earliest days I did not want to believe what was said about the appearance of Luther after his death and his recantation and refutation and that he is only in Purgatory. However, of one thing I was certain: this man [Paul Keck] could not have made up this story by himself. Therefore, I gave the order that he was never to be left alone. I was certain that when he wrote, he could not have plagiarized it. Moreover, I remembered that at one time in Munich, Fathers Fortunatus and Augustine presented the same thesis to me (that Luther is not in Hell), at which time they referred to St. Teresa and Maria of Agreda. On hasty reading of what was written [by Keck], the idea seemed orthodox. Therefore, I considered it at least possible that the case had some foundation, especially

---

[50] Othmar Wirtz, O.S.B. (1831-1874).

since Father Prior and Father Novice Master,[51] who were closer to the seer than I was, vouched for the excellence of his character. The case reached sensational heights in the house, and almost all the fathers were divided either for or against the seer. The most zealous were all for him while the more lax repeatedly came forward with angry misrepresentations or obvious lies against him, and really the hand of God seemed to have touched several persons through this. So naturally, it was impossible for a long time for me to decide what I should think of the matter, particularly since I myself could give evidence that I had become more zealous in good deeds through it, as was also certain to a greater or lesser degree with all his friends. Your Excellency probably knows that I am not a man who is easily misled, but as I said above, while I was on a journey for five weeks, many things occurred that placed the morality of the seer in grave suspicion. When I investigated closer, I soon found out that my good novice master and prior were dominated by him, and that he was not watched over while writing, and that usually he had many breaches of the *Holy Rule* to confess. Soon afterward, my judgment was formed, and I expelled him from the Order. Of course, his friends were very indignant over this, and it caused much irritation in the monastery, but now everything has been in order for a good while. The only thing is that the novice master ran away with this fellow and has not come back yet. Even now, he cannot be convinced of his mistake. That happened on November 10.

On my last journey, the train was derailed over a 65-foot embankment at 7:30 in the evening. I would have taken the morning train, but I could not make the connection since there was about an eight-hour delay. The morning train also derailed only a few miles back from where the evening train ran off the track. Had I been on it, I would certainly have been injured badly since all the passengers sustained serious injuries of varying degrees. I first heard of this at the station where we ate supper. When we continued our journey again, I immediately began to commend myself to my holy guardian angel, when all of a sudden I noticed that the train was falling into a ravine. Immediately after that, the car overturned and everyone fell in disorder on top of one another. It is a wonder, but only one man broke his arm and two others were slightly injured. Although the whole train was involved in the wreck, and the last car even burned (because in this car there was a stove that overturned and caused a fire), the other passengers, including myself, were not injured in the least.

Otherwise, there is not much to report. Nonetheless, I can say truthfully that everything goes well. In Minnesota, the Indians have badly ransacked several

---

[51] The prior was Father Othmar Wirtz; the novice master, Father Wendelin Mayer, O.S.B. (1832-1881).

places, but few Catholics were killed. A short time before, the people of New Ulm had challenged and mocked the Catholic Corpus Christi procession. They had led around an ox instead of a monstrance. Their town was destroyed to its foundations, and hundreds of them were killed. In Chicago, we have to build a new church since the present wooden structure is small and miserable, but building sites are terribly expensive and funds are not adequate. In Covington, we have built a nice convent for the Benedictine sisters. Brother Cosmas[52] built a lovely altar in the church, though we fell short of making a profit from it because we contracted for it too cheaply ($2,400). Presently, with outside help, the brothers are working on an altar (for $5,000) for the beautiful Jesuit church in Cincinnati, as well as on altars for some country churches. From a financial and disciplinary perspective, I am not satisfied with these undertakings. I fear that later on they will fail.

In Lower Canada, we have taken over a college that this year has 45 students, among whom are many philosophers and theologians. There are only three priests, two clerics, and six brothers there, but a fourth priest will soon join them as a French teacher because French is the principal tongue there. It is the diocesan seminary for Detroit and Sandwich. The first year was very difficult since we were just beginning, and many arrangements and repairs were necessary. Only a few students came. (The place had a bad reputation.) This year there is a great problem with money. Currently the American dollar is worth a half dollar in Canada. That makes the loss great. The French bishop constrains us so that he profits but we Germans do not. I took it when the war broke out principally to have a sanctuary in case of emergency.

At home, we have 30 scholastics, five novices, 12 clerics, one subdeacon, and one deacon. There are two clerics in St. Cloud and two in Canada. Therefore, we have a total of 16 clerics. There are also 122 students in the school. Father Alto Hörmann[53] of Texas (who cannot return there for the present) is acting prior. Father Luke Wimmer[54] is subprior. Father Alphonse Heimler[55] is director of the school. Father Francis Cannon[56] is procurator. Father John Sommer[57] is professor of philosophy, chemistry, etc. Fathers Alto and Alphonse are lecturers in dogma

---

[52] Cosmas Wolf, O.S.B. (1822-1894), an artist whose wooden altars and sculptured wooden statues decorated Benedictine churches in Pennsylvania and Kentucky.

[53] Alto Hörmann, O.S.B. (1829-1867).

[54] Luke Wimmer, O.S.B. (1825-1901).

[55] Alphonse Heimler, O.S.B. (1832-1909).

[56] Francis Cannon, O.S.B., a former Franciscan brother, later left the monastic life and returned to his native Ireland.

[57] John Sommer, O.S.B. (1815-1886).

and moral theology. The clerics staff the scholasticate (gymnasium). Maurice Schwab[58] is the music teacher in the college, but he recently suffered a stroke. Father Boniface Krug[59] is the choir director for the scholastics and clerics. In addition, two secular priests help out in the scholasticate. They are here to learn moderation. Also an old pastor from Mainz, Kerchen, gives music lessons. The southern students (who can no longer go home) already owe me $6,000. I will probably never get any of it.

From time to time, we give missions in which Father Gerard, Boniface, Luke, and Paulinus are employed.[60] Father Luke gave an excellent one last week in Ligonier, where every evening the church was filled with Protestants. He is a very clever speaker–considerate, not inflammatory–and preaches only in English.

Our last harvest was very good. Only the corn failed. The brewery had begun to be a significant auxiliary enterprise, but then came the new tax of one dollar per barrel (a barrel equals 32 gallons, a gallon being somewhat more than a bucket). This ruined everything. The prices for clothing are three to four times greater than before. Even the barest necessities are expensive. Besides these, personal expenses are exorbitant. A new draft law is coming that exempts nobody between the ages of 20 and 45, not even priests. Everyone who does not want to serve must pay $300. How this will turn out, God only knows. It can hardly be enacted, however, without universal revolt, especially among the Democrats (to which party I and all my people belong).

We have not had to endure anything of the war itself. There were four brothers drafted into the military. However, the army sent one back as unfit and two left to join our priests in Canada. The fourth was sent back by the War Department after he had been three months in the field, or actually in the hospital.

My Father Leonard Mayer,[61] pastor of the German community in Richmond, was able to write me four times, but he received none of my letters. Because of this, I received a permit from Washington for a meeting with him. Father Emmeran Bliemel[62] (who is in Nashville) tried to smuggle medicine to the southerners in Tennessee, but he was caught and imprisoned. Luckily, he was brought

---

[58] Maurice Schwab (+1875) was a layman who came to Saint Vincent from Munich in 1851 to teach music.

[59] Boniface Krug, O.S.B. (1838-1909) later left Saint Vincent and joined the Archabbey of Montecassino in Italy, where he became archabbot.

[60] Gerard Pilz, O.S.B. (1834-1891); Boniface Krug, Luke Wimmer, and Paulinus Wenkmann, O.S.B. (1836-1921).

[61] Leonard Mayer, O.S.B. (1824-1875).

[62] Emmeran Bliemel, O.S.B. (1831-1864), became a chaplain in the Confederate Army. He was killed in combat during the Battle of Atlanta. See Peter J. Meaney, "Valiant Chaplain of the Bloody

before General Rosecrans, who is a good Catholic, and was sent home to his bishop with an admonition that would do him some good. I received notification of this. I have heard nothing from the four fathers in Texas since January 6 of last year. Father Alto is here.

Brother Gallus[63] was enticed into the military and fought in the three-week campaign in Maryland. He was wounded in the bloody battle at Antietem and had to be hospitalized. He was discharged, however, and is home again. He is from St. Boniface and is now thoroughly cured of his hypochondria. He has a great respect for grenades and shrapnel. The stories of his adventure have provided us with many enjoyable hours.

Emmeran Bliemel, O.S.B. (1831-1864), a chaplain in the Confederate Army, was killed in combat during the Battle of Atlanta.

I have almost forgotten to speak about my finances. It is better for me, however, not to touch upon this difficult matter. I need not pray "Lord, protect me from wealth" for there is no danger from that quarter. God has never punished me with an abundance of riches, and I will not complain about poverty since I have already praised it. Nevertheless, I always receive credit as I need it, since I am an honorable soul who always pays his debts eventually. I am always building and farming, taking in more poor students (and unlucky priests), always giving lodging to strangers, etc. The brewery is paid off, but I must get more barrels. Recently I commissioned Brother Conan,[64] a very capable mechanic, to build a machine that would make trimmed noodles, macaroni, Fadennudeln, etc. Since we have no fish, the fast days (especially the 40 days when we can eat no meat at all) are quite difficult to bear. We have connected this machine to a steam engine that needs only one brother to run it. It easily processes three to four hundred pounds of flour a day. Some of what it produces we will eventually be able to sell. Excluding labor, the machine cost about $100, so there are things we still need money for.

Tenth," *Tennessee Historical Quarterly* 41 (1983): 37–47; and Aloysius Plaisance, "Emmeran Bliemel, O.S.B., Heroic Confederate Chaplain," *The American Benedictine Review* 17 (1966): 206–16.
[63] Gallus Maier, O.S.B.
[64] Unidentified.

Our Father Edward Hipelius[65] also costs me a great deal. Then I have two clerics, Fraters Adalbert and Innocent,[66] whom I would like to send to Rome so that
some day they can return as excellent professors. Unfortunately, they have no
stipend. Other than this, I do not want to mention what sort of plans I have in
mind because it is very disappointing when I cannot carry them out. All of them
are good and reasonable. I desire nothing at all for myself. I have nothing over
and above what is necessary, not even a good riding horse, but it is the Lord's
will. I attract more priests to this country than any bishop. The expenses of this
undertaking are never in harmony with my income. Therefore, as distasteful as
it is, I must renew my annual request for the powerful assistance of the *Ludwig
Missionsverein* and humbly ask Your Grace to see to it that St. Vincent's request
for alms not be overlooked. This is a necessary request, since I will probably not
be able to find time to write to the honorable members of the central committee
to place this request humbly before them, much as I would like to.[67]

Much more could still be done. For example, the *Missionsverein* could furnish
me with traveling expenses so that I might send the Fraters Adalbert and Innocent
to Rome, or even to Munich. It would certainly be good to further their education in one of these two cities. I want to remain quite honest and thereby to see to
it that my people are upright and constantly improving, and that even the young
people studying here receive a healthy education.

Currently we number 62 Benedictine priests. This number does not include the
secular priests we have educated here, most of whom would not have been able
to become priests at all without us. In addition, our sisters—the Benedictine nuns
in St. Marys, Erie, Newark, Covington, Chicago, Shakopee, and St. Cloud—are
doing much good and leading very edifying lives.

The accursed civil war, in which more than 100,000 men have already died,
must, in a short time, cause universal bankruptcy. The war will probably not end
soon because it can easily degenerate into a war between the political parties. This
would be unfortunate for the Catholics. The Methodist preachers and the Reds
of '48 are the instigators of the war. Their plan was to destroy the South, where
most of the Democrats live, and then to attack the Catholics in both the North
and the South. Many spoke of this loudly and stated it unreservedly in their
newspapers. Since most Catholics are Democrats, and this party is now victorious
everywhere, they cannot at present consider persecuting Catholics since public
opinion is against it. Thus, God shows how to derive good from evil. *Ad plurimos*

---

[65] Edward Hipelius, O.S.B. (1836-1900), was studying in Rome at this time.

[66] Adalbert Müller, O.S.B. (1842-1906), and Innocent Wolf, O.S.B. (1843-1922).

[67] As archbishop of Munich, Gregory Scherr was president of the *Ludwig Missionsverein*.

annos! With deep reverence, and asking your holy blessing, I am Your Grace's most obedient servant, Boniface M[aria] Wimmer, Abbot

Ger   oAAM   cASVA   transKB

TO ABRAHAM LINCOLN   **70**

Washington City, June 10, 1863

Dear Sir: Through your very kind favor, I obtained on the 28th of November, 1862, from your Secretary of War,[68] an order by which the members of the Benedictine Order were relieved from military duty because, by the religious belief and doctrine of said Order, it is unlawful to bear arms, and the monks are bound irrevocably to the Order by solemn vows, and are thereby prevented from taking up arms, their mission being a mission of peace.

The poor brothers released by your order, and indeed all of us, will forever be grateful to Your Excellency for this favor. I had no doubt the same would hold good also for the impending draft, because it was expressed in general terms, specifying no number or times, and was coming from the highest authority in the country, and the very same reasons for which it was granted existing yet. However, I am told that the new conscription law made it void, and therefore I am compelled by duty and necessity to appeal again to you for protection, so much more as this time not only the brothers but also the priests and clergymen have been enrolled. Your well-known benevolence admits of no doubt that you would again help us, and certainly if you will, you can do it.

Permit me, dear sir, to give you some reasons, which I trust will justify this humble petition:

First. I cannot believe that the law intends to press clergymen (of any denomination or religion) into military service, because as a general matter these men are very warlike indeed if the fight has to be done with their tongues or pens, but otherwise they keep at a good distance from danger, and what should the Government gain if some hundred cowards were in the army? Then if it had been the intention of the law to press us in the Army, it would not permit us to evade the draft by paying $300, and it is my firm belief you won't catch a single priest or preacher or minister of the Gospel, unless he could not afford paying.

This admitted, I can see no reason why the highest Executive would not let escape such whom the law did not intend to reach, and consequently, I do think

---

[68] Edwin M. Stanton (1814-1869).

you can again grant us exemption; for whether we range under the warlike or like cowards, we are not fit men for military service.

Second. These learned men in Congress cannot well have been ignorant of the fact that nowhere and at no time among civilized nations ever a law existed by which clergymen or monks had been obliged to go to war. Indeed, in the middle ages we find sometimes bishops and abbots in war, but not in their clerical capacity, and only if they held lands from a sovereign. Congress, therefore, could not well have passed a law that is in contradiction with the feelings of the whole world; and this confirms me again in my belief that they did not intend to touch the persons of the clergy, but only their purse.

Third. If the law with regard to the clergy of all denominations does not intend to press them into the Army, and to take them away from the pulpit and the altar, and if it be satisfied if they ransom themselves for a certain sum, it would not make a very great difference whether the money has already been spent for the benefit of the country or shall be spent at the time of the draft. I mean to say, if I had given last year all my fortune, say some thousand dollars, for charitable or religious purposes, not expecting or suspecting that I ever as a clergyman could be drafted, and if, nevertheless, I would now be drafted and had to go to war because I had not so much money any more to pay for my exemption, should the fact that I had given all my fortune for the best of the country not deserve any regard, and excuse me from paying of the $300?

President, this is in fact the case with me. I am a good many years now living in this country. No necessity compelled me to emigrate; it was my own good and free will. I came to devote all I was and all I had to the moral and material aid of my countrymen. I had 19 men with me when I arrived here, and a good many more followed every year to join in our trials, in our labors, and they were no trifles. I bought land and improved it (not for speculation); I built a college strictly for the poor, who have talent but little money or none at all to pay for their own education; took charge and care for orphans, gave shelter to the poor traveler (hundreds of them); established a female branch of our order for the same purpose in several places, from New York to St. Cloud in Minnesota, to Atchison in Kansas, and from Chicago to Texas. I have collected not one cent from anybody in this country for these establishments, but I got every year $3,000 from Bavaria and some years $4,000 and $5,000 and $6,000 (from the ex-king of Bavaria, King Louis, alone more than $15,000); all this money and all that I could earn through the hard labor of my good confreres I have spent in this country for the benefit of this country, more so than I ought to have, for I ran ever into heavy debts. All my confreres who came over from Germany have done the same; have deposited their fortunes into our common stock, little or much as it was, unsuspecting, of course, that we ever could be disturbed in our peaceable and charitable pursuits, the least of all that we ever could be drafted into military service, such a thing being unheard of in the annals of Christian nations; and now the law says, Shoulder arms or pay; and I having spent all my own, all our common money, for the benefit of this country, I must blushingly confess I cannot pay. I have no money, and the law then answers: Shoulder arms. Is there such a law in this country?

Do we not deserve any regard on account of our money spent, though we have at present none to spare to pay the exemption? I do not like to boast or to glory, sir; I am ashamed that I am compelled to say it. I cannot be drafted, I am too old for that; but I must speak for those of my confreres who may be drafted.

Fourth. The question of conscience I will not touch. Suffice it to say that we cannot go in war unless we act in a grievous manner against our conscience.

These reasons I trust will justify this my humble petition for a new confirmation of the former grant or to obtain a new one for the impending draft. I have the English language too little in my power but that I could express myself so politely as I wished I could, and I must in this regard beg for your kind indulgence. But I ask your permission to suggest an idea that might be to the purpose. In the German States, conscription is a regular thing every year, and no able-bodied young man is exempt from the draft unless he buys a substitute. However, with regard to students of law, medicine, and particularly of Divinity, exemptions are admitted in this way: These students are enrolled and drafted like other men of their age, but in order not [to] interrupt their studies, they are indeed kept on the list, but obtain furlough for an indefinite time. Thus the law is complied with and these young men are not [taken away] from their scientific employments. If there is no other loyal way to grant exemption for the members of the Benedictine order, I think this one would not be [objectionable].

But your kind sentiments and your experience in law and life will easily find means and ways in justice or in equity to put us out of trouble and conflict with our conscience. May God bless you for it.

I remain, sincerely, Your Excellency's most faithful and obedient servant, Boniface Wimmer, Abbot of St. Vincent, Westmoreland, Pa.

Eng   oArchives of the United States[69] cASVA

---

[69] Printed in *The War of the Rebellion – A Compilation of the Official Records of the Union and Confederate Armies* (Washington, D.C.: Government Printing Office, 1880) Series III, Volume 3: 333-336.

TO ALESSANDRO BARNABO   **71**

St. Vincent, June 20, 1863

Your Eminence, Most Reverend and Kind Cardinal Prefect: With a great deal of surprise, I received a letter from Paul (George) Keck, our notorious visionary, mailed from Rome. In this letter, he indicated that he had come to the Eternal City, to Prince Hohenlohe,[70] with a letter recommending that he complete his studies. Your Eminence knows that this Paul, whose visions and revelations I once believed to some degree, was expelled from the Order by me in November 1862. His moral conduct had become questionable. He had committed a number of actions that were extremely detrimental to the peace and good reputation of our Order. More than that, there could no longer be any doubt that his visions and revelations were false.

At that time, I reported to Your Eminence that his friends raised a sort of rebellion in the monastery and that he took leave but returned shortly afterward to the monastery and to religious submission.[71] There was one exception: Father Wendelin Mayer,[72] who had been Paul's novice master and spiritual father. He was absent from the monastery for about four months continuously, both without my permission and without my knowing where he was living. He finally returned to the monastery when Paul had made up his mind to go to Rome. Upon his return home, he was received by me like a prodigal son, and although I should have punished him severely, I forgave him everything in order that I might win him by being kind, but in a spirit of perversion he did not want to acknowledge that he had sinned, but rather accused me of unjustly condemning and expelling Paul. He requested that I permit him to go to Rome so that he could defend Paul's cause. I refused to allow such a course of action (1) because such a defense was no business of his, and Paul himself could, if he so desired, defend himself; (2) because such a long journey would have cost a great deal; and (3) because if he chose to do so, he could appeal to the Holy See by letter.

He submitted for a time and remained at home, but he then slyly took advantage of my good will. He requested that I send him to the mountains (with the permission of the most reverend bishop) in order to give the Germans dwelling among the English-speaking people an opportunity to fulfill their Easter duty.

---

[70] Archbishop Gustav Adolph Hohenlohe (1823-1896), later cardinal, of the Roman Curia.

[71] Paul George Keck, after his expulsion from St. Vincent, sought refuge in the Priory of St. Cloud, Minnesota. On Keck's alleged apparitions and their aftermath, see *An American Abbot*, 256-79. Wimmer was eventually forced to repudiate Keck and his "visions."

[72] Wendelin Mayer, O.S.B. (1832-1881).

Not suspecting anything evil, I granted his request, but he used the opportunity of staying five weeks in that region, where he was well known by all, to collect stipends and the money necessary for undertaking a trip to Europe. This he did without requesting a single word of permission, against my will and without my knowledge. He sent back 51 mass intentions (without the stipends) and left me to look after their fulfillment on his behalf and in his place! I have no doubt that he will travel first through Germany and then into Italy to the gates of the Holy Apostolic See and begin to act in the cause of his client, Paul; although I am convinced that Paul, if it could conveniently be done, would prefer to remain hidden rather than defend himself.

I desire to acquaint Your Eminence with this matter, lest perchance I might seem to have sent these unhappy religious who have been discovered to have so little religious spirit. It disgusts me to find fault with confreres or to bring such problems to the Sacred Congregation, but since matters have come to such a pass, it seems necessary to reach a solution so that those who looked upon Paul almost as if he were a prophet, and who still consider him holy and innocent, may be changed. Indeed, some of our people still cling to him and accept his visions and revelations as genuine. Even our excellent Othmar Wirtz,[73] who has been elected prior in Minnesota and who helped me so outstandingly in quelling the rebellion (when I dismissed Paul), is nevertheless attached to Paul, who rushed to Minnesota when he was cast out of our monastery so that he could ally himself with Othmar. Upon my warning not to keep him, [Father Othmar] dismissed him immediately, for he did not wish to act against obedience.

We had two visionaries in the monastery at the same time: this Paul, whose director was Wendelin, and a certain Leo, an upright, elderly, respectable man of our parish, whose director was Father Prior Othmar. It was as though one protected the other and helped the other, but in such a way, that Paul seemed to excel the other in extraordinary gifts. Like Paul, Leo also had visions and revelations, and among them some most beautiful ones regarding the feast of the Most Sacred Heart of Jesus. Both pretended to penetrate the secrets of hearts, and so on. Leo pretended to have an angel under the appearance of a beautiful young man. Paul, in the same way, had an angel in the form of a boy as his teacher and interpreter. After Father Othmar had gone to Minnesota, Leo received from me the recently appointed prior, Father Alto,[74] as confessor. After a short time he no longer had visions, ecstasies, and revelations, and because I would not permit him to follow

---

[73] Othmar Wirtz, O.S.B (1831-1874).
[74] Alto Hörmann, O.S.B. (1829-1867).

Father Othmar to Minnesota, he has only just recently left the monastery and returned to his relatives. He had never pronounced vows.

In both cases, certain remarkable events occurred, through which they acquired quite a reputation for trustworthiness. Since the one supported the other, this concord of two witnesses did much to increase their credibility and acceptance, all the more because there was moral certainty that they were not acting by mutual counsel. In general, Leo seemed to speak more temperately and solidly. While Paul seemed to practice and promote devotion to the Blessed Virgin, the holy guardian angels, and the souls in Purgatory, Leo seemed to practice and promote devotion to the Most Sacred Heart of Jesus and the wounds of the Most Holy Redeemer. Both spoke of the lack of true charity among the brethren. They saw this defect in all those who did not believe them, but they predicted everything good with regard to those who clung to them, as though the whole Benedictine Order in America was to be restored by them to its pristine severity and splendor according to the Cluniac reform. The purpose was to enable the Order to battle most strenuously and successfully against heresies and the Anti-Christ. In this battle some were to become martyrs, others renowned preachers of the divine word with tremendous success at winning souls.

I never put full confidence in them, but in many things I agreed with them, partly because what they said was true, partly because I placed great confidence in Father Othmar, my prior, and in Father Wendelin, the novice master, and partly also because their first adversaries were not particularly good and upright men, and also because they were frequently persecuted with lies and insults. Finally, I was hesitant because the Apostolic See itself seemed to have identified difficulties [at Saint Vincent] when it had first rescinded my election as abbot (which was almost unanimous) and then later postponed a second election to another year. This affected me very deeply, to the point where I almost despaired. I frequently thought of resigning the abbatial office because I thought there was a clear indication in such a reproof that I was unworthy and incapable of bearing the office of abbot.

Hence, I was led into believing that perhaps God had sent young Paul and the old man Leo, although neither was educated or very knowledgeable, precisely for the purpose of further humiliating me, and that I would learn from them the things that I still needed to do for the government of the Order. For Paul especially seemed in fact to assume the government of the whole monastery. He learned from a revelation who should become pastor, who should be the priest in charge of material things (the procurator), who should be director of students, who should be prefect, who should be prior in this or that parish, who should be transferred from one place to another, and so on. The same was true with regard to the lay brothers.

Most certainly I did not do all that he recommended, nor immediately, but sometimes I followed his counsel, if it did not work to anyone's disadvantage, although I would have acted differently if I had relied on my own judgment. In this manner he gradually managed to have his friends in the house in charge of all the important offices, so that in the chapter his opinion (I mean by that, the opinion he espoused) was more readily adopted. Thus, it happened that a candidate who was disliked by Paul was not admitted to the novitiate. Even the clerics in minor orders were not secure if Paul did not approve of them–for which reason they all feared him and did not dare say anything against him.

I knew all this well. I understood also that it was entirely against the divine order for a superior to be governed by an inferior, or for a novice, or one who was scarcely professed in simple vows, to govern an entire monastery and almost the entire congregation. I frequently discussed these matters with Father Prior and Father Master and rebuked them for placing too much confidence in Paul and for accepting him as though he were an oracle, but all to no avail. They pointed to the signs and good results (as they considered them). I, for reasons indicated above, although strongly shaken by doubts, gave in–because I still at that time considered Paul a very pious young man. In this state, I sent that report to Your Eminence in which I still defended Paul, speaking however of my misgivings.

Not long afterward, when the general chapter was over, I had to travel to Minnesota to conduct the election of the prior there. At the insistence of Father Prior, I permitted him to present Paul with two others in minor orders to the bishop of Pittsburgh[75] for ordination to the subdiaconate provided he could pass the examination, for he had learned very little theology. On the journey I received a letter from Father Wendelin in which he indicated to me that the Archangel Michael had appeared to Paul three times and had said to him that in the future neither angels nor saints nor the souls in Purgatory would appear to him, and this was a just judgment and punishment because I had neglected the souls in Purgatory and that I had never received with filial faith the revelations made to Paul nor had I acted in accordance with them except when I approved of them with my own reasoning. Also [the archangel said] that in order that this punishment would be more evident, not only had four lay brothers been drafted into military service, but conscription was to be extended to our entire congregation.

Paul had frequently urged me to send missionaries into two of our parishes to preach to the people wearing cucullas (not ordinary monks' garb). He said that

---

[75] Bishop Michael Domenec of Pittsburgh (1816-1878).

nothing would be accomplished unless they wore cucullas, or so the souls in Purgatory had declared. On his own authority, he had a cuculla made for himself, and imitating him, the novice master and other fathers did the same. The pattern of this cuculla was similar to that which professors in the university usually wear. I replied that I would not admit the cucullas because they were not customary with us and seemed too theatrical. Continuing in this manner, I said, "*I* am abbot of this monastery, not the souls in Purgatory, and if missions must be conducted only in cucullas, they will not be conducted at all." Because of this declaration of mine, the Archangel Gabriel threatened me with this judgment.

This revelation shook my confidence in Paul's revelations, and I was soon able to prove him false. The four lay brothers who were drafted into military service were sent back to the monastery when I remonstrated with the President in Washington. There really was a law passed this year by which absolutely all clerics–non-Catholics as well as Catholics–were to be conscripted into military service and called to arms unless they paid $300. Again, I remonstrated against this law in Washington and obtained promises that everything would be done to ensure that I could either entirely escape the law or that I would certainly not feel its full force.

Shortly afterward, something else happened, an event of so great importance that I had to dismiss Paul. When Paul went with two confreres to Pittsburgh, the bishop refused to ordain him because he considered him an impostor, as did most of the clergy of our diocese. Paul always prophesied that he would celebrate his first mass on the feast of the Immaculate Conception of the Blessed Virgin Mary[76] in the year 1863, and that if he did not succeed in doing so, that is, if the Devil were to prevent it, this would result in the greatest calamity for himself and for the monastery. Over my objection that this simply could not occur because in so short a time he could not absorb the necessary courses in philosophy and theology and because [ordination without a proper educational foundation] was against the custom of the Order, the Church, and the saints, he nevertheless insisted, stating, "The Blessed Virgin will intervene."

After he had been rejected by the bishop, he petitioned Father Othmar to be allowed to go to the Bishop of Erie[77] and receive all the orders from him at one time so that he could become a simplex priest.[78] At first, Father Othmar refused, but

---

[76] December 8.

[77] Bishop Josue Mary Young of Erie (1808-1866).

[78] A "simplex priest" was one who was validly ordained before reaching the canonical age of twenty-four. Simplex priests did not have faculties from their bishop to hear confessions, though faculties to administer all the sacraments (including hearing confessions) were generally granted after the

when Paul stated that I had promised that I would see to it that he would be ordained as a simplex priest, he finally consented. This was a lie. He had repeatedly expressed the fear that the Devil would impede his ordination. I told him that if his spirit was right, there was no cause for fear. In such a case, I would certainly see to it that he would become at least a simplex priest, but not so quickly as he desired.

Without my knowledge, they went to Erie, to the bishop who agreed to ordain Paul if he received dismissorial letters from me. Father Othmar came to meet me on my return from Minnesota in order to obtain dismissorial letters from me, but when he could not find me, he returned to Erie. While he was absent, a grave scandal had occurred.

There were three fathers in our priory [in Erie]. At the invitation of one of our more outstanding parishioners, they met with Paul one afternoon in the parishioner's home. Because Paul is an excellent singer and piano player, the little group had an excellent time, and they remained there until almost midnight. Father Ignatius[79] had returned in due time to the priory before supper, but the other two returned with Paul. Paul was with Father Otto.[80] The other priest accompanied a layman to his home and then returned to the priory, where he went straight to bed. Paul followed Otto into his cell, took off his clothes, and (as Otto said) incited him to impurity, which having taken place, Otto awakened Father Ignatius, who was asleep in the next room, and accused Paul of being an impure man. However, Paul denied everything and accused Otto of calumny. The following day, Paul himself (because the others avoided him) went to the bishop and revealed the whole matter to him, placing the blame on Father Otto. To confirm his accusation, he gave the bishop a letter, sent to him by his friends, but this letter greatly displeased the bishop because it seemed more like a love letter than a letter written by priests.

Upon investigating the matter in depth, the bishop found Paul guilty and rejected him. That same day Paul wrote to me, relating the matter and admitting that on the journey he had kissed Father Otto with the kiss of peace. He also admitted that he had visited Otto's cell and had taken off his clothes because Otto was in a drunken state and could not do so, but he claimed that Father Otto had then tempted him to impurity, and said that because he did not want to consent, he had cried out. He confirmed this statement with an oath. I received this letter

---

priest had reached the canonical age for ordination and had undergone additional theological and pastoral training.

[79] Ignatius Trueg, O.S.B. (1827-1910).

[80] Otto Kopf, O.S.B. (1832-1907).

in Sandwich, Canada, since Paul knew I was to go there on my journey. I also learned of the matter in an oral account by one of the witnesses, Father Ignatius, whom I had summoned from Erie to Sandwich to work in our college there before I knew anything at all about this affair.

Father Otto, summoned by the bishop, put an account in writing and declared that he would sign it with an oath if this was required. When I arrived in Erie a few days later, I visited the bishop immediately. He told me the whole story and recommended that I immediately dismiss Paul. I showed him Paul's account contained in the letter, which the bishop did not believe. Knowing full well what sorrow this affair would cause me, I requested that the bishop investigate the facts more accurately, namely that he interrogate the persons with whom Father Otto and Frater Paul had had supper, and the layman who opens the door to the callers at our house (the porter), to find out whether or not Father Otto was drunk. I also asked the bishop to warn Father Otto of the gravity of the matter and have him take an oath. At the same time, I asked Father Ignatius to provide a written account of what he knew, which he could state under oath.

Then I returned to Saint Vincent. I summoned the chapter and in Paul's presence I read his own account and the report from Father Otto (which had as yet not been sealed with an oath), and I asked Paul what he could say in his defense. I accused him of these points: (1) that without my knowledge and without my consent he tried underhandedly to receive holy orders, and by telling lies, he tried to persuade Father Othmar to assist him in this endeavor and had gone with him to Erie; (2) that in Erie, hoping to be ordained in two days, he had remained until almost midnight with several priests in the home of a laymen and had scandalized the people by singing and playing; (3) that upon returning home, he kissed Father Otto, whom he thought to be drunk, and committed other acts which, according to Father Otto's account, should certainly cast the gravest suspicion on him; (4) that he had communicated the whole affair to the bishop, when he knew perfectly well that I was to come to Erie in a few days; and (5) that although not required to do so, he had attached an oath to his statement. With two exceptions, the other capitulars were friends of Paul. All of them were inclined to believe him, and they refused to believe Otto.

It is true that a comparison of the statements of Father Otto and Father Ignatius seemed to reveal contradictions. Father Ignatius was already asleep when Father Otto and Paul returned home. He saw nothing, heard nothing of what was going on until awakened by Father Otto. Hence, he could testify only to those things he had seen and heard. However, Paul's and Ignatius's testimonies did not harmonize either. I therefore did not dare draw conclusions regarding the impure act, but I did declare in chapter that I would expel Paul from the Order if Otto would attach an oath to his statement.

A few days later, I received a letter from the bishop of Erie stating that he had strictly examined the witnesses, all of whom stated that Father Otto was not drunk. Our lay porter who had opened the door and shown the way with lighted candle stated that Father Otto needed no help and that he was not helped by anyone in climbing the stairs, whereas Paul had affirmed that with no small effort he could hardly lead him up the steps. The bishop also sent the sworn testimony of Father Otto and again declared that he was unable to not accept Otto's testimony as true and rebuked me for supporting Paul so long.

When I received this letter, I dismissed Paul without calling another chapter, because in the meantime I had consulted several capitulars privately. It was from this that the rebellion arose, during which Paul was always with the rebellious fathers. He came to my room with them and always acted by common counsel with them. At that time I myself was scarcely able to believe that Paul was inclined to commit so great a sin (of Onan or of Sodom), but I thought the sworn testimony of a priest was to be respected, all the more so since the bishop insisted. He had been wholly impartial, had not considered Paul an impostor, and would even have ordained him. In fact, witnesses to the contrary notwithstanding, I thought that Father Otto was drunk. Otherwise he would not have permitted Paul repeatedly (so Otto testifies) to have kissed him, to have come to his room, to have taken off his clothes, and so on. Afterward I wrote him a severe letter, full of reproaches, for his disgraceful way of acting, in which he not only received Paul, but even seemed to have drawn him to sin.

I soon learned that even in the monastery Paul was accustomed to embrace his friends most tenderly and to kiss them by putting his tongue in their mouths, as scarcely any chaste friends would do, which I expected all the less because I had already dismissed someone from the monastery for this kind of kissing, which I consider gravely impure. When I recall that he had frequently complained to me that the Devil almost constantly tormented him with the most violent temptations of the flesh, I could not think of these kisses as innocent. Hence, I became convinced that in Erie he really thought Father Otto was drunk and therefore acted more freely with him because he hoped that a drunken man would not remember on the following day anything that he had done in his drunkenness. In reality, Paul's whole manner of acting manifested a certain womanly tenderness and effeminacy, particularly when he sang, for which he was looked upon askance by many laymen and clerics. Nevertheless, Otto, who suspected him with regard to such conduct, admitted his kisses in order to see what he finally would have done, and when the matter proceeded to touches, he cried out. Hence, we have a hypocrite.

Whatever finally turns out to be the case, even though a priest should have induced one in minor orders to sin, the devil caught the devil. Paul was convicted of having sworn to perjury, even if we do not accept the statements, because all the other witnesses contradict him. Hence, I wrote on the testimony that I showed to him, "Since he seemed to be guilty not only of a grave sin against the sixth commandment, but also of perjury, he is expelled from the Order."

What he did after the expulsion does not commend him either. He traveled to Chicago where two priests from our order are pastors of St. Joseph's Parish, both of them very close friends of Paul. Father Wendelin followed soon after, and they so prevailed on the prior, Father Louis,[81] that he went to the bishop[82] and petitioned him to ordain Paul a priest. They almost convinced the bishop to ordain Paul, saying that it was according to my will and consent that he was being presented, but being informed of this new deceit, I warned the bishop not to ordain Paul. Rejected anew by this bishop, the prior in Covington went and tried the bishop there,[83] but he was rejected there because our confreres who are pastors in that city had already notified the bishop about Paul. Still they were not quiet. They went to Minnesota in order to get Father Othmar to plead his cause and with his help obtain the same goal, but Father Othmar, as I stated above, having been admonished by me, commanded both of them to leave, and I notified the bishop[84] that if Paul asked to be ordained, he should refuse him.

From all this, which is written without hatred but out of zeal for truth and justice, Your Eminence will readily perceive what kind of saint Paul is and how worthy a companion he has in the person of this Father Wendelin, his former novice master. Here you have an instance of the blind leading the blind, and it is difficult to say which of them is the more blind. Nevertheless, there is hardly any doubt that Paul blinded Wendelin, whose indiscreet zeal and secret pride were overly flattered when Paul prophesied that he would be a light of the first class, an outstanding preacher of the divine word who would win hundreds of thousands of sinners for God—which this simple man firmly believes. Moreover, because he still believes it, he cannot admit that Paul is a false prophet. Since bad fruit reveals a bad tree, there is no doubt that Paul is an impostor, and a most dangerous one who, if he were ordained a priest, could easily become another Arius and drag

---

[81] Louis Fink, O.S.B. (1834-1904).
[82] Bishop James Duggan (1825-1899), of Chicago.
[83] Bishop George A. Carrell, S.J. (1803-1868), of Covington, Kentucky.
[84] Bishop Thomas Grace, O.P. (1814-1897), of St. Paul, Minnesota.

innumerable souls to ruin. He frequently complained to me that nine devils surrounded him and tormented him. Sadder still, he said that he always beheld one devil among them who exactly portrayed his (Paul's) likeness. I hope this is not an omen. Through this very sad experience, I have learned how easily he can deceive others and how difficult it is to convince the deceived that they are deceived. I do not in the least doubt that even in Rome Paul will make friends, possibly even more influential ones. I thought it best to write to Your Eminence so that to some degree, while preventing new scandals, I may repair the scandal I have given.

If someone were to ask me how I can now assail Paul when only a few months earlier I commended him so highly, I would simply reply that this is not a matter of my inconstancy, and still less is it to be attributed to any passion or malice. Rather, because of the reasons mentioned above and others that it would be too tiring to list, I had doubts and suspicions about Paul's holiness, which I held close like sins spoken in the confessional. My reticence continued even when Paul's actions spoke so loudly that I could no longer doubt. In fact, it continued until those who had had the opportunity to observe him on a daily basis dared to speak against him. Then, all at once, I learned that he was not obedient, not chaste, not a lover of poverty, not humble, not given to mortification, not reverent, not sincere, not meek, truly loving neither God nor his neighbor, but an arrogant, hypocritical, pious impostor. In this judgment, with five or six exceptions, all the confreres now agree with me. There is no need to speak of his visions and revelations since such a man could not possibly be God's messenger, but if the question were asked, I can very easily prove that they are either Satan's illusions or Paul's fictions.

What I want to achieve by this letter is (1) to prevent Paul's deceiving others and (2) to bring about a decision in this matter by which the followers of Paul, especially those in the Order, be converted, particularly Father Othmar, prior in Minnesota, lest perchance, should he continue in his error, he harm others since he is a superior. For if by my fault–and with Michael the Archangel as witness, I never deeply believed in Paul, though for a time I did believe in him–many evils befell the Order because I tolerated and protected Paul and Leo so long, thinking it was possible and probable that they were truly enlightened by God (until the contrary was proved)–how much more evil could another superior cause who sincerely and from his inmost heart and almost from his very nature adheres to this kind of false mysticism and vain fictions!

It seems to me that Paul's principal purpose was to become a priest, and to do so at the earliest moment. Since he could no longer achieve this goal in America, or in Germany, he went to Rome to achieve it there. Possibly, had he been well directed, he would have immediately recognized and repelled this diabolical illusion, but when he saw how much influence he had acquired in so short a time by these fantasies, he used them for attaining his goal. He deceived Father Master and Father Prior first, and through them, me and other simple confreres.

For when he was leaving the monastery, he admitted and explicitly declared that he would not have come to this point if he had been properly directed. Elsewhere he admitted that the visions were diabolical in the sense that when he suffered from irritability of nerves and lassitude, the Devil abused him with this disposition and inflicted these false illusions on him. No one doubts that he tried to throw the whole blame on others, to justify himself, and to induce others to have pity on him. In this manner, perhaps, had he been given to other spiritual directors for training, he might not have been able to deceive them with his hypocrisy and it might have been possible for him to become a priest. In this, however, I was deceived.

This letter has grown out of all proportion, and it is time for me to end it. I beg you most humbly that if I have written anything that is not to the point, believe that I certainly tried to write nothing that was not in harmony with truth, charity, and justice. With great humility, Boniface Wimmer, Abbot O.S.B.

Lat   oAPF   ASVA   transBS

TO ANGELO PESCETELLI   72

St. Vincent, October 19, 1863

Right Reverend Procurator General, Dear Confrere: I have already transmitted this report concerning Frater Paul[85] to Cardinal Barnabo.[86] The press of business prevented me from making a copy for you until now. Meanwhile your letter arrived. It is not what you fear. I have done nothing against Paul. He is not a person of great strength, nor of outstanding morality. I will prove this. Nor does he have true gifts from God. I will prove this too. If he has any extraordinary knowledge, he has it from the Devil, but he knows nothing. He is a bold prophet whose conjectures are sometimes accidentally borne out. For that reason, I do not care if the whole world hears what he said about me and about others. Nobody of sound mind will believe him. He has deceived me for a long time. He has showered me

---

[85] Paul George Keck. See Wimmer's letter to Barnabo of June 20, 1863 (above).
[86] Cardinal Alessandro Barnabo, prefect of the Sacred Congregation for the Propagation of the Faith.

with enough ignominy. He has introduced enough harm to the monastery. It is time that he be shown for what he is, a very clever person. He learned the art of acting well. He has a certain piety, to be sure, but it is false piety. Treat him with caution lest you too be deceived. Father Edward[87] has already been entirely deceived, to such an extent that he wrote a completely disreputable letter against me to one of the confreres, a letter that I intercepted. In it, he says, among other things, that I will be defeated in this affair.

Everywhere one sees the same diabolical fruit: suspicions, bitterness, hostility, contradictions, detractions, divisions. I would prefer that you not speak with Father Edward about our affairs or communicate to him what I write to you in secret. Nevertheless, even if you yourself abandon me, I will still rely on God, and in my just cause, I will fight alone against the Devil.

You know that Father Wendelin[88] went to Rome without my knowledge or permission. You will also learn that Father Boniface[89] has gone there to defend Paul. Both of them, Boniface and Wendelin, were drafted into the army. As soon as Boniface learned of his conscription, he took a ship to Europe. I did not try to stop him because he would have gone in any event and I did not want to seem to be impeding the defense of Paul. By law, however, Boniface cannot return to this country. His mother and I would have been able to pay the bounty, and two lay Irishmen would have gone in his place, but he did not know this.

Father Alto,[90] the prior in Texas, will come with the writings of Paul in order to defend me, and perhaps another person will also come. Try to see if the case can be dealt with here before the bishop and some theologians so that witnesses can be heard. You will hear from me again after the retreat. The Lord be with you. Be well. Clerics are being drafted. Several are already called up, including many secular priests, but we are not without hope. Pray that all will be well. At the next opportunity, I will send you money so that you can cover expenses. Boniface Wimmer

Lat   oASPR   cASVA   transJO

---

[87] Edward Hipelius, O.S.B. (1836-1900).
[88] Wendelin Mayer, O.S.B. (1832-1881).
[89] Boniface Krug, O.S.B. (1838-1909), who became a monk at Montecassino and later archabbot of that ancient Benedictine monastery.
[90] Alto Hörmann, O.S.B. (1829-1867).

TO ILDEPHONSE HOFFMANN 73

St. Vincent, October 19, 1864

Dear Brother Ildephonse: Enclosed I send you the tax collector's receipt, i.e. a note certifying that the taxes for you and Brother Ulric[91] have been paid so that you can vote in the presidential election. I hope you will vote for McClellan[92] so that the war soon will come to an end. We are all well and hope you are too. Father Emmeran,[93] who was serving as chaplain for the forces of the South, died in the battle of Jonesboro near Atlanta. He was struck by a cannon ball. Brother Michael[94] died two years ago in Texas, but we learned of it only a few weeks ago.

Why don't we hear from you anymore? Kindly greet Brother Ulric. Our township paid $23,000 to have us exempt from the draft. We had to pay $1,000. Fortunately, we had just received that much from the railroad company, the profit from the output of our sawmill. Brother Martin and Father Valentine[95] were drafted but were subsequently released. It seems as though you poor brothers must be the scapegoats for us all. This time at the primaries, we had a majority of 7,000 votes, if the soldiers don't spoil it. Now we will also win the presidential election, and then rest and peace will be restored once again.

Please write soon and be convinced that we continuously remember you in our prayers.

With much love, sincerely yours, Boniface Wimmer

Ger   oASVA   transIG

---

[91] Ulric Barth, O.S.B.

[92] George B. McClellan (1826-1885), Democratic Party nominee for President in the election of 1864.

[93] Emmeran Bliemel, O.S.B. (1831-1864). See Peter J. Meaney, "Valiant Chaplain of the Bloody Tenth," *Tennessee Historical Quarterly* 41 (1983): 37–47; and Aloysius Plaisance, "Emmeran Bliemel, O.S.B., Heroic Confederate Chaplain," *The American Benedictine Review* 17 (1966): 206–16.

[94] Michael Böhm, O.S.B. (1822-1862).

[95] Martin Beck, O.S.B. (1820-1889), and Valentine Lobmeyer, O.S.B. (1832-1882).

1865-1869

TO KING LUDWIG I

Rome, April 21, 1865

Most Serene Highness! Most Benign King and Lord! Since Your Majesty has graciously deigned to inquire into my financial conditions, I consider it my humble duty to submit more direct and complete information in this letter. In the beginning, my finances were very bad (1) because the two priories, Carrolltown and St. Marys, which I took over for the sake of the German immigrants, swallowed up much money and brought in nothing, (2) because I had to start out with debts, (3) because in order to build a large monastery, I had to accept more non-paying students than I could feed and board with the income I had, which was low. Thus, my condition was at times very discouraging since I also had many additional expenses for the Benedictine nuns. The worst was that I could not tell any one, not even my own confreres, because they would have lost courage, nor my benefactors and friends in Europe, because they would have considered me an adventurer who blindly ran up debts until they were exorbitant and then sooner or later would run away. They would most likely have left me in the lurch and caused me still greater embarrassment.

Nevertheless, I never burdened myself blindly with debts. At favorable moments, I bought land that now is worth five, ten, and twenty times the value I paid for it. It is land that at first was barren but which later became fruitful. My poor students gradually became priests and could work for God and labor for souls and for the monastery. In addition, I was conscious that I was laboring not for myself or for my aggrandizement, but for spreading our Order whose history I know well. Above all, I had the firm conviction that for such undertakings, God would send me help in due time. With this confidence in my heart, I continued to work until the newly founded monastery had obtained the full sanction of the Church and was raised to the status of an abbey. That this happened ten years ago I owe especially to Your Majesty. From then on, our existence was secure in spite of the debts. It no longer was a private affair because it had grown to be an important ecclesiastical institution.

Meanwhile the land I bought or otherwise acquired was made arable and productive. The stations we had taken over ceased to be burdens on the monastery and gradually began to produce something. The educational institute grew. We could take in not only poor students, but also well-to-do boarders who brought in money. We built a brewery and with that acquired a healthy, nourishing drink–and, on the side, a small income. The two priories, of which St. Marys alone cost over $14,000, prospered and began to pay back something. In this way, I established a regular accounting system whereby, instead of making more debts, I could gradually pay off the old ones without incurring new ones. Had it not been for the war, I would probably have no debts at all now, but I am still a debtor, though also a creditor. I have important claims on the parents of students from the South. If I can receive payment on the outstanding bills, I will have no more debts, that is on the abbey itself and on the two priories in Carrolltown and St. Marys. I may, however, not be able to receive payment for even half of them. On the other priories, I still have heavy debts, which actually are the concern of the respective parishes since they were contracted in building their churches. I must see to it that my priors take care that they be liquidated because the churches are ours since the so-called deeds are made in our name. Thus, the bishops cannot take them from us.

In Chicago, we have a nice German community, which, however, has deteriorated woefully. We have had it for just four years now and have erected a building for the Benedictine sisters and the parish school, with an expenditure of $17,000–all paid–besides $3,000 we had to pay for outstanding debts that still remained on the old church. The new church, dedicated on the feast of St. Joseph [March 19], cost $43,000, and we owe all of this. It could not be helped, however, because the old church threatened to collapse and was too small. A new one had to be built. By means of collections within and outside the parish, with so-called "fairs"–a sort of bazaar where all kinds of gifts (women's fancywork, needlework, toilet articles, etc.) are raffled–the money must be raised. The yearly pew-rent serves the same purpose. Payments on the borrowed money are also considerable. The *Ludwig Missionsverein* is contributing $1,000 this year. In Erie, Covington, and Newark, too, there are still many debts, but not too many.

After this financial report, may Your Majesty be pleased to permit me to write about other monastic matters of concern? I am still abbot only as long as it pleases the Holy See (*ad mentem S. Apostolicae Sedis*), instead of for life as is customary in Germany, even though I need subject myself to no more elections. Nonetheless, should His Eminence Cardinal Barnabo[1] have in mind to take from me the command of Saint Vincent, I would simply be an abbot without a monastery, as is the case in the Cassinese Congregation. Without asking for it (rather, against my will), I was first made abbot by the pope. This was for three years. After that, my own community elected me almost unanimously as abbot for life, but the election was not sanctioned [by the Holy See] because we made a mistake in procedure. I was again authorized, however, to be abbot of Saint Vincent for three years. After the expiration of this term, we received an order, because of the war, to delay the new election for a year, and when that year was over, we were to delay the election again. My confreres then petitioned that I be made abbot for life (*ad dies vitae*), but only *ad mentem Apostolicae Sedis* [at the pleasure of the Apostolic See].

At the last general chapter, we recommended the erection of a second abbey at St. Cloud in Minnesota, and because of these two matters, my presence was required in Rome.[2] This last point will probably fail because I myself cannot defend it since the present prior[3] neglected (at first probably because of lack of means) to construct a respectable building and to direct his confreres toward a single, definite objective. It is a pity that this important project cannot be carried out, for there are now ten priests and ten brothers in Minnesota. We must establish a secondary school there. Otherwise, there will be no recruits for the new abbey. No such school exists in the whole of Minnesota. From St. Cloud, the Northwest of the United States must be supplied with missionaries, and Minnesota will in the future become an independent Benedictine province.

Concerning the first, a principle is at stake. According to our Bavarian statutes, the abbot must be abbot for life, but the Romans do not like to see this. There is an abbot here, Casaretto,[4] who founded the monastery at St. Ambrosio and then

---

[1] Cardinal Alessandro Barnabo, prefect of the Sacred Congregation of the Propaganda Fide.

[2] In addition to the matters of Wimmer's lifetime abbacy and the proposed elevation of the priory in Minnesota to the rank of abbey, Wimmer was summoned to Rome in order to answer questions related to the scandals surrounding the case of Paul Keck.

[3] Othmar Wirtz, O.S.B. (1831-1874).

[4] Peter Francis Casaretto, O.S.B. (1810-1878).

separated himself from the Cassinese Congregation. He is in high favor with the pope, and it is he in particular who insists that abbots should rule for only three or six years. This may work well in monasteries where everything is already stable, but it would not work well in America to have the abbot changed every three years. An abbot must have time for carrying out long-range plans, and it takes from 12 to 15 years at least before a regular abbey can be established. It is not at all in the spirit of our Order to change abbots except in cases of evident inability or unworthiness. St. Benedict founded his Order on patriarchal or monarchical, rather than on democratic, principles. I beg you most earnestly, should Your Majesty perhaps have a chance to see the Holy Father or Cardinals Antonelli[5] or Barnabo, to put in a good word for the American Benedictines with regard to this matter. It will be of great value. Cardinals Pitra, Reisach[6] and several others are already on our side.

I ask this not for my own sake. If it comes right down to it, I am indispensable in one sense, but I do not fear a change because I really do not care much for the onerous office of abbot. As for my personal inclinations, I would prefer rest and quiet seclusion to the pressure of business and external labor, but I cannot leave my young community to themselves and must continue to shoulder the burden a little longer. An abbot, however, needs complete and secure authority; otherwise, he is more or less impeded. For that reason, I must desire for myself as well as for my successors that the papal chair not encroach upon the privilege of our having lifetime abbots, which privilege was formerly granted us.

To come back to our plan for founding a second American abbey, I hope to see to it that if not this year, it will become a reality within a short time, as soon as we are able to erect a more adequate building. Had I not so often already enjoyed Your Majesty's boundless generosity, I would dare ask it on this occasion–but I dare not do so. Nevertheless, because I am very eager to see Your Majesty's celebrated name linked with all the Benedictine foundations that will some day be of historical significance, Your Majesty will pardon me when I most respectfully recommend the idea of founding a second Bavarian American Benedictine abbey to your most high and benevolent consideration. Yet, Your Majesty has already given 3,000 florins for the priory of St. Cloud, and with this money, a wonderful region of almost 2,000 acres was obtained. With this, the foundation for the abbey is already laid and this without any debts. If some outside help could be obtained, it would be possible to erect, before long, the necessary buildings for a monastery and a small seminary.

---

[5] Giacomo Antonelli (1806-1878), secretary of state of the Holy See.
[6] John Baptist Pitra, O.S.B. (1812-1889) and Karl August von Reisach (1800-1869).

We also have a place in San José, near the city of San Antonio in southern Texas, close to Mexico. For the time being nothing can be done there, though it is of great importance for both Texas and Mexico. It will not be long, however, before I can recommend the priory at Atchison as a third abbey, since nice, roomy buildings already exist there, though the monastery is very small.

It seems that in Europe the Order of St. Benedict, like all Orders everywhere, must gradually yield to the Masonic Order. In Catholic Spain, it is completely suppressed. In England and France, the governments do not recognize it. In Austria, it is not safe because of the Jews. In Bavaria, your name covers it like a protective shield, but there too one has reason to fear the legislators and the press. In Italy, only Montecassino and Perugia still exist at present. In America, [the Benedictine Order] develops unhindered by law and government. It seems to be providential that our Order has been transplanted to America in order that it not be totally annihilated. Once before, it saved Europe from barbarism, because the barbarians had more understanding of real freedom and religion than our spoiled, badly educated leaders. Perhaps it is in America, where until this time freedom has been rightly valued, that our Order once more may rise to new life and become powerful enough to overcome the new barbarism that values nothing except what brings money and sensual pleasure, without regard for understanding of or thought for the higher things, and that therefore hates ecclesiastical institutions, persecutes and oppresses them whenever it can, or in its most lenient form, treats them like states treat persons who are in the custody of the police.

However, complaining does not help. We must act and not despair because the Church does not die. Neither can its spirit be suppressed by the spirit of the world. To nip a thing in the bud is easier than to suppress what already exists. This is the reason why I am so terribly eager to spread our Order as quickly as possible and to make immediate plans for priories that in due time may become abbeys. Often, one cannot trust even bishops because some of them are friends of religious only when they cannot get along without them. I do not expect much from mission societies anymore. Though I have been received very cordially, they let me know that they expect that I should soon be able to help myself. So be it. Yet for all that, my oaks and evergreens bear only acorns and pine cones, not dollars, and America is a vast country where in many large states little has been done for the Church. We are scattered in ten states and eleven dioceses; that is, we have made small beginnings and want to achieve something great. May Your Majesty not forget us! We intend to bring honor to our patrons and benefactors.

In most humble reverence, love, and gratitude, I am Your Royal Highness's most humble and obedient Boniface Wimmer, Abbot

Ger   oRAB   cASVA   transGE   Math(164-69)

TO RUPERT SEIDENBUSCH   75

Rome, July 2, 1865

Dearest Reverend Confrere: I have been waiting a long time for an answer to the three letters I wrote you, the last one on June 11. I am
a little anxious about the exchange for 3,000
florins I sent you. Since then nothing special has happened here, except that because
of Keck,[7] I, too, was examined in writing. I
had thought there was no report from him.
The case takes its slow course. Everything
will probably be in order, but not for several
months. I do not know yet whether I shall
stay here that long. In any case, I shall put
everything in order. However, I have made
a precious discovery. Father Othmar[8] has revealed himself as a liar and hypocrite. He had
written me earlier when Father Edward[9] told
him that Paul's[10] visions were repudiated here.
Therefore, he did it a long time ago. This letter is at Saint Vincent and I would like to have
it. It came shortly before my departure. Last
April, however, he wrote Father Wendelin,[11]

*Right Reverend Rupert Seidenbusch,
O.S.B., first abbot of Saint Louis on
the Lake Abbey (later Saint John's
Abbey) in Saint Cloud, Minnesota.*

whom he thought was at Montecassino, something completely different, and even
more came up in a second letter that he sent to Rome. Father Wendelin, however,
had left Montecassino and Rome before the letters arrived, and so they came into

---

[7] Paul George Keck, the false visionary.
[8] Othmar Wirtz, O.S.B. (1831-1874).
[9] Edward Hipelius, O.S.B. (1836-1900).
[10] Paul George Keck, the false visionary.
[11] Wendelin Mayer, O.S.B. (1832-1881).

my hands. From these letters it is evident that Othmar still believes firmly in Paul and wants to establish connections with him again; that he writes to Father Louis and Father Paulinus who plan to join up with him, and also with Father Agatho who will try everything to reach the goal;[12] that they want their own novitiate for Minnesota and are eager to establish a monastery with Cluniac statutes–in short the plan is for the whole swindle of the deceiver to be given concrete reality. Convey to Father Paulinus my great displeasure with the fact that he has had anything to do with such things behind our backs, and have Agatho watched. I am afraid he is just as incorrigible a hypocrite as Father Othmar.

These letters arrived just in time, and I can make good use of them. It was providential that it happened this way. I would have believed everything else but that Father Bernard[13] of Minnesota could be such a hypocrite. All the more reason why I don't feel obliged to give him any further consideration. Wendelin is just as false. Under the pretense that he had to go to Germany because of his poor health, he obtained permission and 300 francs travel money from the kind abbot of Montecassino (who, by the way, gave it to him out of charity because all of them, even Father Boniface,[14] consider him crazy). This was, however, only a pretense. He really wanted to go to Rome and find there the opportunity to defend his Paul, to speak with the pope, and to promote his idea of establishing a monastery, for he, too, wants to be a founder of monasteries! Unfortunately for him, I got in the way. Although he spent six weeks here creeping around town like a fox, visiting cardinals and monsignori whenever he could, he still did not obtain an audience with the pope. Cardinals von Reisach and Barnabo,[15] to whom he complained about me again, laughed at him and thought he was crazy. Barnabo said to him: "You say one thing, but Abbot Wimmer says the exact opposite. Therefore, one of you is a liar. We have known Abbot Wimmer for ten years and there is a cardinal here (von Reisach) who has known him for more than twenty years as an honorable man. Therefore . . . etc."

Therefore, good Wendelin had to leave Rome if he did not want to be jailed. Nonetheless, his earlier lies found their way to the Holy Office, and it is, or was, up to me to refute them. Forced by necessity, I had to tell the truth about him in order to be sure that he would abandon the idea of founding a monastery.

---

[12] Louis Fink, O.S.B. (1834-1904); Paulinus Wenkmann, O.S.B. (1836-1921); and Agatho Stuebinger, O.S.B. (1841-1890).

[13] Bernard Mauser, O.S.B. (1835-1899).

[14] Boniface Krug, O.S.B. (1838-1909).

[15] Cardinal Karl August von Reisach (1800-1869) and Cardinal Alessandro Barnabo (1801-1874).

In addition to this, Father Odilo[16] comes to the pope with a petition for his dispensation. What am I to do? I shall tell the whole truth. I know now what to expect from such people. They must answer for the consequences. In his letter to me, as in the previous ones, he lies again and wants to scare me with the threat of apostasy. Naturally, I am sorry that he has gone so far, but it is his own concern. I will do what is right. You can see that my business here is very sad and very unpleasant. I have to clean up a mess of ten years and fight against the hypocrisy and maliciousness of my own confreres. I banished the Devil from Saint Vincent, but from there he took up refuge in Rome in order to hide behind the authorities. However, I find that the authorities are honest and have good will and will do the right thing and that I have the right to hope that everything will turn out well.

I had some papers, among them the revelations of Keck that he had written down, in my desk drawer. If I did not tear them up, and if you can find them, I would be very interested in receiving them. Do not forget to send me a couple of dozen catalogues and photographs of Covington and Newark. I wrote to Dubuis[17] and Father Aemilian[18] at San Antonio. Meanwhile, I made the latter prior. The bishop wishes to get his two students ordained priests now. Speak to Father Director and see what can be done.

The day before yesterday the pope was at the ceremonies at St. Paul's which were celebrated by a Capuchin bishop. Five cardinals were there, among them Cardinal Deacon Mattaei who had a long conversation with me and who favors us very much. In addition, Archbishop Hohenlohe[19] was there. We all came to pay homage to and have dinner with the Holy Father, who was very gracious. During the ceremonies, I sat right across from him. There was very much festivity but little devotion, just as at the Feast of St. Peter in St. Peter's Basilica.

Nevertheless, at Montecassino I spent five days as if in heaven. There, for hours, I could be in the church at the grave of our holy father. I had so much to tell him, to ask, to beg for forgiveness. I felt very small there. The church is extraordinarily rich in artistic works of marble. Even in Rome, one does not see anything like it. It is a beautiful basilica even if its style is not pure. What is not marble or gold plated is hand-painted. Naturally, there are scenes from the life of St. Benedict and his sons and daughters. The mountain is a thousand feet high. On three sides, it is completely open and so steep that it is impossible to climb it. One has

---

[16] Odilo Vandergrün, O.S.B. (1827-1887).
[17] Claude M. Dubuis (1817-1895), bishop of Galveston, Texas.
[18] Aemilian Wendel, O.S.B. (1832-1901).
[19] Archbishop Gustav Adolph Hohenlohe (1823-1896).

to walk zigzag for an hour. I rode a mule, Father Edward and Anselm[20] each had a donkey. A third donkey carried our luggage. The road to the monastery goes through a long, arched passage (a steep slope) which is in part still formed by the tower in which St. Benedict had his cell. Up many steps, one could see an atrium that forms three beautiful courtyards under which there is an enormously large underground cistern, as large as the church. The courtyards are situated among cliffs and enclosed by buildings on the west, east, and north. On the south, there is a magnificent gallery from which one can see as far as the sea at Gaeta. Then there are many steps leading to the second courtyard, and again several steps to the church standing on the peak of what seems to be an old crater.

The monastery is to the east of the church and has another beautiful courtyard in the cloister. The seminary is to the west. The buildings take up the entire span. The tower rises powerfully and like a ghost from the abyss. Its frightening walls and arches are constructed against earthquakes. The cells too have arched ceilings. They are high but small; however, they have extremely beautiful views. All the other mountains around are higher. The Kairo, which is connected with Monte-cassino, is about 6,000 feet high. The more distant mountains were still covered with snow. It is very cold here in winter. The Cassino is a rough, wild mixture of rocks. Only in a few small places did I see grain, and on the terraces, vegetables. Otherwise, there are only rocks and bushes, which nonetheless form beautiful and artistically landscaped walks.

There are no farm buildings because they are not necessary. The seminary where Thomas Aquinas and St. Ignatius spent 60 days does not belong to the monastery. It is a mile away on a low mountain ridge connecting Cassino with Kairo. The cloister of St. Scholastica is situated in the valley. It is an empty building. The place where she met with St. Benedict is at the foot of the mountain. The abbot is at the same time bishop, and as such, he confirms and has a beautiful palace at St. Germano. St. Germano is small, but has 10,000 inhabitants. At Pentecost, thousands of pilgrims usually come from all lower Italy. This year, because of the abuse of the bandits, only a few could come, about 300 men, all of whom slept in the corridors of the monastery, while the women spent the night locked in an outer court on the grounds. They were all very poorly dressed and wore only sandals. The ones from the neighborhood naturally did not stay overnight. They think very highly of St. Benedict, and they prayed with great devotion. I felt very sorry for them. The people of Italy are very poor and oppressed.

I had to celebrate pontifical vespers in *cappa magna* with seven candles. No protest was of any use. They say it is their privilege. In Rome, they are jealous of

---

[20] Edward Hipelius, O.S.B. (1836-1900), and Anselm Nikes, O.S.B. (1825-1866).

such privileges, but at Montecassino, they were proud of being able to present an American abbot in full splendor. Even the 100 days' indulgence was announced in my name after the blessing. Nobody got it, however, because I protested against it, since I was afraid of receiving a censure. Setting aside this exaggerated favor, I was very pleased to be able to exercise these functions at the source of all abbatial dignity and legitimate succession for American abbots and to pass it on to them. Once I said Mass in the cell of our holy father, which still exists but has undergone changes and has an altar now. I shall bring along some pieces of the mosaic that covers the floor. Exorcism of the possessed still takes place there. Not long ago the devil was exorcized from a woman who could hardly be held by eight men. After that, she perspired as if from a great heat and was healed. Her sweat is still kept there. At both places, i.e. at the grave and in the cell of our holy father, I remembered you and all the confreres, clerics, brothers, and scholastics as best I could. I shall bring many relics from St. Paul's and Montecassino.

Above all, I must praise the fraternal love of our brothers at Montecassino. They do not eat as well as we do here and their wine is worse yet, but they showed attention to us that almost went too far, especially Father Abbot de Vera, [21] although he is a prince by birth. They spend $1,000 a year for guests (not for banquets), which is one third of their income, for there are always some guests there, Catholics and Protestants, learned and uneducated. They have there a beautiful printing shop where they have published Dante's works with notes, and naturally, a beautiful library and many manuscripts, although the French destroyed very much, especially the beautiful vestments, chalices, etc. When I finally decided to leave on Wednesday, they packed and saddled the mule and the donkey, but when we were scarcely a thousand paces from the monastery, a rain came and we were drenched to the skin. Since Father Edward did not catch up with me, I had to wait too and then we sent the animals back with the exception of the pack animal, but we missed the train and had to spend the night in the bishop's palace in San Germano. From the monastery, they saw our misery, and Father Abbot sent a brother to cook and take care of us. We had to laugh about this joke, which we attributed to St. Scholastica. We dried our clothes, shoes, socks, trousers, etc. as well as possible. The next day we said Mass in the house chapel, and Thursday evening we arrived in Rome. If Saint Vincent were in Bavaria, I would send all my people on pilgrimage to Montecassino.

I am very well again, but I have more fleas than our Douglas, and the warmer it gets, the more they multiply. Since the beginning of May we have been eating cherries. We had lettuce earlier, potatoes a long time ago. Now we have figs,

---

[21] Archabbot Carlo de Vero (+1871) of Montecassino.

tomatoes, pears, and apricots. We have had cucumbers for a long time, but they are cooked as vegetables or roasted in sherry. From Easter until now, the festivities have had no end. They cost much money.

With regard to Paul, Father Edward is sound and he is again in favor of St. Vincent. Father Wendelin is considered crazy here, but he is only confused because he has a bad conscience. He is as false as a cat or as a heretic. I gave him the choice of joining a strict order or going to [indecipherable], but he did not want to do that. He wanted to stay at Montecassino, but they did not want him there. Therefore, four weeks ago, I sent him to Munich, but he is not there yet. He is ashamed to show up, but he must come if the Inquisition does not come to him.

Be strict with examinations, especially with the examination of priests. They must have good reports from their bishops. Also, hold weekly conferences. Wendelin blamed me for not having them. If I want to explain satisfactorily the sad ghost story, I cannot leave Rome before November, but perhaps I shall be so far along in October as to be able to depart. There is no hesitation as far as the abbatial confirmation is concerned. I also hope that the second abbey will pass and that we can reasonably expect everything. Kercher appealed to the pope. I had to make a report about him too. He will not have much influence because they know him there.

Father Francis[22] wrote me that Father Mackay[23] invited him to return to St. Vincent. It seems that he wishes to stay longer in Dublin. Upon my reply, however, he offered to go immediately. If you need him, write him to come, but then you must send him travel money. His sisters asked me to let him stay longer. Also, if you need Father William,[24] order him to come home. He can go at the end of August. He will get travel money in Munich. Do not say anything about Father Othmar's letter to the fathers. Perhaps he will trap himself again. His role will soon end, and he certainly will not become abbot. The brothers are probably back from the war. Do not engage in politics; do not vote, for we will have another civil war.

Goodbye. May God give you strength and consolation, and may he lead you. Greetings to everyone at home. The doctor's pills do me good. Greetings to Father Bernard, [25] who is now probably your most devoted confrere. Boniface Wimmer, Abbot

Ger   oASJA   cASVA   transVS

---

[22] Francis Cannon, O.S.B.
[23] Camillus Mackay, O.S.B.
[24] William Walter, O.S.B. (1840-1882).
[25] Barnard Manser, O.S.B. (1835-1899).

TO GILES CHRISTOPH   **76**

Rome, August 31, 1865

Dear Reverend Confrere: I have had your letter of August 6 in hand for several days. It interested me very much since I have heard nothing further from St. Vincent since June 15. Because it is vacation time, no one has thought of me. I am glad that you are succeeding with construction. To be in debt is all right, but nonetheless you ought not to rush into debt. Do not demolish the old house. A dwelling is a dwelling. What is farmer Conrad doing? Who does he need? Father Edward[26] sends his regards to Miss Scanlon.

I did not succeed until this week in getting the Holy Office to make a formal declaration in Keck's case.[27] His visions were formally declared false, and Fathers Othmar and Wendelin[28] are to be closely watched because they are his main supporters and even now continue to be believers and partisans. The Propaganda has not yet been able to consider our other business. Unfortunately, it is no longer opportune to press it, and it will not come up for a decision until December since October is vacation time and nothing much happens in November. Consequently, I cannot think of returning yet. I will probably remain here and go back to Bavaria only when everything is decided. I want to visit your parents since I plan to make several trips to Regensburg.

I recently received a privilege for each of our fathers to bless the Benedictine medal. We may also have a privileged altar in each priory church for 10 years; we may each give the papal blessing with plenary indulgence after a mission or retreat; and we are granted the privilege of establishing a confraternity under the title of St. Benedict, with a black scapular, following the model of the English Benedictines.

Since tomorrow is your namesday, I wish you every happiness and blessing. Do not let yourself be distracted by a huge amount of work and the cares connected with the construction, etc. We are in the first place obligated to ourselves. Unless God builds the house, they labor in vain who build it, and if we look to God, He will look after us. It gives me joy to know that Father Edmund[29] is doing well and equally that the brothers are genuinely willing, industrious, and well-behaved. My affectionate greetings to all. Write me again soon, and if possible tell me about the financial situation. In all charity, your most devoted confrere, Boniface Wimmer

Ger   oASVA   transJM

---

[26] Edward Hipelius, O.S.B. (1836-1900).
[27] Paul George Keck, the false visionary.
[28] Wendelin Mayer, O.S.B. (1832-1881); Othmar Wirtz, O.S.B (1831-1874).
[29] Edmund Langenfelder, O.S.B. (1823-1885).

TO ANGELO PESCETELLI   77

Rome, February 12, 1866

Most Reverend Abbot, My Dear Procurator General: Since I must linger in Rome so long, and since I do not know very much Italian, I have had a lot of time on my hands that I have used to think of ways to promote the honor of our Order and especially the honor of our congregation in America. Seeing the necessity of having a place where I can send my young priests to study philosophy and theology, and seeing that such a place has to be in Rome, I have been thinking of a location in the City where they might live. Since you yourself have said to me that neither St. Paul's nor St. Callistus is suitable, and since I do not want to fall into the hands of Casaretto,[30] I have had to look elsewhere, and by looking, I have found a temporary place. I proposed the matter to Cardinal Barnabo,[31] and he has approved it. Before knowing what the pope thought about my idea, it was useless to speak of it to you, but this evening I learned from Archbishop Hohenlohe[32] that His Holiness received my petition and has graciously approved it (although he again made a joking reference to the brewery). It is now possible, therefore, for me to bring you, my dear friend and procurator general, up to date on the matter.

I do not believe it necessary to justify the need for such a residence. I did not act against my confreres, or against St. Ambrose, or (much less) against St. Paul's.[33] Throughout the discussions, I always spoke about and praised you for giving us your help so graciously. I simply acted on my own behalf and that of my congregation in order to obtain a residence where, without restrictions, I could send my priests and clerics for studies. This is a very great necessity because we now have a college in America, and we must establish more, partly to educate priests for ourselves and for the bishops, and partly (and especially) to have a steady income. Since many bishops send students here to the Propaganda, we must send our students here, too, so that we do not become inferior to them. It is equally clear that it is very inconvenient and a great burden on any monastery if it must always have students from America inside its walls. Therefore, no one should interpret it as something underhanded if I want to have my own residence and college in

---

[30] Peter Francis Casaretto, O.S.B. (1810-1878), reforming abbot of the Cassinese Congregation who established the Cassinese Congregation of the Primitive Observance.
[31] Cardinal Alessandro Barnabo, prefect of the Sacred Congregation for the Propagation of the Faith.
[32] Archbishop Gustav Adolph Hohenlohe (1823-1896).
[33] St. Ambrose and St. Paul's-Outside-the-Walls were Benedictine monasteries in Rome.

Rome. I feared very much that the Holy Father would order us to St. Ambrose,[34] so I attempted to prevent this by saying that we wanted to live in our own house in accordance with our own customs. It was not, therefore, from a separatist or dissenting spirit (as I explained to the Holy Father) that I asked for our own residence, but in order to close the door to Casaretto and maintain both our independence and our affiliation with the Cassinese Congregation. Moreover, if all the monasteries are suppressed (as seems probable), we will still have a presence in Rome. I had Father Edward[35] draw up the petition and send it to the pope. We continue to be very beholden to you, of course, and will never forget all the benefits you continue to obtain for us.

For the time being, we will have the church of St. Elizabeth with its small house (near Sant' Andrea della Valle) as our residence. It is close to all the colleges. It is presently under German administration and has been canonically established. As for the rest, God, who is always accustomed to help those who are not able to help themselves, will provide. If the revolution does not come in the meantime, I intend to send three or four priests here next fall. With God's help, the Order of St. Benedict in America will grow "like a tree planted far from the source of water," provided that we remain good, learned, hardworking Benedictines.

We have passed through fire and water, and we have always emerged more vigorous after the storm. An invisible hand has always opened the way for us and pointed us in the direction we should go. It has corrected what we have done wrong and has furnished what was necessary. It seems to have been at work in this matter too, for I would not have thought of looking for a residence in Rome, nor would I have been able to think of such a thing, if in the tedium and boredom of the long delay the idea had not come to me.

I have communicated this news to Bishop Celesia[36] and would have informed you in person rather than by letter, but because I was detained here, I decided to write you because I well know how eager you are to hear of anything that touches us. I will try to find out if the Spanish church of St. James, together with the house belonging to it, is available, and if so, how quickly I can get it. For that reason, I said above that I have taken St. Elizabeth as a "temporary place." I will try to get St. James and hope that the apostle of Spain will help me in this endeavor. Without money, I will not be able to buy it, but I will find the money if the property

---

[34] The reformed Benedictine house in Rome presided over by Abbot Peter Francis Casaretto, O.S.B.

[35] Edward Hipelius, O.S.B. (1836-1900).

[36] Michaelangelo Celesia, O.S.B. (1811-1904), bishop of Patti, Sicily, and former abbot of Montecassino.

is available, even though I have no idea where to look for the money. You see, then, Most Reverend Abbot, that I am an American speculator, but if I did not speculate, I would not be an American! In one way or another, if God wills it, I will be successful.

Most earnestly commending myself to your charity, and with deepest reverence, I am your most humble servant, Boniface Wimmer, O.S.B.

Lat   oASPR   cASVA   transJO

TO CELESTINE ENGLBRECHT   78

Rome, June 18, 1866

Celestine Engelbrecht, O.S.B.

Dearest Reverend Confrere: This is to let you know that on June 4 the cardinals decided, and on June 16 the Holy Father confirmed: (1) that I am abbot for life; (2) that St. Cloud is an abbey and that the fathers there may elect or propose an abbot who must be confirmed by the Holy Father; (3) that the abbot and all our abbots are also, from now on, to hold the office for the duration of their lives. Now that the three main points have been granted, we have normal status. Thanks be to God! You will hear details when the documents come out and are in my hands. (4) Also, my work for the sisters has not been completely in vain; more about this later. The brothers may no longer take solemn vows, but the solemn vows already taken remain valid. My most humble respects to the right reverend bishop.

It is generally regarded as a great triumph, and this unanimously, that I achieved my point about the abbots being elected for life. Overall, everything I applied for was accepted, with only a minor exception, and we found widespread appreciation for our work. All the damage has been repaired. Moreover, Father Wendelin[37] has been forced by severe punishment to submit himself again, and he cannot be absolved until he has performed penance. On June 20, I will travel with two confreres to Munich by way of Marseille, and possibly, on June 24, I will join Cardinal von Reisach.[38] He is going to Luxemburg, so I may accompany him as far as Lyon. Our friend Prince Hohenlohe[39] will be made a cardinal on June 25. I would like to stay for that, but I have no more time. I am fully occupied now with making farewell visits and with packing. If only the long and troublesome journey were already behind me! I received the message about the happy outcome of the meeting from a friendly cardinal on June 5, as a namesday present. Only after 14 months did I accomplish my goal! Only after 20 years of work, troubles, vexations, and struggles is our congregation firmly established! Our guardian angels have won the victory for us, for the Devil has resisted mightily. Now we will all be more industrious, good, and zealous in the service of God, will we not?

A thousand greetings to the fathers, brothers, and sisters. Farewell, and don't cease to pray for your ever loving, respectful, and most devoted Boniface Wimmer

Ger   oASVA   transGM

TO UTTO LANG   79

St. Vincent, January 28, 1867

Most Venerable Abbot and Honorable Confrere: I enclose a copy of the apostolic brief I received from Rome. Since it praises me, perhaps I should not have sent it. It is possible that vanity has compelled me, but in fact, the document says at the very beginning not *tua opera* but *tua potissimum opera*.[40] Many have helped with the work, as I duly pointed out in my petition to the Holy Father and the cardinal prefect. I am permitted to and must share the praise with you as the president of the mother congregation. For a similar reason, I sent a copy to the *Missionsverein*. I know well enough that when one receives any praise, the honor is due to God. God could have conferred this honor on my predecessors as well

---

[37] Wendelin Mayer, O.S.B. (1832-1881).
[38] Cardinal Karl August von Reisach (1800-1869).
[39] Archbishop Gustav Adolph von Hohenlohe (1823-1896).
[40] Not "your work," but "your work above all."

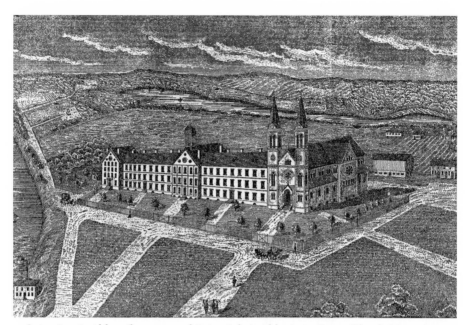

Saint Louis Abbey (later named Saint John's Abbey), in Saint Cloud, Minnesota.

as He did upon me, if He had so desired. I am sending you the document merely because of its historical interest for Metten, for I glory in having once been a priest of the Metten community, *et ab isto monasterio in Americam si non missus, attamen dimissus.*[41] I, therefore, felt ashamed that I could stay only a few days in Metten, because I am attached to it by so many happy memories that neither time nor distance can weaken.

The second brief is of less interest to you. It is about the founding of a new abbey in St. Cloud, Minnesota, which we named St. Louis Abbey in honor of the king. I am also sending a copy of this brief to the *Missionsverein.*

I left Munich on September 1 because Father Edward[42] had not booked passage on the ship as he had promised. On September 10, we 1,300 passengers steamed from Southampton and arrived safely in New York on September 25 after a stormy voyage. From New York, we went to Newark where we rested for three days. The next day, September 29, at 1:30 am, we arrived at a brightly illuminated St. Vincent.

---

[41] "And from this monastery if I was not sent to America, at least I was permitted to go."
[42] Edward Hipelius, O.S.B. (1836-1900).

My next task was to prepare three young fathers for a voyage to Rome, namely Adalbert Müller, Hilary Pfrängle, and Innocent Wolf.[43] All three are American-born. On October 5, I had to attend the Plenary Council in Baltimore. It lasted two weeks. I attended the advisory meetings of the bishops and directed the fourth congregation of theologians as vice president under Bishop Wood of Philadelphia.[44] Meanwhile, my three fathers traveled from St. Vincent to Newark. From there, Prior Oswald Moosmüller[45] accompanied them to Rome. I received a two-day leave of absence from the council to go to Newark to provide them with the necessary recommendations and information. I returned to the council on October 21. That same day, they left New York and arrived in Brest on October 31. On November 1, they were in Paris and on November 2 in Marseilles. On November 5, they reached Civittavecchia. Here they were quarantined for seven days and for that reason could not reach the college on November 5.

On November 12, immediately after the closing of the council, I traveled home. I was caught up at once in all kinds of business. After finishing the most important affairs, I went to Minnesota. There I supervised the election of the new abbot. My prior, Father Rupert Seidenbusch,[46] was unanimously elected by the twelve capitulars. He is now abbot of a large house built in a forest of about 1,330 acres that belongs to the monastery. The election was held on a very cold December 12. In the evening, at the close of the ceremonies, we sang the *Te Deum* with great enthusiasm. A new, large stone building was erected last summer about a mile and a half further south, near a beautiful lake. It was not yet ready at the time of the election, but will be the permanent site of the abbey. The surroundings are excellent. The lake is almost a square mile in area and has many fish. The forest is deciduous. Bordering the creek that runs past the building are a few hundred acres of natural meadowland. Pheasants, rabbits, deer, and bears are plentiful.

I stayed only until the result of the election was three times recorded and copied. Then I returned via St. Cloud, St. Paul, Shakopee, Winona, and La Crosse. At La Crosse, I had to cross the frozen Mississippi while carrying heavy sacks and sprained my arm. It still hurts. From La Crosse I went to Milwaukee and then on to Chicago, where I rested for several days and made a visitation. Erie and St. Marys were the next stops. I arrived at St. Marys [Pennsylvania] on Christmas

---

[43] Adalbert Müller, O.S.B. (1842-1906), Innocent Wolf, O.S.B. (1843-1922), and Hilary Pfrängle, O.S.B. (1843-1909).

[44] James Frederic Wood (1813-1888), bishop of Philadelphia.

[45] Oswald Moosmüller, O.S.B. (1832-1901).

[46] Rupert Seidenbusch, O.S.B. (1830-1895).

Eve and conducted spiritual exercises at noon with the brothers there. After an absence of six weeks, I returned to St. Vincent on January 5.

It was a difficult and expensive trip, but I was amply rewarded for my labor by the sincere love and delight with which I was hospitably received and feted by my confreres (in St. Joseph, Shakopee, Chicago, Erie, and St. Marys) and also by the bishops and secular priests. God be thanked a thousand times for our expansion. A second abbey has been erected, a second abbot elected, and thus a second guarantee given us for the propagation of our Order and our Faith.

I confidently hope that Father Rupert will be a better abbot than I am–that won't be difficult!–and that his monastery will accomplish more for the Far Northwest than St. Vincent did for the East. Father Rupert is young, healthy, robust, shrewd, pious, chaste, good-natured, forgiving, and sincere. He also has the advantage of my experience. God bless him!

My fathers arrived in Rome unexpectedly. My patrons and friends there consider me a schemer. I am known for this fault even in Rome. St. Elizabeth's was not ready when they arrived. Nevertheless, they were gladly received in the college and stayed there until the inhabitants of St. Elizabeth's found another dwelling. Since Christmas, my fathers have been living in their own house. They study philosophy and theology with the Dominicans in the Sapienza.

At home, I am again paying more attention to our seminary. I had left it pretty well to Father Edward. By relieving Father Peter[47] in Texas with another priest, I gained an efficient professor. Now I am preparing a large building for occupancy next spring. The cold winter and the great amount of snow are not very helpful.

I can laugh at my Bavarian confreres. Because I am an American, I can do as I please without waiting for the permission of a royal minister or the president. I am sure of success if I undertake something good and use common sense. However, I do not laugh too loudly, for even here not everything is completed.

In conclusion, I cordially greet Your Grace and my confreres and recommend myself to your pious prayers. With sincerest love and respect I remain, your devoted confrere, Boniface

Ger   oAMA   cASVA   transCZ,CW   *Script*19:72-75

---

[47] Peter Baunach, O.S.B. (1815-1868).

TO SCHOLASTICA BURKHARDT   **80**

St. Vincent, June 5, 1867

Dear Mother Prioress: I am accustomed to keeping my word. Hence, I am lend-
ing you, with pleasure, $1,000 for the purchase of the house. The money will be
ready any day (I have to change gold), but for my golden sisters I gladly give the
golden dollars. I cannot donate them to you since I am not the owner of them.
Complete the transaction quickly, therefore, and let the paper be drawn up and
signed before I go to Kansas, but the purchase means nothing. Since you are not
incorporated, you cannot, as a community, possess property. It will be necessary
that the deed be made out in the name of the "Benediction Society"–note that
it should be called the "Benedictine Society," but in Westmoreland County it is
written "Benediction Society"–until you receive your legal status as a corporation.
It is well that the purchase be made before the new bishop[48] comes, for it is possible that he would demand the deed for himself. If it should be necessary that
I go to Erie because of the deed, I will do so because I am very anxious that you
get this house. The man will have to vacate it soon so that you can accept pupils.
Therefore, get moving and God bless you all. Boniface

Ger   oASBC   cASVA   transGS

TO RUPERT SEIDENBUSCH   **81**

St. Vincent, July 8, 1867

Right Reverend Abbot Rupert: We have eagerly awaited news from you regarding
your arrival in your new home, to which only now can I respond with local news,
but first your requests. I wanted to send out Frater Ulrich with Alexius.[49] Hence,
I held him back, and he stayed very willingly. Today construction begins on the
new barn at the Kuhns Farm. For this purpose, I sent 20 brothers over there in
two wagons at 3:00 a.m. Fathers Ferdinand and Eugene[50] had driven over yesterday evening to be on hand to offer Holy Mass this morning so all would proceed
happily. In two weeks, this new barn will be practically finished. Then our old
barn must get an addition over the hog stalls. That is where the time goes–harvests

---

[48] The new bishop of Erie was Tobias Mullen (1818-1900) who succeeded Josue M. Young (1808-
1866) in 1868.
[49] Ulrich Northman, O.S.B. (1846-1890) and Alexius Edelbrock, O.S.B. (1843-1908).
[50] Ferdinand Wolf, O.S.B. (1834-1914) and Eugene Phelan, O.S.B. (1840-1903).

Brother Ubald Schneider, O.S.B. (1831-1907), carpenter at St. Vincent Abbey.

must be gathered; work on the buildings will continue into the fall. Consequently, I cannot spare the services of Brother Corbinian.[51] You know, of course, that he and Brother Ubald[52] are our only carpenters. Your desire to have everything at once is only a temptation. The round-trip fare to Minnesota would cost $100. For this amount or a little more you can engage a regular millwright. The sawmill on the Ridge cost only $40 (excluding our work). The one in Carrolltown, however, came to almost $1,000. If a brother cannot operate the mill, then the advantage is minimal, especially if you have to buy the pine boards.

Since your departure, Frater Dominic has deserted us and writes me from Pittsburgh for money because he wants to marry and start a business. Father Edward[53] had told him that his vows were worthless since they were pronounced under duress and with a mental reservation that he was making them only for a time! Naturally, I gave a different opinion. During my absence, the same Father Edward stirred up a small revolution in Erie and St. Mary's, Newark, against me. He wrote that he would have to insist on a transfer if I did not remove the prior (against whom, he said, the fathers were roused to indignation) and provide better meals. Naturally, I answered him that I would know how to break up such a conspiracy if there really were one. If the prior simply demands the exact observance of the *Holy Rule*, that is nothing more than his duty. With regard to food, Father Edward cannot complain since he has not been keeping the monastic abstinence. Furthermore, he has endured meals in the college a long time. Since he never takes soup and generally does not eat, but gulps his food down and takes no exercise, it is his own fault that he suffers dyspepsia. Therefore, I refused to grant his demand for a change of residence. After that, he resigned his office and wrote Cardinal Barnabo, and (I suspect because of the presence here of V.R. Drane) he initiated action to go as a professor

---

[51] Corbinian Schiller, O.S.B. (1824-1876).
[52] Ubald Schneider, O.S.B. (1831-1907).
[53] Edward Hipelius, O.S.B. (1836-1900).

to Seton Hall. He wrote a letter from Newark to Frater Lawrence[54] that all was well and that he was in good health. From that, you can see that Father Edward is lost for the Order. The cardinal will certainly not give him another assignment without my knowledge and approval. It is a shame for the institution, but otherwise no loss. Perhaps I am seeing the matter too gloomily. Possibly, in the end, he might perceive that it is better to be a child of this house than a hireling of a bishop. Your most devoted brother, Boniface

Ger   oASJA   cASVA   transAHo

TO UTTO LANG   82

St. Vincent, July 11, 1867

Right Reverend Father Abbot and Most Dear Confrere: If young Meier, whom you recommended, has a real vocation to the monastic life, or if he thinks he is called, he will be received because my chapter voted in his favor in the expectation that the ocean voyage, the change of climate, and the quietness of monastic life would be advantageous to his health. I have no idea what you mean by "culture mechanic." We have plenty of "construction mechanics," a very profitable profession if it means "architect."

August is the best time for traveling across the ocean. After landing in New York, he should take the train to Latrobe, Westmoreland County, provided he has enough traveling money. Otherwise, he should use my letter of recommendation and go to Newark where my fathers at St. Mary's German Church on the corner of High and William Streets will help him out in the event that he is stranded. He will need $14 in paper money or $9 in silver. The trip to Latrobe takes 20 hours.

On June 29, Father Alto Hörmann[55] died after returning here last December with tuberculosis. He died peacefully and resigned to the will of God. Shortly before his death, a scholastic, a fine young man, died, and between the scholastic and Father Alto, Brother Theobald,[56] a very capable stonecutter, died. A few days after Father Alto, our leather worker, Brother Bernard[57] from Eggerdinger near

---

[54] Lawrence Schaeffer, O.S.B. (1847-1871).
[55] Alto Hörmann, O.S.B. (1829-1867).
[56] Theobald Baumann, O.S.B. (1814-1867).
[57] Bernard Eggerdinger, O.S.B. (1819-1867).

Pfakofen, also died, and Brother Placidus,[58] a locksmith, will doubtless follow them in the fall. May they rest in peace.

Abbot Rupert[59] was blessed in our church with all solemnity on Ascension Day by Bishop Carrell of Covington.[60] Immediately afterward, he went to his Abbey of St. Louis on the Lake with a cleric who had just completed his novitiate and another who will be ordained a priest in September. Another cleric and a novice for St. Louis are still here. At the start, there were 12 priests and one cleric in Minnesota. Now they number 18.

The printing of the *Holy Rule* with the declarations and constitutions of the Bavarian Congregation is now completed.[61] I shall send 100 or more copies to Bavaria because I think they are anxious to have them. I had 500 printed in booklet form. At present, we are busy printing the *Rituale* and *Ceremoniale* of our Order on very fine paper using brand new type. I shall send you copies sometime. If you could send me the complete set of the novitiate regulations in Latin, I shall also have them printed. They would be very useful for our novices, both English and German. Ours are written out so poorly that it would not be worthwhile to print them. Our Benedictine Confraternity is established in practically every one of our parishes. I expect much from it.

The address of my father rector in Rome is Rev. Signore Oswaldo Moosmüller, Rettore O.S.B. a S. Elizabeth a via Chiavari No. 77 a Roma. Father Willibald is very well acquainted with the place. It is located across from Sant' Andrea della Valle. So far, there has been nothing but good news from my people there. Cardinals Pitra and Hohenlohe,[62] as well as more than one bishop, have paid them a visit. The abbot of St. Peter's was also there and insisted that they should come to Salzburg during the vacation and stay with him. Cardinal Barnabo immediately made Father Oswald my representative *ex officio*, but I do not want to separate myself from the procurator general[63] because it is important to be on good terms with the Roman Benedictines. It gives me great advantage to have a house in Rome, and for the students it is more than advantageous to be able to follow the Roman courses of philosophy and theology.

---

[58] Placidus Wittmann, O.S.B. (1814-1867).
[59] Rupert Seidenbusch, O.S.B. (1830-1895).
[60] George A. Carrell, S.J. (1803-1868), of Covington, Kentucky.
[61] *Regula sanctissimi patris nostri Benedicti, auspice Reverendissimo et Amplissimo Domino Domno Bonifacio I abbate S. Vincentii et Congregationis Americano-Cassinensis praeside, denuo edita* ([Beatty, Pa.]: Typis Abbatiae S. Vincentii in Penna, 1867).
[62] John B. Pitra, O.S.B. (1812-1889), and Gustav Adolph Hohenlohe (1823-1896).
[63] Abbot Angelo Pescetelli, O.S.B.

At home, we began gathering the harvest a few days ago. Hay and wheat are abundant, as are oats, but corn did not prosper because of the rain. We are under the impression that our steps are taking us forward, but not without struggle and adversity. Our Benedictine sisters are well, though not without burdening me with work and more work. Our general chapter will begin on August 16, and when we finish, a retreat will begin on the Feast of the Guardian Angels. All the priors will attend the chapter. Tomorrow I go on visitation to Covington and Kansas.

Best regards to all my confreres, especially Fathers Placidus, Fortunatus, Xavier, and Ambrose.[64] With affection and respect, I am Your Grace's most devoted Boniface Wimmer

Ger   oAMA   cASVA   transRG

TO KING LUDWIG I   83

Erie, August 10, 1867

Most Serene, Most Benign King and Lord: May Your Majesty be pleased to accept my heartiest good wishes on the occasion of your namesday on behalf of myself and the whole American Bavarian Benedictine Congregation. You have not heard from me for a whole year chiefly because there was too much to do after a two-year absence from my monastery, but may Your Royal Majesty not think that my unbounded love and gratitude have diminished. On the contrary, they grow in proportion to the importance and prosperity of our congregation, fostered by your powerful protection and magnanimous support. Every Monday, I say the Mass for a king and beg God most fervently to grant Your Highness His richest blessings. This privilege I will not relinquish to another. I know by faith that as a priest I have the power to offer to Almighty God the Holy Sacrifice of the Mass as a most efficacious, never-failing means of proving my gratitude, loyalty, and devotion to Your Royal Highness. This is my great consolation, and I hope that God will graciously hear and grant my prayers.

On December 14, 1866, I presided over the election of an abbot for the new abbey. The prior of St. Vincent, Father Rupert Seidenbusch,[65] a native of Munich, was unanimously chosen first abbot. The papal brief confirming the election came into my hands only in May, and the blessing took place on the Feast of the Ascension. Together with the minutes of the election, I sent a written petition to

---

[64] Monks of Metten.
[65] Rupert Seidenbusch, O.S.B. (1830-1895).

Rome that the new abbey be called not St. Cloud but St. Louis as a memorial of our gratitude to Your Majesty. The Holy Father gladly granted the request and had a special protocol concerning it drawn up. I will send you the latter and the plan of the property of St. Louis. There is no reason why it should not reach a flourishing state within a short time. Right now, it has 17 fathers and clerics. With the beginning of the next school year, it will open a secondary school for boys, a boys' seminary. They do extensive spiritual work for the Germans who are near to being a majority of the inhabitants of Minnesota. The abbot is an excellent and energetic young man who as prior of St. Marys and Newark and as administrator of St. Vincent has already given ample proof of his fitness and active zeal. He will probably go to Europe soon to recruit suitable people for his monastery. If until now St. Vincent alone and with very meager means has achieved so much that the Order is already introduced into ten dioceses, it will now with the support of a second abbey be able to accomplish proportionately more.

I also expect a great deal from our house in Rome, which is perhaps as important as the new abbey. Because our work is, in the first place, to educate and train good, efficient priests and to further Catholic learning, I had to keep in mind that I must provide teachers trained in Rome. Many American priests are alumni of the Propaganda, and many bishops (if not all) support students at the Propaganda or have alumni from the Propaganda among their clergy. If we are unable to provide our own Roman-trained clerics, we will not be regarded by the diocesan clergy as equals, but as clergy of minor rank and quality, and our influence as well as our effectiveness will suffer considerably. However, even apart from that, genuine Catholicism is Roman Catholicism alone. The specialized German philosophies and theology at present have been more or less tinged by rationalism.

Besides this, we need a permanent agent in the capital of Christendom, like the old Bavarian Benedictine Congregation, which always had an agent there to protect itself against the infringement of episcopal power. A house in Rome answers both needs and is, therefore, very important and useful for us. To be sure, it takes a significant sum of money to maintain four to six students in Rome, for there is no endowment in Rome itself, but we cannot avoid even great sacrifices when it is a question of such a serious matter.

I am here on my return from a visitation that, according to the statutes, I had to undertake at the priories in Atchison, Kansas, and Nebraska City, Nebraska. Atchison will be the next abbey. It now has five priests and five clerics. Within three years, I hope it will have the required number of capitulars for the formation of an abbey. Both places are on the Missouri River, in the very heart of the United

States, which is still sparsely populated west of the Missouri. I found there, as in the other priories, everything in good order.

To my sorrow, I lost three priests this year through death, and a fourth, it seems, will soon follow them. Five new priests have been ordained. On August 16, we will hold a general chapter at St. Vincent. There is just enough room left to repeat my best wishes. In deepest reverence and with grateful love, I am Your Royal Majesty's most humble and obedient Boniface Wimmer, Abbot

Ger   oRAB   cASVA   transGE   Math(181-84)

TO MARTIN MARTY   84

Covington, November 18, 1867

Very Reverend Confrere: At our recent general chapter, it was proposed and approved by acclamation that the president, in the name of the chapter, extend hearty greetings and welcome to the dear confreres in Indiana. With the greatest pleasure, the president promised to do that forthwith. Immediately afterward, however, there was first the annual retreat, then several time-consuming matters, and trips and other circumstances that prevented him from keeping his promise until now. For the same reasons, the decisions of the chapter could be sent to the respective priories and missions only at the end of October. Hence, I must earnestly beg your forgiveness that only now, on my return from Nebraska, am I discharging this pleasant obligation.

Cordial greetings, therefore, from all of us, and especially from me, to our dear confreres in Indiana! Happiness and blessings, good health and prosperity, success and growth and expansion! Being sons of the same illustrious Father, and children of the same noble family, we have many common interests and aspirations, and consequently we share in each other's successes. It is no longer news to you that we Bavarian Benedictines, fully organized as a congregation with a sure footing, continue developing tranquilly, and that to the first abbey, St. Vincent, we have added a second one in Minnesota. This new abbey is called St. Louis on the Lake in honor of our protector King Ludwig. In Latin, the name is "S. Ludovii sub Lacu," thus serving at the same time as a memorial to the cradle of our Order, Subiaco.[66] All this has been approved by a formal apostolic brief. You must also

---

[66] Subiaco was the site of St. Benedict's monastery. This Italian name derives from the Latin *sub lacu*, below the lake.

have heard by this time that Father Rupert Seidenbusch[67] was elected as first abbot of this new monastery and confirmed as such by His Holiness for life. (Such will be the case with all our abbots in the future.)

From now on there is nothing to prevent our abbeys from multiplying, so long as property and personnel are available. This holds even if all the fathers of a particular community do not live together in the same place, as was the case in Minnesota where 12 fathers were stationed in different locations, only four residing at the place where the monastery was located while four others lived not too far from the monastery. Nevertheless, the abbey now numbers 17 fathers and clerics, though the latter are receiving further training at St. Vincent.

We are sincerely happy to hear from all sides that your priory has developed, as it were, into full bloom and that the number of your confreres has grown to such an extent that you must now consider the question of raising your priory to the status of an abbey. It was only your humility that prevented you from applying to the Holy See for this honor. Apart from my own experience, it appears that we should imitate the practice of the Church in this matter, which seeks to erect as many dioceses as possible. An abbot has more power and influence than a prior. Hence, I would like to advise you not to let modesty go so far as to be detrimental to the Order, but to do even as I had to do, namely, seek permission for an abbey even at the expense of people accusing me of ambition. The general chapter has expressed the same idea.

We are hoping in the not too distant future to establish a third abbey. With you, there are now already more basic elements for such a project than we could muster in such a short time. In saying this, we are looking at your situation as though it were ours. Whether or not the common bond of one congregation will bind us more closely some day remains something for you to decide, but even without following one and the same goal side by side with one another, let us remain bonded together by the bond of sincere, warmhearted, and strong brotherly love.

I suppose you know that we have a house in Rome, whose rector is Father Oswald Moosmüller,[68] formerly prior in Newark. He is at the same time our agent with the Holy See and officially recognized as such by the same Holy See. He will gladly handle whatever affairs or dealings you may have with the Holy See and will try to serve you as best he can. At the general chapter, this house (St. Elizabeth, Via Chiavari No. 77) was declared the property of the whole congregation.

I beg you most respectfully to extend my greetings as well as those of my confreres to the most reverend confreres of your monastery whom I know and also

---

[67] Rupert Seidenbusch, O.S.B. (1830-1895).
[68] Oswald Moosmüller, O.S.B. (1832-1901).

such as are not personally known to me. With this, I add my signature with my special affection and esteem. Your most devoted confrere, Boniface Wimmer, Abbot and President

Ger   oASMA   cASVA   transBB

TO THE *LUDWIG MISSIONSVEREIN*   **85**

St. Vincent, February 25, 1868

To the Board of Directors of the *Ludwig Missionsverein*: It has now been a year since I had the honor to send my last report on our work and our situation, and so I hasten to take up once again the thread of the story at the point where I dropped it last year. I have nothing extraordinary or especially interesting to relate because nothing of that sort readily appears in our work, which is seminary teaching, education, and the general care of souls. The most important event for our congregation was the election of the first abbot, Rupert Seidenbusch,[69] of the new abbey in Minnesota, which I reported last year. His confirmation was confirmed by papal brief on March 15, 1867, and on the same day another apostolic brief granted permission for the new abbey to be named in honor of His Majesty, King Ludwig I, *Abbatia S. Ludovici sub lacu* ("The Abbey of St. Louis on the Lake"), because it is situated on a pleasant lake.

Since the bishops of Pittsburgh and St. Paul were in Rome, the new abbot received the blessing from the Bishop George Aloysius Carrell of Covington in the abbey church of St. Vincent on Ascension Day, May 30. In default of a second abbot, Father Augustine Wirth,[70] conventual prior in Atchison, and I assisted on the occasion. The blessing of an abbot is, of itself, an impressive rite, but this one was even more so for me and for my local confreres who, like me, never saw one, for, as you know, in this regard I came off badly. The Holy Father made me an abbot in a private audience, and though I became an abbot with all the usual rights and privileges, still, at the beginning, it was only for three years because this was the custom in the Cassinese Congregation to which our American Congregation is affiliated. Hence, this was the first blessing of a Benedictine abbot in America.

At the time, I was naturally thinking of the past. When the Benedictine Order was restored in Bavaria by King Ludwig I, I became in 1832 one of the priests who joined Father Ildephonse Nebauer, the prior, and Father Roman Raith, the

---

[69] Rupert Seidenbusch, O.S.B. (1830-1895).
[70] Augustine Wirth, O.S.B. (1828-1901).

subprior, at the monastery of Metten. I was the second to enter Metten, and I witnessed all the difficulties that a monastery has to overcome at the beginning. When in 1834 St. Stephen Abbey at Augsburg was established, I was sent there from Metten and for the second time experienced the same things. When Scheyern was established in 1836, I was sent there, too, to assist until the first novices had been professed, and when in 1840 the Metten Benedictines assumed charge of the Royal Educational Institute in Munich, obedience once again called me there, as though I were especially chosen to observe the introduction of our Order in various places and under differing circumstances in order, so to speak, to study and make use of these experiences in America.

When, after my arrival at St. Vincent 21 years ago, I gave the Benedictine habit to my companions, future prospects were, of course, quite gloomy, and I do not know whether, apart from me, even one of them had the firm expectation that we would bring a monastery into being. Despite many difficulties and dangers from within and without, however, the work we had begun went forward and flourished and became consolidated, once it had obtained papal authorization, and it spread mightily into 11 dioceses and 8 states! Is it not wonderful how here also God is glorified by bringing into being a great work through insignificant means? I say "great" work because if unexpected events do not have a disturbing effect, without any doubt our Order will spread all over America, and through the care of souls and the teaching and training of priests, it will exercise a great influence on the population.

At St. Vincent we now number 53 priests, two deacons, nine clerics, five novices, two of whom are priests (one a diocesan priest, one a theologian educated here), and some 70 brothers. In the school, there are always around 100 students, more or less, because some come for only a few months, for example, to learn commercial bookkeeping. The current number is 96. Of these, there were two last year who paid absolutely nothing and 25 who paid only a very modest fee. This year, 13 pay nothing at all and 35 pay only a part. Last year a local theologian was ordained a priest for the Diocese of Pittsburgh, whereas 27 were studying for the religious state. This year there are 39 candidates for the priesthood.

In addition, there are 50 secondary school students for the Order. They are called scholastics, and their support falls entirely upon the monastery. Of the 53 priests, only 17 (in addition to the two novice priests) are in the monastery. Of these, one is in charge of the parish and three take care of the mission stations that belong to it. The other 13 are officials or teachers. In fact, except for the procurator and me, all the other priests have to teach. Since my last report, six, apart from the priest novices, were ordained to the priesthood and two to the diaconate, but I did not profit very much from this because four priests–Fathers Cyril Eder, Alto Hörmann, Casimir Seitz, and Isidore Walter[71]–were carried off by death in the prime of life. Of the other 36 priests, four are in Rome, as I have already informed you, to become teachers; five are in Newark, four in Carrolltown, four in Chicago, three in Erie, three in Covington, four in St. Marys, and the others in separate missions.

The Abbey of St. Louis on the Lake in Minnesota has 13 priests, 2 clerics, 15 scholastics, and in the seminary 40 students, several of whom are educated *gratis*. Five priests are teachers; the others are engaged in pastoral work. The conventual Priory of Atchison counts 5 priests, one of whom belongs to St. Vincent. All of them work in the care of souls. The five clerics of this monastery are at St. Vincent to complete their studies. Therefore, at present our congregation comprises 72 priests, 18 clerics, 5 novices, and 65 students for the Order, with more than 120 lay brothers. Of the 136 students in the two seminaries, 39 are preparing for the secular priesthood, the other 97 for various other callings. The philosophers and theologians studying here belong to the dioceses of Charleston, Brooklyn, Covington, Erie, and St. Paul.

This is about all I find worth reporting about our work and the situation of our monastery and Order. It goes without saying that the numerous lay brothers also do something. I am sure they will not take it amiss if I make no mention of their building activities, their achievements and improvements in farming, though in both respects they have accomplished much and for the coming spring are ready to build a large addition to the seminary. I will merely note that at the moment our efforts do not permit us to spread further, though we do hope to strengthen our dependent priories so that one father in each one may conduct a Latin preparatory school for boys who seem to have a vocation and talent, in order thus to gain more candidates for the priesthood.

I also hope to give the most capable of my clerics or young priests such a formation in philosophy and theology at Rome that we may obtain really qualified teachers and be able to do for learning more than has thus far been possible. Hence, this year I am again thinking of sending two clerics to Rome, although this entails heavy expenses. I was a bit anxious about my confreres in Rome when there was a cholera outbreak there last summer, but the young ones[72] accepted with pleasure an invitation from the abbot of Montecassino to spend their holidays there, and

---

[71] Cyril Eder, O.S.B. (1842-1867), Alto Hörmann, O.S.B. (1829-1867), Casimir Seitz, O.S.B. (1829-1867), and Isidore Walter, O.S.B. (1838-1867).
[72] Innocent Wolf, O.S.B. (1843-1922), Adalbert Müller, O.S.B. (1842-1906), and Hilary Pfrängle, O.S.B. (1843-1909).

they were thus safer from the attack of the dangerous epidemic. The older priest[73] found an opportunity to go from Rome to Bavaria, free of charge, with a German-American from our parish in Chicago, in order to visit his sister, and in this way he too escaped the cholera that he probably would have contracted since when he left Rome he was already suffering from a severe bilious cholera.

Having mentioned Chicago, I would like to note in passing that we have just built there a very beautiful church in the best basilica style, not (it is true) with marble, but with cast-iron columns and three altars. The two side altars cost $1,700 each, contributed by two benefactors. The high altar is now under construction and will cost between $7,000 and $8,000, which is being donated by a former Bavarian soldier, later a mounted policeman, Herting by name, who after several rough experiences in Chicago became a wealthy man. He also had a side altar constructed for around $1,700. He is active in every good work. He has four sons and a daughter as religious as he is. This congregation in Chicago (St. Joseph's) is made up of only 400 families. It has really made extraordinary sacrifices for the erection of a worthy house of God (which will cost $80,000) and of a school (at a cost of $25,000). In addition, our church in Newark, near New York, is at present being frescoed by the Munich painter Lamprecht.[74] This is being done at the expense of benefactors, each of whom has bound himself to pay a specified sum.

People in Germany have no idea what American Catholics provide for churches, schools, priests, teachers, orphans, and the sick. It is amazing that the zeal does not slacken as needs constantly grow, but experience shows that faith and giving stand in intimate relationship. If a person is careless in making his contributions, something is lacking in his faith, and gradually he falls away completely.

It used to be thought that American boys had no inclination for the priesthood, but this is not so. The sons of wealthy parents, of course, seldom dedicate themselves to the religious state, but this is universal. The poor, however, do so if they find the opportunity, especially in the large cities, where it is frequently difficult

---

[73] Oswald Moosmüller, O.S.B. (1832-1901).

[74] Wilhelm Lamprecht (1838-1902) studied at the Royal Art Academy, Munich, winning many awards as a young painter. In 1867, the Benedictines at St. Mary's Church, Newark, commissioned him to paint a series of frescoes depicting the Blessed Virgin. He remained in the U.S. with more commissions than he could fill, and his paintings and murals were found in churches, seminaries, and hospitals throughout the East and Midwest, particularly New York City; Hartford, Connecticut; Hoboken, New Jersey; Indiana; Ohio; and Illinois. During a period in Cincinnati, Lamprecht co-founded the Christian Art Society, for which he painted his famous *Marquette on the Mississippi* (1869) as a donation to the Society for a fundraising raffle. The painting passed through many hands until Father Francis X. Weninger, S.J., purchased it about 1880 and presented it to Marquette College (later University), where it is now located.

to achieve an independent position. They do not do so as easily in the countryside as in the populous areas. We recruit most of our priesthood candidates from our city parishes where we select the best and most talented boys from the schools for ourselves. All the Orders do the same, and so do the bishops. From my earlier mention of the 39 aspirants for the religious state, it is obvious that we have more candidates for the Order than for the secular clergy. This scarcely needs justification, but in the end, the proportion adjusts itself, for some of our scholastics leave before entering the novitiate or making profession, and become secular priests. Sometimes they make simple profession, but leave the Order before solemn profession or give such indications of a lack of religious vocation that we do not admit them to solemn profession, but turn them over to the secular clergy. In this way, we have sent many secular priests to the bishops–three since last year alone.

Finally, let me mention that I had the *Holy Rule*, with the constitutions and declarations and the life of St. Benedict, printed at our press, [75] and I sent one hundred copies *gratis* to the Bavarian Benedictines. In addition, very shortly, a statistical album[76] of the entire Benedictine Order in all countries will proceed from our press. Boniface Wimmer, Abbot

Ger   oALMV   cASVA   transABi

TO UTTO LANG   86

St. Vincent, April 19, 1868

Right Reverend Abbot and Dear Confrere: Do you really think that Abbot Rupert Seidenbusch[77] is my alter ego? I would not have thought that. It is interesting that Mr. Lebling[78] wrote something similar about him. I always considered our charac-

---

[75] This was the first edition of the *Rule* of St. Benedict printed in the United States, *Regula sanctissimi patris nostri Benedicti, auspice Reverendissimo et Amplissimo Domino Domno Bonifacio I abbate S. Vincentii et Congregationis Americano-Cassinensis praeside, denuo edita* (Beatty, Pa.: St. Vincent Press, 1867). Published at the same time were the constitution and statutes of the Bavarian Congregation, *Statuta Congregationis Benedictino-Bavaricae Sedis Apostolicae dispositione ad Congregationem Americano-Cassinensem extensa* (Beatty, Pa.: St. Vincent Press, 1867), and St. Gregory the Great's life of St. Benedict, *Vita sanctissimi patris nostri Benedicti, ex lib. 2 Dialogorum s. Gregorii romani pontificis. Auspice . . . Bonifacio I abbate S. Vincentii* (Beatty, Pa.: St. Vincent Press, 1867).

[76] *Album Benedictinum, seu Catalogus exhibens seriem sacrorum antistitum ac monachorum hoc superiori biennio ad Ordinen S.P. Benedicti pertinentium*, ed. Eduardus Hipelius, O.S.B. (Beatty, Pa.: St. Vincent Press, 1869).

[77] Rupert Seidenbusch, O.S.B. (1830-1895).

[78] Louis Ignatius Lebling, treasurer of the *Ludwig Missionsverein*.

ters very different. In many ways, he is certainly better than I. Because we worked so closely together for several years, he may have adopted some of my traits, as Mr. Lebling states, perhaps even my faults. My priors were always informed of my plans. I hope he has adopted one good point, i.e., not to look narrowly only to the benefit of his own abbey, but rather to that of the whole congregation. I have always done that, as he has often enough seen from my actions and planning. One gains nothing by such an approach, however, not even a "thank you."

Good candidates for the Order are always welcome. This year I will get some from my own scholasticate, but too slowly in proportion to the needs. The College of St. Anselm at St. Paul's-Outside-the-Walls [Rome] did not open this year because none, or rather only two students, applied. I doubt whether it will ever start. I intend to send two clerics to St. Elizabeth's unless political disturbances interfere. It is favorably located for its purpose. My students can choose their college and professors and live their daily schedule according to their own desire. Father Adalbert[79] will study philosophy for four years at the Minerva or the Sapienza. Fathers Hilary and Innocent[80] will study moral and dogmatic theology for four years. Father Edward[81] occupied himself for the most part with Hebrew and Arabic. Father Oswald[82] is studying canon law. If I send clerics, they must spend one year in college. Then they can attend the Anselmium, but not all the necessary branches.

I do not know if I shall go to the ecumenical council. I have to be invited first. There are financial and disciplinary reasons for not going, for it might be harmful if I were absent from home for a year. Nevertheless, there are important reasons for the trip. God will provide.

You have certainly received 100 copies of the *Holy Rule*, with the declarations and statutes and the life of our holy father from Pustet. I did not want to change anything. When everything is exactly observed, there is no need to change anything. At times, we are stricter than the old statutes require. We are not old enough to determine how everything should be observed, neither are the priories. Therefore, we should allow the old statutes to stand as they are. Many want to introduce clear-cut statutes now, something which lack of room has certainly helped promote. I ordered 500 copies of the statutes printed. I will send 100 of these as a gift to my confreres in Bavaria, and I ask that you distribute them in Metten, Weltenburg, Scheyern, and Munich. Perhaps some would like to read the original

---

[79] Adalbert Müller, O.S.B. (1842-1906).
[80] Hilary Pfrängle, O.S.B. (1843-1909), and Innocent Wolf, O.S.B. (1843-1922).
[81] Edward Hipelius, O.S.B. (1836-1900).
[82] Oswald Moosmüller, O.S.B. (1832-1901).

constitutions and declarations of 1735. The *Rituale* and *Ceremoniale* would have been finished long ago had we received the musical notations on time. Now we are printing the *Album Benedictinum*, for which purpose I bought a new patent printing press and much new type for a thousand florins. We are diligently setting type and printing. The result will be elegant.

We must have the novitiate regulations printed in Latin because some novices cannot read German and others cannot read English. Certain Jansenistic ideas appear at points in the old edition, but we have made the necessary corrections already. In Mallersdorf, I saw the novitiate regulations bound in three volumes, consisting of seven divisions. I copied them but lost the copies. I always thought they were complete in Metten, but maybe they can be found in Scheyern. I could find out nothing about them in Rome. The *Ceremoniale* will be ready soon after the *Album*. I will send you a copy. We received the notes from Pustet.

I am deeply grieved to hear that our magnanimous patron, King Ludwig, went home to his eternal reward and received his well-earned crown in the next world. God took him from this world so that he might not see the sad events in store for Germany and Bavaria. Even the English newspapers praised him. We celebrated the three *requiem* masses for him. I believe he wrote me eight days before his death. I feared a misfortune and was much saddened merely at the thought of it. Some years ago, not far from Newark, the sorceress Lola Montez[83] died as a Methodist, because she ate the bread of a Methodist.

Unemployment is raging in our cities. I must frequently give refuge to up to 20 people going west in order to find work. The high cost for material to make clothing is about to go down, but the cost of grain, especially barley, is still high. You have to pay $2.60 per bushel ($5.60 for the special measure). For hops, you paid $75 per hundredweight before, but now only $40 because much found its way into this country from Bavaria. We drink a lot of beer and cannot brew enough. It costs $11 a barrel (32 gallons), plus a $1 tax. In the cities, they sell it for $14. I do not make much profit from it, but at least we have it for our own table.

Our harvest was good. So far, the winter crop looks promising. I manage to get by because my fathers stationed outside send me the money they have left over after expenses. At present, we are 55 priests, of whom two are novices. Thirty-four are at stations away from the monastery. The rest are at home. (This does not take into account the abbey in Minnesota and the priory in Atchison.) Four of the 34 are in Rome. Consequently, we in fact have only 30 doing pastoral work. Of the

---

[83] The courtesan and lover of King Ludwig I whose relationship with the king had resulted in his being forced to abdicate in 1848. See Bruce Seymour, *Lola Montez: A Life* (New Haven: Yale University Press, 1996).

21 at Saint Vincent, three are doing parish work. The rest are officials and professors. I am the fifth wheel on the wagon, or shall be very soon because of my age. I am a real sit-at-home for the reason that I do not like to travel. Nevertheless, I have to do it more than I want. Recently I was in Richmond for the first time and took formal possession of the German parish there. The trip takes 26 hours on the railroad and costs $20. In a short time, I will have to send a second priest and then a third one. The place is ideally suited for a college, which we will establish when the time comes. Some parts of the city are still in ruins, but that's enough for now. Abbot Rupert landed in New York on March 9 and arrived on April 4 in St. Paul where the German Catholics gave him a most solemn reception. He put three of the students he brought along in the novitiate here. Two younger boys he took with him to Minnesota. He is a beggar, and does a very good job of it.

A thousand greetings to my old confreres. Peace be with you all. With most sincere affection and respect, your most devoted confrere, Boniface Wimmer

Ger   oAMA   cASVA   transRG, CZ, CW   *Scrip*19: 75-77

TO INNOCENT WOLF   87

St. Vincent, July 30, 1868

My Dear Father Innocent: I received your letter of July 8, 1867, only now, and in response I want to tell you that it was altogether unnecessary to present proof that you are in need of books for the reason that the public libraries afford only scant resources and few opportunities for use. I am quite ready to believe this and am glad to give you approval now and for the future to purchase any works necessary or useful to you. I extend this approval also to Fathers Hilary and Adalbert.[84] In fact, I have always expressed myself plainly in this matter and only recently wrote Father Oswald[85] that he could invest $100 annually for books to establish a library. You will know the kind of books that are needed. I certainly don't know that. For exegesis and hermeneutics, you should have the works of Abbot Haneberg; for church history, the later editions of Alzog. Besides this, you must also include sacred scripture, both the Old and New Testaments in the version of Dr. Valentine Loch and Dr. Wilhelm Reichl of Regensburg. These are by far the best and most thorough works, and they cost just a few gulden. Just as the soldier needs weapons, so does the student need books in order to face and defeat his

---

[84] Hilary Pfrängle, O.S.B., (1843-1909) and Adalbert Müller, O.S.B. (1842-1906).
[85] Oswald Moosmüller, O.S.B. (1832-1901).

Innocent Wolf, O.S.B., who served as prior at Saint Vincent, and was later elected abbot of Saint Benedict's Abbey in Atchison, Kansas.

foes, i.e. the examiners. It would be cruel economics for Father Oswald to curtail his budget for books.

Today I forwarded $400 in gold and will also take care of future needs. Since I will be obliged to attend the ecumenical council, no one else will be sent to Rome this year, but next year, if I am still alive, I will send two more. This year I cannot spare anyone because I must part with two priests for Atchison. I will be losing Father Edward[86] because of his persistent discontent, his non-observance of the *Rule*, and his constant ailing condition. He will take over as professor in one of the colleges. He is a man truly unworthy of the name of Benedictine because of his total lack of loyalty to the house that raised him. If you or any of your companions should ever turn out to be of the same stamp, then neither I nor any other abbot will ever feel tempted to send his folks to Rome to finish their education. I hope, though, that Father Edward will prove to be the only instance of such ingratitude and of such perverse behavior and that you and your future conduct will justify my decision to acquire a house in Rome for the American Benedictines.

Father Prior's condition has not improved. Very likely, he will return home. The clerics have been spending two weeks on the Ridge in pleasant diversion. Four of them—two from Kansas and two of our own, Fraters Aloysius and Lawrence[87]—hiked 40 miles in one day over Laurel Hill in 98-100 degree heat. The scholastics and college students are gone. Blackberries and huckleberries abound; a few cherries and apples; chestnuts will be plentiful by all indications. No one has gone

---

[86] Edward Hipelius, O.S.B. (1836-1900).
[87] Frater Aloysius did not persevere in the monastic life, while Frater Lawrence Schaeffer, O.S.B. (1847-1871), did.

farther than Carrolltown for vacation. The harvest is very large and will benefit still more from recent rains. Excavation for the new college building will be completed in a few days. It will depend on weather conditions when construction of the building will begin. Otherwise, there is no news.

I want to remind you not to worry if the results of your examinations do not reflect the effort that you have put forth. It will be comforting enough to me to know that you have applied yourself diligently to study, that you are acquiring a good foundation of knowledge, and that you are preparing yourself for eventual work in our colleges. In the process of acquiring the necessary preparation, you are free to act, and are urged to act, without restriction. If academic honors come your way–and these will deservedly come according to what Father Oswald writes me–this will please me all the more. Take care of yourself also in point of health. My greetings to Fathers Adalbert and Hilary. A thousand greetings from Father Ferdinand[88] and from the other confreres. May God help and bless you. Boniface Wimmer, Abbot

Ger   oASBA   cASVA   transPB

TO RUPERT SEIDENBUSCH   **88**

St. Vincent, September 21, 1868

Right Reverend Abbot: I was waiting for the candidates you sent before I wrote. They arrived three days ago. You know from my experience with what eyes an abbot is watched, for have not my own brethren already lodged complaints against me in Rome? Did not Father Wendelin[89] utter everything that he possibly could, true and false, against me? Do we not also see in the case of the prior of Atchison[90] how men participated in the party and afterwards discredited him alone? Has not one of our fathers said of me, "He's a chronic drinker and has arranged also for a chronic drinker to become abbot in Minnesota"? A bishop wrote that to me. A man's enemies are found in his own house.

Most recently, Father Ferdinand[91] has shown a disposition toward me that I would never have suspected of him. He thinks so ill of my administration, past and present, that at no price will he agree to be an official any longer. "I would

[88] Ferdinand Wolf, O.S.B. (1834-1914), brother of Father Innocent.
[89] Wendelin Mayer, O.S.B. (1832-1881).
[90] Augustine Wirth, O.S.B. (1828-1901).
[91] Ferdinand Wolf, O.S.B. (1834-1914).

rather die than live longer at St. Vincent," he has written and said. I had to relieve him of his distress and name him pastor in Indiana, Pennsylvania, a position that became vacant when Father Utto[92] became professor of moral theology. If the man could reproach me for significant weakness, how quickly would I be accused!

We abbots surely need to exercise caution since we are watched, criticized, and envied more than bishops. For a long time I have been accustomed to every kind of treachery and ingratitude and would be tempted to be a misanthrope if I had not learned to make God alone witness of my intentions and actions. I would restrain myself less if I were not abbot, but nothing is overlooked in the abbot. I would have to be poorly acquainted with my Papenheimer[93] if I thought you did not have some people of the same sort among your numbers. Therefore, be on guard. Let us both be on the alert! "Let no one look down on you" (Tit. 2: 15).

Brother Thaddeus was homesick.

I will place the new candidates on retreat immediately. Brother Dominic[94] allowed me no rest with regard to his inheritance of 1,000 florins. He even wanted the interest ($335), but I would not give it to him. Father Celestine[95] paid him the 1,000 florins. He was already married, and, if we are correctly informed, to a divorced woman. Naturally, he thoroughly inveighed against me about the novices.

We have not yet laid the foundation for the new building because a great deal of excavating was required and rain held this up. Novices and clerics here now number 30, scholastics 62, college students 105. In love and respect, your devoted brother, Boniface Wimmer

Ger   oASJA   cASVA   transAH

TO INNOCENT WOLF   89

St. Vincent, November 17, 1868

Dear Father Innocent: From a letter of Fth. Ferdinand,[96] I learned that you are in a good deal of excitement about him and partly yourself. But you need not bother yourself about Fth. Ferdinand. It was indeed unpleasant for me that he gave me

---

[92] Utto Huber, O.S.B. (1819-1896).
[93] Unknown reference.
[94] Dominic Ziegler, O.S.B.
[95] Celestine Englbrecht, O.S.B. (1824-1904).
[96] Ferdinand Wolf, O.S.B. (1834-1914), brother of Father Innocent Wolf.

I'll try to find time for a letter to Fr. Adalbert. If Abbot Haneberg[107] wishes to stay with you, try to accommodate him. My best regards to our friends and patrons. Yours in sincere love and esteem, Boniface Wimmer

Eng   oASBA   cASVA

TO MARTIN MARTY   **90**

St. Vincent, November 22, 1868

Very Reverend and Dear Confrere: The things you said in your letter to me against the idea of a common novitiate and house of studies marks you out as a true Switzer. It makes me wonder that while you were writing, you did not get homesick and feel tempted to set out bag and baggage to return to your father at Einsiedeln, there to spend all the days of your life at your father's side or at the side of his successor, in a cozy and comfortable life together, just as many of your fellow countrymen do who have never left the valley where they were born or who, if they have left it, die abroad out of sheer homesickness if they cannot return home in time.

That the Order of St. Benedict is patriarchal and monarchical I am willing to grant. That stability is a fundamental stipulation of his *Rule* I also grant. I deny, however, that stability is to be understood only with regard to place, or that it is to be restricted according to your interpretation of it. For you must note that the stability St. Benedict speaks of is also a stability of state. The first kind of stability, that is, of place, does not mean that one must remain for life in the monastery of his profession, but rather that one cannot at will change over to another monastery, etc., except when necessity (in which surely charity and the honor of God must be included) or the command and will of the abbot permit it. Otherwise, how in the world could the Order spread? How could the Benedictines have converted England, Germany, Hungary, Sweden, etc.? What about our St. Boniface, St. Willibrord, St. Otto, and the others? What would we be without them? It was against the gyrovagues and sarabites of his time that St. Benedict introduced stability, not only the stability of place but also the stability of state, so that those who made their profession might not take off their habit and return to the world. (See Calmet's commentary on the *Rule* of St. Benedict, chapter 58.)

If you insist on a one-sided view of the stability of place, what can America expect from St. Meinrad? That it remain as it is now or that it should get a few

---

[107] Daniel Boniface Haneberg, O.S.B. (1816-1876), abbot of St. Boniface Abbey, Munich.

more fathers and with that, period! God forbid such an interpretation of the vow of stability whereby we would be setting up a constraint that would stifle all future development and would disappoint the hopes that young America places in us. Such an interpretation would destroy once and for all every prospect of filling up the gap that exists here, namely the lack of an Order that has as its special objective to supply America with a sufficient number of good priests.

It is certainly not contrary to the stability of place to have a common novitiate and house of studies so long as they exist in accordance with the express will of the respective abbots, just as it is not contrary to the vow if a father goes to a parish to take up duties of some sort or is sent away as a professor. That St. Benedict had a seminary for the Order at Montecassino, and earlier at Subiaco, is now certain, judging from the reliable account of his famous biographer. It was from there, you know, that he sent missionaries to Sicily and to Gaul.

It follows clearly from his *Rule* that he wanted uniformity in certain matters, whereas in other things he left room for differences if the locality required or the abbot desired them. For example, in the matter of clothing and drink and even in things pertaining to the Divine Office. How, therefore, can it be said to be contrary to the spirit of St. Benedict if a general uniformity is sought after in some congregations by the establishment of a common novitiate and house of studies when the individual monasteries are nevertheless permitted to have their own house rules? Moreover, why cannot domestic freedom be preserved in this way? Will there then be no more criticizing, no more murmuring if the novitiate is in one's own house? I know from experience that the opposite is the case.

In my opinion, there will be less criticizing and less murmuring if one realizes that we find the same usages and customs everywhere and that whatever differences may exist can easily be justified on local grounds. What you call "modern experiments" date really from ancient times. As is well known, a certain second St. Benedict[108] in the reign of Louis the Pious was ordered to bring about a uniformity of discipline in all the monasteries of the kingdom. It was hardly a hundred years later that the Congregation of Cluny was formed; again, a hundred years later the Congregations of Clairvaux and Citaux. By order of the Council of Constance, the Bursfeld Congregation was established for all of Germany, from which, after the Reformation, arose the Bavarian, Swabian, Austrian, and Swiss Congregations, and which lasted until the end of the German Empire.

These were not experiments, but, in fact, a consequence of the times and circumstances. Neither were they abuses. Rather they should be understood as natural offshoots, ever fresh and strong, stemming from an ancient rootstock, just as the

---

[108] Benedict of Aniane (c.750-821).

Church in the course of time, though preserving her fundamental, essential, and inalienable character, has, nevertheless, been formed and molded to correspond to the needs of a particular time.

The fact that all modern popes (including Pope Pius IX) pressed for a common novitiate in all religious orders and issued exact regulations on the matter, enjoining their observance under severe penalties, is something we cannot afford to disregard. Did they not have good reason for such regulations? Do not these reasons hold good for us here? Is it not well known in monasteries of monks and nuns that ascetic formation is very deficient and incomplete, if in the novitiate conducted in their own house, there are only one or two novices? How could it be otherwise? Who in the world is going to appoint a special novice master for one or two novices? Even if an abbot does so, how often is the novice master going to be with the novices? How often will they be left to their own devices!

The last abbot of Tegernsee did not send his four novices to the common novitiate. They became open freethinkers and enemies of the Church. One died in Munich excommunicated. In Erfurt and Salzburg, the Benedictines operate flourishing universities with 800 or 900 students as well as several secondary schools. How could the Benedictines maintain these schools without a congregation and a common novitiate, if each one brought along his own peculiar customs and insisted on living according to them?

An absolute monarch (and an abbot), provided he is good and well qualified, can do more good than one whose authority is restricted and curtailed. It is true. How many capable abbots of this kind, however, do we meet with in history? It does not matter at all if the abbot has a court above him and so has to be on his guard. As long as he does what is right, the president and visitors of the congregation can have no objections to make. Calmet[109] has unusual praise for the Bursfeld Congregation and its offshoots, the Bavarian, Austrian, Swabian, and Swiss Congregations. On the other hand, he was not pleased with the Cassinese Congregation.

You are still obsessed with the idea that the president and the visitors have the power to send any father to any monastery in the congregation, or that any father can easily have himself transferred to any place. I deny that that is the case. Every abbot is the ruler of his own men. He has full authority to make appointments in his own house, and only then, when he has a surplus and there is need elsewhere, can the one in need petition him for help. It is, moreover, assumed that the one

---

[109] Antoine Augustine Calmet, O.S.B., a French Benedictine whose commentary on the *Rule* of St. Benedict (*Commentaire littéral historique et moral sur la règle de S. Benoît* [Paris, 1734]) was a standard reference work for Benedictines in the nineteenth century.

having the surplus should help the one in need, for a time at least, but also in such a manner and for such a length of time as he judges to be fitting and proper. Nevertheless, he is under no obligation. Charity should rule, not pressure. After all, there is nothing perfect on earth, and there are two sides to everything, especially when time and circumstances change the whole picture. The best organization can turn out to be troublesome or even harmful.

It is, however, certain that over against other Orders what we can accomplish is of no consequence if our efforts are only sporadic and scattered, if we do not march up, as they do, rank and file, in formation. Yet a congregation cannot exist without a common novitiate and house of studies. By a common house of studies, of course, it should be obvious that we mean only philosophical and theological studies. The gymnasium (secondary school) is not included. There could also be several such rallying points in the congregation.

With the greatest affection and esteem, your devoted confrere, Boniface Wimmer

Ger   oASMA   cASVA   transBB

TO CLAUDE DUBUIS   91

St. Vincent, December 15, 1868

Rt. Rev. and Dear Bishop, My Lord: With great pleasure I learned from the papers that you arrived safely, and with a crowd of Missionaries, too, from Europe in this Country again, where so many of your faithful children were longing after you and expecting you hourly. I, myself, am one of these who counted the days when you would come home, and send you now a hearty welcome.

But at once also I must come out with a conversation about an affair in which Your Lordship, as well as myself, is strongly concerned. I held here in August our third General Chapter. Father Aemilian[110] was invited to be present at it among the Priors. We spoke, of course, much of the Texas Missions, privately and in the Chapter. We weighed and considered maturely all the pro and contra of these Missions, as well in regard to the Mission itself as in regard to ourselves as to the Abbey which has to support it. The result was that we resolved to carry it on (a) if in S. Antonio a house for the Order could be established and a Congregation secured for it, where at least two Fathers at first could live together; (b) if you could find other priests, regulars or seculars, to tend to the missions which we

---

[110] Aemilian Wendel, O.S.B. (1832-1901), of San José Priory, San Antonio, Texas.

had attended to so far. Therefore, also I retained F. Aemilian till you would come home, so much more, as in the meanwhile, the yellow fever had broken out in all the places through which he had to pass if he wanted to return to S. Antonio; and after eights years absence from home it was at any rate a good chance and a kind of necessity to keep him in the monastery and get him again accustomed to monastic life.

A few days since I got a letter from Brother Gamelbert[111] telling [me] that Fth. Eberhard[112] had left Castroville for parts unknown; and a little afterwards he was announced already in Pittsburgh, where he stopped with our Fathers there, and it was said that he left Castroville because some men threatened to shoot him for his refusal to bury a freemason in the graveyard, if I understood him, for I have not yet seen him. Now this step was entirely against my expectation, though I well know that Fth. Eberhard, when he is left alone, is apt to act rashly and precipitately.

Under these circumstances there are only two Benedictines at present in Texas, or, properly speaking, only one: Fth. Columban.[113] For Fth. Theodore[114] is yet with simple vows and can leave us, and I believe will leave us. Two of the brothers died; one would not remain any longer, and the fourth is an old feeble man, left in Castroville. This looks all like a dissolution of the Mission personnel and of the whole concern, and may be repeated again and again (until we could get a regular Priory with at least 3 priests and 2 brothers in one house) to the shame and disgrace of our Order. The distance from St. Vincent to Texas is too great, the communication even by letter too slow, a visitation too costly, the difficulties great and many, the exchange of discarded and disabled or disqualified [monks] too costly and [above all] the exposure of single Fathers, a thing which doesn't suit religious, at any rate not for a length of time. All these circumstances together must always cause a failure. I have Fathers in Kansas, Nebraska, Minnesota, Kentucky, Chicago, New Jersey, Richmond, Va., and all goes right because these places are easily accessible by railroad. I can visit all of them once a year and oftener. I can make changes without trouble. I can gather them to a retreat, etc., and, therefore, they keep good order and purpose.

From this it is evident that Texas is not a fit place for us unless I could send such a number thither that they could constitute a regular community, which I cannot do because I cannot spare so many, and also because it would cost too much. I lost

---

[111] Gamelbert Daschner, O.S.B. (1817-1870).
[112] Eberhard Gahr, O.S.B. (1832-1922).
[113] Columban Schmidbauer, O.S.B. (1832-1868).
[114] Theodore von Grunder, O.S.B. (b. 1834).

two young priests since February, not yet 30 years old, and two more of 38 years, one of whom was Fth. Alto[115] who died the 29th of June from a consumption which he contracted in Texas. I have paid the debts contracted by Fth. Alto up to $2,500 in gold, and $500 I have to pay and will pay them yet. But this is only the capital. The interests amount nearly to the same sum, and I try to pay them also. But these debts are also a great drawback on our mission.

From all this you can easily infer, My Lord, that I have brought great sacrifices and am to bring yet for your Diocese: persons as well as pecuniary. I well know that your Most Rev. Predecessor[116] has also brought as great sacrifices for the same purpose, which have been wasted by unpractical management or the presence of unpropitious circumstances, and the early fruits of our mutual endeavors are simply that four German Congregations were well attended to for a term of 8 years at a time when it would have been scarcely possible to provide priests for them.

Should we not be satisfied now and stop here? Or should we make another onset to make a permanent establishment of our Order in your Diocese under circumstances not a bit more favorable and in several regards more difficult and at the risk of another [failure]?

This is the question I would put before your Lordship now, and which I most humbly beg you to answer frankly. You have brought with you 14 priests, I read in the papers, perhaps some French half-Germans, who you can send to a German congregation. If so, I would be very glad if I could also call in F. Columban, and F. Theodore could also either go to St. Vincent if he chooses, or take dispensation and stay in Texas if you wish it. And everything could be adjusted fairly and satisfactorily.

I think on both sides we have done our best. If we did not meet with the desired success, it is not our fault. We may consider it a sign that it is not the holy will of God. At any rate, you had, for the outlays made, the service of five good priests for 8 years. I have for my outlays nothing but 3 men dead, $2,000 to pay yet, and 8 years labor. Still I hope to have earned some merits in and for the other world.

In conclusion, I wish you a happy New Year and remain in profound reverence Your Lordship's most humble servant, Boniface Wimmer, Ab.

Eng   oArchives of the Diocese of Galveston, Texas   cASVA

---

[115] Alto Hörmann, O.S.B. (1829-1867), prior at San José Priory in Texas, who returned to St. Vincent when he became ill with tuberculosis.
[116] Bishop John M. Odin, C.M. (1800-1870), of Galveston, who had invited the Benedictines to Texas.

TO UTTO LANG 92

St. Vincent, January 11, 1869

Right Reverend Father Abbot and Dear Confrere: Many thanks for your kind letter of November 13, 1868, and the news you sent me. I am satisfied and consent to all the decrees, except those that deal with simple vows. On this point, I disagree. It is better if the novices wait three years after simple profession before making solemn profession. In urgent cases, when it is necessary to ordain them, Rome is willing to give a dispensation. I myself have received three such dispensations already. Each time I had to send in a special petition. I am losing half my clerics because they are not permitted to make their solemn profession immediately. That means a financial loss, as well as a loss of manpower, but I believe the moral benefit is far greater because by waiting, those who do not have a real vocation are sorted out. The law should have been enforced long ago, but as God pleases . . . . I am in favor of waiting the full three years even when the time of solemn vows is fast approaching. With regard to the congregation and representation in Rome, I am in agreement, but am against centralization.

You will have the *Album Benedictinum*[117] before Easter or shortly thereafter. It will provide proof to the Roman prelates that the Benedictines are not yet dead, but that the old stem is flourishing with fresh branches. If I am not mistaken, the English Benedictines are printing their small breviary in greater numbers. Abbot Guéranger[118] decided to publish a larger one some years ago. It must be ready by now. For me, our breviary is good enough. What faults do you find with it? I surely do not want to return to the cold breviary of the Maurists.

I am in good health, although I am now 60 years old. However, I have the feeling that I shall not live much longer. If I live until next fall, and if the Council takes place, I will go to Rome. I will first go to Bavaria in October if the country is open for entry. Whenever something can be done for our Order, I want to be there.

I did not send the copies of the *Holy Rule* to you so that you could sell them. I wanted you to distribute them to your own people, as well as to our confreres in Munich, Scheyern, and Weltenburg. When I left for America, I took along from Metten an old edition of the *Rule*, which I am now returning a hundredfold.

---

[117] *Album Benedictinum, seu Catalogus exhibens seriem sacrorum antistitum ac monachorum hoc superiori biennio ad Ordinem S.P. Benedicti pertinentium*, ed. Eduardus Hipelius, O.S.B. (Beatty, Pa.: St. Vincent Press, 1869).
[118] Prosper Guéranger, O.S.B. (1806-1875), abbot of the French abbey of Solesmes.

If you find a few novitiate handbooks, please send them to me. I will accept them gratefully as the equivalent of my "pious fraud." It seems the *Ceremoniale* for our Order will not be published on time. The editor [Camillus McKay], [a priest] who made simple profession, was later dismissed for drunkenness. Afterward, out of pity, I allowed him to stay on as a guest. He was supposed to edit the *Ceremoniale* because he was an expert on rubrics. He first edited the *Rituale*, which was printed and is on the way to you. Then he was going to edit the *Ceremoniale*, but in November, he died suddenly in his cell without having finished the manuscript.

On September 19, my prior, Father Peter Baunach,[119] died. Then Father Columban Schmidbauer,[120] and afterward a cleric who was a very fine young man.[121] I could not appoint a prior immediately because no one was available. In the face of all this sorrow and misfortune, I could not ask another father to proceed with the *Ceremoniale*, but it will be done.

I send my cordial greetings and New Year's congratulations a little late. Please convey them to Father Prior and all my friends. With sincere affection and deepest respect, I am your unworthy Boniface

Ger   oAMA   cASVA   transRG

TO RUPERT LEISS   93

Munich, October 21, 1869

Right Reverend Abbot and Esteemed Confrere: Summoned to Rome for the Council as president of the Congregation, I had to undertake the voyage again despite my disinclination. On October 1, I left St. Vincent, and on October 2 New York, on the French steamer *Ville de Paris*. On board with me were 12 other priests, 3 bishops, and 110 Papal Zouaves. We were in Brest on October 12 and in Munich the morning of October 15. There I learned of your jubilee and very much regret that I did not know of it earlier. Hence, I must offer my best wishes late. Fifty years in the priesthood is a wonderful thing. May you one day be able to show the Lord not only double, but triple and quadruple the talents He entrusted to you in order to obtain so much the richer reward!

---

[119] Peter Baunach, O.S.B. (1815-1868).
[120] Columban Schmidbauer, O.S.B. (1832-1868).
[121] Timothy Kirby, O.S.B. (1848-1868).

I would not have traveled to Rome so early, but I was again sending two clerics[122] there who had to report before November 1, and I did not want to let them go alone. Last Sunday I sent them on from here to Rome. I intend to go to Metten in the morning and, by way of Regensburg, Weltenburg, Hinheim, and Scheyern, to return to Munich, and from there to set out for Rome in the middle of November.

I am determined to lead a wanderer's life, like our doves in North America. The nest remains at St. Vincent, and every year I make it wider and more spacious so that it is becoming a real dovecote from which the young brood fly away to establish new nests and cotes. Nevertheless, I dislike traveling. I feel a noticeable decline of physical strength and suspect that I do not have much more time, though otherwise I am healthy. My sole desire is to see St. Vincent so well established that it will stand not only as mother but as motherhouse for our Order in America, and especially as Alma Mater in scholarship. Thus, I send my best men to Rome for schooling in order to have a good school at St. Vincent. Of course, this costs me much money, but as usual, it comes in time, even if I am no longer around. I see the distress of our time, the spread of unbelief, the dearth of good priests, and I would like, as far as possible, to stop the misery that must follow.

Last year I had 21 novices (for St. Vincent, St. Louis in Minnesota, and St. Benedict in Kansas) besides 9 clerics and some 50 scholastics. This year there are not so many novices, but the scholastics have increased in number to 70. I had to construct a new building 133 feet long, 40 feet wide, and 3 stories high, and also a chapel 50 feet wide and 40 feet long, in order to gain new space. I also bought 160 acres of land for 26,000 florins, of which 13,000 florins in cash were the down payment. The other half I must pay in two installments, but God blesses all my undertakings. I go deeper into debt, but our means and income grow from year to year despite the enormous debt that always keeps me in a certain peril, to which, however, I am by now accustomed. Even as the debt grows, someone always helps.

I hope to see you soon in the best of health. Meanwhile, I sign with special love and respect, Your Grace's humble confrere, Boniface Wimmer

Ger   oASA   cASV   transABi

---

[122] James Zilliox, O.S.B. (1849-1890), and Xavier Baltes, O.S.B. (1844-1876).

TO *DER WANDERER*   **94**

Rome, December 9, 1869

I hurry to write to you what I remember of yesterday's events. The
Council session was to begin at 8:30
am. Because it had rained all day and
all night, however, it was difficult to
find a carriage. Everyone wanted one.
Hundreds of them crossed the bridges to get to the Vatican. Cavalry kept
good order, but many traffic jams occurred. It took me a whole hour to get
there. We were afraid that we would
be late for the procession, but it did
not start until 9:00 am. This left us
just enough time to don rochett,
amice, cope, and miter. Ten prelates
went to the chapel above the portico
of St. Peter's Basilica and there waited
for the pope. When he came, the procession began, led by the papal cross,
followed by the abbots, bishops, archbishops, primates, and patriarchs, all
with cope and miter and without cro-

The photograph of Boniface Wimmer from the Vatican Council Album Monumentale.

sier. The cardinals were vested beautifully, as if for Mass. All wore the white miter.
The abbots were unaccompanied; the bishops had their chaplains; each cardinal,
a chaplain and a trainbearer. Two German prelates led the long procession. They
were Abbot Boniface Wimmer of St. Vincent, Pennsylvania, and Abbot Utto Lang
of Metten, Bavaria. Alongside them marched a detachment of Swiss Guard garbed
in their picturesque medieval costumes, while on the impressive high steps of St.
Peter's Basilica, the clergy of the city formed an espalier.

Inside the church the procession, singing and praying, moved between a military detachment and an enormous multitude of onlookers on both sides up to the
high altar where the Blessed Sacrament was exposed. There the procession turned
to the right, into the Council hall, a well-known part of St. Peter's. When a Council is held, the right transept is blocked off for that purpose. By the entrance is an
altar on which the cardinal deacon celebrates Mass. At the end of the hall is the

papal throne; to the right and left are seven elevated rows of seats for the prelates, but the center aisle is open. To the right and left behind the seats are the places for the nobility.

It took quite some time for all the prelates to find their seats: the cardinals to the right and left of the pope; the patriarchs, primates, and archbishops according to rank and time of appointment in the upper rows; the bishops in the middle and lower rows; the youngest bishops and abbots in the lowest ones. The general of the orders sat on plain benches; the lesser papal prelates did not find any seats, but took turns sitting on the steps of the altar.

The exact number of those attending the Council has not yet been announced. I did hear the number 914, not including 20 abbots. I also heard there were 940 fathers with miters and about 15 generals of orders in the vestments of their respective orders. However, I am told that there were 600 bishops. Therefore, one cannot go by the numbers I heard.

Imagine the impression one gets looking at that multitude, that forest of prelates among whom are many Orientals wearing a kind of crown similar to those of the old dukes, or like a turban, and dressed in very rich gold and silver embroidered vestments. They wore beards, of course, the number one decoration of the Orientals. Bearded as well are the Occidentals from the Turkish provinces and from overseas countries. There are representatives from all the nations of the world speaking all the major languages, but all, even most of the Orientals, know Latin, so they can converse with each other! Many of them were in the best, or middle years of life. Others were venerable old men who needed a helper or a staff to mount the stairway. The gray hair of most of them bears witness to their mature experience, to hardships endured. They are genuine Catholic senators, representatives of knowledge, of faith, of striving after virtue, of the unity of the faith as only the Church of God can produce.

Once the Holy Father arrived under the baldacchino, Cardinal Patrizi celebrated a Solemn High Mass. Before the blessing, the secretary of the Council, Bishop Fessler of St. Poelter [Austria], carried the gospel book to the altar and placed it on a small throne especially made for the occasion. Then Archbishop Puecher-Passavalli of Iconio mounted the pulpit and gave a fitting sermon in Latin, after which the Holy Father gave a plenary indulgence to all. The cardinal read the gospel from St. John, which ended the Solemn Mass. After that, the ceremony of obeisance to the head of the Church by all the fathers of the Council took place. In a long line, they approached the papal chair. Heads uncovered, with miters in their hands, the cardinals kissed the pope's hand, the bishops his right knee, and the abbots his foot. This took a whole hour.

Then the cardinal deacon asked all to pray. The pope, in a loud voice, read the prayers prescribed for Councils, and two singers intoned the Litany of the Saints, each invocation answered by the fathers. At the petition "that Thou wouldst bless this holy assembly and all orders of the Church," the pope rose and in a solemn voice gave the triple blessing: "That Thou wouldst bless and govern them and preserve them." At the end of the litany, the cardinal deacon sang the gospel passage (Luke 10) of how Christ sent the apostles to proclaim the good news.

I will briefly summarize the Holy Father's address to the assembly as follows: First, he expressed his joy that his ardent desire to convoke a Council had been fulfilled and that he could open it on the Feast of the Immaculate Conception. "I see more bishops gathered around me than ever before," he said. With a strong voice, he reminded the assembled fathers of the dangers that threaten the Church and our holy faith today. "Secret societies confuse sound doctrine and threaten the rights of the Church. Openly and with brazen lies and distortions, they seek to unleash the bonds of public morality and authority. They give free rein to the lowest human passions and seek to uproot the Christian faith, and they would succeed were the Church not stronger than the heavens, as St. John Chrysostom put it."

Then he said, "'Heaven and earth shall pass away, but my words will not pass away.' The words referred to are, 'Thou art Peter and upon this rock I shall build my Church, and the gates of Hell shall not prevail against it.' Although the Church is invincible, it is my duty to oppose these evils and these dangers with all my strength. I knew of no better way to do this than to call all the bishops together for a general council. Despite all obstacles, this has now happily been achieved." He could not withhold his joy at seeing in the assembled bishops the whole flock of Christ, as it were; that is, all the faithful. Vividly he recalled the many and extraordinary proofs of the love and affection they have given and continue to give to him, and he prayed fervently to God that they might be purified and made strong in faith by the trials they must endure. He prayed fervently as well for the unfortunate who have deviated from the path of truth and justice, and he prayed that, following the example of Christ, who came to seek and save what was lost, we would do something to bring them back to the right path. He prayed not less for the Roman people, his own, who have always shown their enduring love, their faithfulness to him. With most special love, he embraced the assembled fathers, recognizing their glowing zeal for intimate union with him. Today, he said, this is more necessary than ever. "Help me, therefore, that to the nations peace may come; to the barbarians, morality; to the monasteries, tranquility; to the churches, discipline; to the clergy, order; and to God, an acceptable people."

After this allocution, the Holy Father intoned the *Veni, Creator Spiritus*, and all the fathers joined in. The opening decree of the Council was then read. All gave their *placet*, and the Holy Father confirmed it. The opening of the next session was set for January 6, which was agreed to by the fathers and confirmed by the pope. The *Te Deum* closed the solemn session, which lasted from 9:00 am to 4:00 pm. The noble guests in the galleries held out to the end. Among them were the queens of Austria, Naples, and Parma; the grand duke and duchess of Tuscany; the king and queen, with the count and countess of Girgenti; the count and countess of Caserta; the count and countess of Trapani; then ambassadors, generals, etc.

It was not easy finding a carriage back to our lodgings as it was still raining. All wanted to ride back. The clerks had to wait half an hour and longer. Stomachs were rumbling. It was an unforgettable day, and one of the most important in history. Abbot Boniface Wimmer

Ger   cASVA   transAHo *Wand* (January 8, 1870)

1870-1874

Rome, February 20, 1870

Right Reverend Lord and Confrere: Some time ago, I sent you a list of all the Council fathers. It has probably arrived. I left Munich on November 22 and did not reach Rome until November 28 because en route I visited the abbots of Saint Peter and Muri-Gries. After that, I was sick for three days, but my homeopathy again saved me and now I feel very well. Eight Council fathers have already died, and several are dangerously ill. Apart from the six abbots nullius, there is no abbot here as such, but only abbots who are presidents of congregations, whom they call abbots general. The abbots nullius are here as quasi bishops, the abbot presidents as quasi generals of an order. The fact that other abbots are not here signifies a loss of privilege, at least de facto, however much justified by lack of space. There would not have been room for all of us. However, we have precedence over the real generals of orders, from a hierarchical point of view.

At the very opening of the Council, the abbot presidents marched at the head of the bishops. We were dressed like bishops, that is, in cope with simple miter and pectoral cross. Abbot Utto[1] and I opened the Council. We moved into St. Peter's and into the Council hall at the head of the procession, whereas the generals of orders only came after the Pope, and were admitted into the hall through a side door. In the sessions also, we are among the bishops, while they have their places

---

[1] Utto Lang, O.S.B. (1807-1884), abbot of Metten.

EMINENTISSIMI ET REVERENDISSIMI DOMINI
S. E. R. CARDINALES
REVERENDISSIMI DOMINI
PATRIARCHÆ PRIMATES ARCHIEPISCOPI EPISCOPI

ABBATES NULLIUS DIŒCESIS
SUPREMI ORDINUM REGULARIUM MODERATORES
QUI CONCILIO ŒCUMENICO VATICANO INTERFUERUNT

The front cover of the Album Monumentale for
the Vatican Council (1869-1870).

on the floor. On feasts when there is a Mass in the papal chapel and the bishops have to appear in cope, the generals of orders are not present, while the abbots nullius are also in cope, though we others are in prelatial dress, that is, in rochett, manteletta, and mozetta with covered pectoral cross. However, this is only by special privilege during the Council.

We have already seen to it that the quasi-episcopal jurisdiction of the abbots nullius will not be curtailed, although the French bishops moved that exemption should be abolished and invited the Germans to support this motion. The latter, however, did not do so. We hear that a great deal is to happen with regard to the orders, but nothing prejudicial to the old orders. We have not yet seen these proposals. Good persons were elected to the commission or deputation for religious orders. Ten of the 24 members of this deputation are former religious. Members from our Order are Archbishop Dusmet of Catania and Bishop Willi of Chur.[2]

The sessions are in St. Peter's, that is, on the right side of the north transept, which is divided off for this purpose from the rest of the church by a wooden

---

[2] Joseph Benedict Dusmet, O.S.B., Archbishop of Catania, Sicily, and Caspar Willi, O.S.B., Bishop of Chur, Switzerland.

partition beautifully painted on the exterior. The result was a hall, 175 feet long, 200 feet high, and 80 feet wide. In the center was an aisle, and to the right and left were seven rows of benches, with writing desks, covered with green cloth, one higher than the other, and on these sat the primates, archbishops, bishops, and abbots. Almost one-third of the area, however, was occupied by a platform, to which one ascended from the aisle by several steps. On it was nothing except, in the middle, tables for the apostolic protonotaries, the secretary and subsecretary, the five cardinal presidents, and, at the far end, an altar where, every day before the beginning of the session, an archbishop celebrated the Mass of the Holy Spirit. In the semi-circle around it sat the cardinals and patriarchs.

It was soon discovered, however, that the speakers could not be understood, and so a portion of the hall was cut off by a curtain, so that now it is only about 125 feet long. Then a cloth ceiling was stretched over the pulpit from one wall to the other, that is, 80 by about 20 feet, and four more benches were placed to the right and left of the aisle and also on the platform (where we abbots now sit in front of the cardinals and beside the patriarchs), so that now every speaker can be understood everywhere, if he speaks clearly and slowly.

Thus far, we have had 26 sessions. Each lasts from 9:00 am to 1:30 pm. Because secrecy has been imposed on us, I cannot tell you anything about them. However, I may say, since it is already known from the newspapers, that the poison spread by Döllinger[3] seems to be operating significantly. There prevails among many bishops, in particular the Germans and French, a spirit of distrust and suspicion of the Apostolic See that is distressing. Much prayer is needed if anything beneficial is to come about. The great majority of the bishops (and, of course, we abbots also) are on the pope's side, but as the speeches indicate, there is still a strong opposition. Hence, the matter is dragged out. There is too much freedom of speech and no profit is apparent in it. The pope is bitterly disappointed and out of temper and seems very tired, but perhaps this has to be, and God will direct all to the best. If things do not change, we will still be sitting here a year from now. Some fathers are for introducing a different order of business, and then things will probably move faster.

Let us pray fervently for humility for the Council. These gentlemen are too clever. However, peace, decorum, and good understanding prevail outwardly. In anticipation of the feast, I offer Your Grace my hearty good wishes for your

---

[3] Johannes Ignaz Döllinger (1799-1890), German theologian and historian who was a leader of the liberal wing of the German church. He had been Wimmer's professor of history at the University of Munich. After the Council, he refused to accept the dogma of papal infallibility and was excommunicated by the archbishop of Munich, Gregory Scherr, O.S.B.

namesday. Otherwise, I might be too late. We have much to do. Please greet the prior[4] and all the dear brethren most warmly. I always pray for you at the tomb of St. Peter. With the request that you remember me before God, I have the honor to be, in deepest respect and love, Your Grace's most obliging, Boniface Wimmer

Ger   oASA   cASVA   transABi

TO *DER WANDERER*   96

Rome, May 15, 1870

. . . On Friday, April 29, the 45th secret session was held. It dealt with the small catechism that the pope will publish. It is to be in Latin and translated into all languages spoken by Christian nations. Its purpose is to teach all Catholic children the world over the same basic tenets of the Church. Strictly speaking, it does not belong to matters of faith but to ecclesiastical discipline. It has been discussed frequently at previous sessions, and several changes have been made. The Latin bishop, Francis Xavier Wierchleuski, spokesman for his deputation, raised the question of changes and recommended that the fathers accept them. Two cardinals and three bishops spoke at length. As there were no other speakers, the subject was closed, and the comments on the infallibility of the pope were distributed in printed form with the announcement that after the primacy of the Holy Father has been considered, his infallibility will come up for debate.

The next day, April 30, session number 46 was held on the small catechism. Three bishops questioned whether it was necessary and practical to introduce it universally. The bishop of Seckan, who represented the Deputation on Ecclesiastical Discipline, also spoke. At the 47th on May 4, Bishop Zwenger continued the discussion of the small catechism. The vote was not unanimous, but there will be no further discussion. A decision will be announced at the next session. It is good to have one universal catechism, especially in our time when people are on the move and families are changing residence. When nearly every diocese has its own catechism, parents and children become confused. The session closed with the announcement of the death of Bishop Bucouroux, the 13th father who has died during the Council.

Soon the Council will deal with the Constitution on the Dogma of the Church of Christ, which refers to the primacy and infallibility of the Pope. The infallibil-

---

[4] Peter Lechner, O.S.B. (1805-1874).

ity question will be difficult because many do not think that this is a good time to define it as a dogma. Although many are of that opinion, they constitute only a large minority. It will not be possible, however, for the fathers to make any suggestions for changes or additions. Whatever the outcome, the faithful can be sure that the question has been discussed and thoroughly tested by the fathers of the Council. Hardly any other teaching of the Church has been so diligently studied, so sharply attacked, so intelligently defended as has infallibility. For several weeks, many old and new publications have been sent to our lodgings, free of charge, to win us over to one side or the other. Many of the publications are very biased and contain almost nothing new, only old ideas in new dress.

One of the latest publications, by Joseph Pennacchi, professor at the University of Rome, is outstanding. It is not polemic, but truly scholarly. He refutes Bishop Hefele of Rotterdam with an irresistible logic in dealing with the much-disputed case of Pope Honorius. I highly recommend his book: *De Honorii I Romani Pontificis causa in Concilio VI* (1870).[5]

There are many empty seats at the meetings because many fathers are sick. If there are dangers outside that may threaten the Council, we know nothing about them.

Ger   cASVA   transAHo *Wand* (June 18, 1870)

TO *DER WANDERER*   97

Rome, July 17, 1870

If I remember correctly, my last report covered the Council up to June 27, that is, through the 76th session. The 77th session on June 27 lasted very long. Since it was the day preceding the Feast of St. Peter and a day of fast, the stomach was not too content. On the feast itself, the Holy Father celebrated High Mass, although he did not feel well. That evening there were fireworks and a magnificent illumination in Rome. The pope was scheduled to come to St. Paul's-Outside-the-Walls on June 30 and celebrate Mass, but he did not come. Instead, he called the 78th

---

[5] Wimmer himself wrote the preface to this book. See Giuseppe Pennachi, *De Honorii I Romani Pontificis causa in Concilio VI. Dissertatio Josephi Pennachii in Romana Studiorum Universitate Historiae Ecclesiasticae Professoris Substituti ad Patres Concilii Vaticani. Praefatus est P. Bonifacius Wimmer, O.S.B., Abbas S. Vincentii et Praeses Congregationis Americo-Bavaricae Benedictinae* (Regensburg: Pustet, 1870). The book's contents are discussed in Oetgen, *An American Abbot*, 310-11.

session for that day. Most Benedictines could not attend the session until 1:30 pm, where one speaker dwelt very long on infallibility.

Suggestions for chapter three were handed out, and there was a vote on the Dogmatic Constitution of the Church. Fifty-three fathers have so far spoken on the infallibility of the pope, and as many more were listed to speak. The fathers did not make use of the right to ask for a closure to the debate in order to avoid false accusations that the fathers had no freedom to express their opinions, an accusation that has appeared in some newspapers and pamphlets. Nonetheless, a change occurred in the 80th session when several of those listed to speak declined to do so. This found approval from all sides. In the 81st session, all relinquished their turn to speak except two, who spoke very briefly. The session closed at 9:30 am. We had several free days until the proposed additions were printed and handed out to the fathers at the 82nd session on Monday, July 11. Bishop Gassen of Brixen was appointed to clear up the doubts that have been raised. He then read the decree on the infallibility of the pope when as head of the Church he makes a declaration on matters of faith or morals. He did this in an excellent address that lasted two hours. In the vote that followed, each of the 601 fathers present was called by name. Quite a few responded "non placet." Sixty-two responded "placet juxta modum," that is, affirmative, providing a few changes are made.

Hence, the vote on the fourth chapter of the First Constitution on the Church of Christ brought approval by a great majority. At the 84th session on July 16, the changes suggested in the 83rd session by the 62 who had voted "placet juxta modum" were considered and evaluated. With the exception of two or three, all those who had voted conditionally now gave their assent. The vote on the whole constitution, which followed, resulted in a still greater majority in favor.

The Holy Father had an announcement made that all those who had asked permission to return home for reasons of business or other matters could do so on condition that they return to Rome by November 11. A good number were excused permanently. The next session was set for July 18. The short interval between the two sessions was due to the war between Prussia and France. The report had reached Rome on the evening of the previous day. All the fathers signed a solemn protest that firmly refuted the lies and calumnies published against the Council by some newspapers.

On Monday, July 18, at 9:00 am, the fourth public session began with a Low Mass celebrated by a cardinal. The Holy Father came in toward the end and said the usual prayers. Bishop Valenziali of Fabriano read the decrees from the podium, asking in a loud voice, "Do you approve?" Then the undersecretary, Monsignor Jacobini, took the podium and read the names of all the fathers, from the cardinals on down to the generals of orders. Five hundred thirty-five of them were still present. Five hundred thirty-three answered "yes," and two "no." One was a Neopolitan, the other an American.[6]

The vote lasted until 12:15 pm. The Holy Father solemnly confirmed the decrees and the canons. There was great jubilation in the Council hall and in the galleries inside the basilica. The door of the hall had been opened, and many in the crowd could see inside the hall. Some could understand what had just been read. During this time, a heavy thunderstorm was over the city.

There would have been several other opposing votes by those who did not think the declaration of infallibility opportune, but they had left Rome after giving the Pope a written statement that they would support the decision of the majority. This is the best refutation one can give to the newspaper reports that the Council members were not free to speak their minds uninhibitedly. Furthermore, it is striking proof of their truly Catholic spirit. Each voiced his view and defended it to the best of his ability. At the same time, they were willing to accede to the decision of the Council. By declaring their assent, unanimity prevailed.

After four hundred years in which infallibility was on the mind of many, a decision has been reached and all doubt has been removed. The same thing happened with the question of the Immaculate Conception.[7]

Ger   cASVA   transAHo *Wand* (August 20, 1870)

TO GREGORY SCHERR   98

Metten, August 23, 1870

Right Reverend Lord Archbishop, Your Grace: May God reward you for publishing the Council decrees by your own authority, thus exposing yourself to the opposition of the whole world. It is a good sign today, even more than before, if our ecclesiastical authorities, while executing their apostolic duties, come into conflict with the secular law and so-called public opinion. In fact, it is not the opinion of the people, who are after all still very Catholic and who do not want to be guided by journalists, but by their own bishops.

---

[6] The American bishop who voted against infallibility was Edward Fitzgerald (1833-1907) of Little Rock, Arkansas. Several other Americans bishops, who felt they could not vote in favor of the decree, had already left Rome.

[7] Pope Pius IX had proclaimed the dogma of the Immaculate Conception in 1854.

I am fully confident that the artificially created agitation will soon subside, provided that ecclesiastical authority asserts itself and shows the plain truth to people so that they can quietly look at it themselves. In most cases it was the misunderstanding presented to the people by exaggerations and distortions that caused the agitation. Few prudent people will be carried away by these deceptions, especially when political events, contrary to every expectation, take a turn in favor of the Church, as will no doubt happen.

Relying on the prophecies of the revered Rosa d'Ascente of Taggia,[8] I have predicted the victory of the Prussians and the fall of Napoleon. Because of the same prophecy, I also expect the fall of Victor Emmanuel and the safeguarding of the Holy Father by the Prussians. I am very sorry that the poor French have to suffer so much for the sake of their emperor, but at the same time, I rejoice over the Prussian victory because that will become the bridge for the reunification of the Lutherans with the Church. This is not just plan making, or wishful thinking. It is something that will happen because God wills it–for the glory of the Church.

At this time I also thank you sincerely for the traveling money, which you kindly granted and which Mr. Lebling[9] sent to me yesterday. After the usual heat in Rome, I find it almost too cold here and must actually close the windows morning and evenings. Perhaps my stubborn head cold causes that.

My monks who remained in Rome left only on August 9 for vacation at Montecassino. Dr. Haber (stenographer at the Council) came safely from Braunburg to Rome on August 19. Next week I must think seriously about returning to America because now, in all probability, the way to Cologne, and from there to Ostende, London, and Liverpool, will be open. Last night we had as guests Professors Greil and Leitl, and this morning many people who made a pilgrimage to Hirnau.

I hope Your Excellency is well and that you find the cold Bavarian August weather more agreeable than I do. Recommending myself humbly to Your Grace's continued kindness and good will, I am Your Excellency's submissive and grateful servant, Boniface Wimmer, Abbot

Ger   oALMV   cASVA   trans IG

---

[8] One of several Italian holy women who were making apocalyptic prophesies during this period.
[9] Louis Ignatius Lebling, treasurer of the Ludwig Missionsverein.

TO ADALBERT MÜLLER   **99**

Metten, October 18, 1870

My Dear Confrere, Rev. Fth. Adalbert!
Hoping that you received my letter
wherein I wanted you to leave Rome
with the two Clerics[10] and to go to Innsbruck, I will inform you now that I am
quite anxious to see you before I leave for
America, but not in Innsbruck. I found
that there was no room for you in the
Jesuit Convict[11] there, and that the Jesuits don't read philosophy. Abbot Utto[12]
thought it better to send all of you to
Ratisbone.[13] I spoke, therefore, to the
Bishop, and he gladly consented to make
room for you in his Diocesan Seminary.
There I want also F. Gerard[14] to join
you. You get a room of your own where
you can stay and sleep. The two Clerics,
though, must sleep with the Seminarians in the common Dormitory, but can
study with you and stay with you during

Rev. Adalbert Müller, O.S.B.

day time. There are 92 Seminarians there and no more room to spare. There is an
excellent Professor at the royal Lyceum for Geology, Minerology & Botany, and
another one for Physic and Astronomy, and there is also an Observatory there.[15]
Besides that, Ratisbone has a much milder climate than Munich and Innsbruck,
and I have many friends and acquaintances in Ratisbone among the Clergy and
laity. Now then, come as soon as you can get ready.

---

[10] James Zilliox, O.S.B. (1849-1890), and Xavier Baltes, O.S.B. (1844-1876).
[11] Community (from Latin *convictus*, community life). The Benedictines had closed their house of
studies at St. Elizabeth in Rome because Italian forces of King Victor Emmanuel had captured the
city from papal forces, and Pope Pius IX had ordered the schools closed.
[12] Utto Lang, O.S.B. (1807-1884), abbot of Metten.
[13] Regensburg.
[14] Gerard Pilz, O.S.B. (1834-1891), who went to Bavaria to study art.
[15] Wimmer had tapped Adalbert Müller to teach philosophy and the natural sciences at St. Vincent.

I repeat again: take your books and vestments with you; pack my copes, etc., in a good trunk or in a box and send it with F. Oswald's[16] and Mr. Hund's trunks. Hund's trunk [is] to be sent to Innsbruck in Tyrol; F. Oswald's and mine to Munich for Ab. Haneberg.[17] But it will be safest to send these things by an Agent, perhaps Spitthover, or some one else. In the "Anima" they know perhaps one for Innsbruck, too. However, if you can take all the trunks with you, so much better, i.e. mine and Fth. Oswald's one; Hund's one may go by itself, or you [will] have trouble with the expenses for the freight. Of course, if he should give you another direction, I will not interfere with him. You know that I paid in full for the *Album Monumentale del Concilio Vaticano*, and did not get one fotograf of it. Since that time 3 months elapsed, and, therefore, then I need not fear any delay, which even by fast freight is often caused. I hope they finished it meanwhile. Therefore, I wish you to take it with you. Should the whole Album not be finished yet, you might take so much of it as has been finished, but don't give up the receipt for the payment in full. The photographic laboratory is at 207 Via di Pan Perna in the Palazzo di Card. Pietro, but the address is Macel de Cervi, No. 29, 1. At all events tell Fth. Abbot of S. Paul[18] (I forgot to do it) that he might be kind enough to tend to the matter if you get nothing of it.

Regarding the furniture, it will be best to have it all together in one place, in the Saloon. Since so many families had to move out of the Quirinale, some one might be glad to move into S. Elizabeth. I offered to the Abb. of S. Paul to make use of our S. Elizabeth for himself. If he won't, you must not omit telling the Cardinal and F. Bauer or Spitthover to take charge of the house. I don't care if they can rent it to some one else. I have paid Casaretti for the *thecae* to put in relics, 67 frcs. in full, but he has not brought home to me a single one. I have also paid him well for the *Agnus Dei*. He has no other charge for me at present. If he can give you the 245 relics, you might give him something reasonable yet for his trouble; otherwise, he has been overpaid by 16 lire you gave him and has the 245 cases (*thecae*), for which I paid, yet in his hands. Give him your address, "Ratisbona in Baviera, Seminario Diocesano," so that he can send the relics and Authentics after you. Write again as soon as you can and come on fast. The lectures begin at Ratisbone on the 23rd. The next year, if Rome is quiet, we shall return to it again. If you come to Innsbruck you may go to the [indecipherable] hotel and ask for Mr. Hund. I am very sorry that we must leave him alone.

---

[16] Oswald Moosmüller, O.S.B. (1832-1901)
[17] Daniel Boniface Haneberg, O.S.B. (1816-1876), abbot of St. Boniface Abbey, Munich.
[18] Francis Leopold Zelli-Jacobuzi, O.S.B. (1806-1875), abbot of the Abbey of St. Paul's Outside the Walls, Rome.

Now then, let us hope that all and everything will turn out well, so as to recompensate us for the trouble wherein we are now. God bless you and fetch you safely in the land of my birth. Kind respects to our friends! Yours, B. Wimmer

Eng   oASPR   cASVA

TO MARTIN MARTY   **100**

St. Vincent, February 17, 1871

Right Reverend Abbot and Very Reverend Confrere: I did not receive your letter of December 9. Nevertheless, I learned from the newspapers that your monastery was made an abbey.[19] I left Munich only on December 1, then sailed out of Liverpool on December 6, landing in Boston on December 18, and arriving at St. Vincent on December 23.

Accept my sincere congratulations both for the elevation of your monastery to the status of abbey and for your own election as abbot. I sincerely hope that you will have a happy reign as abbot for many years to come. Naturally I shall attend your abbatial blessing, health permitting. In the spring I will be busy with visitations in Minnesota, Kansas, etc., so please let me know in good time the date of the blessing so that I can make the necessary arrangements.

It should not be, as has often been the case in the past (sad to say), that the individual monasteries of our Order should live in isolation from one another. Good people, nowadays more than in the past, must band together so that with their united strength they may be able to offer a more powerful resistance to the forces of evil.

With all affection and esteem, devotedly yours, Abbot Boniface

Ger   oASMA   cASVA   trans BB

---

[19] St. Meinrad Priory in Indiana, a foundation from the Swiss Abbey of Einsiedeln, was made an abbey on September 30, 1870. Martin Marty was elected first abbot.

TO GREGORY SCHERR **101**

St. Vincent, March 16, 1871

Most Reverend Archbishop and Patron: Being burdened with so much work upon my return, I forgot all about your approaching namesday until I saw it on the calendar. I humbly ask your pardon for not offering you my congratulations on time. I hope that you will receive them, not as empty compliments, but as my sincere feelings. When asking the Lord to bless you, I do not ask for material blessings on your behalf, because Your Excellency already has attained what praiseworthy ambition permits, but rather I ask that health and a long and fruitful life be granted you. I wish you this with all my heart.

In spiritual matters, it is my special wish that you succeed through energetic action and holy zeal to overcome the Hydra of Rationalism, whether it is secret rationalism or rationalism openly defended, which has revealed itself in the opposition to the Council and has been promoted through rationalistic legislation. Yielding to the rationalists through weakness produces neither victory nor reconciliation. The Trappist abbot of Oehlenberg[20] told me during the Council that all those whom the newspapers mentioned as leading the attack against infallibility were well-known members of the school of Hermes.[21] The abbot himself had earlier been a disciple of Hermes, but he told me that Hermes lost all hold on him when he remembered the lessons he had been taught by his mother, that is, to hold nothing higher than the pope and the Blessed Virgin. These are the true criteria for loyalty to the Catholic faith, and a stumbling block to those who do not believe, as God Himself reveals in *Genesis* about Mary and in the Gospels about the victory of Peter and his successors over the "gates of Hell."

Your Excellency has done a very important and meritorious thing by calling a general meeting at Fulda. This will be a sparkling jewel in your eternal crown. You face the alternatives of the victory of Faith or the victory of sovereign Reason, of Church authority or of individual choice, and consequently the existence or the dissolution of the Church. For this glorious achievement, I offer you today my special congratulations. I shall always support your efforts in the controversy. I pray that you will achieve success and that the adversary will not be able to cause any important damage. You can expect to be the target of aggression, but that will

---

[20] Andrew Zugtriegel, O.C.S.O. (+1893), was a former Benedictine of the Abbey of Ottobeuren, Augsburg, Bavaria, who between 1848 and 1850 assisted Wimmer at St. Vincent.
[21] George Hermes, a German theologian whose writings had been condemned by the Catholic Church before the Vatican Council.

make your name more honored, your fame more eminent, your merit more glorious, your destiny more certain.

Here in America only a few priests in New York showed themselves rebellious, but upon being suspended by the archbishop, they all submitted. All my people accepted infallibility unanimously and with enthusiasm, and they feel proud that Your Excellency, a former Benedictine abbot, has taken such energetic steps to defend it. The archbishop of St. Louis[22] has declared his submission explicitly and in public, and the bishop of Pittsburgh[23] is holding public lectures in defense of infallibility. Americans in general, even the Protestants, do not see any difficulty in believing that the head of the Church is infallible because they are used to accepting the decisions of the Supreme Court as quasi-infallible. In any case, an appeal against the decision of that court is in all practicality out of the question. I have pity on poor Döllinger[24] who at the end of his life, through his obstinacy, is losing all his glory, the affection of all his disciples, and all the merits of the past. Indeed, he has lost them already.

Since my return on December 23, I have had much trouble with the independent priory in Atchison, Kansas. These gentlemen have run themselves into the ground with debts by building a church. They were so deep in the hole that they could not find their way out. I was good enough to give them help. I first ordered an exact financial accounting to compare regular expenses with income. I found nothing but a great burden of debt because they had borrowed money at ten or twelve percent interest. (That is the rate in the West.) I found the financial condition of St. Vincent very sound, even though there was not much cash because in October Father Prior had paid $6,500 for the farm I had purchased. In Atchison, $7,000 was needed immediately to pay the arrears of interest and some other debts. What to do? I sent $700 from my own pocket at once, together with $1,100 that I had received in trust and on which I had promised to pay five percent. I also persuaded Father Boniface Krug,[25] who is here collecting for Montecassino, to lend the proceeds of his collection to Atchison, and I committed myself to repaying the capital and paying the interest rate of eight percent. Furthermore, Father Boniface has promised to lend Atchison $2,000 more that he expects to

---

[22] Peter Richard Kenrick, archbishop of St. Louis, had been one of the most prominent American opponents of the proclamation of the dogma of infallibility.

[23] Bishop Michael Domenec of Pittsburgh had also been an opponent of the proclamation of the dogma of papal infallibility.

[24] Johannes Ignaz Döllinger (1799-1890), a German liberal theologian who led the opposition to infallibility and who was later excommunicated by Archbishop Gregory Scherr. Döllinger had been Wimmer's professor of church history at the University of Munich.

[25] Boniface Krug, O.S.B. (1838-1909).

Rev. Boniface Krug, O.S.B.,
a monk of Saint Vincent
who became archabbot
of Montecassino, Italy

collect. During this time, I also received 2,000 florins from the Mission Society, which I also threw in the pot for Atchison. With that, the greatest need has been met. In addition, I sent three priests to Kansas to do pastoral work in order to provide some financial support for the priory, and I sent a fourth priest out to give missions, with instructions that he was to send his earnings to Atchison. This missionary has already given four missions and has sent $300 to Kansas.

That, however, is not enough to cut down the expenses resulting from such high interest rates. These rates must be lowered to something more reasonable. I am, therefore, busy looking for money in the East, where there is more money and where the interest rates are therefore lower than in the West. I am eager and hopeful about borrowing $10,000 at six or seven percent interest in order to wipe out the $10,000 debt in Atchison, which currently has an interest rate of twelve percent. I am prepared to mortgage our three houses in Newark for that purpose. (I bought these houses for $800, and only a fraction of the debt remains to be paid. They are now worth double what I paid for them.) Without any doubt, I will have to pay the interest on the $10,000 and on the other $7,000 if the priory is to remain in existence and make some progress.

That was my Christmas present this year, but I accepted it willingly for the reason that blessings from above have visibly rested on St. Vincent and are still hovering over us. The other reason I accepted this burden is to teach my fathers and the various communities emanating from St. Vincent to consider themselves as one unit, to help each other in need, and to lay all emphasis on that duty. For that reason, I keep six novices from Minnesota and one from Atchison in the common novitiate *gratis*. For the same reason, I have appointed a novice master and a socius to educate and instruct the novices and clerics in a common monastic observance. There are 13 novices and 12 clerics here.

The novices are entrusted with no other monastic duty than to attend choir and study asceticism deeply. The clerics attend classes in philosophy and theology, but live in the novitiate, though some of them are assigned as prefects and others teach a few lower level classes to the scholastics. I have 57 scholastics, most of them

American-born, in various classes. Five or six of them enter the novitiate each year. Since my return, two clerics have been ordained priests.

German Americans are very glad that Germany has become a unified nation. My congratulations to Your Excellency for not failing to do your share in bringing about this reality. Even as the progressive party advanced, the Catholics did not recede. On the contrary, they won a very strong position and will have much influence if they make use of their prerogative. It seems to me that the Patriots have acted foolishly by dividing themselves into two parties. They engaged in heated debates among themselves at the most inappropriate time, debates that they had avoided for a long time. Now "Health to Prussia." If King, rather Emperor, William knew how high his standing is in my esteem, he would honor me with a decoration. That's for sure. Today he is the only Christian ruler who gives God glory, and for that reason, he can call himself, with every right, king "by the grace of God." He hurled down the greatest enemy of the Church of God, the most nefarious hypocrite, surpassed only by Satan himself, and dashed him to pieces,[26] and he will also castigate that weakling Victor Emmanuel, who carries the name of "Satyr," and will make him an instrument of punishment against Catholic Austria, which with bad conscience and without fear of or confidence in God, has cherished and protected the mob of vipers' bred out of an insane policy that will not escape punishment. Not until Henry Chambord again takes possession of the French throne will peace and tranquility reign once more. Then we shall meet each other again for the closing of the Vatican Council.

That we Benedictines in the United States now have our third abbey is surely known to Your Excellency. The priory of St. Meinrad in the Diocese of Vincennes, Indiana, has been raised to the dignity of an abbey by an apostolic brief dated September 30, 1870, and at the same time the prior, Father Martin Marty, is named its first abbot for life. He will receive his solemn blessing after Easter, and I am invited to assist and have accepted the honor. This abbey was founded not from St. Vincent but from Maria Einsiedeln and belongs to the Swiss Congregation, but that makes no difference in our common work as Benedictines.

Our Atchison priory is still deep in debt, but we hope to extricate it in a few years and after a length of time, we have every hope that it will become an abbey too. The community there consists of 13 priests already. Young Quadt is doing well. He is beginning to study earnestly. Now, beginning as a brief note of congratulations, this has become a long letter of news without my noticing it. I beg

---

[26] Wimmer refers here to Napoleon III of France.

pardon and ask to be permitted to express my sincerest affection, gratitude, and respect. As always, Your Excellency's most devoted and obedient servant, Abbot Boniface

Ger   oAMA   cASVA   trans RG

TO ANGELO PESCETELLI   **102**

St. Vincent, August 7, 1871

Very Reverend Abbot, Procurator General: It is time for me to write you again about what is happening here. On May 21, I was at the monastery of St. Meinrad for the blessing of the new abbot, Martin Marty, by the bishop of Vincennes.[27] The Trappist abbot[28] of the monastery of Gethsemani attended the ceremony with me. I had as my companion Father Lambert Kettner,[29] prior of our community in Covington, Kentucky. The monastery buildings at St. Meinrad are made of wood, as are the church and the college. Many of the priests in the house are involved in pastoral work outside the house. The community is small, but everything is done according to the *Holy Rule*. The abbot is a learned and pious man, and all hold him in great honor and love. No railroad passes near the place, so the college has few students.

After the abbatial blessing at St. Meinrad, I went on visitation to Kansas where I celebrated a Pontifical Mass. I found everything in good order, but the construction of the church has put them deeply in debt. It is not finished, but only under roof. Father Boniface Krug[30] collected $5,000 for Montecassino and lent it to me. I will pay him $400 per year for the loan. It is a hard condition, but not unfair and certainly much better than the ten percent interest rate regularly charged in Kansas. I used this $5,000 for the priory in Atchison and added another $2,000 from my own funds so that we might extract ourselves from the current financial difficulties there. Moreover, I sent two fathers out to give missions, and the money they will collect will go to the Kansas priory. Father Wendelin,[31] whom I also sent

---

[27] Martin Marty, O.S.B. (1834-1896), was the first abbot of the Swiss-American abbey of St. Meinrad in the Diocese of Vincennes, Indiana. He was blessed by Bishop Maurice de St. Palais (1811-1877).

[28] Benedict Berger, O.C.S.O. (1820-1889), of Gethsemani Abbey, Kentucky.

[29] Lambert Kettner, O.S.B. (1831-1896).

[30] Boniface Krug, O.S.B. (1838-1909), formerly a monk of St. Vincent who had joined the Abbey of Montecassino in Italy.

[31] Wendelin Mayer, O.S.B. (1832-1881).

out to give missions, will donate the money he raises to the priory in Kansas. He has already contributed $900. For my part, I will collect no interest on the money lent to Kansas but will continue to pay the interest on the $5,000 borrowed from Father Boniface until the brothers in Kansas have some breathing space. For the moment, I made Father Timothy[32] rector of the college and temporary prior. When I returned home, I named Father Giles Christoph,[33] my claustral prior at St. Vincent, as the new prior in Atchison. I did this to satisfy the confreres in Kansas, who, with one exception, asked me to do it.

From Kansas, I went to Nebraska to see how Father Emmanuel Hartig,[34] who lives alone in Nebraska City, was doing. He formerly had two confreres living with him, but because Bishop O'Gorman,[35] an Irish Trappist, had been less than kind, I recalled them. After taking care of some temporal affairs in Nebraska, I returned to Chicago where I spent some time with Bishop Fink[36] before going to the Abbey of St. Louis on the Lake in Minnesota for a visitation. Everything is flourishing in Minnesota, both spiritually and materially. The monks have constructed a comfortable building of stone and brick next to the monastery. The building accommodates 80 boys, some of whom pursue classical studies, others philosophy and theology. It would be an ideal place if only it did not have mosquitoes and bears infesting the forest. After the visitation, I went with Abbot Rupert Seidenbusch[37] to the city of St. Paul where the bishop[38] resides. The bishop blessed the new church in St. Paul, built by Father Clement Staub,[39] and I preached the sermon to the people. Afterward, all of us (Abbot Rupert, Father Clement, and I) returned to Chicago for the consecration of our Louis Fink as coadjutor bishop of Kansas on June 11. The consecrating bishop was the bishop of Chicago,[40] and the co-consecrators were the bishops of Kansas and of Green Bay.[41] The bishop of Pittsburgh[42] preached in English and I in German. My text was John 3:30, "He must increase and I must decrease."

---

[32] Timothy Luber, O.S.B. (1842-1901).

[33] Giles Christoph, O.S.B. (1830-1887).

[34] Emmanuel Hartig, O.S.B. (1830-1910).

[35] James O'Gorman, O.C.S.O. (1804-1874), vicar apostolic of Nebraska.

[36] Louis Fink, O.S.B. (1834-1904), who had recently been named coadjutor bishop of Kansas.

[37] Rupert Seidenbusch, O.S.B. (1830-1895).

[38] Thomas L. Grace, O.P. (1814-1897), bishop of St. Paul, Minnesota.

[39] Clement Staub, O.S.B. (1819-1886).

[40] James Duggan (1825-1899).

[41] John B. Miège, S.J. (1815-1884), of Leavenworth and Joseph Melcher (1806-1873) of Green Bay, Wisconsin.

[42] Michael Domenec, C.M. (1816-1878).

At length I returned to my abbey on June 21 after an extended journey of 3,700 miles! I was overjoyed by the work being done by the Benedictines in so many places. St. Meinrad in Indiana, St. Benedict in Kansas, and St. Louis in Minnesota are thriving. In the future, with God's help, they will do great things for the Order and the Catholic Church. In a few years the abbey in Minnesota will become what St. Vincent Abbey is now, the mother of other monasteries. Already it is a strong foundation with many monks in the monastery and many students in the college. It is also well situated on the Northern Pacific Railroad. Atchison is on the Southern Pacific Railroad in a state where no other Catholic college exists. (The same is true of Minnesota.) In a few years, Atchison will begin to grow too, unless some calamity strikes. It is a foundation at least as strong as St. Meinrad Abbey, and all its buildings are made of brick.

The location of St. Meinrad Abbey is more suitable for the monastic life than the active life. It has 2,000 acres of land but many debts. By selling some of the land, however, they can pay off the debts. I do not know if they can eliminate the debt altogether, but before they can construct new buildings, they will have to pay off some of the debt. They have good parishes and administer the southern part of the diocese. Their college is the only one in the diocese.

Our academic year at St. Vincent ended on June 28. As you can see from our catalogue, we had 227 students from nearly all the states of the Union. Father Oswald[43] became prior in the abbey. Happily, Father Adalbert[44] will return from Germany in a few days. Father Lawrence Schaeffer,[45] who had been ordained only seven months, died in Pittsburgh from the smallpox. Ten days after being infected, he was dead. He was a young man of excellent character. What a pity! I was at home giving a retreat to the priests, clerics, and novices when he was taken to the hospital of the Sisters of Mercy where he died. Another father, Gregory Bauer,[46] is gravely ill with consumption. Seven novices pronounced simple vows and four scholastics have entered the novitiate. I now have 20 clerics, including James and Xavier.[47]

Our grain crops were abundant, and our harvest was larger than ever before. We finished bringing it in today. Only the corn (from which your *polenta* is made)

---

[43] Oswald Moosmüller, O.S.B. (1832-1901).

[44] Adalbert Müller, O.S.B. (1842-1906).

[45] Lawrence Schaeffer, O.S.B. (1847-1871).

[46] Gregory Bauer, O.S.B. (1837-1873).

[47] James Zilliox, O.S.B. (1849-1890), and Xavier Baltes, O.S.B. (1844-1876), who were studying in Europe.

remains in the fields. This too is abundant because we had a lot of rain. There were no potatoes, however.

In Munich Louis Ignatius Lebling, treasurer of the Ludwig Missionsverein, deposited 1,000 francs (or lire) in my account. You can draw on it if you have to. I hope this will be sufficient, but if you need more, I have written to him to give you as much as you ask for. I do not want you to have any difficulties or to be inconvenienced on my account!

I had to recall my clerics from Regensburg and send them to study with the Jesuits in Innsbruck because in Regensburg they do not teach scholastic theology.

Here everything goes well. The blessing of heaven is apparent to all. In October, I must pay $6,500 for some property I bought before I made the journey to the Vatican Council. Fortunately, I am able to pay despite the many burdens I have—giving alms to the poor, helping immigrants, educating boys *gratis*, not to mention the debt of our priory in Kansas. Although the money I gave to Kansas was a loan, I know that it will not be repaid. But that's all right. I am responsible not just for my abbey but also for the whole congregation and indeed for our whole Order, and when need and utility require something, I depend more on the payment that God will give than on mathematical calculations.

Bishop Fink was sick at the time of his consecration, but he is better now. Probably Father Edward[48] will become my secretary. He has just finished translating into English Alzog's *Church History*.

I am sending you (1) a petition concerning a candidate who is a convert from Judaism, and (2) a petition made in the name of a secular priest. Please submit them to the appropriate authorities. The young Jewish man appears to have an excellent character and spirit. He has lived with us for a year and in that time has patiently and willingly worked with our lay brothers, even though he was trained as a businessman. Perhaps I will accept him as a cleric, if that can be done. The anonymous penitent priest is a pious man. His case is secret and was committed to me under seal for the Sacred Congregation of Penances.

I am also sending you our catalogue since you know English. Perhaps you will enjoy reading what it contains. We are all anxious about the news from Rome. We fear that things have become dangerous, especially for the clergy. May God grant that all will come out well in the end. Father Oswald, who is now prior, has told me that he has written you. He is well. In sincere love and with a thankful heart, I am your most grateful, Boniface Wimmer, Abbot

Lat   oASPR   cASVA   transJO

---

[48] Edward Hipelius, O.S.B. (1836-1900).

TO UTTO LANG   **103**

St. Vincent, November 2, 1871

Right Reverend Abbot, Dear Confrere: Many thanks for the 1020 Mass intentions, which I have received. October 24 was a family feast to be remembered.[49] No one but our bishop and two secular priests from the neighborhood were present.[50] We celebrated for the greater glory of God and in thanksgiving for His infinite goodness. I pontificated, while the bishop attended and gave the sermon. We could not really enjoy our happiness fully because of the recent disaster in Chicago.[51] Our St. Joseph Priory was completely destroyed. The whole parish, without exception, was burned down. Our beautiful church (whose altar alone was worth $8,000), our new priory (for which we paid $17,000), the convent of the Benedictine sisters, and the schoolhouse all lie in ruins.

The fathers saved the monstrance, the ciboria and chalices, the best Mass vestments, and the parish registers. Otherwise, everything was lost except the clothing on their backs. Even $75 in bank notes went up in flames. The sisters could save only their lives because the fire came on the wings of a storm at 4:00 am. It burned everything that could not be saved, beasts and humans. Only the buildings with the strongest structures survived. The fire did not reach the Redemptorists and the School Sisters until 6:00 pm. They managed to save many things by burying them in the garden, but their church, monastery, and convent went up in flames. Only a small part of their large parish, which was not in the path of the wind and the devastating fire, was not destroyed.

We still have a debt of $50,000 on our property in Chicago, but we cannot get a cent of insurance money for the simple reason that all insurance companies have gone bankrupt. Altogether, the damage is estimated at $400 million. Our sisters were taken in by four Benedictine convents [elsewhere]. Two fathers remained with the flock while two others went begging for help, and St. Vincent, the poor St. Vincent, is being bled until its condition is nearly dropsical. I sent $400 immediately and tomorrow I go myself with another $1,000 in order to get a church for our parish and a wooden house for ourselves. The year started with the misadventure in Kansas and is ending with the catastrophe in Chicago. I hope that

---

[49] On October 24, 1871, the monks of St. Vincent celebrated the twenty-fifth anniversary of the inauguration of Benedictine monastic life in the United States.

[50] Bishop Michael Domenec (1816-1878) of Pittsburgh; Father James Ambrose Stillinger (1801-1873) pastor in Blairsville, Pennsylvania; and Father Jerome Kearney (1831-1891), pastor in Latrobe, Pennsylvania.

[51] On October 9, 1871, a devastating fire had destroyed most of Chicago, including the Benedictine church, priory, convent, and school there.

this is all and that nothing else follows. The Lord gives and the Lord takes away. Blessed be the name of the Lord.

Please give the money for the stipends to the clerics,[52] and many thanks for the kindness you have shown them. We have 175 students in the college who pay their way. We also have 80 scholastics who pay little or nothing. There is plenty to eat for everyone, provided we are not visited by fire. Here and everywhere there is talk of nothing but fire. The holy angels will protect us I hope. In Bavaria, another fire is burning away the rottenness. Perhaps in the end it will unite faithful Protestants with Catholics. The most reverend archbishop[53] is doing well, very well, but he is also undergoing his penance for trying to shield Döllinger[54] before and during the Council. When Bismarck has attained his goal, he will become a Catholic, even against his will, because of the urgency of the circumstances. Father Prior and my other Romans kiss your ring in all reverence and send you their best regards. They are all well.

A girl in nearby Latrobe was suffering much from eye infections that made attending school impossible. There was danger she would go totally blind. I gave her mother a little bottle of St. Walburga oil, and the mother made a novena with the child. The girl is lively now and in good health, despite the unsuccessful efforts of the doctors. Why could the saint not also help my confrere? Why has Father Willibald not made use of the oil? In one of our convents a sister was cured from two fatal ailments by the saint, who appeared to her and revealed the spiritual condition of a novice who was about to run off because she did not want to make a good confession. The novice admitted this and cleared herself by making a good confession. Now she has peace of mind and exhibits the best behavior.

Wishing you the best of health, good cheer, and courage, I send you a thousand greetings and remain your most devoted, Boniface Wimmer, Abbot

Ger   oAMA   cASVA   transRG

---

[52] James Zilliox, O.S.B., and Xavier Baltes, O.S.B., who were studying at Innsbruck, Austria.
[53] Gregory Scherr, O.S.B., archbishop of Munich.
[54] Johannes Ignaz Döllinger (1799-1890).

TO ANGELO PESCETELLI   **104**

St. Marys, November 14, 1871

Very Reverend Procurator General and Abbot: I received your letter and asked Father Adalbert[55] to respond since I had little time because of our general chapter, our jubilee, and the grave problems in Kansas and Chicago. Many thanks for your tireless efforts on our behalf. I have not broken the formal financial agreement with Cardinal Hohenlohe.[56] I will pay him all I agreed to pay in the St. Elizabeth contract. Father Salua knows this because he cosigned the contract. I hope that, in the meantime, you have informed Mr. Lebling[57] about the 1,300 francs.

No doubt, you have learned from the newspapers that a third of the city of Chicago was destroyed by fire. Twenty thousand homes were burned and more than 20 churches, including the cathedral and six other Catholic churches. What a sad thing! Our basilica at St. Joseph's Priory and the convent and school of our sisters were among the buildings destroyed. None of our brothers or sisters died, but beyond some clothing, parish books, chalices, and ciboria, nothing was saved. Our parishioners also lost everything, and one lost his life. We have not lost hope and confidence in God, however, nor have we lost our spirit, even though our loss is particularly grave and seems irreparable. All 25 of our sisters have gone to our four convents in Erie, St. Marys, Johnstown, and Carrolltown where they have been warmly received. Father Leander Schnerr,[58] prior in Chicago, hurried to St. Vincent immediately after the loss of the church and priory with a plan to rebuild them. I returned with him to Chicago in order to see with my own eyes what had to be done. I left one father there to look after the parishioners and sent the other four out to large cities to collect alms for the parish. Within a few days, they collected $4,000. As soon as they collected this money, we began the work of building a temporary church, made from planks. We contracted an architect, and in three weeks, we expect to have the church finished, if all goes well. The buildings will include a school and priests' residence as well as a church 40 feet wide and 70 feet long. It will not be on the site of the old church but near it.

At the same time, nearly all the heads of households in our parish have begun to build little houses from planks. At the moment, the city looks more like an Indian camp than a city. The buildings we lost were valued at $150,000, of which $48,000 was paid, but because all the insurance companies have gone bankrupt on account of the fire, we will obtain nothing for our loss. Moreover, many pa-

---

[55] Adalbert Müller, O.S.B. (1842-1906).

[56] Gustav Adolph Hohenlohe (1823-1896).

[57] Louis Ignatius Lebling, treasurer of the Ludwig Missionsverein.

[58] Leander Schnerr, O.S.B. (1836-1920), became the third archabbot of St. Vincent in 1892.

Right Reverend Leander Schnerr, O.S.B., was the prior at Saint Joseph's Priory in Chicago when the city was destroyed by fire in 1871. He became the third abbot of Saint Vincent.

rishioners had lent money ($47,000) for the construction of the church, and that must now be repaid. I myself lost everything I had put into the parish over the past eight years. There is no hope that the parishioners will be able to pay the debt on the church in the next few years since they themselves have nothing and many of them who were wealthy are now paupers. The battle in Chicago must be fought against great odds. We hope that the fathers who are collecting money will be successful and that we will be able to pay what we owe.

In our common misery, we have this consolation: our Catholics have accepted and borne this visitation from God with a Christian spirit, and therefore they feel themselves more closely linked to us than before. There are many signs indicating that this terrible conflagration was the work of an international sect, and it is true that some reckless men fed the fire, but it is also true that nothing can be proved. Probably the authorities do not want to publish what they know for fear that the public will lose confidence and that universal terror will interrupt all business. Otherwise, the calamity affects me less than our difficulties at our priory in Atchison. In Kansas the priory is affected; in Chicago, the parish, or the parishioners. In both places, with the help of God, we can resolve the problems, but not in one year.

Prior Giles Christoph[59] of Kansas was absent from the general chapter. He excused himself saying (foolishly in my opinion) that he had not been invited formally, even though I had invited him verbally when I was in Kansas. At the chapter, we were especially concerned with matters related to parish work. We considered the manner and method of preaching, the common novitiate, help for the poor, the book of ceremonies, attendance at choir, and financial affairs.

On October 24, after the chapter ended, we celebrated the jubilee, the 25th anniversary of the founding of St. Vincent Abbey. On this day 25 years ago I gave the monastic habit to my 19 first companions and initiated life according to the

---

[59] Giles Christoph, O.S.B. (1830-1887).

Rule with them. Of course, this was not the date of the foundation of the monastery properly speaking. We did not own the property at that time. Nevertheless, it was the day we established the spiritual foundation of the monastery because we introduced monastic life that, for the past 25 years, we have continued without interruption. Besides our confreres, I invited no one except our bishop[60] and two neighboring secular priests.[61] I wanted this to be a thanksgiving feast and not an ostentatious display. I sang a Pontifical Mass, and the bishop assisted on the throne. The bishop preached an excellent festive sermon appropriate to the occasion. I did not forget you or all the things you have done for my abbey and congregation. May God reward you!

Enrollment in our college has increased this year, and with the increase, our strength has grown as well. In fact, we are as strong as any Catholic college in America and are stronger than many in terms of number of students, reputation of our professors, and discipline. Thank God!

The clerics James and Xavier[62] are studying with the Jesuits in Innsbruck this year because the Jesuits have an excellent college there. Perhaps you can send me the photograph album through an American student who is returning from the American College or the Propaganda. I do not have any other news. I am in good health, as are all my people. Boniface Krug,[63] however, is in Erie sick from the smallpox, which he contracted in Chicago. I send you a thousand greetings and wish you all prosperity. I remain your most devoted, Boniface Wimmer

Lat oASPR cASVA transJO

TO BONIFACIA STADER   105

St. Vincent, January 7, 1872

My Dear Child in Christ: Thank you very much for your kind wishes for the New Year. It pleases me that you have thought of me on this occasion, and even more that you have assured me that you often pray for me and that you will strive to make me happy by becoming a good nun of our Order. We all need prayer. It is

---

[60] Michael Domenec, C.M. (1816-1878), bishop of Pittsburgh.

[61] James Ambrose Stillinger (1801-1873) of Blairsville and Jerome Kearney (1831-1891) of Latrobe.

[62] James Zilliox, O.S.B. (1849-1890), and Xavier Baltes, O.S.B. (1844-1876).

[63] Boniface Krug, O.S.B. (1838-1909), formerly a monk of St. Vincent who had joined the Abbey of Montecassino in Italy.

therefore very good that we pray for one another. With prayer, we accomplish much because Jesus has promised that he will never refuse us if we pray for good things. I remember you daily at holy Mass and pray that you fight the good fight, overcome every temptation, control and root out every evil tendency, and consecrate your undivided heart to the heavenly Bridegroom. In all likelihood, you will have many struggles to undergo, struggles against flesh and blood, pride and self-will, attachments to your parents and brothers and sisters, etc. You will need special grace to achieve victory, which will come to you through prayer.

It is not difficult to be a good religious. A good religious is a small, and often even a great, saint. A good religious has a humble heart. A good religious is as joyful as a child, as chaste as an angel. A good religious is detached from the world, even from all the good things of the world such as its joys and pleasures. A good religious desires and loves only God. As a good religious, you will seek to please no one, to be of value to no one, but God, and whatever you do, or whatever you suffer, you will do and suffer willingly for God. This, however, is not so easy. One must bring great zeal and patience to the task; one needs much grace. It is certainly a good sign that you have a desire to become a good religious, that you have hope of becoming one. With God's grace, may you never abandon the effort.

Children first learn to crawl, then to stand and walk, and finally to run. They often fall down, but they keep trying until they succeed. It is the same in the spiritual life. It is thus that I want you to progress securely and courageously in the way of the spirit. Do not become fainthearted when you stumble or take the wrong path. As you progress, the way will become easier. Many go to heaven this way. If we are persistent in making progress on our way, we, too, will arrive there and rejoice for all eternity.

May God bless you, may the Holy Virgin protect you, may St. Benedict and St. Scholastica be with you, and may St. Boniface pray for you. With paternal wishes, Boniface Wimmer, Abbot

Ger   cASVA   transJO

TO UTTO LANG   **106**

St. Marys, Pennsylvania, February 7, 1872

Right Reverend Abbot, Most Dear Confrere: I am here to receive the monastic profession of Father Herman Wolfe,[64] the son of a Lutheran bishop of Holstein, a convert, and now a Benedictine, and I am making use of my leisure time during the visit to chat with you. During Advent, and even at Christmas, I did not feel well at all, but now I am better. During the holy season we killed some 60 hogs (most weighing 400 pounds, but one weighing 500 pounds) and ate heartily—sausage, sauerkraut, a couple of gorgeous turkeys (we have quite a lot of these dumb creatures here). We save abstinence for Advent (when we abstain from meat four days a week) and for Lent (six days a week). As you see, we are prudent, like the children of the world, and do not forget that "jackass," our body.

Our affairs in Kansas turned out better than expected. Enrollment in the college is as good as it was before, even better, and as a result, our income there has improved. We might consider it financially sound now, and we can even hope that our folks there can help themselves again. The situation in Chicago is also brighter. My three beggar priests have thus far collected $11,000. The temporary church is crowded on Sundays and feast days, so much so that on Christmas the collection amounted to over $60. Normally it is $10. Everywhere in Chicago, buildings are going up, and for that reason, there is plenty of money on hand. The priest and the Church are not forgotten. Despite the immense damage, the fire brought something good with it. We were able to move the church, which stood at the extreme end of the parish, to a better location. I told Father Prior[65] to buy a better place in the middle of the congregation. This he did after talking it over with me once more. That was Wednesday, a week ago. The property is 218 feet in length and 339 feet in width and is located between two convenient streets. The cost is only $45,000, of which we must pay $5,000 in cash and the balance in eight years, at an interest rate of eight percent. The temporary church, which we built under emergency conditions and which is 70 by 40 feet, we want to move on rollers to the new location. We will do with the temporary church until the people have recuperated and are able to build a regular church. We will sell the old property to pay the debts. It was 244 feet in width, but less than half the length of the new property. It is estimated to be worth $48,000 because it is situated on a

---

[64] Herman Wolfe, O.S.B. (1816-1884).

[65] Leander Schnerr, O.S.B. (1836-1920), prior of St. Joseph Priory, Chicago, when fire destroyed the city on October 9, 1871, directed the reconstruction. Later Schnerr became third archabbot of St. Vincent.

much-used street. I gave $5,000 as an advance for the new place and guaranteed another $2,000. We will have to redeem the old debts and pay some $1,000 on the new place in order to make up for the damage inflicted. Thirty thousand dollars still has to be paid on the old place.

That is the status of the church in Chicago, which I took over 12 years ago. I have to be satisfied with this. It causes me many worries and many inconveniences that are not easily digested, but I am used to all these difficulties. I have been in debt for 25 years, so I don't find it extraordinary. Debts are my trade, my business. They keep me alive. They are my steady exercise in dependence on God's providence. I do not incur debts for the sake of speculation. I have nothing to do with speculation. The debts I undertake are necessary for our Order and for the Church, and it always turns out for the best, provided that things are arranged properly.

By the way, did you receive a Council medal, or are they only for bishops? I did not get one. Did you know that you are a "Doctor Ecclesiae"? I did not know it either until I was told in a dream the day before yesterday. It was a foolish dream, I suppose, because I do not remember one word, nor the cause. However, I do know that members of the Council do not need the doctor's degree because they are *ipso facto* "*doctores ecclesiae.*" Therefore, my good Doctor, do you see that it would have done you good to incline yourself to a more liberal stance in order to be raised to the episcopate of Speyer.[66]

Is everything in order at St. Boniface? Even the "blind ones" have to see the reality about Döllinger by now. It is a pity that this poor man is going his own way and that there is only a faint hope left of his return to the true faith. The Lord goes his own way too, but "my ways are not your ways." Döllinger and his followers want to divide the Church, but God is making use of their attack to bring back the lost sheep to the Church. Döllinger and his followers want to subject the Church to the state, but God is making use of their efforts to liberate his bride, the Church, from the secular government. The Kingdom of God is passing through adversity

---

[66] This sentence seems to be a joke. Daniel Boniface Haneberg, O.S.B., the learned abbot of St. Boniface Abbey, Munich, and a friend and confrere of both Lang and Wimmer, had recently been named bishop of Speyer. Unlike Lang and Wimmer, Haneberg had a doctorate, and along with a number of the intellectual Benedictines at St. Boniface Abbey, he had early on been identified as a "liberal" who sympathized with the ideas of Johann Ignaz Döllinger. Upon the proclamation of the dogma of infallibility at the First Vatican Council and the subsequent excommunication of Döllinger by Archbishop Gregory Scherr, O.S.B., of Munich, Haneberg abjured his earlier views and was named bishop of Speyer. Wimmer seems to be telling Lang in a joking manner that he (Lang) could have been bishop of Speyer if only he had earlier expressed liberal opinions, like Haneberg.

as Bishop Wittmann repeatedly foretold.[67] What seems ruinous, God makes use of. What seems profitable, He despises. I had expected that a victorious Prussia, for its own interests, would protect and unite the Church, but the contrary is happening. Prussia is persecuting the Church, but God purifies and unites it through persecution. Döllinger, Lutz, and Bismarck shall live to see all entirely different from what they intend with their machinations. Without intending to, they will become the instruments of God's plan.

Until January, we had a very dry winter. Since then, especially here in the immense forest, we have had much snow and bitter cold. The smallpox causes great calamity in many places. In the worst cases, it is almost in pestilential form. Until now, we have been spared at St. Vincent. I think everything is going smoothly, more or less. Still, there is reason to pray: "Send us the Spirit, Lord, whom the Blessed Abbot Benedict served." I hope you are in the best of health and ask most sincerely for your kind *memento* before God. Please give my best regards to Father Prior and to all the reverend confreres. I remain in sincerest affection and respect, your most devoted confrere, Boniface

Ger   oAMA   cASVA   transRG

TO DOMINICA RIEDERER   **107**

St. Vincent, July 2, 1872

Dear Reverend Mother Prioress: The graduation and tumult afterwards kept me from answering your letter sooner. What the bishop told you with respect to the election is established in canon law and holds good in Italy. There, both the abbots and abbesses are elected for only three years. This is not the German custom, however, nor is it according to the spirit of our *Holy Rule*. Naturally, the pope can make exceptions, and he often does. As you know, I fought to make sure our abbots would be elected for life, as is the custom in Germany.

If the bishop has not yet been at your place, you may tell him that you will not oppose his order but that it is not in accord with the present custom of your motherhouse nor with the *Holy Rule*, and then beg him not to take action without careful consideration. Should he insist upon his idea, however, and you upon yours, then nothing will remain but that you tell your sisters about it, and if they

---

[67] George Michael Wittmann (1760-1833), bishop of Regensburg, was Wimmer's teacher in the seminary. Wittmann was renowned for his sanctity, and his comments about the future were often taken as prophecies by Wimmer and the bishop's other former students.

are for it (namely, holding to the *Holy Rule*), then they should send a petition to Rome.

My view would be this. Once a convent is self-supporting, that is when it numbers at least 14 sisters, it should have a superior (prioress) validly elected for three years, and even for a second term. Should she be elected three times in succession, she should hold office for life.

A meeting of prioresses might consider the question. Still, my fear is that the sisters in general (even if not in Erie) would prefer repeated elections so that they also can become superiors. The Benedictine fathers in Rome, you know, also wanted three-year abbots so that many could play at being abbot. On the other hand, it would also be well if changes could be made without having to formally accuse and depose a guilty or careless superior.

With all respect and in the unity of prayer, your devoted brother, Boniface, Abbot

Ger   oASBC   cASVA   transGS

TO ANGELO PESCETELLI   **108**

St. Vincent, September 14, 1872

Right Reverend Procurator General, Dearest Confrere: Let me respond immediately to your letter of August 17. Thank you for taking care of my affairs so well. I have approved everything and send you many thanks. We have paid the interest on the $5,000 due on April 1 and October 1–$200 each time. Father Boniface[68] asked us to make the October payment early, which we did. I am scrupulous in making the payments he asks for since he is the representative of the abbot [of Montecassino]. As I wrote you in my last letter, he is now in Cincinnati collecting for Montecassino. He is living with my confreres in Covington (across the river from Cincinnati). How he manages to get the money, I don't know, but until now he has managed to collect $8,000. He says the contract he made with me was destroyed in the Chicago fire, so the prior in Atchison[69] drafted another, which I have countersigned, noting on the document that this $5,000 does not belong to Father Boniface, but to the monastery of Montecassino and that the transaction is approved by the abbot of Montecassino, whose representative is Father Boniface.

---

[68] Boniface Krug, O.S.B. (1838-1909), of the Archabbey of Montecassino, Italy.
[69] Oswald Moosmüller, O.S.B. (1832-1901).

If I understand correctly, the intention is that the money collected here not go to Italy but rather to some secure place where the Italian government cannot confiscate it. Later, at the appropriate time, the money will be returned to Montecassino. The bishops who have given permission for the collections recommended this. Boniface has proven himself a very effective beggar. As long as he has the permission of the bishops, he will without doubt collect a considerable sum. I have concluded an agreement with him to repay the $5,000 in 15 years and to repay it sooner in case of necessity. I wrote and asked you to take any money that remains and say Masses for it. If it should be necessary, you can send 1,000 francs to Montecassino as anticipated payment of the interest, and I will see to it that the Masses are said. If 1,000 francs should be a burden on you, then send what you can (unless the Masses have already been said).

I received the *Album Monumentale* of the Vatican Council yesterday, but Father Kith has indicated that the three keys are still in the New York customhouse. I will have to find out how to get them so that I can open the Album and get the photograph of the Holy Father. What a shame! But at least I have the album.

I am glad that Haneberg[70] has been made a bishop, although I fear that because of his lack of energy he will accomplish very little. I read just recently that ecclesiastical affairs in Bavaria would be better if the bishops exercised more authority over the king and princes, but Haneberg is hardly the man to do it. He reluctantly withdrew his support from Döllinger.[71] Like Döllinger, he thought the decrees of the Vatican Council were not valid. Those people wrote so many lies about the Council in the newspapers that many were induced to accept these errors. Moreover, our German professors, educated in Germany by Germans, followed Hermes and the semi-rationalists and through ignorance opposed positive Catholic dogma. I would like to receive the Acts and Decrees of the Ecumenical Vatican Council. You can use the same agency to send the ancient coins from Montecassino securely from Rome to Munich.

It would be unjust if in the history of our monastery, your merits and services were not duly recorded, but God alone can fully repay you for them. Considering my own weak efforts, it is miraculous that the monastery has become what it is. Without the firm support and help of yourself and others, all would have been in vain! This is very clear to me when I think of what has transpired in the course of these 26 years, and it would be clear to everyone if I could write the true history of the monastery.

---

[70] Daniel Boniface Haneberg, O.S.B. (1816-1876), abbot of St. Boniface Abbey, Munich.
[71] Johann Ignaz Döllinger (1799-1890).

Father Hilary[72] is now director of our college and doing very well. When I was in Rome, I gave $20 to Father Boniface Krug to buy a book about old coins. He gave the money to a friend and asked him to get the book. I did not think the friend had bought it, but now realize that Father Adalbert[73] brought it with him when he returned from Rome. Without it, we will know nothing about the ancient coins you are sending. We have a very extensive mineral collection (donated by a priest friend in Bavaria), a shell collection (donated by the same priest), and a rare plant collection (gathered in our mountains). Father Adalbert has charge of all these collections.

A few days ago, two rich men from Pittsburgh visited me and invited me to sell them the right to extract coal from our monastery lands. They offered $100 for each acre of land (an acre is 40,000 square feet), or $46,000 for 460 acres. This is the price all the farmers in our region have received. I, however, do not intend to sell it for $100 an acre because it is worth at least $1,000 an acre since the vein of coal is 8½ to 9 feet thick, and each acre therefore has (40,000 x 9) = 360,000 cubic feet of coal. Moreover, I cannot sell the rights to the coal unconditionally since we ourselves need great quantities of it. Rumor has it that these rich men intend to bring workers from China (called "coolies") to mine the coal here. A fairly large town has suddenly grown up near our property.[74] Because of the presidential elections on November 5, the politicians are greatly agitated. Everything else goes along peacefully and tranquilly. Would that it were the same in Rome and Italy! My Romans send you heartfelt greetings and with me pray for your happiness. With many repeated thanks, Boniface Wimmer

Lat   oASPR   cASVA   transJO

TO MICHAEL REGER   **109**

St. Vincent, February 21, 1873

Right Reverend Provost, Dearest Friend: My heartfelt thanks for the 1,990 intentions and the 1,011.31 florins in stipends, which I received not long ago. Just before Christmas, and shortly thereafter, we had ordinations to the priesthood. For this, our most reverend ordinary[75] was with us twice, for almost a whole week.

---

[72] Hilary Pfrängle, O.S.B. (1843-1909).
[73] Adalbert Müller, O.S.B. (1842-1906).
[74] The "fairly large town" was Latrobe, which had become a stop on the Pennsylvania Railroad.
[75] Michael Domenec, C.M. (1816-1878), bishop of Pittsburgh

Eight priests were ordained for our community and several others who studied in our college for the dioceses of Pittsburgh, Harrisburg, and Scranton. Our brothers had their annual retreat at Christmas, and after that, we celebrated the first masses, all of which took much time, though it was the cause of great joy and consolation. After that, another wind blew in.

In the course of a single week, two carpenters hurt themselves so badly that they were unable to work for several weeks. A third fell from the windmill of the water pump, a height of thirty-four feet, and broke eight ribs. He died on January 21.[76] He was an excellent religious and a very capable mechanic from Rotthal. The quasi house doctor, Brother Ildephonse,[77] who with two doctors nursed him with the best care, contracted a cold by doing so. The cold developed into pneumonia, and Brother Ildephonse died on January 31. That again took up much of my time, and for that reason, I was delayed in writing until now. Earlier the horses came down with a disease, and for a month, we could not harness 26 of them. We need 150 meters of coal each day during the winter, but fortunately, we had ready a team of six to eight oxen. From among those waiting in the barn for the slaughterhouse, we trained some more. Thus, we were able to take care of the most necessary transportation.

Therefore, we have had joy and sorrow, consolation and sadness, each taking its turn. I, myself, am in pretty good health, except for the trouble with my eyes. You tell me that the bishop admires me and says that I am filled "with fresh energy unhindered by hard work or suffering." That, however, is not the case. I feel as if I am an old workhorse, knowing nothing but the harness day after day. I have the same endurance as a horse, but need to be awakened from time to time with a slap, or the blow of a whip. I do my best but cannot do more than when I was young. The mistreatment is the same. I get used to it and experience little excitement any more.

I did not at all expect what is happening in Prussia because I considered Bismarck a man of prudence. The present situation could be considered Prussia's suicide. I recently read the life of Katharina von Emmerich by Schmöger.[78] What a difference between those times and ours! How different the people from those

---

[76] Colman Reingruber, O.S.B. (1826-1873).

[77] Ildephonse Hoffmann, O.S.B. (1829-1873), the monastery infirmarian, had learned his medical skills as a stretcher-bearer in the Union Army during the Civil War.

[78] Karl Erhard Schmöger, *Das Leben unseres Herrn und Heilandes Jesu Christi. Nach den Gesichten der gottseligen Anna Katharina Emmerich* (Regensburg, 1864). Anna Katharina Emmerich (1774-1824) was a German and stigmatic whose mystical experiences included visions of Jesus' Passion and Crucifixion. Mel Gibson's movie, *The Passion of the Christ* (2004), was based on accounts of her visions. Anna Katharina Emmerich was beatified by Pope John Paul II in 2004.

of our day. It is the same with the clergy and even the bishops. Those of the past were a hundred times better. On the other hand, how deep-rooted, protected, nourished, and powerful was the Protestantism of that time, and how lax it is now, how weak and helpless. What could be in the mind of Bismarck and Falk? The Church has nothing more to fear from them. It will have to enter into a partnership with the Protestants, not intentionally but by force of circumstances. Van Gerlach is depicting the situation as that of two parties fighting each other when a third party is the aggressor. There is already a kind of unity. The real unification has to come soon, and according to the law of nature, the less heavy substance will be absorbed by the heavier one.

Because of its disciplinary regulations, the Church will shine in greater glory before men. She shall be "a city built upon a hill" because she cannot be defeated by her enemies. From every corner, she will be considered and praised as the only secure refuge—she of whom they predicted doom. Prussia is, therefore, on its way to becoming Catholic, but before that happens, one has to expect a great battle. It seems as if the small stone, which is supposed to knock down the Colossus, is being loosed from the mountain and rolling down in Spain. The longer it rolls, the greater will be its force, like an avalanche crushing everything in its way. Prussia, however, is not yet giving up the fight. What Prussia is looking for now is in reality nothing other than Josephinian Febronianism.[79] The only difference is that under the influence of the Catholic Church, the situation will be less dangerous and less grievous than under the Protestant Church. Febronianism in Austria is not yet dead, but the Concordat has taken away much of its life, and the liberal party would like to restore it. I would gladly welcome this, for in order for it to be destroyed at its root, conditions have to become much worse. Then a forceful reaction will come and eradicate the whole plant. In order for that to happen, Prussia will give its assistance in secret, or openly (as I expect), by force and by war. In Italy and France circumstances will arise that will cause it to operate in a different manner.

The American press is definitely opposed to Prussia's policies. Even the Protestant religious papers, with few exceptions (i.e., when their hatred against the Church is at its height), are not in favor of Prussia's legal moves against the Church. The *New York Herald* (whose editor, Bennett, died last year), the most widely read paper in the world, has sharply criticized Prussia. Americans cannot understand such in-

---

[79] Febronianism was an 18th century movement within the Roman Catholic Church in Germany that advocated restriction of the power of the papacy in favor of the episcopate and the reunion of Protestant churches with Catholicism. "Josephinian Febronianism" was the form this movement took in Austria under Emperor Joseph II (1741-1790).

terference in Church affairs by the state. They favor complete separation between Church and state, as we enjoy here, but that cannot be put into practice fully in Europe. It would mean that the state would entirely fall away from the Faith and signal the adoption of the American system. The Devil would then have a principal share because most people would have no faith at all, or they would adopt a faith that suited their taste. The best people would remain loyal to the Church, but they are few in number. The evil ones are in the majority, as are, for the most part, the rich who see no difference between right and wrong. They have power in the government and harm the Church whenever they can, directly or indirectly.

Until now, we have been glad that the state does not interfere in our affairs. It does not take notice when we build churches, schools, monasteries, convents. Sometimes the public school is next to the parochial school. Everyone is free to attend the public schools, without having to pay. Their teachers receive good salaries. For this reason, the public schools have the best teachers. Catholics have to pay the school tax for new public schools and their upkeep, without receiving the benefit unless they send their children there, something that will endanger their faith. Because the better Catholics refuse to do that, they build their own schools, hire their own teachers, and pay for it all with great sacrifice.

If the state were Catholic, necessarily and naturally, the situation would be much better and the loss of souls would not be so great. If the state were Protestant, it would put pressure on the Church. Because the state is without any religion at all, we enjoy religious freedom. In many cases, this is not to our benefit. Innate depravity, the press, bad example, secret societies all cause the catastrophic ruin of many young people, especially in the cities. We have a free Church (free in reality) in a free and liberal state. This is better than having an established church in a zealous or insidious state. The best thing, of course, would be a free Church in a truly Catholic state, which fosters the interests of the Church. Whether that will ever happen, only God knows. We shall never live so long.

Taking everything into consideration, I am convinced that the Catholic Church in Europe, especially in her teaching capacity, is better off today than it was a hundred years ago. In Bavaria, it seems the king is not inclined to follow the Prussian model in everything. Were it done in all honesty, for a good purpose, it might not be without some benefit.

Our severe winter continues. Our Bishop Domenec cannot digest infallibility. I think accusations have been made against him in Rome. Not long ago he printed some of his lectures about the dogma with the intention of sending them to Rome. He asked me to give my opinion, and I told him they sounded Catholic, but not entirely Catholic. He avoids *"sese solo"* ["himself alone"] every time we have a discussion. Otherwise, we understand each other very well.

My deepest respect to His Grace, the bishop. Good health to you. Greetings to my acquaintances. In all love and esteem, your very much obliged, Boniface

Ger   oASVA   transRG

TO ANGELO PESCETELLI   **110**

St. Vincent, March 28, 1873

Right Reverend and Dear Father Abbot: I received the rescript concerning the Masses and have transmitted it to the priest in question. It has consoled him very much. Father Boniface[80] has been with us. He continues to travel and collect money. He received over $300 from our parish here at St. Vincent. In Allegheny City (Pittsburgh) he collected $700. From St. Vincent, he went to Johnstown and Carrolltown, and from there he will travel to Newark, from which he will return to Italy. No one has ever collected so much money in our parish before. The people gave $200 for Chicago, as well as more than $300 for Montecassino. There are about 120 families in our parish, so each one gave about three dollars. Our scholastics contributed twenty dollars, even though they are all poor. Father Boniface was very successful collecting in Chicago, as well as in Covington and Cincinnati. He lent $5,000 of the money he collected to the priory in Atchison, and recently he lent another $10,000 to the priory in Chicago. He charged eight percent interest on both loans, which is a great help to us. While in Chicago, he also helped our sisters build their convent and gave them other assistance as well. His visit has been an example of Benedictine cooperation. No doubt, he will have collected $20,000 before he leaves America. This is more than 100,000 lire.

With regard to the ancient coins, Father Boniface says that the collection is incomplete and suggests that I leave them for now at Montecassino until he can complete it. I agreed to do this. Soon I will send you some money for your immediate expenses on our behalf. We now have a machine for extinguishing fires.

On the Feast of St. Benedict,[81] the question of whether or not to grant licenses to sell liquor publicly was put to a vote in our state. The vote in many places was against selling liquor. (By "liquor," the law understands not just liquor properly speaking, but wine and beer as well.) This law will come into effect if it is signed

---

[80] Boniface Krug, O.S.B. (1838-1909).
[81] March 21.

by the governor and will be in force for three years. Consequently, we are going to have to drink all the beer we made this winter ourselves! The law permits the sale of beer or liquor in barrels, but no one will buy it in barrels, and the law does not permit it to be sold in small amounts. This law ends an important source of income for us and will mean a significant loss in the coming year. Unlike wine and liquor, beer cannot be kept in storage because after a few months it goes bad. This law was put forward in good faith, with the intention of preventing drunkenness among the lower classes, but in fact it was supported by those who make liquor because they want to drive their competitors, who make wine and beer, out of business so that they can later sell more liquor. You can imagine how this law sits with many people–especially with the Germans. The vote was against it in all places where many Irish and German Catholics live.

Grant[82] is not a good president. He is corrupt and venal and feeds public corruption. He has destroyed all sense of justice and honesty in the nation. One finds no patriotism in these Republicans. They are without honor and without shame, Pharisees and hypocrites in the extreme, and when it comes to their private lives, they are whited sepulchers. Many of them are Methodists. It is hard to imagine how corrupt the public spirit of the whole nation has become during the 12 years of the Lincoln-Grant administration! They are attempting to establish their Protestant religion by law, but so far, they have been frustrated in this. As soon as they achieve their goal, they will begin attacking and persecuting Catholics.

Our winter was very harsh. We had five months of ice and snow. Immediately after the beginning of the year, various calamities and illnesses struck us. Two of the brothers died and several others were very sick. Likewise, one priest died and several became gravely ill, both here and in the priories. I am preparing for even more tribulations since I believe they were prophesied in a dream I had on October 30, 1872. I myself would enjoy the best of health if only I were not troubled occasionally by sore eyes and other small ailments.

Everything is going well in the college. Eight of our clerics were ordained priests, and in Minnesota, three clerics received holy orders. As for our temporal affairs, we have suffered a loss of some $3,000, which we hope to make up. The cold weather has caused setbacks in our building program and on our farm. An epidemic struck our horses, and for several weeks, we had to use oxen in our coalmine. Despite all this, however, things go well enough with us.

Tobias Mullen,[83] bishop of Erie, has been annoying our Benedictine sisters in Erie and St. Marys. The sisters in St. Marys have an oratory above the sacristy

---

[82] U.S. President Ulysses S. Grant (1822-1885).
[83] Tobias Mullen (1818-1900), bishop of Erie.

where they are accustomed to say the office, receive communion, and sometimes hear Mass. If there is no priest available to say Mass in the oratory, however, they were able to hear Mass on Sunday through a window that looked from the oratory into the parish church. The sisters in Erie had a greater part of the choir loft as their oratory, where Mass was always celebrated, where they received communion, and where they said their office. Similarly, when a priest was not available to celebrate Mass in the oratory, they were able to hear Mass through a window that opened on to the church. Their choir was well separated from the rest of the choir loft, and as at St. Marys, their window was protected by a grill. The good bishop has decided now to prohibit the use of oratories, which the sisters used for 14 years with full knowledge of the deceased bishop, Josue M. Young.[84] Now on Sundays and feast days the sisters in Erie (where there are only two priests available to say Mass) are obliged to leave their cloister and go through the public street and into the church in order to sit near the altar and attend Mass among the lay people, if they want to hear Mass at all. This is not only very bothersome but also appears most indecorous. If possible, please do what you can to remedy this situation. Before prohibiting the use of the choir as an oratory, the bishop himself wrote to Rome for instructions. Even though he did not receive a response, his passionate zeal for the Lord's house caused him to abolish this "abuse." I do not know whether I should write to the Propaganda or to the Sacred Congregation of Bishops and Religious. It seems to me that this "abuse" should be tolerated because there are few priests here, because their number is not going to increase soon, and because it is not appropriate for our sisters to attend public Mass where they can be gazed at by the faithful. I have seen such oratories in monasteries in Europe, and I would, therefore, ask that you try to get permission for our sisters in St. Marys to attend the parish Mass from their convent oratory above the sacristy and in Erie itself from their choir (which is separated from the public choir loft). Without this permission, the sisters will have to mix with laymen in order to attend Mass. Please do what you can. Be well! Boniface Wimmer

Lat   oASPR   cASVA   transJO

---

[84] Josue M. Young (1808-1866), first bishop of Erie.

TO SCHOLASTICA BURKHARDT   **111**

St. Vincent, March 30, 1873

Dear Reverend Mother: Man proposes; God disposes! We experience that a hundred times. I have been waiting several months for the bishop[85] to take away St. John's so that I can send Father Bernard[86] to St. Mary's. The bishop himself approached me about handing the place over to him for the Jesuits, but that has not happened, and now, all of a sudden, Father Bernard himself walks off and I do not know where he has gone. Then I sent Father Roman[87] in the hope that by saying Mass, he, although physically weak, could render a little service, but he became very ill. I had to call him home, and after he arrived, until three days ago, he suffered such excruciating pains that for days and nights he could not close an eye or even lie down. He received extreme unction, for we believed that he would die immediately. St. Walburga, by means of her holy oil, brought about a change for the better, so that now there is hope. Had these events not occurred, you would have received a third priest, but now I cannot give you one, unless Father Roman gets well again. Therefore, you must pray very hard for this.

In the meantime, however, I wrote the reverend procurator general[88] in Rome and asked him to take steps that would permit you to use the choir again. Still, I have to say that if I were the bishop, I would have reservations too—i.e., I would be hesitant to allow the sisters to leave their chapel to go to the church gallery, since that might lead to bad results. Because of this, the Church wisely prohibited it. If part of the gallery is used for a chapel, this part should be closed off most strictly from the public part of the gallery. I have also frequently criticized the practice of brothers and fathers meeting with the sisters unnecessarily. It is certainly innocent, but it is not proper. We cannot tell what the consequences might be. When I come up again, I will probably have to do the same thing the bishop did. The sisters and the brothers are putting themselves at risk and must be prudent and wise.

The librarian will send you the copies of the *Rule* you asked for. I, myself, will arrange payment for them later. Not long after Easter, I hope to find time to visit Erie. In the meantime, I recommend myself to your kind remembrance at prayer, and I send best wishes, together with fatherly and brotherly love, to all the good

---

[85] Tobias Mullen (1818-1900), bishop of Erie.
[86] Bernard Manser, O.S.B. (1835-1899).
[87] Roman Hell, O.S.B. (1825-1873).
[88] Abbot Angelo Pescetelli, O.S.B. (1809-1885).

sisters (they are all surely good!), especially to my parishioner Sister Antonia. Your devoted brother, Boniface, Abbot

Ger   oASMC   cASVA   transGS

TO UTTO LANG   112

St. Vincent, November 12, 1873

Most Reverend Abbot and Dear Confrere: Please don't stop your correspondence entirely, even if you can't write as often as before. We had a very good year. Last spring we were able to pay for the farm that we bought three years ago, and we could still give Atchison considerable help. Everything is in good condition now. We payed $800 for the library and $700 for the musical instruments. We erected a nice malt house and other buildings and did repair work. Eight clerics were ordained to the priesthood.

For the past four weeks, we have had to struggle through very difficult times. Almost all the banks closed their doors and stopped payments. I had deposited our money for current expenses in two banks and cannot withdraw a cent. What is worse, we cannot get payment for tuition because others are suffering the same hardships. Everywhere there is mistrust, uncertainty, and unemployment. Thousands upon thousands of working people are losing their jobs every day. God knows what they will do during the winter. Times will change. Pride and the desire to have a good time were too great, and now everybody is paying for it.

Threatened by fear of exile, the Bavarian Capuchins wrote me for advice and help in immigrating to America. Our bishop[89] offered to give them a German parish. Shortly afterwards two priests came and took over the parish where they can also establish a community.

Likewise, our sisters at St. Walburga's[90] wrote, and the bishop is also willing to accept them. Our sisters here are doing their best to prepare for them if they have to leave their homeland. I cannot believe that the Benedictines will be expelled because of their hostile attitude toward the government, but if that should happen, we will give them a most kind welcome at St. Vincent. Right now, there is not much available space here, but many can be housed in the various priories. We already have one hundred thousand bricks ready for a new building that we will

---

[89] Michael Domenec, C.M. (1816-1878), bishop of Pittsburgh.
[90] The Benedictine convent of St. Walburga at Eichstätt, Bavaria.

begin constructing in the spring, and I could easily find suitable parochial work for them until they can establish their own houses for their communities.

Einsiedeln is also preparing for the worst. The abbot of St. Meinrad[91] is building a new monastery as quickly as possible. Until now, he has had to be satisfied with a wooden monastery. His daily expenses, I am told, are $120 or $3,600 a month. Since he has no more than seven or eight fathers at home, he must be expecting guests. In addition, two fathers from Engelberg are coming next spring. They have decided to settle in the Far West, near our Atchison, but in another diocese.[92]

Do not lose courage. Be full of hope. The political conditions in Germany and in all of Europe are dark. Ecclesiastical affairs seem little better, but everything is on the right path. It has to happen this way so that Protestantism can be destroyed and the unity of the Faith can be restored. How wonderful are God's ways! What Bishop Wittmann[93] often said is coming to pass. The kingdom of God will pass through adversities. What is happening today appears to be leading toward the destruction of the Church, but in fact, it is merely a trial. Many cannot endure it because they are dry branches on the tree, which is the Church. Those who stand the test gloriously by their example will bring back to the Church those who are in error and will destroy those who started the persecution.

In this country, the bishops are one after another consecrating their dioceses to the Sacred Heart of Jesus. The act of consecration for our diocese is set for December 8. On December 13, 14, and 15 we will have the retreat for our students.

As I have already said, if the worst happens, you and your whole community will be cordially welcome here. You can establish a new Metten here until you can return to the old one.

The new *Ceremoniale Benedictinum*[94] is at the press.

A thousand greetings with most cordial affection and respect from your most devoted confrere, Boniface Wimmer

Ger   oAMA   cASVA   transCZ,CS,RG   *Scrip*19 (77-78)

---

[91] Martin Marty, O.S.B. (1834-1896), abbot of the Swiss-American abbey of St. Meinrad in Indiana.

[92] Conception, Missouri. This community of Swiss Benedictines developed into Conception Abbey. See Edward Malone, *A History of Conception Colony, Abbey, and Schools* (Elkhorn, Nebr.: Michaeleen Press, 1971).

[93] George Michael Wittmann (1760-1833), bishop of Regensburg, was Wimmer's teacher in the seminary. Bishop Wittmann was renowned for his sanctity, and his comments about the future were often taken as prophecies by Wimmer and the bishop's other former students.

[94] Edward Hipelius, O.S.B., *Ceremoniale Monasticum, Jussu Reverendissimi Domini Praesidis Congregationis Americano-Casinensis Editum* (Beatty, Pennsylvania: St. Vincent Abbey Press, 1875).

TO JAMES ROOSEVELT BAYLEY   **113**

St. Vincent, March 3, 1874

Most Rev. Archbishop, My Lord: Father Helmpracht has written to me about the Church in question, and I have answered [that] I could not well take charge of it unless in case if the Benedictines of Bavaria would be compelled to leave Bavaria—which is very probable and expected by them.

After I had received your letter, wherein your Grace expressed a desire to have a house of our ancient Order in Baltimore, I thought it to be my duty to convocate a Chapter and to lay the matter before it. The result of our consultation was then that I, notwithstanding the scarcity of disponible Fathers, should try to find at least one able to take care of the Church of the 14 Martyrs first, and then, if circumstances prove favorable, to commence on a small scale a formal establishment of our Order, if this plan meets your approbation.

Immediately I can not send a priest; however, I will arrange to have one ready about Easter.

With my heartfelt thanks for your present and past benevolence towards our Order, I have the honor to sign in profound reverence and obedience, Your Grace's most humble servt, B. Wimmer, Abbot

Eng   oAAB   cASVA

TO CELESTINE ENGLBRECHT   **114**

St. Vincent, April 19, 1874

Dearest and Reverend Confrere: I shall not be able to attend the 25th anniversary of your ordination because I must go to Chicago to meet Bishop Fink[95] and Father Leander[96] in order to settle the matter of our church property. From there I have to go to Minnesota to make the visitation prescribed by our statutes. I therefore beg you to regard, and to kindly accept, this letter as my representative.

I heartily congratulate you on this beautiful day, which is filled with consoling and uplifting remembrances. Twenty-five years are indeed a considerable length of time in a person's life, but still more so when they are 25 years of service, as in the life of an official or a soldier. What soldier would not be proud to have served his king for 25 years? However, 25 years of service become even more important

---

[95] Louis M. Fink, O.S.B. (1834-1904), bishop of Leavenworth, Kansas.
[96] Leander Schnerr, O.S.B. (1836-1920), prior in Chicago.

when they have been spent in the service of our Lord, and this you have done, Honored Jubilarian!

How many holy Masses have you said during this time! With their merits, you have given joy to heaven, consoled the poor souls, comforted the Church Militant, and averted innumerable punishments from her! To how many innocent children have you opened the gate of heaven through holy baptism in the course of this long period! How many suffering souls have you consoled and calmed on their bed of suffering! To how many dying persons have you granted the assistance they needed in their hour of utter distress and desolation! How many sinners' eyes have you opened! How many hearts have you touched in the holy sacrament of penance so that they stopped walking in the way of perdition and reconciled themselves with God! To how many have you given the bread of life so that they could persevere in the struggle with their evil inclinations, the pernicious attacks of the enemy! How many children have you instructed and through your prudent guidance saved from the snare of temptation!

At the same time, you have continued to fight the good fight and to bring high esteem to your state as a priest and a monk. You have preserved a spotless reputation everywhere. You have selflessly, and with joyful devotion, concerned yourself with the holy interests of the Church, of the Order, and of the parish that has been entrusted to your care. All the churches in which you have served bear witness that you loved the cleanliness, the beauty, and the adornment of the house of God. In addition, I myself testify personally, and feel myself indebted to you, for your faithful attachment to me as your abbot.

You have thus scattered many seeds during this long time, and you have zealously put out at interest your God-given talents so that they will someday be returned to you multiplied by the Lord. Give thanks to the Lord most affectionately for all the gracious gifts of your holy vocation, and beg Him insistently for His continued blessing and protection, for the grace of persevering to the end in those years when, with the decrease of physical strength, there might creep in all too easily a decrease of initial zeal, a cooling of first love, and perhaps, in the joyful awareness of victories won and of laurels attained, a certain dangerous sense of security. May God grant you another 25 years of meritorious service so that the crown destined for you may become all the more beautiful and bright!

With cordial love and sincere respect, I remain your friend and brother, Boniface Wimmer

Ger　　o　　　ASVA　　transGM

TO MARTIN MARTY   **115**

St. Vincent, November 17, 1874

Reverend Abbot, Venerable Confrere: In the hope that Mr. Sigel is still staying with you, I am sending you the enclosed two railway tickets from his father. They cost $30 each. I have also enclosed a letter without an address. I believe it is also intended for him. I received both from Father Kilian, who sent them from Mainz. He told me that "it should be used in accordance with the father's wishes." I can only surmise what those wishes are since there was no accompanying letter to me, except the note asking me to forward the tickets. At your convenience, would you please send me a note confirming that you have received them?

I read with the most extraordinary pleasure the history of our Order which you have presented to the readers of the *Cincinnati Wahrheitsfreund* through Benziger.[97] Writing a small book like this, so brief and compact yet containing all that is essential, is a greater feat on your part than publishing a larger, voluminous work. Nevertheless, the art and industry that makes this work so commendable are small in comparison with the great good that redounds to the Order and the reading public. The more recent orders and congregations, by glamorous descriptions of their merits (which are truly commendable), have for a long time brought things to such a point that people no longer know anything about the Order of St. Benedict except that there used to be such an Order and that there are still some monasteries of that Order in Austria, whose members are anything but monks and hardly even good priests. For that reason our great saints are almost completely forgotten and no longer venerated, a fact that can only result in harm to the people and to the Order as well.

By your work you have restored renown and honor to our Order. Your work has surely brought about a fresh interest in the saints of our Order, promoting anew their veneration by the people. No doubt many young people who come across this book will be inspired with a desire to become members of our Order. It is therefore something very timely, and though small, it still fills a gap in the literature of church history and supplies something that people need. Also, it is a good forerunner to a larger work on the same subject which it is rumored you have already completed. My Father Wendelin[98] has for a long time entertained the idea of writing a history of our Order, but he has never gotten around to it. Besides, he did not go through the course of studies that is necessary for such a project.

---

[97] Martin Marty, O.S.B., *Der Heilige Benedikt und Seine Orden von einem Benediktiner in St. Meinrad, Indiana* (New York: Benziger Brothers, 1874).
[98] Wendelin Mayer, O.S.B. (1832-1881).

I added only eighty-eight feet to the monastery, and it took me all summer to do it. I did it, of course, with my men only. I expect to finish it by Christmas, but it will mean a lot of hard work. Even then the monastery will not yet be finished, which is true of the college as well. Moreover, no steps have yet been taken for building a suitable church, so I am certain I will not be in a position to realize it.

Father Clement[99] completed a magnificent church. He finished it against my advice, for I was afraid that he would have the same sad experience as Father Augustine[100] had with his church in Atchison, namely that he would run too deeply into debt. I am in the habit of building only as much as time and means allow.

I was sorry to hear that the health of Abbot Henry[101] is so bad that they fear his life is in danger. Is there any truth to the story that the Benedictines of Mariastein want to emigrate to Ecuador? I would still prefer California or Oregon. Father Weninger[102] is always after me to go there, but I have too few men. Besides, there is not enough stability in South America. Finally, congratulations on your names-day! With all affection and esteem, I remain Your Lordship's devoted confrere, B. Wimmer, Abbot

Ger   oASMA   cASVA   transBB

---

[99] Clement Staub, O.S.B. (1819-1886).
[100] Augustine Wirth, O.S.B. (1828-1901).
[101] Henry Schmid, O.S.B. (1800-1874), abbot of the Swiss Abbey of Einsiedeln.
[102] Francis Xavier Weninger, S.J. (1805-1888).

1875-1879

TO MICHAEL REGER

116

St. Vincent, January 2, 1875

Right Reverend Sir, Dearest Friend: Not long ago a young man by the name of Andreas Peter[1] came to us from the monastery of Scheyern with the intention of becoming a lay brother. He is 23 years old, born on November 24, 1851 (illegitimate), at Eichelberg near Geisenfeld. He has excellent testimonial letters and recommendations from Scheyern, but because of the regulations of the papal decree, I must also have a certificate of his conduct from the Diocese of Regensburg, so I ask you the favor of sending me one in writing.

I am too late to send greetings and good wishes for the New Year, but I included all my friends in my intentions at the holy sacrifice of the Mass on New Year's Day. I have sent written greetings to no one except our bishop[2] because of my heavy burden of letter writing, which never ceases. Unfortunately, since last winter my eyes have troubled me very much. Only during the day and in my unheated room can I read and write. My eyes cannot stand heated air. Except for the minor inconveniences of old age, however, I still feel well enough, although I must live a life of strict moderation.

I have nothing special to report. In 1874, I made an addition to the monastery 88 feet long and four stories high. This coming spring we will begin an annex to

---

[1] Matthias Andreas Peter, O.S.B. (1851-1908).
[2] Michael Domenec, C.M. (1816-1878), bishop of Pittsburgh.

the college 100 feet long and partly four and partly three stories high. This is all I can do without incurring debts, for I must carefully manage our economy.

In Chicago, we will have to be satisfied with a frame church for some years to come, but this summer we built a large schoolhouse, 100 feet long, 50 feet wide, and four stories high. We use the ground floor, which is 17 feet high, for weekday Masses and the Sunday Mass for the children. The next two stories are the school. The fourth floor is used exclusively for meetings of the sodalities and for fairs. The cost of the building rose to $21,000. It is the property of, and taken care of by, the parish. Naturally, it will take time until the debt is paid off. The priest has to know how to manage things so that he can get money from the people whenever possible, even through innocent entertainments and fairs to which people flock from other parishes (and Protestants as well). That is the way we help ourselves in America. We had to have this building, knowing full well that the debt would be between $10,000 and $12,000. The parishioners are still poor because of their heavy losses in the fire, and times at present are not good.

On November 3, we had our state elections. The Democrats were victorious again, so we hope to see a better government. My nephew, Sebastian Wimmer, won on the Democratic ticket and was elected to the Pennsylvania House of Representatives. In some state elections, the Catholics won the upper hand.

How are things over there? Is what I predicted gradually happening? Many Protestants might now be ready to awaken. Through the dissolution of the church-state relationship is not a bridge being built for the unification of the better elements? Bismarck has suffered an awful setback in his church policies. In Spain, he received a slap in the face because of the defeat of Serrano and the Republic. On the other hand, the pope received support he never dreamed of. Garibaldi might overthrow Victor Emmanuel. That would mean another fallen pillar for Bismarck. It will soon come about that instead of being helped, he has to help. Through all this, it is inevitable that everything will become very confused, but from the chaos, the Church will arise victorious and glorious and will be in great demand. Germany will be united in the Faith.

With deepest respect, I send greetings to His Grace, the bishop, and wish you health, long life, and God's blessing and protection. B. Wimmer, Abbot

P.S. I could make use of some stipends, in the event that you have any left over.

Ger   oASVA   transRG

TO MARTIN MARTY   **117**

St. Vincent, January 24, 1875

Right Reverend Abbot, Venerable Confrere: A few days ago, I received with profound sorrow the news of the death of Abbot Henry[3] and was reminded of your short letter, which lay before me for a good while awaiting a reply.

I fully agree not to admit, except with your recommendation, any who have run away from you or who have been dismissed by you. Besides, I do not think much of people of that kind. Nonetheless, there are times when you have to feel pity for such people, if you see that it is possible to save a vocation that otherwise might be lost.

I never had great hopes for Father Rhaban.[4] When I was with him, I was on the verge of sending him away because he was so headstrong and short-tempered. Hence, I had to remove him from Covington and transfer him to Newark. There are nevertheless some very good points in his favor. For example, he is very good at what he likes to do.

In your history of the Order,[5] I found something I did not like and about which I must express disagreement. It is something of special interest to me. You say that St. Boniface was killed by the heathens because they wanted the wine he had brought with him. Such an observation concerning my patron saint seems rather scandalous, as though because of it, he deserved the crown of martyrdom. I have never read anywhere of this particular detail. We have here the latest edition of the *Acta Sanctorum*, and in it, no mention whatsoever is made of the circumstance you bring up. If I were the *censor librorum*, I would order it to be stricken out!

Father Ignatius,[6] my director of music, has tried to persuade me to introduce Roman chant since we are running short of hymnals and those that are available (from St. Emmeran, Salzburg, and Scheyern) are so widely different from one another. I myself at one time toyed with the idea of introducing the Maurist breviary, but in Rome, they practically accused me of heresy because of it, and so I gave up the whole idea. I was prepared for proposals of this kind at the Council, but the matter did not come up for discussion. The monks of Beuron sided with Gueranger,[7] a staunch conservative. At present, as long as we can have both Benedictine breviaries and missals, I do not want to give them up. However, I am

---

[3] Henry Schmid, O.S.B. (1800-1874), abbot of the Swiss Abbey of Einsiedeln.

[4] Rhaban Gutmann, O.S.B. (1845-1928).

[5] Martin Marty, O.S.B, *Der Heilige Benedikt und Seine Orden von einem Benediktiner in St. Meinrad, Indiana* (New York: Benziger Brothers, 1874).

[6] Ignatius Trueg, O.S.B. (1827-1910).

[7] Prosper Guéranger, O.S.B. (1806-1875), abbot of the French Abbey of Solesme.

having an antiphonal printed in octavo size so that it can be available everywhere. Until now, the novices always had to transcribe it, each one his own. Two of the three parts of the *Benedictine Ceremonial* have already been printed.[8] Uniformity is a nice thing, but variety also has its charm.

You are building at a faster pace than we are. I am always building, it is true, but I have still not got a church and will hardly live to see one built. Last year I added 88 feet to the monastery. This year I will add 100 feet to the college building. It is hard going, but I am doing my best.

My prior, Father Oswald,[9] was made prior in Atchison. Father Innocent[10] is taking his place here at the abbey. Abbot Rupert[11] will probably be made a bishop. With sincere affection and esteem, your most devoted confrere, B. Wimmer, Abbot

Ger   oASMA   cASVA   transBB

TO JOSEPH MEYRINGER   **118**

St. Vincent, April 19, 1875

Right Reverend Canon, Dearest Friend and Cousin: Last evening I received your letter dated March 28/29; hence, this sign of life again. If you imagine, my dear friend, that I can write as often as you can, you are sadly mistaken. That's not so easy for me. I have more to do than you think, and the work continues to increase. Seldom a day passes that I do not write at all, and often I have three, four, five letters to write. Besides, I am pressed with other obligations that require much time and thought. I have no opportunity to rest except when traveling–if you can call it resting to be on a train day and night for several days, thrown out of one's routine and often embarked on some unpleasant business or other.

Moreover, I cannot rest because everything is in a state of development and growth. I am always looking for means to do the work. I often make mistakes, which cannot be avoided, and then have to change things again. I have to take

---

[8] Edward Hipelius, O.S.B. *Ceremoniale Monasticum, Jussu Reverendissimi Domini Praesidis Congregationis Americano-Casinensis Editum* (Beatty, Pennsylvania: St. Vincent Abbey Press, 1875).

[9] Oswald Moosmüller, O.S.B. (1832-1901).

[10] Innocent Wolf, O.S.B. (1843-1922).

[11] Rupert Seidenbusch, O.S.B. (1830-1895), first abbot of St. John's Abbey, was ordained a bishop and made vicar apostolic of Northern Minnesota in 1875. He was the first of three of Wimmer's monks to become a bishop. The others were Louis Fink, O.S.B. (1834-1904), bishop of Atchison, and Leo Haid, O.S.B. (1849-1924), vicar apostolic of North Carolina.

into consideration not only my fathers, but also my sisters. In addition, I feel the burden of advanced age and suffer small annoyances even when I am extremely careful. For example, for quite a long time I have had to abstain from anything cold in food or drink as well as anything stimulating. Tea and coffee are my only beverages unless I want to catch a cold in my stomach or experience the old affliction in my chest.

Despite all this, however, I enjoy a good appetite and can observe the latest regulations concerning the Lenten fast without real discomfort. I do not take much exercise. In the evening after compline, from eight to nine o'clock, I walk up and down in my room praying and meditating. I cannot read or write by candlelight, at least very seldom and not for very long. I do not leave the house often, but when I do, I go for a short walk in the woods in the afternoon. That's been the case for a long time. I do not feel strong enough to go for a long walk. The old misery around my heart, or near it, has lately become stronger. It will kill me one day. If it doesn't, then I shall succumb to some other enemy after it causes me much pain and torment. I don't worry about that. The thought of death occupies my mind daily.

It is certain that I shall not finish building my monastery since I need five more years to do it. Meanwhile, I labor tirelessly for the growth of the community, but that too is going slowly. Among the many students, only a few achieve the goal. That fellow Bluty from Hierheim is working in a cigar factory. Such is often the case with others. Satan is screening and screening the chaff. Most fail. If only pure wheat would be left over! The kingdom of heaven always suffers violence. Nobody wants to force himself, but despite it all, thanks be to God, we are still making progress, though slowly and with much pain and patience, though also with consolation and joy.

Abbot Rupert[12] from St. Louis in Minnesota became a bishop. He is vicar apostolic for Minnesota. I will have to go there twice this year, once for his consecration and the election of a new abbot, and a second time for the blessing of the new abbot.

It's strange. I was thinking of Mr. Stern for the past few weeks. I felt myself admonished and intended to write him, but then postponed it because of too much work. I forgot about his being sick. Then last Thursday I read in the paper that he had died. Your letter tells me the day.

The boxes are intended for me on the condition that we say 200 masses and that I pay for packing and shipment. That was the legacy he signed on May 29, 1871.

---

[12] Rupert Seidenbusch, O.S.B. (1830-1895).

He told Father Adalbert[13] that he would send along with the snails and conches the respective books and drawings and perhaps his magnifying glass. May I ask you to please help us by going to a dependable forwarding agent in Regensburg with the order to bring the cases bequeathed to me from Stauf to Regensburg and then to ship them via Bremen to New York with the Bremen agency of Anton and John Unkraut. They are well known to me. I will take full responsibility for the shipment. The boxes must be packed with the utmost care. Tell them to fit them with iron hoops to protect them against rough handling and from being broken to pieces. The address is: St. Vincent College, Westmoreland County, Pennsylvania, United States. The contents have to be declared: land and sea insects, various books, illustrations, a magnifying glass. Ask his sister for help identifying the contents. If the declaration is not correct, everything will be confiscated. The college does not have to pay duty, but if the shipment is sent in my name, I will have to pay. Now is the best time to ship the boxes because there is less danger of storms in May and June. In the event that the books and illustrations belonging to the collection have been left out of the legacy, I will buy them. I will also buy the magnifying glass.

Would it be too much to ask that you go along with the agent to Stauf and look after the packing so that nothing is left out? The collection is of great value to us, especially because of its variety. It would be a shame if anything were lost. The books and illustrations should also be included. Please take some interest in this matter. The agent should defray the expenses for packing immediately. That and his own expenses will be refunded by Unkraut in Bremen. He will deal with an American agent who will later transact business with me.

Best regards to the sister of Mr. Stern. I will write her myself because I am anxious to have more information about his death. Here we shall have a solemn funeral service for the dearly departed. My two priests[14] have returned from Innsbruck to Rome for graduation. Next fall they will be back at the abbey. Many greetings to the provost at the cathedral and to all my friends and acquaintances. In cordial love and remembrance before God, I am your sincere friend and cousin, B. Wimmer, Abbot

Ger   oASVA   transRG

---

[13] Adalbert Müller, O.S.B. (1842-1906).
[14] James Zilliox, O.S.B. (1849-1890), and Xavier Baltes, O.S.B. (1844-1876).

TO UTTO LANG   **119**

St. Marys, December 16, 1875

Right Reverend President,[15] Dearest Confrere: Unfortunately, I could not answer your letter of September 24 sooner because I did not have enough time until now. I was neither surprised nor offended that they did not trust me in that money matter. We Americans have the reputation, I suppose, of being swindlers and reckless gamblers. Thank God it turned out for the best.

Father Oswald[16] is saving $1,500 a year in interest. Because of the insistence of the bishop,[17] I sent a petition to the Holy Father right after Christmas asking that the priory in Atchison be elevated to the dignity of an abbey. I gave as reasons that very soon we might not be able to communicate with the Holy See [because of political developments in Italy] and that time and necessity required immediate action in the matter of raising the priory to an abbey.

I had to name the new abbot of St. Louis on the Lake, just as you had to do at Scheyern. Because the new abbot is young (thirty-three years old) and rigorous and was *factotum* in the college (which caused some to fear that his election to the abbacy might take him away from the college), a small majority was not in favor of his becoming abbot. Instead, they elected my prior, Father Innocent,[18] with thirteen of twenty-five votes, even though I told them at the start that I would not consent to either Father Innocent's or Father Oswald's election. Therefore, I voided the election and gave them Alexius Edelbrock[19] who received eight votes on the first ballot and eleven votes on the third. Two young priests and one older one objected, and I sent their protest to the Holy Father with the election returns and my own report. The Holy Father approved and confirmed my decision, which satisfied everyone.

The new abbot is a native of Westphalia. He came as a child to America and as a boy went to Minnesota where he was a rather unruly fellow until our Father Alexius Rötzer[20] took him under his supervision and taught him good behavior. Because of his gratitude and affection for Father Alexius, the boy took his name in religion. Young Edelbrock ran away from his father, who was a rough man, and came to St. Vincent with the intention of studying here. He made good use of his exceptional talents and studied hard. He finished with distinction and returned

---

[15] Lang was president (or *praeses*) of the Bavarian Benedictine Congregation.
[16] Oswald Moosmüller, O.S.B. (1832-1901), prior at St. Benedict's Priory, Atchison, Kansas.
[17] Louis M. Fink, O.S.B. (1834-1904), vicar apostolic of Kansas.
[18] Innocent Wolf, O.S.B. (1843-1922).
[19] Alexius Edelbrock, O.S.B. (1843-1908).
[20] Alexius Rötzer, O.S.B. (1832-1860).

to Minnesota. Under Abbot Rupert[21] he devoted himself to the foundation and improvement of the college, of which he became director. He enjoys good health, a strong constitution, and intelligence, and he is ready, I trust, to use his talents for the greater honor of God and of our Order.

Abbot Rupert left him a great deal of work to be done. He (Abbot Rupert) brought from Europe plans for a church in Riedl which he wanted to build in St. Paul. The plan was executed in all its details, against my repeated verbal and written warnings. The church is built of stone and has two beautiful towers and a church in the basement for the winter. It is a magnificent building–but the debts, the debts! So you had better send me some money right away–say, 50,000 florins. You see, your *Projektenmacher*[22] is still at it.

I have finished the monastery building, which is nearly 400 feet in length and four stories high, not including cellars. It faces east. Another wing faces north and is 200 feet in length and three stories high. In finishing the building, I have incurred no debts. I build only when necessary and only when I have the money, people, and means to do so. I build for necessity first and for comfort afterwards. Thus, last summer, because we did not have enough water, I constructed a water-works. Now a steam engine pumps water from the well in the valley through two-and-a-half-inch iron pipes. The water is pumped 150 feet up and for a distance of 1,600 feet and put into three cisterns, which provide all the water we need, and even supply the brewery, to which the water is carried through earthen pipes down the hill to the north of the monastery.

Not a few gentlemen are beset with the idea of building quickly and in a gran-diose manner. They are not concerned about paying debts, or if they are, they suffer from the presumption that they can pay them off easily. This year one of my priests burdened me with the obligation of paying several thousand dollars. The reason some act in this way is that they think the good times of the past will continue in the future. They have also been able to depend on the liberal support of the people, who never leave their priests in the lurch. In recent years, however, things have changed. Money is scarce, and anyone who speculates on the future is making a bad mistake.

This year I have 103 poor students, scholastics, who can pay little or nothing for their education. There are only 147 students in the college. Payments are coming in very slowly. Money is extremely scarce. Everywhere you hear that there is no

---

[21] Rupert Seidenbusch, O.S.B. (1830-1895).

[22] *Projektenmacher*, plan-maker or visionary. This was the derogatory nickname some of Wimmer's confreres at Metten had given him in the 1840s.

commerce, no wages. Grant[23] would like a fight with the Catholic Church to win votes from the Methodist bigots and other religious sects so that he can rob and corrupt the land for three more years. Just as in the old country, one hears the old song of how Catholics are dangerous to the state, but here we have freedom of the press, and the chief executive (Grant) is daily represented in the press (without suffering fine or imprisonment) as an imposter, swindler, and thief, which he really is. The old song is even carried into the Congress, which is Democratic. We will have troubled times here until the next presidential election, with one party battling the other.

Nonetheless, we proceed tranquilly, finish the work on our buildings, improve our farms in order to secure our sustenance, properly educate our young people, and take in as many as we can, giving them lodging and food. At St. Vincent we have thirty-five clerics and at St. Louis (I think) fifteen. Abbot Rupert erected several important buildings for the monastery and college, which Abbot Alexius will extend. In Kansas, Father Oswald is developing a very extensive field of work. After my death, I don't want to leave behind a treasury filled to the brim, but rather few debts and, as much as possible, a monastery and college in the best of condition, to be a fortress against hostile aggression, a protection for the holy Church, with a small army of well-trained fighting men and many outposts in the priories, which in due time, like Atchison and St. Louis, might become real fortresses.

My health at present is not as it was a few years ago. I cannot take beer or wine but only tea. My old agility has entirely left me. Traveling is no longer a pleasure but only a burden, and I do it only when necessary. When at home, I seldom leave my room, and when I do, it is only to go to the choir or to the refectory.

The agenda of the general chapter is at the press. Alzog's *Church History*, a summary in English, is ready for the press. The Bible translated by Father Peter Lechner[24] is being prepared for publication by Father Edward.[25] Let us pray to God for grace and let us hope with all confidence that we shall all do His holy will in the coming year. With true affection, your most devoted confrere, Boniface Wimmer, Abbot

Ger   oAMA   cASVA   transRG

---

[23] President Ulysses S. Grant (1822-1885).
[24] Peter Lechner, O.S.B. (1805-1874).
[25] Edward Hipelius, O.S.B. (1836-1900).

TO ALEXIUS EDELBROCK   **120**

St. Vincent, February 13, 1876

Right Reverend Alexius Edelbrock, second abbot of Saint Louis-on-the-Lake.

Right Reverend Father Abbot: I received your letter of February 3. We must continue in Iowa. On February 2, I clothed Father Harrison,[26] a priest from Iowa who seems to be a very nice and efficient man and who has been asking to be received for a long time. If he perseveres, as I have no doubt he will, I am sure he will draw other Irishmen after him, and we will soon have a branch of Irish Benedictines. This would favor the spread of the Order in America, Canada, and Ireland in a few years and will be the salvation of many Irishmen. We must therefore zealously do our part. As the initiative was taken by Minnesota, and as you have proportionately many more men available, you have to continue, and for you it is easier to do so. I have seven, and with Father Oswald[27] there are eight fathers and three brothers in Kansas; so it is very difficult for me to keep another father in Iowa.

Actually, I am at a great loss right now. Because Father Bruno[28] brought the sisters to Washington Heights against my will, I have the choice of either keeping a resident priest there or sending one there from Chicago every day. Otherwise, the sisters will be cheated, for they bought a home there for $16,000 and are dependent on a boarding school for their livelihood. Now that he is gone, I had to take Father Suitbert[29] from Chicago for the time being. Because of his absence from Chicago, there can be no 6:00 am Sunday Mass for the congregation any more, and that means, besides the considerable moral harm, considerable material loss

---

[26] Unidentified. He did not persevere in monastic life.
[27] Oswald Moosmüller, O.S.B. (1832-1901).
[28] Bruno Riess, O.S.B. (1829-1900).
[29] Suitbert de Marteau, O.S.B. (1834-1901).

as well. Because of this, please send to Chicago in place of Father Bruno a father who is at least able to say Mass. By the way, Bruno belongs to Minnesota.

When he came to Chicago years ago, I accepted him because he was downright confused, but he has been neither formally dismissed from Minnesota nor formally accepted here. He can be used for the care of souls neither in Minnesota nor here. He does not understand his moral theology because he was ordained too soon and never made up for the studies he missed; therefore he does harm in the confessional where he demands from ordinary people a life according to the Jansenists. Likewise in his sermons. He gives exclusively "mission" sermons. He attracts to himself a little flock of pious souls–girls and old women whom he visits frequently and from whom he learns the secrets and scandals of all the families. Then he makes use of this information in the pulpit and thus makes many enemies within a short time who eventually chase him out, after having first invented and then burdened him with all kinds of malicious stories. He has a great natural eloquence, so he is fit to be a missionary and for making collections, but not for the regular care of souls. I would not trust him very much as far as the other sex is concerned. He dares too much and is consequently in danger of falling. We will still have much trouble with him. Maybe it is a good thing that he cheated me so terribly in Washington Heights. At least he has been shamed and humiliated by his action.

During the summer, Bishop Gibbons[30] offered me a small parish in North Carolina and, in addition to that, a farm of five hundred acres. Recently he asked me for an immediate answer, whether I was willing to accept it or not. My chapter unanimously advised me to accept the offer. Father Herman[31] will go, but another man has to go to Richmond to replace him. Your sick father[32] there is no help. He also does not seem to improve, but I cannot free anyone to go!

If you would take over Creston (Iowa) and send Father Boniface[33] another English-speaking father so that Father Placid[34] could return to Atchison, then I would take Father Theodose[35] from there and in this way could help myself. Even if there were then only an invalid in Chicago to say one holy Mass, either at the sisters in Washington Heights or in Chicago itself, I could manage until the next

---

[30] James Gibbons (1834-1921), bishop of Richmond (1872-1877) and later archbishop of Baltimore (1877-1921). While bishop of Richmond, Gibbons was also vicar apostolic of North Carolina.
[31] Herman Wolfe, O.S.B. (1816-1884).
[32] Placid Watry, O.S.B. (1851-1876).
[33] Boniface Moll, O.S.B. (1840-1910).
[34] Placid McKeever, O.S.B. (1840-1896).
[35] Theodose Goth, O.S.B. (b. 1849).

ordination. The sisters in Washington Heights will give board to the former as their chaplain and to the latter because he takes care of their garden.

I have four foreign priests at St. Vincent, two Germans and two Irishmen, all young and intelligent men, but I do not need them here, and in a place like Chicago one cannot put too much confidence in them. My Father Maurus[36] is here too, but suspended. He can still not be trusted, and all the others are in the harness.

Returning again to the subject of Father Bruno, I must correct my former statement. I have just been reminded that he did not vote at the election of the abbot. That means he was regarded as belonging to St. Vincent. Consequently, if you cannot or do not want to give me anybody in exchange for him, at least temporarily, I will have to recall him.

Be glad that you are an abbot. An abbot can learn and merit much. As a rule, an abbot is little esteemed by people, but certainly by God. An abbot needs much patience, however, which he acquires only bit by bit–also great caution in judgment because he so easily deceives himself, or is deceived, if he does not investigate matters thoroughly or if he does not heed advice and listen to all sides. Likewise, an abbot should make people feel as little as possible that he is abbot, except when he has to be serious, because he is easily envied as well as easily hated. In truth, he is not to be envied.

In spite of all this, however, it is beautiful to be the head of a group of good, pious, and well-educated men who, put in the right place, accomplish much good together and who, despite their weaknesses, possess many precious gifts and complement one another. The most disagreeable thing for me has always been, and still is, the fact that our means are in no way proportionate to our desires, and it takes so long to accomplish only a little. In 30 years, I have not even completed one monastery! Also for this cross, the proper means are patience and humble resignation because one recognizes that we may be glad if God has made use of us as instruments to accomplish even a single small work of mercy.

Bishop Krautbauer[37] offered me some small parishes that together include more than 300 families. He offered me the "fire area" for a monastery because more land would be available for purchase there. I asked him to approach you. I am so short of personnel that I cannot undertake anything significant. I am hardly able to keep up the places we have, and as for finances, I have been made lame by

---

[36] Maurus Lynch, O.S.B. (1831-1887).
[37] Francis X. Krautbauer (1824-1885), bishop of Green Bay, Wisconsin.

Washington Heights. Therefore, patience! Remember me! With special love and esteem, your most devoted confrere, Boniface Wimmer

Ger   oASJA   cASVA   transAHo

TO BENEDICTINE ABBOTS   **121**

St. Vincent, May 1, 1876

Right Reverend Abbots and Prelates of the Order of Our Holy Father St. Bene-dict: Greetings in the Lord! What a happy and joyful occasion it will be for the international family of St. Benedict when in four years we mark another centen-nial feast of our holy father. Since such an event occurs so rarely, it is certainly incumbent upon us to celebrate it in a special manner. After considering the matter thoroughly, our general chapter, which met last year, decreed with won-derful unanimity, after careful consideration, that a committee be established in our congregation to organize a worthy and dignified celebration of this feast, and that this committee be delegated to oversee all aspects of the solemnity. When we decided this, we did not have in mind to restrict our endeavors to narrow ends but rather to encourage all students everywhere of our great patriarch to join in these pious efforts.

At the time of the chapter, we considered giving the honor of leading this en-deavor to some more ancient monastery of our Order, but in the end, we decided to take the initiative ourselves for two reasons. First, we had already reflected on the matter, and others had received our many efforts with general applause and praise. Second, we considered that the wonderful freedom of our American Republic (which we pray God to preserve) would favor our administering the initiative. In any event, we are prepared to undertake the work ourselves, but if our boldness should offend anyone, we declare ourselves ready to correct our error by surrendering the glory of beginning the undertaking to others. Therefore, if I may be permitted to do so, let me provide the right reverend abbots and prelates with some details about the suggestions made by my confreres for the centennial celebration.

First, it is appropriate that all the congregations and monasteries of our holy Order should be invited to participate in the celebration of this feast. Then, in order that the auspicious event might be brought about and concord and harmony among all our members be achieved, we think that the superiors of each of the congregations and monasteries should appoint several capitulars to undertake the work of planning and that when they have organized celebrations with the consent of their superiors, they should report their plans in writing to:

Rt. Rev. Abbot B. Wimmer, O.S.B.

St. Vincent's Abbey

Beatty P.O.

Westmoreland Co., Penna.

United States of North America

The members of our collegiate institute have designated as the patron of our work the distinguished son of our Holy Father St. Benedict, Cardinal John Baptist Pitra,[38] and they have suggested that the right reverend abbots and prelates also consider asking Cardinal Pitra to accept the patronage of the worldwide endeavor to mark the centennial celebration of St. Benedict. Moreover, my confreres have considered proposing the following to the right reverend abbots:

(1) That students of the whole Order be invited to participate in a poetry contest to celebrate the praises of St. Benedict in centennial poems written in Latin;

(2) That all the sons of St. Benedict versed in rhetoric be invited to write a Latin panegyric in honor of our holy father;

(3) That those who compose the most outstanding poem or the best panegyric be given an honor and a prize;

(4) That a contest and a prize be established for a short hymn appropriate to the feast;

(5) That the winning poem, panegyric, and hymn be published in a new edition of the *Album Benedictinum*;

(6) That a sung Mass in honor of St. Benedict be composed and a prize be awarded to the composer;

(7) That a diploma be granted by the most eminent patron and judges of the competition as a complementary prize to each of those who participate in the competition;

(8) That one person who is known for his sound doctrine and literary knowledge, but who is not competing for a prize, be selected by the most eminent patron from each congregation, and from any monasteries that do not belong to a congregation, to serve on a panel of judges;

(9) That one or several Benedictine students write an epitome or summary of the history of our Order, not to exceed 600 pages, in any language;

---

[38] Cardinal Jean Baptiste Pitra, O.S.B. (1812-1889), a monk of the French abbey of Solesmes who became cardinal in 1863 and prefect of the Vatican Library in 1869.

(10) That the Holy Apostolic See be petitioned to grant certain spiritual benefits, such as the opportunity to receive a plenary indulgence on each day within the octave of the feast of our Holy Father Benedict;

(11) That a memorial medal, funded by the whole Order, be minted in honor of our Holy Father Benedict, and that everything having to do with the minting of this medal (including its inscription) be the responsibility of the Right Reverend Angelo Pescetelli,[39] Abbot of Farfa and Procurator General of the Cassinese Congregation;

(12) That a votive gift be offered by the whole Order at the tomb of our Holy Father at the Archabbey of Montecassino, and that the type of gift be determined by the right reverend abbots when they consult with one another at some future time.

We ask that the distinguished prelates of our Order receive and consider our well-intentioned suggestions, and that they send any questions or further suggestions to me as soon as possible, for although the feast might at the moment seem in the distant future, nevertheless when one looks at all that must be done, he can easily see that there is not much time left to make the necessary preparations.

We, ourselves, will accept the responsibility for publishing a new edition of the *Album Benedictinum*, and we have assigned the editorship to the secretary of our college who will explain the plan for the new edition in a separate letter. Because the cost of publishing this work is not insignificant, I respectfully ask the right reverend abbots to indicate to me as soon as possible how many copies they wish to order.

I am confident that the great love we all share for our holy patriarch will result in widespread and generous support for this undertaking and that our purpose will be accomplished.

In conclusion, I pray that the good Lord grant all Benedictine abbots and prelates His blessings and His graces. Boniface Wimmer, Abbot of St. Vincent and President of the American-Cassinese Congregation

Lat   cASVA [printed circular letter]   transJO

---

[39] Angelo Pescetelli, O.S.B. (1809-1885).

TO MICHAEL REGER 122

St. Vincent, August 7, 1876

Right Reverend Dean, Most Respected Friend: As soon as you see this letter, you will say to yourself, "He must need something again; otherwise he wouldn't write." You are right. I could use more stipends again, if any are available and if other poor priests or communities are not in need of them. I could use a thousand or more since we have many priests. If it can be done without prejudice to others, please be so good as to send me some. The money should go to Louis Ignatius Lebling[40] in Munich, the intentions directly to me.

How is your health? I am at times as well as ever, but at other times, I have all sorts of ailments. Since May the pain on the left side of my chest, which oppressed me for so many years, has completely disappeared. Because of this pain, I abstained from beer, wine, and strong coffee for over a year and restricted myself to tea. Then one day, because of the intense heat, or rather to quench my thirst, I had a nice pitcher of lemonade made and drank it to the last drop without a care for the consequences. The next morning all pain was gone, and it has not once come back. That was indeed a precious discovery for me in the great heat. I do not, however, believe that my ailment was completely cured by this "treatment." Good enough that it is no worse.

You will, of course, have received the catalogue. This year we had fewer paying students, but more poor ones. Those who paid did so sporadically; that is, they remained in debt to us because money is scarce here among the people, even among those who own property. There is simply no business. It will be even worse next school year. There are plenty of poor students, but fewer students who can pay. Thus it is.

The Dear Lord has granted us a truly bountiful harvest. All went well, and without delay, in getting it into the barn and the bin. We have never had so much hay, wheat, and oats. The maize also stands beautifully. The potatoes and vegetables had too little rain, but they can still amount to something. We will, therefore, have sufficient food. The beer also held out despite the terrible heat. It brings a pittance of cash into the house, and the boss has need of it. A father in a small parish built me an expensive church, and I had to shell out $3,000 to avert evil consequences.

I have personally taken possession of two new poor places that cost me considerable money and will cost me even more. In the state of Alabama, Diocese of Mobile, I assumed responsibility for a German colony and bought a thousand

---

[40] Treasurer of the *Ludwig Missionsverein*.

acres of land for $3,440. I will, however, get back this money since I sold most of the land to new settlers. I retained only 300 acres, which will be debt free if the settlers pay me my original $3,440, as agreed, for the 700 acres. In addition to this, however, the initial negotiations and the trip (about 800 miles) cost several hundred dollars, and once construction gets underway, far more money will go into the project.

The second piece of property is in North Carolina, in the apostolic vicariate of North Carolina under the jurisdiction of the bishop of Richmond.[41] The entire state, with a population of about 100,000, has only 1,600 Catholics scattered around in nothing but small parishes, of which several together cannot maintain a resident priest. An old priest offered us a farm of 500 acres.[42] The bishop advised me to accept it since he thought if we were to establish a Benedictine house there, we could make a living from it, and from there look after the poor parishes, i.e., several of them, without remuneration. I accepted it even though I know that we cannot live from farming alone. Furthermore, the land is poor, and there are many Negroes around who do little or no work but steal everything they can. Nevertheless, we will try to establish a school there since there is no Catholic school within a radius of 300 miles. We hope in this way to meet a great need and eventually to obtain some income. Of course, at the outset a substantial expenditure will have to be made for construction and that sort of thing. Already since April of this year, the place has cost me $1,600.

Otherwise, things are going well enough, except in Chicago where the effects of the great fire are still weighing heavily upon us and our parish. The independent priory at Atchison, Kansas, was, upon my recommendation, elevated to an abbey by the Holy Father on April 7 of this year. Consequently, an abbot must be elected. I have not yet set the day for the election since I could not get away during vacation. During the summer holidays, the fathers travel to the priories for vacations. Consequently, the abbot has to stay home with a few monks to keep the choir going. In addition, the clerics and novices are permitted vacations by turns at our villa on the "Ridge," during which time a couple of fathers are in charge as chaplains and prefects to make sure freedom does not get out of hand and to maintain some degree of monastic life. Since the harvest is also ready and construction of buildings must proceed and guests arrive almost daily, I am for the moment kept busier than usual. From August 13 to 17, we will have our retreat. After that, I must make assignments. Then the students return. Once everything

---

[41] James Gibbons (1834-1921), bishop of Richmond (1872-1877) and later archbishop of Baltimore (1877-1921).

[42] Father Jeremiah J. O'Connell (1821-1888), who became a Benedictine oblate.

is in order, I will have a little time and can then go to Kansas for the election. As soon as the abbot is elected and the choice sent to Rome for confirmation, I will, if my health permits, go to North Carolina to investigate on the spot what must be done there.

It is a great comfort to me that we now have a third abbey, which means we now have a real congregation, the American Benedictine Cassinese. As you know, in order to have an exempt congregation, three monastic communities are required, and according to our Bavarian statutes, three abbots also, of whom one is the president (or, as they say in Rome, the "abbot general") and the other two, visitators. It took ten years for St. Vincent to become an abbey, ten years likewise for St. Louis on the Lake in Minnesota, and eighteen years for Atchison. Eternal thanks be to God for all this. All three abbeys have healthful and favorable locations, for themselves, for their external work, and for wider dissemination of the Order, provided that God, on whom all depends, gives His blessing.

We are afflicted this year with much sickness among the brothers and priests. Four brothers have died since last November, three of them after very short illnesses. Of the priests, the two last Romans, Fathers James and Xavier,[43] and Father Prior Innocent Wolf[44] are sick, and won't be able to work during the coming school year. That causes much inconvenience and necessitates many changes.

The approaching presidential election is the subject of much discussion. Since in this country the ruling party appoints the officials, naturally all who are holding office or who hope to obtain an office are very deeply interested in the election, as are their adherents and friends. In the electioneering, every effort is expended and all available means used by both parties to win votes. The Democrats, among whom most Catholics are numbered, hope to win the election. Then better times might come again. Need is very great in big cities and in factory areas, where the price of food is exorbitant despite the abundant harvest. Many people think if a big war were to break out in Europe, we would profit from it. I myself believe this, but I do not on that account wish you a war, although it appears to be the only way after great revolutions to reestablish a sensible order on a clean slate and also to verify known prophecies. I am in any case happy that I am in America where we enjoy complete freedom. The *Kulturkampf* over there is gradually losing its charm and exhausting itself. Gradually the battle between capital and labor will occupy center stage, and I fear that it will be dramatic. Still, God rules the world.

---

[43] James Zilliox, O.S.B. (1849-1890), and Xavier Baltes, O.S.B. (1844-1876), were the most recent monks from St. Vincent to have studied in Rome.

[44] Innocent Wolf, O.S.B. (1843-1922).

He alone knows His intent and will dispose all things in the best interests of His children.

The students who came from Regensburg are all in good health and to date are doing well. Please convey my respects and best wishes to His Excellency, to Spiritual Director Amberger, to my friend Leitl, and to all my good friends and acquaintances. In addition, please extend a most friendly greeting to your house-keeper, and now and then please remember me in your prayers. With special love and respect, your old friend, Boniface Wimmer, O.S.B.

Ger   oASVA   transAH

TO UTTO LANG   123

Creston, Iowa, September 24, 1876

Right Reverend Abbot, Most Esteemed Confrere: It is high time I write you again since a letter from me is past due. I am here on my journey to Atchison. Creston is a new place, fairly large and growing fast because the Burlington Railroad line from Chicago to California passes through it. It is the junction for railroads in various directions, a central point for traveling. We intend to establish an Irish priory here. At the moment, there are only two fathers stationed here, but at St. Vincent there are two priest novices for this place. Our priests do pastoral work in small villages and among scattered families within a radius of 40 or 50 miles. The prior is Eugene Phelan,[45] whom you met at Metten. The other priest is from Atchison.

Tomorrow I am going to Atchison (150 miles away) where on September 29 the election of an abbot will take place. After the election, I will pay a visit to Bishop Fink[46] in Leavenworth and to the new bishop of Omaha. (Our house in Nebraska City is located in his diocese.) His name is James O'Connor,[47] and he is the brother of Bishop O'Connor,[48] who was always a personal friend of mine. After that, I will return home via Chicago. The trip should take four weeks and cost $100. Abbot Alexius Edelbrock[49] of St. Louis Abbey is also coming to the election, after which we shall have an important visitation in order to put the new

[45] Eugene Phelan, O.S.B. (1840-1903).
[46] Louis M. Fink, O.S.B. (1834-1904).
[47] James O'Connor (1823-1890).
[48] Michael O'Connor (1810-1872), first bishop of Pittsburgh.
[49] Alexius Edelbrock, O.S.B. (1843-1908).

administration on a sound footing. The apostolic brief establishing the abbey is dated April 7, but I could not find the time to travel so far for the election until now.

I think I told you in my previous letter that I have taken over two new places in the South. One reason for this is to make room for the growing number of young Benedictines. Another reason is to help the poor bishops in this part of the country in their efforts to attend their forsaken sheep, both white and black. I was able to make a beginning in both places with only one father and three brothers. I myself went to the Diocese of Mobile in Alabama because I had to buy a parcel of land there. In order to get established, I immediately paid $3,440 for 1000 acres.

In North Carolina, we received a farm of 500 acres as a donation from an old priest,[50] on condition that we keep him there for life. After the presidential election in November, I am going there to have a look at the place and to make the necessary arrangements. There is a gold mine on the land that was worked until the discovery of gold in California. After that, the work ended. The land is not very good for agriculture. I took it for the sake of the poor Catholics. In the whole state, there are only 2,000 of them. The South itself has four million Protestants and pagan Negroes. Despite the gold mine, I will have to send my extra money there each year in order to make something out of it because the Catholics are too poor to support the Church.

In general, things at St. Vincent go satisfactorily, though we have been afflicted with much sickness and death. Since last November, four brothers were taken by death: a miller, a carpenter, a cook, and a blacksmith.[51] What is worse is that sickness took its toll among my Roman doctors. Since last spring, Prior Innocent[52] and Father James Zilliox[53] have been unable to teach, and on September 2 Father Xavier Baltes[54] died at the home of his relatives in Hastings, Minnesota, and was buried at St. Louis on the Lake. On the advice of his physician, he went to his people to recuperate and lived there for only two weeks. James went to a seaside resort near Newark and is feeling better. He is now master of novices and prefect of clerics. I sent Innocent to Kansas and from there to Colorado where he got his health back to a certain extent, but there is hardly any question of his recovering completely. As a consequence of all this, I had a very troublesome vacation

---

[50] Jeremiah J. O'Connell (1821-1888).

[51] Notker Heil, O.S.B. (1816-1875); George Held, O.S.B. (1821-1875); Godehard Nadermann, O.S.B. (1819-1876); and Corbinian Schiller, O.S.B. (1824-1876).

[52] Innocent Wolf, O.S.B. (1843-1922).

[53] James Zilliox, O.S.B. (1849-1890).

[54] Xavier Baltes, O.S.B. (1844-1876).

and had to make many changes in personnel. Often I did not know how to help myself, but despite everything, my health did not break down. The machinery is still going.

We have as many students this year as last, but this year I took in an even greater number of poor students to make sure God continues to bless us. The college building, 100 feet in length and four stories high, is almost under roof. I have made no new debts except for the purchase of land. This is a great advantage. The harvest was very good, though it came up shorter than we expected because of the terrible heat. Nonetheless, the beer did not go sour despite all the heat. We held three retreats over three weeks during the vacation so that the fathers stationed in the missions could attend. The young abbot of Minnesota[55] is a very good man, an excellent manager of money, and an excellent superior.

Who will be elected abbot in Atchison? It is a big question. I anticipate that Father Oswald[56] will receive a plurality of the votes, but because he has declared repeatedly that he will not accept, another might be elected instead, or I might have to step in and name the abbot, as I did in the election at St. Louis in Minnesota. In any case, I am very grateful to the Holy Father for responding favorably to my petition to have the priory raised to the dignity of abbey. With this, our congregation is complete and formally established. If I should be called from this world today or tomorrow, I leave everything in order–at least externally. There is more to be done internally, with regard to discipline, studies, etc.

Next year I will build a large new barn at the foot of the hill and finish the college building. Only after that can I think of building a new church, provided that God grants me life and means to do it and permits me to make use of those means. This year, only two priests were ordained. Next year, just one will be ready, but the year after that, there will be eight priests ordained and in each of the subsequent years we expect to have several ordained. This year we have five priests in the novitiate: three Irish and two Germans. I failed to mention that a pious young man, a very capable priest whom we educated from childhood, became so scrupulous that his talents were wasted. That caused me much embarrassment.

As you see, I do not lie on a bed of roses. If I did not have the disposition to take everything more or less lightly, trusting in God, it would sometimes turn out rather badly, because often disagreeable and irksome matters arise and give me no rest. I cannot thank God enough for that disposition of mind and for my bodily health, for I still feel strong in my advanced age. Generally speaking, there is nothing wrong with my health, and sometimes I feel as healthy as a child. At

---

[55] Alexius Edelbrock, O.S.B. (1843-1908).
[56] Oswald Moosmüller, O.S.B. (1832-1901).

other times, I do not feel so well. For more than a year, I have not taken beer or wine because I happened to notice that beer and wine stir up the old trouble in my chest and make it worse. I have, as usual, a good appetite and eat whatever is on the table, though I drink only water or tea or (for the last three months) lemonade. By chance, I discovered that lemonade is good medicine for angina pectoris, and it has freed me from this ailment entirely. I do not exercise very much, except in my room where after Compline, I walk up and down praying the rosary, thinking over the events of the day, preparing for the next day. It hurts my eyes when I try to read or write by lamp light. Moreover, I see much better when I do not drink beer. In any event, I see very clearly that I shall not last much longer. My end is very near.

I am sure it was my duty to be a good Benedictine. Whether I was called to propagate our Order in this country is something I am not so certain about. I know only that I felt a very strong call to do so. I think, I know, that my intention was to bring honor to our Order, to advance the greater glory of God, and to contribute to the salvation of souls. In fact, the Benedictine did not do so well. Perhaps I propagated the Order, but I did not do much more than that. For this failure, you gentlemen in Metten, my confreres, are a hundred times guilty because you should not have trusted such an important work to a reckless confrere, but rather should have done it yourselves. However, there is nothing to be done about it now. I hope you will keep me in your fervent prayers while I live and after I am dead. When the election is over, I will write you again. With a thousand greetings, your most devoted confrere, Boniface Wimmer

Ger   oAMA   cASVA   transRG

TO JAMES F. WOOD   **124**

St. Vincent, November 9, 1876

Most Reverend Archbishop: Allow me to introduce [to] Your Grace the bearer of these lines, the Rev. Innocent Wolf, D.D.,[57] my former prior here, who has had the misfortune of having lately (Sept. 29th) been elected abbot of our new abbey of St. Benedict in Atchison, Kansas. Indeed he is not yet confirmed as abbot by the Holy See; however, as his election met with no opposition, the Papal confirmation is sure. He is on his way to see some of his friends and acquaintances in the East, before he has to go West, and as he has been raised from boyhood at St.

---

[57] Innocent Wolf, O.S.B. (1843-1922).

Vincent's, and is therefore a lamb of Your Grace's flock (although he spells [his name] Wolf) and has never had the honor of getting known to you, he thought he would not leave the Archdiocese without having paid you his visit and asked and obtained your blessing.

On this occasion, I most humbly beg leave also to introduce a petition, which I hope Your Grace will not find unreasonable. A rather strange case has lately been brought before your tribunal: two Bishops fighting for a parcel of my Benedictine Sisters, each one claiming them as his own, viz., for his Diocese. Although I have no authority over our sisters, both the Rt. Rev. Prelates appealed not to my tribunal indeed, but to my judgment or sense of justice and knowledge in the matter. After I had heard the case, I decided in favor of my Rt. Rev. Ordinary, the Bishop of Allegheny,[58] and the sisters acted at once accordingly, i.e., they left East Liberty and the new Bishop of Pittsburgh[59] and returned to their own old Bishop of Allegheny. Therefore, without having [been] sued, I voluntarily plead guilt to the case.

My humble petition is now [that] Your Grace may deign to listen to me a little and to hear what I would wish to say in the matter, not as a Benedictine Abbot but as an old monk and confrere of those sisters who takes a natural interest in their temporal and spiritual welfare. I abstract entirely [from] the interior merit of the case. I stick only to that point which concerns the sisters most.

Bishop Tuigg has declared [that] if the sisters remained in his Diocese, in East Liberty, he would cut them off from all connection with the sisters in Allegheny Diocese. So I am at least informed, and I believe the information is correct.

Now the consequences of this [separation], viz., separating those five or six sisters from their superior and Motherhouse in Allegheny Diocese, would necessarily be that they would be at once constituted as a Religious family of [their] own, as a formal convent of Benedictine Nuns. As such the Bishop would either give them a Mother Superior (not local), or they would have to elect one from their own [number]. They would also at once have to open a Novitiate and also a school for Candidates. And also, if they would [constitute] a convent, they would be obliged to say the Office in the Choir. How could they do all these things? It is a sheer impossibility!

In the first place, Canon Law does not acknowledge a lot of sisters as a Religious family of its own as a Regular Convent unless they are at least 12-14 in number, because so many at least are necessary for the Choir and other religious duties in the House. Sisters in America must live either from teaching in schools or Acad-

---

[58] Michael Domenec, C.M. (1816-1878).
[59] John Tuigg (1820-1889).

emies or [from] land work if they won't starve or beg alms. Those five sisters in East Liberty could not have kept up even a common parochial school last year. Dr. Hune, their confessor and Pastor, really notified them of the necessity that they must get a good German teacher or leave. Mother Superior implored me to intervene for them at the larger convent in Erie or St. Marys to get, at least for one year, the help of a good German teacher. To avert disgrace from them, I took just in Winter the trouble to go to Erie and St. Marys, where I got and took a German Sister, able to teach, with me to East Liberty. How then could the five sisters, left to themselves, cut off like a limb from the main body of the sisterhood, keep a good school for their own candidates in the different branches, in music, needlework, etc.?

The Novitiate, and a good one indeed, is the first thing needed in every house, or there will be no discipline, no contentment, no religious life in it. The Decrees of different Popes are, therefore, [very] strict and severe with regard to the Novitiate. But what [kind of] a Novitiate could these five sisters have had if [they] were cut off? Their poor novices would even not learn [*the Rule*] and not at all practice what their *Rule* requires. This is evident, for there was no sister there who had the time or the knowledge to teach them, and religious exercises as practiced in a regular convent could not be practiced by so few sisters.

The Benedictine Sisters are bound [by] Stability, like the Fathers. They must have therefore at least some property of their own. They had nothing of that kind in East Liberty and not the slightest prospect either of getting property. For these and a good many more reasons I could easily allege, I beg Your Grace not to permit that the Benedictine Sisters be any longer kept in suspense or disturbed in the place where they are now living, in Manchester, Diocese of Allegheny, where they share a connection with their Motherhouse and [are] under their regular Mother Prioress, and are watched and cared for and assisted.

Asking your blessing and recommending myself and my large religious family to your gracious benevolence, I remain most sincerely, Your Grace's most humble servant, Boniface Wimmer, Abbot

Eng   oAAP   cASVA

TO MICHAEL REGER   **125**

St. Vincent, November 12, 1876

Right Reverend Dean, Dearest Friend: I have received the intentions and the corresponding money, i.e., 232 florins, 30 kroners for 361 intentions, and 1,096 florins, 9 kroners for 2,007 intentions, for which I cordially thank you. I will have the Masses offered as soon as possible. There are 33 priests here; therefore, satisfying the obligations will go rather quickly.

I have realized for some time that your housekeeper had something to do with the Way of the Cross. She did the right thing. One must help where one can. It always comes back to the donor. One would have to do it otherwise in any event. I am glad if the poor young girls are helped in this way, at least for a while. They cannot do very much with 200 florins.

I just returned from a three-week trip to Atchison for the election of the abbot. It did not turn out as I had expected in the choice of the Atchison prior Father Oswald Moosmüller.[60] Rather, my own prior, Father Innocent Wolf, D.D.,[61] was elected abbot. I have already received word from Rome that my request for confirmation was presented immediately to the Holy Father and that the confirmation will soon arrive here. Then I must undertake another long winter journey for the blessing.

We have been in a state of great excitement these past several weeks throughout the country over the impending presidential and state elections. At last, on November 7, the battle was fought. Since 1860, the Republicans have been at the helm and have run the country in an abominable way. They have perpetrated without punishment numerous great deceptions involving millions of dollars and have undermined the general freedom. As they caused the four-year civil war over slavery, so they would also have gladly conjured up a religious war and would have suppressed immigrant Germans and Irish. They have, however, been conquered at last. The South will be free again. The Democratic president received 300,000 more votes than the Republican candidate.[62] At St. Vincent, we gave 107 votes to the Democratic slate. The Democrats in the United States are, in fact, the true republicans, whereas the Republicans are the pseudo-republicans. Consequently, more Catholics by far are Democrats, as are my folks and myself. The election

---

[60] Oswald Moosmüller, O.S.B. (1832-1901).

[61] Innocent Wolf, O.S.B. (1843-1922).

[62] While the Democratic candidate, Samuel Tilden, did indeed receive 250,000 more popular votes than the Republican candidate Rutherford B. Hayes, the returns in several southern states were disputed and the Republican-controlled Congress declared Hayes the winner.

represents a victory of truth over deception and a victory of Catholics over the powerful sect of Methodists, to which belong President Grant and the majority of current officials and office holders. Thanks be to God.

I am not permitted to drink lemonade in winter. Neither my stomach nor my lungs can endure anything very cold. I am still free of the malady, which has weakly announced itself only a couple of times. Come mid-January I will be 68 years old. You are two years ahead of me. Our college is well attended again, but people do not want to pay, i.e., they are always deferring payment. Many are cheating me by leaving the lads here for months and then taking them home without paying. We have lost thousands of dollars in cases where people, of whom such behavior was not expected, did this.

Many greetings to my friends Leitl and Meyringer, your housekeeper, and others. Remember me. I entirely forgot your namesday. Forgive me. With heartfelt affection, your most obliged friend, Boniface Wimmer, Abbot

Ger   oASVA   transAH

TO JAMES F. WOOD   126

St. Vincent, December 29, 1876

Most Rev. and Gracious Archbishop: I know that from the very beginning the Division of the Diocese of Pittsburgh, as it has been made, found no grace with part of the Clergy of Pittsburgh for several reasons, and particularly also because Westmoreland County has been made a part of Allegheny Diocese. On the very day of the consecration of Bishop Tuigg,[63] one of the priests came out very hard against me into my face because he thought I had had something to do with the Division.

Meanwhile the agitation has been going on among the Clergy, and I am told that protests and petitions have been tendered to Your Grace to the purpose to get the Division of the Diocese so modified that Westmoreland would be dismembered from Allegheny and left with Pittsburgh.

It is not my business to meddle with such arrangements. Yet, if Priests and Pastors of Congregations as such have a right to demonstrate or petition, I presume, as a Priest and Pastor, not to trespass against modesty if I beg leave [that] Your Grace may deign to hear also my opinion in this matter.

---

[63] John Tuigg (1820-1889), third bishop of Pittsburgh.

It appears to me there is much passion, and perhaps only passion, at the bottom of the whole movement, at least as far as Westmoreland County is concerned. My name appears in the Catholic Almanac among the Counselors indeed of the Bishop, but he never has asked my advice or consulted me in any way whatever. I know nothing more of the affairs of the Diocese but what I learn from the papers or from rumor. Neither do I want or desire to know more, for I have plenty to do if I mind my own affairs as Abbot of St. Vincent and Abbot General of the Benedictine Congregation. Therefore, I have nothing at all to do with the Division of the Diocese in general or in particular.

But I confess [that] the Division, as far as Westmoreland Co. is concerned, has my fullest approval. For all the stations occupied by Benedictine Fathers in this part of Pennsylvania are in Allegheny City, in Indiana County, and in Cambria County, in the Diocese of Allegheny. There are ordinarily 6 Fathers in Allegheny City, 2 in Johnstown, 4 in Carrolltown, while one attends from St. Vincent twice a month to Saltsburg in Indiana County, and one to Bolivar and Florence. It is, therefore, a great advantage for us if the abbey also belongs to the Allegheny Diocese because very often the Fathers on the above stations get assistance from the abbey or must be exchanged vice versa, and it would be troublesome if they were not of the same diocese on account of the faculties.

But not only the abbey is benefited by this Division. It is also in the interest of the Faithful. A small river is not a practical line for a Diocese if the Catholic population is thin. If Westmoreland Co. should belong to Pittsburgh, the Northern line of the Diocese would be the Kiskiminetas and Conemaugh River, on which some small Congregations are located, which would then be divided each into two, to their great detriment, particularly Saltsburg and Blairsville, which would be entirely ruined if divided. Therefore, I never heard any complaint against the arrangement of the Diocese made by laymen. The opposition is merely on the part of the Clergy, or rather of a few priests. I considered it always as spitework [*sic*], as far as St. Vincent's Abbey and Westmoreland Co. is concerned. St. Vincent's Abbey, particularly, is in some way almost necessary for Allegheny, on account of the college, at least for some years, since the Bishop[64] has no seminary yet while the Bishop of Pittsburgh[65] has one.

Of course, I abstract entirely of the persons of the respective Rt. Rev. Bishops. I take my view of the case from the point of utility and convenience for my abbey and for the new Diocese and for the Faithful, and from this standpoint I find the arrangement well made, and in the interest of my house I would protest against

---

[64] Bishop Michael Domenec, C.M. (1816-1878), of Allegheny.
[65] Bishop John Tuigg (1820-1889) of Pittsburgh.

any contemplated alterations as detrimental to it. But, of course, I submit cheerfully, nevertheless, to the disposition the Holy Apostolic See will find proper to make.

I should by no means wish to be drawn into the feud that is going on between Pittsburgh and Allegheny, but I thought it to be just to say that much [which] I said above, when others who have no real interest in the matter at all come forward with complaints and remonstrances against a measure which has, no doubt, met first with the approval of Your Grace and has obtained the signature of the Apostolic See afterwards.

On this occasion please deign to accept my heartfelt good wishes at the turn of the year and the assurance of profound reverence, in which I sign, Your Grace's most humble servant, Bonif. Wimmer Abbot

Eng   oAAP   cASVA

TO ALEXIUS EDELBROCK   127

St. Vincent, January 4, 1877

Right Reverend Father Abbot, Dearest Confrere: Thank you very much for the congratulations you sent me in your letter of November 20. I know from experience that congratulations that come from a sincere heart are as great a profit for the one who extends them as for the one who receives them. In a few days, I will be 68 years old. Thanks be to God! Like autumn in the cycle of the year, so is old age the most beautiful time in life! The young ones do not want to believe this, and yet it is true. In growing white, one also grows wise, or at least wiser than one was. I am glad the hot season of my life has passed. I would not want to go through it again even if I could. A burnt child, you see, shuns the fire!

When I think of the past, I do not know whether to laugh or to weep. I think I might do both, depending on the moment and circumstances. It may well be that I had the vocation to bring the Benedictine Order over here; otherwise, I could not have done it. This is a great grace. But! But! But! In this case, laughing and weeping are very close akin. In many cases, I do not see the spirit of the Order, nor genuine love for the Order, nor zeal for the honor of the Order, and this moral defect will be reckoned to my account! ("The abbot must, therefore, be aware that the shepherd will bear the blame wherever the father of the household finds that the sheep have yielded no profit."[66]) At least a great part.

---

[66] *Rule of St. Benedict*, 2: 7.

Prairie du Chien [Wisconsin] was first offered to me. I did not want it and could not accept it. I consoled the bishop[67] with "perhaps in two years." Then he approached you. For you, it is a fitting place, but a hard place—Frenchmen, Irishmen, Germans, Bohemians. I doubt that your Father Anton[68] is the right man for prior, unless he has entirely changed. I hear that Lawler[69] is very capricious and makes high demands on priests and professors because he himself is a scholar. There should be no scandals, especially not in the beginning. I could acquire a college in California for $20,000, possibly for $15,000 or even for $12,000. It can accommodate 200 students, and 30 thirty acres of the very best land belong to it. I would buy it if I had the money.

As for Father Bruno,[70] I do not know of any place here, but I will take him home if you cannot make use of him any longer. Maybe he would be welcome in Kansas. Yesterday Father Eugene[71] came with the complaint that Father Oswald[72] recalled his Father Placid[73] because you recalled your Father Boniface.[74] Father Eugene cannot do without Father Placid until Father Anselm Harrison[75] has made profession (on February 2) and then only with difficulty. Please write Abbot Innocent[76] and ask if he will take Bruno for Boniface so that Placid can stay in Creston. Then three priests will be there.

The confirmation for Abbot Wolf arrived here on December 18. Last week he traveled from here to Chicago in order to go to Atchison from there because Father Oswald wants to go home. Bishop Fink[77] gave him a crosier, a ring, a pectoral cross, and a miter. I gave him shoes and $100. Dalmatics, etc., will come from the sisters and others. Father Oswald accomplished this at least: in the financial statement, a balance has been achieved. He even has $100 more income than expenses. The blessing will not take place before April, probably April 22.

I had to take over Elizabeth City [New Jersey] recently in order to free Father Henry[78] from the pastorate. He wants to retire and he should. Father Athanasius[79]

---

[67] Francis X. Krautbauer (1824-1885) of Green Bay, Wisconsin.
[68] Anton Capser, O.S.B. (1841-1898).
[69] Unidentified.
[70] Bruno Riess, O.S.B. (1829-1900).
[71] Eugene Phelan, O.S.B. (1840-1903).
[72] Oswald Moosmüller, O.S.B. (1832-1901).
[73] Placid McKeever, O.S.B. (1840-1896).
[74] Boniface Moll, O.S.B. (1840-1910).
[75] A diocesan priest in the novitiate at St. Vincent.
[76] Innocent Wolf, O.S.B. (1843-1922).
[77] Louis M. Fink, O.S.B. (1850-1912), of Leavenworth, Kansas.
[78] Peter Henry Lemke, O.S.B. (1796-1882).
[79] Athanasius Hintenach, O.S.B. (1838-1923).

relieved him. This happened at a bad time for me because there are many debts and sisters. After the feast, I wish you much luck and prosperity for very many years! Let us pray for one another daily and ardently, especially at the altar. With most sincere love and esteem, I am your most devoted confrere, Boniface Wimmer

Ger   oASJA   cASVA   trans AHo

TO RUPERT SEIDENBUSCH   128

St. Vincent, January 14, 1877

Most Reverend and Dear Bishop, My Lord: You are a little late, my Lord. It is not the 68th but the 69th birthday I celebrate today, for I have now completed 68 years and am entering my 69th. *Deo gratias!* It is a great blessing to grow old. I am pretty well still; indeed my health is better than it was years ago. By abstaining from beer, wine, strong coffee and teas, and using instead only weak tea and in summer lemonade, I have lost that suspicious pain I used to feel over my heart.

My stomach has also improved considerably and has lost the sensation of cold. My eyes are much better again. In short, my general state of health has improved to my advantage, but there is still an infirmity there that is rather annoying and that I knew nothing of, or only a little, in my younger days. It is the exercise or practice of patience—or rather the occasion for it.

I do not like to travel any more unless duty or necessity calls for it, and I will not see Rome any more unless I am called (God willing) for the continuation of the Council. For you, of course, it would be of interest to go there and see our great good Pius.[80]

Abbot Innocent[81] received his confirmation on December 18 and left soon afterward for Chicago and Atchison. Father Oswald[82] goes home and then will likely have to go to Savannah where Bishop Gross[83] wants me to accept 865 acres of land some miles from Savannah, but in a very healthy location, for a Benedictine establishment.

---

[80] Pope Pius IX (1792-1878).
[81] Innocent Wolf, O.S.B. (1843-1922).
[82] Oswald Moosmüller, O.S.B. (1832-1901).
[83] William H. Gross, C.Ss.R. (1837-1898), bishop of Savannah.

All fall and winter, I intended to go to North Carolina, but the trip did not material-ize. I am glad about it now. Father Herman[84] writes that they have had plenty of snow and cold there, just as we have had here. In the spring, I must go to Kansas. The blessing of Abbot Innocent will take place on the feast of St. Joseph.[85] Bishop Fink[86] found a miter, ring, and crosier for the abbot. I found shoes and a few other things. I also gave him $100 more income than expenses for last year! They have only $58,000 in debts!

Father Henry[87] wanted to retire and offered his resignation to the bishop,[88] who gladly ac-cepted it and prevailed upon me to take the place. I did so ad interim and sent Father Athanasius[89] to take it. Father Henry was sorry that he had resigned, but the bishop took him at his word and so he moves away on January 17 for Carrolltown or St. Vincent–I do not know which. We have plenty of students here but little money.

Father Herman Wolfe, O.S.B. (1816-1884), a convert from Lutheranism and a veteran of the Confederate Army, became the first prior of Maryhelp Priory (later Belmont Abbey) in North Carolina.

I feel my end rapidly approaching. The past often appears to me like a dream. Sometimes I feel like Adam before Eve was made. I see nobody like me. I am sur-rounded only by young folk. I am like an old tree in the middle of young under-wood. I am much alone, all the time at home. Writing and answering letters are my chief occupations, yet I participate regularly in the choir, etc. All seem to live in good harmony, and recreation is often lively. Nobody gives me much trouble. All seem to regard me, but they do not approach me very often. In many ways, I consider myself happy, more happy by far than I could ever expect. There are disappointments, of course, but I have it so good that I often apprehend great troubles or calamities ahead because I have so little to suffer. Some years ago,

---

[84] Herman Wolfe, O.S.B. (1816-1884).
[85] March 19.
[86] Louis M. Fink, O.S.B. (1834-1904), bishop of Leavenworth.
[87] Peter Henry Lemke, O.S.B. (1796-1882).
[88] Michael A. Corrigan (1839-1902), bishop of Newark.
[89] Athanasius Hintenach, O.S.B. (1838-1923).

we had our hardships, our trials, our difficulties, but we did not mind. Except for a few cases and a few people, though, I never had much to complain about; and where are those who were not sincere, not true to our work? They were not blessed. As for the rest, faults were committed both inside and outside the walls and then made good again, and each of us both receives and commits faults.

Your record stands well with me. You have deserved what you are, and I am heartily glad of it. I, too, was upright and true toward you (and indeed toward all). I know well that the success of our enterprise has been largely because of you. May God grant you many years and all the blessings necessary and useful for your apostolic office and career. My warmest thanks to you for your good wishes. All I wish for is a happy end after a perilous and agitated life. With sincere and profound reverence, I remain Your Lordship's affectionate father, brother, and son, B. Wimmer

Ger   oASJA   cASVA   transAHo

TO UTTO LANG   129

St. Vincent, February 1877

Right Reverend Father Abbot, Esteemed Confrere: In the event that you have some stipends to spare, please send some to me. We have 36 priests, six of whom are priest novices: one for the Irish priory in Creston, Iowa, three for St. Louis on the Lake Abbey in Minnesota, and two for St. Vincent. Mr. Lebling[90] continues to handle my business affairs.

The new and first abbot of Atchison[91] left us just before the New Year to take possession of his abbey. The same thing that happened to Your Grace on the feast last September happened to him. His farewell was something not to be forgotten. He wept like a child. He came to our place as a boy of ten. He is really an offspring of our monastery, related to and intermingled with everybody in the house. He must leave us now to establish his home far away from here and to take upon himself, under very great difficulties, all the responsibility of administration. He is not even in good health and is subject to a throat condition that is not without danger. I, myself, was very much affected by his departure because he has a special knowledge of theology, because he possesses a deep religious spirit, and because he gave me much helpful assistance. On his journey, he paid a visit to his mother

---

[90] Louis Ignatius Lebling, treasurer of the *Ludwig Missionsverein*.
[91] Innocent Wolf, O.S.B. (1843-1922).

and brothers in Chicago. He arrived in Atchison on January 8. We received the confirmation of his election from Rome only on December 18. Thus, it is in bidding farewell to this world. Only the tomb remains for me.

I am glad that Atchison is now organized on a solid foundation. It will certainly be an important place, a starting point for the Benedictines in the Southwest. I feel certain that Abbot Innocent is the right man in the right place, and I have the sincere hope that God will give him good health. He combines many impressive characteristics in his person.

We had a very severe winter and have never before had so much snow as we had this year, although by last week, the ice had melted and the deepest snow had gone so that we could use the sled. Because of the weather, I could not go to North Carolina as I had intended. I had to postpone the trip for an indefinite period because next spring (April 22) I have to be present for the abbatial blessing in Atchison.

Like you, I am extremely grateful for the age I have reached. I am now in my 69th year, but I have no rest and there is no standing still for me. Under current conditions, there is always more work. For us, it is a time of growth, of development. Even if I do not know where to put them, I must take in as many candidates as I can find lodging and food for in order to be able to use them when necessity requires. Either I will make use of them or my successor will. That is clearly understood here. We do not ask for priests simply to continue what we are doing. We feel the need to expand and, therefore, take in as many as apply. (Naturally, we do not take those who are unfit.) That is the reason I never get any rest. Something new is always turning up. We are not unlike speculators who have good luck and see their assets swell. Speculators, however, work because of greed and selfishness. We work because of our zeal for the greater honor of God and of our Order.

Unfortunately, things are not proceeding quickly enough. One has to overcome many obstacles and often we do not have enough people or material resources. One also often finds himself deceived and cheated, so one needs much patience in order to avoid a bad or hot temper. We disagree with the old saying "one needs manure, not prayer." In our case we say, "Instead of manure, let us pray."

Rumor has it that Father Celestine[92] will not accept the episcopacy. Who can blame him? Being a bishop in Bavaria at the present time cannot be very pleasant. Still, I thought he should have accepted, even if he had good reason to refuse. Catholicism's struggle is just beginning. The Italians are now showing their true colors. We have to prepare for the worst, as the venerable Sister Rosa de Foggia

---

[92] Celestine Feiner, O.S.B. (1818-1887), of Metten.

has prophesied. I am afraid that the Holy Father will experience many unhappy events, which are still in store for him.

I just received a couple of weeks ago the protocol you mentioned in your letter. We are all satisfied with it. It is much easier to collect the German material for the Album[93] in Germany than here. As for the printing, we will have no difficulty whatsoever in doing it here. We can get the information regarding the Benedictines in America, Australia, and Brazil. With regard to those in England, the current prior of Erdington, Father Placidus Wolter,[94] is the best person to collect the information. Abbot Maurus Wolter[95] has contacts with the French and is in the best position to provide an accurate report about the French monasteries and the new congregations. However, before anything is done, it is absolutely necessary that the abbots form a committee that, like a central organization, has full authority in the matter. Otherwise, we cannot expect success. I took the advice of the committee we have established here and will send over the printed results to the 14 abbots in session at Salzburg, as well as to the others, as soon as possible. We feel very happy that our proposal has met with approval and has awakened enthusiastic interest. There are enough capable men in our Order to ensure that something worthwhile will come of the proposal, provided our "forces" are properly organized. If others help with collecting the information, I will have time to undertake the printing, after I have accomplished the great undertaking of printing all or most of the immortal work on the Bible by Father Peter Lechner.[96]

With regard to the Lechner Bible, I need your expert knowledge and advice. I want to print the Latin text on one page and the German translation on the other. Father Peter's commentary will be below the Latin and German texts. Since he, himself, did not do a German translation, I want to reprint the one by Allioli because it has the *imprimatur*, but I have serious doubts about whether I can do this without permission from the publishers. Do I have to purchase the right to reprint the Allioli translation? As you know, at least three different publishers printed the Allioli Bible. May I ask you for an authoritative response to this inquiry at your earliest convenience? Father Peter's work is not intended for lay people but rather for scholars, i.e., those versed in Latin, Greek, and some Hebrew. For

---

[93] The second edition of the *Album Benedictinum*, which was published at St. Vincent in 1880.

[94] Placidus Wolter, O.S.B. (1828-1908).

[95] Maurus Wolter, O.S.B. (1825-1890), abbot of Beuron.

[96] Peter Lechner, O.S.B. (1805-1874). Wimmer refers to Peter Lechner's commentaries on the Old and New Testaments, published at Saint Vincent between 1881 and 1884. *Die Heilige Schrift des Neuen Testamentes nach der Vulgata und dem Grundtext erklärt* (Beatty, Pa.: St. Vincent Press, 1881); and *Die Heilige Schrift des Alten Testamentes, nach der Vulgata und dem Grund text erklärt* (Beatty, Pa.: St. Vincent Press, 1882-1884).

that reason, it will not sell well. Still, it has the *imprimatur* of an archbishop and is an outstanding scholarly work. We will begin with the New Testament within the next few weeks. It has already been redrafted by hand. The edition will be very beautiful. I have bought new Greek type and excellent paper for it. If God preserves my life, I will see it through to the end.

Our Bishop Fink[97] has given the new abbot[98] an *infula*, a ring, a crosier, and a pectoral cross. I myself gave him the abbatial vestments: sandals, mantelet, rochette, and chain. I also gave him $180, and the priories gave him another $160. Benziger Brothers have donated the pontificals. His blessing will be a fashionable Benedictine feast.

Our chaotic political situation turned out in the end to be more peaceful than expected. My health is fairly good. It is enough that I am alive, but with regard to drink, I can have no water, no beer, no wine. Only tea. That's all. Our financial condition could be better. People are not paying money anywhere, but, nonetheless, I am holding on. We have just as many students as before. Otherwise, I have nothing to report except that Bishop O'Connor[99] of Omaha very much wants a Benedictine monastery in his diocese in Nebraska. For the moment, I cannot comply with his wishes because I have no people to send.

How is my good old Father Xavier?[100] I have heard nothing about him. My musicians are half crazy about their chant and often make me angry with "nothing else but chant." They are like our teetotalers, i.e., throwing out the baby with the bath water. I think I should stop now. *Ne quid nimis. Vale et Dominus tecum.*
Boniface Wimmer

Ger   oAMA   cASVA   transRG

TO BENEDICTINE ABBOTS   130

St. Vincent February 8, 1877

Right Reverend and Distinguished Lord Abbot: The letter[101] we recently sent to all the abbots and prelates of the Benedictine Order, in which we proposed a celebration in honor of our most Holy Father Benedict, was warmly received and ap-

---

[97] Louis M. Fink, O.S.B. (1834-1904), bishop of Leavenworth.
[98] Abbot Innocent Wolf, O.S.B. (1843-1922), of St. Benedict Abbey, Atchison, Kansas.
[99] James O'Connor (1823-1890).
[100] Francis Xavier Sulzbeck, O.S.B. (1807-1881), prior of Metten.
[101] See Wimmer's letter to the world's Benedictine prelates and abbots (May 1, 1876), page 392.

plauded by many. Indeed, all the responses we have received clearly demonstrate that the right reverend abbots of our Benedictine monasteries are entirely in favor of our proposal and are delighted to assist in the effort to worthily celebrate the centennial of our holy father.

Among those who have joyfully approved of our proposal are the right reverend abbots of Austria and Bavaria. These abbots, who have, in fact, already taken the first steps to mark the centennial, not only honored our undertaking with words of praise but also made some suggestions of their own that elicited our immediate approval.

A few months ago, when these right reverend prelates gathered in Salzburg for the consecration of the new archbishop, they took advantage of the occasion to discuss how the celebration of the centennial ought to proceed and came to some conclusions that they reported to me in a letter of October 24, 1876. After praising the suggestions we had made, they said that in their opinion the principal place for undertaking the celebration should be in Europe where, after all, the roots of our holy Order are found. Likewise, they said that in their opinion it was more desirable that the Benedictine Album suggested by us in our earlier letter be published either by Frederick Pustet in Regensburg or by Benziger under the auspices of the monks of Einsiedeln. We are extremely pleased by these suggestions and gladly give our support to them.

Since the suggestions we made in our previous letter seem to have been generally accepted by all, we have decided to test the good will of the distinguished prelates once again, and in light of the suggestions made by the Austrian and Bavarian abbots, we earnestly and respectfully propose that the administration of the centennial celebration be handed over to the right reverend abbots of Europe, who will receive all the necessary support from the rest of us. Moreover, we suggest that a committee be established, made up of European abbots known for their wisdom and prudence, and that this committee oversee all aspects of the celebration of the feast of our great patriarch.

In addition, if we might be permitted to suggest something further, we propose that the right reverend archabbot[102] of St. Martin's Archabbey, Pannonhalma, Hungary, who is well known for his devotion to our Holy Father Benedict, be named chairman of this committee, and that he be assisted in his work by Right Reverend Gunther John Kalivoda[103] of the Austrian abbey of Raigern in Moravia, who has proven himself to be an especially energetic and eager supporter and champion of this project.

---

[102] Chrysostom Kruesz, O.S.B. (b. 1819).
[103] Gunther John Kalivoda, O.S.B. (1842-1928)

When these two venerable abbots have discussed the matter between themselves, they will then invite and choose certain other abbots, however many in their prudent judgment might be needed, to participate in the management of the celebration. It seems to us extremely important that this select committee of a few abbots take immediate charge of the celebration and begin in such a way as to ensure a happy outcome. Finally, we think it important that the right reverend members of the committee ask His Eminence John Cardinal Pitra[104] to be the patron of the entire enterprise.

These, then, are the matters that we believe must be taken up by the right reverend abbots. Nothing remains except to ask your careful consideration of our proposals. Your Grace's humble servant, Boniface Wimmer, O.S.B., Abbot of St. Vincent and President of the American Cassinese Congregation.

Lat   oASVA   transJO

TO GREGORY SCHERR   131

Newark, February 25, 1877

Most Reverend Archbishop, Your Grace: As your holy namesday approaches, I must not and cannot forget you, for you are among those whom I remember with love and happiness and gratitude. First, I thank God with all my heart that you are still alive and, as I hope, in the best of health and as full of good cheer as advanced age, with all its demands, permits. May the Lord be pleased to grant you the age of our Holy Father[105] so that after all the years of worry and trouble you may see and enjoy days of gladness and peace.

There is no doubt that the struggle against the Church and divine institutions caused by non-Christian cultural forces cannot last much longer. As Bishop Wittmann[106] of happy memory predicted, the purgation process will take a long time and only after it is completed will the body become healthy again.

Your Excellency has already passed 70 years. I myself am still in my 60s. A few months ago, I was 68. My Father Henry[107] is already 80. A short time ago, he built a small Irish parish in Elizabeth City about five miles from here. Because he could

---

[104] Cardinal Jean Baptiste Pitra, O.S.B. (1812-1889).

[105] Pope Pius IX (1792-1878) was eighty-five years old.

[106] George Michael Wittmann (1760-1833), bishop of Regensburg.

[107] Peter Henry Lemke, O.S.B. (1796-1882).

not work any longer, the bishop[108] hinted that I should recall him and take on the parish myself. This I did, sending Father Athanasius[109] to Elizabeth City and recalling Father Henry. I am here in Newark in order to get more information about the place, to clear up some debts, and to collect tuition due to us. Money is very scarce. I have six fathers here who conduct a preparatory school, which this year has 40 students who pay $60 a year and five who pay nothing at all. My priests are taking care of the German parishes in the city and attending one rural parish on Sundays. It is not good for the monastic life that most of our priests are engaged in pastoral work, but it has to be this way since the bishops are in need of priests and prefer those from religious orders. Besides, we have to make our living.

At present, we have 76 priests, though only 26 are living at St. Vincent. All the others are assigned to stations along the Atlantic coast from New Jersey to Florida, in virtually every state. You will find my people in Delaware, Maryland, Virginia, North Carolina, and Georgia (though not in South Carolina). They are also in Alabama. It is very consoling to know that in some cases these small places, where at the beginning only two fathers are assigned, will become important fortresses and centers for the expansion of our Catholic religion. In the southern states, the Catholic religion is represented by a very small group of Christians. There is often not one Catholic among a thousand inhabitants. For that reason, these states have no more than eight or ten priests each. Half the population is Negro, and these people have been brutalized with respect to religion. One finds plenty to do there. All my people have to support themselves, at least at the beginning and for several years afterward, but it seems predestined for our Order to convert the heretics and the pagan Negroes in this part of the country. We most earnestly want to respond when called upon by the bishops.

I have 40 clerics and 12 novices at home. Next year, I shall have 18 novices. We have 116 scholastics in the college and 200 students. It is naturally a great burden to take care of so many people, even though the burden is divided among various people. The college and scholasticate each has its own director, and the directors are assisted by two priests and by clerics who serve as prefects. Father James Zilliox[110] is master of novices and prefect of clerics. His companion, Father Xavier,[111] I regret to say, died last summer.

If nothing is achieved with these young people, it will not be our fault. We offer them the best possible education and training. I have made more additions to the

---

[108] Michael A. Corrigan (1839-1902), bishop of Newark (1873-1880).
[109] Athanasius Hintenach, O.S.B. (1838-1923).
[110] James Zilliox, O.S.B. (1849-1890).
[111] Xavier Baltes, O.S.B. (1844-1876).

college building, but still it is not enough. In order to complete the work, I must build a much larger building. God never deserts me. I always find the necessary means, which is something miraculous because the expenses are enormous. There is no doubt about it. God intends to do something extraordinary here with our Order.

Abbot Marty[112] of St. Meinrad Abbey in the state of Indiana, Diocese of Vincennes, (which was founded from Einsiedeln) has been working since last September with a father and a brother among the wild Indians far up on the Missouri River. Father Isidore Robot[113] from the French monastery of Pierre-qui-Vire has been appointed apostolic prefect for the Indians living in the Indian Territory between Kansas and Texas. Many of these Indians have already tasted civilization, and in addition to converting some, he has the task of keeping many in the faith. About 5,000 of them became Catholics in earlier times but have been without a priest for many years. Our three abbeys–St. Vincent, St. Louis (in Minnesota), and St. Benedict (in Kansas)–have taken care of the Germans up until now. They have educated hundreds of priests for the spiritual welfare of the Germans and have done pastoral work for Germans in far-flung places (without neglecting the English-speaking people). Now, because there are enough priests to do the job and because the field of education is adequately attended to, I feel obliged to turn to the South where Protestantism, with its hundred sects, has not been aggressively challenged and where the Negroes, many of whom are in the fullest sense pagan, must be converted.

As a rule, I can count on eight or ten new priests each year. I have to put them to work, and the only field, or the easiest to find, is the South. I repeat, I must act because our Order is still growing. To hold it back is to kill it. I really do not know where to place all my people, but I do not care. I take in everyone who asks to be received, everyone who seems to have a vocation, as many as I am able to house. I educate them in the best possible way–for the care of souls, to teach in schools, or to dedicate themselves to the missions in accordance with their talents and abilities. I am convinced that they will find a field for their work here or there. I have a vision that not a few of them will establish monasteries because it is my firm belief that Protestantism will fall into ruins and that its better part will be converted in great numbers by means of our Order, just as Arianism was defeated in Spain and southern Germany through the efforts of the Benedictines.

In any event, that is the reason I was sent by Your Excellency and by the Mission Society to America, and for 20 long years I have worked to transplant the Order

---

[112] Martin Marty, O.S.B. (1834-1896).
[113] Isidore Robot, O.S.B. (1837-1887).

to this country and to educate priests for the Germans. I have done it, I am still doing it, and I shall continue to do it as long as I live. My successors will have to do the same because it is absolutely necessary for the existence and propagation of our Order. Without question, it is divine providence that calls us to bring the most prudent and wise plans to fruition.

Personally, I cannot do much any more. I feel my age very much. Traveling, even traveling by railroad, exhausts me. The extensive correspondence and constant worries tire me. My body and mind long for rest, but in vain. I do not make plans any more. I see clearly the work I must do, though I keep wondering why God has given it to me. I am often afraid that the work is beyond my abilities. I do what is necessary but get no satisfaction from it. I think that God has chosen a foolish and weak person, but what can I do? Still, it is my work and I cannot neglect it. I have to keep going, as well as I can. My only consolation is that those who benefit from our work offer many prayers for me.

Please excuse all this nonsense. I must, however, tell you about the prospects and efforts of our Order because I know that you want to hear about anything that brings honor to our calling, just as I myself am always ready to seek its praise and glory, even it if might seem that I am seeking my own praise and glory. However, that is not the case. Still, I can boast that no one surpasses me in love and zeal for our holy Order.

Wishing you all happiness and health, and asking for your blessings for my dear St. Vincent, I remain with deepest respect, as ever, Your Excellency's most grateful and devoted, Boniface Wimmer

Ger   oAMA   cASVA   transRG

TO UTTO LANG 132

St. Vincent, April 4, 1877

Right Reverend Father Abbot, Most Esteemed Confrere: Many thanks for the 2,100 intentions, for which I received yesterday, through the kindness of Mr. Lebling,[114] exactly 1,860 marks and 90 pfennigs. Likewise, I send sincere thanks for the information about the printing of the Bible, even though it is not altogether clear what we should do since here in America a copy is not legally considered a reproduction. In any event, I do not want to reproduce the text in exactly the

---

[114] Louis Ignatius Lebling, treasurer of the *Ludwig Missionsverein*.

same manner as it was published in Germany. At least, now I know what direction I have to go.

With regard to the centenary celebration, I have heard nothing from Montecassino except that we made a great mistake by proposing Cardinal Pitra[115] as patron without first asking him if he was willing to accept the honor. Perhaps it was too presumptuous on my part. According to the rumors I heard, it seems that a certain amount of "deal-making" resulted in Cardinal Bartolini's[116] being appointed Protector of the Order of Saint Benedict instead of Cardinal Pitra.

At the urging of Prior Boniface Krug,[117] Montecassino is preparing for the centenary celebration by restoring the tower in which St. Benedict lived, as well as the crypt. The restoration has begun and will cost $50,000. It will be done in accordance with the designs of the artists from Beuron who had worked there earlier. They expect to raise the money abroad from us abbots, but whether or not we will be able to collect so much is still to be determined. I sent a few hundred dollars immediately and have promised at least a thousand, but I am not able to give more until times are better. The college has not been bringing in much money lately. People are not paying their debts, especially the bishops, who are the worst when it comes to meeting their obligations. Not all of them, but a few.

Father Henry Lemke,[118] who is 80 years old, finally returned to the monastery. To help him, I had to take over his parish, which is five miles from Newark, by sending a younger father there. Father Henry has been here for a few months and seems satisfied.

Father Oswald[119] and his companion, Father Maurice Kaeder,[120] do not have an easy job in Georgia. Their efforts to convert the Negroes, a difficult task in itself, are made even more difficult by the opposition of different Protestant sects. Father Maurice is an excellent preacher and lecturer in English. He tends not to neglect the white people. Fathers Oswald and Maurice have no income and depend entirely on St. Vincent. This is not a profitable business for me, but we do the work on the one hand because of pity for these entirely neglected Negroes and on the other hand because of the need to find new fields of activity for my young people. We must spread out and expand in the South, where there are very few Catholics. Indeed, this region, which has no more than one Catholic for every thou-

---

[115] Cardinal John Baptist Pitra, O.S.B. (1812-1889).
[116] Cardinal Dominic Bartolini (1813-1887).
[117] Boniface Krug, O.S.B. (1838-1909), prior and later archabbot of Montecassino.
[118] Peter Henry Lemke, O.S.B. (1796-1882).
[119] Oswald Moosmüller, O.S.B. (1932-1901).
[120] Maurice Kaeder, O.S.B. (1837-1892).

*Br. Rhabanus Conoge,
O.S.B., the first African-
American Benedictine
in the United States.*

sand people, must be our new field of labor. I am confident that within a short time we will have Negro Benedictines, male and female. Already we have one Negro brother. Divine providence is urgently calling us to live and work in this mission field among pagans, quasi pagans, and Protestants of various sects. We are being called whether we want to respond or not. So naturally, you see, we have no choice but to respond.

How wonderful! I am staggered with dizziness. I am too glad to do it and would like to do even more for the salvation of souls, the honor of God, and the propagation of our holy Order. However, I am old, weak, and near death. I do not know how to govern my monastery, how to supervise and direct so many of my priests who are stationed away from the monastery. I do not have to worry about Minnesota and Kansas any more, of course, since they are both abbeys now; but St. Vincent forms an axis from which we are spreading 500 miles east and west and a thousand miles south. I must even turn west again. Five thousand Bohemians are waiting for a Bohemian priest in Nebraska. I will send them one, and he will have to select a place for a real monastery. That is the desire of the bishop of Omaha, James O'Connor,[121] and I have promised to help him. He attended the blessing of the abbot[122] in Atchison with Bishop Hogan[123] of St. Joseph, Missouri, and Bishop Seidenbusch.[124] Bishop Fink[125] of Leavenworth presided at the blessing. Nothing like it has ever occurred in America before. Present were two Carmelites (originally from Straubingen), a Jesuit superior, three vicars general, and 30 secular priests. Thanks be to God a thousand times that, externally, all is well, though internally I fear that I am not fit for the task. God will help me. Like everyone else, I carry too many heavy burdens, but I depend entirely on the help and protection

---

[121] James O'Connor (1823-1890).
[122] Innocent Wolf, O.S.B. (1843-1922).
[123] John J. Hogan (1829-1913), first bishop of St. Joseph, Missouri (1868-1880), and first bishop of Kansas City (1880-1913).
[124] Rupert Seidenbusch, O.S.B. (1830-1895), bishop of northern Minnesota.
[125] Louis M. Fink, O.S.B. (1834-1904).

of God and on the prayers of my friends. I am grateful to them for all the success we have experienced. With sincere affection and deep respect, I am Your Grace's most grateful confrere, Boniface Wimmer.

P.S. Bishop Seidenbusch is going to Europe this month. It seems that Abbot Alexius[126] will go with him. I am glad I am at home. Unless there is real need, I do not intend to cross the ocean any more. Greetings to Prior Placid, Father Xavier, Father Fortunatus, and Father Willibald.[127]

Ger   oAMA   cASVA   transRG

TO GREGORY SCHERR   133

St. Vincent, August 27, 1877

Most Reverend and Gracious Lord Archbishop: On August 18, Abbot Alexius Edelbrock[128] arrived in Newark. He was here on August 23, but he remained only two days so that he could return to his monastery as soon as possible. I expected a packet of letters, but he arrived with only a bushel of greetings.

I am very happy that the vacation is over because almost all the fathers went to the priories or to our villa in the nearby mountains for vacation and left more work for me. I had my vacation in the spring, in April and May. For four weeks, I made the longest trip I have ever made through the entire South. We have three new stations in the dioceses of Mobile, Savannah, and Wilmington (in the states of Alabama, Georgia, and North Carolina). I wanted to visit them so that I could see personally what to expect and what to do for them. Even though we traveled by train, the journey was very tiring, but it was a good trip and gave me much satisfaction. The stations will be quite a burden on St. Vincent for many years, but they open a wide field for the Order and promise rich results. With God's help, I expect to be able to take care of their expenses until the stations need more priests, rather than more money, and we ourselves will prepare the priests. Last year, I had only four new priests ordained, and this year only three were added to our number; but next year, God willing, eight will be ordained, and then for a number of years we will have the same number or more.

---

[126] Alexius Edelbrock, O.S.B. (1843-1908).
[127] All monks of Metten and former confreres of Abbot Boniface. Placid Lacense, O.S.B. (1802-1887), Francis Xavier Sulzbeck, O.S.B. (1807-1881), Fortunatus Braun, O.S.B. (1806-1893), and Willibald Freymüller, O.S.B. (1807-1890).
[128] Alexius Edelbrock, O.S.B. (1843-1908).

In Savannah, Father Oswald[129] has undertaken the work of establishing an institution for the conversion of Negroes. He had many difficulties to overcome because the Negroes on the island where he planned to erect the institution were mostly bigoted, ignorant Methodists and Baptists. He succeeded, however, in building a large house with the help of the Negroes, and he has one Negro cook already and another as a student. Bishop Gross[130] gave us 800 acres of excellent land on the island. The institution, as well as the people living in it, will be supported from the produce of this land. I hope this can be done. Our plan is for the young Negroes to work for their own support. This was the plan I had for St. Vincent (but with whites), though in smaller measure, i.e.,

Father Maurice Kaeder, O.S.B. (1837-1898), a renowned preacher and musician, was an early Benedictine missionary in Georgia.

with the scholastics, but it was not possible to carry it out. I take great pleasure in this institution for the Negroes. It is, of course, only a small beginning, but with God's blessing, we will accomplish much good.

Since February, the station in Georgia has cost me $1,000, but now Father Oswald has gathered in the harvest, and he recently wrote that he is able to get along without extra help. He has another priest with him now, Father Maurice Kaeder.[131] Father Maurice is a traveling missionary, as were the wandering bishops of old. He goes everywhere, to any place that does not have a pastor (there are only a dozen priests in the entire diocese of one million people) to seek the scattered sheep, to support them, and to convert Protestants. He gives lectures on religious truths, which are attended by the most renowned people. He is a very talented man, a good theologian, and an extraordinary preacher, a Rheno-Prussian educated at St. Vincent. There are good prospects for him to make a number of conquests for the Church, especially in the small town of Thomasville where in the July heat of 105 degrees he delivered three lectures in the town hall. The entire class of better citizens of this town filled the auditorium, and there were

---

[129] Oswald Moosmüller, O.S.B. (1832-1901).
[130] William H. Gross, C.Ss.R. (1837-1898), bishop of Savannah (1873-1885).
[131] Maurice Kaeder, O.S.B. (1837-1892).

many requests afterwards for catechisms. In this manner, we plan to attack the devil in his own realm. In the southern states, there is hardly one Catholic among a hundred souls. I have plenty of plans, but until now, I could not realize even one because I was called to help in the North too often. Naturally, everything depends on the grace of God, who must provide the right people and right means, and must point out the proper circumstances. Everything has arranged itself properly without my searching for it.

The work, however, is becoming too difficult and too much for me to cope with. The years are weighing heavily on me. In general, I am well, perhaps even better than before. My chest pain is gone. I felt it only twice in the last year. However, my strength is no longer there. I am dead tired by the time I have prayed Matins, offered Mass, made meditation, prayed Prime, and drunk my cup of coffee. After the mid-day meal, I have to take a nap. My appetite is good, but I drink only tea and only at table. If I go outdoors in the summer, I perspire too much, so I seldom go outdoors. I do not enjoy riding either, and I have done so only twice in 15 years. I take my exercise after Compline, from 8:00 to 9:00 pm in my room, where I pray, make plans, examine my conscience, and so forth, and thank God a thousand times for having led me so graciously, borne with me so patiently, and supported me so faithfully. If I write of my accomplishments, I do not do so out of pride. I know and confess that it is the greatest miracle that any good at all has happened through me. Nevertheless, it has happened, and if I am so blessed that our college has become a kind of small *"Propaganda Fide"* for spreading the Benedictine Order, and does so, it is also the will of God. It is a special grace of God.

These days I count 46 scholastics, whom we feed and clothe entirely *gratis*. Before the year is half over, we will have 50 more. The other 100 students pay something, but not much. Add to that 40 or 50 clerics and novices, 25 priests, 78 brothers, 50 workmen, poor travelers and friends, the new institutions, and the continuous building. Yet, we have enough. I promised and have already given $1,000 to Montecassino for the restoration of the tower of our Holy Father Benedict. I could have used the money myself for Kansas and elsewhere, but thought, "The poor you will always have among you." St. Benedict can find the money when I need it, and this happens often enough.

Perhaps I have gossiped too much, although I am convinced that Your Excellency is pleased at all times to hear from me. I really did not want so much to give information as to make a request. My Mass stipends are running out, and I would like to ask for more, if your diocese has some on hand and can spare them. With 30 kreuzers, one cannot jump very far here, but many of them soon amount to a sum with which something can be accomplished. Here and in the new places, we receive no stipends. I beg, therefore, if other priests who are poor are not deprived, that you kindly send me a number of intentions. The stipends can be sent to us through Mr. Lebling.[132]

Bishop Domenec[133] divided the Diocese of Pittsburgh into two dioceses: that of Pittsburgh and that of Allegheny. He kept the latter, and Pittsburgh went to his favorite, Tuigg.[134] They disagreed, however, about sharing the debts. Other complaints were added, and as a result, Bishop Domenec had to resign. Bishop Tuigg remained bishop of Pittsburgh and became administrator of Allegheny. I do not yet know how he will fare. I had nothing to do with it. My sympathy is with Domenec.

I hope and heartily desire that you are well, and I sign with deepest reverence and gratitude, Your Excellency's most grateful servant, Boniface Wimmer, Abbot

Ger   oAMA   cASVA   transIG

TO ALEXIUS EDELBROCK   **134**

St. Vincent, December 29, 1877

Rt. Rev. and Dear Father Abbot: Your letter with the $20 came to my hands and the dollars were at once handed over to the Procurator, but the good wishes I kept for my own self, and I thank you heartily for the blessings wished. As regards long life, I beg to amend so far that it is a good life, a better one [than] it was till now, or it would be of little use. Often it seems to me that I have been living too long already. My habitual sins–taking everything easy–I [still] commit often enough yet, and the consequence thereof will be, I am afraid, a great lack of order and regularity, or bad discipline.

Of course, you speak only in a complimentary way if you call me an ornament to the Order. I ought to be one. Indeed, every Abbot ought to be one, and those thousands of Saints of our Order were mostly all of them Abbots, and as such ornaments to the Order and to the Church. But alas, after a 45-year-long life in the Order, I am farther away from the lowest grade of perfection than I was when I joined. Therefore, it is that I cannot do anything in the administration of the Abbey and its Dependencies for which I am not more or less sharply censured, cer-

---

[132] Louis Ignatius Lebling, treasurer of the *Ludwig Missionsverein*.

[133] Michael Domenec, C.M. (1816-1878).

[134] John Tuigg (1820-1889).

tainly for the reason that I never hit the nail on its head. Of course, I don't mind this, nor do I wonder at it, but often the thought comes into my head that I am not the man for the office. To be sure, an Abbot's duty is not [to] please people but to rule them. Still, as he ought to rule so that they gain thereby, it is to be feared they are not well ruled if they complain about me, and this fear is a grave one.

In a few days I am going into the 70th year of my life. Only one of those 12 Fathers who joined the Order in Metten in its first period is living yet, and me–P. Xavier Sulzbeck.[135] Of course, I am aware that the end of my career must soon be here. I am not attached to life so much that I would not gladly die any day it may please God to call me home, but for the fear of judgment. A certain success and prosperity or good luck is no sign of Predestination. It is a poor consolation for me that I succeeded in getting up one monastery aided by the Mission Society, by King Louis[136] and other good friends. The great question will be if in that Abbey and in the abbeys descended from it the spirit of St. Benedict is at home or not, or only little, perhaps very little.

People may think I have done great things, and God may judge I have greatly failed in doing what I chiefly ought to have done! Not to speak at all of my private life as a priest and a Religious and an Abbot! I often think I should not have undertaken such a work at all because to do it right would require not only an energetic, assiduous, and wise man, but a holy man. I am none of that. For this reason I am afraid of death, but likewise of long life, since it is very doubtful if I can or will do much better.

Father Eberhard[137] has written to me for a place, or at least for advice. The latter I gave, sincerely, honestly. For the rest, I offered him my house to live here if he will conform himself to the rule. He wrote from Ottawa, Ill. He wrote reverently and humbly.

Weather was constantly so nice that we could till now go on in the building of a large barn, the mason work of which we have more than half finished. Barley and hops cheap. Beer good.

Wishing you in return every happiness, I remain truly, your unworthy confrere, Bonif. Wimmer, Abb.

Eng   oASJA   cASVA

---

[135] Francis Xavier Sulzbeck, O.S.B. (1807-1881).
[136] King Ludwig I of Bavaria (1786-1868).
[137] Eberhard Gahr, O.S.B. (1832-1922).

TO ALEXIUS EDELBROCK   **135**

St. Vincent, March 14, 1878

Right Reverend and Dear Confrere: At present, I cannot spare another priest. Father Suitbert[138] did not want to leave Chicago to go to Allegheny. When he heard that I needed a priest in the South, he offered to go there because he is suffering from a throat ailment that he thought would subside in the South (Alabama), but because I had already assigned Father Matthew[139] there, I offered him a place in Covington. I had recalled Father William[140] from there and sent Father Maurice[141] in his place because the people complained that they did not have a good preacher. I also needed someone to remind the church trustees to settle and present their accounts. Father Maurice managed to do this.

Perhaps Father Suitbert does not like being under, or close to, Father Maurice. I do not know. Perhaps he does not like being under Father Luke either, whose accounts I asked him to take care of. I do not know. However, I cannot make him pastor, or first assistant, since he cannot preach because of his throat ailment. At least he cannot do so without danger.

Write to him and say simply that he should first approach me about this matter and that you cannot give him an answer before this is done. It has been suggested to me that he be made pastor and that Father Maurice be moved to Huntsville, Alabama, which I am supposed to take over after Easter. Maurice would like to go there. However, if Suitbert cannot preach, this will not work.

I am just now negotiating with Father Baasen[142] to take over his places in Alabama. It is not good to have only one priest in St. Florian, but there is not enough work for two. Baasen will not give us anything (even though he has so many stations to take care of that he seriously neglects them) unless I buy his house in Tuscumbia for $3,000. The house, however, is not well suited for us. Father Matthew is there now because Father Benedict[143] became ill and is, for the time being, in Covington to recuperate. He is strongly urging me to buy the house from Father Baasen so that the people do not perish. He says two or three fathers would have enough to do there. I probably will have to do this, but then the sisters must go there, too, and we will have to take care of ten counties.

---

[138] Suitbert de Marteau, O.S.B. (1834-1901).

[139] Matthew Stuerenburg, O.S.B. (1828-1888).

[140] William Walter, O.S.B. (1840-1882).

[141] Maurice Kaeder, O.S.B. (1837-1892).

[142] Father John B. Baasen was a diocesan priest in Tuscumbia, Alabama, who assisted the Benedictines when they arrived in the state.

[143] Benedict Menges, O.S.B. (1840-1904).

In addition, I committed myself in Louisiana for the sisters' sake, so that they would have a priest as chaplain. They want to open an institute in Covington, in Tammany Parish, close to Lake Pontchartrain, in a very healthy, high area with many woods and excellent medicinal springs. If I can send another priest, the two of them will have the whole parish (county) to take care of. It is populated by Frenchmen, Englishmen, and Germans, and they will have to speak three languages. For the time being Father Bernardine[144] is designated for Louisiana. If I am in good health, I will go with him to North Carolina and Savannah after Easter; from Savannah to Mobile to see the bishop;[145] then to New Orleans to speak with the archbishop[146] about Covington. After that, I will go to Covington, Kentucky, to see the glories and improvements at Monte Cassino, then home again to prepare for the General Chapter that is scheduled again this year.

What mischief old Father Magnus[147] has done! So much that he is suspended. Now he wants to do penance at St. Vincent. I cannot take such a character into our house! He has no right to expect it and offers no hope that he will improve. I want to know what he has done and ask you as visitator to get reliable information and report to me.

Since the middle of February, we have had much sickness here, and it is not over yet. Frater Justus[148] would have become a really good and reliable priest, and Brother Damian[149] is almost irreplaceable as carpenter. Brother Gregory[150] is still in great danger, and Fathers Paulinus[151] and John[152] have been very sick. I always have something to suffer, but never anything dangerous. Right now, I have a problem with my left knee. Since September 1877, I have not been able to drink anything cold, only warm tea. For the past few days, I have been taking a little lemonade again.

Father Edward's[153] dispensation has arrived, but he did not accept it because no bishop accepted him. Remember me at the altar. Have you already responded to

---

[144] Bernardine Dolweck, O.S.B. (1828-1905).
[145] John Quinlan (1826-1883), bishop of Mobile (1859-1883).
[146] Napoleon J. Perche (1805-1883), archbishop of New Orleans (1870-1883).
[147] Magnus Mayer, O.S.B.
[148] Justus Leithaeuser, O.S.B. (1845-1878).
[149] Damian Jacob, O.S.B. (1820-1878).
[150] Gregory Kalmes, O.S.B. (1832-1912).
[151] Paulinus Wenkmann, O.S.B. (1836-1921).
[152] John Sommer, O.S.B. (1815-1886).
[153] Edward Hipelius, O.S.B. (1836-1900).

the archabbot of St. Martin (in Hungary)?[154] With special affection and esteem. B. Wimmer

Ger   oASJA   cASVA   transAHo

TO ISIDORE ROBOT   **136**

St. Vincent, December 11, 1878

Rt. Rev. Abbot and Prefect Apostolic, Rt. Rev. and Dear Sir: With the greatest pleasure, I read in the papers that you have been honored with the title of an Abbot by our Holy Father Pope Leo XIII so as to make the number of Abbots now 7 in the U. States. I congratulate you heartily [on] this well deserved distinction, and wish you every success in your great enterprise, the preservation of the Catholic faith among the Indians and the conversion to the Catholic faith of those who are not Christians, or outside the Church in the Indian Territory. And I hope confidently [that] you will be made Bishop, too, in order to be enabled to do more yet for that Territory, if the Episcopal power and authority is added to that of an Abbot.

It is certainly not by accident that a Benedictine Abbey just now is growing up in your Territory, another one in Kansas, another one to be erected in Nebraska, and certainly in a not distant future one also in [the] Dakota Territory, which is also to be erected into a Vicariate Apostolic, while Northern Minnesota has already an Abbot and a flourishing Abbey, too.

Yielding to the invitations and instances of the respective Bishops, I have accepted places in North Carolina, Georgia, Alabama, and Louisiana, with a view to draw the Negroes into the sphere of our missionary labors, and in Georgia, indeed, to work exclusively for their Conversion. We have given up Isle of Hope and have left it to the Bishop, partly because the location is not at all suitable for a Religious House, and partly because we could not get a good title to the property there. But Father Oswald[155] moved over to the Island Skidaway, only 3 miles distant from the *terra firma*, where he has 4 white Brothers and a Cleric, and a few colored Brothers and boys gathered around him. By this way, almost all the Atlantic and Gulf States, and, likewise, all the Border States, are occupied by Benedictines, and indeed not in consequence of a preconcerted plan, but as it were accidentally, in a

---

[154] John Chrysostom Kruesz, O.S.B., archabbot of St. Martin's Archabbey, Pannonhalma, Hungary.
[155] Oswald Moosmüller, O.S.B. (1832-1901).

providential way. May it please God in his infinite goodness to awake in us once again the spirit which the blessed abbot Benedict exemplified, so that in every way we might promote the glory of God, the salvation of souls, and the glory of our Order!

Perhaps you know that in the year 1869 we have got printed in our own typography an *Album Benedictinum*, containing all the information we could collect about the monasteries of the Benedictine Order. Of the French Congregation we had only three monasteries: Solesmes, Ligu16, and the Priory of S. Magdalen in Marseille. We intend now to edit an American Benedictine Album, or rather an "overseas" edition, which should exhibit the names of all the American (also Brasilian) and Australian Benedictine houses, and we would be happy to get in your Abbey, too, and, therefore, I beg you to fill up the Rubrics of a Schema, which will [be] sent to you one of these days for this purpose by the Secretary appointed. If one of the European Abbots, as we expect, will cause an Album of the whole Order to be printed, our American Album will be a part of it. If nobody cares for the edition of a universal Album, ours will stand on its own merits as a work in honor of St. Benedict on the occasion of the 14th Centennarium of his birth.

I hope the testimonies for Mr. Rieman have arrived. He is a good man, but his sight is so poor that a majority of the Chapter decided not to admit him to profession here. He is a good classical scholar and a good Catholic. As he mentioned in his letter that he was very poorly set up in clothes, I would send him some clothes if I could make sure he would get them either by freight or Express.

Perhaps you wonder what became of O'Lorne. He was some months in Atchison, but sent off by the Abbot,[156] he went to the Irish Priory of S. Malachy in Iowa. When the Prior[157] did not want to keep him longer, he begged me to receive him and came about a month ago hither. I did not then receive him in the Order, but gave him a chance in the College to study Theology, and there he is yet among the secular students. D. Sullivan, who was at Isle of Hope with good Fth. Bergier,[158] is here in the Scholasticate, studying the classical course. Pardon this lengthy letter. I wish you a happy new year and beg you to accept the assurance of sincere and profound esteem, in which I sign, your devoted Confrere, Boniface Wimmer, Abbot

Eng   oASVA

---

[156] Abbot Innocent Wolf, O.S.B. (1843-1922), of St. Benedict's Abbey, Atchison, Kansas.

[157] Eugene Phelan, O.S.B. (1840-1903), prior of St. Malachy's Priory, Creston, Iowa.

[158] Gabriel Bergier, O.S.B. (1830-1876), a French Benedictine who had made an unsuccessful attempt to establish a monastery in Georgia.

TO UTTO LANG 137

St. Vincent, December 16, 1878

Right Reverend Father Abbot, Dear Confrere: I wish you a very happy new year from the bottom of my heart. May you have patience and perseverance until the end. Life in this world is nothing but a struggle, a battle, and the only thing we can do is wish each other perseverance and patience so that we will enjoy peace in the next world. Because I did not find your name on the list of those attending the consecration in M[unich], I suspected you were probably not feeling well. I hope it was nothing serious. My health is better this year than it was last year. Patience is the main virtue I strive for.

I was very worried about the yellow fever because Father Bernardine[159] is stationed near New Orleans, and Fathers Matthew, Joseph, and Benedict[160] are only 150 miles from Memphis. If I had lost one of them, I really would not have known how to replace him. The wonder is that Father Bernardine's parish was not affected at all by the fever, though the parishes of the other three were. In Father Joseph's parish only Protestants became ill. In Huntsville, Decatur, Tuscumbia, and St. Florian, they fought it courageously, but many people died, all fortified by the sacrament of extreme unction. We gained many converts and brought many obstinate sinners back to the Faith. None of the priests in Alabama became sick.

Father Bernardine, while in a neighboring parish taking the place of Father Gratz who had succumbed to the malady, caught the fever just before the epidemic ended. Fortunately, he knows a good deal about homeopathic medicine and cured himself with aconite, belladonna, arsenic, and vegetable carbo. None of our sisters, who live in one house, contracted the illness. In a second convent, just at the end of the epidemic, some were afflicted. In a third convent, in New Orleans, all except one came down with the fever; but all escaped death, thanks be to God.

In August, we had a General Chapter. I had the two abbots and all the priors around me for almost two weeks. Abbot Innocent[161] had to erect a new building to enlarge his college, for which I promised him $3,000, which I gave as "mutual assistance." In Chicago, finally, the new parish church was completed, replacing the one destroyed by the great fire of 1871. The new one is 168 feet long, 64 feet wide, and 67 feet high, but the tower is not yet finished. The cost is $30,000,

---

[159] Bernardine Dolweck, O.S.B. (1828-1905).
[160] Matthew Stuerenburg, O.S.B. (1828-1888); Joseph Keller, O.S.B. (1847-1907); and Benedict Menges, O.S.B. (1840-1904).
[161] Innocent Wolf, O.S.B. (1843-1922), abbot of St. Benedict's Abbey, Atchison, Kansas.

cheap enough. It is a solid building, but burdened with debts. At the consecration (performed by Bishop Foley),[162] Bishops Fink, Seidenbusch, and Krautbauer[163] were present, as were the three abbots.[164] It was a great festivity. I was away from home for two weeks. Shortly afterwards, I went to Monte Cassino near Covington, Kentucky, where I remained ten days because many things had to be attended to. A lot of money is involved in that undertaking.

I would have forgotten about the *Album Benedictinum*, but Father Ildephonse,[165] the dean at Einsiedeln, wrote me twice at the behest of his abbot[166] saying that I should get busy with a new edition; otherwise, it would not be done. Similarly, Father George[167] sent me some points for consideration about the album that a committee appointed by the abbot had drawn up. These included some modifications of our proposal. My answer was this: I would be willing to collect material for the album from the overseas Benedictines, i.e., those in North and South America and in Australia. I would put this material at the disposal of the archabbot[168] in the event that he or someone else would prepare the new edition. If no one else is willing to publish the album, I am willing to do it, if that is agreeable with everyone,[169] and to gather information from Einsiedeln and Engelberg, the motherhouses of St. Meinrad and Conception here in the United States, and from Metten, the motherhouse of Saint Vincent. If the English want to cooperate, they can do so, and include their offshoots in Australia and elsewhere. Recently we got a new abbot in the United States. He is the Frenchman Isidore Robot,[170] prefect apostolic of the Indian Territory, who comes from Pierre-qui-Vire.[171] At the mo-

---

[162] Thomas Foley (1822-1879), coadjutor bishop and apostolic administrator of the diocese of Chicago (1870-1879).

[163] Louis Fink, O.S.B. (1834-1904), bishop of Leavenworth, Kansas; Rupert Seidenbusch, O.S.B. (1830-1895), vicar apostolic of Northern Minnesota; and Francis X. Krautbauer (1824-1885), bishop of Green Bay, Wisconsin.

[164] Innocent Wolf, O.S.B. (1843-1922), of St. Benedict's Abbey, Atchison, Kansas; Alexius Edelbrock, O.S.B. (1843-1908), of St. John's Abbey, St. Joseph's, Minnesota; and Wimmer himself.

[165] Ildephonse Huerlimann, O.S.B. (b. 1826).

[166] Basilius Oberholzer, O.S.B. (b. 1821), abbot of Einsiedeln.

[167] George Ulber, O.S.B. (b. 1818), novice master at the Swiss abbey of Einsiedeln.

[168] Nicolaus D'Orgemont de la Fontaine, O.S.B. (b. 1826), archabbot of Montecassino.

[169] In fact, Wimmer did publish the second edition of the album, as he had the first. See *Album Benedictinum, Nomina Exhibens Monachorum qui de Nigro Colore Appellantur, Locorumque Omnium, Quotquot Innotuerunt, Hac Aetate Florentium, O.SS.P.N. Benedicti, Quod ad Annum a Nativitate Ejusdem Ss. Patris MCCC* (Beatty, Pa.: St. Vincent Abbey Press, 1880).

[170] Isidore Robot, O.S.B. (1837-1887).

[171] The story of the abbey in Oklahoma founded by French monks from the Abbey of Pierre-qui-Vire is told by Joseph Murphy in *Tenacious Monks: The Oklahoma Benedictines* (Shawnee, Okla.: Benedictine Color Press, 1974).

ment, I am unable to commit myself to printing the album as requested, which would be cheaper than contracting an outside printer, because I am busy printing Lechner's Holy Bible[172] and an antiphonary in octavo, which we will use here.

We will have to wait to hear what Einsiedeln says about this. Please tell me your opinion in your next letter. I will write England in a few days. I have already notified the archabbot. Father James Zilliox[173] is acting as secretary of the project because Father Edward[174] was granted a dispensation from the vow of poverty in order to help his unfortunate sister. No one should take my actions amiss. I am the oldest abbot, and Saint Vincent is the oldest abbey here. It is certainly no presumption that I take the lead in this matter. The archabbot himself proposed that the album be divided into two parts: one (the principal part) for Europe, the other (an appendix) for the overseas houses; in other words, the old stem and the new branches. However, if the first part does not appear in print, then the second one will, even after the celebration, though not in an extravagant form.

We have 12 fewer students in the college in these difficult times. Last year I began building a new barn, the largest in the country, 220 feet in length, 68 feet wide. On the ground floor, there are stables for 30 horses and 120 head of cattle. From floor to roof, the barn will be 21 feet high, with four floors and four doors. It will have oak beams above the stables and the floor will be paved with stone. The barn itself will be of brick. We had completed it up to the roof when winter set in. Now we are busy finishing the stables. The roof will be plank board covered with tiles. We will not finish it before spring. Overall, it has been a very expensive undertaking.

On the hill west of the monastery, we built a cistern 40 feet in diameter with natural vaults. In reality, it is nine cisterns with nine openings on top. We pump water 130 feet up to the openings by means of a steam pump. I allowed my painters and photographers to build a small house for themselves near a natural spring in the garden. All this has emptied my treasury. Two priests broke their feet; one in Kansas has had a bad fever for a long time; another was spitting blood; another contracted typhus from a scholastic who died from it. An old brother died, as did a deacon. Seven clerics were ordained to the priesthood. We have 17 novices, 34 clerics, and six subdeacons. My music master, Father Ignatius,[175] wanted to transfer to Beuron. Without hesitating, I gave him permission and $150 in traveling

---

[172] Peter Lechner, *Die Heilige Schrift des Neuen Testamentes nach der Vulgata und dem Grundtext erklärt* (Beatty, Pa.: St. Vincent Press, 1881), and *Die Heilige Schrift des Alten Testamentes, nach der Vulgata und dem Grundtext erklärt* (Beatty, Pa.: St. Vincent Press, 1882-84).

[173] James Zilliox, O.S.B. (1849-1890).

[174] Edward Hipelius, O.S.B. (1827-1910).

[175] Ignatius Trueg, O.S.B. (1827-1910).

money. I pity him for his foolishness, but I wish him the best. Perhaps he will gain in monastic spirit. I am again in need of stipends. If you can spare some, can I ask for them?

December 17: I just received news that Father Bernardine left his sick bed too early and has become ill again. He is now sicker than before. At the General Chapter, I was denied authority to establish independent priories with the consent of the bishop alone, without papal approval. I submitted the question to our procurator general, Abbot Pescetelli,[176] who brought the matter before three congregations, including the Congregation of Bishops and Religious. The decision was that every abbot is entitled to establish independent priories with episcopal approval. Only in the case of the foundation of abbeys is papal approval required.

I have received a photograph of the Madonna with Child in the pilgrimage chapel at Metten. The sculptor created a terrible work of art. It is a wonder that the pastor of Neuhausen did not protest.

In three weeks, I shall be 70 years old. You are much older. Fathers Xavier, Ambrose, Willibald, not to mention Father Prior Placidus,[177] are even further along, thanks be to God. It is an extraordinary grace to be able to count so many years. May they all have many more years in this world, a short time in purgatory, and unending happiness in heaven. Let us pray for one another. With sincere affection and deep respect, I remain Your Grace's most devoted confrere, Boniface Wimmer, Abbot

Ger   oAMA   cASVA   transRG

TO PLACIDUS WOLTER   **138**

St. Vincent, January 31, 1879

Right Reverend Lord Abbot, Most Esteemed Confrere: I thank you kindly for the directory you sent me. I read that you have become abbot of Maredsous. I should have sent my best wishes, but am always burdened with correspondence, and in meeting routine obligations, I sometimes forget other duties, or put them off until it is too late, as has happened in this case.

---

[176] Angelo Pescetelli, O.S.B. (1809-1885).

[177] Francis Xavier Sulzbeck, O.S.B. (1807-1881); Ambrose Vischer, O.S.B. (1808-1878); Willibald Freymüller, O.S.B. (1807-1890); and Placidus Lacense, O.S.B. (1802-1887) were all monks of Metten.

It does seem that our holy Order really will have a great future–not great in a worldly sense, but great because of its call, strengthened by God's grace, to address the needs of the Church in the missions and in education. Here, the Right Reverend Isidore Robot of Pierre-qui-Vire became apostolic prefect and afterwards abbot in the Indian Territory. North of that territory is our monastery at Atchison, in Kansas. Next to Kansas is Nebraska, where we have two stations, one in Nebraska City and the other in Omaha. Adjacent to Nebraska is the Dakota Territory, where Abbot Marty[178] has a number of Indian missions. East of these missions and east of the Missouri River, our brothers from St. Louis on the Lake are in Dakota and in Minnesota. South of Minnesota we have a mission in Iowa, and south of Iowa, in Missouri, the Swiss monks from Engelberg have a community, a very fine group under a remarkable prior. Further south, in Arkansas, are other Swiss under Abbot Marty from St. Meinrad. Thus, we have a strong foothold in all the border states. We also have two Benedictine bishops.

In the Gulf States, we began settlements three years ago. We now have Benedictines at Maryhelp near Charlotte, North Carolina; on Skidaway Island near Savannah, Georgia, for Negroes; in Alabama, eight counties along the Tennessee River; and in Louisiana, on Lake Pontchartrain, near New Orleans, in Covington and Tammany Parish (or County). This year three of our fathers in the Gulf States survived a siege of yellow fever; only one contracted it. He cured himself by means of homeopathy. In all these places, everything is proceeding steadily, despite the cost in money, people, patience, correspondence, and traveling.

At home, we try to advance as much as we can. We are always building. At the abbey, almost all the monks are professors. Only one is a parish priest; another is his assistant. Sacred music almost brought discord to our monastery. Father Ignatius[179] did not want anything to do with polyphonic hymns. Perhaps you remember what I wrote you about Gregorian chant. In my opinion Gregorian chant belongs in the choir and in the conventual Mass, but not at parish Masses or at pontifical Masses (except when there is no other music). However, nothing helped. We could no longer have a patterned Mass. I let him have his way, but this exclusiveness created much opposition from other modern music teachers, whom we could not banish because of the college. There was constant friction until Father Ignatius left. I was happy to give him travel money and wished him well. Now we have as much chant as before, but we also have other music as before.

Increase in personnel is not going as well as I wish. Although we have 120 scholastics, we seldom have more than six new priests a year. We have among

---

[178] Martin Marty, O.S.B. (1834-1896).
[179] Ignatius Trueg, O.S.B. (1827-1910).

them many Bohemians, and we would like to found a monastery for Bohemian-speaking monks. Thousands of these poor people, indeed most of them, will be lost because of a lack of priests.

With regard to the celebration of the Jubilee in 1880, nothing seems to be developing. I decided to publish an album of overseas Benedictines and include the English Benedictines. Then I was asked to publish once again an album of the whole Benedictine Order, which I will do if I possibly can.

But what will the future bring? Another terrible revolution? Are you safe in Belgium? May God grant that you are! The Red danger is going around again, and how easily we could become martyrs of the Church and thus see her completely cleansed. God will provide. May God guard and bless you! With sincere love and respect, Your Grace's loyal brother, Boniface Wimmer, Abbot

Ger   oASBM   cASVA   transIG

TO UTTO LANG   139

St. Vincent, July 2, 1879

Father Abbot, Most Esteemed Confrere: I cannot go over the mountains today with the Blessed Mother of God, but I would like to cross the ocean and knock at the door of Metten for a short visit. We are again badly in need of stipends. I would ask if you could spare some. We do not have any here. We receive very few and the need is very great.

Our exhibition, or distribution of prizes, has passed, and vacation has started. The harvest began with the feast of St. John, June 24, and so manual labor has taken the place of intellectual labor. Everywhere in America, there is as much wheat as is needed. Oats are not overly abundant and there is hardly any hay at all, but there is still enough to meet our needs. The corn crop, here as elsewhere, is not exceptional. Frost killed all our fruit (apples, pears, peaches, etc.). The beer, however, is very good and of high quality. Several thousand dollars in tuition payments from our students are delayed, and some of it, no doubt, will be lost entirely.

Yesterday I bought a new reaping machine. It is already in operation and is breaking all records. It cuts perfectly and cleanly. It binds the bundles together with a very thin wire. Using it, three men and three horses can finish the whole harvest. The machine cost $250 and will pay for itself in no time. The local farmers are coming here to see it work and watch in astonishment as it operates. I have become a real farmer.

We have the largest barn in the country, with up-to-date stables. We also have a wonderful steam engine, the best possible, which pumps the water below the monastery building up a distance of 150 feet to a vaulted cistern 40 feet in diameter. The water flows into nine connected cisterns from which it runs to all the buildings, including the stables. The brothers grow old and their number is steadily declining. For that reason, we have to find laborers from somewhere. Perhaps our Republicans will come and take away all our nice things and use them for some entirely different purpose. Who knows?

From May 19 to June 11, I was on canonical visitation in Chicago and Minnesota. I learned to my great satisfaction that Abbot Alexius Edelbrock[180] is an eminent economist and abbot. During his short regime, he has had some outstanding achievements. One can hardly recognize his monastery. At present, he is building a monastic church, of which the lower church, or basement, is already finished. It is the custom here that during the cold season, when the weather is harsh, the people and school children attend Mass in the basement, a kind of crypt (as at St. Peter's). Only on Sundays and feast days are the divine services held in the upper (or real) church. The 400,000 bricks he has ordered are already on the site. He has also improved the farm.

St. Louis on the Lake is capable of becoming a first class place. Until now, they have had to send a freight wagon every day from the monastery to the town of St. Joseph to haul things from the train station. This is a journey of two hours, but now the railroad has agreed to build a depot, on its own land, half an hour from the monastery–like Beatty Station near St. Vincent. The railroad has laid the groundwork for a small town there, a self-contained community with its own income. This will be a real advantage for the monastery and college.

Abbot Alexius has also started a mission among the Chippewa Indians, near the source of the Mississippi River, at a place called White Earth. The mission is flourishing and shows promise for the conversion of those Indians and others farther north. Unfortunately, he is not in the best of health. He suffers from an obstinate bronchitis as well as a chronic sore throat, with signs of an inflammatory infection. Not long ago he was spitting blood.

During my journey, both going and coming, I visited Bishop Seidenbusch.[181] I stayed with him only briefly, however. In Chicago, I remained with my people

---

[180] Alexius Edelbrock, O.S.B. (1843-1908), abbot of St. Louis Abbey, Minnesota.
[181] Rupert Seidenbusch, O.S.B. (1830-1895), vicar apostolic of Northern Minnesota.

for a whole week. I transferred the prior, Father Giles,[182] to Covington, Kentucky, and brought the prior of Covington, Father Suitbert,[183] to Chicago.

The sad financial business of the old archbishop of Cincinnati[184] has brought all the churches of that city and its neighborhood, including ours [in Covington, Kentucky], into great trouble and embarrassment. No one knows what the outcome will be. Many families have lost all their property, and with that, their Faith. The burden the churches must carry is heavy. They have no credit, and nothing is left to replace the $4 million. Only God knows what will happen. Even the bills are missing.

I feel better now than I have for two years. In fact, I am often in excellent health as before. How long this will last only God knows. How are you? I got rid of the arthritis in my left knee by rubbing juniper spirits on it. Perhaps you should do the same for the pains in your face.

I have received a great many contributions to the *Album Benedictinum*. One even came from East Bengal, from Bishop Jordanus[185] of Thanasia (*in partibus infidelium*), who wrote me a very kind letter. I became acquainted with him in 1866 at Subiaco and in 1870 at Rome. I had actually forgotten him until he wrote. He is a native Prussian from a Belgian monastery. We have not received anything from Salvado[186] or from the Brazilians.

Our Bishop Fink[187] has been ordered by Rome to gather our Benedictine sisters into a non-exempt congregation. On August 4, all the superiors of the various houses of sisters will meet in Covington, Kentucky, in order to discuss the statutes that Bishop Fink, all by himself, has drawn up. I, myself, am requested to be present as an advisor (the fifth wheel on the wagon).

It seems a change has taken place in the political situation of the whole world, not in the way we desired, but slowly. My confidence in the "Mettenbucher" story, as I have heard it, is not great. It is very hard to believe. Our people in St. Marys, Elk County, are drilling for oil on our monastery property. They will go down 2,000 feet, if they don't strike it sooner. They found some after drilling for ten hours. The test drilling cost $2,400. If the first drilling fails, they will try a second one, for which money is available. They have already gone down 200 feet.

---

[182] Giles Christoph, O.S.B. (1830-1887).

[183] Suitbert de Marteau, O.S.B. (1834-1901).

[184] John B. Purcell (1800-1883), archbishop of Cincinnati (1850-1883).

[185] Jordanus Balsieper, O.S.B. (b. 1835), vicar apostolic of East Bengal.

[186] Rudesind Salvado, O.S.B. (1814-1900), bishop of Port Victoria, Australia.

[187] Louis Fink, O.S.B. (1834-1904), bishop of Leavenworth, Kansas.

I hope this letter finds you in the best of health. I sign in true respect and sincere affection, Your Grace's most devoted confrere, Boniface Wimmer

Ger   oAMA   cASVA   transRG

TO JAMES ZILLIOX   **140**

St. Vincent, July 29, 1879

Rev. James Zilliox, O.S.B.,

My Dear Father James: I myself have received a petition from St. Marys Help[188] to remove Fth. Herman.[189] It had been written by Fr. Julius[190] and was very likely also conceived by him, or inspired by one who wishes to be in Father Herman's place. It looked very like to the result of a Conspiration, with reasons that were no reasons and accusations not containing any quick at all. I gave therefore to the young fellow, in whose mouth such a petition sounded particularly wrong, a good scolding and to Fth. Stephen,[191] who timidly had seconded it in a letter of his own, a warning; and since that time I heard nothing more of it. Of course, I told nothing of it to Fth. Herman in order to save him the cruel disappointment of finding two enemies and supplanters in the very confreres he supposed to be his sincere friends. I was much exasperated against that boy Julius for his insolent running down an old man of

---

[188] The Benedictine monastery in North Carolina (Mary Help of Christians, later Belmont Abbey) founded by monks from St. Vincent Abbey in 1876.
[189] Herman Wolfe, O.S.B. (1816-1884), prior at the monastery of Maryhelp in North Carolina.
[190] Julius Pohl, O.S.B (1857-1924).
[191] Stephen Lyons, O.S.B. (b. 1850).

60 years after he had scarcely got warm in his house, for which he certainly had deserved a good whipping.

Now, my dear Father James, if your petition dates from the same time–I forget: Nov. or Dec. of last year–please tear it into pieces or burn it lest someone might read it and be scandalized by it, unless it would contain other material but that which I got. But if the fellow can give facts and proofs of facts that make a change necessary, or very desirable, then let me see it. I have inquired into the accusations laid before me, but they were found groundless. God will[ing], I can go to see N. Carolina and Georgia this fall yet. Ahead of me, I sent yesterday Fth. Melchior[192] to Skidaway.

Just about the retreat I got a letter from Gethsemani notifying me that a cleric had made application there, with the remark [that] others would go to Europe. On inquiry, I found out that my good P. Magister[193] himself wanted to be of the party. Truly, if I had not been in silence, I should have given him a good march in old style Gregorian chant. But I soon cooled off, throwing all the blame on Fra. Diabolo. Still I thought it safer for him and for me to remove the *occasio proxima*, considering at the same time he had really too much to do, and plenty yet if he taught his theology, etc., and thought about the editing of the Album, which will give a good deal of work. Therefore, I accept your resignation as Master of Novices so that you can breathe easier in vacation, without fear of being sent South or West or [to] a parish, although there has been opened a fine home for us at Wheeling quite lately.

I have engaged a lay printer from Pittsburgh to print the Album here. Your Sisters can be in the same bundle with us. Abbot Wolter[194] has sent all the Belgian convents. It will make a nice exhibition of the strength of the female branch of our Order.

We had 2 terrible storms here of late, but passed without great harm.

The novices are under the care of Fth. Sebastian.[195] I am almost left alone with Fths. Paulin, Timothy, Casimir, and Boniface.[196]

---

[192] Melchior Reichert, O.S.B. (1852-1940).
[193] Novice master, i.e. Zilliox.
[194] Placidus Wolter, O.S.B. (1828-1908), abbot of the Belgian abbey of Maredsous.
[195] Sebastian Arnold, O.S.B. (1847-1916).
[196] Paulinus Wenkmann, O.S.B. (1836-1921); Timothy Blasius, O.S.B. (1855-1898); Casimir Elsesser, O.S.B. (1854-1902); and Boniface Wirtner, O.S.B. (1855-1928).

Spend your time profitably for your health as long as you can. Kindest regards to the Fathers, and also to your own father and brother. Yours in sincere love and esteem, Bonif. Wimmer, Abbot

Eng   oASVA

TO UTTO LANG   **141**

St. Vincent, October 6, 1879

Right Reverend Father Abbot, My Esteemed Confrere: As you can see from the enclosed circular, my good, old, and trusted Brother Wolfgang Beck[197] died on September 19, 1879. I saw him for the last time on Pentecost Tuesday in St. Cloud, Minnesota, where like Brother Gamelbert[198] before him, he was cook in the rectory. He worked diligently for the foundation of St. Louis Abbey and previously for St. Vincent. He was a good religious. May God abundantly reward him for his labor and toil. He lived at both places during their hardest times. Compared with those days, our times are very easy. I do not know any details about his death. It must have come rather unexpectedly because last June he was still in fair condition.

There is not much news from here, but in the Dakota Territory Abbot Marty[199] has been made vicar apostolic. His neighbor to the west is our vicar apostolic, Rupert Seidenbusch.[200]

The state of North Carolina has a million people, but there are only 1,800 Catholics there. The state belonged to the Diocese of Richmond but is now a vicariate apostolic. Not long ago, a priest of the vicariate, Father Mark Gross, who was working in the city of Wilmington, became vicar apostolic. This new vicariate is not without importance for us since our monastery of Maryhelp is located there. We started a small institution with six pupils in North Carolina. We now have 26, but whether we can sustain it with tuition at $130 is doubtful. Still, everything must have its beginning.

We have received all the expected contributions for the *Album Benedictinum* and have already started to print it here in the house. Our intention is to print

---

[197] Wolfgang Beck, O.S.B. (1805-1879).
[198] Gamelbert Daschner, O.S.B. (1817-1870).
[199] Martin Marty, O.S.B. (1834-1896), first abbot of St. Meinrad's Abbey, Indiana.
[200] Rupert Seidenbusch, O.S.B. (1830-1895), vicar apostolic of Northern Minnesota and former abbot of St. Louis on the Lake Abbey, Minnesota.

2,000 copies. I intend to go to Kansas next week for visitation. I wanted Abbot Edelbrock[201] to conduct the visitation, but he is ill. The Masses for the intentions you sent have all been said. We are now celebrating Mass "for the treasury of the Church."

This year we have plenty of chestnuts, which grow wild in our forest. For that reason, our students, with drums beating, are marching to our villa on the nearby ridge. They will collect the chestnuts and camp overnight. A four-horse wagon laden with bread and meat is following them. It will be a real *"gaudeamus"* celebration. We are experiencing beautiful weather, as we usually do in the fall, so we are continuing to make bricks and proceeding without hindrance to construct buildings.

On September 23, a crazy young man who imagined that the monastery belonged to him sneaked into my room, or rather tried to get into it, with the intention of murdering me. I subdued him and kept him tied until I got help.

I send you cordial felicitations, *post festum*, for your namesday. At the time, I was visiting Wheeling, West Virginia. With a humble request for your prayers, I remain, in deepest respect, your most devoted confrere, Boniface Wimmer

Ger   oAMA   cASVA   transRG,GZ,CW   *Scrip*19:81-82

TO UTTO LANG   142

St. Vincent, December 22, 1879

Right Reverend Father Abbot, Dear Confrere: I wish you a happy New Year, good health, patience, cheerful courage, perseverance in striving for perfection, and God's blessing for many years to come in spiritual as well as temporal affairs. We will see what the new year of 1880 has in store for us. What a change has taken place in the world since 1780, especially with regard to our Order. Prelates of those days would certainly be surprised if they were to rise again and visit their fine abbeys. If the world still exists, I wonder how conditions will be in the year 1980. Monasteries of the old style will most likely not rise anymore, for that is not really necessary. Whether large monasteries rise again in great numbers is another question. Life according to the evangelical counsels cannot be suppressed, for such a life is an essential part of the Church. Still, the different orders may be suppressed or cease to exist. I personally feel that the spiritual orders will be greatly multiplied. In other words, women will embrace the monastic life in great

---

[201] Alexius Edelbrock, O.S.B. (1843-1908), abbot of St. Louis on the Lake Abbey, Minnesota.

numbers, while men who want to devote themselves to teaching will hardly be able to support themselves as long as the state prescribes the kind and amount of studies for its teachers.

Here in the United States we are better off, for the state requires no special studies for teachers. The only requirement is some specialized knowledge for lawyers, doctors, and teachers. The European system, however, is strongly favored here. So far, however, there is nothing to block the founding of monasteries as long as they can support themselves by teaching, missions, regular pastoral work, and literary work.

In Europe conditions will change when the people again become Catholic. Then the good and the bad will be separated. Now the poor become Christians, and the rich, pagans and infidels. I think this opposition of the two groups is more or less the condition for suppression or persecution, even for the so-called license of the wicked. God will provide!

We received the circular letter from Montecassino and will celebrate the feast[202] as best we can. I do not know how the Benedictine medal will turn out since we cannot give much. The *Album Benedictinum* will be ready on time. If you can spare Mass intentions, keep the stipends in payment for Atchison and send us only the intentions. Our weather has been so mild that we have not had to heat the buildings. We will have a green Christmas if it does not snow tomorrow or the day after.

Again, I have my old knee malady, which causes me a lot of inconvenience. Thank you for all your favors this year. I remain with sincerest love and respect, your most obliging, Boniface Wimmer, Abbot

P.S. Please also extend my New Year's greetings to all the fathers, and especially to Fathers Prior, Subprior, Willibald, Fortunatus, and Rupert.[203]

Ger   oAMA   cASVA   transCZ,CW   *Scrip*19:82-83

---

[202] The 1400th anniversary of the birth of St. Benedict, scheduled to be celebrated in April 1880.
[203] Prior Placidus Lacense, O.S.B. (1802-1887); Subprior Bernard Hoegl, O.S.B (1813-1886); Willibald Freymueller, O.S.B. (1807-1890); Fortunatus Braun, O.S.B. (1806-1893); and Rupert Mittermüller, O.S.B (1814-1893).

1880-1884

TO MICHAEL REGER 143

St. Vincent, March 14, 1880

Very Reverend Cathedral Dean, Dearest Friend: I received your letter with the 1,386 Mass intentions, for which I am very grateful. The intentions were very welcome because I have not received any for a long time, and those I received from Metten have long ago been taken care of. I thought that when you had relinquished the position of vicar general, you had also given up the distribution of stipends, and because I did not know your successor, I did not want to ask him. Indeed, I was also reluctant to bother you because of your severe illness, since I knew that any work at all would be very difficult for you. It appears that Mass stipends are decreasing all over Bavaria because of the great poverty. I suppose you sent the 1307.45 marks to Mr. Lebling,[1] whom I had earlier asked to keep such money until I had decided what to do with it.

I only wonder how you have been able to bear this terrible suffering so long, and with such submission. Indeed, your suffering is a gift and a sign of special favor from Heaven that will increase your merits for eternity. My health is fairly good provided I take it easy. During Lent, we completely abstain from meat except on Sundays, and fish we have only once in a while. I manage, but may not take cold plum soup, and my beverages must always be warm, i.e. coffee or tea.

---

[1] Louis Ignatius Lebling, treasurer of the *Ludwig Missionsverein.*

Shortly before your letter arrived, I took a trip of five weeks (less two days). I was invited to the episcopal consecration of Abbot Martin Marty[2] of St. Meinrad in Indiana, who was appointed vicar apostolic of the Dakota Territory. I could not refuse the invitation, although I was suffering from rheumatism in my left knee. It is a long trip: 40 miles to Pittsburgh; from there 300 miles to Cincinnati; from there 120 miles to Louisville; then 180 miles by steamboat on the Ohio to Troy; then 15 miles by covered wagon over very poor roads to St. Meinrad. However, I made it. Since I had gone that far, I wanted at the same time to visit our mission stations in the South, where I had not been for two years. After the consecration on February 1, I returned to Troy, from there by steamboat for another 80 miles to Evansville. There I took a train to Nashville, the capital of Tennessee, then further on to Decatur in Alabama, where I visited my three fathers in St. Florian, Tuscumbia, and Huntsville, partly by train, partly by buggy. From there I went northeastward for 100 miles to Chattanooga in Tennessee; from there to Atlanta in Georgia and then through the whole state to Savannah on the Atlantic Ocean; from there by boat to Skidaway Island, where we have a Negro mission. Then I returned to Savannah to take the train home, stopping in Charlotte, North Carolina, near which for three years we have had a college for small boys. This is the only college for Catholics in the whole state and has an attendance of only 24 young people. Lack of space prevented us from accepting more, so I had to plan for a new building. From North Carolina, I went northward to my people in Richmond, Virginia; then by way of Washington to Baltimore, and finally I returned home. On only two days of the whole trip was I not feeling well. The rest of the time I managed well and returned home in good health, though very tired. Lent made traveling even more difficult, but my energy is gone. I am no longer half the man I was, and my strength is diminishing daily.

Now I am expected to travel to Europe right after Easter in order to celebrate Pentecost at Montecassino with many or most of the abbots of our Order and to participate in discussions and consultations. I think, however, I should not do that, partly because I dislike traveling and partly because it is not good for my monastery if I am absent for so long a time. In addition, I hesitate to spend so much time and money for the trip and cannot see that my presence at Montecassino would be of much advantage. Moreover, it would not be good for my health. Nevertheless, my people encourage me to go so that I will be present at the discussions and can represent our monastery. I do not know what to do, but in the end, I will probably go.

---

[2] Martin Marty, O.S.B. (1834-1896).

Father Benedict Menges, O.S.B. (1840-1904), an early Benedictine missionary in Alabama, became abbot of St. Bernard's Abbey, Cullman, Alabama.

You have probably heard that this year we celebrate the 1400th anniversary of the birth of St. Benedict. The feast will be postponed until after Easter because it falls on Palm Sunday. The day fixed for it is the Tuesday after Whitsunday. The Pope has given us permission to celebrate the solemn Mass of St. Benedict on three consecutive days, namely Whitsunday, the following Monday, and Tuesday, the feast itself, that is, April 4, 5, and 6. Since Pentecost falls on May 16, I will have to begin the trip at the end of April, if I go at all. I would take the shortest route through France to Rome and return home as soon as possible, if it is God's will. I must consider it a pilgrimage, which I should undertake as a penance because of a special devotion to our great and holy patriarch. On my return, I would most probably see you, but only for a short time. If possible, I would like to be, and should be, home again in three months.

I must do much building this summer. In the last two years, I erected a number of farm buildings. Now I must take care of the college. If I am not here, things do not go well. I experienced that once again during my recent trip. The paterfamilias of so large a family may not be absent. The most capable substitute cannot fully replace him.

May the dear Lord give me a sign so that I know what to do. Naturally, it would please me very much to see Rome and our ancestral monastery again, to show my reverence to the Holy Father, to visit my few old friends again (especially you), and to be able to support good measures for our Order. However, I am not merely the fifth, but the fiftieth superfluous wheel on the wagon. Therefore, I believe things would go just as well without me. Reunions are followed by separations, which are always painful.

I thank you sincerely, for your many kindnesses and favors, which for so many years you have bestowed on me and my monastery. The stipends you have sent me amount to many thousands of dollars, which otherwise I would have been deprived of. I can always use money. Immediately after my trip, I sent $500 to

Father Oswald[3] for his institution for Negroes, and $75 to the poor community of Huntsville (under Father Benedict[4]), where during my last visit I left $40. I also gave $90 to Father Oswald. Tomorrow I will send $100 to Charlotte for a piano, which they need to give instructions. At my own monastery, I must support the young members in formation so that they will grow and develop faster and better.

Through the intercession of St. Benedict, the Lord will certainly reward you richly here and in eternity for all the good you have done. I never forget to pray for all my benefactors at holy Mass in general, and for some of them in particular. Now I bid you farewell. I hope we will see each other soon, if it please God. With sincere love and respect, your most obliging friend, Boniface Wimmer

Ger   oASVA   transWM

TO UTTO LANG   **144**

On Board the S.S. Arizona, April 26/27, 1880

Right Reverend Father Abbot, Dearest Confrere: Induced by my fathers, I am making the journey to Montecassino. On Sunday evening, April 18, I traveled from Latrobe to Newark where I arrived the following day, Monday, and met Bishop Seidenbusch, Abbots Wolf and Edelbrock, and Father Peter Engel,[5] who were all ready to set out on the journey. On Tuesday, April 20, at 2:00 pm, we departed New York and made 298 miles the first day. On Wednesday, we made 345 miles; on Thursday, 341 miles; on Friday, 318 miles; on Saturday, 375 miles; on Sunday, 342 miles, and today, 376 miles. We hope to be in Liverpool Wednesday night. For the past 20 hours, we have had terrible weather. We still have 400 miles to go before we reach Ireland.

From Liverpool, we will travel together to Paris, which we hope to reach by next Saturday. We will separate in Paris. The bishop will go to Augsburg. Abbots Alexius and Innocent will go directly to Rome. Father Subprior and I will go to Lourdes and from there to Marseille and Rome. The trip by train from Paris to Lourdes will take 24 hours. We will remain in Lourdes at least two days, so this

---

[3] Oswald Moosmüller, O.S.B. (1832-1901).

[4] Benedict Menges, O.S.B. (1840-1904).

[5] Rupert Seidenbusch, O.S.B. (1830-1895), vicar apostolic of Northern Minnesota; Innocent Wolf, O.S.B. (1843-1922), abbot of St. Benedict's Abbey, Atchison, Kansas; Alexius Edelbrock, O.S.B. (1843-1908), abbot of St. Louis on the Lake Abbey, Minnesota; and Peter Engel, O.S.B. (1856-1921), sub-prior and future abbot of St. Louis on the Lake.

little excursion will cost us three days and some \$30, but now or never! This is the only way I can satisfy my strong desire [to visit Lourdes]. It would be entirely out of the way on the return trip. I do want to make this pilgrimage.

Because I have traveled so far, I hope that Your Grace will also make the trip to Montecassino. I cannot say what business will be conducted there, but perhaps the Holy Spirit will inspire one or the other of us to propose something of importance for the common good. It certainly is not a mistake for so many of us to meet. Surely, St. Benedict and St. Scholastica will intercede for us and ask for graces and blessings upon our conference.

Upon my return, I would like, with your permission, to stay with you and be your guest for at least a week. My intention is to compare our discipline with yours. I will do the same at Einsiedeln because there is not much difference between our statutes and theirs. I have no special business to conduct and will not remain for an extended period in any one place. I plan to return to America on July 17, aboard the same steamship we are currently traveling on, the *Arizona*.

By now, you should have received the first part of the *Album Benedictinum*. The second and third parts will appear shortly after Pentecost. With the best will and despite our efforts we could not do it earlier. I hope you will be much better satisfied with the form and contents of this edition than with the previous one. It required a great deal of work and much money. In it, you will find a true picture of our Order, as it really is, because the female communities are listed. I am filled with hope that the publication will lead to greater unity and mutual support, as well as a higher reputation in the outside world.

I have four deluxe editions, bound in fine leather, with me. One is for Pope Leo and one each for Cardinals Pitra, Bartolini, and Simeoni.[6] Six more will follow, and I hope to give them to six other friendly cardinals when I reach Rome. I ordered 2,500 copies printed because many people were interested in receiving them. I will have to see if I can dispose of them all. I will have to give many away as presents.

If you receive this letter, it is a sign that I have landed safely in England. I would be very glad to see you at Montecassino. It was a real sacrifice for me to make this trip, but I could not resist my people who insisted that I not be absent from the meeting where there might be discussions of great importance. Therefore, against my own will, I put myself in the hands of God and went for the love of our holy father, St. Benedict.

---

[6] Jean Baptiste Pitra, O.S.B. (1812-1889); Dominic Cardinal Bartolini, prefect of the Sacred Congregation of Bishops and Religious; and John Cardinal Simeoni, prefect of the Sacred Congregation for the Propagation of the Faith.

Best regards to Father Prior, Father Subprior, and all the fathers. I remain in sincere affection and deep respect, Your Grace's most devoted confrere, Boniface Wimmer, Abbot

Ger   oAMA   cASVA   transRG

TO ANDREW HINTENACH   **145**

Montecassino, May 20, 1880

Andrew Hintentach, O.S.B.

Reverend and Dear Father Prior: I suppose my letters to you, Father Paulinus, the subprior, and Father Hilary[7] arrived in due time. With today's mail, you will receive the published brochure of the celebrations that just ended here. Let me add that I could not celebrate the pontifical high Mass *coram cardinale in throno* on the third day, as I was scheduled to do, because the consecration of the sanctuary, with its seven altars, lasted until 1:00 pm. It would have been too much for the cardinal, so I had only a low Mass, the conventual Mass, at 1:30 pm.

On Sunday, the archabbot[8] celebrated a high Mass with all solemnity in the presence of all the archbishops, bishops, abbots, and delegates, and I, as senior abbot, was entrusted with giving the response to his remarks in the name of the August assembly and in their presence. I did my best, emphasizing what the archabbot did not refer to, namely, that we came here, not only because of devotion, but also with the hope of holding a conference to deliberate about whatever is best for our Order.

The Pope answered our telegram by assuring us of his good will, but adding that we should keep in mind that "the wisdom and virtue of the ancient fathers should be restored." There were many lectures, but I do not know what the outcome will

---

[7] Paulinus Wenkmann, O.S.B. (1836-1922); Subprior Adalbert Müller, O.S.B. (1842-1906); and Hilary Pfrängle, O.S.B. (1843-1909).
[8] Nicholas D'Orgemont, O.S.B. (1826-1896), archabbot of Montecassino.

be. In our response to the Holy Father, we stressed our sincere desire to obey him and to do whatever he thinks best.

All the branches of our Order were represented: Cistercians, Trappists, Camaldolese, Olivetans, Vallumbrosians, Sylvestrians, Montevergines, and Mechitarists. Everything took place in the spirit of brotherly love in the church, at table, in the discussions. Everyone marveled at the possibility of such a conference. Everyone was overjoyed. You could see the spirit of belonging together, which could lead to real unity, in case that is the wish of the Holy Father.

These were very laborious days. We were busy from early morning until late in the evening. I caught a bad cold last Tuesday and still have it. Prior Vaughan[9] of Fort Augustus was taken ill by the so-called cholera morbus but was healed by Abbot Alexius's[10] homeopathy. Abbot Alexius, himself, feels much worse. An old priest of Montecassino, Father Claudius,[11] almost died. Nothing like this celebration at Montecassino ever occurred before, and will not easily happen again.

The possibility has emerged that the archabbot of Montecassino will be called "*Abbas abbatum,*"[12] a title that will probably have no meaning. Still, the Beuronese have published a memorandum supporting the appointment of an Abbot General over all the monasteries. We, the German abbots, held our own conference at which I, as the senior abbot, had to preside. We discussed the Beuronese proposal, and everyone, including myself, voiced opposition to it.

Today all the German-speaking Swiss left, as did Rupert and Alex.[13] I will stay here until I have the coins. During the last few days, it was impossible to speak with the prior.[14] Like the abbot, he was much bothered with, in fact tormented by, all the guests. This lasted up until today, but by this evening all the strangers will be gone, and then I can speak with him. When the reports of the festivities are published, I will send them to you.

As for business, please note that Abbot Rudolph of Goettweig[15] paid me for 25 albums (at eight francs each, or 200 francs); Michelbeuren paid for five (40 francs); St. Peter's, Salzburg, for seven (60 francs); and Seitenstetten, for 20 (160 francs). The abbots of Seitenstetten and Goettweig will receive albums in accordance with what they have paid.

---

[9] Jerome Vaughan, O.S.B. (1841-1896).

[10] Alexius Edelbrock, O.S.B. (1843-1908), abbot of St. Louis on the Lake Abbey, Minnesota.

[11] Claudius Buzzoni, O.S.B. (b. 1804).

[12] "Abbot of abbots."

[13] Rupert Seidenbusch, O.S.B., and Alexius Edelbrock, O.S.B.

[14] Boniface Krug, O.S.B. (1838-1909), a former monk of St. Vincent Abbey and claustral prior at Montecassino, where he had transferred his vows in 1864.

[15] Rudolph Gusenbauer, O.S.B. (b. 1827), abbot of Goettweig (Austria).

The archabbot of Martinsberg[16] is disappointed that we did not show him belonging to the Cassinese Congregation, and that we showed Zelowar as being in union with the Austrian Congregation. He said that Martinsberg always enjoyed the closest of unions with the Cassinese and that the archabbot of Martinsberg is *ex officio* president of all the abbeys under the Hungarian crown, whether affiliated or associated. Zelowar is associated. The rest are affiliated. Perhaps this should be noted for a future edition of the Album. I should send him the bill since he seemed willing to pay.

I hope to be in Rome by Saturday and will send the coins and medals from there, a gross of them, directly to the U.S. The port-of-entry will be the Customs Office, Pittsburgh. The medal of St. Benedict was minted in Rome and is an outstanding work. I bought 800 francs worth for 350 francs.

From Rome I will go to Salzburg, Metten, Regensburg, Munich, Einsiedeln, Oehlenberg, England, and then home—although I am inclined to accept various other invitations.

I have hardly been able to find time to say my prayers, but now it is becoming easier. During the three days of the festival, it did not rain, but it is now raining again and is very cool. I have had to stay inside for eight days. Fortunately, my knee held up during all those days of kneeling on the floor. How happy it would make me not to be stuck here, but the fact is that at Montecassino I have found much courtesy and love. Everyone gave me the warmest welcome. The Beuronese are leaving in the next few days.

A thousand greetings to everyone. I have been away from home for more than a month already. With love and respect, your most devoted confrere, Boniface Wimmer, Abbot

Ger   oASVA   transRG

TO RUPERT SEIDENBUSCH   146

Munich, July 3, 1880

My Dear Lord Bishop: Your card found me in the hospital here. I had suffered for three weeks in Ratisbon and in Metten from a cold in the stomach, and a terrible cough tormented me day and night [so] that after all I made up my mind to return to Munich and go to the hospital where I now already am for the third day,

---

[16] Chrysostom Kruesz, O.S.B. (b. 1819), archabbot of St.Martin's Archabbey, Pannonhalma, Hungary.

to my great satisfaction, under the hands of Dr. Gietl, who pays me every attention possible, and I do not leave before I am in good health again.

Therefore, I cannot go to Augsburg to celebrate the 4th [of] July, nor can I be on the 15th inst. at the Hotel Adelphi in Liverpool as Abbot Alexius[17] wanted me to be. I must postpone my return to America at least for two or three weeks, the last three weeks having been almost entirely lost on account of ill health. I always had to sleep sitting in a chair, not in bed.

I follow rigidly the [prescriptions] of my old physician, who with the greatest care on three different days knocked and listened to every spot of my torso in order to discover a fever, but found only 100 beats of the pulse and a big catarrh of the stomach, and [he] makes me cough to get the *materia peccans* [out] and makes me drink much mineral water.

There was a registered letter for you in Metten from Tirschenreuth for a good while. They expected you there, but when you did not come, gave the letter to me, and I gave it to Bro. Constable[18] for you, who expects you to come once more to Munich.

It seems my P. Bernard[19] is desirous of returning with me to America. All right, of course, but I advised him to use the Springs since he is not out here, and then return to America.

I hope to hear your plans about your voyage across the Atlantic. I think your friend from Minnesota[20] should also use the Springs or go to a good hospital, at least and submit himself to a good doctor, like old Dr. Gietl, and only then think about starting for home.

In a letter from Rome, I read that the Encyclical of the Pope in regard to our Order shall soon appear, and that it is the Pope's intention next winter to convoke [from] every Congregation two men to deliberate with him in Rome. In such a case, it is far better going first to the mountains for fresh air, spending October in Italy, and waiting until the trumpet sounds for the abbots again. Next week I am for sure in town, even if I am already dismissed from the hospital.

My kind regards to Dr. Unsinn. I am sorry not to be able [to accept] your and his visitations. I feel a good deal of anxiety for our Abbot Alexius resp[ecting] his health. Abb[ot] Innocent[21] is well. He left Salzburg on the 20th [of] June for Vienna.

---

[17] Alexius Edelbrock, O.S.B. (1843-1908), abbot of St. Louis on the Lake Abbey, Minnesota.
[18] Constable Enders, O.S.B. (1800-1885), a lay brother of St. Boniface Abbey, Munich.
[19] Bernard Manser, O.S.B. (1835-1899).
[20] Probably Abbot Alexius Edelbrock.
[21] Innocent Wolf, O.S.B. (1843-1922), abbot of St. Benedict's Abbey, Atchison, Kansas.

My love to you, your brother Jacob,[22] and the other confreres who know me. Of course, particularly the Rt. Rev. Abbot.[23]

In true reverence, Your Lordship's humble servant, B. Wimmer

Eng   oASJA   cASVA

TO UTTO LANG 147

Munich, July 27, 1880

Right Reverend Abbot, Dearest Confrere: My stay in the hospital lasted 19 days. My physician would have liked me to stay longer because he was afraid I would have a relapse of the bronchitis without another week of rest, but in fact, I am fairly well restored to health. I do not cough any more, can sleep well, and have regained my good old appetite. I can even take a glass of beer if it is not too cold. My voice is the same as before, thank God. I did not know that I had a steady fever of 100 degrees, which I could not rid myself of for a long time. No doubt, I brought it along with me from Montecassino. I was advised to take the baths at Scheftlarn in order to strengthen my legs and cure myself of difficulties when urinating, which I have experienced lately. I have been delayed for a week, but tomorrow I expect Canon Meyringer.[24] He and I will go together to Schaeftlarn for a couple of weeks.

So my return to America is postponed. I checked in Rotterdam, Antwerp, and La Havre and discovered the only way to travel is from La Havre, but not before August 14. I will probably leave on August 21. Otherwise, I cannot take the baths. Regaining my health is my strongest desire. Nobody can blame me for that. It is a desire rooted in nature.

I would like to go to Metten for the celebration of your 50th anniversary. The celebration will take place whether the Lord Abbot wants it or not! However, I will probably not be able to attend if I am to take the baths. I would also like to visit Regensburg, where they want to see me, but I can hardly find the time, unless the baths help me very quickly. If circumstances prevent me from attending your celebration, please forgive me and accept my congratulations in writing for this extraordinary feast. I will offer a Mass of thanksgiving for the many graces and blessings, past and present, you and those connected with you have received

---

[22] Jacob Seidenbusch, O.S.B. (1825-1892), a monk of St. Stephen's Abbey, Augsburg.

[23] Raphael Mertl, O.S.B. (1820-1889), abbot of St. Stephen's Abbey, Augsburg.

[24] Joseph Meyringer of Regensburg, Wimmer's cousin.

during your 50 years in the priesthood, and I will ask God to grant that you guide your community, with honor and blessings, for many years to come.

Yesterday I received a letter from Abbot Wolf[25] who wrote from Prague. He said that he would arrive at Metten on July 26. He does not know about the celebration, but I am sure he will want to take part in it as soon as he learns of it and that he will remain in Metten if at all possible. He is not having any luck on his begging trip and may decide not to go to Fort Augustus, Scotland, as he planned. He may decide to return to the United States with me. Abbot Alexius[26] is supposed to land in New York today, and Bishop Seidenbusch,[27] I believe, is at the moment being rocked by the waves in the English Channel.

In Rome, the president of the Cassinese Congregation,[28] the procurator general,[29] Cardinal Bartolini,[30] and Cardinal Pitra[31] all refer to papal plans for reforming of our Order. The fear is that the matter will be put in the hands of Schiaffino[32] (bishop of Nyssa and abbot general of the Olivetans), Abbot Maurus,[33] and the archabbot of Montecassio.[34] All of them would like to win the Holy Father over to their plans. What are their plans? That remains to be seen, but I have no doubt that they all (particularly the archabbot) have the best of intentions. I doubt there is much reason to fear because insofar as the fundamental points of the *Rule* are concerned, nothing can be changed. Thus, I begin to make plans for my journey home, confident that nothing really compels me to stay, or to return, since I know full well that those things can be taken care of without me. It is strange, though, that many of the abbots look on good Abbot Maurus with suspicion. Perhaps it is the same with me in those cases where I am not well known.

I would be very pleased if I could attend your 50th anniversary celebration. I certainly hope that on that memorable day your happiness will be great and that the many congratulations you receive will bring you fathomless good, for good wishes are prayers and prayers will be heard.

---

[25] Innocent Wolf, O.S.B. (1843-1922), abbot of St. Benedict's Abbey, Atchison, Kansas.
[26] Alexius Edelbrock, O.S.B. (1843-1908), abbot of St. Louis on the Lake, Minnesota.
[27] Rupert Seidenbusch, O.S.B. (1830-1895), vicar apostolic of Northern Minnesota.
[28] Francis Leopold Zelli-Jacobuzi, O.S.B. (1818-1895).
[29] Angelo Pescetelli, O.S.B. (1809-1885).
[30] Dominic Cardinal Bartolini, prefect of the Sacred Congregation of Bishops and Religious.
[31] Jean Baptiste Pitra, O.S.B. (1812-1889).
[32] Placidus Schiaffino, O.S.B. (1829-1889).
[33] Maurus Wolter, O.S.B. (1825-1890), abbot of Beuron (Germany).
[34] Nicholas D'Orgemont, O.S.B. (1826-1896).

Once again, may you have many years in the best of health. With sincere affection and deep respect, Your Grace's most devoted confrere, Boniface Wimmer, Abbot

Ger   oAMA   cASVA   transRG

TO LUKE WIMMER   **148**

St. Vincent, September 20, 1880

Rev. Luke Wimmer, O.S.B.

Dear Confrere: I am sending you good Father Thaddeus[35] who will make his simple vows tomorrow, so that you will have some pious company. He is to recuperate there if at all possible. He is only ten years younger than myself and is suffering from serious liver trouble. He is a very learned man.

Your letter was the first one I read upon arriving here. My sincere thanks for what you said. I undertook the journey very unwillingly because of its difficulties and because of the things that had to be done at home, but having been urgently requested to go, I consented. I considered it a penitential pilgrimage made to honor our holy father Benedict. Under the circumstances, the other abbots would have excused my absence. I was cheerful and kept my spirits up until I reached Montecassino. When I arrived there, I was honored to such an extent that I often blushed with shame and felt myself obliged to protest.

---

[35] Thaddeus Wardy, O.S.B. (1819-1880), had been ordained in 1845 and entered the novitiate at St. Vincent in September 1879. He died in Covington, Kentucky, a little more than two months after Wimmer wrote this letter.

On both Pentecost Sunday and Monday a pontifical high Mass was celebrated by an archbishop assisted by Cardinal Pitra[36] *in throno*. On the main feast, Tuesday, when the tower of our holy father, its seven chapels, and seven altars were consecrated, I was supposed to celebrate the Pontifical High Mass as was announced in the printed program. The kind archbishop of Catania (a Benedictine)[37] congratulated me and said, "Father Abbot, this is your day because you have instigated the whole celebration." The Cassinese abbots were not jealous of me because Montecassino has gained much high esteem because of the festival. I protested with all my power but, nonetheless, felt very happy.

I was under the special care of the papal master of ceremonies, Monsignor Cataldi, but was afraid because of my pride and the jealousy of strangers. I prayed to St. Benedict before his grave to prevent me from taking part in the celebration, but rather to make me humble, and it worked! The consecration of the tower lasted so long that there was no time for a Pontifical High Mass, and I was asked instead to say the last conventual Mass in the main church, above the holy sepulcher.

That day I developed a fever, and because it did not seem serious, I took it with me to Munich where it broke out anew. Throughout my visit to Bavaria, I was sick and did not enjoy myself at all. Then, when I landed in New York, I felt bad and went in misery to Newark where during the first and second day I got worse. From the time I left Montecassino until my return to St. Vincent, everything went wrong, except that we were offered the hospice of St. Elizabeth's, which was ours some years ago.

The ocean voyage was, of course, delightful, but I could not get a first class reservation and had to travel second and third class, which was not very enjoyable because of the many immigrants. I am very glad that it is over and that I am back home again.

Yesterday I assigned the subprior, Father Adalbert;[38] two young priests, Fathers Vincent Huber[39] and Philip Kretz;[40] and two clerics, Fraters Clement Stratman[41] and Robert Monroe[42] (from Covington), to make the expedition to Rome. Father Adalbert is the most suitable man to be rector. The cost for their settling in and for the first year's expenses will clearly be no less than $2500. The investment we are

---

[36] Jean Baptiste Pitra, O.S.B. (1812-1889).
[37] Joseph Benedict Dusmet, O.S.B. (1818-1889), archbishop of Catania, Sicily.
[38] Adalbert Müller, O.S.B. (1842-1906).
[39] Vincent Huber, O.S.B. (1855-1941).
[40] Philip Kretz, O.S.B. (1857-1905).
[41] Clement Stratman, O.S.B. (1859-1935).
[42] Robert Monroe, O.S.B. (1860-1889).

making rests upon the solid calculation (I hope) that it will be a source of blessings for St. Vincent, for the Order, and for the Church.

I am very happy that you will enjoy a good vintage and harvest because it will put an end to the heavy obligation of the debt payment due next spring. You will be able to pay the debt from the proceeds of the sale of the wine. You must devote all your effort to that purpose.

Mrs. Gruber visited me for ten days in the house of Canon Meyringer[43] at Regensburg. This was shortly before my departure. The canon and I visited her home for one day. She is a good, pious soul who prays very much. She is also praying for both of us. She and the wife of Johann, together with our many relatives, send you a thousand greetings. Likewise, many of your fellow students at Munich.

It seems that good spirit and good will prevail among certain of the young fathers—better than before.

I said many holy Masses for your intentions. With the inconveniences of travel, etc., I surely performed no small sacrifice for the good cause. You can be sure of that. I hope that it has pleased God. How long it will last is known only to Him. His will be done in everything, his most holy will. May God bless you and keep you in His Grace. Your devoted, Boniface Wimmer P.S. The small picture is blessed by the Holy Father.

Ger   oASVA   transRG

TO CHRYSOSTOM KRUESZ   **149**

St. Vincent, November 4, 1880

Right Reverend Abbot, Dear Confrere: I was very pleased to receive your letter, which arrived at 1:00 pm today, and I am answering immediately. I was in the hospital from July 1 to July 19, in a private room as I stated earlier to Your Lordship. Then I spent 12 days at Schaeftlarn where I received news from Monsignor de Waal, rector at Campo Santo, that St. Elizabeth would again be available to rent whenever I wanted it, a decision that was easy to make. I set August 29 as my departure date from La Havre for America. I hurriedly made preparations and left Bavaria without allowing myself time to visit Scheyern, St. Stephen's, or Weltenburg. A spell of sickness overtook me, acute bronchitis, inflammation of the windpipe and the adjacent area of the lungs, accompanied by an alarming fit of coughing that tortured me day and night and allowed me no sleep except in a

---

[43] Joseph Meyringer, Wimmer's cousin.

sitting position on a chair or sofa. This was a bitter experience that made it impossible for me to visit any of the places I was interested in, and when I got well, I had to hurry my travel plans in order to return home, find men for Rome, and send them on.

On August 22, I went from Munich by way of Lindau to Basel. The next day I was in Oehlenberg, and on August 24 in Strasbourg. From there I went to Paris and La Havre, arriving on the afternoon of August 25. Regrettably, I arrived too late to obtain first class passage, so I had to be content with poorly equipped and very uncomfortable second-class accommodations. The trip lasted from 3:00 am, August 28, until 6:00 am, September 8, when we reached New York, but we could land only at 8:00 am, and we got our baggage only a few minutes before noon. I went at once by rail to our confreres in Newark, and on the second day in Newark, the illness struck me again. I went to St. Vincent where it finally wore itself out. Since then I have been as well as I was before the journey, thank God.

I immediately selected two priests and two clerics to go to St. Elizabeth's house of studies in Rome, supplied their needs, and sent them to New York on September 26. They departed New York on October 2 at 4:00 pm, and reached Antwerp on October 18 in the morning. From there they traveled by way of Cologne to Munich, Metten, and Rome. In Rome, they will attend lectures at the Apollinare. They are being led by Father Adalbert Müller[44] who was in Rome during the time of the Vatican Council. The group consists of talented, nice young fellows. I have rented St. Elizabeth's at 1500 lire for only the next three years. The house has been repaired and improved considerably. Earlier I asked Abbot Pescetelli[45] to make the necessary improvements, and he writes me that he has done so. He has also provided a cook and servant. This is a very costly venture. My people took with them the sum of $2100, which should cover their costs for half a year.

I am eager to receive their first report from Rome. According to the letters of Monsignor de Waal, there is room for more people, but I could not send any more this year. If I live until next year, I will send at least two more men. If I had my way, St. Elizabeth would become the nucleus of a Benedictine college in Rome. I think that a worthy objective, one that would contribute significantly to the renewal and prestige of the Order.

I regret to note that the Albums have not yet arrived. They were sent from here on August 30 to the Frederick Pustet Company in New York. From there they were forwarded by steamer to Frederick Pustet in Regensburg, to be distributed to

---

[44] Adalbert Müller, O.S.B. (1842-1906).
[45] Angelo Pescetelli, O.S.B. (1809-1885), Roman procurator for the American-Cassinese Benedictines.

all the monasteries and places in Europe, including St. Martinsberg in Hungary. They were not lost at sea, so they must have reached Regensburg. It is very annoying that Father James[46] made the blundering references, calling Your Excellency a *Praeses*, which implies a congregation, and placing your monastery in an incorrect relationship with respect to other monasteries.

We accidentally heard criticism from Bavaria about how the women's convents were included in the Album. It is true that one finds no mention of French or Spanish convents and that the others are merely named with their locations given. If I ever publish the Album again, I will correct many things, but I am afraid that I will not be able to publish it again, at least not soon. The project takes too much in the way of pain and money, and it does not pay well because circulation is small and most monasteries take only a few copies. I have sent 50 copies to Father Adalbert. To the Holy Father and many of the cardinals we sent bound volumes, which took a long time to reach Rome. I gave away many more copies as gifts than I sold. I achieved my purpose in publishing the Album, however, by making it widely known that the Order is a force in the Church, which one can see by simply looking at the figures in the summary at the end of the volume. These figures show that the Order is alive, that it thrives, and that given the freedom of action, it could accomplish great things.

It was no small satisfaction for me to learn that in Italy alone there are 260 Benedictine nuns living in 32 convents; in Bavaria, 74; in Belgium, 172; in America, 482; in England, 26; in Australia, 64. This gives a total of more than 1000. In addition, there are Benedictine nuns living in 44 French convents, eight Swiss convents, and 17 Austrian convents. There are certainly many nuns and devoted women in other convents not accounted for here, totaling at least 5000, exclusive of those in Spain. That represents a power of prayer that cannot be underestimated, in spite of the Masons and Jews and others who turn from God. Over and above this are many other religious communities of nuns who are not Benedictines.

Had the festive celebration at Montecassino been in the charge of one who was better equipped, it could have been an occasion for important and fruitful deliberations. I was very sorry that Your Lordship could not be present. It was my objective in addressing the meeting of non-Italian and German abbots and delegates to stimulate interest. I was very much concerned about reactions to the proposal of Abbot Wolter[47] for an abbot general whose position in the Order would be analogous to that of the Pope in the Church. No one, including myself, expressed

---

[46] James Zilliox, O.S.B. (1849-1890).
[47] Maurus Wolter, O.S.B. (1825-1890), abbot of Beuron (Germany).

approval. Abbot D'Orgemont,[48] however, showed some interest in being called "Abbas abbatum"—a title which, after all, does not imply very much—but I made it plain to him that our constitution calls for government that is representative (federal), not centralized.

Something of importance was accomplished at the gathering, however, for the meeting effected a greater, more universal and united expression of honor for the name and memory of St. Benedict. The cause would not have been helped by mere local celebrations held around Easter time. The idea was for all branches of our Order (except for the Camaldolese, who were not represented) to manifest a devout intention for vigorous, formal union in acknowledgment of St. Benedict as our common Father. In any case, the Holy Father will not find any difficulty in his effort to unite the small branches with the older one and to join the two Italian congregations into one. I have no regrets about having gone to Montecassino. A volume of photographs has been made, and copies are available at Beuron or Emaus.[49]

The presidential election has ended here, and the pseudo-Republican, liberal, moneymen and bigots once again defeated us Democrats. The outcome depended on New York, and the Democrats committed a folly by presenting a Catholic candidate for mayor of the city of New York. New York City is Democratic and Catholic and has a Democratic majority, but upstate New York is Republican. The Democratic majority of the city was not large enough to offset the rest of the state's vote, and so it was that the presidential vote went to the Republican candidate.

Dr. Matthew Gietl, a private physician in Munich, has cured me of my bronchial condition with his prescriptions of mineral waters, taken very warm, and Apollinaris, taken very cold, and chest tea. Even now, I cannot take beer or wine, but only tea (green or black Chinese, and occasionally chest tea). I also found out that honey and milk with sugar helped my chest and throat very much. I must wear a small white band under the collar to keep my throat warm. I take nothing cold, fluid or solid, and as a result, I feel sound and well. I drink warm water in the morning. I take the Apollinaris when I am thirsty, to offset the coughing and to ease the expulsion of phlegm, which has been very heavy. Earlier I took the Apollinaris cold but now naturally cool. In Hungary, they have very good mineral waters, Broadcy etc., but in my experience, it is eating and drinking warm things that benefits the lungs, if they are affected. I have just two months before my 72nd birthday, and nine months before my golden jubilee.

---

[48] Nicholas D'Orgemont, O.S.B. (1826-1896), archabbot of Montecassino.
[49] Benedictine monasteries. Beuron in Germany, and Emaus in Prague.

With prayer and good care, Your Lordship should be able to overcome your trouble. You cannot imagine my disappointment at not having seen you. If I had not become ill, I certainly would have hurried to Hungary. In Bavaria, I met, besides Abbot Utto,[50] only a few good friends in Regensburg. I am not interested in sightseeing, not even in Rome, but for you, though we live far apart, I will always cherish a warm regard. I prize our friendship very highly in view of our mutual efforts on behalf of the centennial celebration and the *Album Benedictinum*, which has brought us into a kind of business relationship. Without your collaboration and help, the great celebration would not have taken place at all, nor would the *Album Benedictinum* have been successfully launched. Both these projects, in my opinion and in the opinion of others, should have far reaching results for Montecassino, for the Order as a whole and, best of all, for the glory of our great founder St. Benedict. He was almost a forgotten man. How much honor has come to him all over the world because of these festivities! How great the recognition our Order has received from unbelievers and Protestants! Moreover, how vigorous now is the spirit of renewal and the spirit of cooperation in the fields of scholarship and asceticism and the desire for renewing the spirit which our father Abbot Benedict served! Before, we were unaware of what others were doing, but now the entire family is aware of its communal existence and is seeking to restore what was long forgotten or disregarded: a new brotherhood, its teaching, and its promise.

Then there is poor Montecassino, the cradle of our Order. Even though it was plundered and impoverished, it has once more gained recognition and sympathy even from those who helped plunder and sought to destroy it. Thus, it happened at the recent festivities. Nicetero attended these festivities, a fellow who has placed his son in the abbey to be educated there. He offered the abbot a monastery near Turin that had been left unharmed by the marauders. Therefore, the prayers of devout Catholics everywhere will rise in prayer that to Jerusalem will someday be restored the cloak of gladness.

Then the meeting itself! One cardinal, four archbishops, seven bishops, 148 prelates and delegates of prelates of all colors from Europe, Asia, America, Australia! It was a joy to see them all together in beautiful order and harmony at the altars, at table, in the house, all assembled as children of their Father in fraternal unity. It was a sight never to be forgotten by those who were present, one that must have given joy too to St. Benedict and his holy confreres in heaven. Now then, I suppose both of us may, without any presumption, take some credit for the undertaking and arrangement of these festivities. This was in fact done at Montecassino in a public way. I think and believe firmly that spiritually you stand before

---

[50] Utto Lang, O.S.B. (1807-1884), abbot of Metten.

God a worthy servant, worthy of reward and deserving of the special protection of St. Benedict. We have gained merit, you and I, for what was accomplished.

For this reason, I am more obliged and attached to you than to any of the other abbots and confreres. I do not know any other abbot to be more obliging and zealous for the common good of our holy Order, more ready to work and make sacrifices, than Your Lordship! For this reason, I will cherish your fellowship in a special way, because I am of the same mind, and I deeply deplore the lack of such characteristics in otherwise estimable persons. I would have preferred much more to have had half a day with you than to attend all the conference's festivities. It was not to be so, however, and I will have to think of it as one of the penitential afflictions, of which there were not a few, which the dear Lord allowed to come to me during my journey. Now, I hope you have a long life and that you will survive me for a long time, and my prayers for you will always be for that end.

Abbot Innocent[51] has not arrived yet, but he recently wrote from Downside (Bath), England, that he will soon be here. He did not act wisely in making the begging trip. Anyone could have told him what the outcome would be, but he did not believe me. He will have to help himself now, and he will do so if he makes a start in the right direction. I am ready to help him too. I have given him $5,000 since he became abbot, and I took care of his scholastics and novices without charge. Naturally, however, I do not want him to rely altogether on me. I have many irons in the fire, and I stand in need of God's help, too, so that I do not burn them up.

We have had an excellent harvest with an abundance of oats, wheat, and corn. We likewise had a good harvest of hay, fruit, and wine, and we were successful in the sale of beer. There was a shortage of potatoes. Attendance is good at the college, which I strive to put in flourishing condition. We are all in good health, with the exception of Father James Zilliox. He was the editor of the *Album Benedictinum* and has had to put aside his class work for a while. One of our good brothers passed away during my absence.

I must close now. You see, I am inclined to overindulge when chatting with you. Do not allow yourself to be overcome with frustration and gloom because of ill health. It is well and good that we prepare for death, but your illness will pass. After my spell of illness, I was in such a weakened condition that I could hardly walk a thousand paces. Now I move about like a youngster. I suppose I will die of a stroke some day.

Be that as it may, let us strive to serve God faithfully as long as we can and as well as we can in our holy Order, with patience and trust in God. A thousand

[51] Innocent Wolf, O.S.B. (1843-1922), abbot of St. Benedict's Abbey, Atchison, Kansas.

greetings. May God keep and bless you always. In sincere love and esteem, Your Lordship's devoted confrere, Boniface Wimmer, Abbot

Ger   oAPH   cASVA   transFF

TO SCHOLASTICA BURKHARDT   **150**

St. Vincent, December 31, 1880

Dear Reverend Mother and Sisters: You must not die before I have seen you and given you the spiritual blessing. Just hang on to our dear, eternally good Lord and Savior so that He will keep you that long. He'll do that all right. But I cannot come immediately. Nor can I say just when I can come, first of all, because I have so much to do on account of the southern missions, to and from which there is much correspondence, and secondly, because I cannot travel on account of my feet. I cannot go when the cold weather afflicts them. Up until now, I have warded off severe rheumatism, but just recently it has settled in my knees and the pain attacks me, now here, now there, so that at times I cannot walk at all. That's my problem, and I have other problems as well, big ones and small ones, that are not in my feet!

Well, I too will soon have to die, and that is why I would like to see you once more. If I cannot go with you, I would like to give you all sorts of messages to take along with you. O Mother! What will happen? I think often enough about this journey to eternity, but I never start the journey except in my sleep. I have often dreamed that I was on my way, going here and there, even ready to sail on a ship, except that I have no money or can't find the right place or the right door. And thus I wear my pitiful self out until I wake. Perhaps my trip to eternity will present the same difficulties. If I cannot make things right here, how much will I have to atone for there? It may be, however, that I shall have to plough away here on earth for a while longer, contending with various unbearable annoyances, idiosyncrasies, sicknesses, and pains, because until now (I am seventy-two years old) I have had only good days, while you and so many good souls have had to suffer from illness.

In many respects I am better than I was before the last trip, but my strength has diminished and is diminishing rapidly. I am now only an old crow, not worth much more than the sparrows that sit in my alcove waiting for me to feed them because they cannot find any food in so much snow. I hope that the bitter cold will soon give way to milder weather. Then I'll try to get to Erie. Who knows but that I shall even bring you good health and that you will recover so that you will be the better able to fill the wedding lamp for the final arrival of the heavenly bridegroom, and share the oil with others without danger of your own lamp being extinguished. Let us pray and hope that the new year will be a blessed one for us and all the good sisters and brothers and mothers and fathers—and, for that matter, for all Christians while we still have to tarry in this valley of tears, until we can celebrate on the other side.

May God bless you with His graces so that you will be richly garbed for the wedding feast and enter into the heavenly home with great rejoicing when the time comes. I shall remember you in my daily Mass in a special way. Your devoted brother, Abbot Boniface Wimmer

P.S. Hearty wishes to all the sisters for a blessed New Year.

Eng   oASBC   cASVA

TO MICHAEL REGER   151

St. Vincent, January 8, 1881

Right Reverend Dean, Dearest Friend: I should have written you earlier but was unable to do so. I am very sorry that I could not see you for more than a few minutes. I had looked forward to being with you, but the dear Lord did not want me to have that satisfaction. For five weeks, He held me back by illness, but when that was over, no one could hold me back. I rushed urgently back to St. Vincent since I had to make arrangements for sending some students to Rome where the school year was to begin on November 1. I could not delay my return home. I had to select and prepare the students so that they arrived in Rome on time.

I was determined to embark from La Havre on August 28, and for that reason, I could not visit Metten again. Likewise, I had to miss Weltenburg, Scheyern, St. Stephen's, and Eichstätt entirely. It was not even possible for me to visit Einsiedeln again, but I took in the Trappists of Oehlenberg on the trip to La Havre. I arrived in New York on September 8 and went immediately to my confreres in Newark where I became sick again. Nevertheless, after five days I returned to St. Vincent, where I arrived on September 15, and felt miserable for several days.

The joy of sleeping in my own bed after five months away and of being with my own people, however, restored me to health, and since then I have felt fine, have had no pain, can eat and drink (except anything cold), sleep soundly, can attend choir, and otherwise can do what my duties call for. I do not think I could travel far, but in any event, I do not have to travel because I am always at home. I have no other exercise than walking around the house and, in the evenings, walking in my room while I say my Rosary. Sometimes I experience weak spells, which is nothing to laugh at since they are more or less serious.

I say Mass every morning after choir at 5:00 am, then meditation, then Prime, and after that, two cups of coffee with a slice of bread. Then I go to work, which consists mostly of writing letters. I think often of you and of how well I have it in comparison with you because I have always enjoyed good health. I am often afraid that the dear Lord might, for the little bit of good I have done, reward me with temporal happiness and in the end not allow me to reach heaven. Then I recall that I may still have to suffer here on earth. It is up to Him to know what is best for each of us. There is no question that I have to be in good health because St. Vincent is no place for a sick abbot. Therefore, I cannot thank the Lord enough for my health.

It is not so easy to explain, humanly speaking, why I could not experience what you might call interior satisfaction in either Germany or Rome. Certainly, I did not go there for that purpose, but I did not expect that I would get no pleasure out of the journey at all. I deeply regretted not being able to spend time with you, since I feel certain that this was the last opportunity we will have to be together in this world.

I had bad luck on the steamship and had to be satisfied with second-class accommodations, which made for very uncomfortable traveling. The festival at Montecassino was worthwhile and justified the extended trip. May the dear Lord, with the intercession of St. Benedict, pour out His spirit on all His children and awaken them to a new and holy life in the midst of the terrible and universal destruction brought on by the spirit of the modern world.

I wish you at the beginning of the new year, from the bottom of my heart, everything that is best for your welfare: plenty of patience so that you may persevere in obeying the holy will of God to the end, a daily increase in a holy life in Him, and a full measure of reward in heaven for all your trouble and work in the service of God and for the many difficult things you have had to suffer, by which you have earned your martyrdom.

I include you everyday, not only in general with all my friends and benefactors, but in a special manner, in the holy sacrifice of the Mass, and I hope you will not forget me when you are in joy and sorrow and need, as I do not forget you. With sincere love and respect, your friend, Boniface Wimmer, Abbot

Ger   oASVA   transRG

TO ALEXIUS EDELBROCK **152**

St. Vincent, July 15, 1881

Right Reverend Father Abbot, Esteemed Confrere: A thousand thanks for your beautiful letter for my namesday. May God make everything true and reward your love! The general chapter will take place on August 3, 4, and 5. I am very glad we will come together again and am convinced it will not be without profit. Will you be able to hold visitation here immediately afterwards?

Do not expect any solemnities on August 1. I have firmly forbidden them, but will be happy to see my confreres around me, as many of them as want or are able to come. Please let Father Benedict[52] come. He has asked to be present and has always proven himself a sincere confrere. I am sorry that Father Clement[53] is so ill. That priest who is waiting for his dispensation wrote to me from Covington, where he is staying with our fathers. They think that his vocation is not yet decided. I gladly allowed him to stay there for the time being. Your priest-novice is getting along very well, as are the others. We have had extremely hot weather here for some days. Today it is cool. Most of the harvest is in already and is very good. All are well.

My health is good for my age. I can, and actually do, follow the whole schedule of the day, but I can no longer manage the correspondence because I am so weak that I must sleep nearly every afternoon and thereby lose a good deal of time. I also have to be very careful that I do not become distrustful and suspicious because I realize time and again that many are dissatisfied with my administration, or that they work against it.

A good, strict visitation will be necessary. By the way, this is good for me since it saves me from pride and helps me towards humility. Therefore, I do not want any solemnities because in many cases the enthusiasm would be only a show. Such experiences lead beautifully to the effect that in everything one does, one considers only God's pleasure, and one learns to bear more easily disregard or even contempt. In this manner, one also practices salutary penance.

I have accomplished some good things. Or rather, God has accomplished them through me. This cannot be denied, but one can maintain (with proofs) that I did not do well enough, so that the results are not good, and perhaps even bad. If a monastery is a good monastery, it is, of course, good. However, if it is not a good one, it is not good, and possibly even bad. Thus it can happen that the founder is admired and exalted by people who are not thoroughly aware of the reality,

---

[52] Benedict Haindl, O.S.B. (1815-1887).
[53] Clement Staub, O.S.B. (1819-1886).

and that at the same time good people, who are better informed, can think in all seriousness (like rats on a sinking ship) of leaving the monastery and complaining to the Pope about the founder, or at least they denigrate him everywhere. Such an experience could have a very depressing effect. If what they say is true, it would prove that the whole course of one's life has been a failure. To fear this (even if one does not necessarily believe it) is sad enough.

Therefore, you see that my mood is by no means festive. However, it is not morose because I have always tried to be detached and indifferent to how people talk and judge me. Until we meet again! All good wishes for your namesday! With sincere love and esteem, your most devoted confrere, Boniface, Abbot

Ger   oASJA   cASVA   transAHo

TO CHRYSOSTOM KRUESZ   **153**

St. Vincent, August 30, 1881

Right Reverend and Dear Archabbot, Your Excellency: I received your letter of April 2 on April 22 and have not yet answered. Now I am finally going to attend to it today, and what do I have to say? I have become the victim of a special kind of conspiracy, and you, too, Your Excellency—please do not be offended—seem to have been involved in the plot. Before I could give any thought to the matter, the local newspapers announced that the abbot of St. Vincent would celebrate the golden jubilee of his priesthood on August 1. I took exception to this and strictly forbade my confreres to arrange any kind of celebration, or even to agree to one, because I wanted to celebrate the occasion in a quiet manner. When I heard no more about it, I continued to believe that I could plan something for a small circle of local confreres and those in the neighborhood with a low Mass, while a young priest just ordained could say his first Mass in the same way and thus we could have a double festivity on the day. Since the general chapter was to be held this year, the two abbots[54] asked me to schedule it close to August 1 because they wanted to be present for the anniversary and did not want to make the trip a second time. I could not easily deny their request, so I scheduled the general chapter for August 3, 4, and 5, so that the abbots and priors, too, could be included and the entire family, therefore, could be represented by their leaders. I issued no other

---

[54] Alexius Edelbrock, O.S.B. (1843-1908), abbot of St. John's Abbey, Minnesota; Innocent Wolf, O.S.B. (1843-1922), abbot of St. Benedict's Abbey, Atchison, Kansas.

invitations except one to Father Nicholas Balleis[55] of St. Peter's Abbey, Salzburg. I had followed him to America a few years after he, himself, had come to the United States to labor in the mission fields, but he never attempted to found a monastery. He has lived for many years in Brooklyn, has a small parish there, and will celebrate his golden jubilee next December. I invited him with the promise that if he attended my celebration, I would, in turn, be present for his.

As the day of the celebration drew near, I noticed that the fathers had not heeded my order, but had quietly arranged for a public celebration of the day in the church and in the house, which I could not easily avoid. Invitations were not sent out, but the report of the coming celebration got around by word of mouth, so many uninvited guests were on hand. They all knew they would be welcome as usual. Our two bishops, Fink and Seidenbusch,[56] attended. Fink is from Leavenworth, Kansas, and Seidenbusch is vicar apostolic of Northern Minnesota and a former abbot in Minnesota. Also Bishop Marty,[57] vicar apostolic of the Dakota Territory and a former abbot in Missouri, and Abbot Frowin Conrad[58] from Engelberg, Switzerland, who is abbot of Conception Abbey, Missouri, the youngest abbey of the Swiss-American Benedictines. Also Father Nicholas Balleis.

Throughout the whole day, telegrams kept coming in. Our Benedictine sisters, of course, could not be present, but they sent an entire bazaar of things, costly articles for the sacristy and altar, and also letters and notes expressing their pledges of Masses and prayers and rosaries to be offered for me. Our neighbors, the Sisters of Mercy, did likewise, as did the Bavarian Dominican sisters of Brooklyn, who came to America from Regensburg at my request 30 years ago and who, since that time, have spread as far as California, all on account of some little favor I might have done for them or for what I might still be able to do for them.

My own people presented me with a rich set of pontifical vestments and a gold miter, which must have cost at least $1,000, with the request that I bless these on the day of my celebration. Bishop Marty, at whose consecration I had the honor to give the sermon, preached the sermon for me in return on this occasion. He is a very learned and very devout prelate and had a very inspiring message on the wonderful ways of divine providence. The three abbots and the priors assisted, while our clerics, novices, and scholastics rendered a Cecilian Mass. Then came the meal, a plain meal, in the college refectory where there were toasts, readings

---

[55] Nicholas Balleis, O.S.B. (1808-1892).
[56] Louis M. Fink, O.S.B. (1834-1904), bishop of Leavenworth, and Rupert Seidenbusch, O.S.B. (1830-1895), vicar apostolic of Northern Minnesota.
[57] Martin Marty, O.S.B. (1834-1896), vicar apostolic of the Dakota Territory.
[58] Frowin Conrad, O.S.B. (1833-1923), abbot of Conception Abbey, Missouri.

of the telegrams received during the day (we have telegraph service in the house), and a very attractive entertainment by the brass and string band.

Now all this was very nice, and the gaiety went off in beautiful order, but I sat there as if on pins and needles and did not know whether to laugh or to weep. It was too much of a good thing. I was all of a sudden marked as a patriarch, and I had to listen to stories of exploits carried out in the line of duty of which I knew nothing, or of "extraordinary" deeds, which were nothing, more than ordinary daily acts of charity or zeal performed for the honor of God and His Church. One thing there was, though, that pleased me very much during the celebration. It was not just a family feast, but turned out to be a regular Benedictine feast of unity because of the participation of the Swiss. Bishop Marty especially emphasized this in his sermon when he noted that besides our own Bavarian-American-Cassinese Congregation, there is also another Benedictine congregation in America, the Swiss Congregation, which already has two abbeys and one priory. The Swiss Benedictines, he said, would not be in America today had it not been for the effort first made by the Bavarians and for the two visits I paid to Einsiedeln when I vigorously urged Abbot Henry[59] to establish a Swiss foundation in America. As a result, he said, they likewise derive their beginnings from us and would have it thought of in that way.

I was deeply moved that the bishop, Abbot Frowin, and another Swiss Benedictine, the vicar general of St. Joseph, had made a journey of 1,000 miles to be at the celebration. The second abbot of St. Meinrad's[60] wrote to express his regrets that he could not be present. All this strengthens the bonds of union among us. Everyone knew that I wanted only a family festivity and had, therefore, refrained from sending any invitations. The gathering made a deep impression on everyone here, and it will not soon be forgotten, but will continue to have beneficial results for the future. The two congregations will have more opportunities to meet in friendship and brotherhood and, thereby, mutually help each other in their common interests.

Your own kind and cordial letter of friendship had arrived, as did those from Metten and St. Boniface Abbey. An announcement of these letters was made, but I forbade the reading of them for reasons of modesty. It was said that another message would come from Scheyern, but no one knew what it was about. So it was a thrill for me and for all of us when a few days ago a beautiful album arrived showing the entire Bavarian Congregation. Soon afterwards the multilingual album, presented by Father Placid Mathan, arrived, as did the exceedingly rich album

---

[59] Henry Schmid, O.S.B. (1800-1874), abbot of Einsiedeln.
[60] Fintan Mundwiler, O.S.B. (1835-1898).

from the Austro-Hungarian monasteries. These gifts and their unexpected arrival made a profound impression on me that I cannot describe.

I deeply appreciated the fact that my old friend and confrere, the abbot of Metten,[61] remembered me. Years ago, I was honored with membership at Metten, and it is something I still cherish. Even a friendly little letter from you would have been welcome because you have often greeted me most cordially with short notes, but when a collective ovation from all the Austro-Hungarian abbots arrived, that was unexpected! I cannot think of anything more satisfying because I am well aware that I have never had occasion, remotely or casually, to meet any of these wonderful persons.

I know very well that these expressions of honor do not come to me personally, but only because of the fact that I was the first Benedictine to introduce the Order here, and under favorable circumstances, and that I have helped establish it and caused it to spread. I, too, express my joy that it pleased God, at a time when the very existence of the Order was in danger in the Old World, to find new life and vigor for our Order in the New World.

It is natural for Benedictines to be joyful about anything that is good and meritorious in the Order and that is conducive to its well-being, and I share in the joy of my fellow Benedictines. Nevertheless, I must confess that I cannot claim any special merit in bringing these things about, for to God alone is all honor due and from Him alone proceed the merit and worth of our deeds. You and all my right reverend confreres have an estimate of me that is far above my deserts. If you or any of my confrere abbots had been in my place, with your zeal, learning, experience, understanding, and character, you would have done far more in my position than I.

My best friends, that is, those who knew me best, tried to dissuade me from the undertaking when I was ready to set out for America with the announced purpose of founding one or more monasteries that would become training centers for the Order and for future missionaries. Because they knew me, they did not conceal their conviction that I would return very shortly without having accomplished anything or that bad things would happen. Father Müller,[62] the royal chaplain in Munich, and Bishop Ziegler of Linz,[63] whom I consulted by letter with regard to my project, were the only ones to offer me encouragement in my efforts, proof again that God can make use of the poorest instruments in attaining His ends,

---

[61] Utto Lang, O.S.B. (1807-1884).

[62] Joseph Ferdinand Müller (1803-1864), chaplain to the court of King Ludwig I of Bavaria and treasurer of the *Ludwig Missionsverein.*

[63] Gregory Thomas Ziegler, O.S.B. (1770-1852), bishop of Linz, Austria.

because He used me, the least of my brothers at Metten, to take up this mission. I am therefore quite undeserving of any honor or distinction and was taken aback when in your address you featured me before friends and confreres in a garb so implausible. It was attractive enough for the delight and applause of those present, but it was an abomination in the eyes of the all-knowing God.

Undoubtedly, what the fathers did in arranging this celebration was done with the best of intentions. For that reason, I want to offer my sincere thanks. They all wanted to please me by manifesting their feelings, good wishes, and congratulations and to further the interests of the Order and to assure me of their willingness to help me with whatever God may have in store for me in the remaining days of my life. I will continue to live with that thought as long as I can. These assurances have given strength to my soul, and not only to me but also to those who help at my side, strenuously and loyally, while I continue to sit at my desk arranging for the work ahead.

I do not know to whom I am indebted for the devoted and honorable things that were written about me in the album, but, as I have said at the start of this letter, I have the suspicion that Your Excellency was the chief "conspirator." Therefore, I express my deepest appreciation to you above all. May I ask you, in all humility, to express these sentiments of appreciation to all the right reverend confreres? I will also write to the Bavarian confreres who were responsible for the album and multilingual book.

Of course, I will be most happy to accept the books printed to mark the centenary and will place them in the library. You can send the money for the 50 albums to Metten rather than to Pustet because I am constantly in touch with the abbot there.

At the moment, my health is good. The harvest was excellent—wheat, oats, hay. The corn has a beautiful stand. There is little fruit, and wine production is somewhat skimpy. We have lost three priests to death since spring. I fear that the many honors and joys are forebodings of sadness and suffering. The former I have not sought; the latter I will try to accept with resignation.

Again, my thanks to you for your expressions of love and friendship. May God bless you with continued health for many years to come. Please do not be too critical of these rambling lines. I have been repeatedly interrupted while writing this letter. In sincere love and esteem, Your Excellency's unworthy and devoted confrere, Boniface Wimmer, Abbot

Ger   oAPH   cASVA   transFF

TO FROWIN CONRAD   **154**

St. Vincent, December 25, 1881

Right Reverend Lord Abbot and Brother: First, I want to wish you a very happy New Year, good health, patience, good cheer, and God's blessings on all your work and endeavors. On December 6, I celebrated with Father Nicholas Balleis[64] of Newark his 50th anniversary as a priest. The celebration took place at our priory in Newark. Perhaps you met Father Nicholas at St. Vincent. It was a beautiful day.

I have rented St. Elizabeth's in Rome for our men there, three priests and four clerics. The cost is $300 a year. There is a small church and a house large enough for a dozen men. It is located in the middle of the city and belongs to Campo Santo because it is a German foundation. It is not far from the Roman College and the German College. It costs me $200 a year for each person. Because so many Roman doctors are running around, I thought we too should have a few so that our college will be secure. I have three already. I still hope to see a Benedictine college in Rome. Maybe that will happen one day.

Our novitiate is in good order, and our clerics are well behaved. If they misbehave or cause trouble, it is not my fault. The three schools and the overcrowded conditions are obstacles to keeping good order. You will find that out too. Overall, I cannot complain. With the exception of two or three of them, more than 100 fathers do what is required of them and are industrious. I must admit, however, that they do not devote enough attention to the spiritual life. This is difficult or even impossible to change if they themselves do not want to change. On the other hand, there are those who are overzealous and do not want to take into account the conditions we face. They want to live only a contemplative life. I believe that there is no justification for living an exclusively contemplative life here and that the poor people need us, especially the young.

My own prior[65] is of this company. He looks to Beuron where he thinks he can find his paradise. However, I am quite certain that the monks of Beuron will one day lose all that their life stands for if they do not take up the care of souls as priests or missionaries and undertake the education and development of young as well as older people. I am convinced that we must take an interest in the missions as the mendicant orders and congregations do. I would have done more for the missions long ago if it had been possible, but I did not have enough men because the college required them.

---

[64] Nicholas Balleis, O.S.B. (1808-1892).
[65] James Zilliox, O.S.B. (1849-1890).

In the same manner, a press is absolutely necessary. I was very disappointed when Frater Heinrich[66] was not accepted for the priesthood by our chapter because as a typesetter he could have done much for our press. The idealists were also at fault here. The Paulists are a good example of what can be done with a press, as are our brothers at Montecassino.

What I said about the suffering I expect to experience referred to suffering that God might deign to send as a penance or a trial, whether we do our duty or not. Until now, things have been too good for me. May you remain in good health, and may God bless you and your house! With sincere love and reverence, Your Grace's most devoted, Boniface Wimmer, Abbot

Ger   oACA   cASVA   transIG

TO JOSEPH MEYRINGER   155

St. Vincent, January 22, 1882

Esteemed Reverend Canon, Dearly Beloved Friend and Cousin: Yesterday I received your letter dated November 22 from Louisville where the sister of Mr. Schrem lives with her husband. The Schrems must have passed St. Vincent on the express train. They could not stop in Latrobe without making their ticket for Louisville invalid. Louisville is about 500 miles southwest of here. He sent the letter by mail. I am not sure how it happened.

For many years, I have made a memento at Mass for my friend Geltinger, who I thought was dead, but then last year I learned that he was still alive and taking care of a parish. I was delighted to receive his photograph. Father Aschenbrenner is dead? So soon after his jubilee! I shall surely not forget him at Mass. For a long time, I had not thought of Schau and Mullner because I did not know them very well. Lately I received greetings from Pollauern through a brother candidate. I did not imagine so many of those ordained in 1831 were still alive. Without a doubt we will all be dead soon. I accept it as a special grace that we are still among the living.

How much time has passed since the death of Father Pius Bacherl![67] It happened that I was at his deathbed. I could see clearly that the devil attacked and

---

[66] Odilo Heinrich Beyer, O.S.B., was a printer who had entered the novitiate at St. Vincent in 1880. At the end of his novitiate he was not accepted by the chapter for simple profession. He went to Conception Abbey in 1881, but he did not persevere as a monk.

[67] Pius Bacherl, O.S.B. (1805-1844), had been in the novitiate at Metten with Wimmer.

terrified him shortly before he died. I tried to help him and to fortify him with words of consolation. I urged him not to believe the devil, but to have faith and trust in Christ's redeeming blood and grace. I made the sign of the cross over him and sprinkled him with holy water until he quieted down. Shortly after that, he died peacefully. I think Father Scheweiger died before that. I never saw him again after our pastoral examination. He comes to my memory often, but I never heard where he died. I often make a memento for him. When will my turn come?

My health is not stable. I am no longer robust, but I am all right because I take care of myself. I felt the effects of the sickness of 1880 for a long time. I am still not able to drink or eat anything cold. Not even fruit, when it is cold. I can take practically no beer or wine or even water. In the morning, I have coffee, at the noon and evening meals, tea. During the day, I drink nothing. I enjoy a good appetite but cannot take any heavy food without having a bad night.

I jump out of bed at quarter to four on the dot. There is no heat in my bedroom. At 4:00 am, I am in choir. At 5:00 am, I say Mass in my private chapel. Then I meditate until 6:00 am, when we pray Prime. Then I have coffee, after which I often feel tired, so I rest for a few minutes and then write until 9:00 am, when we have the Little Hours. Then I write again until 11:00 am, at which time I make my particular examination of conscience for 15 minutes. Then we have lunch at 11:15 am, followed by adoration of the Blessed Sacrament. After that I read the papers or write letters or give audiences until 1:30 pm. Then, if I am not disturbed, I nap in my armchair until Vespers at 3:00 pm. After that, when the weather is good, I visit the brothers and workmen or keep myself busy with reading until 6:00 pm, when we eat supper. After that, I give audiences etc. until 7:30 pm, when we have Compline. Then from 8:00 until 9:00 pm, I walk up and down in my room saying the Rosary and thinking over what happened during the day and what might happen [tomorrow]. Then I go to bed. That is my daily routine when I am at home. Even if the bishop or someone of my acquaintance happens to be here, I wish them "good night," with the excuse that I can no longer stay up in the evening, and go to my room. That is the way I keep fit and preserve my health! During the winter, when the weather is bad, I do not go out of the house for weeks at a time. I get enough exercise in my room between 8:00 and 9:00 pm. I cannot do much reading by candlelight because my eyes hurt. I never have much time because I am usually busy.

George is in the best of health and looks good. He is growing a lot. He likes to work and makes himself useful everywhere. He is good-hearted and will help his mother as much as he can. Conrad Mittewerder is behaving himself. I put both of them on their conscience to send their savings home, as the young Irishmen are doing, so that they will receive greater blessings for supporting their parents, but they are both doing this spontaneously, freely, and gladly. The dear Lord disposes everything in the proper manner. Stay in good health and keep up your good spirits. Peace be with you. Boniface Wimmer, Abbot

Ger   oASVA   transRG

TO ALEXIUS EDELBROCK   **156**

St. Vincent, March 23, 1882

Right Reverend Abbot Alexius Edelbrock: The following complaints have been sent to the Sacred Congregation for the Propagation of the Faith, or rather to the Pope, by Fathers James Zilliox and Maurice Kaeder.[68] I answered them today, and depending on the circumstances, I will have to request that you come as soon as possible after Easter in order to make the visitation here *ex officio*. The denunciation was made very shortly after the general chapter. With all esteem and love, Boniface Wimmer, Abbot-President

P.S. Father Edwin[69] has come back and brought the $1,000 I lent him. The money (about $500) he had in the bank, however, he spent on studies in St. Louis, where he acquired the title of medical doctor. He humbly asked to be forgiven and to be received again, which I granted him on condition that he improve. However, I sent him to Richmond the next day to make a retreat during the whole of Lent. Now I have to report his case to Rome and wait for their reaction.

After Edwin left, I succeeded in inducing all the professors to participate again fairly regularly in the morning office, even Father Maurice (who objected most of all), although Father Maurice agreed only after he got the message that I intended to deprive him of his professorship, which Father Prior had offered to accept. Now he also says Mass, which before he sometimes failed to do for a whole week. I also asked the prior of Metten[70] for his opinion about this matter. He defended, as I do, the position that in our monasteries all the fathers, including the professors, are obliged to attend choir, and especially the morning choir insofar as they are not prevented from doing so. This is the practice at Metten.

That novice (Reverend Henry Joseph Kraemer) came only as far as Chicago. He never did show up here.

---

[68] James Zilliox, O.S.B. (1849-1890), and Maurice Kaeder, O.S.B. (1837-1892).
[69] Edwin Pierron, O.S.B. (1846-1930).
[70] Rupert Mittermüller, O.S.B. (1814-1893).

[Attachment] [Lat]

Most Reverend Father: The Sacred Congregation for the Propagation of the Faith has been informed of several things that, if true, would indicate that the regular discipline at St. Vincent Abbey has not only been relaxed but also completely abolished. It is reported that the monks do not observe any law of enclosure, that they go out and wander here and there, that they talk and feast with women outside the enclosure, that sometimes they go to the city to visit the theater, and that they receive women within the enclosure (even in the dormitories of the abbey). It is further reported that as a result of these things, the monks are considered most scandalous, ensnared in shameful habits, pursuing earthly not heavenly things, and that matters reached such a point that one took flight so that the civil authorities would not put him in jail. These and similar things have been reported which are unbecoming not only of monks but even of ordinary Christians. Even though I believe that all this is false or exaggerated, I would like nevertheless to inquire about the accusations and ask that you diligently investigate whether any of these abuses exist among your subjects and whether any of the monks lead a life that does not seem to be in accordance with monastic profession. Please write to me and tell me the whole truth so that I am not in doubt and uncertainly about a matter of such gravity. Farewell in the Lord.

Devotedly,

John Cardinal Simeoni, Prefect
S. Masotti, Secretary
Rome, Sacred Congregation of the *Propaganda Fide*
February 25, 1882

Ger   oASJA   cASVA   transAHo

TO INNOCENT WOLF   **157**

St. Vincent, April 7, 1882

Right Reverend Abbot and Confrere: I write the following in answer to your letter of March 28. I sent the answer to the charges only on Easter Monday. I presented my answer objectively, without any reference to the accusers or what they had to say. The coarsest allegations were made, characteristically, by Father Maurice.[71] The others were signed by the prior[72] as well as by Maurice. Naturally, Maurice's recital is far more harmful. Now he seems to be ashamed, but he is a dangerous person, full of pride, as you have said.

The story of Father Edwin[73] is not so bad. He swears under oath that he had no improper relations with the woman. Nor did he lead her astray, but rather she ran after him, much to his own disgust. They did not discuss marriage, though she wanted to entice him into marriage. His error is that he made many visits to her house and that in general he led a very unspiritual life. He made a very good retreat in Richmond and afterward, as I trust, a good confession. I demanded, however, a profession of faith, as the Councils of Trent and of the Vatican prescribe, as well as a written recantation of his blasphemous joking, as when he spoke at table of St. Mary Magdalen being the beloved of Jesus. I explained further that I would not tolerate a scoffer of religion in the house and that he would have to change his ways in this respect. He promised to do so. His letters sound very contrite and humble. I have not concealed my own misgivings, however, and I still do not trust him altogether. One does not change so suddenly and completely. He is much to blame for the disorder here.

Everyone now attends choir without opposition. Even Father Maurice attends. Only Louis, Albert, and Timothy[74] sleep in with any frequency. Especially Timothy. Nevertheless, they have to get up at 5:00 am when I rouse them myself so that they can say Mass. The nocturnal silence, broken most frequently by Maurice, is now well observed, as is, to a great extent, the particular examination of conscience. I hope now by earnest effort and with patience to restore order everywhere.

The prior offered his resignation, which I cannot accept just now since he has been in office less than a year. I delayed my answer to Rome until I was entirely cooled off, and for that reason, I am not making any recriminations. In the event that they reject my statement as coming from a judge on his own behalf, I have asked that the monks at St. Elizabeth's be asked for their opinion, or that a visitation be ordered, or that the *Propaganda Fide* give an official judgment. I hope this is enough, but if not, let come what will. I could give evidence against James and Maurice that would quiet them for all time. I wrote it down but did not send it

[71] Maurice Kaeder, O.S.B. (1837-1892).

[72] James Zilliox, O.S.B. (1849-1890).

[73] Edwin Pierron, O.S.B. (1846-1930).

[74] Louis Haas, O.S.B. (1855-1936); Albert Robrecht, O.S.B. (1851-1897); and Timothy Blasius, O.S.B. (1855-1898).

to Rome. I leave the retribution to God and accept their efforts against the monastery and me as my own punishment.

Do not take any money at ten percent. Mrs. N. at St. Clair had $500 she offered to lend Father Paulinus[75] at four or five percent. If you think you can accept her offer, we can have the money. Write me soon about this. The former Marian brother, I.M. Raufenberger in Kulmbach, near Bayreuth, wrote and offered to lend 1,000 Austrian marks. He wanted to know the rate of interest and the security for such a loan. I replied that we could offer him four percent with security, or even five percent, and suggested that you might be willing to offer five percent since you were trying to retire some capital debt for which you were paying seven percent. I urged him to send the money. We should be able to gather enough money to repay Dietl.

We had to pay $1,800 for ice so that we could keep up brewing operations during the summer. We will earn this back again, of course. An Easter frost in Covington, Kentucky, did much damage there. Four hundred and ninety-two Mass intentions have arrived from Metten. Unfortunately, they are dated as far back as October 9. Some of our professors often fail to say Mass. This situation was made known to me just recently. Lebling[76] will let Munich have $15,000 in the near future. I have heard nothing since December from Father Balleis.[77] Next week I will go to Savannah. Father Pirmin[78] returned only during Lent. I will be obliged to recall Frater John[79] from Rome because his studies cause headaches. May God keep you faithful and well, and may He be your refuge and strength in all things. Boniface Wimmer, Abbot

Ger   oASBA   cASVA   transPB

TO JOSEPH MEYRINGER   158

St. Vincent, April 21, 1882

Right Reverend Friend, Dear Canon: Because I am about to take a long journey, I am trying to answer old correspondence and do not want to neglect your letter

---

[75] Paulinus Wenkmann, O.S.B. (1836-1922).

[76] Hugo Lebling, son of the late Louis Ignatius Lebling, treasurer of the *Ludwig Missionsverein*.

[77] Nicholas Balleis, O.S.B. (1808-1892).

[78] Pirmin Levermann, O.S.B. (1829-1899).

[79] John Kops, O.S.B., a cleric of St. Vincent who did not persevere in monastic life.

of March. I received the death notice of our friend Reger[80] from someone else, so I did not mention it in my last letter to you. I took it very much to heart because I had received many favors from him. I did not think that 12 veterans of the class of 1831 were still alive. I am the youngest of them, being 73 years and three months old.

Oh, my dear friend! If you are trembling at the thought of judgment, what shall I do? You had only parochial duties, but I...! You were always a much better student than I. I give thanks to God each day for calling me to the secular priesthood and the religious state. What would have happened to me otherwise? Therefore, every day I say an Our Father in respectful memory of Bishop Wittmann,[81] that God may reward him for what I owe him. He was the cause of my entering the monastery, which I was thinking about even when I was at the Gregorium.

Humanly speaking, we have behaved ourselves more or less worthily, but what about God's judgment? Who knows what that will be? I was told the story of an old monk who walked up and down the corridors of the cloister repeating, "Dear Lord, you are good. Do not reject me." He had frightful thoughts in his mind. That is the pitiful case with us too. The sins of youth and ignorance, especially the sins against our neighbor, we seldom think about until we are old, but it is well that we remind ourselves.

This latter type of sin, i.e. sins against one's neighbor, I am especially afraid of. Not long ago an old monk died here, an Irishman.[82] He felt so happy that he could die in the monastery. He was not afraid of death. He could speak of it lightly. I received him in the monastery when he was already an old man. He could not do much more than teach, and that only for a short time. As a result, he had few responsibilities. I console myself, like that monk, with the immense goodness and mercy of God, which we priests enjoy more than other people.

Next week, I am going to Baltimore, Richmond, Charlotte (in North Carolina), and Savannah and Skidaway Island in the state of Georgia. I will remain four days in Georgia, then travel northwest from Savannah to Chattanooga, Huntsville, and Tuscumbia in the state of Alabama; then to Wetaug near Cairo, Illinois, where two large rivers, the Ohio and the Mississippi, join each other; then to Covington, Kentucky, and afterward home, via Pittsburgh. If the trip proves too much for me, I will come home directly from Savannah or Tuscumbia, but I think

---

[80] Michael Reger, one of Wimmer's correspondents and a seminary classmate.

[81] George Michael Wittmann (1760-1833), bishop of Regensburg and one of Wimmer's seminary professors.

[82] Aurelius Peter McMahon, O.S.B. (1819-1882), became a novice at St. Vincent in 1868, when he was 49 years old.

I can make it because I can rest when I am with my people. The distance between each of these places is only one-day's travel by steamboat or railway, but the whole journey is still 3,000 English miles.

I was able to keep the Lenten fast (no meat except Sundays) without special hardship. I am not as strong as I was in years past, but my health is satisfactory, thank God. We did not get much ice this year. I had to buy some for the brewery at a cost of $1,800. Then on Easter Tuesday, we had an inch of ice, which ruined all our early fruit and damaged the corn.

I am afraid that I cannot write anything good about George this time. I hear many complaints about him. He does not obey, he is not studious, he does not economize but spends his money foolishly, and he likes his beer too much. Today I heard he plans to leave here if he finds a job somewhere else, but that won't work. He says that the $5 a month he earns here is not enough. Nonetheless, he is making $60 a year (150 francs), and he has no heavy work to do. You had better admonish him and bring him back to his senses. Tell him to pray or he will have nothing but disappointments.

I will not return home in less than four weeks. I think this will be my last extended trip. Cordial greetings to all our friends and to Mrs. Wimmer. Your staunch friend, Boniface Wimmer, Abbot

Ger   oASVA   transRG

TO RUPERT SEIDENBUSCH   159

St. Vincent, June 11, 1882

Right Reverend Bishop, Loyal Supporter: Things often turn out better than one expects. I have an excellent offer of half a lot with a house on it in Carrolltown and entirely free. Now a decision must be made. It is not true what you say. Father Henry[83] was well paid. I thank you heartily for your congratulations. I know how sincerely you mean them.

The complaints to Rome did not reach their target this time. Cardinal Simeoni[84] did not believe them even before he spoke with Bishop Tuigg,[85] who testified strongly on behalf of me and my people. Thus the affair is settled. I have received a

---

[83] Peter Henry Lemke, O.S.B. (1796-1882).
[84] John Simeoni, cardinal prefect of the Sacred Congregation for the Propagation of the Faith.
[85] John Tuigg (1820-1889), third bishop of Pittsburgh (1876-1889)

very friendly letter from Cardinal Simeoni. Still, it is very annoying to have people say such things. Something always sticks.

I have had many misfortunes this year. Father Valentine[86] is near death and will not recover. Father William[87] has also been given up. I must go to Newark tomorrow. Father Benno[88] has a serious spinal injury. Father Richard[89] will hardly recover. He is now in critical condition.

Financially, things are somewhat better. In Carrolltown, someone has bid $80,000 for the timber on the Hopper tract. The coal there is in three layers. I can finally buy the land in Chicago. With regard to my health, everything goes downhill. Nevertheless, I feel fairly well. The wastrel Sebastian[90] has gone overseas for three months—to carry on his fight with Baron Kessling and to learn better German!

Hoping your health is good and will remain so, I remain in deep respect and love, Your Excellency's devoted servant, Boniface Wimmer, Abbot

P.S. Hugo Lebling[91] loaned $10,000 from his estate to Abbot Innocent.[92] The loan is at four percent and will continue until Lebling's children come of age. The abbot was thus able to pay back half his debt to Metten. The money has been sent to Europe.

Ger   oASJA   cASVA   transHW

TO EDWIN PIERRON   160

St. Vincent, December 2, 1882

Reverend and Dear Father Edwin: I had a hearty laugh when I had gone through your welcome letter dd. Oct. 24, which, however, I received only after my return from Minna., where I had to go for the triennial Visitation and the dedication of the new church there. On my way home, I stopped for four days in Chicago, went then on to Wetaug, our latest colony, and saw further Covington for 2 days.

---

[86] Valentine Lobmeyer, O.S.B. (1832-1882).
[87] William Walter, O.S.B. (1840-1882).
[88] Benno Hegele, O.S.B. (1837-1885).
[89] Richard Wolpert, O.S.B. (1839-1882).
[90] Sebastian Wimmer, the abbot's grandnephew.
[91] Son of Louis Ignatius Lebling, late treasurer of the *Ludwig Missionsverein*.
[92] Innocent Wolf, O.S.B. (1843-1922).

Now as to your report about your College,[93] I believe you are correct in general. I opposed the acceptance of that place from the first, yet the chapter decided against me, and we have it now and must make the best of it we can. In the Deed we got from the Doctor[94] is only the condition of his decent support, and of [our] keeping a "school," as I refused inserting "college." Therefore, if we keep a school there, we fulfill the condition. It was Father Stephen[95] who made it a "college," a complete college. I never anticipated for the next time a great frequency of this College [sic], unless we wanted [to] open it to the Sects as well as to our Catholics. Still, I expected, nevertheless, a reasonable number of pupils. But I told already the then Bishop Gibbons,[96] and repeated also to the present Vicar Apostolic,[97] that we must get the Congregation of Charlotte or we could not get along. Msgn. Gibbons promised it; Bishop Northrop did not speak out his mind. To be sure, the Christian Brothers in Richmond, Wilmington, and Charleston will be some drawback, but not one so great that we could on that account not go ahead with a college on a small scale. Still, it will take some time till a fair prospect may appear.

I find the reason of the sudden decrease of the number of students chiefly in the increase of the pension to be paid. P. Herman[98] charged only $130, could offer only very poor accommodations while the number increased. P. Stephen charged $150 and still got more pupils. Now I find it gone up to $170, and the boys have to fetch yet their bed along. That is too much for the poor southern fathers. It is equal to our $180, and they cannot afford paying it.

Since Bishop Gross[99] has to charge the same amount and has neither such a staff of professors nor such accommodations as we have, he is no competition for us. Last spring, when I was in Savannah, he tried personally and by another priest to persuade [me] to take (accept) his college, buildings and everything, since he cannot run it without running every year deeper in debt. Of course, I declined since I have already one elephant. The Jesuits in Mobile have a flourishing college,

---

[93] St. Mary's College, Gaston County, North Carolina.

[94] Father Jeremiah J. O'Connell had donated to the Benedictines the land in North Carolina that became Belmont Abbey.

[95] Stephen Lyons, O.S.B. (b. 1850).

[96] James Gibbons (1834-1921), who was vicar apostolic of North Carolina at the time Benedictines from St. Vincent established the monastery and college that became Belmont Abbey.

[97] Henry P. Northrop (1842-1916), vicar apostolic of North Carolina (1881-1883) and later bishop of Charleston.

[98] Herman Wolfe, O.S.B. (1816-1884).

[99] William H. Gross, C.SS.R. (1837-1898), bishop of Savannah, had recently opened Pio Nono College in Macon, Georgia.

but they (1) have a great name and fame, (2) were the first to start one there, (3) have Mobile itself [and] New Orleans to recruit [from], (4) have a healthy [place] and fine grounds.

But I cannot see why the Carolinas could [not] support a college also, with some accession from Va., and Ga., and Tennessee, if the r. road over the mountains once will be finished. Everything must have a time to develop if it should grow. What was S. Vincent for many years? All depends on how a thing is done; e.g., our "college" in Newark had many pupils when [it] started because P. William[100] coaxed parents to send their boys. After they got Christian Brothers, our pupils decreased in number, dwindled down to some 30, because the following director did not hunt up pupils. I scolded P. Mellitus[101] etc. hard for their indifference. They again sought pupils and got them, a good number last year already, and more yet this year.

The Canadian French stole 25 Pittsburghers last fall away from us. The priests of the Holy Ghost in Pittsburgh practice the same—and get scholars. Why should we not get pupils by doing the same? The *Freeman*[102] has not so large a circulation and contains numbers of renowned old colleges easier accessible (by sea) than ours. You better stop that advertisement in the *Freeman*. Traveling is the thing needed. We must teach as good as others and must do it cheaper and for some *gratis* or almost *gratis*.

In your letter to P. Leo[103] you run down the South, as if nobody could go there and nobody would go there or remain. They don't like to see greenhorns move in who want to see nothing but fine wheat and corn and can raise nothing else. I have seen those settlements you mention. Of course, if shoemakers, tailors, etc. from large cities move on poor land, they starve. But intelligent farmers, they won't. Go to St. Florian and Tuscumbia, Cullman Settlement.[104] You find there Germans who do very well. If they raise not such large crops of wheat, etc. as they did in Ill., Mich., or Minna., they raise fruit, wine, cotton, and sell their butter so well that they get nicely along, need less shoes, clothes, less coal, less horse shoes, etc, don't suffer from [illness] and have less work to do, and feel content and happy if they have a church and school and priest too.

Therefore, no doubt the South will get immigrants plenty in not a far off time, Irish and Germans, if they find priests and schools. Good priests make converts

---

[100] William Walter, O.S.B. (1840-1882).
[101] Mellitus Tritz, O.S.B. (1847-1891).
[102] The *Freeman's Journal* of New York, edited by the Catholic layman James A. McMaster.
[103] Leo Haid, O.S.B. (1849-1924).
[104] Settlements in Alabama where the Benedictines from St. Vincent had established missions.

too, and we have a future also from this side. Our people in K[ansa]s had this year 400 b. of wheat grown out in the fields, etc., and the rest stacked so badly that it was wet when they threshed it. Are your 130 bushels not almost quite as good or better? Corn looked very well in May when I was there. If earlier planted, very likely it would have grown at least a middling crop. "When in Rome do as the Romans." Of course, the brothers, too, must learn going with the season as it is in the South. I charged them to sow cow peas and Lucern clover. I don't know if they have done so and in due time, but I have seen in Charlotte blue grass one foot long in May, and cow peas, a double crop in Tuscumbia, and fine Lucern clover in St. Florian, and Rev. Merriweather of Columbia told me with 4 acres in that clover he supported a whole Ursuline Convent, viz., he could feed cows so well that milk and butter was so [plentiful] as to support a house. I also saw last May near Macon and Atlanta large fields of the finest wheat and nice corn too. But the South is not chiefly for wheat and corn, I concede. It is for cotton, tobacco, wine, fruit. Cotton wants no rain when once up. Scoppernong, the best wine in the world, grows only in the South. Vegetables of every kind too, far better than in the North, with God's help.

They coined last year 2,000,000 [dollars] of Georgia and S. Carolina gold. Never mind, our plantation has gold too. There exist documents to prove it. The old Mint is still standing in Charlotte. But this is a digression from our point. I admit that St. Mary's has for the [near] future not very fair prospects, but I hold that you look at things under a too black view. I am convinced you get no pupils with a pension of $170, and only few if you do not seek them. I also believe it would be enough for now to keep only a commercial school with a good English course, whereby one or a few boys could still be started in Latin, if they should desire, and learn some music; and I believe 3 good diligent professors would be enough. This was my own original intention. I wish the advertisement in the *Freeman* to be stopped, and so also in other papers. But someone should see Augusta, Columbia, Charleston, etc., during vacation to get pupils.

As for this year, you can now see if somebody (a professor) can be spared. It won't pay keeping a proper prefect for 17 boys. We had in Munich 126 and no prefect exclusively for them. We, the professors, had to watch them in turn. True, 3 scholars need a professor as well as 30, but for that reason it is not necessary that the professor is there exclusively for 3. I know from my own experience that a professor can teach two small classes without loss to the scholars and without much trouble to the professor.

I wish first to get your precise opinion about this point: who eventually could be spared? I mean at present, because I need one or two priests. As to Fr. Leahy, I am sorry that he loses his time. Nobody here understands how it came to happen that he at once got into an aversion against being a religious and (I guess) a priest, too. Of course, I don't want to persuade him over again, but if he has no chance to study, he loses a whole year for whatever he wants to turn to afterwards. In some way, Fr. Conrad is in the same fix. He advanced in years but not in learning, except what perhaps he studies by himself. Still if it should be in your opinion a great harm to the repute of the college, I will let things go on as they [do] now, unless compelled by necessity.

Of course, men who like the South and the place must be considered more suit[able] because they are reasonably expected to take more interest in it, but with a man of principles, that should make little difference, if any. Duty and the interest of the Order are motives enough for everyone engaged there to do all he can on and for the place. I am not at all disappointed, nor disheartened. All good enterprises meet with difficulties.

I see in *Rand Atlas* that in N. Carolina the Methodists, Baptists, Presbyterians, and Lutherans have a college, and besides a state university. Let us have our college also! But corresponding to our wants.

Bear your exile well—for everything [there] is an end. All [are] well here except Rev. Taylor, the novice. The 7 years banishment from choir of instrumental music is over too. Yours sincerely, Bonif. Wimmer

Eng   oASVA

TO CHRYSOSTOM KRUESZ   **161**

St. Vincent, December 12, 1882

Right Reverend Abbot and Dear Confrere: I am ashamed of myself for having delayed so long in answering your letter of February 22. I should have answered at once, especially since I knew that you were convalescing from a serious illness. One of the reasons I did not answer, I suppose, was that the contents of your letter do me entirely too much honor. You seem to want to make me out as a vessel of election in the hand of God, while it is my constant fear that I have driven myself into undertakings for which I am not capable. However, let us not think of that any more. You are a good soul, a heart full of understanding and charity, eager to discover in every poor confrere some fine quality. In your charity, you exaggerate the efforts of others. I thank you for the good opinion you have of me and for the spirit of benevolence you always show me. If I have not deserved this, it will be my constant effort for the rest of my days to justify it, with the help of God and according to my poor powers.

I hope that you have completely recovered from your illness and that by now you are enjoying good health. I myself have been in good health during the past year, despite some minor ailments that were irksome but not of a serious nature. In a way, I am in better health now than ever before. I believe I can attribute this to the use of electric homeopathy, but this year I have been kept very busy with some annoying matters.

Shortly after Easter I made a visitation to our southern missions in Baltimore, Richmond, Charlotte, Savannah, and Skidaway Island, and from there by way of Macon, Atlanta, and Chattanooga, I went to Cincinnati and Covington. The Negro mission is very close to my heart. If this work is to be successful, lay brothers are needed, but they do not have much interest in the work, very likely because of the heat in Georgia, which at times is very oppressive, and because of the climate, which is not very healthful. It is more difficult to get men from St. Vincent to go south nowadays than it was to find men in Metten and Munich to come to America.

From time to time, I have to contend with a spirit of indifference and faint-heartedness in moments of stress and trial, but this does not mean that all my people display this spirit. It is in the nature of things that we show a readiness and interest when opportunities and circumstances are encouraging. The finger of God will point to possibilities and opportunities. We receive frequent invitations to undertake new missions, and we receive many attractive offers of land, but often the motive behind these offers is speculation, even when the offers come from bishops. For our part, we take note of the needs of the faithful, the interests of the Order, and our own capabilities, and of course, we must consider the constant problem of money and availability of funds.

The North no longer offers many promising opportunities for monastic establishments. Almost all the orders are now represented here, and there is much competition among them. The mendicant orders manage quite well precisely because they are mendicant, while we have to live by industry and activity, but the mendicants are careful to avoid the South, where there are few Catholics, so there is room for us in the South. There is a lot of work to do there, but not much income except from the land, which we cultivate, and from education. The poor Negro is virtually abandoned, or else he is in the hands of the Methodist and Baptist sects.

Only in the large cities of the South are there enough Catholics to form parishes and parish schools. In Savannah, we have built a church. Father Oswald Moosmüller[105] undertook this work and put it into fine condition. He has also built a beautiful school where the Sisters of Mercy teach the children. On Skidaway Island, about twelve miles distant from Savannah, we have erected an agricultural school for Negro boys where they are now receiving instruction in all the regular school subjects, in accordance with their talents, so that they themselves will eventually become teachers or serve in business positions or work for the government, as peace officers for example. We are looking forward to receiving brothers from among the Negro students. Providence has already provided us with three professed Negro monks. I have great hopes for this Negro mission, but we must deal with many difficulties. One serious problem we have there is the high frequency of fever, which causes the work to go slowly. I expect to return to Georgia in the spring to see what needs to be done and then take the necessary steps for further action.

On October 21, the abbey church at St. John's, Minnesota, was consecrated. Among those present were Bishop Krautbauer[106] of Green Bay, Wisconsin; Bishop Grace[107] of St. Paul; his coadjutor, Bishop Ireland;[108] and, of course, Bishop Seidenbusch,[109] who performed the consecration. Abbot Wolf[110] and I consecrated the two side altars. The church is 143 feet in length and 64 feet in width and is built in Romanesque style. There are two beautiful towers and a basement church as large as the main one for use in winter. It is indeed a beautiful structure. The cost was $30,000, and it was completed in three years. The consecration took place on the 25th anniversary of the arrival of the Benedictines at the headwaters of the Mississippi River in Minnesota. I took advantage of my visit to make the regular visitation so that I would not have to make the thousand-mile journey from St. Vincent a second time.

After the visitation in Minnesota, I went to Chicago where I stayed over All Saints Day with Prior Suitbert[111] who had just completed a new priory to replace the one destroyed in the great fire of 1871. From that time until now, the fathers have lived in a temporary frame house. Only the top floor, i.e., the fourth floor,

---

[105] Oswald Moosmüller, O.S.B. (1832-1901).
[106] Francis X. Krautbauer (1824-1885).
[107] Thomas Grace, O.P. (1814-1897).
[108] John Ireland (1838-1918).
[109] Rupert Seidenbusch, O.S.B. (1830-1895), bishop of Northern Minnesota.
[110] Innocent Wolf, O.S.B. (1843-1922).
[111] Suitbert de Marteau, O.S.B. (1834-1901).

remains unfinished. Thus, the damage done by the terrible conflagration has been repaired, though we must still pay the debts.

From Chicago I went to Wetaug, near Cairo at the confluence of the Mississippi and Ohio rivers in the southern part of the state of Illinois. We have two fathers and three brothers there. It is a beautiful farm, with 180 cultivated acres and 500 acres of woodland. This property, together with Chicago, should eventually become fine locations for an abbey. The site and terrain are ideal, the soil very productive. The day I visited, there were floods because of high waters from the spring rains. We have built a neat little church for the small parish, which up until now has been without the services of a priest. The cost of the church was $4,000, of which a wealthy Protestant and I each contributed half.

From Wetaug I proceeded to Cincinnati, Covington, Pittsburgh, and back to St. Vincent after an absence of three weeks. Weather conditions during my journey were fair. Since December 8, we have had severe cold, which has provided a good harvest of ice. We need about 200 tons of ice, which we harvest from our ponds and haul to storage. Last year we had no ice at all, and I had to pay $1,700 for it in order to cover the needs of our brewery and kitchens.

Since Easter 1881, eight priests and one priest novice have died, and ten priests have been ordained. The harvest was very good. Corn production was somewhat low, as was the potato crop. There was no fruit, and wine production was about half of what it normally is, but the quality was good. The times are very prosperous, and the political situation has improved because of the Democratic Party's victory at the polls. The Democrats are the people's party. The Republican Party represents money and liberal interests.

You must not think that I have forgotten you. The first part of the biblical commentary of Father Lechner[112] must be in your hands by now. The second part will reach you after the New Year, and the last part you will receive in the course of the New Year.[113] This has involved a great deal of work, more than you can imagine.

Good luck to you. May you experience God's grace from above. With sincere love, I am Your Excellency's devoted confrere, Boniface Wimmer, Abbot

Ger   oAPH   cASVA   transFF

---

[112] Peter Lechner, O.S.B. (1805-1874), *Die Heilige Schrift des Neuen Testamentes nach der Vulgata und dem Grundtext erklärt* (Beatty, Pa.: St. Vincent Press, 1881).
[113] Peter Lechner, *Die Heilige Schrift des Alten Testamentes, nach der Vulgata und dem Grundtext erklärt* (Beatty, Pa.: St. Vincent Press, 1882-84).

TO INNOCENT WOLF 162

St. Vincent, March 4, 1883

Dear Confrere, Dearest Father Abbot: To the best of my recollection, I never said you need not expect anything from me or Abbot Alexius[114] for your projected building. I simply did not make any promises. With regard to Minnesota, I merely expressed a well-grounded fear that there would be nothing coming from there. In the near future, I will have to pay $2,500 on our vineyard [in Kentucky]. I already have this money in hand, but it is borrowed. In addition, I have other debts I must soon pay. In the end, there will be something left for you, but I am hesitant at the moment to say how much that will be. Next fall I will have to advance $600 to the sisters in Allegheny for their property. The sisters have done well enough this year to pay the entire amount. Last year I had to advance them $1,000. This year's payment, however, will depend on help from the *Ludwig Missionsverein*, which I asked for and hope to get.

You will do well to appeal to Munich yourself for $1,000 or thereabouts. If you have not already done so, make your appeal soon because the allotments are always made in April. Archbishop Steichele[115] is a very important person on the board of the *Missionsverein*. He is a friend of the Benedictines, and you can make your appeal to him. I also know Dr. Kagerer very well. He, too, supports us. I will write him soon and try to interest him in your project. I have to write him anyway within a few days. But hurry! Later, when the meeting is over, it may be too late. Last year I received about $860 for the sisters. You should be in line for that much, too.

We have made progress with the disciplinary measures taken after my indignant address to the chapter. I do not like to employ punitive action against priests. We have clerics and novices here, and public penalties have a way of impressing everyone when imposed on clerics in the presence of their teachers. That is what I want, and that is what should have happened. No one took the initiative, however. Now Father Prior[116] shoulders the burden and takes action calmly and deliberately.

As for the priests, the negligent are denied recreation and must spend that time in choir praying their office. Recently, three of them failed to rise in the morning. Afterwards, two went to choir during recreation because of the stinging notes they received. The third asked for pardon today and yielded by attending to his choir duty during recreation. I feigned ignorance of the fact that earlier they did not

---

[114] Alexius Edelbrock, O.S.B. (1843-1908), abbot of St. John's Abbey, Collegeville, Minnesota.

[115] Anthony Steichele, Archbishop of Munich.

[116] Michael Hofmayer, O.S.B. (1838-1901).

Father Michael Hofmayer, O.S.B. (1838-1901), was prior of St. Vincent and administered the abbey after the death of Boniface Wimmer in 1887.

attend their choir duty during recreation. If this occurs again, they will be dealt with more severely. It is not easy to remove priests from their jobs and send them away. That would be my last resort since these lazy fellows would simply continue their evil practices in the priories. They hate the idea of eating at second table, and especially of missing recreation, but making them eat at second table imposes an unfair burden on the cooks, who must work harder because the lazy ones are being punished. According to the *Rule*, everyone should encourage each other to wake up in the morning. Until now, I have done this myself. The prior does it now. It takes considerable rousing to get some of these fellows up. Otherwise, he gets no results. Since I have begun to insist that they fulfill their duty, however, only eight have failed to say Mass regularly, and these have had some excuse for their failure.

The opinion of Father Maurice[117]—that it is no sin not to say Mass and that the professors need not attend choir—would mean the collapse of all order. Thus, I had to be firm in my insistence that observance of the *Holy Rule* is a matter of moral duty so long as there is no directive to the contrary. Nowhere does the *Rule* mention that priests must celebrate daily Mass because that was the actual practice. There was no need to make special mention of it. In Bavaria, I never heard of a priest failing to say Mass except for reasons of sickness. For pastors, and for professors at the gymnasium and especially in monasteries, there was no need for legislation, except for prescriptions concerning time. However, in the declaration on Chapter 50 pertaining to travel, there is this directive: "They must not fail, without serious cause, to say Mass." From this, one can conclude that the obligation applies even more to those who are lazy or idle. Such failures cause serious scandal for the brothers, and scholastics will lose their vocations if they see this as common practice. The responsibility to attend choir is almost as serious a duty because it is the principal occupation of monks.

---

[117] Maurice Kaeder, O.S.B. (1837-1892).

Anticipation of the office does not appeal to me, so I insist the former practice be retained. Personally, I would be in favor of meditation in common. This was a practice maintained for three years in my seminary days, and I learned to love it. Here they are reluctant to lose a quarter of an hour of their recreation time. I should also give some thought to the matter of confession. A cleric of ours, Frater Alexius,[118] did not go to confession for many months in spite of much urging. I called him in one day and told him I would not allow him to proceed to ordination and that I would send him to North Carolina, as a cleric, where he would be the cause of less scandal. At other times, I spoke kindly to him about the matter, but still he would not go to confession. I called him in a second time. After that, he obeyed, went to confession, and has continued faithfully in the practice since then.

We are now well-ordered, at least exteriorly, and there is peace and harmony since music has once again taken its place in the liturgy. We must continue to practice, of course, and more regularly than before, especially the clerics and novices, though not exclusively them. Overall, there is good spirit among most of the community, though in the case of some there is clearly a lack of good spirit in the matter of prayer and mortification. This may improve when they get older or, please God, after a visitation.

Your novice[119] died very suddenly. I learned of his serious illness just a few days before the end came. When I arrived, I found no pulse in his forearm. He was a good man, and I regret his loss. We were in doubt about the matter of Masses to be said for him. The novice master thought he was entitled to have a Mass from each one of us because he had been allowed to make his profession before he died. I am of a different opinion. By his mere profession, he receives a considerable advantage from the prayers of the brethren of our Order, as well as from his closer union with the saints of our Order to which he was admitted. He also receives the indulgences connected with the profession and with all the religious services and obsequies both here and in Atchison. If each priest were to say one Mass, it would mean an offering of $100, and that was not my intention. This is also the judgment of Father Prior and the rest. Father Cuthbert Taylor[120] also died as a novice (on December 8) and did not receive such an offering, although he made profession before death. I may be mistaken in the matter, however.

---

[118] Alexius Grass, O.S.B. (1860-1918).
[119] Aloysius Wagner, O.S.B. (1859-1883).
[120] Cuthbert Taylor, O.S.B. (1829-1882), an English secular priest who died less than a year after entering the monastery at St. Vincent.

I have not yet spoken to Father Louis.[121] It would be better if he remained where he is. I am afraid our plan to abandon Creston will not proceed smoothly. It also seems to me we should consult first with Bishop McMullen[122] to find out if he approves of the action we have in mind. Dr. Bernard Smith[123] could also give us counsel. He told me in 1880 that if he had known what I had in mind with re-spect to an independent priory in Creston, he would have voted otherwise. I have done nothing in the matter until now and would willingly reopen the case. Do you expect me to write, or will you? It is a rather touchy problem to petition the pope to reverse his earlier decision. Because I was afraid something like this would occur, I was opposed to an independent priory. It happened against my will. Now it will come to nothing. The mess should be laid at the feet of Father James,[124] and it should be his responsibility to make matters right again. The papers follow. May God keep you in good health and good cheer. Boniface Wimmer

P.S. I am so constantly troubled about my own salvation that I can hardly pray for sheer distraction. The terrible lukewarmness and lack of spirituality among almost a third of the priests is killing me because of the thought that they will be lost and that I cannot prevent it and have likely caused it because of my indulgent ways. I have now made up my mind to try anticipating office by having *Matins* at 6:45 pm, followed by evening prayers. At 4:00 am, we will have *Lauds* and *Prime*, then common meditation in choir so that I can be sure it is done. Lamps will be kept burning so that they will be able to read the meditation or, if they wish, some material from scripture. Afterward, holy Mass, etc. I am starting with this next week.

I have also been thinking about how to make sure that everyone goes to confes-sion. I am still not clear as to how this can be enforced, unless it be by appointing confessors. I would do this reluctantly because I do not wish to restrict freedom of choice, but if we specified confessors, lists could be given them that would show each month the number of confessions heard by each father, and in that way, we would be able to reach and admonish those who neglected this duty. Frater Alex-ius did not go to confession for half a year, in spite of all urging. I called him to task a number of times to no purpose, although I always appealed to him in a fa-therly way. Finally, I made it plain to him that he would not be allowed to advance to ordination next summer, and, in fact, not at all (nor would I have allowed it),

---

[121] Louis Haas, O.S.B. (1855-1936).
[122] John McMullen (1832-1883), first bishop of Davenport.
[123] Bernard Smith, O.S.B. (1818-1892), an English Benedictine and professor at the Roman college of the Sacred Congregation for the Propagation of the Faith.
[124] James Zilliox, O.S.B. (1849-1890).

and that I regretted he had already made solemn profession. I also told him that I would send him to North Carolina in order to prevent the scandal he was giving, or at least to minimize it. As a result, he now goes to confession. I am sure Fathers Timothy and Albert[125] do not go to confession at all, or seldom do. They never make meditation, and if they boldly insist on saying Mass, matters are worse. I believe, therefore, that I can and must insist that they receive the sacrament. What is your opinion in this matter? I maintain steadfastly that if one or the other acts defiantly, severe punishment will eventually have to be applied, including expulsion. They must change.

Go ahead with your building project, but construct only the most essential buildings in order to avoid too much debt. Take it step by step. That was what I did here. At one point, building operations went no further than an extension of two windows, but you will know what is best for you to do.

Ger   oASBA   cASVA   transPB

TO NEPOMUCENE JAEGER   **163**

St. Vincent, April 10, 1883

Reverend Father Nepomucene, Dear Brother: Next Saturday I will go to Newark for the blessing of the new priory, which takes place on Monday. From there I will travel to Baltimore, Richmond, Charlotte, and Savannah for visitations. On the way home, I am going to Alabama and Wetaug for the same purpose. I will not return home before the middle of May.

I have written the bishop of Charleston[126] concerning the ordination of Father Ulrich.[127] I hope to receive an answer before I leave. In any case, he will be ordained as soon as possible so that he can help you. I am sorry that I had to overload you with work, but I could not help it. I have appointed you pastor of the Polish parish because Father Hyacinth[128] became ill and needed rest. Although he has improved, he cannot take charge of the parish because his affliction is such that it can easily recur and could become incurable. Therefore, you must conform to the will of God and remain pastor of the Polish parish until we can transfer you,

---

[125] Timothy Blasius, O.S.B. (1855-1898), and Albert Robrecht, O.S.B. (1851-1897).
[126] Henry P. Northrup (1842-1916).
[127] Ulrich Simeth, O.S.B. (1859-1885).
[128] Hyacinth Lanz, O.S.B. (1843-1892).

in any case until the bishop[129] returns and I myself can speak with him. I presume that the Polish people, or at least many of them, would rather have a Polish-born pastor, but besides Father Hyacinth I have no Polish priest and, therefore, cannot give them a Polish pastor. No doubt, Father Hyacinth would take the Polish parish again if I were to demand it, but the doctor says he might soon become ill again, and then we would lose him. Thus, I cannot send him, as I said before.

I know you are doing all you can to take care of Poles, preaching the word of God, hearing confessions, instructing the children, anointing the sick, burying the dead. If you still cannot please everyone, you must patiently bear with it. I hope, however, that the people appreciate it and will be satisfied. I fear only that you will

Rev. Nepomucene Jaeger, O.S.B.

succumb to so much work and collapse. Therefore, do not overdo it. It is a great misfortune that Father Hyacinth became ill, but we cannot help that. It is also a great blessing that we have you. Otherwise, the large Polish parish would not have any priest at all for a long time.

I wanted to speak with you in person but have no time left to come to Pittsburgh. Please pray for me that I may return safely from this trip! United with you in the Sacred Heart of Jesus, I am your most devoted brother and abbot, Boniface Wimmer

Ger   oASVA   transIG

TO HENRY P. NORTHROP   164

St. Vincent, June 4, 1883

Rt. Rev. and Dear Bishop, My Lord: A while ago, I was traveling to visit the southern stations occupied by fathers of our Order, sci., Richmond, St. Mary's

---

[129] John Tuigg (1820-1889), third bishop of Pittsburgh (1876-1889).

College near Garibaldi [North Carolina], and Savannah with Skidaway Isle near it. I had my procurator, F. Paulinus Wenkmann,[130] and the prior of Richmond, F. Benno Hegele,[131] with me. It is the fourth time that I made this route, and I watched carefully the development of the latter two places. I had also taken the two fathers with me to give them a chance of seeing the state of things and to enable them to judge about them and give me candidly their own views.

Well, we found reasons [for] being well contented with things as they are at St. Mary's. I had opposed the acceptance of that place when it was offered because I saw it would cost much and would for many years not bring much, and particularly from fear the "old gentleman,"[132] whom we have to support for a lifetime, could give us immense trouble. Yet when I saw that most of the fathers of the chapter were in favor of acceptance, I gave my own consent also.

My reasons for this act were that good management could make the farm productive enough to support in connection with a small college or school, a small convent, and chiefly because I thought we could and should do something to help Catholicity in that poor state, where it is scarcely known, by giving the boys a chance of a good education. Of course, considering the dwindling minority of 2,500 Catholics to 1,400,000 Protestants, I could not expect a great [influx] of Catholic pupils of the state to our school, but looking at the map and the locality of the place between two railroads (one of which is indeed not finished yet, but if finished will open Tennessee, too, and bring it in close connection with St. Mary's), I could not help hoping the college was much needed for the Catholic youth there and would have a future. Therefore I did all I could do for it, and I have laid out on it already over $9,000 cash, not counting traveling expenses and many household goods, etc. And I am not sorry for it. But after a mature reflection, I came to the conviction that in order to secure success it is necessary to make the place independent as a small abbey. As things are now, the prior, the fathers, and the brothers would not consider themselves as permanently belonging to St. Mary's and do not perhaps take the same interest in its prosperity as they might if they considered it as their real home, but if there would be a community under an abbot, matters would be different, particularly with regard to the college.

To secure to the abbot at least some reliable revenue, I would join Richmond with St. Mary's because Richmond is a good congregation and the order owns in the city itself several lots leased in deed but which bear a regular rent of some hundred dollars annually without any expense.

---

[130] Paulinus Wenkmann, O.S.B. (1836-1922).
[131] Benno Hegele, O.S.B. (1837-1885).
[132] Father Jeremiah J. O'Connell, who donated the land in North Carolina to the Benedictines.

And also I would unite with it our house in Savannah with church and appurtenance so as to make St. Mary's the center of the Benedictine missions in the Atlantic states. Certainly for the first, St. Vincent will have to give personnel and material aid to the new abbey. Still, these missions will undoubtedly faster grow and prosper if they are free than if they were appendices of St. Vincent. At least this is my conviction, and I trust it is correct. I have seen the working of the system at least on three other places with the same result. But even if the arrangement should not work as quickly in the South as it did in the North, since in the North religious institutions have the advantage of being surrounded by large Catholic congregations, while in the South the Catholic element is insignificant and the population is in general opposed to the growth of such institutions, it is enough if it worked only well, steadily and solidly and noiselessly.

Now, my dear Lord Bishop, it would be a great consolation for me if my views in this matter would meet with your approval, for something must be done. The Benedictines have not asked for being admitted into the vicariate. They have been asked to come by the then vicar apostolic, the present archbishop of Baltimore.[133] We have followed the invitation. If we have not been able to do so much so far, we have at least shown that we are in earnest to do something. Of course, the good will of the bishop, his benevolence, is absolutely indispensable if religious should work with success in a diocese. Your Lordship has on every occasion yet expressed your kind and gracious sentiments towards us. Therefore, I hope you won't refuse my prayers to give me in writing a few lines which I would send with my petition to the Propaganda to the purpose that you approve in the interest of religion and of the Order of St. Benedict the erection of an abbey in your vicariate near Charlotte. By granting this request you will greatly oblige me and, as I hope to God, do a good work in many ways. Confidently expecting to receive a favorable answer, I remain Your Lordship's most humble servant, Boniface Wimmer

Eng   oADC   cASVA

TO BENEDICT HAINDL   165

St. Vincent, June 19, 1883

My Dearest Confrere: Thanks be to God that you remain in good health and are able to work so zealously in the care of souls. As for me, things are not getting

---

[133] James Gibbons (1834-1921), archbishop of Baltimore (1868-72), invited the Benedictines to North Carolina when he was vicar apostolic of North Carolina and bishop of Richmond.

Rev. Benedict Haindl, O.S.B.

better. I can still attend to my duties at home fairly well, but am no longer able to go out. Thank you for your kind wishes. God's will be done. I pray for a good end. That is my one worry and fear.

Between April 14 and May 11, I once again visited the East and the South. In Newark, we have built well and can now establish a small abbey there. I also hope to establish an abbey for Richmond, Charlotte, and Savannah. A little later, we will establish one in Alabama and another in Illinois (Chicago). For St. Vincent, I will keep only Pennsylvania (Erie, St. Marys, Carrolltown, Pittsburgh) and Covington.

Nevertheless, I am an old house that no longer has a good roof. The rain comes through everywhere. The tower and the windows are of no further use. I am of little use and am failing in every way. I cannot count on many more years to live, yet in my position I cannot do otherwise than I am doing. I look over these distant places but cannot govern them very well from here. They must have their own superiors; then they will do better. St. Vincent will remain a large monastery, and the new abbeys will in time become large monasteries if God wills it.

We have had a good year. Our priories are all advancing in temporal affairs. The same is true of St. Vincent and of our sisters. It really is wonderful. The new bishop of Nashville, Joseph Rademacher,[134] is a former student of St. Vincent and much attached to us. Fathers Giles, Andrew, and Suitbert[135] attended his consecration. I could not go because of graduation exercises. If we could only improve ourselves by adopting a correct spirit! It is a mistake to keep changing from this to that. They reproach me for being too soft, and I believe this is true, for that is my nature and my conviction, i.e., that you can win more with kindness than with severity. I have no doubt been sharp at times and perhaps kind too late. Spare me, O Lord! The dear Lord has been patient with me and all my life has shown me

---

[134] Joseph Rademacher (1840-1900), bishop of Nashville (1883-1893) and later bishop of Ft. Wayne (1893-1900).

[135] Giles Christoph, O.S.B. (1830-1887); Andrew Hintenach, O.S.B. (1844-1927); and Suitbert de Marteau, O.S.B. (1834-1901).

much mercy with his loving patience. Thus, I cannot do otherwise than remain patient and merciful, as much as I can. Yet I am very worried about death, and more so about the judgment. You who live after me, please do not forget me. May God keep you healthy and in His holy love, and may He bless your work. Your sincere friend, Boniface Wimmer, Abbot

Ger   oASJA   cASVA   transHW

TO UTTO LANG   166

St. Vincent, November 3, 1883

Right Reverend Father Abbot, Dearest Confrere: Many thanks for the thousand Mass intentions, which help me very much, particularly now. Some of our fathers really depend on them, especially those in the South. We have a small college [in North Carolina] called Maryhelp. That is the name we gave our farm there. This year we have 15 students and five professors. The 15 students are from the five states of Georgia, North Carolina, South Carolina, Virginia, and Maryland. The number of Catholics in these southern States is very small, and their average income is below the median. We therefore had to lower tuition from $180 to $150 a year. Consequently, there is not much left to support the professors, who therefore depend on stipends. The same is the case with our Negro college on Skidaway. Naturally, if there is not enough to keep these places open, the abbot of St. Vincent must come up with the money. No one is anxious to have these places. Without brothers to do the work, we could not keep them, especially if we expect any fruit to come of them in the future.

We must erect the necessary buildings and make the land productive. The motherhouse has to keep putting money into them until they can stand on their own feet. Many of the fathers do not like it, but for me it is a real joy, though also a burden, because the Catholics in the South cannot help themselves because of their poverty, and they would be entirely lost if they were deserted by everyone. Later, when the Catholics there increase in number, we shall see these places in better condition. Most of the people have good will and show their gratitude.

It has been difficult for me this year to adjust to winter. This seems to be a sign that I will not survive it. There is not a single part of my body where something is not wrong. For three weeks, I have had a sore throat that prevents me from leaving the house, and for the past three days, I have not been able to go to choir because I cannot talk. My throat ailment is getting better but still remains.

Who knows if I shall die before December 29?[136] It often happens that gentlemen in holy orders die suddenly. In any case, if I should still be alive, it may be that I am in very bad health, or that something turns up that spoils the pleasure, the peace of heart and mind. Without question, it is a special grace to have been in the monastery and a member of the Order for 50 years. I was the first person after the restoration of our Order in Bavaria to whom this grace was given.[137] Thanks be to God if I should live longer to make amends for the sins of my life.

Abbot Wolf [138] is building an addition to his college. In order to help, I sent two of my master carpenters so that the four-story building can be occupied by the new year. The housing problem in Kansas is grave. This year they have more students than ever, and many had to be turned away because of lack of space. The abbot is over-burdened, and, besides, he has to teach theology even though he suffers from bad eyesight.

Father Bonaventure Ostendarp, O.S.B. (1856-1912), a priest at St. Vincent, later of St. Mary's Abbey, Newark. He studied art in Munich and became renowned for his eccle-siastical art in the Beuronese style.

Lately we have been swamped by German students, mostly poor Bavarians. We do not appreciate people sending us students without giving us any notice at all. Many come without money. Often they have failed in their careers. They seem to think St. Vincent is such a big and rich seminary that we can receive anyone who comes, give them an education, and feed and clothe them *gratis*. In addition, many are in poor health. We have our painter Bonaventure[139] to thank for this.

---

[136] December 29, 1883, would be the fiftieth anniversary of the abbot's monastic profession.

[137] In fact, Wimmer was the second in order of monastic profession at the restored monastery of Metten. Gregory Scherr, O.S.B. (1804-1877), preceded him in pronouncing vows on December 29, 1833, but Scherr had died before reaching his fiftieth anniversary of profession.

[138] Innocent Wolf, O.S.B. (1843-1922).

[139] Bonaventure Ostendarp, O.S.B. (1856-1912), recently returned from Munich where he had studied art.

With cordial greetings to the confreres and best wishes for your health, I remain in sincere affection and deep respect, Your Grace's most devoted confrere, Boniface Wimmer, Abbot

Ger   oAMA   cASVA   transRG

TO JOSEPH AMBERGER   **167**

St. Vincent, December 4, 1883

Very Reverend Chancellor, Your Grace: I just received a draft from Pustet for $369.07 in exchange for the 1,554 marks you kindly sent me for Mass intentions. The last 300 marks, for 300 Mass intentions, are included in this amount. Heartfelt thanks! We will diligently say the Masses.

Since October, I have been more or less troubled with a sore throat, but it seems finally to have been cured by electric homeopathy. At present, we have spring-like weather. In the middle of November, we had excessive cold for three days, but before and after that it was mild and there was no snow. For many people here Advent is hard because we fast during the week. Moreover, Monday, Wednesday, Friday, and Saturday are days of abstinence. We do not see many eggs (even though we have chickens in great number) and fish is not easy to obtain.

Speaking of chickens, I am reminded of a joke. About a thousand miles from here, out West, in the state of Nebraska, there are many Bohemian immigrants for whom, at the request of Bishop James O'Connor,[140] I have sent two priests and two brothers to undertake the pastoral care. Recently I received from the younger priest a letter in which he describes the people and the country. He tells me that their house is about half the size of one of our chicken coops. (Not far from our barn we have two fenced-in areas, and in the middle of each garden there is a chicken coop where the chickens live, lay, and hatch. One belongs to the monastery, the other to the college. This is to avoid any dispute about eggs. The houses are pretty large, with 300 to 400 chickens in each.) Our small Bohemian monastery in Nebraska, near the city of Pilsen, is comprised of three buildings and is the smallest of our monasteries at present. Its growth will depend on circumstances. We have students here of both Polish and Bohemian nationality, and we have a Polish and Bohemian parish in Pittsburgh.

In Nebraska, as is general west of the Missouri River, there is no timber except for perhaps a few trees on the side of creeks. For that reason, the settlers have to

---

[140] James O'Connor (1823-1890), vicar apostolic of Nebraska and later first bishop of Omaha.

plant trees, mostly poplars and cottonwoods, which grow very fast but which are soft and fibrous. Consequently, they have to live in miserable huts built in the cities and brought to the country and set up there. Some people dig caves deep in the ground over which they put a cheap roof for protection.

May the good Lord preserve your eyesight and grant you good health so that you will be able to continue your good works. Happy feast days. Asking for a memento in your holy Masses, I am your most devoted, Boniface Wimmer, Abbot

P.S. Father Wilfrid[141] is in good health.

Ger   oASVA   transRG

TO WENCESLAUS KOCARNIK   **168**

St. Vincent, December 16, 1883

Reverend and Dear Confrere: So you are thinking it is time to take steps to establish a Bohemian monastery—but who do I have for that? It is easier to make a foundation without money than without people. In this case, both money and people are lacking. The Bohemian students are constantly leaving, most recently a certain Blend. He was in the upper class when he suddenly announced he did not have a vocation to the religious life. There are young Bohemians here who speak the Bohemian language well and who are healthy and quite good. We hope they will persevere. We also have some German Bohemians who know little or no Bohemian.

You say I should send Father Nepomucene[142] to you, but in that case, I would have to call Father Ulrich[143] home and you would not gain much. Besides, Father Nepomucene is not very strong. The Bohemian parish in Pittsburgh is now operating satisfactorily. Because of the school, many Bohemian children have been won for the Catholic Church who otherwise would have been lost. It would be unwise to take the priest away from them. I cannot permit Father Siegfried[144] to go since I need him here to care for the Bohemians, Poles, and Slovenians who come for confession or to get married. If only another priest could be ordained, we would have three and could start a monastery. "*Tres faciunt collegium.*" ["Three make a college."]

---

[141] Wilfrid Frins, O.S.B. (1860-1936).
[142] Nepomucene Jaeger, O.S.B. (1844-1924).
[143] Ulrich Simeth, O.S.B. (1859-1885).
[144] Siegfried Klima, O.S.B. (1851-1893).

I fear we made a great mistake by going too far west. The monastery should be farther east—in Michigan, Minnesota, or Wisconsin where many Bohemians have been living a long time and have already acquired some wealth. They can therefore afford to educate their sons, and we could help each other. A monastery cannot survive from farming alone, unless it has a mill and a brewery (or vineyards). What we have at St. Vincent cannot be easily copied elsewhere. That would take years. A small farm is necessary, with some horses and cows. It is also important to have a few good parishes and a college not far from the railroad and a large city. Omaha should have the monastery. Students come from the city, and so does the money.

If I send Father Nepomucene, he would have to take over Omaha again. Do not forget that. It would also be necessary to build another church, not a dance hall.[145] Naturally, we would have to have one or two reliable priests there, and if the monastery could also be there, that would be even better (as in Atchison). Omaha is centrally located to Iowa, Kansas, Dakota, and Minnesota. From all these states, there are railroads to and from Omaha. You must not give up that place. You must have a home there. However, if we begin in the country where you are now located, or at Cedar Hill, that will also be good. You can work and gain an income, and you will be close to a railroad so that you can communicate easily with Omaha. The beginning must be modest and you cannot contract many debts. Our college in North Carolina cost only $6,000. It has a basement 60 by 37 feet and three stories above that, and it is large enough to house 60 students. First, you must build a suitable rectory that, if necessary, could be enlarged. It could be, for example, 40 by 40 feet with a hallway through the center of the house. In the basement you would want to put the kitchen, the refectory, the cellar, and the par-

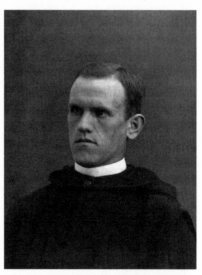

Father Daniel Hefti, O.S.B. (1853-1883), early Benedictine missionary in Georgia, died tragically on Skidaway Island, Georgia, in 1883.

---

[145] The first Benedictine church in Nebraska was a converted dance hall. See Vitus Buresh, *The Procopian Chronicle: St. Procopius Abbey 1885-1985* (Lisle, Ill.: St. Procopius Abbey, 1985), 6; and Jerome Oetgen, *An American Abbot* (Washington, D.C.: Catholic University of America Press, 1997), 351.

lor; on the first floor six small cells; on the second floor, the same. You could then add as much as you want if necessary.

Joseph Poleska may be a good young man. He was a good person when he was here, although he was so scrupulous that he became deranged. I would not trust him too easily. If he perseveres, you will be able to tell whether you can trust him. The Bohemian who is in the kitchen here would have been allowed to make profession, but he did not want to take vows and most likely will return to the lay state.

Our Father Daniel[146] accidentally shot a load of bullets into his abdomen so that his intestines hung out. He died 30 hours later after having been anointed. With the butt of his rifle, he tried to strike a dog that he wanted to chase away, but which he should have shot. The gun went off and killed him. He was a zealous and very good priest who had already converted many Negroes. His death was edifying—but so unnecessary. I wish you a happy New Year and remain with love, your devoted, Abbot Boniface

Ger   oASPA   cASVA   transIG

TO LUKE WIMMER   **169**

St. Vincent, January 19, 1884

Dearest Confrere: It does not matter if you keep the $1,000 loan from Mr. Schmid that was entrusted to you. Keep it in the safe. Soon we will have to pay $21,000 for the vineyard. Keep the money for that purpose. I will then have to send that much less. Our first concern must be to pay off the mortgage. Who knows? A panic may occur, and our creditors could make plenty of trouble by recalling our money all at once, though they could not bankrupt us. They would be smart not to give us a judgment note for the money, but a promissory note or a simple note of deposit.

There is no doubt that I would not be sorry if I had tried to become a saint. I certainly strive for sanctity and try to be holy. Becoming a saint is an entirely different matter. I am afraid I never thought of that. On the contrary, I fear that I might not even be saved because a man in my position is in great danger of committing a mortal sin before he realizes it. As for the present (it would be presumptuous of me to think beyond the present), I prefer to remain a simple

---

[146] Daniel Hefti, O.S.B. (1853-1883), was working at the Benedictine school on Skidaway Island, Georgia, when he died.

abbot. I want to live a holy life and keep everything in order, but I do not think I could govern like a saint. Being in a position of responsibility, I am not a saint. I have heard that said often enough over the past few years, during which so much disapproval of my monastery became evident. Complaints were brought to the pope. Of course, all that was cleared up. Our bishop[147] and others who know us emphatically denied the charges against us, and the jubilee celebration made it clear (indirectly) that things had been cleared up. Still, no one who attended the jubilee thought to mention that I had governed the monastery like a saint. If I wanted to do that, I would have had to learn how to do it in my youth.

I have done many good works—with the grace of God, of course—and I have averted much wickedness. No one can deny that. I am still doing much good and preventing much evil. I do not labor for myself, for my honor or comfort, or for any temporal benefit, but I insist on order in the house. I am a man of peace, a friend of the poor. In all my undertakings, I never craved for money, but rather I looked out for the salvation of souls, the necessities of the Church, and the prosperity of the Order. My motto is, "Everything through the Order for the Church to the greater honor and glory of God." They praised me as a good man. That means a good-natured man who is inclined to do works of charity. That is a gift of nature for which I am grateful and which I try to cultivate as a virtue, but that in itself is not sanctity.

Since the beginning of Advent, things have become better at St. Vincent. Earlier, some individuals presented great obstacles to order and progress. Last fall I cleaned them out, though not altogether. I could hardly control my anger, and I thought very seriously of taking powder and dynamite and going to extremes, but I held myself together and tried kindness once more. And what a success! Those who from the beginning were against me and spoiled so many undertakings are uprooted now. If it only remains this way, St. Vincent will be an ideal monastery.

Just this moment Brother Anton[148] died. Last night he had a second stroke. He was a good brother.

The pope, through Cardinal Bartolini,[149] answered a telegram we had sent on the feast day. He sent us his blessing.

The mother prioress[150] in Newark is dying.

---

[147] John Tuigg (1820-1889), third bishop of Pittsburgh.
[148] Anton Faber, O.S.B. (1824-1884).
[149] Cardinal Dominic Bartolini of the Sacred Congregation of Bishops and Religious.
[150] Philomena Spiegel, O.S.B. (1833-1884)

We drank the "Herbaraut" wine during the recent visit of Bishop Dwenger.[151] Like the "Northan" wine, it is delicious.

Anton[152] is in a hopeless condition. Pray for him and pray for me. I always remember you at the altar. With paternal affection, Abbot Boniface Wimmer

Ger   oASVA   transRG

TO CHRYSOSTOM KRUESZ   **170**

St. Vincent, February 21, 1884

Right Reverend Archabbot and Dear Friend: Your Excellency's letter of December 13 is still on my desk, and has been for a long time, awaiting a reply, while pressing matters always appear and prevent me from taking action! My outside stations make many demands on my time, especially when it is a question of making changes or making decisions about new construction. The interests of large families require the full attention of the father if all is to go well. However, the advancement of age and the frequent ailments that accompany it are bound to take their toll. I am especially troubled with an ailment of the throat. As a homeopath, I am my own doctor and take care of myself as well as I can, but my success in treating myself is limited.

Recently I celebrated the golden jubilee of my profession. This caused quite a commotion. I could not avoid the celebration. Like the celebration two years ago, this one took on far greater dimensions than I imagined. Secular priests who had attended our seminary took charge and made it an occasion for a big ovation. They wanted to show their devotion to St. Vincent and the Order and to recognize what we have done for them. Our two bishops, Seidenbusch and Fink,[153] as well as two other bishops, Rademacher of Nashville and Watterson of Columbus,[154] led them. They began the planning early in the summer. It was only two days before the celebration that I heard anything about what they were doing. The only persons officially invited were Bishops Rademacher and Watterson, who had been educated at St. Vincent. I became their captive and had to surrender.

---

[151] Joseph Dwenger (1837-1893), bishop of Fort Wayne.

[152] Anton Wimmer, a nephew of the archabbot.

[153] Rupert Seidenbusch, O.S.B. (1830-1895), bishop of Northern Minnesota; and Louis M. Fink, O.S.B. (1834-1904), bishop of Leavenworth, Kansas.

[154] Joseph Rademacher (1840-1900), bishop of Nashville (1883-1893) and later bishop of Ft. Wayne (1893-1900), and John A. Watterson (1844-1899), bishop of Columbus (1880-1899), both former students at St. Vincent.

There were four bishops and some 50 secular priests present. Our own bishop[155] had suffered a stroke and could not attend. It was a fine family affair and went off in an orderly manner. It was a reunion of priests who had not seen each other for many years. They came from many dioceses and assembled once again in a fraternal spirit. They recalled old times, the crosses and hardships borne, and troubles that had disappeared long ago. They wanted to make me feel good in a large crowd of fine men, many of whom have achieved honor and distinction, who have gone forth from St. Vincent and now openly profess their gratitude to the Benedictines for all that they have achieved. I thank God for the blessing that has come to all our priests who have done honor to their high station in education and priestly life. A German bishop who was unable to attend the celebration wrote me: "You have no idea how much good you have accomplished through the priests you have educated and trained." He himself has seven priests educated by us in his diocese. One is his vicar general.

All that was fine and proper and in order, but then the congratulatory addresses came and were altogether too full of praise. They made me deeply self-conscious. That is the customary way to make speeches nowadays. Then there was the presentation ceremony. They gave me a pectoral cross on a gold chain, which altogether cost $800. That was truly out of order. What will a poor American abbot do with a cross of gold and a ring set with diamonds? What will an old man on the edge of the grave do with them? If Your Excellency were to appear on state occasions with such insignia, it would be quite in order, but I would be ashamed to wear them.

There was more! These gentlemen presented a petition to the Holy See to grant the abbot of St. Vincent, upon the intercession of the Cardinal Protector Bartolini,[156] the title and dignity of archabbot. So there you have it. In addition, my own confreres petitioned the Holy See through the Cardinal Protector to confer the honor of the Cappa Magna on me. I discovered these plots only two days before the celebration and was much disturbed by them. My first thought was, can these outward, undeserved, unexpected, unsought distinctions be the earthly reward for my efforts and labor? I believe I have expressed this fear to Your Excellency before—that my eternity may be found wanting because the reward has already come to me in earthly honors. Honors and distinction, however, have never been my aim. Thus the jubilee passed.

The weather since November has been quite cold, and I have hardly been able to go outside because of my throat ailment. I received many messages of congrat-

---

[155] John Tuigg (1820-1889), third bishop of Pittsburgh.
[156] Cardinal Dominic Bartolini of the Sacred Congregation of Bishops and Religious.

ulations, many of which did not require acknowledgment. They were in their way good will offerings of a spiritual nature, and more precious than the valuable objects that the world admires. They were offerings of holy communions (spiritual and actual), of rosaries and prayers, all of which I surely stand in need of in order to lead a good life and to have a happy end, which very likely is not too far off.

I did not intend to write so much about the celebration. The newspapers, to my distress and confusion, have already written all there is to say. You wanted a short, firsthand report. I intended to give you that, but it has become longer than I wanted it to be.

Portrait of Archabbot Boniface Wimmer in the Cappa Magna.

I have received an invitation from Cardinal Bartolini to suggest the names of one or two fathers who would be willing to occupy themselves with historical research according to the intentions of the papal encyclical of August 18, 1883. Unfortunately, I cannot help. My people have, until now, had very little time to make any significant literary contributions, although there is no lack of good will on their part.

I am much pleased to hear that you are well. I hope and pray from my heart that you will continue to enjoy good health in order to continue your generous and efficient work in the interests of church and state.

We suffered no disastrous losses during the recent floods. All is well, but death has again taken (on December 10) one of our fine young priests, and at about the same time two of our brothers.[157] May God bless you. With cordial love and esteem, I am Your Excellency's devoted, Abbot Boniface

Ger   oAPH   cASVA   transFF

---

[157] The young priest was Daniel Hefti, O.S.B. (1853-1883); the brothers, Blase Mager, O.S.B. (1846-1883) and Anton Faber, O.S.B. (1824-1884).

TO JOSEPH MEYRINGER   **171**

St. Vincent, May 3, 1884

Right Reverend Canon, Dearest Friend and Cousin: Just a short answer to your two letters of March 5 and 27. George, as I have written, is still here and working as a farmhand on our farm. He is a good young man, much better than the young men of his sort in Bavaria. It would not be just for anyone to make a great stir about his small failures. He likes to be with horses. He plows and drives and behaves himself. Because he is still young, he needs our prayers so that he will keep himself under control and not become loose, fun-seeking, or wanton. I certainly hope he will become an upright man. I am not so foolish as to believe and accept as the truth every kind of report coming to me. I know how it goes on such occasions.

I forbad all exterior solemnities for my jubilee, but I made the mistake of not issuing a formal veto. You must admit that it does not often happen that a monk celebrates the golden jubilee of his priesthood and profession. That was the reason for the extraordinary demonstrations to which I had to submit myself. Because Nannie has complained that she heard practically nothing about the festivities, I am sending you the *Wahrheitsfreud* of Cincinnati, which published everything in detail. Please let her know about the celebration. This will give her great pleasure. She is deeply attached to me, like a child, has no children, and often feels alone and miserable.

It is extraordinary, almost miraculous, the way the good Lord has led me. Not that there is anything outstanding in me, or anything that should make people think that I am somehow special. Rather, it is extraordinary that He has given me such an expansive field in which to work and labor, and the achievements will have even greater significance if my people do not deviate from the right path. Not only Germans and English, but also Bohemians and Poles are in the fields of our activity now, and they will depend on us for many things in the future. My 109 priests (who belong to St. Vincent, not including the other two abbeys) are working in 13 dioceses and at home, and many of these places will eventually become abbeys. In addition, the Negroes are part of my concern. They already have an educational institution founded and operated by us, and we already have some Negro brothers. All this has been accomplished through God's providence, rather than by me. The harvest time has arrived, but there are few laborers. When they are ready, they can immediately go to work.

You can imagine what kind of troubled and "crucified" man I am, with no end to plan-making and worrying, inside and outside the house, with a great deal of embarrassment and disappointment. When anything is lacking, everyone looks to the abbot, writes to him, and the abbot has to be ready at every moment with people and money, with advice and decisions, and, in the event he cannot help, with words that are consoling, comforting, encouraging, strengthening, and hopeful. This is especially true now, when much is just beginning and when in many places one does not find the right man or capable, experienced, and tested people, where the *nervum rerum* is too often weak. The poor abbot must be made of iron, a real "archabbot," if he is to please everyone and if, above all, he is to bear the heavy responsibilities of being spiritual father to such a large spiritual community. Nevertheless, nothing will change. If I tried to resign, they would not accept my resignation. As long as I am able to work, I will not stop. I trust that the Lord will give me strength to hold on. In all honesty, as they say, I shall at least be valiant for as long as I am able and have the strength.

Please do me the favor of giving the enclosed note to the honorable Dr. Amberger[158] as soon as possible; and do not forget me in your prayers. Your old friend, Abbot Boniface

Ger   oASVA   transRG

TO BONAVENTURE OSTENDARP   172

St. Vincent, May 14, 1884

Dear Reverend Confrere: I still have not answered your letter of March 26 because I had a lot of correspondence to take care of. I did order the easel to be sent to you immediately, however, and hope you received it. I instructed Brother Norbert[159] to gather the art material and store it in the library. I will take it from there to my private office until I can find a better place.

Father John[160] put the valuable old paintings in the same box where he stores things for the scholastics. One of the scholastics took them out and gave two of them to Brother Bede[161] to hang in the cellar! I knew nothing of this. Neither did Father John, but when Brother Norbert told me about it, I ordered him to bring them all to me. I now have them in my private office. Nothing is safe here. Father

---

[158] Joseph Amberger, cathedral rector in Regensburg, a friend of Wimmer's, and a benefactor of the American Benedictines.
[159] Norbert Kell, O.S.B. (1864-1931).
[160] John Sommer, O.S.B. (1815-1886).
[161] Bede Hoeffner, O.S.B. (1831-1911).

John is the last person with whom I would want to entrust anything. I will make a thorough examination of all these things myself and then send you whatever you need.

Your concern for paintings is like that of others for books. They want all sorts of books. They buy them and put them in bookcases where they like to look at them! Such people want all kinds of books because they assume they will find some use for them, but then usually they do not use them and in fact do not need them at all. Certainly, a monastery should have works of art, as well as rare books, even though both will be used rarely at best, perhaps not at all.

It is said quite frequently that you will never become a painter because you lack precision, because you are not exact and steady, but rather too much in a hurry and always do things too quickly. As the saying goes, you are not faithful in small things. People say, "He does not finish anything" or "He makes a plan and then discards it" or "He does not take the necessary time to work out the details even in the smallest of his paintings; for that reason he does nothing right." Such a person is discredited and soon has a bad name. Great is the failure there! Indeed, it is usually the same in life. He who is not thrifty in little things will never gain a fortune. He who does not watch his pennies will accumulate few dollars. He who does not use the time given to him will not bring his work to fruition. It is the same in the spiritual life. He who is not faithful in small things will never become perfect because he will also be unfaithful in great things. He who does not shun little sins will also commit big sins. "He who despises small things will fall little by little."

No craftsman can deliver a good product if he is not careful about the details of his work. This is even truer of works of art, machinery, etc. Care and precision. These are the things that make a work perfect. Brother Randolph[162] of Munich, who painted the picture over our altar, complained bitterly, with tears in his eyes, that Abbot Gregory[163] pressured him into hurrying to get the work done. Of course, a painter who has much experience can work more quickly than one who has had less experience. Even the master painters, in works of lesser importance, did not give evidence of great precision when they had to do them in a hurry. You are not yet a Raphael and surely cannot expect to be. Raphael did not do things by halves, for one can observe the master in all his works. It was the same with Rubens, Albrecht Dürer, and others.

Never drop anything that you have not really finished and carefully brought to perfection. People want something worthwhile for their money, even if there is

---

[162] A monk of St. Boniface Abbey, Munich.
[163] Gregory Scherr, O.S.B. (1804-1877), abbot of Metten and later archbishop of Munich.

nothing special about the composition. As St. Benedict says in chapter 62 of the *Holy Rule*, "One should not wish to be called holy before he actually is so. He should first be holy that he may truly be called so."

With all love and due respect, Abbot Boniface

Ger   oASVA   transBB

TO AUGUSTINE PUCCI   **173**

St. Vincent, July 3, 1884

Right Reverend and Honorable Lord Abbot, Dear Confrere and Procurator General: I wrote you on June 27 that I had sent a petition to His Holiness (a copy of which I enclose) asking that the priory in Newark be raised to the dignity of an abbey. At the same time I sent a second petition asking that three other missions, which are under my jurisdiction and now self-supporting, be joined together and that the community comprised of these three missions be made an abbey. These missions are Richmond, the priory of St. Mary Help of Christians near Charlotte, and a school for the education of Negro children on Skidaway Island near Savannah, Georgia.

Recently I went to Newark and remained there for eight days, but I had no time to write. When I returned home, I sent you a check for 253 liras to cover the expenses of the business you must transact with the Holy See on behalf of our Congregation and of St. Vincent monastery.

Now with regard to these two new abbeys, it is hardly necessary for me to say how important it is for me and the whole Congregation that the Holy Father grant our petition. As for the first abbey, to be established in Newark, I have no doubt that our petition will be granted. As for the second, however, I am afraid the Holy See may perhaps doubt whether the time is ripe for the Priory of St. Mary, Help of Christians, to become an abbey.

You must realize that in America things develop more rapidly than in Europe. The number of monks, now small, can easily grow. The income of any foundation seems small at first, but it increases so quickly that it becomes sufficient to support a much larger community. At this moment, seven novices are ready to make their simple profession, nine clerics their solemn profession and 15 scholastics have been accepted for the novitiate. There are 15 clerics in simple vows, three in solemn profession, and six who have been elevated to the priesthood—and all for St. Vincent Abbey! If, therefore, you are consulted about the matter, please do what you can to see that permission is given for the Abbey of St. Mary, Help of Christians, in the vicariate of North Carolina, because it will be a great asset for the Order of St. Benedict to have a foundation in our southern states.

There are 114 priests in the chapter at St. Vincent Abbey. If two new abbeys are created, two new abbots will also have to be elected (for life, in accordance with our statutes) from among the entire community of the mother abbey (excluding myself). There are 114 in all, not counting myself. Since many who live in priories far away from the monastery and who are engaged in the care of souls or in teaching in colleges will be unable to attend the election, it is necessary that they be permitted to cast their votes through procurators. Perhaps a special faculty from the Holy See is needed for this, and if so, I shall write to His Eminence, Cardinal Simeoni.[164] On the other hand, if you have the opportunity, please obtain the indult for me.

On April 19, I sent you 500 liras for Abbess M. Liboria Braccia, and 176 liras on April 30 for Abbess Fiumi. I hope you received the money.

My most cordial greetings to Abbot Pescetelli.[165] I trust he is still in good health. As for myself, my health is quite good except that my memory has become rather weak and unreliable.

With greetings to Abbot Zelli[166] and the confreres at St. Paul's, and trusting in your continued friendship towards me and my confreres, I remain with sincere esteem and reverence, your humble confrere in Christ, Boniface Wimmer, Abbot

Lat   oASPR   cASVA   transBB

TO PLACIDUS LACENSE   **174**

St. Vincent, August 21, 1884

Dearest Reverend Confrere: After traveling nine days from Bremen, Father Gamelbert[167] arrived in New York. Next Monday he is going with Frater Wilfrid Frins,[168] nephew of the Right Reverend Dr. Joseph Amberger, to Richmond as

---

[164] Cardinal Giovanni Simeoni, prefect of the Sacred Congregation for the Propagation of the Faith.

[165] Abbot Angelo Pescetelli, O.S.B. (1809-1885).

[166] Francisco Leopold Zelli-Jacobuzi, O.S.B. (1818-1895), abbot of the abbey of St. Paul's Outside the Walls, Rome, and president of the Cassinese Congregation.

[167] Gamelbert Brunner, O.S.B. (1850-1908).

[168] Wilfrid Frins, O.S.B. (1860-1936).

assistant to Father Willibald Baumgartner[169] from Wolfrathshausen. The pastor in Richmond, Father Benno Hegele,[170] a native-born American, will remain here. He is sick and suffering very badly from bronchitis. During the vacation, Father Rudesind Schrembs[171] from Regensburg was ordained. He will go with Frater Wilfrid and a lay brother from Richmond to St. Mary's Priory, near Charlotte, North Carolina, 300 miles further south.

Father Gamelbert was delighted by the tender and paternal attention you paid him. I am not surprised. Nor do I wonder at the fact that one day you, at the age of 83, walked to Posching, and from there to Michaelsbuch, and then back to Metten in the same day. I do not think I could do that, and I am only 76! My legs, from the calves to the soles of my feet, are weak as a result of some unnecessary experimental exercises I did back in 1866. The problem showed up after my return from Europe that year.

Now let us talk about several things. First, the celebration of the jubilee of my profession. Because of that extravagance (which I did not desire) I will have to suffer a long time in Purgatory. Whether it will do me any good to live longer, I do not know. The faults of my past are still not expiated, and new ones will be added. In comparison with you, the sharpness of my mind, like the vigor of my body, has declined very much. I cannot work by candlelight, and only a little during the day. I have to take an hour's nap because I feel tired much of the time. I cannot depend on my memory, and this frequently causes me to feel embarrassed or to commit sins of negligence when attending to my duties. Beginning many years ago, I laid many crosses on myself, and now I have to finish the work. Perhaps nothing has been done correctly or as it should have been. "I will be afraid because of all my works," as the saying goes. Fear oppresses me. Being praised is no help at all. It is, rather, a poor and cold comfort.

Secondly, your new abbot.[172] He is precisely the right man for the job. It is only too bad that he is so short of stature. If I had had his intellect and talent 38 years ago, St. Vincent would have been an entirely different place from what it is today. I am convinced that I came to America through God's holy Providence. The Benedictines were not yet here, and that left an unfortunate and regrettable vacuum. This made it possible for me to follow St. Boniface and become a "plan-maker" for St. Benedict. I have been here 38 years, and my monastery is still not finished.

---

[169] Willibald Baumgartner, O.S.B. (1853-1930).
[170] Benno Hegele, O.S.B. (1837-1885).
[171] Rudesind Schrembs, O.S.B. (1860-1908).
[172] Benedict Braunmüller, O.S.B. (1825-1898), had recently succeeded Utto Lang, O.S.B. as abbot of Metten.

There is never enough space, never enough room. The buildings are certainly not grand. I erect them without an architect. I build only what is necessary, and I have the brothers, with very few exceptions, do the work. This year we are building a five-story building, 138 by 44 feet, in order to connect the monastery and college on the south side and to gain more space for the college.

I have to worry about providing priests not only for the Germans, but also for the Bohemians, Poles, and Hungarians, because nobody is anxious to tackle this tremendous undertaking. Thousands upon thousands immigrate, and most of them are going to the Devil because nobody on this side of the ocean is helping them and taking care of them. We already have one Polish and two Bohemian parishes. We also have 20 Bohemian students in our house, but unfortunately only two Polish students because no others applied. In addition, two Hungarian students have applied. Our Bohemian and Polish priests are helping the Slovenians with whom we come in contact. The Swedes, Norwegians, and Danes must also be taken care of, but no one bothers about them, and our 11 million Negroes are utterly neglected. In my opinion, the Benedictines are called to awaken America, just as they did in Europe, but real zeal is lacking. Not a few of the younger generation are looking for a good table more than for immortal souls.

I would like to have you here as my guest for a few weeks. Then I would take you on a tour to show you all our places in New Jersey, Delaware, Maryland, Virginia, North Carolina, Georgia, Alabama, Illinois, Missouri, Kansas, Nebraska, Iowa, Minnesota, Indiana, and all around Pennsylvania and Kentucky. St. Vincent is a monastery *sui generis*. Everyone admires our college. The college, the mill, and the brewery (which needs improvements) are the three sources of our income. On them, for the most part, depends our corporal well-being. The principal thing, which I had to plan for from the beginning, is the education of priests for the Order and for the diocesan clergy. That is why I was not able to give the monastery my full attention.

I occupy a room in the corner (like the seniorate at Metten) with three separate cells, one of which, more often than not, serves as a guest room. The rooms are good enough for everyday use, all facing east. The corridor is about 400 feet in length, divided in the middle by the church and choir. Half the floor is for the fathers, the other half for clerics and novices (including the museum). On the ground floor, we have rooms for guests, the brothers' hall, the pharmacy and dispensary, rooms for meeting visitors, etc. The library is above the choir. Half the third floor is reserved for the college. The new building will also be for the college. The brothers' dormitory is on the fourth floor. Some of the brothers have individual cells. Some sleep near their workshops outside the *clausura*. The miller and brewmaster sleep in the mill and the brewery. The workers in the stables and barn live in a nearby building with the overseers.

Third, Atchison. Atchison is doing very well since its abbot[173] was elected. The abbot is doing everything he can to eliminate the debt. He is at the same time erecting new buildings and engaged in parochial work. Lowering the interest on the debt has been very important, but still the burden is heavy. The big mistake they made at the beginning was not accepting young men for the scholasticate. That is the reason they do not have enough priests now. St. Vincent is large because of the scholasticate. In this, it has become a model for others, such as the Redemptorists.

I will send your bill to Abbot Innocent, and he will pay it with Mass intentions. Not long ago he asked me for 500 intentions. I could not give him any because I myself was in need of them, having very few.

I felt very bad that I could hardly talk to you at all when I visited Metten in 1880. I know that I will never go to Metten again. Unless you come to America for a visit, there is not much hope we will see each other again.

I am weary of living and awaiting the end when we must leave everything behind and be deserted by everyone. The pictures of old Fathers Ildephonse and Roman[174] are hanging in front of me. How often I think of them. Not many of my contemporaries and fellow soldiers remain. Most have already left. Who would not understand that I long to be united with them? My grave was prepared long ago in the middle of the cemetery. Yes, let us pray for one another that we all come together in a good place.

Our resolution must be to carry the cross as long as we live, in patience, in the service of the Crucified, faithful in small things even if we cannot do great things. Greetings to His Grace and all the confreres. In sincere affection and respect, your most devoted, Abbot Boniface Wimmer

Ger   oAMA   cASVA   transRG

---

[173] Innocent Wolf, O.S.B. (1843-1922), elected abbot of St. Benedict's Abbey, Atchison, in 1876.

[174] Ildephonse Nebauer, O.S.B. (1789-1844), and Roman Raith, O.S.B. (1788-1856), the two monks who restored Benedictine life at Metten in 1830. Nebauer was prior at Metten when Wimmer entered the novitiate there in 1832.

TO JAMES GIBBONS **175**

St. Vincent, August 30, 1884

Most Reverend Archbishop, Your Grace: In answer to your favor dd. Aug. 24, allow me to say: I always thought that something should be done for the poor priests who were under censure or without faculties; had no place where to go to or where to stay or to reform themselves; and were almost forced to apostatize or to tramp through the country begging from their brother priests and from good Catholics alms or shelter for a short time in order not to starve or to perish on the street. I learned from a German Catholic in Newark, N.J., that a good many such unfortunate priests were working in the leather factories there. I know that others worked on railroads, others, who acted as school teachers, *lecto nomine*. Such are of the better class of these unfortunate men, but many lead a miserable and scandalous life, in no way better than real tramps, in many ways worse yet.

I spoke to several bishops about this matter. I found them generally in agreement with my own sentiments, but they knew not how to help, and some would say nothing could be done because these priests were too unruly and would not allow themselves to be confined in an institution or in a house of correction and would perhaps go so far as to draw their bishop before the court if he wanted to send them to a house of correction, etc. Of course, that might be true, if they would be incarcerated in a kind of penitentiary, but this I had not in view, although I think a charter could be obtained for a corporation which could use some coercive measures against unruly penitents in case of necessary, e.g., strict enclosure inside the walls of the institution for a certain time, or at least as long as they wanted to remain in the institution.

In 1866 at the last Council in Baltimore M[onsignor] John T. Sullivan, vicar general of Wheeling, brought in a formal motion in this regard, which I heartily seconded. It was then decided by the prelates that such a house of refuge should be established, and I consented to find a suitable building in St. Marys, Elk Co., Pa.; and it was stipulated that each priest in the ecclesiastical province of Baltimore should be obliged to pay annually $5 for the support or maintenance of the institution. Father Foley[175] (afterwards bishop of Chicago) was appointed treasurer. But nothing was done. The Vatican Council followed. Archbishop Spalding[176] died. V. Rev. Foley was made bishop, etc. I was almost a whole year absent in Europe on account of the Vatican Council. Everything remained as it was.

---

[175] Thomas Foley (1822-1879), coadjutor bishop and apostolic administrator of the diocese of Chicago (1870-1879).

[176] Martin J. Spalding (1810-1872), archbishop of Baltimore (1864-1872).

Meanwhile Rev. Sagerer arrived from Bavaria with a few Brothers of the Order of St. John of God. Bishop Shanahan[177] received him in his diocese. He wanted to establish a house for penitent priests in the city of Lancaster, Pa., but went too fast, ran into debts, and failed, and everything went to nothing again. So matters stand now. I am very glad that the Apostolic See takes now an interest in the matter, and I trust something will now be done.

In my judgment the first requirement is money, which can be obtained by voluntary contributions of the clergy and laity, by collections, and also by annual obligatory subsidies of the clergy, or by legacy, etc. With money, in each archdiocese a suitable house or property can be acquired which should be located not far from a R.R. station in a county mostly settled by Catholics. If a religious order should have to take care of such a house of correction (better to be styled perhaps a "Retreat for Destitute Priests" or something similar), likely the order would build the retreat at its own expenses, if provision would be made for its maintenance by the contributions from the clergy, etc., and many scandals could be prevented, much good could be done, many priests' souls be saved which otherwise go lost.

My dear, most reverend archbishop! I am an old man, nearly 76 years behind me. I can promise little because I cannot live much longer. Besides, I have on several places, particularly in the South, houses of my own Order which claim all my solicitude and the little activity and energy which I yet have, and also all the money I can spare. Still, I am willing, as far as it depends [on] me, to do what is in my power to assist in this enterprise. Indeed, I have all the time since I am in this country, made my house a refuge for such poor priests who asked me to give them a temporary home for months, and in a few cases even for years, till they found again a bishop willing to receive them. Over a hundred such priests have been our guests. Last year again I had four here at one time: one for over a year, one nine months. One old German priest is already over 20 years here, half blind, unable to say Mass. An Irish priest is here several years, doing very well. One is here two years, also doing very well, and there are two at the priory in S. Marys, Elk Co., Pa. I never asked nor did I receive anything for their maintenance. However, many years ago some ones earned their boarding by teaching the boys, and of late Bishop Chatard[178] paid for one $200 per year.

But should I be obliged to engage myself for keeping a certain number of destitute priests, I would have to raise a proper building for this purpose because it is too inconvenient and even injurious to the discipline to have them in the convent,

---

[177] Jeremiah F. Shanahan (1834-1886), first bishop of Harrisburg (1868-1886).
[178] Francis S. Chatard (1834-1918), bishop of Vincennes, Indiana (1878-1918).

although separate from the members of the house. We felt this so much that at the last Chapter General the proposition was moved and carried that no secular penitent priest should be received any more. Still I made, as above stated, exceptions against this statute again.

To make it short, I say (1) that if something definitive will be decided by the coming Council, I will, as far as I can do it without harm to my own religious family, occasionally receive one or two of these unfortunate priests; (2) if by the decrees of the Council provision be made for establishing retreats for penitent priests, and if no other religious family is found to take charge thereof, I will do my best to find a suitable locality where a certain number, say 6 or 12, could be received, and that I trust to obtain for this purpose the consent of my chapter.

In Bavaria, the Brothers of St. John of God have such an institution in the city of Neuburg, wherein not only penitent, but also *bene meriti* but destitute, feeble priests, are cared for, and everything works very well. I believe such brothers, or the Alexian Brothers, would be most qualified for this task.

Asking your blessing, I remain in profound reverence, Your Grace's most humble servant, Bonif. Wimmer, Archabbot

Eng   oAAB   cASVA

TO BENEDICT BRAUNMÜLLER   **176**

St. Vincent, December 20, 1884

Right Reverend Father Abbot, Dear Confrere: A most happy New Year 1885. I wish you the best in the new year, all that is best for the welfare of your body and soul now and for many years to come. May you be filled with merits! I returned from the council[179] held in Baltimore on December 9. When I got back, we held a General Chapter, and the two other abbots[180] held a canonical visitation of my monastery. With all this, I had five very busy weeks, so I could not write until now.

The Plenary Council lasted more than four weeks. We had sessions each day from 10:00 am until 1:00 pm (sometimes later). We ate lunch at about 2:00 pm, on Sundays even later. Then in the afternoons, we had sessions from 4:00 pm to 6:00 pm and ate at 7:00 pm. Thirteen archbishops and 60 bishops (some

---

[179] The Third Plenary Council of Baltimore.
[180] Alexius Edelbrock, O.S.B. (1843-1908), abbot of St. John's Abbey, Collegeville, Minnesota; and Innocent Wolf, O.S.B. (1843-1922), abbot of St. Benedict's Abbey, Atchison, Kansas.

Archabbot Boniface Wimmer, O.S.B., with Benedictine and Trappist prelates at the Third Plenary Council of Baltimore, November 1884. Left to right: Abbot Fintan Mundwiler, O.S.B., of St. Meinrad Abbey, Indiana; Bishop Rupert Seidenbusch, O.S.B., vicar apostolic of Northern Minnesota; Wimmer; Abbot Benedict Berger, O.C.S.O., of Gethsemani Abbey, Kentucky; Abbot Alexius Edelbrock, O.S.B., of St. John's Abbey, Minnesota; Abbot Innocent Wolf, O.S.B., of St. Benedict Abbey, Kansas; Abbot Frowin Conrad, O.S.B., of Conception Abbey, Missouri.

represented by others) were present, along with one Trappist and six Benedictine abbots. In addition, there were eight domestic prelates, three secretaries of the chamber, 35 superiors of religious orders, 12 seminary directors, and 76 theologians. Most of the religious superiors and seminary directors also served as theological consultants, but they did not attend the routine sessions in the assembly hall. Of the seven abbots, only three were entitled to a decisive vote, but everyone subscribed to the decrees by signing the document on the altar during the last session. This session was open to the public. Those with the right to a decisive vote (including the presidents of congregations) signed by writing *"Definiens subscripsi."* All the others merely signed their names. The document placed before us, with all the decrees, comprised some 90 pages of small print. The decrees dealt with ecclesiastical matters. The whole affair was somewhat tiring, especially for participants of advanced age.

We Benedictines, three bishops and six abbots, were lodged in our brand-new rectory.[181] The rectory has nine rooms, so the pastor[182] had to move to a nearby building. At table, we were normally joined by the pastor and two theologians—12 of us altogether—but in the evening we generally had visitors, and there were 15 or more of us then. Every morning, 16 Masses were said in the church. That is something that certainly does not happen very often. We had to go two English miles to the cathedral or seminary, where the sessions were held, but we could reach the place in 35 minutes by taking for ten cents a streetcar pulled by horses. We spent two hours every day coming and going, except for Sundays when there were no sessions. Good order was maintained. The organization of the sessions was good. Everyone was on good terms, and there were seldom disagreements.

There were 12 delegations, each one headed by an archbishop and consisting of four or five bishops with abbots and theologians. They deliberated for two hours on certain days over the proposed points before submitting them to the Council. On such days, no session was held in the afternoon. The weather was ideal. It could not have been better. Still, a few became sick, and one theologian died. A bishop has taken the decrees and resolutions to Rome for approval and publication when they are ratified. It might be some time before they are authorized and become a *fait accompli*.

Baltimore is a large, beautiful city with over 300,000 inhabitants, but it is not a metropolis like St. Louis, Chicago, Philadelphia, Boston, or New York. I left the rectory only twice, once for a short trip to St. Vincent. Otherwise, I saw nothing of the city except for the streets along which I traveled to and from the sessions. We have a small parish in Baltimore with a pretty church and a beautiful and large courtyard for the rectory. The rectory is supposed to house a small community that will conduct a high school we will establish, if it is God's will. Five Benedictine sisters are also there to educate girls and small boys.

I petitioned Rome to make an abbey in Newark, a city on the ocean. I have given Elizabeth and Wilmington to Newark, and have kept Baltimore for St. Vincent. The other southeast stations (Richmond, Virginia; Charlotte, North Carolina; Savannah, Georgia, with the Negro island, Skidaway) I have joined together to form a small abbey, with the seat of the abbot at the place called Maryhelp, near

---

[181] The rectory belonged to Fourteen Holy Martyrs Parish, a dependency of St. Vincent.
[182] Meinrad Jeggle, O.S.B. (1834-1926).

the city of Charlotte. I have received a letter from our procurator general[183] that my petition was approved and granted in September. I am expecting the apostolic brief any day. We will then have to elect two abbots. After that, I will not have so much to worry about any more. These places will grow far better when they are governed by their own abbots. Naturally, I will still have to provide people and money.

I have been preoccupied by these matters for a long time. Later, when Alabama and Illinois are established as abbeys, St. Vincent will not be so handicapped. It will be more easily governed if it has fewer dependencies. I am too old and not strong enough to take the necessary energetic action.

Many thanks to you for all the signs of friendship during the past year, especially for your kindness in sending Mass stipends.

Perhaps you have already received the last volume of Father Peter Lechner's Bible commentary.[184] I am so happy that I have lived to see the completion of this monumental work. Some of my professors have expressed their intention of translating it into English because no work of this kind in English can be found in print. I had to endure much trouble and spend much money to bring the work to light. May this undertaking harvest for good Father Peter[185] a special reward in heaven and obtain for me, a poor sinner, the mercy of God.

Please give special regards to my old friend Father Placidus.[186] Likewise to the rest of my dear confreres, especially to Fathers Willibald, Fortunatus, Rupert, and Bernard,[187] who are better known to me than the younger ones. May you enjoy the best of health, be happy in the Lord, and steady in fraternal love. Let us pray for one another that we might be saved and united in heaven. Your Grace's most devoted confrere, Abbot Boniface Wimmer

Ger   oAMA   cASVA   transRG

---

[183] Augustine Pucci-Sisti, O.S.B. (b. 1810).

[184] Peter Lechner, *Die Heilige Schrift des Alten Testamentes, nach der Vulgata und dem Grundtext erklärt* (Beatty, Pa.: St. Vincent Press, 1882-84).

[185] Peter Lechner, O.S.B. (1805-1874).

[186] Placidus Lacense, O.S.B. (1802-1887).

[187] Willibald Freymüller, O.S.B. (1807-1890); Fortunatus Braun, O.S.B. (1806-1893); Rupert Mittermüller, O.S.B. (1814-1893); and Bernard Högl, O.S.B. (1813-1886) of Metten.

1885-1887

St. Vincent, January 4, 1885

Your Eminence, Most Reverend Cardinal Prefect: The Most Reverend Patrick A. Feehan,[1] archbishop of Chicago, has in his see city three Bohemian churches, called here congregations or parishes. The largest of these is the church, or parish, of St. Procopius. A year ago, he gave this parish in trust to the Benedictines because he could find no Bohemian priests to staff it. Indeed, good Bohemian priests are rarely found in America.

Now, as the archbishop makes clear in his letter (of which I enclose a true copy), he desires very much that the Benedictines permanently take charge of the care of souls in St. Procopius Parish, on condition that we always staff it with priests who speak the Bohemian language and that we care for the souls of its faithful and administer its property in accordance with archdiocesan regulations, just as other religious orders do. For us, this parish is in fact a burdensome donation. Nonetheless, several grave reasons caused me to accept it.

The brick church, built only a few years ago, is large and solid enough for the present. It has a debt of $30,000, with an annual interest rate of six percent. The parish school, which was the former church, is a frame building that is beginning to show signs of weakness and in any event is not large enough to accommodate the large number of pupils. The church has a house for the pastor, but is not suf-

---

[1] Patrick A. Feehan (1829-1902), first archbishop of Chicago (1880-1902).

ficient to accommodate an assistant because by American standards it is too small and entirely unsuitable for a large city.

Therefore, in addition to the debt that already exists, the parish will have to take on additional debt in a short time to build a new school and a new parochial residence. In an Irish or German parish, this would pose no problem because the Irish and Germans in America are accustomed to contributing liberally to their parishes. They give to their priests whatever is necessary for churches, schools, and parochial residences. The Bohemians, however, do not.

There is a more serious difficulty. In order to staff this large church, it will be necessary to have constantly at hand a sufficient number of priests who understand and speak the Bohemian language. Until now, a single priest has generally had charge of the church, sometimes two. It is entirely impossible, however, for one or two priests (even if they are the best and most energetic men available) to do the job adequately and to attend to the spiritual needs of the people. Three are hardly sufficient. Four or five are required, but where will they come from?

The number of parishioners in this parish can be deduced from the fact that there are 900 pupils in the parish school. Many others go to the public schools. It is said that there are 30,000 Bohemians in the city of Chicago.

At present, I have five priests who speak the Bohemian language. Sadly, I lost a sixth to premature death. Of the five, one lives in the monastery; another has charge of a Bohemian parish in Pittsburgh, and three are assigned to the parish of St. Procopius in Chicago. I am not able to send more to Chicago at the present time, and even if I could, there would be no place for them to live because the house is so small.

It was, therefore, with great reluctance that I accepted the church of St. Procopius, because I am not sure that I will always have enough priests to staff it. I do hope, however, to be able to overcome this difficulty. Certainly for a long time I have had pity on the Bohemians because of their spiritual destitution, and I have accepted all the poor Bohemian boys and talented young men who have applied to our seminary (which we call the Scholasticate) in order to educate them for the priesthood. Nevertheless, even though many have been accepted over the years, only a few have remained to complete their studies. Nonetheless, in addition to the five priests I mentioned above, I have two Bohemian students of theology, four students of philosophy, one novice, five scholastics in the upper classes of the gymnasium, and several younger boys, several of whom show promise of continuing their studies for sacred orders.

Confident, therefore, of the assistance of Divine Providence in this extremely important matter, and obedient to the wishes of the archbishop, I will permanently accept the offer of the church of St. Procopius in the city of Chicago, under the specified conditions, provided that the Holy Apostolic See deigns to approve and confirm the transaction. I humbly request that Your Eminence grant my petition.

If things go well, it would not be a surprise if after a few years a Bohemian monastery and college were to be erected next to St. Procopius Church, because the Bohemians are very ambitious and will do whatever is necessary to promote the honor of the Bohemian nation. They will, therefore, probably contribute liberally to the establishment of a Bohemian educational institution. Such an institution, without doubt, will contribute not a little to the increase of the number of Bohemian priests, because in the city of Chicago there are many young men who are seriously considering choosing the clerical life and would be able to do so if they could find a place to pursue their studies.

With grateful thanks for your many kind favors, and hoping that you will receive many blessings from heaven in the New Year, I am, in deep reverence and obedience, Your Eminence's most humble servant, Boniface Wimmer, Archabbot

Lat   oAPF   cASVA   transJO

TO INNOCENT WOLF   **178**

St. Vincent, February 17, 1885

Right Reverend Abbot and Dear Confrere: On February 10 and 11 elections were held here for abbots for Newark and Maryhelp, North Carolina. There were 115 eligible voters. Some, however, waived their right to vote, and a pair lost the privilege because their proxy was improperly filled out. Thus, nine votes were thrown out, leaving a total of 106 votes, of which 64 were present. I voted and was proxy for Fathers Maurice and Benedict.[2]

We had completed the necessary arrangements by Tuesday morning. At 8:00 am, the prior[3] celebrated high Mass. Then everyone assembled in the choir for the election. Before we started, Father Alphonse[4] stood up to protest the entire procedure of the election. He called it meaningless and condemned it as foolish and said he felt he could therefore not take part in it. I said only that I had proposed

---

[2] Maurice Kaeder, O.S.B. (1837-1892) and Benedict Menges, O.S.B. (1840-1904).
[3] Michael Hofmayer, O.S.B. (1838-1901).
[4] Alphonse Heimler, O.S.B. (1832-1909).

that both abbots be elected by all the capitulars of St. Vincent and that they come from St. Vincent because in neither Newark nor Maryhelp was there a clearly established community of monks definitely committed to each place. I noted that since everyone could not be present for the election, I had also proposed that those who were absent should be able to vote by proxy. I said that Rome had accepted and approved this procedure and that Father Alphonse's objections were, therefore, not directed against me alone but against the Holy See itself. He then placed his written protest on the table to be forwarded to Rome and left the assembly in a huff. No one followed him.

Bishop Leo Haid, O.S.B. (1849-1924), first abbot of Maryhelp Abbey (later Belmont Abbey), North Carolina, who was ordained bishop when he was named vicar apostolic of North Carolina.

Next, three tellers were chosen— James, Hilary, and Andrew[5]—and the work of the election began. The printed ballots had the names of all the eligible candidates in alphabetical order, and as with the election of the tellers, each elector received one ballot. The first election was for Newark. Father James received 47 votes on the first turn and 62 on the second. (Fifty-four were required for election.) The announcement was received with applause; a show of hands made it unanimous. This happened at 12:00 noon. Father Gerard,[6] I think, received five votes. Father Hilary was just behind James with 20 votes. Fathers Leo,[7] Michael, and Andrew also received votes.

At 2:00 pm, we turned to the election of an abbot for Maryhelp. On the first ballot, Father Oswald received 55 votes amid great applause. Father Placidus,[8] who was present, received only a few. Giles,[9] Hilary, Andrew, and Leo also re-

---

[5] James Zilliox, O.S.B. (1849-1890); Hilary Pfrängle, O.S.B. (1843-1909); and Andrew Hintenach, O.S.B. (1844-1927).

[6] Gerard Pilz, O.S.B.(1834-1891).

[7] Leo Haid, O.S.B. (1849-1924).

[8] Placidus Pilz, O.S.B. (1835-1911).

[9] Aegidius (Giles) Christoph, O.S.B. (1830-1887).

ceived a few. It all ended in good order and with good feelings, exactly . . . [the remainder of this letter is missing].

Ger   oASBA   cASVA   transPB

TO ADALBERT MÜLLER   179

St. Vincent, February 20, 1885

Reverend and Dear Confrere: So Father James[10] and Father Oswald[11] are now abbots elect. Father James accepted at once, but Father Oswald answered by telegram, "Thank you for the honor, but cannot accept." On February 16, I wrote him a strong letter saying, "If you were unable or unwilling to accept, why did you not say so earlier so that we could have elected someone else?" The election cost several hundred dollars and untold care and trouble, so that I became quite sick and still am. Now we will have more trouble and expense because of Oswald's changing moods. Yesterday I received a letter from him (dated February 16) in which he says, "I received your telegram of my election and answered 'Thank you for the honor but I cannot accept.' I hereby repeat the same in writing." So it appears that he really is serious and in earnest, but he had not yet received my letter when he wrote. I shall wait to see what he has to say in answer to my letter. It would be terrible if I had to recall the 115 capitulars to elect an abbot for Maryhelp a second time, just because Father Oswald is too timid or too humble to accept the office. He is quite capable of pulling a trick like this, however, so he may indeed not be the man for the office. Such an outcome will exasperate me and will inevitably meet with disfavor at Rome.

I take hope that everything will eventually turn out all right. Oswald would be better off in the South than James in Newark, which is our troublesome place. The men in Newark (some of them) are not well thought of. I feel certain, however, that it will go well when a virtuous man takes hold there. Several men in Newark want to come home. Others, many of them from St. Vincent, want to go there. Everything will remain *in statu quo* until Rome has spoken.

Because Gross[12] is to become archbishop of Oregon, some irresponsible individuals surmise that Oswald thinks he has a sort of right of succession to the see

---

[10] James Zilliox, O.S.B. (1849-1890).
[11] Oswald Moosmüller, O.S.B. (1832-1901).
[12] William H. Gross, C.SS.R. (1837-1898), fifth bishop of Savannah (1873-1885) and third archbishop of Oregon City (1885-1898).

of Savannah. That is hard to believe. His extreme modesty and timidity has caused him to refuse the abbacy, but if he puts these aside, he will get it. The important thing is that we have the abbeys. We will find the abbots, although I would not for any price want to go through another election. *Pax tibi.* Abbot Boniface

Ger   oASBA   cASVA   transJO

TO NEPOMUCENE JAEGER   **180**

St. Vincent, April 14, 1885

Dearest Reverend Confrere: I am pleased that you are doing everything in your power to establish a monastery for Bohemians in Chicago. Of course, it need not, at first be a formal abbey, but can begin as a priory and in time become an abbey, like St. Mary's in Newark and St. Benedict's in Kansas. The first thing required is that the church be incorporated in our name. Until now, you have had only the word of the archbishop[13] in an ordinary letter, nothing more. The second thing is to raise the money to build a monastery. So far, we have only $2,700. The $5,000 and the $2,500 are just promises and not yet in the treasury. It might be a long time before our desires are fulfilled. The third thing (and strictly speaking the most necessary) is that we have to have the proper people—priests and brothers—whose number until now has been very limited (very much so). It seems that we will not have enough members for years to come.

It would not be right to neglect our current responsibilities. We must keep providing the respective bishops with priests because it would not be right to abandon the people. Above all, the Bohemians at St. Procopius must give real proof of their desire to have a monastery. They cannot fail to make some sacrifices if they are to have one. That is the reason we must proceed with caution and avoid making promises until we have a real prospect that we can achieve.

On the other hand, we should not be too timid about the possibility of success. Our pledge is to do something good, to work for the greater honor of God, for the salvation of thousands of immortal souls, for the honor and expansion of our Order. Thus, we can be confident that God will help us if we ask for His help and do our duty. I know this from my own experience. Moreover, you find proof in the whole of Church history. We may not give orders to God, however. We have to let Him decide how soon and how much help He will send us. We must submit

---

[13] Patrick J. Feehan (1829-1902), archbishop of Chicago (1880-1902).

ourselves to His will. God's ways are not ours. He does not work in double quick time.

I would like to go to Chicago immediately to see with my own eyes how things stand since one can hardly give an opinion or make a decision without seeing things himself and becoming acquainted with the details, but it is practically impossible for me to travel because of my infirmities. Let me tell you one thing. I think you should acquire more land near your church, provided you can get it under favorable conditions, because you need ground for buildings. You cannot erect buildings in the air. I asked Father Sigismund[14] to explain to me where the four lots reserved for the church are located. I think you made a sound decision, and, therefore, I have no objection to buying the property. The $2,700 that Father Wenceslaus has in the bank should be used for that purpose. You should sell the houses standing on the lots because they are useless to us. You should do this at once. Then have the deed for these lots made out to the corporation of St. Joseph's Parish until you can establish your own corporation with the understanding that the property title will rest with the Bohemian religious family.

St. Joseph's is no longer in financial danger. The debt has been reduced to $48,000 and is diminishing every year. Because I asked Father Choka to buy two lots (in addition to the other five he had in mind for his church), I must pay $2,500 and hold them at my own risk. For this reason, you must take the $2,700 for Chicago. I do not want to break my word to him and bungle the purchase of the church property for the congregation since it is clear that he will have a large Bohemian parish. However, I cannot give the property away as a donation. Give me time to think it over.

In Newark, we sold two houses when we took over the parish, but for that reason, the congregation had to pay rent because they did not build a rectory. The rent was due yearly. With that rent, with the $8,000 for the houses, and with our own savings, we paid off the debt of the purchase itself little by little. Lately I gave permission to the congregation in Newark to build a rectory at their expense. This rectory will be partly built on our property, which is now the abbey. This is the way we should proceed in Chicago.

The college building in Newark cost over $14,000 (without the lot) and belongs to us, but the debt has not yet been paid off. Until recently, the day school did not make a profit. If it had not been for the stipends and other income the professors received from the city's English churches on Sundays and Holy Days of Obligation, we could not have continued to operate the day school. Because the Bohemians do not offer stipends, a day school will not be successful. For that

---

[14] Sigismund Singer, O.S.B. (b. 1860).

reason, we cannot think of starting one at the beginning, even if we had professors available, but we do not have professors, and we cannot expect those doing pastoral work to be at the same time professors. Eventually, however, we can and must have a day school.

Another point that you should seriously consider: you need more than four lots if a formal priory and a day school are to become realities because there must be a place for recreation. In addition, we cannot think of buying St. Pius church. People, priests, money are all sorely needed for such an undertaking. Much prayer, firm faith, discretion, and prudence will bring the blessing of Heaven. Cordial greetings to Fathers Wenceslaus and Xavier.[15] *Pax vobis.* Your most devoted confrere, Abbot Boniface

Ger   oASPA   cASVA   transRG

TO GIOVANNI SIMEONI   **181**

St. Vincent, July 17, 1885

Most Reverend and Distinguished Cardinal Prefect of the Sacred Congregation for the Propagation of the Faith: I, hereby, most respectfully transmit the official protocol of the election held at St. Vincent Monastery on July 14, in which the Reverend Leo Haid[16] was elected abbot of the new abbey of St. Mary Help of Christians in the vicariate apostolic of North Carolina.

As far as possible, all prescriptions of the sacred canons were carried out in order that the election from every point of view might be legitimate and valid. In order to avoid the necessity of convoking all the capitulars belonging to St. Vincent Monastery, I deemed it better to establish for the new abbey its own community, and, accordingly, I found eight qualified fathers who were willing to transfer their profession from my monastery to this new abbey. I could have found more, but decided not to do so since it seemed to me more advisable to leave this matter to the future abbot, preferring to add to this number some clerics who could help carry out the office in choir until the number of monks grew larger. I hope, therefore, that the small number of monks does not cause any offence.

The abbot-elect is indeed a person highly regarded and deserving of recommendation. He was born in our parish on July 15, 1849. His parents were of German descent and of good character. He was educated in the monastery from

[15] Wenceslaus Kocarnik, O.S.B. (1845-1912), and Francis Xavier Traxler, O.S.B. (1860-1934).
[16] Leo Haid, O.S.B. (1849-1924).

boyhood and became an excellent student. He then entered the Order, and on October 5, 1872, made his solemn profession. He was ordained to the priesthood on December 21, 1872. From that time on, he has always been stationed at the monastery and has taught in the college. He principally taught those subjects needed by boys who wanted to become doctors, lawyers, judges, merchants, etc. He was, moreover, chaplain and spiritual father in the college, an office in which he gave evidence of the highest performance, with fruit equal to his zeal. He is a good monk, a good priest, a good man loved and highly esteemed by all. Thus, he seems to have all the good qualities needed in an abbot of a new abbey.

I therefore earnestly recommend to Your Eminence the newly elected abbot and most humbly entreat that the petition added to the protocol for the confirmation of the election and the abbot-elect may meet, in accordance with your usual good disposition, with your very kind favor and support.

For this new favor, I shall always be indebted with the most profound reverence and gratitude. Your Eminence's most humble and obedient servant, Boniface Wimmer, Archabbot and President of the American Cassinese Congregation

Lat   oAPF   cASVA   transBB

TO JULIAN KILGER   182

St. Vincent, July 18, 1885

My Dear Father Julian: Because you wanted to remain in Newark, I knew you would find it difficult when I did not comply with your wishes. I am therefore, not surprised by your letter of July 13. As your superior and your friend, I have hesitated to let you go. This does not mean, however, that eventually you will not be able to go to Newark since such a transfer is possible in the Congregation, is permissible, and may even be advisable. I will not live much longer, and times change. For the time being, however, you will have to return to St. Vincent, and you will have to do so immediately after the blessing of the abbot[17] because I need and want you here.

For the moment, I am not able to speak of the plan you mention of returning to Metten or Munich or your home in order to organize the affairs of your parents and make things "comfortable for them." It would take a long time for me to respond, and I do not have a lot of time just now, but I do want to say that this

---

[17] James Zilliox, O.S.B. (1849-1890), who was blessed as first abbot of St. Mary's Abbey, Newark, on July 22, 1885.

plan does not come from the Holy Spirit, is not based on good reasoning, and, in any case, cannot for the moment be carried out. It is a plan that you will change when you reflect on it quietly.

You must renew your faith in Divine Providence, which wisely and miraculously directs and orders everything, even the smallest event, and which brings about our temporal and spiritual well-being. When you are as old as I am, you will become more convinced that for those who love God, all things will lead to the best, and that a life under obedience or under the *Rule* is one of the greatest blessings that God can grant to anyone. We cannot do stupid things except when we deviate from obedience to the *Rule*, since the *Rule* gives us the surest guarantee for peace and assures the final attainment of our goal and destination. The fact that we sometimes think we would be more at peace and happier if things happened according to our own desires has its origin in the fact that we lack the experience of a life of true freedom, or else those who have had this experience have paid too little attention to it.

When you write that many people have ridiculed you, I must answer that to my knowledge no one has spoken ill of you; but I can say that you show a great tendency to develop into a peculiar person, and some have more or less given voice to this observation. Community and singularity are opposites and cannot coexist without causing disturbance and friction. These peculiarities are weaknesses in your character that you seem to have inherited. One of your sisters also has this character, as your father and mother bitterly complained when they visited me. We cannot free ourselves completely from our peculiar traits, but with sincerity and practice and God's grace we can rid ourselves of them to a great extent, or else turn them to our benefit.

The worst of our peculiar traits derives from pride. Those afflicted by pride consider themselves more intelligent, better, and more noble than others. They have not learned to live in harmony with others but demand to be taken as models, or at least be left alone. However, temperance and order acquired through Christian principles (such as humility, fear of God, love of neighbor) can become and can remain a great help in developing a firm and determined character. It can rightly be said that "*Omnis sanctus pertinax.*"[18]

It was God's design that you rid yourself of these and similar bad habits through your promise of *conversio morum*,[19] and by appropriate conduct change them into

---

[18] "Every saint is stubborn."

[19] *Conversio* [or *conversatio*] *morum* was the second of the three traditional "Benedictine vows" [RB 58: 17]. It is usually translated today as "fidelity to monastic life." See *RB 1980: The Rule of St.*

virtues and thereby become a saint. Even the diamond needs polishing. Otherwise, it remains only a rough stone without glow or sparkle. If Father Julian is willing to undergo such polishing, then the negative characteristics that aggravate and hurt those with whom he comes in contact will disappear. He will then be very different from what he is now and will not only be considered a gem by all, but will really be one. *"Non velle dici sanctum antequam sit, sed prius esse quod verius dicatur."*[20]

To wish to be esteemed and loved by others, while at the same time looking down on others, makes no sense. The tools of good works[21] contain many good lessons. By adhering to them, an unpolished gem can become a precious stone. If you practice and observe them diligently, you will soon see that everything goes much better.

We are Benedictines by profession, just as we are Christians by baptism, but since neither the name "Christian" nor baptism by itself can make us true Christians, but rather can merely point us toward a Christian way of living, so also neither the monastic habit nor monastic profession by themselves can make us true Benedictines. Only faithful observance of the *Holy Rule* does that. Indeed, we know that no Christian is perfect. None of us is without shortcomings. We also know that no Benedictine follows the *Rule* exactly. We do not expect it because it is not possible. It is, however, both expected and required that we strive to follow the *Rule* as well as we can. There will always be disappointments, but they will never disturb our peace significantly or for a long time. Disappointments will further our salvation, not endanger it.

I embrace you with fatherly love and bless you, and I remain with great respect, your devoted fellow monk, Abbot Boniface Wimmer

Ger   oASVA   transIG

Benedict in Latin and English with Notes, ed. Timothy Fry (Collegeville, Minn.: The Liturgical Press, 1981), 268, 457-66.

[20] "Do not aspire to be called holy before you really are, but first be holy that you may more truly be called so" (RB 4:62).

[21] The reference is to chapter 4 of the *Rule of St. Benedict*, "The Tools [*Instrumenta*] for Good Works."

TO JOSEPH AMBERGER   **183**

St. Vincent, January 15, 1886

Dear Canon: Today I received your letter of December 17 with the 2,000 Mass intentions enclosed. I immediately gave them to Father Prior[22] to enter in the Mass intention book and for distribution to the fathers. They were very welcome since we did not have many Mass intentions left.

I thank you cordially for your kind remembrances for the New Year. This season I received many good wishes, but I cannot acknowledge all of them because I just do not have the time. From November 22 until almost Christmas, I was on a journey to the South. On November 26, the new abbot[23] (that is, the first abbot) of Maryhelp Abbey in North Carolina was solemnly blessed in Charleston, the see city of Bishop Northrop,[24] ordinary of South Carolina and vicar apostolic of North Carolina. For that important event, four Benedictine abbots[25] had to be present *honoris causa*, even though the journey was very long and not very pleasant. I had to travel by express train the whole night, the following day, and again the next night from Latrobe to Charleston. That meant a trip of 31 hours without a break, except for brief stops for lunch.

Bishop Northrop is a young gentleman, American-born, who made his studies in Rome. He is a friend of our Order and has a keen interest in the new abbey. November 26 was celebrated as a public Thanksgiving Day in the United States. It is almost like a Catholic feast day. For that reason, Abbot Leo selected that day for his blessing, in order to give the Catholics of the city and the secular priests the opportunity to witness the holy function, which would not have been possible on a Sunday. Nothing like this has ever happened in the South before. You can imagine the sensation it caused for Catholics no less than for Protestants. Bishop Rademacher,[26] who studied in our college, gave the festive sermon, and the newly-blessed abbot delivered a lecture in the evening on the topic "Monasticism in the Catholic Church" in order to dispel the prejudices of the Protestants. In the afternoon, a wealthy Catholic took all the clergy on his steamboat to Fort Sumter where the first cannon was fired to signal the beginning of the great Civil War.

---

[22] Michael Hofmayer, O.S.B. (1838-1901).

[23] Leo Haid, O.S.B. (1849-1924), first abbot of the Abbey of Mary Help of Christians (later Belmont Abbey), North Carolina.

[24] Henry P. Northrop (1842-1916), bishop of Charleston and vicar apostolic of North Carolina.

[25] The abbots who were present were Alexius Edelbrock, O.S.B. (1843-1908), abbot of St. John's Abbey, Minnesota; Innocent Wolf, O.S.B. (1843-1922), abbot of St. Benedict's Abbey, Kansas; James Zilliox, O.S.B. (1849-1890), abbot of St. Mary's Abbey, Newark; and Wimmer himself.

[26] Joseph Rademacher (1840-1900), bishop of Nashville.

The next morning we abbots went to the new abbey (near Charlotte, North Carolina), about 300 miles from Charleston. We remained there for two days because the other abbots had not yet seen the place. Everyone was pleased. We found 39 students in the college. Our hope is that the abbey will become an important center of Catholicism. At the time of its foundation, I faced much opposition. For that reason, I was eager for the abbots to see for themselves the condition and prospects of the place. It gave me great satisfaction to see that after they had made their inspection, they admitted that the small monastery offers all that is required for a speedy and prosperous development and that its prospects are better even than were those of St. Vincent at the beginning. Likewise, the abbots of Kansas and Minnesota had to struggle for years.

We were together at Maryhelp on Saturday and Sunday. Then on Monday, the abbots of Newark, Atchison, and St. John's went north via Richmond. The new abbot and I traveled 400 miles south to Savannah, Georgia, where I showed him his possessions—a fine frame parish church for whites and blacks, with a rectory, a schoolhouse, and a large field around the church ready for more buildings. I handed the parish over to him. Then we sailed to Skidaway Island, 12 miles from Savannah, where we have 700 acres of land with an industrial school for Negroes. We stayed there four days. On Skidaway, the young Negroes are instructed in domestic work and farm work and learn the habit of work. They also learn fishery, which is the main work of the island and their livelihood. During an excursion in the bay, the abbot caught 200 fine fish in a large net with one draught. The Negroes have lived on the island since before our arrival. The fathers have already entered 114 Catholic baptisms in their sacramental registry.

Afterward we returned to Savannah where the abbot wanted to meet the notable Catholics in order to recruit students for his college. After that, we went west to Atlanta, a famous manufacturing town in the western part of Georgia and only 300 miles from our monastery in North Carolina. In Atlanta, three Catholic priests are occupied with pastoral work. It took us from 9:00 pm to 7:00 am to reach Atlanta, where we parted company. Abbot Leo went north towards home while I went west to Chattanooga in the state of Tennessee, and from there to Huntsville, Alabama, where I arrived on December 7, dead tired after ten hours on the train.

In Huntsville, I met Father Benedict Menges[27] with whom I celebrated the Feast of the Immaculate Conception on December 8. On December 9, I went with him to Tuscumbia where two fathers are stationed and where there is a small

---

[27] Benedict Menges, O.S.B. (1840-1904).

convent of Benedictine sisters. I had sent word to Father Joseph,[28] stationed 12 miles farther away, to meet me in Tuscumbia so that I could be spared a trip into the countryside. From there I took a train to Decatur, and from Decatur I traveled from morning until 6:00 pm via Nashville to Cincinnati and Covington, where I remained for three days. Then I rushed home via Pittsburgh.

My journey took me across the length of Pennsylvania through Maryland, Virginia, North Carolina, South Carolina, Georgia, Tennessee, Alabama, Kentucky, and Ohio. During the whole circuit, I had to remain overnight only once in a place where no Benedictines were stationed, i.e. in Charleston. Thanks be to God! In Pittsburgh, I saw Father Wilfrid.[29] He is in good health, is satisfied with his work, and enjoys great popularity. In general, I found my fathers doing their pastoral work with great zeal. They are held in high esteem by their congregations, lead exemplary lives in their parishes, and are experiencing great success in their work. *Deo gratias!*

Let us pray for one another. The cost of the trip was about $100. I left about $200 with my confreres where help was needed. With all love and respect, Your Grace's most devoted and very much obliged, Abbot Boniface

Ger   oASVA   transRG

TO AMANDUS KRAMMER   **184**

St. Vincent, October 15, 1886

Reverend and Dear Confrere: The two sisters arrived at the abbey at 11:00 am in a fine carriage driven by young Donnelly. I took care that they had something to eat and drink, that they saw the college, and that at 2:00 pm the driver took them to Latrobe. They intended to collect money there and return home by evening. Once again, it cost me ten dollars.

It seems that it has caused ill feelings at St. Boniface that Father Wilfrid[30] replaced Father Sigismund.[31] I expected Father Celestine[32] here all last week. Something must have delayed him because he will arrive only next week. He is going

---

[28] Joseph Keller, O.S.B. (1847-1907).
[29] Wilfrid Frins, O.S.B. (1860-1936).
[30] Wilfrid Frins, O.S.B. (1860-1936).
[31] Sigismund Singer, O.S.B. (b. 1860).
[32] Celestine Englbrecht, O.S.B. (1824-1904).

Rev. Amandus Krammer, O.S.B.

to Chicago because he has never been there before. I hope Father Prior[33] will not remain in the East for long. Abbot James[34] was here for ten days and left yesterday for Wilmington. He looks well but has only half a lung and is very weak because he hardly eats anything. He felt at home here.

In Cincinnati, two young Negro men are editing a good newspaper, not a party paper, but an independent paper, *The American Tribune,* formerly the *Ohio State Tribune.*[35] It is a Catholic paper, a weekly, small in size, and costs $1.50 per year. Archbishop Elder[36] gave them $100, and the bishop of Columbus,[37] $25. As a friend of the Negro people, I also made a small contribution because the beginnings cost much and neither one of the publishers is rich. They asked me for ten names (and addresses) of people who I think would subscribe to the paper. They want to send it to them in the hope of attracting subscribers, but I do not know anyone in our neighborhood who would subscribe to an English Cincinnati newspaper.

Could you send me some names and addresses of people who might give a few dollars each year to support the Negro press? The newspaper publishes the news briefly and concisely, and I like it very much. If you give me names (first name and surname) and addresses, I will send them to the young men and they will send trial copies to them and in that way publicize the paper. In this way, you would further a good cause. The two publishers are upright and well-informed men who could do much good among the Negro people because the paper is a good politi-

---

[33] Michael Hofmayer, O.S.B. (1838-1901).

[34] James Zilliox, O.S.B. (1849-1890), abbot of St. Mary's Abbey, Newark.

[35] *The American Catholic Tribune* was published in Cincinnati by Daniel Rudd and his nephew John R. Rudd between 1886 and 1894. See Cyprian Davis, *The History of Black Catholics in the United States* (New York: Crossroad, 1995), 164-67.

[36] William Elder (1819-1904), archbishop of Cincinnati.

[37] John A. Watterson (1844-1899).

cal one. I receive it and will have it sent to Allegheny so that Brother Rhabanus[38] can enjoy it and perhaps help spread it. A paper by Negroes, edited by practicing Negro Catholics, can do much good among these people. It can prevent them from joining the sects and can instead bring them to the Catholic Church. Do your best. The more names the better. If the paper is sent to you, do not send it back! With heartfelt love, Abbot Boniface

Ger   oASVA   transIG

TO BENEDICT BRAUNMÜLLER   **185**

St. Vincent, October 26, 1886

Right Reverend Father Abbot, Dear Confrere: Just after sending you my last letter, I received a letter dated October 10 from George Redlbacher, who wrote from Riedenburg. He said that he cannot find any relief in the old country, and for that reason he will return to America with his family immediately after the feast of the Dedication of Consecrated Churches [October 22]. He will pay a short visit to me to thank me for my help. I ask you, therefore, to return to me his promissory note for the loan I made to him so that I can give it to him when he repays the loan.

Yesterday, October 25, the first group of orphans from the county home—five children—arrived. I took them in our carriage to the farmhouse, located an hour from here, that I had prepared for that purpose, and placed them with a reliable woman and her daughter. She will be the orphans' mother until the orphan family grows larger and a proper house with sisters becomes necessary for their livelihood and maintenance.

Each county in America has a poor house where destitute people live with their small children until they reach a certain age. The law requires that each young man, when he comes to legal age, must pay a poor tax to cover the expenses of the poor house. In some cases, parents who want to take an orphan into their family receive from the director of the poor house a child who will stay with the family until he or she reaches legal age. (This practice is different from adoption.)

In our county [Westmoreland, Pennsylvania] there is an abundance of bituminous coal, which hundreds of immigrants from Hungary, Poland, Bohemia, and Italy dig from the mountains for highly prosperous companies. Often the father

---

[38] Brother Rhabanus Cononge, O.S.B. (1849-1920), one of the few black members of the St. Vincent community.

of a family is accidentally killed when doing this work, with the result that his wife and children end up in the poor house. In such cases, the Methodists, etc., entrust these poor children to Protestant families, and consequently the children receive a Protestant education. We have already lost about 20 children to this practice. I could not see this happening without doing something to prevent it, so I sent a protest to the county officials and pointed out that Catholic orphans should be placed with Catholic families because Protestant families would not educate the children in the Catholic faith. I stated that our charter authorized us to accept all Catholic orphans who were not being kept at the orphanage and that I had paternal love and responsibility for them. Thus, I have become a father of orphans.

Not all my confreres agreed with me about taking in the orphans, but I met no strong opposition. Moreover, Divine Providence blessed the plan. An upright childless family (a husband and wife in their seventies) donated their property (land and buildings) to us, on condition that they would live there for the remainder of their lives. They wanted the property used for a school run by sisters, but they made their donation without any formal conditions attached. My intention is to use this property as a foundation for our orphanage, and I hope to get more benefactors. In any case, no child will lose his faith through my fault! This work cannot be done without much money and much worry, however. Thanks be to God!

Redlbacher is a native of Geiselhoering, it seems, but grew up in Weihenstephan.

I humbly ask you to remember me in your prayers. With sincere affection and deep respect, I am Your Grace's most devoted confrere, Abbot Boniface

Ger   oAMA   cASVA   transRG

TO INNOCENT WOLF   186

St. Vincent, November 2, 1886

Right Rev. Confrere, Dear Father Abbot: Our rt. rev. confrere Abbot James Zilliox[39] has resigned his office a second time, and his resignation has been accepted in Rome, and an election of a new abbot has to be held as soon as convenient. Here I have made Father Prior[40] also novice master at the [request] of P. Andrew[41]

---

[39] James Zilliox, O.S.B. (1849-1890), abbot of St. Mary's Abbey, Newark.
[40] Michael Hofmayer, O.S.B. (1838-1901).
[41] Andrew Hintenach, O.S.B. (1844-1927).

that he might be relieved of his office. P. Eusebius[42] at the same time has been appointed socius of the master.

P. Celestine[43] is now prior in Chicago in place of P. Bernardine.[44]

Hoping you are well and asking a share of your prayers, I remain truly yours, Abbot Boniface Wimmer

Eng   oASBA   cASVA

TO HILARY PFRÄNGLE   187

Newark, November 17, 1886

Dear Reverend Confrere, Abbot Elect: Yesterday you were elected abbot with nine votes out of 14 on the third ballot. At first, the votes were very scattered, but you had the highest number of votes from the very beginning. Your nearest competitor was Father Benedict.[45] Father Ambrose[46] had two votes while Father Placidus[47] had only one. On the last ballot only you (nine votes), Father Benedict (three votes), and Father Ambrose (two votes) remained. You were then elected unanimously by acclamation. In previous abbatial elections, every vote was announced, in accordance with the ceremonial, so that everyone present knew for whom it was cast. This time, however, following the suggestion of the electors and the advice of Abbot James,[48] and in accordance with the *Handbook for Religious*, I showed the ballots only to the tellers, each of whom noted down the name. I had only to announce "No majority." After the third ballot, I merely proclaimed the election of Father Hilary, without mentioning the number of votes. It was for this reason that in my telegram I merely announced your election and said nothing about the number of votes. I did this very reluctantly because I feared unpleasant results, but the most recent authorities require it, and I followed them.

Your refusal caused great consternation, and still more, your second answer to the telegram of Father Prior.[49] Father Prior alone is responsible for that telegram, as he sent it on his own authority. He, however, meant well. He merely

[42] Eusebius Geiger, O.S.B. (1861-1917).
[43] Celestine Englbrecht, O.S.B. (1824-1904).
[44] Bernardine Dolweck, O.S.B. (1828-1905).
[45] Benedict Menges, O.S.B. (1840-1904).
[46] Ambrose Huebner, O.S.B. (1848-1941).
[47] Placidus Pilz, O.S.B. (1835-1911).
[48] James Zilliox, O.S.B. (1849-1890).
[49] Ambrose Huebner, O.S.B. (1848-1941), was prior in Newark.

wanted certainty. He, as well as all the other electors, feared that if another election should become necessary, no one would receive a majority so that I, the abbot [president], would have to select an abbot. They would not have liked this, and neither would I, even less than they. I think you should spare them and me the trouble and accept the election. You will quite certainly be a candidate for abbot of St. Vincent when I die. It is possible, however, that I may still have a few years to live. In your position, you are also a candidate for bishop, but in our diocese, there is no prospect in the near future. A brilliant future cannot be expected for Newark, but in a small diocese, an abbot is an important man. Under a good abbot, the small abbey has a promising future. Since there are so many *Romani Doctores*[50] in the East, the abbot should be a man who can lend dignity to his office.

Right Reverend Hilary Pfrängle, O.S.B., second abbot of St. Mary's Abbey in Newark, New Jersey.

If I should be compelled to appoint an abbot, I cannot appoint one of the resident fathers. That much I have learned from the people here. They want no Newarker, though this does not reflect badly on anyone. Even Abbot James was not popular for this reason. The monastery, too, will suffer if you refuse the abbacy. It will be a reflection either on the local fathers, because it is rumored that Abbot James did not get along well with some of them, or on the abbey itself.

An abbot, however, must not be so sensitive, and the fathers in Newark are not so bad. In fact, there is beautiful order in the monastery, much better than at St. Vincent. They attend choir regularly; they do not neglect Mass; they do not miss chapter, waste time, or talk after recreation, etc. As far as I can see, they get along well with each other and they work diligently. In fact, it is a nice little monastery, and the food is good and sufficient. I cannot see why a good monk should shrink from assuming the government of such a community. I expect, therefore, that you

---

[50] "Roman doctors." Pfrängle had earned a doctorate in theology in Rome.

will not allow previously conceived prejudices to prevent you from accepting election to this office. It is my wish that you notify me of your consent by telegram so that I am not detained here unnecessarily but can return to St. Vincent by Saturday or Sunday morning.

That I do not like losing you is evident from the fact that I refused your repeated requests to be relieved of your office. I am willing, however, to make the sacrifice for a good cause. It is easier for me to find a director of the college than for St. Mary's to find a good abbot.

Hoping that you are willing to make the sacrifice and that you will lend a willing ear to my representations, I remain with sincere love and respect, your devoted confrere, Abbot Boniface Wimmer

Ger　　　oANA　　　cASVA　　　transCB

TO CELESTINE ENGLBRECHT　　　　　　　　**188**

St. Vincent, December 14, 1886

Dearest Confrere: Thank you very much for the deep sympathy you have expressed for the suffering that befell me on the evening of December 1. The ailment causes me difficulty in urinating, so much so that sometimes for a whole day, I am unable to pass a single drop of water, or only a few drops and am forced to use the catheter. Otherwise, I am well. Only my appetite is sometimes bad, and my thirst great because I am afraid to drink anything. So far, there is no danger of death, but there will be if I do not improve. This, however, is unlikely in such an old body.

Oh, well. The Lord is God, and He is the Lord of life and of death. He has kept me healthy for 78 years. Can I complain now if he leaves my lazy old body to take care of itself? Of course, pain hurts, and one struggles against it, but if it does not let up, one must bear it patiently as long as it pleases God.

I am up all day, writing or praying. I am also able to sleep fairly well during the night, and I no longer expect anything better concerning my health. I am sorry that it is necessary for me to trouble the brothers.

How did my two missionaries get away?[51] Father Rhabanus volunteered for the mission, but later he grew fainthearted.

---

[51] Fathers Rhabanus Gutmann and Eusebius Geiger, who had departed St. Vincent for Colorado the previous week, had stopped at St. Joseph's Priory, Chicago, where Father Celestine Englbrecht

I wish you a happy New Year, good health, all efficacious graces for the fulfillment of your duties! Let us pray for one another in life and in death! With kind regards to the reverend confreres, your most devoted, Abbot Boniface

Ger   oASVA   transGM

TO LUKE WIMMER   189

St. Vincent, January 24, 1887

Dearest Confrere: I received your letters today and will send them to Sebastian in New York. He wrote me today asking for money for Anton, whom he refused because he himself is so badly in need that he can hardly meet his expenses. It seems from Sebastian's letter that Anton left Newark secretly, and, as one might have expected, "forgot" to pay his debts.[52]

Father Gerard[53] tells me in his letter that he could have sold some land, but insisted on more than 10 percent and failed. It would have meant $2,000, of which he would have needed $1,000 to pay off Mr. Radl for the land. The balance ($1,000) would have been his to build a home and have something left over to live on for a while. He could have gotten at least that much and become a well-to-do man, but you see, that is not the way it turned out. He must work and stop speculating, stop running up so many debts, even if it means he must experience some want and distress. He always relies on Sebastian and me.

The driver I am sending is a very trustworthy fellow. He has been with us for ten years already. He will be very good in Covington, and is a most competent man in the opinion of our brothers, but he himself is not a brother and receives wages like other workmen. Sebastian is coming here next Sunday, as you read in his letter. He is a hard worker and for that reason is held in honor and esteem by everyone.

Father Leo Haid,[54] abbot of Maryhelp, will become bishop and vicar apostolic of the vicariate North Carolina. At least I received a letter today from Cardinal

---

was prior. The Benedictine mission in Colorado eventually became Holy Cross Abbey. See Martin Burne, "Holy Cross Abbey—One Hundred Years," *ABR* 37 (1986): 423-32.

[52] Sebastian and Anton Wimmer were, like Father Luke Wimmer, the archabbot's nephews.

[53] Gerard Pilz, O.S.B. (1834-1891), had been sent to Hernando County, Florida, in April 1886 to establish a Benedictine mission in the German community of San Antonio. The mission eventually became St. Leo's Abbey. See James Horgan, *Pioneer College: The Centennial History of Saint Leo College, Saint Leo Abbey, and Holy Name Priory* (St. Leo, Fla.: St. Leo College Press, 1989).

[54] Leo Haid, O.S.B. (1849-1924), abbot of Maryhelp Abbey, North Carolina.

Simeoni[55] saying that he had been proposed. I was requested to express my opinion about his selection. Otherwise, nothing could be done. I sent my approval off to Rome today. It will become a reality. With that, the abbey, which is not held in very high esteem, and for the sake of which I had to swallow a lot of sarcasm and ridicule, will become the center of Catholicity in the whole state of North Carolina and a real Benedictine mission. The money spent and all the trouble I had to suffer will be an investment not to be despised. God is good. Everything for His greater honor. Please give my best regards to Brother George.[56] Begging your prayers, Abbot Boniface[57]

Ger   oASVA   transRG

TO BERNARD SMITH   **190**

St. Vincent, February 14, 1887

Rt. Rev. dear Fth. Abbot, Rt. Rev. and dear Confrere: The last mail brought me today your favor d. S. Callistus, January 30th, with another letter from his Emin. Card. Jacobini[58] and a packet containing printed documents in relation to the intended restoration of the College of St. Anselm.

I have a good chance to distribute the documents without delay since next Thursday, Febr. 17th, the new abbot[59] of St. Mary's in Newark, N.J., will get here the abbatial benediction through our Bishop Coadjutor R. Phelan,[60] as Bishop Wigger[61] of Newark consented he should do because he himself could not come out to St. Vincent's, and I could not go to Newark, being visited by a very great affliction that hinders me to travel. On this occasion, then, all our abbots will be here, and we can speak about this important matter and consider how we best may be able to execute the wish of our Holy Father the Pope.

---

[55] Giovanni Simeoni, cardinal prefect of the Sacred Congregation for the Propagation of the Faith.
[56] George Schnitzler, O.S.B. (1827-1907).
[57] Father Luke Wimmer made the following notation on the bottom of this letter: "This letter was written by the Right Reverend Archabbot himself. He is a sick man but still very active, in his seventy-ninth year, exhibiting the first signs of senility but very capable of writing, although it shows itself from time to time. Father Luke."
[58] Cardinal Ludovico Jacobini, papal secretary of state.
[59] Hilary Pfrängle, O.S.B. (1843-1909), second abbot of St. Mary's Abbey, Newark.
[60] Richard Phelan (1828-1904), coadjutor bishop of Pittsburgh.
[61] Winand Wigger (1841-1901).

The time is not very propitious for doing much for the purpose indeed, because I had to introduce in our college and church and monastery steam heating at an expense of $17,000 cash, and had to strain every nerve to make that amount. Abbot Edelbrock[62] of St. John's, Minn., and Abbot Wolf[63] of Atchison, Ks., have been raising large additions to their colleges, while the other two abbots[64] have just commenced opening their Institutes, but I trust, with God's help, we may still succeed in making up a fair amount, if not at once, at least in phases.

I have passed 78 years and enjoyed until lately good health, although I felt my strength slowly sinking. Therefore, I was desirous [of] finishing the Abbey and College, and [of] leaving everything in good shape and form. The College is for us the *nervus rerum*.[65] By the College we make ourselves most useful, and from it we derive also chiefly our income, and at the same time from the College we draw our recruits. For this reason, we commence in such places, where we wish to establish a monastery, with a school, which we gradually enlarge. By this way, our little abbeys sprang up. Our College at St. Vincent's is one of the largest in the country and has a good name in every way and deservedly, too. But the American is not only for learning and good manners, etc., but likes comfort too. For this reason, I was obliged to introduce steam heating without regard to the terrible expenses. They will be refunded by a greater frequency [i.e., larger enrollment].

Last year (July) 12 secular theologians of our College were ordained priests, and 8 clerics O.S.B. also were made priests. I keep 100 boys *gratis* in boarding and tuition. A few of them pay something for their boarding; others only their books, stationery, and clothes; one third nothing at all so as to absorb the small payments of the others too, and I have really nothing left for me or the abbey. But out of these boys I get my professors, priors, and abbots. Some of our older stations pay well enough. The priors must send in their annual accounts, and the balance belongs to the Abbey, but a few stations must be upheld by subsidies from the Abbey, and when we take charge of stations, it requires every time outlay from the Abbey, at least for some years, for raising buildings, etc.

Thus we can of course not get rich. Still we get a little rich of lands, which after some time become valuable by [agri]culture, and this is the way how I could establish abbeys which for a good while used to be rather poor, though, but with the increase of the number of priests can get along nicely.

---

[62] Alexius Edelbrock, O.S.B. (1843-1908).

[63] Innocent Wolf, O.S.B. (1843-1922).

[64] Leo Haid, O.S.B. (1849-1924), abbot of Maryhelp Abbey, North Carolina; and Hilary Pfrängle of St. Mary's Abbey, Newark.

[65] "Nerve or center of things."

It would be a mistake if people would believe us to be rich. We do not collect. All we own we own by our own industry, every year generally some more than what we need; but this is to be spent again in the propagation of the Order, for necessary new buildings, etc., for the poor, for aiding charitable institutions. If we want to do something worthwhile, we must, of course, do less for other purposes even of our own, or even run into debts, which we are sure afterwards to pay.

I tell this to you that you understand how we stand and how we manage our affairs. Europeans don't understand us so easily, thinking Americans are mostly all rich. [There are] plenty poor people here, plenty begging, plenty distress, plenty debts on church property.

After all, you may assure Msgr. Dusmet[66] we'll do all we can. A Benedictine College in Rome was always a favorite idea with me. I will pray to God that He may deign to bless our great sovereign Pontiff for his good disposition for our holy Order, and that He may give him means and time to carry out the measures he intends to make for its benefit.

It would be a disgrace if the Benedictines themselves would not understand the great advantages which for them must flow from such an institution established in the center of the Christian world, and principally and first for the Cassinese proper [*sic*] in Italy, but more [or] less for all other Congregations.

Of course, we wish soon to learn the times when our contributions should be sent in, or whether the Holy Father wants only to know how much we could contribute. At all events we will consider the matter at once among ourselves and then with our chapters, and will set out then to work accordingly.

I am exceedingly sensible for the honorable trust the Holy Father has put in me and for the Apostolic Benediction he has deigned to send me and which I hope will supply and make up for the want of natural energy, lost through bodily infirmity and high advancement in age.

I am happy to express my sincerest sentiments of respect, fraternal love, wherewith I remain truly yours, Boniface Wimmer, Archabbot

Eng   oASPR   cASVA

---

[66] Joseph Benedict Dusmet d'Amours, O.S.B. (1818-1894), archbishop of Catania, Sicily, whom the pope had placed in charge of collecting funds for the Collegio di Sant' Anselmo, the proposed Benedictine college in Rome.

TO LUKE WIMMER   **191**

St. Vincent, February 23, 1887

Dearest Confrere: I would not subscribe in every detail to what you wrote earlier about relatives. Religious perfection does not require that you be concerned at all about the welfare of those living in the world. Nevertheless, you should help them in temporal affairs, as you are able, but without neglecting the spirit of the monastic rule, and you should do it not because they are your relatives, but because they are your neighbors. St. Benedict built a convent for his sister and made her superior there. St. Placid took his sister and some relatives to Sicily where they suffered martyrdom. St. Bernard brought six of his brothers and their friends to the monastic life. St. Boniface, with Wunibald and Willibald, followed the same vocation as ours. Peter Damian would have remained a swineherd without the help of his brother, a cleric, towards his education, and if I had not accepted you, God knows what your fate would have been. One can be solicitous about relatives without committing a sin. It might even be a great merit and an obligation, as well, because the Church sometimes obliges religious, having been dispensed from solemn vows, to provide for their impoverished parents and close relatives (brothers and sisters). Nevertheless, some just take the burden on themselves and leave religious life. There is no excuse for that because another way may be open. The main concern is charity. As St. Paul explains it, charity derives not from blood, but from God.

I do not know whether I am getting well or not. Some people say I am, and even some doctors believe it. I still can do some work, but not with much energy. I am in miserable condition and sometimes suffer great pain, especially during the night when I cannot sleep after midnight and walk around my room like a ghost. This started to happen lately. In any event, some are beginning to tell me that under such conditions one gets very old and begins suffering from the gout, etc. I have submitted myself entirely to God. He guided me from earliest childhood with paternal love even until now, and He will lead me with all security according to His holy will. With this I am satisfied.

The pope puts a lot of work on my shoulders. He wants to restore the defunct College of St. Anselm in the monastery of St. Callistus as a central educational institution for us Benedictines. He is contributing to this himself, but he expects all black Benedictines in every country to do their share—especially us Americans. Upon his command, the Italians had a meeting with Archbishop Dusmet[67] of Catania presiding, and they promised, despite their own needs, 50,000 lire. Arch-

---

[67] Joseph Benedict Dusmet d'Amours, O.S.B. (1818-1894), archbishop of Catania, Sicily.

bishop Benedict Serra[68] wrote me from St. Paul's saying that I, as president [of the American Cassinese Congregation], should be the leader in raising as much money as possible. He sent me a pile of printed documents for distribution to the American abbots. The Holy Father himself directed a special letter to me through his secretary of state, Cardinal Jacobini,[69] telling me about his particular concern for this college and, knowing my personal interest, asking me to do everything in my power for the success of the undertaking. With this purpose in mind, he sent me the apostolic blessing, for he is anxious that I remain among the living and not die yet. Naturally, I cannot refuse him, and I shall do everything possible, but how much writing I must do because of that! Shortly afterwards the same archbishop, a Benedictine, sent me through Abbot Smith[70] a list of six of our fathers from which I was to choose some to be professors for his college and send them [to Rome]. Thus, my life is not carefree, but rather burdened with work—much work, troubles, and suffering. In sincere affection, your devoted confrere, Abbot Boniface

Ger   oASVA   transRG

TO BENEDICT BRAUNMÜLLER   **192**

St. Vincent, March 12, 1887

Right Reverend Father Abbot, Dear Confrere: Perhaps they will arrive late, but I want to send you my cordial congratulations on your approaching namesday. I wish I could be at Metten for a few hours on that very day. Fortunately, I am still able to say Mass every day, and I never forget you. I will remember you especially on the feast of our most holy father [St. Benedict, March 21]. I know well what brings joy or suffering to an abbot, so I will ask the dear Lord to bless all your steps and mercifully guide you.

Often I feared that God had already fully rewarded me in this world for my work. I have always had good fortune, enjoyed good health, and never had to suffer much, but now I am saturated with suffering, as much as I can bear without breaking. My suffering has already entered its fourth month, and I no longer hope

---

[68] Joseph Benedict Serra, O.S.B. (1810-1886), retired coadjutor bishop of Perth, Australia, and founder of the Oblate Sisters of the Most Holy Redeemer in Spain.
[69] Cardinal Ludovico Jacobini.
[70] Bernard Smith, O.S.B. (1818-1892), Roman procurator for the American Cassinese Benedictines.

that it will end or that it will change its course. I am very much run down because I cannot sleep at night and have no appetite. The doctors tell me that everything will be all right, that I only have to be firm in hope and faith, but I cannot be convinced that I will improve. What can I do but leave everything in the hands of the Lord? I sit, sit, sit, like a solitary sparrow in his nest, like a hermit in his cell, doing nothing but reciting my office, saying holy Mass, taking care of my correspondence, receiving the prior and the procurator in order to chat with them. Christmas was a very sad time for me, but it was not without interior consolation, which has not been denied me during my illness.

On February 17, Abbot Hilary Pfrängle,[71] who has replaced Abbot James Zilliox[72] of Newark, received his abbatial blessing here at St. Vincent from our coadjutor bishop, Richard Phelan.[73] Two bishops, four abbots, and many priests attended the celebration. I myself could not be present either in the church or in the refectory or in the choir. Nowhere! On February 24, I had a turn for the better. This lasted for 12 days. After that, everything got worse, more than before. Now it seems to be getting better again.

I have become very sensitive and touchy because of the many things that are troubling my mind—things that in the past have not bothered me at all and that have been, but light burdens on my shoulders. The College of St. Anselm keeps me very busy. Abbot Bernard Smith[74] has sent me a pile of printed documents regarding the college by order of Archbishop Dusmet[75] of Catania, with instructions that I should send the material to all the American abbots immediately. In addition, I received a letter from the secretary of state, Cardinal Ludovico Jacobini, with a special mandate from the Holy Father to me as president of the American Cassinese Congregation directing me to do everything possible with regard to the reestablishment of the college, a goal to which he is deeply committed. He expresses every confidence that our young and flourishing congregation will do more than other congregations. Then came another letter from Abbot Smith with a list of priests who are desired as professors for the new college. He left the selection up to me. All this is killing me, an old, sick man.

The cardinal noted that the Holy Father knows well how personally committed I am to establishing the college, and he expects me to collect a great deal

---

[71] Hilary Pfrängle, O.S.B. (1843-1909).

[72] James Zilliox, O.S.B. (1849-1890).

[73] Richard Phelan (1828-1904), coadjutor bishop of Pittsburgh.

[74] Bernard Smith, O.S.B. (1818-1892), Roman procurator for the American Cassinese Benedictines.

[75] Joseph Benedict Dusmet d'Amours, O.S.B. (1818-1894), archbishop of Catania, Sicily.

of money. I have none! Last year I spent more than $20,000 on buildings and improvements in order to put our college in the best possible condition. The young abbots have just started building and expanding their abbeys and colleges. The convents of our nuns are dependent upon them, and I have to help them in many ways, with people (priests and brothers). Minnesota alone is able to lend a helping hand. Kansas is laboring mightily to free itself from debt. At the various priories, buildings must of necessity be constructed. How can I be expected to do anything under such conditions? I can do nothing. I am the father who must provide bread for the small mission stations that have nothing. Nevertheless, we shall do whatever lies within our power, even if we have to borrow money. We cannot abandon the pope. We must confirm and strengthen his good intentions and friendly sentiments towards our Order as much as we are able, even through sacrifices. I am an old, sick, half-dead man. I am not eager to take upon myself such an important matter.

The unexpected *intermezzo* had not ended when another unexpected blow came upon me. Father Giles Christoph,[76] one of my oldest and most useful fathers, the prior in Covington, died there on March 6. He was a native of Barbing. His father was the personal coachman of Bishop Sailer.[77] He himself was a very strong, active, and practical man. He had been a priest for thirty years and had given the most fruitful service to the Order and the monastery. His death was in some sense his own fault. He overworked himself, caught a very bad cold, and like a real Prussian did not pay attention to his illness, but kept performing his duties in the confessional, visiting the sick, etc. until he collapsed. Still he expected that his strong constitution would take care of him until it was too late and the doctor could not help him any more. Typhus caused his death in a few days. We did not even know about his illness. I took his death very hard. Bishop Rademacher[78] of Nashville attended his funeral. His own bishop[79] was by his side for the last five hours. He and my Father Michael[80] and 50 other priests were at the funeral. So I do not have him any more. One affliction after another assails me. Suffering knocks at my door and summons me.

Otherwise, everything is in order. The young Abbot Leo[81] of Maryhelp in North Carolina has been proposed as candidate for the vicariate apostolic of North Car-

---

[76] Giles Christoph, O.S.B. (1830-1887).
[77] Bishop Johann Michael Sailer of Regensburg.
[78] Joseph Rademacher (1840-1900).
[79] Camillus P. Maes (1846-1915), bishop of Covington (1885-1915).
[80] Michael Hofmayer, O.S.B. (1838-1901), prior at St. Vincent.
[81] Leo Haid, O.S.B. (1849-1924), abbot of Maryhelp Abbey, North Carolina.

olina. That is, he will become a bishop, though he will not be replaced as abbot of Maryhelp. I wonder if that is best for his monastery. He already has 74 students and, naturally, has to build additions to his monastery and college. The source of his revenue is the college itself.

Abbot Wolf[82] went through very difficult times, but they are over because he has managed to lower significantly the rate of interest, and his debts are being quickly paid off. Your Grace contributed very much to this happy outcome.

It is the will of God that our Order prosper again, that it return to its old glory. If all turns out well and I live a few months longer, I will see our Bohemian Priory of St. Procopius in Chicago become an independent priory. Not long after that, it will become an abbey. At Metten, and generally in the old country, they cannot imitate what we are doing here because under all circumstances they insist on keeping the status quo intact.

My Father Constantine Leber[83] is presently in Baden in order to settle his inheritance. Doubtless, he will pay you a visit at Metten. *Ad plurimos annos!* With a thousand greetings, Your Grace's most devoted confrere, Abbot Boniface

Ger   oAMA   cASVA   transRG

TO POPE LEO XIII   193

St. Vincent, April 2, 1887

Most Holy Father: Prostrate at the feet of Your Holiness, I, Boniface Wimmer, archabbot of the American Cassinese Congregation in the United States of America, humbly make the following known to you. The Most Reverend John Moore,[84] bishop of St. Augustine in the state of Florida, has in his diocese a colony called San Antonio, located in Hernando County and inhabited by people from various nations. For more than a year, the sons of St. Benedict have had charge of the care of souls in this colony because the bishop himself did not have multilingual priests to send there. Now the bishop desires

Pope Leo XIII

---

[82] Innocent Wolf, O.S.B. (1843-1922), abbot of St. Benedict's Abbey, Atchison, Kansas.
[83] Constantine Leber, O.S.B. (1848-1927).
[84] John Moore (1835-1901), bishop of St. Augustine.

that the colony and county be given to the Benedictine Fathers permanently, on condition that the priests of our Order take charge of the churches and provide for the spiritual care of the faithful who live in this colony and county, according to the regulations of the diocese. Since the transfer requires the sanction of the Holy See, I humbly beg Your Holiness to grant the necessary faculties, for which I would be profoundly grateful. Your Holiness's most humble and faithful son, Boniface Wimmer, Archabbot

Lat   oAPF   cASVA   transJO

TO PATRICK A. FEEHAN   194

St. Vincent, April 7, 1887

Most Reverend Archbishop, Your Grace: Since the time Your Grace transferred St. Procop's Church and congregation to the Order of St. Benedict for Pastoration [*sic*], and the Apostolic See has approved and confirmed this transfer, the thought struck my mind that by doing so Your Grace [has] really laid the foundation for a Bohemian monastery and (in connection with it) a Bohemian college, the working of which could be of infallibly beneficial influence for the religious life of these poor people in the United States.

And further, when I observed the progress our fathers at St. Procop's Church made only a couple of years in the congregation, particularly with regard to raising (without collecting money) a stately building large enough to accommodate a considerable number of priests, I convinced myself that it would not be very difficult to go at once to build or erect such a monastery and college there, provided this undertaking would meet Your Grace's approval and sanction.

Of course, I spoke of this matter to several of my fathers here to learn what they thought about it, and found that most of them were not in favor of my views, but wanted St. Procop's Priory to remain what it is now, a dependency of St. Vincent Abbey, so that in case if I should die before something was done in the matter, the whole thing might collapse and go to nothing. But it is very probable that I cannot live many months more, for I am nearly 79 years old, and I am already 7 months visited by a dire affliction which can end my life, if it should be aggravated, in a few days. For this reason, I am very anxious to go to work at once, lest it might be too late.

It is true, St. Vincent's Abbey would gain if St. Procop's Priory remains dependent from it, but Chicago city and diocese and the Bohemian nationality in the

United States would (in my opinion) suffer very much. My prayer, therefore, would be that Your Grace may deign to assist me in making St. Procop's Priory a real monastery, even an abbey (with a Bohemian college), if the idea meets your approval, by giving me in writing a declaration that Your Grace would wish the Priory should become a monastery with a college chiefly for Bohemians, since they have in the United States no such institution and consequently no way to raise a numerous Bohemian clergy for themselves in their many congregations scattered over the country and cities, to the great detriment of souls who go lost without pastors. I would write then a petition to the Holy Father, and I am pretty sure the petition will be granted.

Of course, it will then take some years yet till the monastery and college can be put up in a decent way, but the fathers can go to work for this purpose at once. They have already an embryo of a college—20 boys—and will add to it two classes more for the next year, and I can send to them at once the necessary staff of professors and monks.

I have at my disposal seven Bohemian priests, but one of them must stay in Pittsburgh and one other at St. Vincent. Then I have two subdeacons who can soon be ordained. Then I have 7 clerics in minor orders who can be used for teaching and for choir, all in all besides 3 novices and several scholastics who I raised in our college here for the Bohemians, so as to make sure that in 2-3 years there will be 15-17 monks at St. Procop, just not too many to find room in the house. All of them speak English and German too and are therefore qualified to help also the English- and German-speaking Catholics.

Now, dearly beloved Most Reverend Archbishop, I lay the case before you for no other motive than to do something for God's greater honor and glory, for the benefit of the Bohemians without doing harm to any other race or nationality, for no personal advantage, but with great confidence that you will receive my petition graciously and do what you think right. I can only say, I shall die with much consolation if I shall be so happy having been instrumental in accomplishing this work, as I know it will be truly a good work.

In profoundest reverence and submission, I remain, Most Reverend Archbishop, Your Grace's most humble servant, Boniface Wimmer, Archabbot

Eng   oAAC   cASVA

TO JOSEPH KAGERER 195

St. Vincent, June 28, 1887

Most Honorable Canon: I received the check for $5938.24 from the widow Arnold. Not all of the money goes to St. Vincent, however. One part is to be given to Sister Mechthild Binder of St. Marys, one to the Benedictine sisters in Covington, and only the third (but largest) part to Father Sebastian Arnold,[85] subprior at St. Vincent, and through him to the monastery. This is not an entirely unexpected donation, and it comes at just the right moment because we had to make a great sacrifice of $8,000 to the College of St. Anselm in Rome. I would be pleased if you could find an equally generous benefactor for your Benno church.

My affliction remains the same, but from an acute inflammation, it has developed into a chronic bladder inflammation that makes the daily use of the catheter necessary. For six months now, I have not had a good night's sleep. In other words, no rest day or night! If this does not improve considerably, my death will surely follow soon. I do offer holy Mass, however, carry on correspondence, and pray the Office. I am a real hermit because I can neither pray with the community nor go to the refectory nor participate in any other community exercise.

I have often wanted to know how the blessed Archbishop Gregory[86] was treated, and how he suffered, since he was afflicted, I believe, with the same ailment I have. I bear this affliction with patience and ask for nothing else but patience and to be able to bear it as long as God wills. I am, however, very depressed.

We have generally had good fortune and advance little by little. In the near future, we shall have an independent Bohemian priory in Chicago with a Bohemian college. In a short time the priory will develop into a nice little abbey next to St. Procopius Church on 18th Street on the west side of the city. We already have a good building there large enough to house 13 fathers. We also started a college for about 20 students. Four Benedictines serve the rather large parish. One cleric and two subdeacons from here are there (all Bohemians) and already increase the number during vacation time. Also two clerics, five novices, and 12 scholastics (all Bohemians) are willing to join them. I hope the dear God will not let me die before this institution rests on a solid foundation. There are two more places, one in the South and one in the West, that could and should become abbeys in the near future. God has blessed our Order here with a special blessing.

---

[85] Sebastian Arnold, O.S.B. (1847-1916).
[86] Gregory Scherr, O.S.B. (1804-1877), abbot of Metten and archbishop of Munich.

Bishop Peter Schumacher,[87] a German Vincentian from Portoviejo, Ecuador, South America, has been with us for a few days. He would like to take some Benedictines from here to his terribly neglected diocese, but I am not able to give him any at this time because I cannot spare any priests or brothers. Nor can I spare any money. However, I could possibly send him some student theologians who want to become diocesan priests. He already received two of them last winter and is well pleased with them. He has only seven priests.

I do not believe our professors will permit your candidate to study for the priesthood because in the past we have not been successful with persons of his age. As a candidate for the brotherhood, however, I can accept him, but if he is not in good health, we are taking a risk. We do need good brothers, but if they are not healthy, what can one expect of them? We have a number of easy jobs in the house, however, which do not require great strength, although they do require good health.

Let us pray for one another that we shall be saved. It has pleased the good Lord to use me, unworthy as I am, as an instrument to bring our Order to America. He chooses the weak and the foolish of the world in order to confound the mighty. Still, as you know, I must not rest on that and am often in great anxiety about the end of my life. Nevertheless, I trust in His infinite mercy and in the prayers of so many devoted, good souls, especially religious women for whom I opened the door to the religious life.

Your two honorary posts in Constantinople and Jerusalem may not especially impress you, but they are a testimony to the many years you have devoted to the missions of the whole world. For that, your reward will be great, since you did not receive a monetary one. St. Vincent and its abbot head the list of those who owe you much gratitude.

At holy Mass, I never forget the committee members of the Mission Society who faithfully and constantly supported me when I needed so much help! May God bless those in Munich and Rome who are still living and bless and comfort those who have already died, and may He bring us all together in heaven. With most sincere love and esteem, your grateful and most devoted, Abbot Boniface Wimmer

Ger   oALMV   cASVA   transIG

---

[87] Peter Schumacher (1839-1902), bishop of Portoviejo. See L. Dautzenberg, ed. *Bischof Peter Schumacher, Oberhirte der Diözese Portoviejo, Ecuador (1839-1902)*. Regensburg: F. Pustet, 1908. Monks from St. Vincent went to Portoviejo to establish a priory in the summer of 1888, less than a year after Wimmer's death.

TO JOSEPH BENEDICT DUSMET   **196**

St. Vincent, July 14, 1887

Most Reverend Archbishop: I have received your circular letter dated June 12, as well as the letter you sent from Montecassino on June 25. I would have responded sooner, but I am suffering from a serious illness. From the very first, I have intended to do all in my power to assist the Holy Father in the generous and noble work he has undertaken for the benefit of the Benedictines. I have, therefore, willingly accepted his instructions to provide not just money, but also professors and students to the extent that I am able. I will, therefore, send two professors and two students to the College of Saint Anselm in Rome.

Your Excellency nominated three of our monks to become professors: James Zilliox,[88] Oswald Moosmüller,[89] and Adalbert Müller.[90] However, Father Zilliox has such a weakness of the lungs that he is unable to teach this year. It is the opinion of his doctors that to do so would endanger his life. Father Oswald is an excellent priest and monk, but no one in our monastery would propose him as a professor. Moreover, for the past ten years he has worked with great success in the diocese of Savannah, Georgia, for the conversion of the Negroes. At the moment, he is alone in this work. He has gathered the Negro Catholics in the city of Savannah into a congregation (parish) and has built a church, a school, and an orphanage for them so that they will continue to adhere to the apostolic faith. The bishop of Savannah[91] would be severely inconvenienced if I were to recall Father Oswald. Nevertheless, I would not hesitate to recall him from Savannah and send him to the Holy Father for the new seminary if I thought he was qualified to be a professor. Father Adalbert, on the other hand, has fully recovered his health and will go to Rome to teach philosophy or theology. Even though he is of short stature, he has a brilliant mind.

I hope to find someone to send in place of Father Oswald or James, someone who can teach classical languages, Hebrew, or one of the theological disciplines. Your Excellency speaks also of other monks who can give lessons, but what lessons? In what disciplines? Perhaps I will be able to find someone here in our college.

This is all I can say in response to your letters. I hope to be able to satisfy your expectations and those of His Holiness. In three months, if I live so long, I will

---

[88] James Zilliox, O.S.B. (1849-1890), resigned abbot of St. Mary's Abbey, Newark, New Jersey.
[89] Oswald Moosmüller, O.S.B. (1832-1901).
[90] Adalbert Müller, O.S.B. (1842-1906).
[91] Thomas Becker (1832 -1899), bishop of Savannah.

complete my seventy-ninth year, but I have little hope of living much longer. My health is failing. I have constant pain day and night. Your Excellency's most humble servant, Boniface Wimmer, Archabbot

P.S. If Father Oswald is positively required, I will send him.

Lat   cASVA   transJO

TO CELESTINE ENGLBRECHT   **197**

St. Vincent, July 24, 1887

Beloved Confrere: So you are a prior again—and the anticipation was the least of it! I will do my best to see that Father Adalbert[92] goes to give a retreat at your priory.

Forty-one years ago, this was a busy day for me.[93] I was working from early morning until late at night, preparing for the trip to the "promised land." Today you and I are the only surviving clerics [of the original band], and, if I am not mistaken, of the brothers only three are still alive. Near to death and slowly dying, I naturally think quite often about the days gone by and wonder how things turned out the way they did. No one imagined us capable of accomplishing anything significant, and yet we *did* accomplish something. God's grace was obviously with us. Our chief object—the establishment of the Order in America—has been achieved, and our second major purpose—training and providing a sufficient clergy for our German Catholics—is well underway. May unbounded thanks be given to God a thousand times, for He chose and made use of us as instruments for the execution of His designs. For many, our foundations have had serious defects, but it could not have been otherwise without a miracle, and I firmly believe that things can be made better, once a well-regulated order is established in our abbeys and priories.

Hence, we do not want to become faint-hearted or discouraged. Rather we want to work on confidently and courageously as well as we can. Inasmuch as things have come this far only with the evident protection and grace of God, so may we not expect from ourselves success in the future, but again only from the grace and protection of God, who cannot fail us so long as we work, not for ourselves, but for Him, for His holy Church, for the Order, and for souls.

---

[92] Adalbert Müller, O.S.B. (1842-1906).

[93] On July 25, 1846, Wimmer and nineteen companions (including the addressee of this letter) left Munich for Pennsylvania, in order to establish the Benedictine Order in the United States.

I thank you most heartily for your loyalty and affection, for your zealous service, for all your difficult labors that God will surely reward richly in His time. I thank God that He also sent me afflictions in order to test me, to purify me, and to punish me in this world. May he not cast me away in the next life, as I might well deserve. Peace be with you. Your grateful friend and confrere, Abbot Boniface Wimmer

Ger   oASVA   transABu

TO RUPERT SEIDENBUSCH   **198**

St. Vincent, August 27, 1887

Most Reverend Bishop: I hear that you are planning to go to Rome soon on business. I would like to remind you that in Rome all the congregations are closed for vacation during the months of September and October and that you will not be able to do any business then. Our procurator general, D. Bernardo Smith[94] (formerly Dr. Smith, now Abbot Smith), will also be on vacation, as he wrote me, and so you will not be able to see him in Rome either. You would, therefore, arrive early enough if you go in November.

I am sending Father Adalbert,[95] Father Robert,[96] and three clerics to Rome for the Collegium S. Anselmi. They will not leave before November. We were told that we would receive word by telegram of the day the pope will open the Anselmum. Today I heard that some English Benedictine students, who for a long time have lived in private homes, have moved into the building for converts on the Piazza Scossa Cavalli, not far from St. Peter's. Certainly, this is with the knowledge and permission of the Holy Father. From this we may conclude that there will not be a solemn opening of the Anselmum because there will not be many students present.

I hope that, in any case, you will pay us a visit on your way to Rome. Meanwhile, I greet you warmly and hope that your health is better than mine is. I remain in deep esteem and respect, Your Grace's most devoted, Abbot Boniface Wimmer

Ger   oASJA   cASVA   transAHo

---

[94] Bernard Smith, O.S.B. (1818-1892).
[95] Adalbert Müller, O.S.B. (1842-1906).
[96] Robert Monroe, O.S.B. (1860-1889).

TO ANDREW HINTENACH   **199**

St. Vincent, October 14, 1887

Dear Confrere: Your latest letter changes things in Sheffield and Tuscumbia significantly—perhaps completely. Now listen. For my part, I am satisfied with whatever decision you make, provided you have spoken to the others and have had a serious conference among yourselves. My opinion, however, is still that you should not worry about spending a couple of thousand dollars if in your judgment you must do so. Better to start at once building a college and a church. I think I can help with money if necessary, so long as there is a real foundation for a bright future.

We did not speculate in Tuscumbia, or in the German colony of St. Joseph's, or in Decatur, or in Cullman. It just happened. It was the same recently with the land close to the town limits in Florence. It was all donated, and without future obligations. So let us follow the hint of Divine Providence. As far as possible, I am willing to help and I shall help. We labor for the Church, for our Order, for the conversion of our fellow-citizens of different religions. I have complete confidence in you.[97]

My health has taken a critical turn. Things have not changed significantly, though I am somewhat better. With cordial affection and a request for your prayers and those of the confreres, I am your devoted confrere, Abbot Boniface Wimmer

P.S. Bishop Seidenbusch, Abbot Edelbrock,[98] and three fathers from Minnesota came here on their way to Rome. It turned out that none of them had the information they needed. I convinced them in the end, so they gave up their plan to travel to Rome and all gladly returned home. At the same time, Father Eberhard[99] came. He deposited $300, made a retreat, and went back, with my permission, to his old place. So we might not lose him for the Order after all. He will stay for a while in Chicago.

The Bohemian monastery at St. Procopius is approved. It will be the sixth abbey and can be declared so at any time. Already it houses six fathers, two deacons, and several clerics. It has been formally declared a monastery of the Congregation and is entirely separate from St. Joseph's Priory [Chicago], which will remain a dependency of St. Vincent, but St. Joseph's, too, will become an abbey. This is a

---

[97] The Alabama missions, the principal subject of this letter, became St. Bernard Abbey in 1891. For a history of the community, see Gregory Roettger, *An Historical Overview of St. Bernard Abbey 1891-1991* (Cullman, Ala.: St. Bernard Abbey Press, 1991).

[98] Rupert Seidenbusch, O.S.B. (1830-1895), vicar apostolic of Northern Minnesota; Alexius Edelbrock, O.S.B. (1843-1909), abbot of St. John's Abbey, Collegeville, Minnesota.

[99] Eberhard Gahr, O.S.B. (1832-1922).

great blessing for the Congregation. It will become the seventh monastery, but we are not in a rush and can take our time.[100]

This is a great consolation for me. I did not want to die without seeing it. I have the authority to erect the monastery of St. Procopius, which will have its own novitiate. That is a necessity. I am doing everything in my power because I am deeply impressed by the thought of other foundations coming from that Bohemian monastery. Sheffield and Tuscumbia will turn out to be important places too. Let us take advantage of that. With cordial affection, your devoted confrere, Abbot Boniface Wimmer

Ger   oASVA   transRG

TO MAURUS KINTER   **200**

St. Vincent, October 15, 1887

Dear Reverend Editor: It has been a long time since I wrote you. During this time, much has happened of extraordinary importance. I will be brief. We now have two [new] monasteries—real monasteries. You know that I have been seriously trying to establish a Bohemian monastery ("with all rights, privileges, and immunities") because I was convinced that it would be of great importance not only for the Bohemians in Chicago, but also in general for the West. Now I can tell you that we do have such a monastery in Chicago, and even more than that, we have two. Namely the monastery of St. Procopius and one for the city.[101] I sent my petition to the Holy See in April but received the approval much later because the decree could not be drawn up at once.

To be brief, I will say that the Bohemian Fathers had a space behind the rectory of the church of only 54 feet on which to build. On this front of 54 feet, there is now the monastery of St. Procopius. It has three stories. If you count the

---

[100] St. Joseph Priory, Chicago, never became an independent priory or abbey, though it sponsored the establishment of St. Bede Priory and College, Peru, Illinois, in 1891, which became St. Bede Abbey in 1910. St. Procopius Priory in Chicago became St. Procopius Abbey in 1894. For the history of these two communities see, Theodore Fuertges, "The History of Saint Bede's Abbey and College, Peru, Illinois, 1889-1941" (M.A. thesis, Catholic University of America, 1941); and Vitus Buresh, *The Procopian Chronicle: St. Procopius Abbey 1885-1985* (Lisle, Ill.: St. Procopius Abbey, 1985).

[101] The "one for the city" was St. Joseph Priory, Chicago, which itself never became an independent priory or abbey, though it sponsored the establishment of St. Bede Priory and College, Peru, Illinois, in 1891, which became St. Bede Abbey in 1910.

American basement, it really has four, because the kitchen, refectory, etc., are above ground.

The monastery is already known as St. Procopius because it is Bohemian. The other one also exists after the fact, but it is not exclusively for Bohemians.

Recently, I wrote you three letters. If you have not received them, please note what I wrote above [*sic*].

St. Procopius is a real monastery, but it is not exclusively Bohemian as I have said. It is, however, a real monastery, large enough for 15 priests, clerics, and brothers who are already living there. So we have the monastery of St. Procopius near the church of St. Procopius for the Bohemians who belong to this church, and we have 18 priests, clerics, and novices who occupy the monastery near St. Procopius and who also form a complete monastery.

But there is also a monastery in Chicago of the American Cassinese Congregation, and as such the sixth and seventh abbeys have their start, but not only for Bohemians. [This letter, the last written by Archabbot Boniface, was not completed and never sent.]

Ger   oASVA   transRG

INDEX